STRANGE GROUND

AN ORAL HISTORY OF AMERICANS IN VIETNAM
1945-1975

HARRY MAURER

AVON BOOKS ◆ NEW YORK

AVON BOOKS
A division of
The Hearst Corporation
105 Madison Avenue
New York, New York 10016

Copyright © 1989 by Harry Maurer
Maps designed by Paul J. Pugliese
Front cover photograph by Photri, Inc.
Published by arrangement with Henry Holt and Company, Inc.
Library of Congress Catalog Card Number: 88-13382
ISBN: 0-380-70931-7

The Henry Holt and Company edition contains the following Library of Congress Cataloging in Publication Data:

Maurer, Harry.
  Strange ground : Americans in Vietnam, 1945-1975, an oral history
  / Harry Maurer.—1st ed.
  p. cm.
  Includes index.
1. Vietnamese Conflict, 1961-1975—Personal narratives, American.
2. Vietnam—History—1945-1975. 3. Americans—Vietnam—Biography. I. Title.
DS559.5.M38   1988
959.704′33′73—dc19   88-13382
                                                                         CIP

First Avon Books Trade Printing: October 1990

AVON TRADEMARK REG. U.S. PAT. OFF. AND IN OTHER COUNTRIES, MARCA REGISTRADA, HECHO EN U.S.A.

Printed in the U.S.A.

OPM   10 9 8 7 6 5 4 3 2 1

For Heather, who hung in;
for the memory of my father, Bob;
and for the fighters

Contents

Acknowledgments

My deepest debt and warmest thanks go to the 100 or so men and women who were interviewed for this book but do not appear in its pages. They gave unsparingly of their time and memories, and they all helped—for better or worse—to make the book what it is. If there are some who feel hurt that their contributions are not more evident, I offer an apology. It simply wasn't possible, in assembling a volume covering thirty years, to include everyone.

Good leads are the lifeline of an oral history. Nearly every speaker in this book led me to someone else, often to several people. Other leads came from a crowd of friends and family who would remember, often at odd moments, that they knew someone who had once told them a memorable tale about Vietnam. Among those who steered me, housed me on the road, or kept me going in other ways are Maureen Shea Aspin, G. I. Basel, Mike Blecker, Barbara and Doug Brown, Grant Brown, Kevin Buckley, Jim Calio, Jean Christie, James Credle, Ann-Marie Cunningham, John Donnell, Margo Dougherty, Andrea Eagan, Dave Elder, Todd Ensign, Frances FitzGerald, Dr. David Forrest, Mike Gillen, Paul Gregory, Jim Hebron, Gerald Hickey, Perdita Huston, Ann Jones, Sean Kilcoyne, John Love, Don Luce, Mark Lynch, Charlo Maurer, John McChesney, Bob Minnich, Hallee Morgan, Archimedes Patti, Ron Perez, Col. Larry Pickett, Steve Reichl, Benito Romano, Lionel Rosenblatt, John Rowan, Lynn Schnurnberger, Terry Selzer, Bill Simon, Scott Smith, Mike Uhl, Keith Walker, Joanne Wallace, Steven Young, and Jane Yusko. Thanks to all.

Others went far beyond the call of duty. Diana Gubbay helped talk out the original ideas. Brennon Jones provided files and advice and infused me with some of his passion about Vietnam. Ciro Scotti, my boss at *Business Week*, granted two long leaves of absence. Milly Klingman, as always, kept me (relatively) sane. George Hagman and Kai Bird were there whenever I needed to talk. Jack Robbins never stopped believing. And Mike Gold, head of veterans' affairs at the City University of New York, was simply and modestly indispensable. His encyclopedic knowledge of the veterans' movement and his unfailing generosity with time and energy have helped build dozens of projects—organizations, marches, monuments, and books. He is one of a kind.

The editor who signed up this book, Natalie Chapman, also helped shape the proposal—and then gave much-needed encouragement through the rough spots. Tracy Bernstein's sharp eye and pencil coaxed a book out of a seventeen-pound manuscript. And the Writers Room, that blessed haven in Greenwich Village, allowed me to flee distractions and draw strength from the other scribes.

Whatever you have seen, maybe it is
for the good of the people you have seen.
—*Black Elk Speaks*

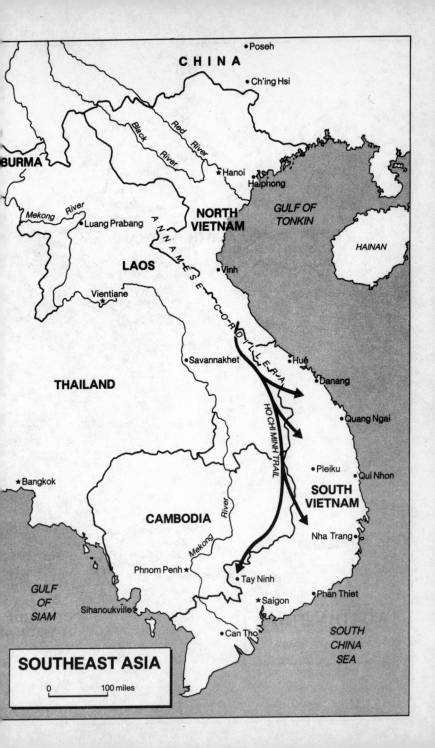

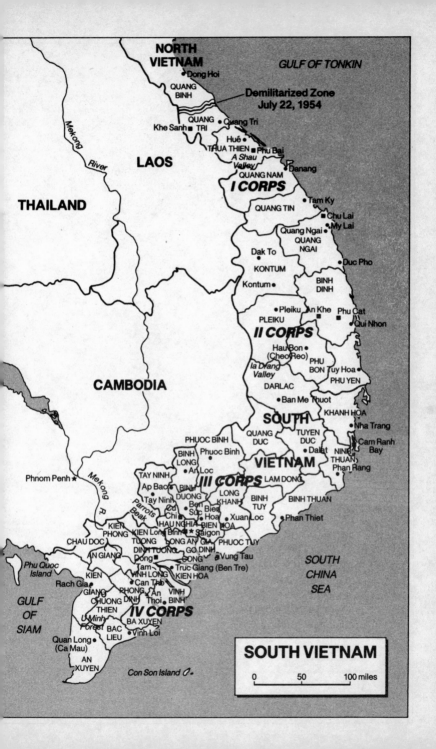

STRANGE GROUND

AN ORAL HISTORY OF AMERICANS IN VIETNAM 1945-1975

INTRODUCTION

Let's get it out of the way: I am a draft dodger.

In the spring of 1970 I graduated from Columbia College. I was twenty-one. At the graduation ceremony, a few hundred students and professors walked out and held a "counter-commencement" at the chapel on campus, their protest signs reading "Stop! Think! Walk out!" The reason was that U.S. and South Vietnamese troops had invaded Cambodia a month before, on April 29. Five days later the Ohio National Guard shot dead four students who were demonstrating at Kent State University. Ten days after that, two students were killed by police at Jackson State College in Mississippi. Columbia, like some 450 other colleges, shut down. It made for an ugly mood on cap-and-gown day.

But then, much of my college years passed in an ugly mood—and the reason, if it can be summed up in one word, was Vietnam. As a sophomore, I was arrested after occupying a building for a week in the famed Columbia "riots." As a junior, after a brief sit-in, I got a letter threatening expulsion unless I asked the dean's forgiveness and promised to behave. I did, not ready to join various friends who had already been expelled. And six months before graduation, I sat with a group of classmates and watched TV for hours as representatives of the Selective Service System's Youth Advisory Committees plucked little blue capsules with numbers in them from a big glass bowl. The numbers held a clue to our futures. They ran from 1 to 365, one for each day of the year. If your birthday fell on the day that drew number 1, you were first in line for the draft the following year. If you drew 365, you were last—and almost certainly the quotas would not reach that high. Suddenly some of my friends were free from the sword that had hung over us for four years. I drew 157—not good enough.

1

I say "a clue to our futures" because none of us had any intention of going into the armed services, low number or high. Those with 300-plus simply knew they could relax. The rest of us had to find another way out. During the late '60s, draft counseling had evolved into a high art. Everyone I knew had seen counselors to map out the best escape route. I lacked credentials for conscientious objection. I had no obvious medical disability. That left the more creative methods. For years my cronies and I had passed on stories of how to fail the physical. Full-scale drug addiction, with needle marks to prove it, worked—but merely going to the physical stoned on downers didn't. Pretending to be crazy or homosexual might work—but simply showing up in drag didn't. Starving yourself to beat the minimum weight limit worked—but the minimum was extremely low, and losing so much weight could be dangerous. And so on.

Through a friend, I learned about an antiwar psychiatrist who wrote letters for people. I made an appointment. He asked about my history, my family, my problems. A week later I got a three-page letter, directed "to whom it may concern." It made me sound like a borderline basket case. One passage implied that I might have homosexual tendencies. The summing-up paragraph consisted of one sentence, saying I suffered from a "character disorder" that could well be aggravated by military service.

I stayed awake all night before the physical; some people did this for three nights running. The rumor mill said that I would have to persuade an army psychiatrist, and I figured lack of sleep would help to play the character I had decided upon: someone withdrawn, depressed, and barely able to communicate. I didn't shave for several days. I didn't bathe. I wore the most pathetic clothes I had. I was scared.

The New York headquarters for the Selective Service was on Whitehall Street. The number of potential recruits amazed me; there were many hundreds, perhaps thousands. The crowd seemed about half white, half black and Hispanic. And of the college boys around me, almost all white, every one had some ailment that was going to keep him out of the army. This one's doctor had providentially discovered a heart murmur. That one had a severe case of conjunctivitis. This one had a trick knee. Young men were displaying X rays and medical reports the way they might show off a new car. Whereas the blacks and Hispanics, and the less privileged whites, were empty-handed. They looked resigned. We were told—I can't remember whether officially or by rumor—that the examiners would reject 50 percent of the candidates. It was obvious who the future grunts were.

The rest of the day had a surreal quality—long lines of near-naked young men standing in halls, clutching papers, being poked and palpated by indifferent doctors. Finally I arrived at a long hallway where low tables were stretched end to end, with men in white coats sitting behind them. I waited until I was called. The doctor looked at the results of my physical exams. No problems there. He said, "Is there any reason that you shouldn't be inducted?" I said yes and handed him my letter. He opened the envelope, flipped to the last page, and read only the last sentence. Then he made an X in a little box on my forms next to the words "character disorder." "Okay," he said, "you can go." I said, "I don't have to see a psychiatrist?" He looked at me. I decided to take no for an answer.

Not long afterward I got my new draft classification: 1-Y. Unfit for duty for psychiatric reasons.

So someone was drafted instead of me. Looking back after eighteen years, I have mixed feelings about that. I am happy that I did not go to fight in Vietnam. If I had passed the physical, I would have resisted the draft in some more extreme fashion: moving to Canada or refusing induction. I hated the war and thought that the army fighting it was a diabolical league of war criminals. And it was clear from my day at Whitehall that the army didn't want me either, or anyone like me. By 1970, military morale in Vietnam and Stateside had been devastated. The last thing the army needed was more troublemakers fresh from campus, so they washed us all out and took who was left. But the ease of it still troubles me. I paid no price. Aside from my foot-soldier role in the peace movement—marches in Washington, protests at Columbia—I did little to stop the war. I took my deferment and went on with my life. That now strikes me as less than honorable.

This book, in a sense, grew out of that day and that dilemma. The idea took shape in the mid-1970s, when I was traveling around the country interviewing Americans who were out of work. At the unemployment centers I met veterans who told me that sometimes they didn't get jobs because they had been in Vietnam. Employers were leery of vets, saw them as drug addicts or potential crazies. It occurred to me that I knew nothing of the men who fought the war, nor of the fighting itself. I had not gone to Vietnam; not a single person I knew in college had gone; I had never even talked to anyone who had gone. And despite my antiwar sentiments, I knew little of the history. There was some feeling of having "missed my war," that rite of passage American males are supposed to undergo. But there was something else: I wanted to know what had happened. How did it begin? How had my country gone so wrong? What had it been like to be there?

This book, then, is a group portrait of Americans who served or worked in Vietnam during thirty years of conflict. It is not a history of the war or of American policy as it was created in Washington. It does not deal with the antiwar movement, except insofar as its members traveled to North Vietnam. It touches only briefly on the experience of coming home from 'Nam, which for many veterans was as painful as the war itself. It ends with the fall of Saigon; though some Americans have visited or worked in Vietnam since then, and though their role in helping the refugees has often been heroic, the U.S. intervention effectively ended in 1975. And while I considered interviewing Vietnamese, I ruled it out for several reasons. First, I speak no Vietnamese, and I was hesitant to interview in English or through an interpreter. I suspected I would miss too much. Second, my curiosity was more nakedly nationalistic, even patriotic: I wanted to learn what *we* had experienced in that baffling war.

There are sixty-two interviews in this book. Some 2.7 million Americans served in Vietnam. These few were chosen largely at random: Friends introduced me to friends, who in turn passed me on. In certain cases, especially those from the early days, I read about specific people and undertook to find them. Most of the candidates I called were willing to plumb their memories for my tape recorder, though often not without a palpable uneasiness, an intake of breath. And some would have nothing to do with me, or were so heavily guarded when we talked that I couldn't get near their bunkers. Others asked how I would portray the war, and declined when I admitted: Probably not as a noble cause. A few buried their reluctance more deeply. One Green Beret who did three tours in 'Nam said he'd be happy to talk. He missed three appointments before calling me to say, "Look, I guess I just don't want to get into it right now."

For reasons that will be obvious, four speakers in this book remain anonymous. All the others agreed to be identified, which I wanted to do partly as a way of screening out tall tales. William Broyles, in an *Esquire* article called "Why Men Love War," remarks that "I have never once heard a grunt tell a reporter a war story that wasn't a lie, just as some of the stories that I tell about the war are lies." He goes on to say: "Not that even the lies aren't true, on a certain level. They have a moral, even a mythic, truth, rather than a literal one." I am not much convinced by that argument, so I have done my best, as many vets advised, to "keep my bullshit detectors out." Stories, even whole interviews, do not appear here because they did not ring true. But I have not tried to check these accounts. Some, undoubtedly, stretch the facts. I hoped that by asking people, in effect, to sign their names to what they said, I would minimize the "mythic truth" and stay close to what happened.

If serendipity assembled these speakers, something else unites them: a stay on strange ground. One of the first things that struck me when I began interviewing was the great gulf that divided Americans from the Vietnamese. The locals remain a shadowy presence in this book, seen entirely through American eyes—but what is glaring is how poorly we saw them. Vietnamese language, culture, and outlook were utterly foreign. The first Americans posted to Vietnam after World War II had to look at a map to figure out where it was. That problem passed as the war heated up, but the place remained an enigma—thus dooming our effort, for how could hearts and minds be won when we had so little idea how they worked? And inscrutability was by no means a monopoly of the East: To the Vietnamese, the big white men with the gross manners were no less mysterious.

There were exceptions, of course—Americans who lived in Vietnam for years and came to know the Vietnamese in all their otherness. The gulf could be bridged. But the great majority made little effort, or, to be fair, had little chance. Heavily armed soldiers, nineteen years old, fresh from the cornfields or the mean streets, scared and enraged, counting off their 365 days in-country, could hardly be expected to practice the sensitivity of anthropologists. For them, Vietnam was not even "the world." It seemed as alien as science fiction. The impression left is often one of loneliness in a hostile landscape. Pete Mahoney, a young officer advising an ARVN battalion in 1970, speaks of a night he and a squad of ARVN were strung out along a road. Three enemy soldiers appeared and walked through the entire ambush without one of the ARVN firing a shot. Mahoney remembers thinking: "It's the Vietnamese against the Americans out here now, and you're the only American. I had this incredible feeling of being alone."

Certainly the most frustrating puzzle was the behavior of "our" Vietnamese, who often showed less than a burning zeal to defend their country. From grunts to generals, Americans talk about the ARVN's maddening reluctance to fight. General Bill Fulton snorts: "You run into people who say, 'The South Vietnamese are very noble, and they fought a hell of a battle.' But they never really put it on the line. . . . They were never willing to find the lion and beard him in his den." And if we never solved the riddle of the apparently lacka-daisical South Vietnamese, we misjudged the will of the enemy even more seriously. Part of the reason for that mistake was simple arrogance. A refrain constantly heard in Saigon during the early years was "Yeah, but we'll win anyway." Ogden Williams, who first went to Vietnam with the CIA in 1956, recalls that "We had the feeling we could do anything. For Americans in Vietnam, the question wasn't, 'What is the reality here?' The question was, 'What reality are we supposed to create here?' "

And for many, the answer was, a little America on the Mekong. Loren Baritz, in his book *Backfire*, traces the country's crusading zeal to the vision of ourselves, first enunciated by the Pilgrim John Winthrop, as "a city upon a hill." Baritz writes: "The myth . . . implies that America is a moral example to the rest of the world. . . . It means that we are a Chosen People, each of whom, because of God's favor and presence, can smite one hundred of our heathen enemies hip and thigh." And, one might add, set our friends on the true path of democracy and free enterprise. The U.S. sent first a trickle, then a torrent of advisers to show the Vietnamese better ways of running their government, political process, bureaucracy, courts, schools, military, police, farms, ports, communications, transport, public health system, and almost every other institution. The teaching was well meant and had some impact. But in countless cases the effects were superficial. The Vietnamese set up sham structures to please the pushy Americans, and went on with business as usual.

The U.S. also poured in billions of dollars in aid and products ranging from computers and cranes to hot dogs and hair spray. One marine who unloaded supplies at Danang told me he decided that America was trying to graft its consumer culture onto Vietnam, as though Kools and Coke would somehow implant the right ideas. In a way, it worked. The flood of cash and goodies wrecked the traditional economy and made many Vietnamese frantic to copy the American way of life—by theft, if need be. But the primary U.S. export to Vietnam was high-tech violence. A fantastic arsenal of destruction ravaged much of the countryside, tearing apart a peasant society. "We had to destroy the town in order to save it": The famous remark of an American major after a battle became a metaphor for all Vietnam.

Once the war was running full tilt, most Americans arriving incountry soon realized that something was drastically wrong. Bob Boettcher, a young Foreign Service officer assigned to the pacification program: "Within a month I knew that this was a futile crusade." Warren Wooten, a marine grunt, took longer, probably because he fought early on, in 1965–66. Yet nine months into his tour "I knew we weren't gonna win the war in this fashion. It felt like a hopeless cause." For the grunts, the Tet offensive finished off any dreams of victory; from then on, the new troops, or "cherries," were taught that the point was not to win, but to survive. Even in Saigon, the cocky "we'll win anyway" attitude was stood on its head; now, if someone reported progress, someone else was likely to joke, "Yeah, but we'll lose anyway."

Hearing tales of disillusionment again and again, I wondered how the war kept going at all—why the machinery did not shudder to a halt, clogged by the sludge of gloom. Part of the answer, of course, is that it was simply too big to stop. Another reason was duty-honor-country, the ingrained code of military men who are trained to take orders, and who are unlikely to give up on a war while their Commander-in-Chief still thinks it is winnable. And there was simple careerism, whose role in prolonging the war can hardly be overestimated. It was careerism that turned pessimistic reports into optimistic ones, that inflated the body count, that smothered doubt in silence. The troops and the low-level advisers may have known that Vietnam was a loser, but their higher-ups also knew that sending bad news up the line rarely brought promotion. General Harry Kinnard, who took the 1st Cavalry Division to Vietnam in 1965, concluded by the end of his tour that the prevailing strategy was doomed. Nevertheless, "I felt it was important for us to hang in there, and I thought if I said we were losing, it would be more ammunition for people who wanted to fold us up. I had made my decision to stay in the army. I wanted to have my shot at being promoted. So I went along with the party line."

A similar silence helped protect American boys whose deadly impulses carried them beyond an ill-defined line. What makes the My Lai massacre astonishing is not that it happened at all; while it may have been the worst such incident, it was far from unique. Rather, it is that almost no one in Charlie Company did anything to stop the killing that day or to press for an inquiry afterward. The army suppressed the facts for a year. Only the persistence of an ex-GI who had not been at My Lai finally forced an investigation. On a smaller scale, the same phenomenon appears in this book. Yoshia Chee, a Green Beret who carried out "snatch" missions, reports that in a strange village in the dead of night such outings could take on an imprecise quality: "If we found the guy in the house, we'd try to take him alive. Maybe he wouldn't be there, or it would be the wrong house. . . . Sometimes if there were four houses in a row, and we weren't sure which was the right one, we'd kill everybody in the four houses." Dick Rutan, who in 1986 piloted the *Voyager* around the world nonstop, flew reconnaissance missions over North Vietnam. Often, trying to confirm the bombers' claims of destroyed trucks, he would find instead a village in flames. "I'd report it back, and nothing would happen. Remember, here I am a lowly captain."

One ingredient in such events was racism. All sides in all wars dehumanize their enemies; whether Americans took it to unusual lengths in Vietnam is debatable. But there is no question that contempt for backward little yellow people made it easier to kill them. Jim Duffy, a helicopter door gunner, watched as the wind from his ship's rotors blew a five-year-old boy under a truck's wheels. "My gut reaction was one of horror. I looked toward the ass end of the ship, and my flight engineer had been watching the same thing. All of a sudden we both started to laugh about it. Ah, we got another gook."

Did Vietnam brutalize its combatants more than other wars? Was it, in some way, fundamentally different? Describing life as a foot soldier, the grunts in this book sound much like the doughboys of World War I or the dogfaces of World War II: the same terror, rage, exhaustion, excitement; the same homesickness; the same bad food and physical miseries; the same acts of daily heroism; the same sense of madness; the same loss of innocence; the same thousand-yard stare. Combat is combat is combat.

Yet Vietnam was different, too. What made it different was the political dimension of the war—the one that Americans understood the least. From top to bottom, the U.S. military was not prepared to fight a war in which the enemy and the civilian populace were often the same, and where the prize was not territory but allegiance. A Kansas boy in a Mekong delta village had no way to pick out the friendlies: he couldn't even speak the language. But he could tell that the villagers weren't glad to see him. They seemed resentful and afraid. He naturally concluded that, for practical purposes, there were no friendlies. This meant that he never felt completely safe. Any Vietnamese over the age of five was a potential assassin. Stories circulated about sudden death from unexpected quarters: the shoeshine boy, the Coca-Cola girl, the whore. It also shattered the moral underpinnings for committing acts of war. If the people we were trying to save were trying to kill us come nightfall, what was it all for?

Politics also governed the way the war was fought. Because President Johnson feared the outcry that would result from calling up the reserves, the troops in Vietnam were mostly teenage draftees. Their average age was nineteen, compared with twenty-six in World War II. And to appease the wrath of the middle class, its sons were granted loopholes like the student deferment. Troops in Vietnam served for a year (marines for thirteen months), a tacit admission that they had no personal stake in the war. The one-year tour meant that soldiers were individuals; they arrived in-country alone, and they left alone, not as part of a cohesive unit. For officers, the tours were even shorter: Six months in a combat command was the norm. The idea was to get your "ticket punched" for promotion purposes. As soon as an officer learned something about the 'Nam, it was time to go home. The troops paid the price for green leadership.

Finally, the strategy of attrition meant that a grunt in his year might see more combat than a GI who served three years in World War II. There were no climactic battles in Vietnam, with long pauses before and after. Search-and-destroy kept the line companies moving, patrolling, sometimes spending sixty days at a stretch in the field. Often the grunts had only a vague idea of where they were, or why, or where the choppers would take them the next day. A typical patrol passed without a shot being fired. But the danger was always there: an ambush, a booby trap, a sniper, a mortar attack. Men were wounded and killed in ones and twos and threes on everyday operations. "I saw a lot of battles," says Angel Quintana. "I can't even remember my first firefight, there were so many. After a while you get used to it. They attack you, and people die, and it's a normal thing. You fight and kill people and wound people, and it seems normal."

And after a year, at the ripe old age of twenty, the grunt came home—to a nation bitterly divided over what he had done. Again, Vietnam has much in common with other wars: the shell-shocked soldier finds family and friends reluctant to listen. There is a kind of embarrassment about his experience, and a need to pretend that the man who came back is the same as the boy who left. But in the case of Vietnam, embarrassment was joined by anger and contempt. Much of the country felt the war was not only a mistake but a crime. Young people especially, the vets' peers, the women they might date, detested the war and did not hesitate to blame the warriors. How could they have been so stupid as to go? Did they like killing women and children?

Some vets cracked under the pressure. Having fought a war that napalmed their most basic beliefs—in their political leaders, in America's infallibility, in their own goodness—they now found themselves ignored at best and reviled at worst. And their memories would not rest easy. Nor would their rage against a society that had double-crossed them. Stories of "crazed vets" started popping up in the news and in TV dramas. Several of the men in this book have suffered from "post-traumatic stress syndrome," a medicinal-sounding term for symptoms that can show up years after an event the mind can't digest. They tell of heavy drinking, drug abuse, nightmares, flashbacks, social isolation, deceit, thrill-seeking, flirtations with death. Some are clearly still caught in Vietnam's coils.

Yet the great majority did as soldiers have always done: They came home, found jobs, married, raised families, got on with life. They didn't talk much about the war, even to their spouses; an amazing number of the people I visited said that this was the first time they had told their stories. But if Vietnam haunted them, it seemed a minor ghost. Some vets have risen to heights of power and fame as politicians, business leaders, movie stars. A few were troubled enough by the war that it sparked careers battling the Establishment. But others simply say the experience tested and tempered them. Walter Mack, a marine company commander in 1967, is now a top prosecutor in the Federal Attorney's Office in Manhattan. He reports: "I'm one of those masochists who feels that Vietnam was very good for me. It was a training ground. I don't think I'd be in this job today without it."

Julie Kayan, a secretary in Saigon, has still another angle: "I had fun there. I loved it for most of my tour." She is far from the only American who had what might be called a swell time. Especially in the early days, Vietnam was the classic colonial paradise: cheap servants, superb food, gorgeous beaches, and a laissez-faire morality. Robin Pell, an AID public-relations officer, thinks that sex played no small part in keeping Americans in Vietnam. "The French had a name for it: *le mal jaune*, yellow fever. The great attraction of Indochina to the West. The beauty, the seductiveness, the opium, and above all, the women."

Some Americans left without a second glance. Others didn't leave until they had to, and have not stopped looking backward. I was struck by the many people I interviewed who seem snared by Vietnam as if by an old love affair that still aches. These are not soldiers who saw too much at a tender age, or even generals whose last war tainted their careers. These are people who were touched so deeply that Vietnam now owns part of them. Ogden Williams did his first tour in 1956–57, spent much of the '60s in-country, and flew to Saigon in the last weeks to help friends escape. He talks about the early military advisers, but clearly includes himself: "These guys would fall in love not only with the country but also their unit and their job. At the end of their tour, you had to take them out of there in chains, practically, because this was the best duty they'd ever had in their lives, and they believed in it more than anything they'd ever done." Mike Benge, an agriculture adviser who nearly died during five years as a POW, went straight back to Vietnam when he was released in 1973.

· · ·

In the end, though, it didn't matter that some Americans cared. Their passion was not enough. South Vietnam fell anyway. In the process, nearly 58,000 Americans died, with more than 2,000 listed as missing. About 2 million Vietnamese were killed, some 5 percent of the population—the equivalent of 11 million Americans in 1975. The U.S. economy has yet to recover fully from President Johnson's decision to fight the war and fund the Great Society at the same time without raising taxes. The Vietnamese economy is a disaster area, making the country one of the poorest in the world. Blunders by dogmatic leaders after the war did not help matters, but fifteen years of battle had already left Vietnam prostrate. Huge tracts of the countryside were defoliated and remain barren. Many of North Vietnam's cities and towns were bombed into rubble. Unexploded munitions still litter the land, killing and maiming hundreds every year. A generation of young men was decimated. When South Vietnam finally collapsed, perhaps one-third of its people were refugees, and most of them had been driven from their villages years earlier. The social fabric in the South had been torn to shreds by the fighting—and by the presence of so many Americans with so much money.

Seen in the light of the South's defeat, such destruction seems horribly absurd. But could the outcome have been different? Should it have been? There is no consensus in this book on those questions, just as there is no consensus in America. Some think the U.S. should not have intervened at all. Others regard the cause as worthy in theory but doomed in practice. Still others see it as a duty that the U.S. cravenly abandoned.

Many of the soldiers I interviewed, from grunts to generals, are convinced they could have won the war had the politicians let them do it. A common GI proposal is that the army should have started at the bottom of Vietnam and simply swept north, covering every inch of ground and flushing out the bad guys all the way to the DMZ. This is simply a revenge fantasy, as are the other notions of how the U.S. could have prevailed with one swift stroke. If Johnson had declared and waged all-out war, he certainly could have "beaten" North Vietnam—assuming China stayed put. But the memory of Korea was fresh. The President and his advisers thought they could win at far less cost and risk. And even if they had successfully invaded the North, what then? Would Ho sue for peace—or take to the mountains, leaving the Americans in the position of the French, an occupying power in hostile territory? How long would it take to snuff out that guerrilla war? How many men would be needed? How long would they have to stay afterward? No one could guess.

Another approach was to do what the military was already doing, only more so. Essentially, this is what Westmoreland proposed in 1968, when he asked for 206,000 troops in addition to the half million he had. The request had much to recommend it. The southern guerrillas had been slaughtered in the Tet offensive. Pacification was starting to make headway. It was clear that a big American army could keep South Vietnam alive indefinitely, and a bigger one would secure even more ground. The problem was that Tet had stunned Americans at home, who were tiring of the war. There seemed to be no end in sight. And that impatience was North Vietnam's trump card. Leaders in Hanoi often said so, as in Premier Pham Van Dong's comment to French journalist Bernard Fall: "Americans do not like long, inconclusive wars—and this is going to be a long, inconclusive war. Thus we are sure to win in the end." He was right. Westmoreland's request was denied, and the slow exit began.

Recently, writers such as General Bruce Palmer and Colonel Harry Summers have argued that another strategy might have been conclusive: The army should have cut the Ho Chi Minh Trail by invading Laos, thus choking off supplies for enemy troops in the South. General William De Puy, the man who invented search-and-destroy, is a believer: "It would have been a big fight, no question about that. The North Vietnamese might have thrown in their entire army. But at least . . . they would have had to fight." Would they, though? Given the North's tenacity, it is hard to imagine it would not have found some way to flank a blocking force. In any case, Washington vetoed such a move, and the generals made little protest.

The argument over what could have been, of course, is really a dispute over what to do in future. The United States left Vietnam like a child that burned its hand on a stove: not seriously hurt, but with a new sense of danger. Coming on the heels of Cuba, which slipped out of our orbit almost through inattention, the war showed that even when America staked enormous blood and treasure, it could be beaten by what Kissinger called "a third-rate power." That ended the feeling of invincibility that had pervaded the country since World War II. In President Nixon's 1970 speech announcing the invasion of Cambodia, he railed against the U.S. becoming a "pitiful, helpless giant." But with that phrase he spoke a truth that eclipsed the rest of the speech. The fact is that America had become a helpless giant in Vietnam. And after the final debacle in 1975, policymakers were left puzzling over what role such a giant could play in the world.

Some strategists argue that the U.S. scored a geopolitical success simply by staying in Vietnam as long as it did. They say the American presence in the region provided an underpinning for the 1965 rightist coup in Indonesia, and gave other countries—Thailand, Malaysia, Singapore—time to shore up their defenses against insurrection. Not many dominos have fallen, after all. It is even argued that by losing, we won—that our exit from Vietnam divided our enemies by encouraging China's split with the Soviet Union. But many of the speakers in this book find little consolation in such ideas. For them, the damage Vietnam did can be easily read in the list of countries that have since moved into one hostile camp or another: Angola, Mozambique, Ethiopia, Iran, Nicaragua—with the Philippines tottering.

What to do in future, then? Two ideas come up again and again. One is that America should enter no wars unless the public is united—indeed, passionate—in support. The other is that the wars should be short and crushing, with no half-measures, no gradual "escalations." So far, Washington has hewed close to the first precept. Various temptations to dispatch marines have been passed up, and one foray in Lebanon was quickly abandoned. U.S. aid has kept a regime in power in El Salvador and another in trouble in Nicaragua, but few Americans have gone into combat. Ironically, the technique of arming and training local forces to fight local wars grew directly out of Vietnamization. Enunciated as the "Nixon doctrine," it was widely derided at the time. But sometimes it gets results. "Take El Salvador," says General De Puy. "I think we have been pretty smart there. I don't think there's anything wrong with giving them support with money and training and communications and intelligence and engineering and all that, as long as we don't Americanize the war."

As for the second notion, that we should go for broke in any war we do fight, it has only been tested on a Lilliputian scale—in Grenada. It proved a big hit for President Reagan.

One can hardly find fault with the idea that wars should not be fought without full backing from the public. But as a major "lesson" of Vietnam, it falls short. In the right circumstances, war fever is all too easy to whip up; even Vietnam was popular at the beginning. True, Lyndon Johnson did not declare war, call up the reserves, put the economy on an emergency footing, and broadcast fireside chats about the dire threat to the nation. His advisers were intrigued by fighting a war in "cold blood," without arousing hysteria. Yet the Tonkin Gulf resolution passed by 416–0 in the House and by 88–2 in the Senate, winning editorial acclaim from coast to coast. So enthusiasm at the outset is no guarantee of victory—or of a good cause.

A deeper question must be asked when the U.S. contemplates war on foreign soil: What will we be fighting for? Ultimately, that problem was the weak link in Vietnam, not flawed strategy or tactics. It underlay every other obstacle: the enemy's stubbornness, South Vietnam's frailty, the GIs' plummeting morale, the erosion of support at home. American goals seemed either muddy or misguided. In part, that was because our leaders lied about them. It was also because the goals didn't match the situation.

The Vietnam War was actually various wars. It began as a battle for independence against France. But when the colonial power was beaten, it became a civil war—and a revolutionary war. Most Vietnamese agreed that the hated French must go, but the shape of a new society was another matter. Into this political maelstrom dropped the Americans. Those who arrived after the Geneva Accords naturally saw themselves as utterly different from the French. They were helpers looking to the future, not exploiters clinging to the past. The problem with this stance was that the U.S. had done everything short of dropping atomic weapons at Dien Bien Phu to rescue the French. If we were so different, why had we wanted them to win so badly? Edmund Gullion, the second-in-command of our Saigon embassy in the early 1950s, points out that the U.S. never seriously pressured France to grant independence. "With the Korean War, Washington came to the view that the French were doing in Vietnam the same thing that we were doing in Korea. We were both fighting a war against Communism, and therefore, full faith and credit to them."

So the U.S. was compromised from the beginning. It had backed the colonizer. Now it was backing Ngo Dinh Diem. Many Vietnamese could be excused for seeing Americans as simply the latest foreigners bent on dominating their country. What's more, Vietnam was now divided, and the Americans seemed to like it that way. But South Vietnam was a phony country, created by the French just a few years before to produce the illusion of independence. Thus the issues of nationalism and xenophobia—both powerful forces in Vietnam—were handed to the North. For the entire course of the war, Hanoi would inspire its soldiers by saying they were fighting to unify the fatherland and free their southern brothers from the clutches of the American "pirates." A common euphemism for the war was "the anti-U.S. task." And the North had Ho Chi Minh, the man who drove out the French, a kind of warrior father-figure.

Against these advantages, what could the U.S. put forward? It said it wanted freedom and democracy for South Vietnam. There was some truth to that, but it was hardly a persuasive argument given the regimes we supported. The Diem and Thieu autocracies allowed more "freedom" than in the North, but only marginally. The gap between U.S. claims and reality was obvious to the Vietnamese, the GIs, Americans at home, and the rest of the world. Thus the endless search for the elusive "third force"—leaders who stood somewhere between the extreme right and the Communists, and who could capture the allegiance of South Vietnam.

Why did the third force never blossom? France, in its ninety years as a colonial power, made little effort to develop Indochina. In 1950 the country closely resembled what it had been in 1850: a semi-feudal peasant realm, with a tiny, wealthy class of rulers and merchants— except that the peasants had been stripped of their land in the interim. The French built up a few profitable industries, such as rubber and mining. But their educational system and the backward economy left almost no room for Vietnamese to advance. Of the handful who did, some became "more French than the French." Others became nationalists and revolutionaries. There was almost no middle class of the sort that anchors a Western democracy. Nor was there any democratic tradition.

For all practical purposes, the "third force" did not exist. The U.S. slid smoothly from an alliance with the French to one with upper-class Vietnamese. Many were genuine nationalists, to be sure. But most were also Catholic and highly Westernized. They had prospered under the French. They might be eager for independence, but they did not want many other changes. A peasant revolution of the sort that had just swept China terrified them. Yet out in the countryside, in the traditional hamlets and villages, the Viet Cong were whispering of drastic measures: land reform, local rule, an end to crushing taxes. The hatreds of a century were spilling over.

So it was not simply a question of freedom. It was a question of change. And on the whole, Americans came down on the side of the status quo. The cornucopia of aid projects never threatened the dominance of an urban elite over the mass of villagers. In any case, development aid made up a small fraction of total U.S. spending in Vietnam; even during the early Diem years, before fighting broke out again, 90 percent of our assistance went to the military. Land reform, a key measure, was decreed by Diem in 1956 at the urging of Americans, but little land was ever turned over to tenant farmers. And throughout the war, the Saigon officials who were imposed on the villages invented new ways to bleed them. So along with the crusade to drive out the foreigners, the Viet Cong had another advantage: They could sell themselves accurately as the agents of a more just order in the countryside. Despite floods of propaganda, the South Vietnamese and the Americans could not.

Since the dedication of the Vietnam Memorial in 1982, Americans have talked a great deal about "healing the wounds" of Vietnam. Just how hard that would be was suggested by the nasty fight over the memorial itself, with conservative veterans calling it a disgrace, a "black gash of shame." But the wall touched a nerve. The desire—perhaps the need—to see it has even spawned "traveling walls," small-scale replicas that have drawn crowds across the country. The austere granite and the relentless scroll of names finally allowed a nation to mourn. Of course, the healing taking place is largely due to the vets' own efforts. They formed the first rap groups, where buried hurts and guilts could be exorcised. They fought for a network of vet centers where troubled comrades could find help. They dreamed up the memorial and built it, and they have built others and staged parades in dozens of cities and towns. On the blustery November afternoon that the Washington memorial was dedicated, I sat in a grandstand and marveled at the loving response of the onlookers to the ragged army of vets marching along Constitution Avenue. When the New York delegation passed and a friend beckoned, I joined the marchers—a draft dodger happy to be among men I once saw as babykillers. And in the years since, at parties and meetings held by Vietnam vets, I have noticed a rare softness, a tenderness with one another. They have walked with death and learned something about caring for the living. Many are stronger for it. Some even manage to be funny.

Slowly, warily, Americans who served in Vietnam edge toward forgiveness of their compatriots who stayed at home—and vice versa. Still, the healing has not gone far enough, for the country owes a debt that is not merely emotional. The GI Bill for Vietnam-era vets was a shadow of its World War II equivalent, so relatively few made use of it when they came home. While most are now past the age when they might attend college, an extension of the eligibility period would greatly help some. Congress has repeatedly refused. The network of storefront vet centers, which should be expanded and better funded, is under constant fiscal pressure—though so far it has survived attempts to axe it altogether. The settlement of the vets' Agent Orange lawsuit against private companies is proving pitifully inadequate, and distribution of any money is still being held up in the courts, four years after the $180 million fund was established. And in the absence of conclusive evidence that soldiers were harmed by Agent Orange, the Veterans Administration refuses to treat most vets whose ailments may be linked to exposure. It would not be hard to design a program that gave gravely ill men the benefit of the doubt. As long as these and other needs go unmet, the word "healing" has something of a hollow sound.

In another realm there has been little healing at all. The U.S. and Vietnam have no formal diplomatic relations. Psychologically, the two countries remain at war. The fault lies first with Vietnam: In 1977, when President Carter was disposed to resume ties, Hanoi's negotiators miscalculated. They publicly produced a letter that Nixon sent them at the time of the Paris Peace Accords, promising $4.75 billion in aid. Nixon had no authority to make such a promise, and after the fall of Saigon it was a political impossibility. The demand for dollars outraged Congress. The talks soon broke off. By the time the Vietnamese understood their error, it was too late. Boat people were leaving by the hundreds of thousands, Vietnam was about to invade Cambodia, and the U.S. was cozying up to China, Vietnam's oldest and newest enemy. A ten-year freeze ensued that only recently shows signs of thawing. But both sides remain prickly, and the issue, as always, is complicated by superpower rivalries. Washington insists that Vietnam vacate Cambodia, but meanwhile supports the guerrilla armies keeping the Vietnamese pinned down—including the Khmer Rouge, who murdered perhaps 2 million Cambodians. One can only conclude that the U.S. is happy to see a Soviet ally caught in its own quagmire, and that a formula could be found if there was a will to do so. Diplomatic ties would nudge along the healing process by marking a final end to the war. Vietnam and the U.S. could explore a new relationship. And a rapprochement would make it easier for vets to visit the battlefields of long ago, helping to quiet private demons.

Still, in all the talk of healing, there is something worrisome—for what, exactly, does "healing the wounds" mean? Is it actually a code phrase for forgetting, for painting history in prettier colors? At the marches and parades, as speakers praise "our boys who made the ultimate sacrifice," there is often the sense that Vietnam is being turned into a solid, patriotic rallying point like World War I or II—that the sting is being removed, that a false unity is being constructed. Certainly the men and women who served in Vietnam are due an apology and a warm welcome back into the fold. But they are due something else: an honest recollection of what they saw and did. If healing means, as some would have it, that the U.S. should "leave Vietnam behind" and "regain its confidence," then we are not listening to the people who were there. Take Harry Behret, who served his tour as an army meteorologist. "The only thing I got out of it," he says, "is that my five-year-old son ain't gonna do what I did. I think there's been a Behret in every fuckin' war in this country's history, but there ain't gonna be no more Behrets in no more wars." The bitterness he tasted in-country also infused the debate at home. Those wounds have not healed, will not heal, and should not heal. As long as the memory of Vietnam stays fresh, America may think carefully— very carefully—before stumbling again onto strange ground.

AN EPIPHANY

CAREY WEATHERFORD

He was an Army Signal Corps technician in Qui Nhon. He is also the first person I interviewed for this book. I liked this story.

We called the Vietnamese police the White Mice. They wore gray trousers and white shirts and gray hats like bus drivers, and they carried .38 Specials. They were civilian police, but they would mix it up with somebody once in a while. They were corrupt as hell, always on the take, forever busting people. They were particularly after American civilians living with Vietnamese women. They would come by and threaten to make life miserable for these men, and would take payoffs.

One night I was on guard. I was up in a tower. I had a pair of binoculars. All of a sudden a couple of White Mice came down the road on a Honda. There was a little blue Renault sedan parked alongside the road. They jumped off and jumped into the car. Two other guys jumped out and ran off down the road. One of the cops took a couple of shots at them with his pistol. I had an M-60 machine gun up in the tower, and I threw a shell in it and got ready for whatever the hell was about to happen. But he just shot at these guys twice, both guys got away, and the White Mice got back on the Honda and drove off in the other direction.

I never did find out what went on. But the thing that struck me was that they didn't jump on their motorbike and take off after these guys. They just took two shots at 'em, got on the bike, and rode off. What the hell kind of sense does that make? But I didn't speak the language, so I wasn't about to ask any questions. It was their country, so what the hell.

BOOK ONE

DRAGON'S TEETH

CHRONOLOGY
1940–1965

<u>1940</u>

September: Japanese armies conquer Indochina but leave a Vichy-ite French administration in place.

<u>1945</u>

March 9: The Japanese oust the French government in Indochina and assume direct power

July 16: The OSS "Deer" team parachutes into the jungles of northern Vietnam to work with Ho Chi Minh and the Viet Minh.

August 6: The United States drops an atomic bomb on Hiroshima.

August 15: Japan surrenders. Ho's men rush to occupy Hanoi. The Viet Minh also move to take power in Saigon.

August 17: De Gaulle appoints Vice Admiral Georges Thierry d'Argenlieu high commissioner for Indochina.

September 2: Ho declares Vietnam an independent nation. No other countries recognize his regime.

September 13: British troops land in Saigon to disarm the Japanese. General Douglas Gracey, ignoring his orders, soon allows the French to take control of the city. After some fighting, the Viet Minh withdraw from Saigon in October.

September: 200,000 Nationalist Chinese troops under the command of General Lu Han occupy northern Indochina, pursuant to Allied agreements. Months of political maneuvering between the Viet Minh, the French, and the Chinese ensue.

1946

February 28: The Chinese agree to withdraw from Indochina in return for the French giving up concessions in China.

March 6: Ho makes a deal with a French official, Jean Sainteny: Vietnam will become an independent country within the French Union, but 25,000 French troops will occupy it for five years. A referendum will be conducted in southern Vietnam to determine its status. But the accord is never put into practice.

March 18: French troops occupy Hanoi.

June 1: Contrary to the terms of the March 6 agreement, d'Argenlieu proclaims a Republic of Cochin China in southern Vietnam.

July 6–September 10: Ho attends Fontainebleau Conference in France to discuss terms of Vietnamese independence. The conference is a failure.

September 14: Ho signs *modus vivendi* agreement with French Minister of Overseas Territories Marius Moutet.

November 20: French ships shell Haiphong.

December 19: War breaks out in Hanoi.

1947–1948

The war smolders as Ho continues to seek a negotiated solution and the French try to persuade Emperor Bao Dai to head the government of a nominally independent Vietnam.

1949

March 8: Bao Dai signs the Elysée Agreement, under which Vietnam becomes an associated state of the French Union. However, the French maintain control over every important governmental function.

October 1: The Communists triumph in China.

<u>1950</u>

January 18: The People's Republic of China recognizes Ho Chi Minh's government, the Democratic Republic of Vietnam.

January 30: The Soviet Union recognizes the DRV.

February 4: The U.S. recognizes Bao Dai's government, the Republic of Vietnam.

February: The Viet Minh attack the French border stronghold of Lao Cai.

June 26: North Korea invades South Korea.

September: The first contingent of the U.S. Military Assistance Advisory Group (MAAG), Indochina, arrives in Saigon.

September–October: The Viet Minh capture a series of French forts in northern Vietnam, gaining control over the border region.

December 7: General Jean de Lattre de Tassigny is named High Commissioner and commander of the French Expeditionary Corps.

<u>1951</u>

January–May: General Vo Nguyen Giap, the Viet Minh military commander, launches three major offensives against the French in the Red River valley. The Viet Minh are decisively beaten, and for two years the war is a stalemate.

<u>1952</u>

January 11: De Lattre dies of cancer.

July: The U.S. upgrades its diplomatic representation in Saigon from a legation to an embassy, with Donald Heath as ambassador.

<u>1953</u>

April: The Viet Minh mount successful attacks in Laos.

May 28: General Henri Navarre takes over from General Raoul Salan as head of the French armies in Indochina.

July 27: An armistice is signed ending the Korean War, which allows China and the Soviet Union to boost military aid to Ho Chi Minh.

November: The French occupy Dien Bien Phu. The Viet Minh soon besiege the base.

1954

March 13: After long preparation, Giap begins the final Viet Minh assault on Dien Bien Phu.

May 7: The French surrender at Dien Bien Phu. On the next day, the Geneva Conference on Indochina's status begins.

July 7: Bao Dai names Ngo Dinh Diem premier of South Vietnam.

July 21: The Geneva Accords are signed after a deal between France and Ho Chi Minh is brokered by Chou En-lai. Vietnam is to be partitioned at the 17th Parallel until elections to unify the country in 1956. The South Vietnamese and U.S. representatives do not sign the accords, though the U.S. says it will abide by them.

September–October: Under the slogan "God has gone South," 850,000 North Vietnamese emigrate to South Vietnam; 80,000 southerners move to the North.

October 9: Viet Minh troops enter Hanoi.

1955

March–May: Diem defeats the Binh Xuyen gangsters in Saigon and consolidates his power.

October 23: Diem stages a referendum and reports that 98.2 percent of South Vietnamese voters favor the deposition of Bao Dai and the creation of the Republic of Vietnam. On October 26 Diem formally takes office as President. He also announces that he will not hold the elections called for by the Geneva Accords to unify the country.

December: Sweeping land reform begins in North Vietnam; thousands killed.

1956

Diem initiates campaign of repression against former Viet Minh cadre and sympathizers.

1957

Hanoi decides to renew guerrilla warfare in the South; campaign of sabotage and assassinations begins.

1959

July 8: Two American military advisers are killed by guerrillas in a raid at Bien Hoa.

1960

May 5: The U.S. announces that its Military Assistance Advisory Group will grow from 327 men to 685.

November 8: John F. Kennedy wins U.S. presidential election.

November 11: Diem defeats an attempted coup by ARVN units.

December 20: Hanoi announces the formation of the National Liberation Front.

1961

October: Walt Rostow, a State Department official, and General Maxwell Taylor visit Vietnam and recommend the introduction of American combat troops. Instead, Kennedy sends more advisers and aid. By year's end, the U.S. has 3,200 military men in Vietnam. Diem steadily builds up his army.

During the year, Viet Cong guerrillas assassinate some 4,000 low-ranking South Vietnamese officials.

1962

February 6: The Military Assistance Advisory Group is replaced by the Military Assistance Command, Vietnam (MACV).

February 27: Diem escapes an assassination attempt by two South Vietnamese pilots who bomb the presidential palace.

The strategic hamlet program, designed to group peasants in villages fortified against the Viet Cong, begins. It soon proves to be more show than substance.

1963

May 8: South Vietnamese police fire into a crowd of Buddhists demonstrating against Diem in Hué, setting off a powerful protest movement.

June 11: A Buddhist monk immolates himself; others follow.

June: South Vietnamese generals accelerate their plotting against Diem, with the encouragement of some American officials.

November 1: The generals depose Diem and murder him and his brother the following day.

November 22: John F. Kennedy is assassinated.

U.S. military advisers in Vietnam now number 16,500.

1964

January 30: Another coup in Saigon; General Nguyen Khanh takes power. The period of the "revolving-door governments" begins.

August 2: North Vietnamese gunboats, replying to South Vietnamese raids on ports, attack the U.S. destroyer *Maddox* in the Gulf of Tonkin.

August 4: The *Maddox* reports a possible second attack. Later inquiries show that it probably never occurred. U.S. jets bomb North Vietnam for the first time.

August 7: Congress approves the Tonkin Gulf resolution, which gives President Johnson virtual carte blanche to conduct war in Southeast Asia.

August–September: The military junta in Saigon undergoes a crisis, and a triumvirate of generals, led by Khanh, assumes control.

November 3: Lyndon Johnson defeats Barry Goldwater in U.S. presidential election.

December: The Viet Cong launch a series of attacks that decimate some fifteen ARVN battalions over a period of six months. South Vietnam appears to be facing collapse. During the year, some 10,000 regular North Vietnamese Army troops infiltrate the South.

1965

February 7: The Viet Cong attack a U.S. base at Pleiku, killing eight Americans and wounding more than 100. Johnson orders retaliatory air raids against North Vietnam.

March 2: Johnson initiates Operation Rolling Thunder, the sustained bombing of the North. It continues until November 1968.

1

"WELCOME TO OUR AMERICAN FRIENDS"

It began in a jungle clearing in July 1945. Six parachutists—three Americans, one Frenchman, and two Vietnamese—landed near the village of Kim Lung, in the remote mountains of northern Indochina. The team's leader, Major Allison Thomas of the OSS, made a short speech. And he met a tiny, sickly man named C. M. Hoo—an alias for the alias by which the world came to know him: Ho Chi Minh.

Since then, the tall tales and half-truths about the beginning have multiplied. Did Americans train a Viet Minh army that later took over Hanoi and beat the French? Did Ho bamboozle the OSS into backing him, then use that support to grab control of the nationalist movement? Did the U.S. tragically miss the chance in 1945 to help Indochina claim its independence and avert thirty years of war?

The cliché answer to the last question is yes. After Ho marched into Hanoi in August, and during the nearly eighteen months of his edgy negotiations with the French—who desperately wanted their colony back—Washington could have pushed hard for Paris to set a timetable and, finally, let go. Instead, the French seized power in Saigon and began moving troops into the north, many of them on American ships. In November 1946, French gunboats in Haiphong harbor shelled the city. A month later, fighting broke out in Hanoi, and Ho's men fled to the jungle. Throughout, the U.S. either protested mildly or connived in the French action.

But did Washington really have any choice? Most Americans in the government who cared about Indochina favored its independence. President Roosevelt himself did not want to see France return. But Roosevelt died, and Truman faced serious troubles in Europe. General de Gaulle was proving to be a prickly ally, if he was an ally at all. The Soviets were expanding. It was no time to be flirting with a Vietnamese rebel of highly suspicious background, no matter how many letters he sent to Washington proclaiming his admiration and pleading for help.

Besides, Indochina was a small, backward country—and very far away.

MAJOR ALLISON THOMAS

I parachuted into a tree.

It was a forested area, bamboo forest on a mountainside, with a rice paddy down at the base. I went out of the plane first. We were all supposed to land in this paddy area, a nice soft landing. But I had a problem on the way down. I could see this tree coming up at me, and I was taught by the parachute specialists at Poseh that if I pulled on the front cords I could get some distance and go forward. I pulled frantically on those cords, and I missed the top of the tree, but I got snagged on a far branch and hung there. It turned out to be the sacred tree of Kim Lung village.

There I was, dangling about thirty or forty feet above the ground. I didn't have the vaguest idea how to get down, so I waited for somebody to help me. Three Vietnamese started to climb up the tree to cut me loose. Before they got up there, Zeilski came along. He says, "All you gotta do, Major, is pull out your reserve chute." We had a reserve chute on our chests. I pulled that out, took my knife blade from my boot, and cut myself free from the big chute. The reserve was fastened to the main one, so I just slid down the reserve chute and got on the ground, thanks to Zeilski.

There were maybe 200 guerrillas there, lined up. They had antique weapons, old French weapons and maybe a Bren or a British Sten. I was asked to give a welcome speech. The substance of it was, "Well, we're all together, fighting the war against the Japanese." I was either speaking in English or French, I'm not sure. An interpreter translated for the troops.

It was very celebratory. Everybody was real excited. We were glad to be on the ground all safe and sound. There was a big bamboo arch that we went through on the way to the hut they had built for us. It said, in English, "Welcome to our American friends." And we had a very fine meal that night. They had some Hanoi beer that had been captured from the Japanese, and they butchered a cow in our honor. We were happy to be there.

I met Ho right away. He welcomed us. Then, the next day, I had quite a conversation with him.

He is a big, white-haired man in his seventies, wearing a jacket and tie and horn-rimmed glasses that give him a scholarly look. His speech has a midwestern cadence. He practices law in the town where he was born: Lansing, Michigan. We talk in his den in the basement. One wall is completely lined with books, mostly on Vietnam, and the room is filled with Vietnamese memorabilia. There are photographs of himself, mustachioed, and several other young Americans lounging about a bamboo hut; peasant tapestries, including one given him by Ho Chi Minh; a Mauser pistol he "liberated."

He was drafted in 1941. After the war began, he joined the OSS. He went to London, then to France with Patton's army. With the war in Europe nearly over, he was sent to China. In the spring of 1945 he arrived in Kunming, where he met then-Captain Archimedes L. A. Patti, who supervised OSS activity in French Indochina. Thomas was placed in command of a team of Americans code-named "Deer." Its mission was to train a guerrilla force and infiltrate Indochina to operate against the Japanese.

About all I knew is that it was called French Indochina. I knew vaguely that it was a French colony and the missionaries came over first, followed by the French soldiers. I knew the French had rubber plantations, and they took the profits out to France. That's about it.

The "Deer" team had seven men. Myself as the leader. René Defourneaux as my assistant, a second lieutenant. A man by the name of Paul Hoagland was our medic. Everybody says he saved Ho Chi Minh's life. I think that's a little exaggerated. There was Aaron Squires, who went along as a photographer and handyman. There was Sergeant Larry Vogt, our weapons man. There was Zeilski, our radio operator. And Henry Prunier, a PFC who had taken some Vietnamese language training.

I guess you could say we were supposed to do three things. First, set up a guerrilla team of fifty to 100 men to attack and interdict the railroad from Hanoi to Lang Son, going up into China. We didn't know what the reason for that was at the time. It turned out that if the Americans didn't use the atomic bomb on Japan, they were going to land forces on the southern coast of China. By blowing up that railroad, we could prevent the Japanese—I think they had several thousand troops in Indochina—from going up into China. But we didn't know anything about the invasion plan.

Second, we were supposed to find targets for our air force—Japanese military bases and depots. And third, send back what intelligence we could.

The question was how to do it. We started out by flying from Kunming to a town called Poseh, which is in southern China, not too far from the border. From there we went to a town real close to the border called Ch'ing-Hsi, where we ran across quite a few Frenchmen. The story on the French is this. When the Japanese entered Indochina in 1940, they took it over but let the French run the civilian administration. But in March of 1945, the Japanese could see the handwriting on the wall. They were afraid the French might start to attack them. So the Japanese swooped down on the French and took over the government completely. Some of the French escaped to China, but many didn't, and those were put in jails.

So here were these Frenchmen in China champing to do something. But they had no money and very few arms. They had some Annamites—we didn't call them Vietnamese. That word was not heard by me or anyone else until much later. The French had trained what they called the Garde Indigène, the local guard, and some of them were loyal.

We tried to make arrangements with the French to have a combined expedition to go into Indochina and attack the Japanese. There was no idea in the beginning of contacting any Vietnamese guerrillas in place. We didn't know they were there. The idea was either to get some Frenchmen and the Annamites who were with them, or to get some Chinese troops to go in.

Well, this turned out to be a worrisome thing. In Poseh I met a French officer named Revol. He said, "Now, wait a minute. We have no business going back there unless we know the Viet Minh are going to cooperate with us." That's the first time I ever heard the words "Viet Minh." I said, "Who are the Viet Minh?" He told me it was a guerrilla force that had been organizing in Tonkin for the last several months. They claimed later they had 3,000 armed men throughout Tonkin.

Then I met another man named Simon Yu. He was working with an independent group that operated a network inside Indochina with Free French civilian agents. He knew a lot about the political situation. He advised me that if we went into Tonkin with any Frenchmen it would be a disaster, that the Viet Minh hated the French, had absolutely no use for them. It would be a plain and unmitigated disaster. Now, bear in mind that we had a small OSS detachment in Poseh. They had a radio. Our messages were sent from the field to Poseh, and from Poseh to Kunming. The Americans in Poseh got real chummy with the French, and of course they couldn't understand why I was opposed to sending all these Frenchmen in. It later turned out that Simon Yu was absolutely right.

At first the idea was to try to walk in across the border. We couldn't find any guides to do it. I kept sending radio messages to Patti, and he'd send messages back. But while we were off in the hinterlands, Patti was in contact with Ho, and Ho said, "Wait, I can help. I offer you my services." So Patti recruited Ho as our agent—to help us, you might say. In turn, Ho was recruiting us, you might say. As a result, an AGAS lieutenant, Dan Phelan, parachuted into Ho's camp about two months before me. He was sent in to help return any American pilots who were shot down. And there was another American there— Frankie Tan, who had been living in Haiphong and who escaped the Japanese. He had walked back into Indochina with Ho from China. The two of them helped coordinate our drop.

Finally I got the word that we would parachute in and work with the Viet Minh. We'd been trying since May to walk in. Now here it was July, two months later, and we were finally going to get some action. I hadn't had any parachute training, so we practiced by putting a rope on a big tree branch and getting up on a balcony, swinging out and dropping. The main thing in parachuting is to be able to land properly—keep your feet together and roll. We practiced dropping and rolling.

I also made the decision to have a French officer named Montfort parachute in with us, along with two of his Annamite soldiers—a man by the name of Phac, and another named Logos, who was half French. The purpose of bringing Montfort was to see whether any Frenchmen would be welcome. The French didn't believe they couldn't go in. They wanted to get in there in the worst way. They wanted the colony back. So they wanted to go with us.

We parachuted in on July 16, 1945. Three of us from the "Deer" team—myself, Prunier, and Zeilski—and Montfort, Phac, and Logos. The French were concerned that Montfort and these other two might be shot at when they were parachuting down if they looked like French soldiers. So they wore American helmets. But we weren't trying to deceive Ho. There's so much literature to the effect that Montfort tried to pose as an American. The only thing we were trying to do was prevent him and Phac and Logos from being killed when they came down from that airplane. Obviously we couldn't fool Ho, because we came in with two Annamite soldiers. Where did they come from, if not from the French army? And Montfort didn't speak any

English. It turned out that some of Ho's guerrillas recognized him, so they knew he was French from the moment he hit the ground. But they would have known anyway, because I would have told them.

The next day, when I had my first talk with Ho, he told me in no uncertain terms that the French were not welcome, and Montfort couldn't stay. Ho said, "The French think we are bandits. But to show you we're not, we will escort Montfort and the others back to the border." He also said that Phac and Logos were welcome to stay and join his group, but he doubted the French army would release them. That was true, the French wouldn't. So they made their way back on foot and rejoined their French outfit in China.

When I parachuted in, I had still never heard of Ho or Giap. All I knew about was the Viet Minh. I got out of the tree, and the first person that spoke to me was Frankie Tan. I just couldn't get over it. This Oriental-looking man walks up and says, "Hi, how are you? We've been expecting you."

Then I met Ho. He was calling himself "C. M. Hoo" at that point. It wasn't until I got to Hanoi that he told me his name was Ho Chi Minh. Much later I found out that was an alias, too.

Physically, Ho was frail. His eyes were piercing. They were his most important feature. Whether that was due to malaria or fever of some kind, I don't know. Extremely piercing eyes. He had the Oriental wispy beard or goatee. Very high forehead. Black hair. And he was quite weak. At one point I saw him being carried in a sedan chair. I don't know what he was suffering from, maybe a host of diseases. Dysentery, malaria, maybe dengue fever. He had walked down from China, and he had been living in the jungle for a while. Later, when our medic came, he gave Ho some sulfa pills and quinine. It may have helped, it may not. Who knows?

We talked about politics, and we talked about our military mission. Ho told me the grievances the people had against the French. He said the French had shot and gassed many political prisoners. They had heavy taxes. They had a monopoly on salt and alcohol, and they forced people to buy opium. There were more prisons than schools. There was no free press. No more than five people could assemble without a permit. A whole litany of things. We were speaking English. Ho wouldn't speak French unless it was absolutely necessary, and his English was very good. The story goes that he spent about three years as a kitchen helper under Escoffier at the Carlton Hotel in London.

It was obvious he was well read and well educated. But bear in mind, I didn't know he was a Communist. I had no idea he spoke Russian, I had no idea he'd been to Russia. I had no idea he was one of the original members of the French Communist Party in 1920. I had no idea he'd been to the Versailles Conference in 1919 and asked Clemenceau and Wilson for freedom for his country. I did feel he was very sincere. He was always soft-spoken. He seemed like a man of iron determination. He knew what he wanted. But he indicated to me and to many others that he wanted to work moderately toward independence. He wanted to work with the French. He needed their help as technicians. He wanted the support of the Americans. He recognized that Vietnam was a very poor country. I think he would have opted for a gradual approach rather than a bloody approach. The reason I feel strongly about that is that he sent a message over our radio. It talks about independence in five to ten years.

Also bear in mind that I wasn't on a political mission. It was purely military. I was a little bit suspicious of Ho, because his troops used the clenched-fist salute. But I talked to Dan Phelan and Frankie Tan about it, and they both felt strongly that he was not a doctrinaire Communist, that he was a true patriot. And there was no evidence that he was under the influence of the Russians. He was his own man. He devised his own strategy. There were no Russians there, and no Russian weapons that I could see. So was he more of a nationalist than a Communist? Well, who knows? All I can say is he was both.

You could see how he could be very impressive to his people, almost like a Gandhi. He didn't dress in fancy clothes. He wore sandals and shorts, maybe a khaki shirt or a white shirt. Very simple, almost ascetic. But how could he impress our group too much? He was a very thin man with no pretense, nothing elegant about him. He didn't have the looks of a Franklin Roosevelt or a de Gaulle or a Reagan. Nothing impressive about the guy physically. There was an inner confidence, an inner force that you could feel. But still, here were a few guerrillas in ragged outfits with poor weapons, and here's a frail little old guy, y'know. . . .

On the military side, he said the Viet Minh had about 3,000 guerrillas under arms. He would help us but not the French, and he wouldn't help us if any French were with us. He said he'd pick out 100 men so we could train them, and he suggested a different target. He said the road and railroad line that the OSS picked out had been frequently bombed by the American Air Force. The Japanese were strong in that area, so he proposed a different road that we could start with.

I was friendly with him, and why shouldn't I be? After all, we were both there for the same purpose, fighting the Japanese, and he was responsible for our safety. Everybody keeps telling me, "Well, when you found out he was a Communist"—but that wasn't my job, to find out whether he was a Communist or not. We were fighting a common enemy.

I was there for about two weeks before the rest of my team came in. I took some reconnaissance trips. The villages seemed to be all in Ho's corner. Finally the team got there and we started the training. We showed them how to use grenades and mortars and bazookas. But the main training was learning how to shoot a rifle. The M-1 was an automatic rifle, and the American carbine is different from a French rifle. The Viet Minh troops were very young, with very little training.

That's another myth I'd like to explode. Some writers have said we furnished hundreds of machine guns to the Viet Minh. It's just not so, at least as far as the "Deer" mission is concerned. And I don't know of any other OSS mission that amounted to anything. It was all small arms—carbines, M-1s, a couple of mortars, a couple of bazookas, and hand grenades. There might have been one or two light machine guns, but not hundreds. It was a very small quantity of arms, parachuted to us in containers.

Another thing people keep saying to me: You trained these people in tactics, and as a result they became leaders of the Vietnamese army that beat us. Well, that's a bunch of baloney, too. We didn't start training until we had the weapons there. It probably took a couple of parachute drops. You can't put many weapons in a parachute container, I'll tell you. So we didn't really start until about the first or second week in August. We trained for a week, and then we heard over the radio: the atomic bomb. The Japanese surrendered on August 15, and we moved out on August 16. So how could we train somebody to win the war in a week? It's ridiculous on the face of it.

People also say that as a result of our support, Ho came to power. I don't believe that for a minute. I'm sure Ho tried to use the fact that the Americans gave him some equipment. He led many Vietnamese to believe that we were allies. But there were lots of reasons why Ho came to power, and it wasn't because we gave a few arms for 100 men or less. One reason was that the Japanese surrendered, and when Ho marched into Hanoi, they offered no resistance. The French had gone. And Ho was very astute. He saw there was a power vacuum. He was going to get into Hanoi just as fast as he could. It was a bold move on his part. This was the opportunity he had been waiting for all his life, and he was going to take advantage of it.

On August 16 we organized our team together, and Giap led us and his men out of the camp at Kim Lung. He took us over the mountain paths and down the slippery slopes to Thai Nguyen. It took three or four days. In the little villages we'd go through, and especially in Thai Nguyen, there were Viet Minh flags all over. Those flags didn't just appear in a minute. They had to be made sometime and hidden away. So Ho was pretty well established already. The Communist Party had been working there for years. Look how strong it was in Saigon, hundreds of miles to the south. The Viet Minh practically took over Saigon, and Ho wasn't even there. If the British hadn't come in and released the French who were in jails, I think Saigon would have fallen right then.

That walk through the mountains was when I was closest to Giap. I was about thirty at the time, and he was maybe three years older. At one point he told me that his wife and his sister-in-law had both died in French prisons. He had a very strong feeling against the French. He was an intense man, no question about it. The French called him a snow-covered volcano. He was always in control of himself, and obviously very bright and well educated. His troops looked up to him. I liked him.

When we got to Thai Nguyen, Giap asked the Japanese garrison to surrender. They were in a regular old French fort, and they weren't about to surrender right away. There was quite a firefight. I don't know if anybody was killed, but I remember there was a lot of noise for about ten or fifteen minutes, and sporadic fire for a while afterward. Giap had given a Japanese woman a note to deliver to the garrison in the fort. She disappeared over the wall and was never heard from again. Giap made another try to tell the Japanese that the war was over and there wasn't any point in having more bloodshed. Finally, after four or five days, everything was peaceful. The Japanese apparently discovered that what we were saying was true. The war was over, and Japan had surrendered. So a truce was arranged and they were allowed to walk into town. They looked at us, and we looked at them. . . . And neither of us said a word.

Patti ordered our team to stay in town until it was wise for us to go to Hanoi. He sent me a message that said, in effect: "You better stay out of the city, we want to be neutral." I was quite put out about that. I felt, Why can't we take some surrenders? We had risked our lives, and we wanted to take surrenders. But we cooled our heels for about two weeks in Thai Nguyen. He was probably right. It had all been arranged at the Potsdam Conference: The Chinese would come in and take over to the 16th Parallel, and the British south of that.

I didn't get to Hanoi until September 9, so I missed Ho's declaration of independence. We spent a week waiting for transport out. Just before I left on September 16, I was invited to a private dinner. It was Ho and Giap and myself. I can't remember much of what was said. But one thing I remember very clearly. I asked Ho point-blank if he was a Communist. He told me, "Yes. But we can still be friends, can't we?"

KENNETH LANDON

A woodsy street on the outskirts of Washington, D.C., with large old houses on a hill overlooking a ravine. Inside, the reception is gracious, befitting a diplomatic household: I am ushered to a study and offered coffee and cookies. He is eighty-two, a small man with a sharp eye and a hearty laugh, proud of his accomplishments and his acquaintance with many of the major figures of his day. Ten years as a missionary in Siam, beginning in 1927, made him an expert on that part of the world. So in 1941, with the U.S. on the verge of war, he got a call from "a Colonel Donovan. He wanted me to come right away to Washington and make a report to the President on the Japanese in Indochina. Which I did.

"You'll be amused to know that the first day I was in Washington to work with Donovan, August third of 1941, I walked into this office in the Triangle Building and threw the door back and hit something. I looked and there was this tall, bald-headed man, saying 'Good morning, sir. My father sent me over to see if I could be of some help to you. I'm James Roosevelt.' I said I'd like to know what the U.S. government knows about Southeast Asia. So he took me in one of these big black limousines to meet a Major Pettigrew. The major was told by James Roosevelt that the President would like him to reveal his Southeast Asia files to me. They had file cabinets marked Southeast Asia, but when we opened them, there was only one folder. I looked in, and there were four articles from Asia magazine—all written by me. I asked the major, 'Suppose you wanted to know something. What would you do?' 'Oh,' he said, 'we'd ask our allies.' "

By the end of the war he was working for the State Department, and in early 1946 he was sent to "find out what was going on in Southeast Asia. I spent about four months and met all the top brass everywhere. I was in a beautiful position. I had a book of travel orders, and I was the authorizing officer. I could order myself to go hither and yon—signed, Kenneth Landon."

I went over to Saigon and met with Admiral d'Argenlieu and his beautiful mistress. He had been a monk, and General de Gaulle had hauled him out of the monastery to make him high commissioner of the Indochina states. He decided that if he was going in for things of the flesh, he'd go the whole way, so he brought Mme. Galsworthy. The French do this sort of thing right.

D'Argenlieu's line was that they wanted American support to get themselves reestablished. They knew that our policy was not to help any colonial powers take back their colonies. But the State Department by that time was preoccupied with the French in France and didn't want to buck them in Indochina. It was a period of searching things out. The aid we were giving to France, we knew they were putting it in their left pocket and taking it out of their right pocket to use in Indochina. Still, our policy was firm—not to help any colonial power return. I know because I drafted it. But d'Argenlieu pointed out that the war was over and it was high time we got back to reality. We were helping the French in France—why didn't we see that France was an empire, and this was part of the empire?

I went to Thailand for a while, and then I got instructions from the department to see if I could head up to Hanoi. So I made another trip to Saigon and talked to the admiral. D'Argenlieu said that one of his generals, General Salan, was going up to Hanoi the next day, and I could ride in his plane if I chose to. I said I'd be delighted. An aide of General Salan told me I should be at the airport at seven in the morning. The airport was well out of Saigon. Salan was very crude—he offered me no way to get out there. So I bribed a Vietnamese with a dilapidated car to take me. I got there at six-thirty, and I was the only person at the airport. Hadn't had a cup of coffee or anything to eat. I was still the only person there at ten. The plane sat there, an old C-47 with bucket seats. All of a sudden, Salan turns up with his entourage. He looks at me, nods his head, climbs in. I hauled my trunk out and piled it in. They revved up the engine by going down the runway—that's why we got to calling it Air Chance. If the engine was warm by the end of the runway, you took off.

We made a stop in Laos. I was left at the plane while they all went off and had lunch. Salan was most unfriendly. He was a tough guy, and to hell with any Americans. Of course, the French were very suspicious of us. We were dangerous people. But in Salan's case it was just because he was a son of a bitch. We didn't get to Hanoi until about four. Still nothing to eat or drink. The general gets off with his crowd. He's met by an entourage of cars. They all pile in and go off. I'm left at the airport, miles from Hanoi, on the wrong side of the river.

I hauled my little steel trunk off to the aerodrome, about 100 or 200 yards away. And I smelled something cooking. I went around the corner of the building, and there was a Chinese GI squatting over a charcoal brazier, cooking his supper. I sat down right close to him. I said in Chinese, "Brother, I'm starving to death. Will you sell me some of your stew as a brother?" He seemed completely unsurprised that I could speak Chinese. He said, "This is all the stew I have. This is my stew." I said, "There's a lot of it there, and you wouldn't starve to death if you shared it. I'd be happy to pay you well." He wasn't interested in the money. He said, "No, and anyway, I have only one bowl and one pair of chopsticks." I said, "Brothers don't need more than one pair of chopsticks." He looked at me, laughed, poured the stew into this big bowl, and scooped some into his mouth. Then he handed the bowl over to me. I took his chopsticks and ate. Back and forth, right to the end. Oh, God, it saved my life. I thanked him and thanked him. He was amused.

Then I said, "Can you get me into town?" He said, "Well, we'll see." We went out to the edge of the road, and after a little while along comes this great big lorry with about thirty or forty soldiers standing up in the back. There were even people hanging on top of the hood. He flagged 'em down and said he had this redhead who wanted to go into town, and would they take me. They fumbled around and finally got another guy up on the cab top and hauled me in, standing on my trunk and looming over all these black heads. We bucketed into Hanoi. The bridge had been bombed out—and I had selected it as a target when I was working for the Board of Economic Warfare. I looked it over and thought we did a pretty good job.

They dumped me in front of the Hotel Metropole. There were no Americans in Hanoi except a graves mission looking for the bodies of lost American flyers. I slept on the floor of the hotel under a mosquito net I had in my trunk.

The next morning I cleaned up and called on Ho Chi Minh. He was right across the street in the high commissioner's palace. I sent in my card, and we sat down and talked. He was quite pleased, delighted even. I was the first State Department officer he had ever talked with. He thought maybe I was the answer to his prayers. Here I was, a guy who could speak Chinese and Thai. We could have talked in Chinese, but he spoke flawless English, radio English, without any accent. Incredible English. I asked him if he spoke Thai and he denied it. But I knew he was lying, because he went to Siam the same year I did. He posed as a priest. Shaved his head, put on a yellow robe, and lived in the hills of northeast Thailand, where he later set up Communist camps. He had gone there as the roving ambassador of the Comintern in 1927.

At our first meeting, he asked how long I was going to stay. I said, "Well, I'm just looking around to see what's going on and how General Lu Han* is handling the surrender of the Japanese." I was supposed to discuss that with Lu Han, which is another reason I'd been sent. And I was looking into opening up a consulate. So I told Ho I was going back on the next plane, in a week. He said, "Why don't you stay longer?" I said, "Well, if you wish." But I said I had no place to stay. The Hotel Metropole was jammed up because the Chinese were occupying it. They were also going around town buying up everything that glittered with phony Vietnamese money printed in Shanghai.

Ho said, "I'll fix it up." He put me in the same quarters with the graves mission boys. All of them had mistresses, one or two each. I moved into this big villa, and it was highly amusing, because the boys were gone all day in the jungle and I had a whole houseful of women. They took a great interest in me until they saw I had no interest in them.

Ho also provided me with a little car and a chauffeur. The car was about as wide as this chair and as long as two chairs back to back. A one-seater, really. You couldn't get two in the backseat. The chauffeur spoke no French, nothing but Vietnamese. I think Ho did that deliberately to see how ingenious I was. So I got a map of Hanoi from one of the mistresses. I'd sit right behind the driver and point out where I wanted to go. I got along beautifully.

For the ten days I was there, I had one meal a day with Ho Chi Minh. Sometimes two meals. He was a very able man, very widely read. I had taught one course in political philosophy, and I thought I had covered the waterfront fairly well. But this was a man who had far out-read and out-thought me. And he was smart. He had picked up all the fluff from the French Revolution and French democracy and the American Revolution and the American Constitution. He quoted them all, thinking that he'd please everybody. He handed me the same line he'd given Patti, that he wasn't a Communist, that he was really a socialist at heart. That he'd been branded a Communist, but he wasn't really. I knew he had been an ambassador for the Comintern, and that he was a familiar in Moscow. So I didn't believe he was just a nationalist, because the Communists don't work that way. But I just listened. I was there to listen. You don't tell a guy you think he's lying when you're trying to find out what he thinks. You let him think he's convinced you.

*Lu Han: Nationalist Chinese general who commanded the Allied Occupation Force for Indochina, assigned to accept the Japanese surrender north of the 16th Parallel.

One day a delegation from the American-Vietnamese Friendship Society called on me. I think the organization had just been set up. It was led by a man who told me his name. I was quite impressed by him personally. We talked for a while. I asked him if he would write his name in my little book that I carried with me so I'd have the spelling correct. So he wrote the name of the society and his name: Le Duan.* But oh, no, he wasn't a Communist. Oh, no, Ho wasn't a Communist. If they dabbled with Communism, it was just for nationalist reasons.

Ho and I talked about Plato, Locke, democracy, fascism, and whatnot. His point was that he had gone through every political philosophy to find one that would enable him to organize his society and throw the French out. He knew the French were never going to yield self-government and independence just to be nice, because they weren't nice. So he had studied and examined. The democratic approach wouldn't work against the French, because he'd never get the opportunity for a vote. He saw the trend in India with Gandhi, but he didn't think that approach would work either, because the French weren't British. The British had a conscience. The French didn't.

So he had tried this, that, and the other. He talked about Communism at length. But he always said, "We're accused of being Communists, and we may use Communist concepts to organize our people. But our aim is strictly national."

His line at this point was that the French would be perfectly willing to let him dominate the north and the central area—in other words, Tonkin and Annam—if he would agree to their dominating the south, Cochin China. The French also wanted to be responsible for Laos and Cambodia, and for all of Indochina in military matters and foreign affairs, that sort of deal. Of course, Ho knew that meant no kind of deal for him. He was not willing to settle for less than extension of his political influence over Cochin China. That was the gut issue: the south. Cochin China was the most profitable end of Vietnam. The French felt that once Ho and the Viet Minh got entrenched there, that would be the end.

My reaction to all this was simple: that he was a good Communist. I was very much against Communist concepts personally. And I had no doubt that if he dominated the political scene it would be a Communist country. I wouldn't be happy about that. But he was the only person of really outstanding ability I met there, and I met 'em all: Le Duan, Pham Van Dong, Giap, the whole column. Ho stood out. A

*Le Duan: Lifelong revolutionary who succeeded Ho Chi Minh as the most powerful figure in North Vietnam.

shrewd guy with a gentle eye that covered an absolutely ruthless determination. I knew that as early as the 1930s his goal was to replace the French and be in control of all the Indochina states, including Laos and Cambodia. That was the goal from the founding of the Viet Minh. But his line was that the three states would become independent and self-governing.

As for the French, I thought they were a nasty bunch of people. D'Argenlieu was a man of culture, but I didn't think the others were. A mean-spirited people. They talked about *gloire* and *honneur*—how the French *honneur* was at stake here. They respected Ho's ability and his dedication, but they were doing everything they could to frustrate and destroy him. They would have killed him if they could. But Ho was well protected. He had all these troops, very smartly dressed troops. My God, they were well dressed. Blue shirts and shorts, blue kepis, knee-high blue socks and black shoes. And well armed. At every big intersection in Hanoi, you had one corner sandbagged with Ho's forces and the other sandbagged with Lu Han's men.

Of course, I didn't think the French should get back Indochina. But I also knew that was a losing position under the American government in 1946. It was perfectly obvious that as we strengthened the French in Europe, they were using those resources to strengthen themselves in Indochina. And the European Office boys were 100 percent for it. They couldn't conceive of the European powers not regaining their own. I've always believed that in diplomacy, your policy is what's possible. I've never believed in hopeless policy. If you're not going to get anyplace, why beat your head?

But I didn't say anything like that to Ho. My job was to find out what he thought and wanted and what he hoped to do. I wasn't in a position to offer him anything. I had no goodies.

Before I left, Ho gave me letters to President Truman and the secretary of state, the usual kind of guff that he handed to everybody. I brought them back and did what you'd expect me to do: I filed them away. Because our government was just not interested.

ABBOT LOW MOFFAT

He was born in 1901 into an old New York State family. From 1944 to 1947, he was Kenneth Landon's boss in the Division of South-East Asian Affairs of the State Department. Now he is retired after a long career spent mostly in foreign countries with the World Bank and various entities of the government. We talk in his office on the second floor of a big house near Princeton. The house is full of light, impeccably clean and ordered, and decorated with Orientalia: screens, scrolls, vases. He is a man of medium height and build with a kindly, patrician face and white hair, dressed in a tweed sportcoat, tie, and slacks. He moves carefully because he was recently given two artificial knees after arthritis made it nearly impossible for him to get around.

I became head of the Southeast Asia division on July 1, 1944. At the time, Siam was the most active problem. We had our forces in there at the end of the war, and the division was heavily involved in negotiating the peace treaty. But we were also following Indonesia and Indochina. In both places the war had brought a terrific upheaval. The people had seen the white European colonialists thrown out by the Japanese. The economies had been all switched around. Now the Japanese were leaving, and of course all this added to the turmoil of nationalism

Roosevelt wanted to keep the French away from Indochina. He had a strong feeling that they had done a wretched job there, which I think is true. He wanted some sort of international trusteeship; he once noted on a memo, "F.I.C. [French Indochina] under trusteeship." But he had no way of implementing it. And the European division was taking the other point of view, that we must back the French in whatever they wanted.

In my case, I never could see that colonialism has any justification in the modern world. I mean the exploitation of another people. I was a Republican in those days, but a fairly liberal Republican. I could see that the nationalist movements were spreading, spreading, spreading. In the case of Indochina I was really concerned that if the French didn't recognize the problem, we were all going to be in trouble. No, that's too strong, because I didn't think the United States would get involved. Nor did I feel that we could turn around and support the nationalist movement and break with France. But I did think the French were being very short-sighted. They wouldn't recognize what was coming. They thought they were right back where they were before the war, so they could just take over. It was tragic, and what was even more tragic was that they had just been released from the heel of the conqueror, and here they were wanting to put their heel right down.

None of us were out to take any colonies away from the French. But I thought if they didn't make any concessions, in the long run they would suffer very badly. Whereas if they could settle this thing, they could keep a lot of their influence. If they gave the Vietnamese some powers and the trappings of self-government, they still had the advantage of the language ties and many years of contact. It's a little bit what de Gaulle did later on in West Africa. But at that time he just didn't see it. They all wanted to hold this "jewel." Actually it was an awful liability for the French except for the Banque de l'Indochine. Everybody else in France rather suffered, because you had to have your big navy, your army, and so on.

What I wanted was for us to keep putting pressure on the French to play honestly with Ho, who was a terrific father figure over there, and to stick to the agreements they made with him. I think I was considered very much of a radical by the European desk. One day I was talking to Jim Bonbright, the French desk man, and I kept saying that fighting was going to break out in Indochina, really serious war. I thought we should be figuring out our policy on it. He looked up and said, "Why, you really mean it. I thought you were just being an ideologue." And another very senior man, I remember him saying one day, "If I'd had my way we'd have sent in American troops and put the French back in power."

Then Roosevelt died and Truman came in. Well, Jimmy Dunn was head of the Western Europe Office. He drew up a paper on Indochina policy and sent it over to us. He didn't propose even to tell Truman anything about what Roosevelt's policy had been or why. The paper merely said the Western Europe Office thought the time had come to give military aid to the French. A complete reversal, without even letting the President have the background. I thought that was a little improper. So we sent an opposite memorandum. No action was taken for weeks. Finally, at a policy committee meeting—which starts at the level above me, I was only a division chief—Joe Grew* said, "Now, we have two papers on Indochina. Frankly, I've read them both, and I agree with the Far Eastern paper." Bill Phillips was representing Jimmy Dunn, and Bill had Far Eastern experience. He said, "Well, I've read them both and frankly I agree with the Far Eastern paper." Which was very shocking for the European boys, I think. So Joe said, "We've got to have one paper that everybody can agree on. You can't have two papers. Get this redrawn."

Bill appointed Sam Reber from the Western Europe Office and me from the Far Eastern Office. Sam and I sat down and argued this thing through to get a single policy paper. He felt he had given up a great deal, and I felt I had given up a great deal. We therefore probably had a fairly good compromise. And Jimmy Dunn just scrapped it. Nothing doing.

*Under secretary of State, 1944–1945.

So there was no policy paper and no policy when I went out there in December of 1946. I wanted to go see my whole area, get to know the people I was dealing with. First I got to Saigon, where there was no atmosphere of crisis. But as I went around, I was impressed with the basic hatred for the French. I felt that by sheer military force, they might be able to hold the cities, but they could never hold that country. There would be constant guerrilla war from then on. Oddly enough, I was also impressed by the number of really competent and dedicated French officials I met. Four or five really top-notch people, very interested in the country, very fond of the Vietnamese. I gathered there were plenty of the other kind, too, but I didn't happen to run into them.

Then I went up to Hanoi. I spent several days there. This was about two weeks after the French had shelled Haiphong harbor. Ho Chi Minh was still in control of Hanoi, but the French were itching to take over. I started to meet Vietnamese for the first time, and they were terribly tense over the Haiphong business. They had a feeling of frustration because whenever they had something agreed upon, the French would run out on it. Of course, I think that worked both ways. The Vietnamese weren't all that pure. It wasn't simply the pure rising up against the wicked.

You knew something was going to happen soon. Every night a lot of people would leave the city, afraid that fighting would break out. In the morning the streets would be torn up with ditches. I don't know if they were supposed to be trenches or what, but they were making the streets less and less passable. And you'd hear sporadic firing nearly all night. The general consensus was that the fighting would start in a week or so.

There was a cocktail party for me at the American consul's house. I was given to understand that this was the first time since the massacre in Haiphong that the French and Vietnamese had mingled. The American consulate was neutral territory. Most of them hadn't seen one another for a couple of weeks. And they were all so glad to see one another again. There was quite a warm personal feeling among a lot of these people. I remember talking to a French general when Giap came up. Their French got too fast for me. I couldn't follow it, so I stepped back about two or three feet and was just looking at them. The Frenchman was quite tall, and Giap was quite short. They were good friends, you could see that. And I remember thinking, "Is it really true that these two men and all their followers will be trying to kill each other in about three days?"

I had hoped that instructions would reach me in Hanoi as to what

I was to say to Ho. They didn't reach me in Saigon, so I was hoping for them in Hanoi. In Washington, I had prepared instructions that I *wanted* to have sent out. But nothing had cleared by the time I left, so I was hoping the boys would get it cleared with minor modifications. I didn't know what the State Department was going to do, because we weren't in a position to make any commitments to Ho. We were still dealing only with the French officially. But I was hoping they would decide on something that would give Ho a little hope about American policy. In any case, I obviously ought to have instructions about what to say.

But they didn't come. So when I went to see Ho I couldn't say anything. I requested the meeting through our consul. The French were upset, though they knew I had come to see Ho. When I saw him he was sick in bed. He was an impressive person even then, lying there. It's hard to define how you find somebody impressive, but he was. There was something about him, an aura, if that's the right word. I thought I was talking to somebody who really was a great person. I suppose we must have talked for fifteen, twenty minutes. I had to talk about the weather and how pleased I was to meet him. I couldn't go beyond banalities. I think he told me the usual, that he hoped America would recognize him, the usual line. And I'm sure it was painfully obvious I didn't have instructions. Because if I had anything to say, I had plenty of time to do it, and all I did was talk about the weather.

Then when I went back to Saigon, I got the cable. To me, it was that cable that closed the door. It was the beginning of the hard-line policy that was followed from then on. The cable began: I ASSUME YOU WILL SEE HO IN HANOI AND OFFER SUMMARY OF PRESENT THINKING. KEEP IN MIND HO'S CLEAR RECORD AS AGENT INTERNATIONAL COMMUNISM, ABSENT EVIDENCE RECANTATION MOSCOW AFFILIATIONS. . . . I was bitterly disappointed when that cable came out. I thought the boys would be able to hold their own. I didn't think such a decision would be taken at that time. But the die was cast. We were going to follow the hard line on Communism wherever it put up its ugly head. I thought we were right back in the wars of religion.

What did you do after you got the cable?

I think I got drunk.

2

LA SALE GUERRE

The first interview in this chapter ends with ragged Viet Minh troops slipping quietly out of Hanoi. The last one ends with them marching back in—"all freshly uniformed, with pith helmets and rubber sandals and greenish combat uniforms." In between came eight years of what the French called *la sale guerre*—the dirty war.

For a time, the war only smoldered. Neither army had the troops or equipment for major campaigns. The French rushed in more men, mostly Legionnaires and colonial units. But France's leaders were already divided, sometimes along surprising lines. General Leclerc, after a fact-finding mission, reported: "In 1947 France can no longer put down by force a grouping of people which is assuming unity and in which there exists a xenophobic and perhaps a national ideal." On the other hand, a socialist politician, Marius Moutet, blustered that "Before any negotiations it is necessary to have a military decision. I am sorry, but one cannot commit such madness as the Vietnamese have done with impunity."

Meanwhile, Ho and Giap organized. In hamlets and villages throughout the north, and to a lesser extent in the south, the Viet Minh pressed the peasants to resist and trained them in the techniques of guerrilla war. Traveling commissars recruited soldiers for the militia and the army, along with support cadres of every stripe, from spies to food-carriers. Giap later wrote that by 1947 he commanded 1 million men, though only a small percentage of those belonged to the People's Army. Soon the war settled into the classic stalemate: France held the cities, the populous areas of the Red River delta, and a network of forts; the Viet Minh held perhaps two-thirds of the countryside.

As late as 1949, Ho still hoped for a deal with the French, who had installed Bao Dai as the puppet leader of an "independent" Vietnam. But a quick series of events made compromise unlikely. In October, Mao Tse-tung triumphed in China. He recognized Ho's regime in January, and the Soviets soon followed. Giap now had a source of modern armaments, as well as training and advisory support. The French cried louder for help from Washington, and their claims to be single-handedly fighting the Communist tide took on more weight. Asia hands in the State Department continued to warn against hitching ourselves to a doomed policy. But the Francophiles had a new bulwark: the policy of "containment." In June 1950, a few days after the Korean War began, President Truman sent the first American military aid to the French army in Indochina.

The United States and France now embarked on an awkward *pas de deux*, with the partners not altogether sure they should be dancing together. The French wanted aid and more aid, but suspected the Americans of harboring designs on Vietnam. The Americans wanted to beat Ho Chi Minh, but thought the only way to do so was to grant the Vietnamese real independence—or at least a real timetable. Yet each time Washington applied pressure, the French would huffily hint that they might just pack up and leave. The bluff always worked. Again and again, Washington swallowed its misgivings and accepted the latest French scheme for military success. And the tab got bigger. By 1954 the United States had pumped nearly $3 billion into the Indochina war, more than France had received under the Marshall Plan.

The American envoys in this chapter lived out their country's contradictory policy. They favored Vietnamese independence and sensed that the French would lose. But they loved France itself. Jim Crane, the young USIS man, hoped to be posted to Paris. Instead he got Saigon. "All of us were full of the Four Freedoms in those days," he says. "Self-determination, Roosevelt's policies, anticolonialism. But we got out to Vietnam and were told in effect to pimp for the French." Edmund Gullion, second-in-command of the Saigon mission, argued bitterly with his boss that France should be pressured more firmly. But no one saw Ho as a desirable head of state. Gullion was a dissenter, not a fellow-traveler: In 1950 he cabled his opinion that "most of the colored races in the world will, in time, fall to the Communist sickle if Indochina is taken over."

In late 1953 the French presented yet another plan for American approval. It called for occupying a remote valley named Dien Bien Phu. The French commander, General Henry Navarre, hoped that a French force there might draw Giap into a major battle. He got his wish.

The French war, of course, uncannily foreshadowed the American effort. Perhaps the most telling parallel was France's stubborn inability to imagine that it could lose. Even the catchwords of the American years strongly echoed those of earlier days. The "domino theory" so hotly debated during the 1960s was first put forward around 1950 to justify backing the French. General Navarre, presaging countless successors, glimpsed victory just ahead: "I can see it clearly, like light at the end of a tunnel." Jim Crane remembers looking for—and, to his delight, finding everywhere—"third-force nationalists" who might offer an alternative to Ho. The "third force" became a will-o'-the-wisp the United States never stopped pursuing. And the marvelously named "Vietnamization" of the Nixon years was prefigured by France's tardy decision to build up a Vietnamese army—a policy called *jaunissement*, or "yellowing."

The French lost 74,000 soldiers in Vietnam. More than three times that many Vietnamese died. The numbers bring to mind a chilling remark that captures the basic political equation of Vietnam's long bloodletting. As the war began, Ho told a Frenchman: "You can kill ten of my men for every one I kill of yours. But even at those odds, you will lose and I will win."

JAMES O'SULLIVAN

A low-slung dog, barking frantically, greets me at the screen door of the condominium. Then his master appears, a smallish, avuncular man with a soft voice and hair mostly gone to gray, nattily dressed in beige slacks and a navy blue golfing jacket; he has, in fact, just come from the links. He lives in Kentucky and retired in 1986 from teaching political science at the University of Louisville. We meet at his summer home near Stratford, Connecticut.

He was born in 1916 and joined the Foreign Service just as World War II began. After working in Montreal and the Caribbean, he was posted to Chungking, the seat of Chiang Kai-shek's government. "I was low man in the embassy, and I just didn't want to stay around and be an administrative officer, with everybody telling me what to do and nothing to do it with. So I tried to figure out how I could escape. By this time I spoke a fair brand of French. The counselor of the embassy said, 'I'm writing to John Carter Vincent'—who was head of Far Eastern Affairs—'so write me a memo and tell me what you want to do.' I wrote a short memo proposing that I be sent to Hanoi. Not that I knew anything about Hanoi, nor did anybody else, or about what was going on in Indochina. I just wanted to get out of the embassy. Three or four days later a telegram came in giving me the assignment.

"I got there in April of 1946. We flew from Chungking to Kunming, and then from Kunming to Hanoi. I remember landing at the airport in Hanoi on a very hot day. The pilot knew somebody who was coming out to meet him, and this guy gave me a ride into the city. There was nobody there to meet me."

The State Department had nobody in Hanoi. The only Americans there were with a graves registration team that was looking for flyers who'd been shot down over Indochina. And there was an army team in Haiphong loading out Japanese POWs, about 35,000 of them. I was supposed to set up a listening post and keep an eye on what was happening up there. I had the rank of vice-consul class A, I think it was. There were eight classes above that—FSO 8 through 1. I was about as far down the totem pole as you could get.

First I went to the Hotel Metropole and got myself a room. Then I went and talked to the graves registration guys, who told me where Ho Chi Minh was located. He was right across the street from the Metropole in the governor's residence. Captain Farris, who ran the team, had been seeing Ho pretty regularly about finding areas where it was safe to search. But after the French came in, things got pretty tense in the countryside. The team had gotten into some areas where they'd been shot at. So instructions came down: Play it cool, boys, there's no point in getting killed looking for bodies. When I got there, they were killing time, just hanging around.

A complicated game was going on in Hanoi. You had the Chinese occupation troops, supposedly under the control of a very urbane general, Lu Han. But he didn't control these guys. He only controlled a corporal's guard. The rest were taking orders from various headquarters in Nanking, Kunming, and Chungking. The Chinese didn't know quite what they ought to do. They didn't like the French particularly. And they didn't like Ho, because they recognized him as a possible ally of the Chinese Communists. Meanwhile, the French were doing their best to get the Chinese out. In February the French agreed to give up their old concessions in China and give the Chinese some rights in Indochina. And the Chinese agreed to go home, though they didn't actually leave until July.

When the French reached those agreements with the Chinese, Ho promptly made a deal with the French, because he realized he couldn't play one off against the other. That was the March 6 deal—the French recognized Vietnam as an *état libre* within the French Union, and Ho agreed to let them bring 15,000 troops into northern Indochina. The French sent in the 2nd Armored Division, commanded by General Valluy, and a lot of other units. They had troops in Hanoi, Haiphong, Lang Son, Thai Binh, and at a couple of places along the Hanoi-Haiphong road. So when I got there, you had troops from three armies at every major intersection in Hanoi—the Chinese, the French, and the Tu Ve, Giap's local security force. They'd stand around looking at each other and at you. Little skirmishes kept breaking out.

I don't remember my first meetings with Ho. The Viets obviously were interested in American help, and Ho was very happy to see official American representation there. Nor do I remember my first meetings with the French. But there were lots of parties, celebrations of this and that, where Ho and the French would both show up. There wasn't much in the way of diplomacy. There were only three foreigners in the consular corps—myself, Trevor Wilson, who was the British consul, and a Chinese. They'd trot us out for almost all occasions.

In the early months the city wasn't particularly tense. There was no feeling of preparation for war, though the Viets were getting their hands on all the matériel they could. One way was by organizing the prostitutes around the Citadel. They told the French soldiers they wanted to be paid in hand grenades and pistols and bullets, not money. So they were organizing. They had big parades—I remember a huge one on the anniversary of Ho's declaration of independence. He did have a genius for organizing. And he was pretty steadily destroying any opposition to the Vietnamese Communist Party, which wasn't called the Communist Party then. His main enemy was the Viet Nam Quoc Dan Dang, which was the Vietnamese equivalent of the Kuomintang. It was pro-Chinese and I guess supported by Chiang Kai-shek. One of Ho's favorite tricks was to catch opposition elements with counterfeit money. Everybody had counterfeit money, because that's something the Chinese do well. Ho used that as an excuse. If his men picked up somebody, he'd always be carrying counterfeit money. Or you'd read in the newspapers that the Tu Ve had raided some Quoc Dan Dang place, and they had found counterfeit piasters. Then maybe they dug around and claimed they found skeletons, so these people were treated as obvious criminals. For all I knew, they were. An awful lot of thugs were roaming around that part of the world. But it was also part of a consistent pattern of liquidating the opposition. These guys would be arrested and then disappear. It was pretty widely accepted that Ho was having them killed. Maybe he wasn't doing it, but he certainly knew it was being done, and he wanted it done.

Ngo Dinh Diem was in Hanoi, hiding out in a monastery. I used to go out there and see him once in a while. I'd go to Mass and drop by afterward to talk to him. I'm sure that Ho knew he was there. I'm sure Ho could have had him killed if he wanted to. Ngo himself said that when he turned down Ho's request to be part of the government, he wondered whether he was going to walk out alive. So there was restraint on Ho's part. Here was a potential opponent, one who had the background and power to be a rival. Ho could have had him killed, but he didn't.

Ho was a very long-headed man. Looking back on the guy's career, you have to admire his ability to achieve what he set out to do, going back to the time when he tried to talk to Woodrow Wilson at Versailles about the independence of Vietnam. I think he was really anguished about going to war with the French. But he didn't see any way out. I didn't realize it until years later, but he correctly estimated the French. They were very consistent in their policy. They knew that what they gave to Indochina today, they would have to give to the empire tomorrow. And it worked out very much the way they feared. Two years after the battle of Dien Bien Phu, Morocco and Tunisia became independent. Two years after that, de Gaulle held the referendum on the French Union. And in 1960, practically all the African possessions became independent.

So I think Ho read them clearly. They were not going to give him independence. That's what he had his mind set on. I remember him saying, "The French aren't the ultimate threat. The ultimate threat is the Chinese. They've been here a lot longer. The French are passing. They're going to have to get out." He was right—the Vietnamese and the Chinese are at it again today.

Ho kept hoping the French would see that they wouldn't be able to win a war. But he sensed that they were trying to smother him. And the people around Ho were even more impatient. They knew the *état libre* was a front, at least the way it was evolving in the spring and summer of '46. But there were no real negotiations going on. The French thought they had signed everything they needed to in the March 6 agreement, and there was such political turmoil in France that any movement was difficult.

My own feeling was that the French weren't facing up to their problems. Maybe forty years have given me a little more wisdom, because the Americans won't face up to a lot of their problems either. But I felt the Viets were going to get their independence one way or another, and the French were going to have a bad time. I didn't see how they could hang on when you had the Philippines becoming independent, then Burma, then India and Pakistan. I thought the French should get out while the getting was good.

U.S. policy toward Indochina was pretty much to leave it alone. We had China on our hands, and Europe. We were occupying Germany. The Marshall Plan was being put on its feet. Europe was devastated, and we had to do something about it. If we didn't, we were in real danger of the Russians taking over. So Indochina was a long way away from the major theaters of concern—not only in Europe but in China. Obviously who won the Chinese civil war made the fate of Indochina pale by comparison. It was very much a sideshow, even for the French.

Another thing that must have been a real problem for the French— at one point I counted nine different intelligence agencies operating in Hanoi. I think they split them up deliberately for fear that if they only had one or two, they'd be penetrated by French Communists and betrayed. So they deliberately had all these agencies reporting to different headquarters in Saigon and Paris. One was working for the customs people, one for the financial people, one for the high commissioner, one for the air force, one for the navy, one for the army, and so on. I remember one of them was getting appropriations in French francs and taking them over to Hong Kong to trade on the black market, so they could get more money to expand their operations. [Laughs.] So it was very hard for the French government to have a clear view of what was happening in northern Indochina.

Toward the end of June, Ho left for Paris. He was hoping to flesh out the March 6 agreements and find out what the French were prepared to do. The negotiations went nowhere. Some of Ho's delegation even left before he did. Finally he said, "You can't let me leave emptyhanded, I have to have something on paper." So they signed a *modus vivendi* in September that didn't settle anything.

The atmosphere changed after Ho got back. He came by train from Haiphong in October. I was at the railroad station with Trevor Wilson and the Chinese consul. I don't know how many hundreds of thousands of people were lining the streets from the station to Ho's headquarters. Both sides of the street were solidly packed with people, and it's about two miles from the railroad station to the Metropole. It wasn't spontaneous—obviously the government had brought them out. It showed you what the Viets could do if they wanted to.

After that, the tension really began to mount. It was only a question of time before the collision. Under the *modus vivendi* the French were supposed to have free circulation through northern Indochina as of November 1. That never happened. In early November the Viets started cutting the roads out of Hanoi. They put up barricades manned by Viet troops, and they wouldn't let anybody through. The idea was to contain the French, prevent them from roaming around the countryside. The barricades were made out of dirt, railroad ties, torn-up buildings, brick, concrete. They were big, sometimes twenty feet high. But the French didn't try to clear them.

In late November the French attacked the Viets in Haiphong and shelled the city. At that point it was clear there was going to be war. On the fourteenth or fifteenth of December, I went to see Ho with Abbot Low Moffat, who was visiting Hanoi. I think we were the last non-Asians to see him before the fighting broke out. Ho looked like hell. He was in bed, a sick man. Given the life he had led, he could have been sick with dengue fever or malaria or half a dozen things. I remember him lying back in bed, looking really distressed. Abbot and I talked about it later, why he looked so bad. Was it just the stress? Because by that time the Viets had made up their minds to attack.

The civilians were already clearing out of the city. I think the evacuation began in earnest about a week before the attack. It was systematic. People were just ordered out. I don't know how they went, but they went. Mostly at night. I guess they walked or rode bicycles. Day by day, there were fewer Vietnamese around. The streets got more and more empty. You could feel that something was going to blow.

General Morlière, the commander in Hanoi, gave me a rundown later about how things built up in the days before the attack. He had confined French troops to barracks because of a firefight in town. Everything got straightened out and he let them out, but there was another firefight. He confined them to barracks again. Then the Viets came to him and said, "Look, as a means of cutting tensions, don't you think you ought to let the troops out of the barracks?" The movie theaters and bars were downtown, maybe a mile and a half away from the Citadel, across the railroad tracks. Morlière told me, "I thought about it, but it was three o'clock in the afternoon, and I decided I didn't want to change my mind again. So I kept them in the barracks. If I had let them out, they would have all been downtown, and a lot of 'em would have been just coming back at the time of the attack." The Viets were trying to get them out of the barracks so they could ambush them.

On the night of December 19, I was at home. By this time I had a house with a guy from the Standard Vacuum Oil Company. Our street was right near the Citadel and near the governor general's palace. There was a French post right behind us, across a wall. We were pretty well surrounded by French troops. They had blocked off the area. We had just gotten through eating. It was eight o'clock. There were three bursts that sounded like heavy mortars. Then the lights went off. About two minutes later the attack began, with shooting all over the place. Morlière said later that when the lights went off, he sent an aide to call the electrical plant to find out what had happened. The telephone exchange was in the hands of the Vietnamese. The operator said, "What do you want?" The aide said, "I want to find out why the lights went out." According to Morlière, the answer was, "That's the least of your worries."

During the first night we stayed in the house. We had a couple of guns, so we went up on the roof, made ourselves some drinks, and watched the fighting. We stayed up there till two or three o'clock in the morning. The Viets were burning all the villages on the outskirts of Hanoi. They burned for three or four nights. We'd sit up there on the roof and see this wall of flame all around the city.

One of the anomalies of the attack was that the Viets had put a lot of mines in the sewers. The idea was to blow up the streets when the French tanks started moving around. The mines were electrically discharged. But the first thing they did was to blow up the electrical plant, so they couldn't explode the mines. They forgot to coordinate. There was also a railroad line that cut the city in half. The French troops were mostly on the west side of it. The bulk of the city was on the east side. About seven-thirty on the night of the attack, the Viets brought in a big train loaded with rocks and all sorts of debris. They stopped it where it blocked all the crossings, so the French wouldn't be able to get their tanks through the main streets. Well, one of the French officers happened to know how to run a locomotive. He got in it and moved the train out and opened up the crossings.

I don't know whether the Viets really thought they could overrun the French, but they certainly gave it a shot. They also attacked in Lang Son and some other places around the delta. But it was obvious the next morning that the French would be able to hold the city. I hopped over the fence to talk to the French soldiers and asked them if things were safe around there. They said, "Yeah, they're probably all right." But there was a lot of sniping going on. And it took a couple of months to completely clear the city. After a few weeks they had it cleared to the outskirts, with the exception of the Chinese quarter, where the Viets were really dug in. The French didn't want to take a lot of casualties, so they didn't attack that. They didn't completely surround it, either. They left a hole for the Viets to escape through if they wanted to. One day the Viets invited Trevor Wilson, the Chinese consul, and me for a dinner in the Chinese quarter. We had to climb over these huge barricades built up between the buildings, with machine guns behind the barricades and people covering them from the buildings nearby. We had dinner with the commander. He gave us shrimp and all sorts of other things they had smuggled in somehow. It was a propaganda stunt. But the French finally got the Viets out of there. They made it hard for them to get supplies and ammunition, so they left.

Around the end of February the city was finally clear. I remember a cleanup that took place on a warm day, so it probably would have been sometime in March. They were gathering the bodies of the people who had been killed. The smell of death was all over the city for months. And there were still a lot of snipers. The AP correspondent got killed by a sniper in the city that winter. Another sniper kept firing into the main French shopping street. He was hiding in a tower that had louvers in it, and he would poke his gun out and shoot at people down below. Finally somebody spotted the gun and sent some soldiers in for the kill.

After Hanoi was cleared, the French gradually started pushing into the countryside. They pretty much fought a holding action until two new divisions arrived in mid–1947. The garrison at Thai Binh was under siege for a couple of months until the French had a parachute drop at four o'clock in the morning, which I thought was pretty hairy stuff. But an intelligence officer told me, "Well, it was the best we could do. The Viets weren't expecting it, and it worked." When the new divisions came in, they were deployed along Route 4, the one that runs parallel to the Chinese border, through Lang Son and up toward Cao Bang. The idea was to stop the Viets from crossing the border and getting arms from China. Southern China was under the control of the warlords, not Chiang Kai-shek. The Chinese being who they are, they'll sell arms to anybody, just like the Americans. [Laughs.] The French saw that if they were going to contain the war, the border had to be sealed.

The French military problem was that there was no place they could force the Viets to fight and die. Ho's government could move around, controlling the countryside and the army without a fixed base where the French could trap it. And the Viets were very tenacious fighters. I remember a canal about halfway down the road to Haiphong. It must have been 150 yards wide. On the far side the Viets set up a machine-gun nest to hose down the convoys as they went through. Well, the French chased the Viets out, but they'd just pop up somewhere else. And they were always planting mines on the railroad. The trains would run over them and get blown up. So the French started putting a railroad car loaded with stone in front of each locomotive to blow the mines. But the Viets figured out a way to trigger the mines by pulling a cord. They'd have somebody out in a rice paddy to wait for the locomotive to run over the mine, and they'd blow it. So there was all sorts of intricate fighting going on, and the Viets were giving as good as they got. Of course, their intelligence was superb. They were stealing French secrets all over the place.

They also had a scorched-earth policy. They were very tough about it. If they couldn't hold a town, they would destroy it. When the French first tried to punch out of Hanoi, they went south to Ha Dong. I went along to take a look. This was in March or April of 1947. The Viets had leveled practically every building in the town. The typical building, a government office or schoolhouse or church, would be made of brick. What they did was to beaver it about three feet above the ground. They just knocked out a layer of bricks, and the whole building would collapse. The point was to make life more difficult for the French, so they wouldn't have any place to barrack their troops or house their vehicles. Make them rebuild everything that they needed. And all the people who lived in the towns were chased out.

By the time I left at the end of '47, I could see it was going to be a long war. For the next couple of years I was the Indochina desk officer at the State Department. Then I was moved to the Indonesia desk, after Indonesia had been given its independence. I never was sure why I was moved, but I think somebody decided to get me out of the line of fire. I thought the French were going to lose. In the long run, nationalism was going to beat them, not Communism. Independence had to come. In the face of what was happening all over Southeast Asia, the French were an anachronism. But there were real problems for anyone saying that. The Cold War had started. We were very dubious of any extension of the Communist system. So independence for Vietnam was not to be recommended. The only way you could advocate it would be to go to Congress and say, "Now look, there are good Communists and there are bad Communists. Ho Chi Minh is a good Communist. Those guys in Europe are bad ones." And that simply wasn't in the cards.

JIM CRANE

In 1951, as a young man with a new graduate degree in political science from the University of California at Berkeley, he was hired by the State Department to study public opinion of U.S. foreign policy. "After a while that seemed like a dead end, so I got itchy feet and slid over to

*the United States Information Service, which was the easiest way of
getting abroad. They said, 'Where do you want to go?' I said, 'Paris,
of course.' They said, 'Well, we can get you pretty close. We'll send
you to Germany.' That sounded okay. Then they changed their minds
and sent me to Vietnam.*

*"They kept telling me it was the Paris of the Orient. But I had this
image of living in a house on stilts with the 'natives' surrounding me.
It would probably be a health hazard, I wouldn't be able to get the
right kind of food, and there'd be complete confusion. I hardly knew
where Vietnam was. It was called Indochina then. A very obscure place.
You'd heard of the Philippines, but not this kind of French, half-hidden
country. Indochina. Was it India, or was it China? I remember flying
in and looking down at the rice paddies and wondering what the hell
I was getting into. My wife probably even more so. As it turned out,
we were there two years, and our first two kids were born in the Clinique
St. Paul, a French hospital."*

*Now he lives in a comfortable suburban house in Santa Clara, Cal-
ifornia. He is about sixty—white-haired, stocky, self-effacing. He is
retired but does volunteer work, much of it to help out the elderly
people in town.*

When I got out there, USIS had about eight people. And the whole
embassy had maybe thirty. Then there was a MAAG. I was assigned
as a public affairs assistant, which means a jack-of-all-trades. We had
to pump out everything we printed—newsletters, newspapers, publications—in five or six languages, because we were dealing with all
the Associated States. You had Laotians, Cambodians, and Chinese—
lots of Chinese people—plus Vietnamese, French, and English.

My job was the flunky job, distribution officer. I was supposed to
make sure that all our publications got to the so-called audience
throughout the Associated States. One of the best ways was to go out
on mobile unit tours. We'd go out in the country in these big things
that looked like tanks, with a generator and a projector on top for
showing movies. We had 'em piled high with publications that we'd
give to everybody in sight when we showed the movies. Everybody
in town and from the fields nearby would come. We'd set up a screen,
and they'd sit on the ground. I have certain vivid impressions of it.
One is that it was a total waste. It was asinine. And it was cruel. These
people were dead tired. They were rice peasants, leaning over all day
sowing rice, and the local officials would say, "Here come the Americans with their mobile unit, bring in all the folks to see the movies."
I don't think they gave a thought to whether it was worthwhile. So I

felt self-conscious about that. I wondered what the hell we were doing.

And the movies. . . . The idea was to tell these folks about the dangers of Communism. That was the idea. But we couldn't get enough good movies, certainly nothing they could absorb. They'd sit there with their mouths open. All the little kids. . . . They liked anything that moved, anything that was different, anything to get away from pulling weeds. But they were tired. This was late at night. It had to be dark so you could show the movies outdoors.

Since we couldn't get the right kind of movies, or any kind to speak of, in desperation I used to show Laurel and Hardy over and over again. It needs no commentary. The people would laugh. There's a universal sense of humor, and they liked it when Laurel and Hardy would climb a ladder to paint a house, and fall over. These peasants in a totally alien culture thought that was funny. Or I would get Walt Disney–type cartoon movies on public health—how to make a privy, or something like that. But the regular stuff—there was a movie that the agency in Washington was so proud of, called *The Peanut*. It taught you how to grow peanuts. As far as I know, they don't grow peanuts in Vietnam. It meant absolutely nothing. But the word was, you've got to show this movie because it's agricultural and it'll get to the rural people. We got more sophisticated as the years went on, but Washington was totally unselective in those days. They'd send the same movie to every post in the world, with very little audience evaluation as to what we were doing and why. None of these movies were made for a foreign audience, let alone for Vietnam in a war situation.

And by the way, there was a war on. People always say to me that Vietnam must have been nice in those days, but the Viet Minh were around. I got into danger twice. One time I was going up to Phan Thiet by train, and the train was mortared. The other incident ended up in *Time* magazine. I had been on a mobile unit tour to Cap St. Jacques, at the mouth of the Saigon River. There was a French base with a lot of Vietnamese employees. I made arrangements to show a movie—maybe *The Peanut*. [Laughs.] Some armed people came in dressed as Vietnamese soldiers, but they were Viet Minh. They leveled the place with machine-gun fire. The command center where we were going to show the movie got shot at. It was kind of a campground, under a roof, an open-air place. The Viet Minh came in and shot up the place. Twenty-five people were killed. *Time* called it the Cap St. Jacques massacre.

All of us, certainly including me, were full of the Four Freedoms in those days. This was right after World War II. Self-determination, Roosevelt's policies, anticolonialism. But we got out to Vietnam and were told in effect to pimp for the French. We used to grouse all the time and mumble at meetings. Any time the French policy would be mentioned, we'd mutter, "Fat chance" or "They don't mean it" or "They're just supporting the *colons*." But not too loudly, because Lee Brady, the chief public affairs officer, was known to be a Francophile, and if you wanted to get promoted you wouldn't get on his bad side.

Frankly, I think most of us used to look for dirt under the rug— anything that would enhance our preconceived ideas about why the Vietnamese had to fight. I was flat-out pro-nationalist and anti-French, full of fervor. I never visited the prisons, but we heard stories of torture. Stories about the Sûreté, and how the Vietnamese were copying their French masters. There was an island called Poulo Condore, kind of like a penal colony, where they dragged all the political prisoners. Vietnam was like any other police state. You'd hear from the Vietnamese themselves that they were told what to do, that it wasn't their country, that they were being bled dry of all their resources. Stories that all this money was being sent back to France, not put back in the country. A typical colonial policy of sucking the country dry.

I believed in the dangers of Communism, but I figured that the salvation for Vietnam was third-force nationalism. I'd go out looking for people like that, and sure enough, I'd find 'em all over the place. Asians are clever that way—they'll tell you what they think you want to hear. In no time at all I found several important provincial Vietnamese who said, "We want independence. We don't think much of Communism, but we think we should have self-determination. And you Americans can probably nudge the French on that." They were telling us, "Everything will be all right, don't worry, there won't be any Communism. We'll take care of that." I said, "Well, who? Is there somebody?" Ho Chi Minh was this mythical, charismatic figure. I'd say, "Who else do you have in mind?" And they all said, or most of them, "Ngo Dinh Diem." No question about it. I said, "Who the hell is he?" It was just a name to me. They all said he was an anti-Communist and a nationalist. They didn't say anything about his being a mandarin and an autocrat.

His brother was the bishop up in Vinh Long. So I took it upon myself to go up there. I was one of the few people in the embassy who got out in the country. In the first place, nobody wanted to. It was uncomfortable. Second, it was a bit dangerous. Third, it was my job, not their job. So I went to see Ngo Dinh Thuc without authorization. And I got the same story: that Diem was probably the hope of Vietnam, that the Communists are no good, and what we need is to get out from under the French in a respectable way. He wasn't vicious about it, he didn't want to start a revolution. He just wanted the French to leave. I sat there saying, "Of course, of course," taking notes. [Laughs.] That's exactly what I thought the French should do, too.

Thuc was like a wise Asian. Quiet. Looked you in the eye, however. He wasn't evasive. Quiet and purposeful. I went to see him out of ego, frankly. He was a contact, an important person, and no doubt if I could report that I'd seen Thuc, then *ooh*, it would enhance my chances of being promoted. What a clever fellow, to go see Thuc.

But finally I got in trouble for it. I went off to Hué on a trip and talked to some officials up there along the usual lines: self-determination, getting rid of the French. I wrote a report on it, although it wasn't my job to write political reports. I thought, Hell, since I talked to this guy, I might as well let the embassy see it. Now, remember, I was the lowest of the low. And the ambassador himself called and said, "I want to see you, Crane." I went in and he sat me down. It was a short meeting. He said, "I want you to know what our policy is here." Then he told me what the policy was, which I knew. Protect the French flank. Get them into the European Defense Community, and in due course the Vietnamese would get their own nation. The French had promised that, and so forth. It was indicated to me that they didn't want any underlings wavering from the party line. In my report, I hadn't said whether I believed in what these Vietnamese told me. I just reported it. But the ambassador figured that I believed what they said, which I did. [Laughs.] And his message was, I don't want any more of these reports on Vietnamese nationalism.

I got the hint.

Otherwise, I enjoyed Vietnam.

EDMUND GULLION

He is seventy-four and retired after a long career, first in the Foreign Service and then as dean of the Fletcher School of Law and Diplomacy at Tufts University. He lives with his wife in a big colonial house in Winchester, a wealthy suburb of Boston. We talk in his study. Vietnam has marked him twice: first as chargé and then second-in-command in the U.S. Embassy in Saigon from 1950 to 1953, when he was known for advocating that France move faster to grant the Vietnamese independence; and second during his years in academia, when some students attacked his support of U.S. involvement in the war and burned down his office. Though he can still be diplomatically vague when it suits him, it seems clear that the latter episode was painful. But he has not changed his mind. "People who knew how I felt about the French, I think in later years wondered why I was not at all an antiwar fellow in the American conflict. The main reason is that I was quite aware of the consequences of defeat. The defeat has been disastrous for this country. It is today, even."

Before he went to Saigon as a young Foreign Service Officer, he served in Marseilles, Thessaloniki, London, and Helsinki. At one point he was ordered to Singapore, though he never arrived because Pearl Harbor intervened. "I remember when I first heard I was going to Saigon, after serving in Europe during the war. I told the chief of personnel: 'But it's so far!' He said, 'So far from what? It's closer to Delhi than Washington. It's closer to Tokyo than Paris.' [Laughs.] It was a good lesson in relativity."

Vietnam was not a place of importance to Americans. There was little trade in that area. We only had a consulate in Saigon. The French, of course, saw it as their baby. But after they set up the Associated States of Indochina, with Bao Dai as head of state in Vietnam, we decided to recognize him and upgrade the post to an embassy. That had a lot to do with the so-called loss of China, too. Washington sent a couple of missions out to Southeast Asia to look things over. There was a tide of interest in "containment." So at the beginning of 1950 I was tagged to go to Saigon and set up the mission. I guess it's standard practice to have a young fellow secure the terrain.

The change took effect when I presented letters of credit as chargé d'affaires. That was the opening of diplomatic relations. For the first nine months, I was in charge of the embassy. I was accredited to all three countries in Indochina—what France called the Associated States. I went to see Norodom Sihanouk in Cambodia and Prince Savang in Laos. I presented credentials, and the embassy kept officers in Phnom Penh and in Vientiane. I would send them up on rotation.

Through all this was France's lingering fear of the Anglo-Saxons, as de Gaulle put it. A lot of their policy was influenced by distrust or complexes vis-à-vis the Anglo-Saxons. They were not altogether happy about our opening up an embassy. It was all right for us to go out and present our letters of credit to Cambodia and Laos, but they didn't want us making a constant circuit of it. I remember the *conseiller diplomatique*, Roger du Gardier, used to give me a little friendly caution: "Oh, it's so unusual to want to see the chief of state once or twice a month." It was friendly, but he was suggesting that I was seeing Bao Dai too often. So there was always an underlying tension with the French, which sometimes surfaced in petty and annoying ways. They were always looking over our shoulders. We made agreements for direct military assistance to these countries, and the French were worried about that. They insisted on provisions that limited the role of our MAAG basically to selecting and verifying the supplies that we delivered. There were no training missions that I recall.

When I was first out there, our tendency was to push the French. Two questions dominated the period: Was it possible to create a self-sustaining, self-confident Vietnamese nation and national spirit? And what was the link between that creation and the timing of the change in their relation to France? There were great differences of opinion in the State Department, doubly so in the embassy, about the timing. One issue was the so-called evolutionary statement. Some people thought that France should make an early statement saying, "Here's a real timetable for independence." But the French desk was against that. One argument was that if you do that, you emasculate the possibility of French military pacification, because where is the incentive to fight or stand if you know that the game is already given away, and you're going to leave over time? The French desk was powerful in the State Department. It was a center of European affairs, with great prestige. So the doctrine was that an evolutionary statement was premature, because you wouldn't have control of the pace if you immediately pulled the rug out from under your forces.

I went to Saigon thinking there was a lot of logic in that position. But in three months I sent back a telegram renouncing my stand, because I could see it was probably already too late and not enough. It wasn't working, and it wasn't going to work. I traveled around the country. I went up to the Red River delta. I was impressed. The French did appear to have it under control—"le Tonkin util," as General Carpentier called it, "the useful part of the delta." But it just seemed to me the French were doing too little, too late. In the first place, they had heavy negative ballast from years of colonialism. And I didn't think they had begun the process of independence soon enough. I didn't think the grants of power were sufficient. I thought the reserve powers that France kept were too great. I thought the people who were selected as leaders didn't have credibility.

I remember talking to my colleague Jim O'Sullivan on the South-East Asia desk before I went out to Vietnam. He had spent years there in the '40s. I knew very little about the place. I was a European hand. I said, "I can't understand it. Here's France, a power with a great military tradition. They know the score out there. Why can't they handle this thing?" He said, in effect, "They could, but they won't. There's no will to do it." After I'd been there awhile, I knew he was absolutely right. He meant that it would require a major effort, and the French were war-tired. They no longer had a taste for empire. The war was unpopular in France. It was a *sale guerre*, a dirty war. France just didn't have the resources or the willpower to do it.

One milestone was the decision to create a national Vietnamese army. There were some Vietnamese units in the French army, but the officers were almost all French. Finally an army was created. I used to have arguments with Bill Leonhart about this. He was head of the political section in the embassy, and a very able man. He was less optimistic than I was, much less inclined to see Vietnam as a going proposition. He thought it was too late after 1945 or 1946. I thought we were right on the cusp of the crisis, at a point where we could still pull it off. He thought it was too late to create an independent army and the rest of it. I thought it might work.

As I say, after three months I announced in my telegrams that I was not on board for an evolutionary statement. I thought the French were headed for doom and disaster. The problem was that we had no real alternative policy, except to keep pushing the French for real concessions and early ones. The whole idea was to find a nationalist solution that wasn't Ho Chi Minh. You had lots of different elements in Vietnam. The idea in later years that we were always fighting against the guys with the white hats, and all the black hats were on our side— that was not true back then. True, the feeling about Ho Chi Minh was: Well, he is Vietnamese, after all. And the Vietnamese got a kick out of seeing him beat the French here and there. But that was a long way from his being the national choice of the Vietnamese at the time. And certainly not in South Vietnam.

That was another factor—the difference in attitude of Cochin China, or South Vietnam, from that of Annam and Tonkin. The three had lived in dissociation probably as long as they had lived in association. There was even a school of thought in Cochin China that was willing if necessary to see the country partitioned. They didn't feel they had that much in common with the north.

I wouldn't say there were lots of alternatives to Ho. And it wasn't enough for us to find one, it had to be somebody believable. Anybody who was a French product was tarred by association. I remember the United States had a lot of hope for Bao Dai's new prime minister, Tran Van Huu. I went to see him just after he took office. He said to me, "Well, now, I know you Americans probably think of me as a creature of the French, brought up by the French and in the pay of the French. But you see, I'm not." And the way he proved it was by saying, *"J'ai épousé une des plus grosses fortunes en Indochine, et je l'ai fructifié de mes propres efforts."* [Laughs.]

I think the real watershed was when the Korean War began. Up to that point we were preserving our free will and independence of policy vis-à-vis the French in Vietnam. And we were putting pressure on them. Not as much as I might have liked, because there were bitter divisions in the embassy and the government. But with the Korean War, Washington somehow came to the view that the French were doing in Vietnam the same thing that we were doing in Korea. We were both fighting a war against Communism, and therefore, full faith and credit to them, and let's stop this business of being half-hearted in our support for the French. This coincided with the arrival of Donald Heath, the new ambassador, and of General Jean de Lattre de Tassigny, the new French commander. Ambassador Heath was much more pro-French than I was, and de Lattre was a most majestic and commanding figure. I think we abdicated the kind of role we could have had in influencing the French to bring about a solution.

I remember de Lattre's advent in Indochina. He arrived at Tan Son Nhut airport. The French turned out the *corps constitué*, all the high dignitaries of the ministries and the army and the judiciary and the diplomats, to greet the great general. And a large number of troops. I was told that de Lattre had indicated he liked the custom of a nineteen-gun salute, even though it was American, not French. So they had this salute laid on. The plane circled, and it landed precisely at the hour and the minute scheduled. It rolled to a stop. They pulled the ramp up to the door. He walked out onto the platform and stood there at the top. No waving. He just stood there in profile, with his kepi, and he slowly put on these white gloves. Then he came down the ramp. The symbolism was not lost on anybody: He had come there to clean up this mess, with his white gloves. He got to the bottom of the ramp and they gave the salute. There was a group of people waiting there. De Lattre said to one of them, "You're relieved of duty. Go home." The fellow apparently needed a shave. Another general who was supposed to be friendly with de Lattre got into a disagreement with him during the first hour, and he was sent home. [Laughs.] De Lattre knew what he was doing, you see, with the white gloves and all.

From then on, our main contact was de Lattre, and de Lattre was a mesmerizer. He was like a more sophisticated MacArthur. A tremendous figure, a great actor, and an absolutist. An example: the little villages around Hanoi are wall-to-wall with each other. One of them might be dominated by the Communists, and the next one not. But they used the same well, and they had the same wallows for their water buffalo. There had to be contact and cooperation. Well, the French intelligence took advantage of that. The contact made it easier for them to infiltrate. But I was told by the head of French intelligence that de Lattre was furious about it. He saw it as dealing with the enemy, confusing the issue. "It's us against them, let's not fool around with this back-and-forth stuff!" I remember once he addressed the Lycée Chasseloup-Laubat, the big school where doubtless there were a lot of young Vietnamese who wanted to go out and fight the French. He said to them, "Be men. If you want to go fight us, go." He'd just dare them to go and do their worst.

He energized the place, there's no question about that. I was much taken by him as a character, and I was fond of him. And he did have some military successes, where he enticed the Viet Minh to attack in the Red River valley and mowed them down. He even lost a son in one of the battles. But I don't think I ever believed he could bring it off, because there just wasn't enough real support at home. And he wanted the Americans kept in their place. He was giving us hell. As I remember, we were going to open up a USIS library at one point. De Lattre was invited to the ceremony. Instead of opening the library, he closed it down. "Information service? We don't need that around here!" It shows you how independent Vietnam was, when the French general could shut down an American library.

All in all, it was a difficult assignment. There were strong differences of opinion in the embassy. I campaigned for my point of view by telegram, but I was the second-in-command. I couldn't send out telegrams over my signature. In briefings, of course, I could say what I thought. To his credit, Heath didn't interfere with that. If prominent people came through, I spoke freely. I keep saying "I," but I think a majority of the people in the mission felt the same way I did, that our policy was too supple, too compliant with the French. Still, the Foreign Service is collegial. We all got along. I think Heath put down some of my views to my relative lack of seniority and experience. It's true, I think I might have been more effective had I been older. I probably would have done better by not openly disagreeing with him.

Finally I came back to Washington. I remember seeing the plan for the Dien Bien Phu operation, because at that time I was still in the picture to some degree. It was the so-called Laniel-O'Daniel-Navarre plan. Laniel was the French premier, General "Iron Mike" O'Daniel was head of MAAG in Vietnam, and Navarre was the new French commander, because de Lattre had died of cancer. The plan had three flags on it—Vietnamese, French, and American, with a handsome cover. I remember saying, "The only thing good about this is the cover." It called for deployment way-the-hell-and-gone up there close to the Chinese border. It was the stupidest damn thing. But I guess they thought, Well, the Viet Minh will have to come out, and we can get 'em. De Lattre had had those early successes by staking out a position where he could get a field of fire and then inviting an attack. The idea was to repeat that on a vast scale. But it was just the kind of position that I predicted in a cable the year before. [Reads:] ". . . We will find some months from now a French group of at least division strength cut off from its bases of support in mountain defiles." That's what happened.

Dien Bien Phu need not have been the end. The French still had a large army in place. They could still have had a military victory, but the home front wouldn't support it anymore. I think that French policy was responsible for the whole catastrophe, but the French as soldiers I rather admire. There's an oversimplified argument that says military solutions never work, that you've got to get the hearts and minds of the people. That's partly true, but it's not all true. It is possible to have military solutions, even in guerrilla wars. Look at the British in Malaysia and Aden, or Pershing in the Philippines. It's perfectly possible to do things by military means. The trouble is that you have to have a home base that supports you. And there's the question of timing. If you're going to be military, you have to be military from the beginning, and you have to be ready to provide bottomless pockets and unlimited forces.

While Dien Bien Phu was going on, the secretary of state had regular morning meetings on Vietnam. This was John Foster Dulles. I remember him saying one day, in effect, "Well, the French have done this and that, they're turning over these ministries, they've created an army. The process is good." I spoke up from the back of the room and said, "Mr. Secretary, Vietnam is not independent. They don't have their own currency. They don't command their own forces. They don't command their own jurisprudence. They don't command their own central bank." I had other examples I can't remember now. But it irritated him. So I was disinvited from that series of meetings. [Laughs.] I appeared for the next one, and I was told by a friend who was the secretary's adviser: "This is by invitation. And you're not invited." I remember being so goddamn furious. I walked around the State Department like Hector being pursued around the walls of Troy, trying to decide if I should quit this organization or not. As it turned out, I didn't quit—and I never regretted it.

HOWARD SOCHUREK

The small office in a high-rise on New York's Fifth Avenue is crammed with equipment, cartons, magazines, luggage. Papers and boxes of slides are piled a foot high on most surfaces of the desk. The resident is a freelance photographer sixty-two years old, a heavyset man with a tie hanging loosely from his unbuttoned shirt collar. His voice is growling, and he likes to tease. We talk four times, spread over a year because of his constant travels. Much of his work these days involves high-tech photography such as medical imaging; blow-ups of the brightly colored, almost abstract photos hang on the walls. But he reveals a certain nostalgia for his days as a war correspondent.

In 1950 he was a staff photographer for Life, *based in Singapore. He parachuted into North Korea to cover the early months of the war there. "In the fall I got a wire from my boss, saying, 'The Korean War looks to us to be pretty well over. But all hell is breaking loose in Indochina. Start coverage immediately with a major story on de Lattre. Signed Thompson.' So I packed up and headed for Saigon."*

The French problem in Indochina got a lot worse after mainland China fell to the Communists. Ho Chi Minh quickly made an arrangement with Mao to get supplies. There was no love lost between China and Vietnam, but for purposes of the moment, Mao supplied artillery and small arms and so forth. That was the beginning of the end of the French operation. Until then, the Viet Minh was a ragtag bunch that Ho held together in the jungles in the north. The country is very rugged up there. You could hide divisions and nobody would ever find them.

But as soon as Ho made the deal with Mao, in the fall of 1950, he staged attacks on the French border posts manned by the Foreign Legion—Cao Bang, Lang Son, That Khe, Dong Khe, and Mong Cai. Since Mong Cai was right on the ocean, it always remained in French hands. The navy could come up and control that territory. But the rest of the posts were destroyed. Thousands of men were killed. And the refugees, the Legionnaires who had not been killed or wounded or taken prisoner, started filtering out of the jungle in October and November.

It was a disaster for the French. Because of it, they appointed a new commander, General Jean de Lattre de Tassigny. De Lattre was a famous French resistance general. He had tremendous credentials.

Came from a fine family. A very important figure. It was like putting MacArthur in charge of the operation. So *Life* wanted a story on de Lattre taking command.

Back then, Henry Luce was the dominant force in all Time Inc. publications. The managing editors of *Time* and *Life* and so forth had autonomy, but Luce was the editor. His beliefs were followed. They were his magazines, right? His views were always very strategic, very big-picture. He didn't want to hear the details of how the French soldiers were goofing off in the field. He'd say, "The basic American interests lie with the French. Preventing the inroads of the Russians in Europe and having the French support us in NATO are far more important than what's happening in Hanoi." And that was that.

I got to Saigon at almost the same time as de Lattre. I met up with Eric Gibbs, who was the Paris bureau chief of *Time*. We attached ourselves to de Lattre. He was interested in publicity because that was part of his mission. We flew with him to Hanoi, toured the Red River delta, talked to all the officers, went up on a flying mission to look over That Khe and Dong Khe to see what remained. We watched him meeting with district officials, trying to get the support of the Vietnamese, trying to make contact with Ho. He even traveled with Bao Dai, who was the head of state they had installed.

De Lattre had tremendous personal magnetism. He was a portly man, not too tall. He had a flushed, reddish face, and a fantastic pointed nose. Not a handsome man, but a man of extreme dignity and command, with a military kind of pompousness. Impeccably dressed. Beribboned with every medal given by the French military for the last fifty years. Beautifully tailored shirts and shined shoes. He was a towering figure. I would attend dinners at which he would give long, inspiring toasts to the grandeur and the glory of France and the French military. He wasn't a small-talk man. His manner was somewhat remote. He didn't pat anybody on the back. He pushed the idea of patriotism and the professional military. He was a military man, and he was going to solve the military problem.

Traveling around with him, I could see why the French didn't want to give up Indochina. Colonial life was very grand. There was the Cercle Sportif, which was the club. It was restricted to the top *colons*— the most wealthy, the highest members of the government. As journalists, we were given guest memberships. These clubs were in all the major cities. Each of them had a beautiful swimming pool, lockers, a dining area, a horse track in some cases, a massage room, tennis courts.

In the private homes, the French traditions were carried on. If you went to dinner, it was always formal. You dressed in a white jacket and black trousers. The generals and the top military of course observed this very strictly. So if you attended a dinner thrown by de Lattre it was usually in a chandeliered governor's house, with many, many servants, great long tables, the finest of cutlery and glassware. It was like something out of the past. The women were some of the most exotic in the world, mixtures of French and Vietnamese. Fantastic creatures. They would all come dressed to the hilt, driving up in their Citroëns. Nobody worked very hard. All the finest imports were available—caviar, French wines and champagnes. A fantastically easy and gracious way of life, because of the tremendous number of servants and the wealth they got out of the rubber plantations and the trading of rice and the other businesses. In 1950, they still had all that.

Even the military had a beautiful way of life. The French defense was based on forts, which I visited with de Lattre or by myself. If you were invited to lunch, as we often were, you'd arrive in the morning, do your work, make the rounds, see the troops, inspect the fortifications, and then at one there'd be this fantastic lunch in the officers' mess. If de Lattre was there it was really superior, but even if he wasn't, they ate extremely well. You'd always start with an apéritif at the bar. Cinzano or sherry or cassis, which was the favorite of the French. Everybody would stand around and have drinks. Then the head of the mess would formally announce the lunch. All the seats were assigned. There were little nameplates for the visitors. All elegantly set up, with crystal. This is in the middle of the jungle. Then there would be an officer who would announce *le menu*. He'd stand at the head of the table and say, "The menu for August 14 at 1:00 P.M. Gentlemen, the menu is . . ." Then he'd recite. "We will begin with soup. Then we will have fish. Then we will have *entrecôte*. Then we will have a salad. Then we will have a tart. Then we will have coffee." The menu was always printed up. Meanwhile, on the perimeter the damn mortars are going off. This went on up until the very end. I'll bet you the last meal at Dien Bien Phu, they still sat down and had somebody announce the menu. That was how it was done.

De Lattre staved off panic, especially in Hanoi. I got there three or four weeks after the border posts fell, and the first survivors were just trickling out of the jungle. The panic built up as the stories came out. The *colons* started flooding the airport to get out of Hanoi. I remember taking pictures of them. But de Lattre turned it around. He said, "We're going to stay here. I'm going to bring more troops in, and we're going to win." He instilled confidence, and for a while he was successful.

I interviewed survivors from the border posts. The basic story was always the same. Some of these forts had 350, 400 men. The walls were thick, with parapets, like in a Foreign Legion movie. They'd have regular French houses inside the perimeter. The commandant's house would be quite nice, with bedrooms and toilets and running water. They usually had some Vietnamese troops there, but some were strictly Foreign Legion. Big barracks, with long rooms for sleeping. The men all slept in bunks. A shower or washroom on one end. Another building for storage of rifles and ammo. Then you had towers where you'd stand watch, and machine-gun positions on the perimeter. But the forts were separated by great distances from any support. They were sitting out there all by themselves. The French had very few helicopters and almost no air force. It was incredible, how little they had. So these guys couldn't call for reinforcements. They had to sit there and fight. If they won, they won, and if they died, they died.

The Viet Minh would attack around midnight. First they'd fire a barrage of heavy mortars. They had very few 105s or 155s, but they had a lot of 80mm mortars. There would be a terrific barrage. It was usually very accurate, because they had a good idea of where your positions were. They infiltrated the forts. All the forts had servants, and the servants came from outside. So they knew where the machine guns were, where the mortars were, where the towers were. They could zero in.

The Legionnaires would get to their defensive positions. They'd look out and see masses of soldiers in palm hats. The helmets of the Viet Minh were made out of palm leaves, a thatched helmet like a pith helmet. It wasn't any good against a bullet, but it was their uniform. You'd see thousands of these guys out there. Usually the first line of defense was barbed wire. The Communists would come with bamboo ladders that they'd put on top of the barbed wire. Your machine-gun positions could just keep spraying 'em and killing 'em, and they'd just keep coming. Just like little ants that you couldn't possibly wipe out. They gave the impression that casualties meant nothing. If somebody got killed, they just rolled him off into the barbed wire and kept coming. The machine guns would get so hot that they'd misfire or blow up.

You would defend and defend, and they'd just keep coming. They'd go through your first barrier and through your trench barrier, and they'd come up to the wall. They used ladders and ropes to scale it. The walls were clay, with big bamboo spikes on 'em, so when these guys got to the top they had a spike to climb over. But they'd come over, and there would be so many of them that at some point, even if you were told to fight to the last man, you'd try to bug out. Usually there was one escape route from the fort, maybe a path that went down to a river. A lot of the forts were on rivers, so the escape route would be to get out the back door and down the path and into a dugout. Or maybe you'd just grab a log and float.

I remember one guy said that when he saw the thing was hopeless and everybody was wounded or dying, he got out the back door with fourteen other guys. They made it to the river, where they had some small canoes. Fortunately the Viet Minh were so busy attacking the camp that they didn't pay any attention. These guys slowly straggled and walked all the way out. By the time I saw them, they were all terribly emaciated. They had been living off the jungle, sometimes for as much as thirty days.

Later on in the war, I visited some posts after they'd been taken. The Viet Minh never stayed around. They would take all the weapons, destroy everything else, and by ten o'clock in the morning, by the time anybody could get there by road or plane or helicopter, the place would be completely deserted. All you'd see was a bunch of bodies. Nobody alive. The place would still be smoldering and burning, but there wouldn't be a Communist there. They'd leave their flag flying. They always took away their own bodies. You never saw a Viet Minh body, even if they suffered tremendous casualties.

The French soldiers were very realistic. They would just hope that they weren't in a post that the Viet Minh decided to attack. As long as the fateful night didn't come, everything was grand and glorious and peaceful. They'd go on patrols during the day to pacify the countryside, and there were ambushes and firefights, but not massacres. The big fear was to be in a post on the night of an attack. If you avoided that, there was no big problem.

After I did my story on de Lattre, I went back to Singapore. A magazine like *Life* wasn't going to run a Vietnam piece every week, so I would go in, spend some time, do a story, and then go back to Singapore and rest up. In 1951 the Viet Minh attacked some outposts in the delta, but this time de Lattre was ready for them. They got slaughtered and didn't make much headway. That was a boost for the French. Then de Lattre got sick and went home. He was replaced by a general by the name of Navarre. He was a whole different kettle of fish. He didn't have the political or popular support that de Lattre had. His field commander in the north was named René Cogny, and the two of them became bitter enemies. So here was Navarre, the overall commander, and Cogny, the tactical commander, completely disagreeing on how to proceed. That caused a lot of problems. They also had problems with metropolitan France, where the government was constantly changing. There was very little support for the policies out in Indochina.

My next big story resulted from the fact that David Douglas Duncan, who was well known for his pictures of the Korean War, had come through Indochina. He had suggested to *Life* a story on the French army. I was on another assignment, and frankly I was glad to get out of there for a while. It wasn't an easy beat. You were constantly under fire, riding around in lousy airplanes that could crash at any moment. And it wasn't going anywhere. Nobody was winning, nobody was losing. It was a tough story to cover.

Now, Henry Luce was living in Europe at the time. His wife was ambassador to Italy. He left New York in the hands of his capable editors and moved to Rome. He was courted by the French a good deal. He knew them socially and was very pro-French. He told Duncan to go ahead with this story.

Duncan went in and spent about a month. He knew a lot about the military. He had been a marine captain in World War II. He knew what he was doing. He traveled all over the country, went to various French outposts in the north and the south. And he came back with a very anti-French story. He said they weren't fighting, they were living it up, they were having siestas, they weren't really defending their positions, and the whole thing was a disaster. Now, Luce was in Europe, and *Life*'s managing editor, who knew what Luce wanted and what Luce didn't want, was on vacation. He assigned a deputy editor to run the magazine the week of the Duncan story. And Duncan is a very strong personality. He pretty much bulldozed the story through as he saw it. He laid it out, he wrote it, he insisted on certain captions. It was a hard-line story. So *Life*, with all its clout, publishes it. And of course the French are absolutely furious. Luce gets calls from the prime minister and all his buddies in the French government: "How can you do this to us?"

Luce immediately called Duncan to Rome for a meeting. It was one of the classic stories of Time Inc. Duncan is a handsome, Hollywood version of a *Life* photographer. Articulate, sharp, an ex-marine officer, ramrod straight. Always with a beautiful girl on his arm. He has this meeting with Luce in the ambassador's residence. Luce grills Duncan about why he ran this story. Doesn't he see the real national interest lies with France? After the meeting they come out, and Bob Neville, the bureau chief, is there. Both Luce and Duncan look very grim. Neville asks Luce, "How did it go?" Luce looks at him, with his shaggy eyebrows, and says, "Well, at least Duncan didn't fire *me*."

Then I got a wire in Singapore saying, "Stop everything. Luce is furious. Proceed immediately to Vietnam to continue your coverage." The implication was that Luce had promised the French more coverage to show that they weren't all goofing off. So I went out and did mainly combat stories. I got to know General Cogny very well. He was an impressive guy. It was hard to do a negative story on Cogny. He was six feet four, spoke fluent English, and he had a manner about him. He had warmth. He'd throw his arm around you and look at you in a penetrating way. A man of stature, and a serious man. His troops loved him. He was a field man, he was out there. And he knew how to handle the press. He just took me into his retinue. [Laughs.] I got the royal treatment. I'd find out something was happening because his aide-de-camp would call me at two o'clock in the morning. There was a chateau where all the press stayed in Hanoi, an old French house. The aide would call me and say, "I'll pick you up at four-thirty." We'd go in his staff car, a black Citroën, to Gia Lom airport, and Cogny would be waiting at the plane. We'd jump on. Maybe it would be a mission, maybe just a reconnaissance.

I did a lot of stories in '52 and '53. The Viet Minh kept nibbling away. By late '53 the French didn't hold much but the delta. The Communists were threatening Laos and Cambodia. Navarre and Cogny wanted to prevent the fall of Laos. There was one main invasion route that went from east to west. It led from Ho's jungle hideouts north of the delta through the jungle to the border. It so happened that astride this route was a huge valley called Dien Bien Phu, where all the main roads came together and crossed a little river and proceeded west. Because of the mountains, the only way of moving large forces into Laos from Ho's positions was through this valley.

So Navarre came up with a plan to put paratroops into Dien Bien Phu, which had been held by a regiment of Ho's troops for a long time. The plan was to put in some battalions of paratroops, to seize the Viet Minh regimental headquarters, and build a fortress to stop any infiltration into Laos. Navarre also thought it would be a good thing to publicize—"We're really on the offensive, and we've stopped these guys." The military always thinks in those terms. You've got to have a success.

I went in the first day. Cogny's aide woke me up at four. I jumped in the car, taking my combat gear and cameras. Around six Cogny shows up at Gia Lom. He was doing a reconnaissance of the area. It was about an hour and a half's flight by C-47. On the plane he briefed me on what was happening. I said, "How am I going to get in there? I want to jump with them." He said, "I've got a better idea. We're going to watch the first jump, and then I'm going to land you at Lai Chau, where I have a helicopter. General Gilles* and you are going in by helicopter, and you can be there before the second wave comes down." Lai Chau was the nearest French base, about twenty minutes from Dien Bien Phu by helicopter.

The troops were landing by nine. I remember when we flew over in Cogny's plane, there was some ground fire coming up at us. Not heavy antiaircraft, but small-arms fire. And we could see Communist troops doing exercises on the airstrip. They evidently thought we were just a reconnaissance plane.

After Cogny gave the signal we went back and landed at Lai Chau and got into the helicopter. I was with General Gilles and a French correspondent by the name of François Sully, who was later killed. He was my translator. The helicopter was an old Sikorsky. We talked to the first wave of paratroops from the air, and they said, "It's secure, it's secure." They put up a smoke grenade, and we landed in the middle of the perimeter they had established. Troops were dropping all the time, wave after wave. I think they sent in five battalions that first day.

We moved out from the helicopter. The wounded were already coming in. I photographed the wounded being loaded into the chopper. We went to a command post. Then I went with a column that was moving out toward the Viet Minh headquarters building. We got there and found all the regiment's papers. I went down to the river, and just as I got there, about six or eight members of the headquarters staff were trying to make a getaway across the river. The squad I was with shot them. Then I went to the drop zone to photograph more troops coming in. You could still hear firing on the perimeter as the troops moved out to grab as much of the valley as they could. I heard a woman screaming on the second floor of one of these native huts. We went up and she was in labor. So they called a corpsman, a paratroop who had never delivered a baby before. He did his best, and in the first hours of battle, a baby was born.

The first thing was to fix up the airstrip. A little bulldozer was airdropped in. By the afternoon, C-47s were landing and taking wounded out. There were quite a few wounded, not extreme cases. Then we holed up. They set up a little command headquarters in one of the huts and we slept on the floor. I stayed over the first day, and then I wanted to get the story back to *Life*. So I waited for most of the injured to get out, and there were some seats left the second day on

*Brigadier General Jean Gilles, commander of the French airborne forces in Indochina.

a helicopter going back to Lai Chau. Then I flew back to Hanoi and got the film out.

At the time, it looked like a big success for the French. Again, it was this fortress mentality. You set up a big fort, give 'em artillery, give 'em air support, put an airfield in the middle of it, string barbed wire. And because of the remoteness of the place, they thought Ho Chi Minh could never amass the troops and firepower to destroy such a strong position. Over the next few months, they made a tremendous buildup there. But Ho decided, "If you guys go in there, I'm gonna wipe you out." So he got mortars and heavy artillery from the Chinese, built roads through the jungle, dragged the guns over mountains, took every unit he had, and infiltrated the valley. Then he attacked.

When the French came under attack I asked Cogny if I could parachute in to cover the resistance. I didn't have any idea the place would fall. None of us thought it would fall. The French still didn't think it would fall. So Cogny agreed. I got in a C-47 with John Mecklin, who was the *Time* correspondent in Hanoi. We were going to land at night because it was a little safer. We flew from Gia Lom and went in at around 3,000 feet. Suddenly there was tremendous ground fire from the surrounding hills. All the hills just opened up. There seemed to be a lot more going on than anyone had reported. The pilot decided he wasn't going to land. As soon as he started taking all that fire, he gained altitude as fast as he could and headed back. Thank God.

After that night, it became obvious to me the place would fall. Here you were out in the middle of a jungle, and you have extremely heavy antiaircraft fire coming from positions that we didn't believe the Viet Minh could establish or maintain. We thought no one could put heavy weapons in there except the French, who had flown them in on C-119s and C-54s. But the Viet Minh, who had no air, had somehow put in 105s and 75 millimeters, and heavy mortars and all the rest of it, in what we thought was impenetrable jungle.

This hadn't been reported before we saw it with our own eyes. We also saw that a lot of the airdrops to the French were outside their positions. At various times, flares went up, so you could see from the air this pockmarked valley with thousands of white parachute canopies on the ground outside the perimeter. A large percentage of the supplies for the besieged forces were going to the Viet Minh. And as the perimeter shrank, they were getting more and more.

That was the last time I saw Dien Bien Phu. After that, they didn't allow reporters in, because Cogny knew that if you went in, you wouldn't get out. Our information deteriorated. There were no foreign reporters there. Nobody was sending messages out except the French military correspondents, and they weren't letting on how disastrous it was. De Castries* was cabling every day that his position was hopeless, and what should he do? Should he surrender? But I didn't know that at the time.

It got worse and worse. They lost post after post after post, and the place shrank, shrank, shrank. The atmosphere got more and more grim in Hanoi. Cogny was furious. The only hope was that America would come in with air power. We had the capacity to go in there and destroy the surrounding area by heavy bombardment. If Eisenhower had decided to commit our air power, the French could have survived. But the decision was made not to commit American forces. When that happened, the whole thing went down the tubes.

By that time, the decision had been made to have the peace conference in Geneva. I think the decision not to intervene was based on the hope that Dien Bien Phu would hold, and the Geneva Conference would solve the problem. But Dien Bien Phu fell the day before the conference opened, so it was a debacle.

After that I stayed in Hanoi covering what was left of the war. The French still held the delta. We didn't know what had happened to the survivors of Dien Bien Phu. We kept asking, "Where are the survivors? How do we get to talk to them? Can we fly anywhere? Are they at Lai Chau?" It turned out that they were marched through the jungle to the coast. The Viet Minh couldn't keep them prisoners forever, because they didn't have enough supplies. But it wasn't easy to release them, because the Viet Minh held all the territory up there. I don't know why they didn't let the French fly in and take them out. Instead someone decided to march them to the coast and let the French pick them up there. But that's one hell of a long walk. They had some trucks for the officers, so the officers rode at times. And a few people were taken out by air—the doctor and the nurse, and de Castries and a couple of the top officers. But the rest of them walked out. And the losses on that march were terrible. In the first place, you're marching people who had just gone through one hell of a battle. Many of them were wounded. The Viet Minh had no supplies in the jungle, and they were in a very remote area. So the thirst, the hunger, the dysentery, the injuries—they caused fantastic losses along the way.

One afternoon I got a call to go to Haiphong. I went with some French correspondents. In Haiphong we got into some small surplus American LCTs, which stands for "landing craft/tank." We pushed off at about six o'clock and headed south along the coast. We traveled

*Colonel Christian de Castries, the commander at Dien Bien Phu.

all night in that flat-bottomed boat, bobbing around. I'll never forget it, I was so sick. In the morning at first light, we landed at a place called Dong Hoi. Remember, the French just held the delta, so as you moved south you were in Communist-controlled country. There were all these red flags flying. The Viet Minh had built a little settlement at Dong Hoi up a small stream. We pulled in maybe 300 or 400 yards from the ocean and beached the LCTs. There was a clearing in the jungle, and ten or twelve long, thatched huts, just a roof and some poles. They had set up canvas cots, and on these cots were the survivors of Dien Bien Phu. All of them looked terrible—emaciated, with dysentery and malaria. It was a horrible scene of sick soldiers, some of whom I had met that first day at Dien Bien Phu, or even before. I found some of my friends and asked about the others. Obviously our little LCTs couldn't take out all these sick and wounded and starving paratroopers. So the commander of our force asked for more ships to evacuate everyone. I think it took three or four days.

In the meantime, this was a hell of a story, and we asked if they could get some of us out so we could take the story back. I stayed just one day. It was very sad. The Viet Minh couldn't even take care of their own people. They had very limited medical supplies, and very few doctors. They had some girls who acted as nurses, but they had no medicine. You either got better by yourself, or you died, so most of them died. A lot of the fellows that were picked up in Dong Hoi died later, they were in such bad shape.

After that I left Vietnam to cover the Geneva Conference. When I came back, it seemed like business as usual in Hanoi. Maybe there was a sense of "Thank God, it's over. We're not going to fight and lose men anymore." There was still some patrolling, and once in a while somebody would get killed. There was a battery of 105s near the Cercle Sportif swimming pool, so you'd be swimming and suddenly 105s would fire off a barrage at some distant target. We left the *campe de presse* and moved into the Hotel Metropole as people started taking off. The electricity worked, and people still ate well. There was no direct threat militarily. The road to Haiphong was open. So life was quite normal in terms of creature comforts. People were still walking their poodles. The restaurants were open, and the traffic was bustling. People were getting their money out, but until the time the French actually left, the city was active and prosperous.

The very last day before the cease-fire, I took a Jeep between Hanoi and Haiphong. We were on the main road. The car in front of us was a Citroën with army officers in it. All of a sudden, *psshew!* A mine went off under their car. The Viet Minh would dig up the road in the middle of the night, plant a mine, stretch a wire, hide in the paddy field, and when they saw a target they'd let go. Four people in that Citroën were blown to smithereens. I did a story about it—the last Frenchmen killed in the north.

I stayed and watched the French military leave Hanoi. Everybody who had money had gotten out by that point. A few Frenchmen stayed. There was a very fine university, and some of the professors had spent their lives there. Other people were studying archeology or the language. Some of them just didn't want to go. They had their libraries and their friends, and they were sure Ho Chi Minh would maintain the school system, which he did. But the businessmen left. The people who ran the good French restaurants left, because there wouldn't be anybody to go to them. They all took off and reestablished in Saigon.

The night before the takeover, Cogny held a ceremony at the main French military cemetery in Hanoi. It was very moving. The French had been there for 100 years, so there were tombstones of soldiers who had died fifty, sixty, seventy years before. Because of the heat and humidity, a very thick green moss covered all these headstones. In the setting sun you saw the moisture glinting on this moss. And there were three flags flying over the cemetery. The tallest flagpole had the French national flag on it. The shorter ones had the Vietnamese flag and the military flag.

Cogny was in charge of the ceremony. There was a small military band and a battalion of Legionnaires all dressed in their white kepis, those little round hats, with beautifully shined black boots and red sashes. They had drawn up to attention with their rifles. Cogny gave a short but moving speech. He said, "No member of the military is ever forgotten by his brothers. They will always be remembered. They gave their lives for France and what they believed in. And they did not die in vain." Tears welled in his eyes. As a soldier played taps, first the two side flags came down, and then the French flag. They very carefully folded it and gave it to Cogny. Then he took the salute of the battalion commander and got into his Citroën and drove off. The last French troops left during the night.

The next day at 6:00 A.M., the Viet Minh troops started marching into Hanoi. They were all freshly uniformed with pith helmets and rubber sandals and greenish combat uniforms. I must say the Vietnamese in the town didn't show any exuberance. There were some kids waving flags, but no great outpouring of, "Gee whiz, the millennium has come." I was surprised. The soldiers paraded around, and there were people on the streets, but it was not an overpowering display of affection. Why, I don't know. Maybe everybody was just tired out.

3

"A PUPPET WHO PULLED HIS OWN STRINGS"

The phrase comes from an anonymous American in Saigon, quoted by Stanley Karnow in his book *Vietnam: A History*. The man it describes, of course, is Ngo Dinh Diem. In a sense, he was a puppet created by another puppet: Bao Dai, the playboy "emperor" of a regime the French installed in 1949, appointed him prime minister on June 18, 1954. But Diem proved too hard for any of his patrons to handle. He soon angered Bao Dai, and in 1955, at the suggestion of American advisers, Diem staged a plebiscite on the question of whether to depose the emperor and declare South Vietnam a republic. Diem won with a tidy margin of 98.2 percent, tallying more votes in Saigon than there were registered voters. In 1959 he won an equally sweeping—and fraudulent—victory in American-inspired elections to set up a national assembly. But just four years later, he had so alienated the U.S. that it cut the strings altogether—and Diem died a bloody death in the back of an armored personnel carrier on a dark Saigon street.

So Diem was not a creature of the United States, though he had spent years in exile in New Jersey, and though Bao Dai elevated him in hopes that he would draw the Americans in deeper. During Diem's first months, some Americans in Saigon even argued that he should be replaced. But he was tougher and more wily than they expected. After the spring of 1955, when he crushed the Binh Xuyen gangsters in Saigon and came to terms with the armed religious sects in the countryside, the doubters fell silent. Diem was our man: "Sink or swim with Ngo Dinh Diem." In American eyes, he had many virtues: He was passionately patriotic, anti-Communist, Catholic, Western-oriented, brave, and personally incorruptible. And there was the dilemma that stumped the U.S. for two decades—if not Diem (or, later, Thieu), then who?

That question became more pressing as Diem's flaws emerged. Ogden Williams and Douglas Pike make clear in this chapter that those flaws were substantial. One wonders, in fact, why more policymakers did not conclude that if Diem was the best South Vietnam had to offer, the country might not be a good bet to survive. In the first place, he was a mandarin, with a mandarin's sense that he ruled by divine right. His Catholicism, so congenial to Americans, was a disadvantage in a country 95 percent Buddhist. He was austere, shy, rigid, autocratic, a poor administrator. Worst of all, he was a clumsy politician and apparently a mediocre judge of character. Rather than building ties with the myriad factions of Vietnamese political society, he governed largely through a small group of Catholics and his family, including his conspiratorial brother Nhu and Nhu's cartoonish wife.

He ran the country badly. But for a time, running it at all seemed miracle enough. Diem successfully resettled 850,000 northerners, mostly Catholics, who had come south after the Geneva agreements; they provided him with a crucial political base. And having refused to endorse the Geneva terms, he felt no compunction about declining to hold the elections to reunify the country that had been scheduled for 1956. The North was in no position to insist, having plenty of problems to contend with at home. It was recovering from eight years of war, and it was now cut off from its food supply in the Mekong delta. In 1955, Ho Chi Minh launched a land reform drive that even he later admitted was riddled with "errors." Pressures to identify and expropriate major landlords—of whom there were few in the North—led to chaos in the countryside. Peasants were murdered and jailed by the thousands, and a revolt broke out in Ho's home province. Meanwhile, in the South, Diem embarked on his own repressive campaign, decimating the Viet Minh cadres who had stayed behind—and sweeping up sympathizers, relatives, and innocents in the process. Both sides began to look toward full-scale civil war.

And more Americans arrived, stepping into the vacuum left by the French. The most important was Edward Lansdale, former advertising man, now an air force colonel, psychological warfare expert, and reputed nation-builder extraordinaire, having helped Ramon Magsaysay suppress a Communist insurgency in the Philippines in the '40s. Lansdale spent countless hours listening to Diem's monologues and nudging him to create a South Vietnam in the image of the United States. Other Americans trained the army, instructed civil servants, built schools, dug wells, did studies, and variously helped to spend the $1 million a day that Eisenhower lavished on Diem's government. Some fell incurably in love with South Vietnam—and the attraction did not lie simply in the adventure of a country being born. There were also the lush climate, the charming southerners, the colonial lifestyle, and the easily available women.

But Americans found, too, that when they pushed, Vietnam did not necessarily budge. The country was deeply exotic. Initiatives had a way of mysteriously evaporating or turning into something else. And the advisers began to discover the drawbacks of the short tour, a problem that plagued the U.S. until the end of the war. John Cushman, then an army colonel advising a Vietnamese division in the delta, says it took him months to understand the importance of the parallel Viet Cong government in the countryside. To fight it, he revived an old French pacification technique known as the "oil spot." Did it work? "Well, I left Vietnam," he says with a laugh. He doesn't know whether his successor followed up.

And Diem kept pulling his own strings. By 1959, when Hanoi ordered its cadre in the South to step up guerrilla operations, his regime already showed the paranoiac quality that rapidly got worse in the early '60s. He sidestepped American pleas for more democracy, serious land reform, less corruption among his cronies. His strategic hamlet program was largely a sham, and where it did succeed in moving the peasants off their lands into fortified villages, it enraged them. He promoted generals on the basis of loyalty, not talent. Predictably, the insurgency mushroomed. President Kennedy's response was to send more advisers, who soon went beyond advising. And another American pattern was set—that of pessimism in the field clashing with optimism in Saigon. As the number of advisers topped 10,000 and then 15,000, it became inconceivable that we could "lose" Vietnam. Yet many majors and colonels sensed that Diem was losing it for us. Their reports were not welcomed; nor were press stories to the same effect.

Diem finished digging his political grave with his repressive campaign against the Buddhists in the spring of 1963. In June, Kennedy appointed a new ambassador, Henry Cabot Lodge, who saw his first task as ousting Diem. The coup came three weeks before Kennedy's own death. Some Americans still argue that helping to overthrow Diem was a catastrophic mistake, because it robbed South Vietnam of the only figure with stature enough to resist the Communists. Douglas Pike thinks the fall was inevitable. "Over three years," he says, "I watched Diem alienate one element of the society after another. . . . It wasn't a coup in the usual sense. It was a collapse."

Collapse followed upon collapse for nearly two more years, as juntas came and went. During 1964, according to Karnow, the Viet Cong doubled in size, to 170,000 men, and late that year the first regular

North Vietnamese units arrived in the South. The Tonkin Gulf incident in August allowed President Johnson to rush a resolution through the Senate giving him virtually unlimited powers to make war in Vietnam. In February 1965, he began sustained bombing of the North. But he and his advisers already suspected that bombing alone would not win the war. With the Saigon government barely hanging together and the ARVN fighting poorly, the Communists seemed poised to take over. Kennedy had irrevocably committed the U.S. to South Vietnam's defense. American prestige was at stake. That alone was enough to convince Johnson that he must take the next step.

OGDEN WILLIAMS

His career in Vietnam spanned twenty years, from his first tour in 1956 until a visit just before Saigon fell. Now he is retired from the government and living in a small, book-strewn apartment in Washington.

"I had been in World War II in the air force. I got out in 1946 and went to Harvard Law School and became a lawyer in New York for about three years. About that time I got an invitation from an older friend whom I respected greatly to come down to Washington to be interviewed by somebody for something. It was going to be very exciting, he said. I said I'd give it a try. Sure enough, it was the CIA. Now, the CIA in those days was the most exclusive club in town, and the most prestigious agency in Washington by far. That would have been 1950. The whole place looked like the New York Social Register. The secretaries were liable to be Vassar graduates. It was like the OSS, all terribly on the inside track.

"I was attracted to the idea of the CIA. My father had been a very successful New York lawyer, and I knew what that life would be. It would be very disciplined, doing good work, riding the subway every day, getting one month's vacation in the summer, making a lot of money in the end, and dying. That was what it was going to be. He'd done that, and he'd done it far better than I probably could. So what was I doing there? Try something new."

After a tour in Germany from 1951 to 1953, I had a chance to get out of Washington again in '56, which I welcomed. That was because a guy named Ed Lansdale, who was a big shot in Vietnam in those days, was President Diem's primary adviser. Lansdale needed somebody, so I got a chance to go. I said, Great.

This was the Cold War period. The Cold War was not an abstraction or a theory or a psychosis. It was something we perceived as being very real and very physical and right there. For example, at the end of the war the Russians took over Eastern Europe. That was fresh in our minds. The U.S. reacted with the Marshall Plan. Then the Communists started to take over Greece and the eastern Mediterranean, and we reacted with the Truman Plan. Then Truman ordered the Soviets out of Iran, and they left because he had the bomb and they didn't. Then, going down the line, there was Korea, 1950. So the issue of Communist expansion was not something people debated about.

The U.S. under Roosevelt had opposed French colonialism reimposing itself in Vietnam. But by 1949, when the Communists won in China and opened up a flood of arms to Ho Chi Minh's people, we began to take a different tone.

After the French defeat, along comes little South Vietnam and says, in effect, "We fought against the French, too, and we don't want to be colonialized. But we also don't want to be Communized." They wanted to be a third force, and they turned to us for help. For the U.S., as the leader of the free world, it was entirely natural in the context of the 1950s to say, "Well, of course. Obviously. That's what we stand for. We have to man the ramparts wherever they are." Furthermore, we had a feeling in the '50s that the U.S., having come out of World War II the only really successful nation on earth, which totally believed in itself and was totally believed in by everybody else, that this was our normal mission in life. We had the feeling we could do anything. For too many Americans in Vietnam, the question wasn't, "What is the reality here?" The question was, "What reality are we supposed to create here?"

There I was, brand-new, never been to the Far East before, and knew nothing about it. They just put me on Lansdale's team. I suppose I was going to fit in wherever he could use me. It turned out he could use me for an interpreter. I speak French, and the Vietnamese spoke French in all their offices.

Lansdale was just the kind of man to learn from, because he'd had so much experience and insight. He had been successful in the Philippines working with Magsaysay. Then somebody—it might have been John Foster Dulles—had hand-picked him and said, "Do for Vietnam what you did for the Philippines." He was assigned there in 1954 and threw his weight behind Diem. In very short order he ingratiated himself to the point that he had Diem's full confidence. He also had a direct line to Washington and was able to pull strings fast. And he was quite a personality. He dominated the scene in those days.

Lansdale ran his own show with his little team—not more than ten of us, maybe eight. Down in the embassy, there was also a regular CIA station. There was no love lost between them and Lansdale. He regarded them as a bunch of fuddy-duddies, and they regarded him as an uncontrollable wild man, not subject to them, which automatically made him bad. Furthermore, he had much more talent than they did. On the other hand, they had much more discipline. So there was a natural kind of bureaucratic confrontation.

Lansdale had the energy of two or three men, but in many ways the mind of a woman. I'm not talking about his sexuality. Women notice what you're wearing, what you're thinking, the little mannerisms you have. Whereas when a bunch of American men meet, they look at the business on the table. All the thought is on the business, the plan, the concept. Lansdale hears all that, but like a woman, he's observing these people. He's psychoanalyzing them and figuring what makes them tick. He rapidly figured out that Diem had two passions. First, the reason Diem kept Madame Nhu around was to guarantee a family dynasty. Diem was a bachelor, but his brother Nhu and Madame Nhu had children. Diem was very dynastic. He no doubt thought that in due time he'd groom his family to succeed him in government.

The other thing Diem was interested in was photography. And I think Lansdale helped him set up a darkroom. That would mean more to Diem personally than getting a million-dollar loan.

Our idea in Vietnam was: This is a new nation being born. It has to be something. And naturally, we Americans were convinced that the "something" should be our system of representative government, the best in the world. Furthermore, we were the guys who were there. We had the sense of mission. We were the nation that had won World War II and was honored throughout the world. To serve the United States overseas was a dream in those days, because you had very high standing—even low-level Americans did. We had enormous prestige in that period, which we didn't lose until everything blew up.

And Vietnam was an ideal place. It was enormously attractive in those days. It even stayed attractive to many people forever, including me. There was that sense of a young country, which was very inspiring. It was a small country, which meant you could identify with it as a project. There was a very graceful, traditional culture, an enormously pleasant way of life. Saigon was an elegant city. The beautiful tropical foliage, the flamboyant trees, the cabarets, the lovely slim women in those gorgeous ao dais. The whole thing was just elegant and romantic as hell. It was a dream country if you left it alone. Very seductive. So when you combine the seductive ambiance with the idealism of what people were trying to do—well, my life in Vietnam was life in Technicolor, as opposed to black-and-white. It was always an enormous letdown to come back to the States.

South Vietnam had been a country, legally speaking, for several years. In June 1956 the last French troops marched down Rue Catinat and got on the boat and left. I saw that. It was the end of an era. Diem had been consolidating his power against the various warring factions. By '56 he was fully in control and there was no war going on in the country. You could go from one end to the other without anybody shooting at you. Picnic in Dalat, if you wanted to. The war hadn't been turned on by Hanoi yet. And in this period of peace, a hell of a lot got done. South Vietnam was recognized by dozens of foreign countries. Embassies all over the place. Black-tie dances. I remember going in a black tie to hear Piatigorsky play the cello in the Dainam Theater.

But Diem had problems, obviously. He had to pick up the marbles and organize the country. Basic nation-building. Lansdale said, "Okay, what kind of government are you going to have?" We were trying to promote, among other things, something like an American legislature, a national assembly. This was all new to the Vietnamese. They had had monarchies and colonial experience. Getting up a modern political state was a new ball game. We had a lot of sympathy for that, and sometimes a lot of frustration because it wasn't easy to put across. How do you do the elections? How about the judicial system? Do you leave it just the way it was under the French? What do you do about agriculture? What do you do about land reform? What about voting procedures? It wasn't just us—Michigan State University had all kinds of people there, political scientists. Very big on public administration. AID had a mission in there doing everything from teaching English to building hospitals and bridges to figuring out what kind of seed you should plant. Helping the young state get going.

I spent endless hours with Diem, because Lansdale did. I went along as a fairly second-rate interpreter. It wasn't too hard, because Diem was a monologuist. He would sit you down, and no matter who you were, from the janitor to the king, he'd talk for hours about whatever was on his mind. Some of those sessions were duller than hell, and it was hot as hell, and the president was a chain smoker. He'd sit there and smoke. When he wanted an opinion, it'd be: "Ah, Colonel Lansdale, I wanted you to come in because I want to ask you something. What's your advice on this?" He'd get right to the point. Then: "Ah, yes. Now I understand. We'll do that." Very decisive. No problem. End of subject. All over in ten minutes. Then after that: "Well, now, you see. . . ." And he'd just start talking. Smoke going up, we're sitting there nodding: *"Oui, M. le Président."* After two or three or four hours, he'd say, in effect, "Thank you very much, it's been really interesting, now you can go." So I didn't have to do a lot of interpreting. Just translate for my boss what was going on.

It gave people pause about Diem—he spent so much time doing this, they'd wonder how he could have time to run the country. He'd spend all day talking to anybody who would listen. But Lansdale had great patience. He could go on all night if Diem wanted to.

Lansdale did something else that was extraordinary for that time. He's an extrovert from the word go. A great public relations guy. He was comfortable with the Filipinos, who are the same way—very outgoing, very warm, full of gimmicks. He brought a lot of Filipinos over to Vietnam, and he would try to get Diem to act like a modern Filipino politician. Being carried around by a crowd, shaking hands, doing all the things a mandarin would normally never do. Trying to develop the popular touch. Diem tried and tried. He learned how to march and smile and pat babies and so forth, but basically he was not that type of man. He was more austere. Lansdale tried to make a Magsaysay out of him. You couldn't do that. But he went a certain distance. There was some nonsense in that, because the Vietnamese are not Filipinos. It was something of a cross Diem had to bear, I think. Lansdale would bring in Filipino experts to help write the constitution, do this and that, but Diem at first regarded Filipinos as people who play in jazz orchestras, and that's all.

I had mixed feelings about Diem. I didn't easily cotton to a very conservative, fanatical Catholic type. A man who if he hadn't been a politician would have been a priest or a monk. Very prissy. Very authoritarian. Rather pompous, as I thought. Though he also could be very endearing and outgoing in a personal way. But I respected the man. I think in Vietnam he wasn't particularly popular, but he was always respected. He was a man of courage, too. What he was, he was. But he was very narrow. It was evident even that early. He wouldn't reach out like an FDR or a Jack Kennedy to try to win over elements who were patriotic but not Catholic, not from his background. He would treat them with suspicion, and they would resent it.

I remember him talking about the National Assembly. I can't remember the timing exactly, but I think it had just gotten elected and Diem was confronted with the reality of this thing. He said, "I'm worried about this. I know these people. They're a lot of dilettantes. I know what the country needs, and I know what we ought to do. I want to get on with it. These people are just going to sabotage the whole thing and cause me endless headaches." And Lansdale said, "First of all, *M. le Président*, it broadens your government. It gets more people involved. And as far as its difficulties, every democratic president has a problem with his legislature. Part of the art of being president is manipulating and leading and making deals and otherwise getting your way. Even Franklin Roosevelt had to manage his Congress."

Diem went "Hmm," and he had a little Oriental smile. It seemed obvious to me that he was twisting what Lansdale said to his own mindset, which was, in effect, "Ah, we're talking about a puppet assembly. We're talking about something I can manipulate and control. It'll look good on paper, and it'll satisfy the Americans, but I don't have to take it too seriously." I mentioned it to Ed later. But we were overwhelmed with work, and nobody ever went back and said, "When we said Roosevelt managed the Congress, we meant he persuaded them." So there was undoubtedly slippage in these lessons in democracy as you tried to translate them into an Asian framework. I daresay, though I can't prove it, that Diem's way of controlling the National Assembly was hardly the same as Franklin Roosevelt's. It was an autocratic state, which didn't make us comfortable, but nevertheless it was a hell of a lot better than what was going on up north.

Then there was the problem of the so-called elections. According to the 1954 Geneva Accords—which the South Vietnamese delegation had objected to—elections were supposed to happen in 1956 to reunify the country. But it wasn't one country. South Vietnam was already a country before the Geneva Conference. Two years before that, they'd been given their autonomy and had their own government. They sent their own representatives to Geneva. It was de facto two countries, two adversaries, two systems. It was two countries, just like East Germany and West Germany. Diem would talk about this and say, in effect, "Look, we could have these elections if they're in our interests, and not if they're not. We're not bound to do it. And I'm not going to do it for the following very simple reason. North Vietnam has more people than South Vietnam, and they're all under total control. They're going to rig the vote in the North. They'd have to win for that reason alone, even if I could control the voters down here, which I can't. So why should South Vietnam be asked to deliberately commit suicide? Why should we have the elections?"

No Americans differed with him on this, as far as I could tell. Eisenhower didn't, nobody did. Quite the opposite. For one thing, the South Vietnamese had objected to the idea at Geneva. Second, the Americans had merely said we won't object to it, but with the proviso that this represents the will of the people. And it obviously didn't in South Vietnam. So it presented no legal or ideological issues for us. I don't think anybody in Saigon gave two seconds' thought to it. It wasn't as though there would have been an honest plebiscite. The whole election thing was a farce, as far as we viewed it. Why kid ourselves?

We saw the real issue as a race against time—to get South Vietnam built up strong enough and get its institutions in place well enough for it to resist what was obviously going to be a threat someday. No question about that—it was just a matter of when it would come under attack. And in just the two years of my tour, '56 and '57, South Vietnam started to boom. It was exporting rice, which it had done before the French war. Rubber was going out. It was a free-enterprise state, so naturally along with the embassies came foreign corporations. Foremost Dairies set up a big milk-products operation. These gorgeous resort places like Nha Trang and Vung Tau were beginning to be eyed by people as tourist attractions. Everything was beginning to boom. The country was becoming so delightful, so prosperous, so well recognized internationally that the Communists had to knock it off before it got too strong. That's why they started the war again. And that's why guys like me fought to the end to stop them.

In those days, when you had U.S. military advisers and that's all, no combat troops, these guys would fall in love not only with the country but also with their Vietnamese unit and their job. At the end of their tours, you had to take them out of there in chains, practically, because this was the best duty they'd ever had in their lives, and they believed in it more than anything they'd ever done. They were helping to build a little professional army which had a mission against a ruthless, cruel, determined, well-organized enemy. It was quite clear that there were good guys and bad guys. And the good guys needed help. That appeals to something in human nature; it did particularly to Americans in those days. It's not a good analogy, but why wouldn't a scoutmaster become deeply emotionally involved with the Scout troop he's training? Or a schoolteacher with his students? Well, an American adviser would be entranced by the country and his job. You could have staffed the whole place with volunteers.

DOUGLAS PIKE

"I've heard every question on Vietnam that's conceivable—and some that are inconceivable," he says, with the timing of someone who has made the joke many times before. He is another old hand—one of the

State Department's experts on the enemy, the author of Viet Cong *and other books on Vietnamese Communism. From 1960 to 1975 he was stationed in-country almost continuously, though he was also a tireless traveling spokesman for American policy: "I gave something like 2,000 lectures in forty countries on Vietnam." Now he has settled in Berkeley, where he runs the Institute of East Asian Studies. He is about sixty, stocky, rumpled—a bit of the absent-minded professor. Prominent on his desk is a sign with the motto, "I know you believe you understood what you think I said, but I am not sure you realize that what you heard is not what I meant." It oddly mirrors what he has to say about Vietnam.*

I got there in 1960, about the time the National Liberation Front was being formed. I was a Foreign Service officer, and I was interested in social movements as channels of communication, how ideas get around. The jobs I had in Saigon varied. I did studies on communication and public opinion. I wrote some movie scripts for USIS. I was a kind of freelancer in the embassy. When the ambassador needed a speech, I'd write it. If they had a special project, I'd run it. More and more my jobs had to do with the other side. First the Viet Cong and then the North Vietnamese.

I started collecting material on the NLF—propaganda leaflets and so on. There were only about 400 Americans in Vietnam at the time, so I became known as the person who was following the Front. The CIA had nobody tracing it. Their people in the field would send me leaflets when they found them, or they'd capture documents or get them from the Vietnamese. Then they'd come over and pick my brain once a month about what these people were up to. But they weren't really that interested. They kept saying, "This doesn't amount to anything. It's a shadow organization." I'd say, "Yeah, but they're fleshing it out. It's becoming reality. You can't just write it off." A year or two after they started blowing up bridges, they were systematically distributing leaflets all over the country. That took some organization. Particularly since the South Vietnamese government was no dummy, they'd go after these people and scarf them up.

In the early days we did a series of what were called minimal-needs studies. We'd send teams of Vietnamese interviewers out to villages. The basic question I wanted to answer was, Is it possible for the South Vietnamese to win this struggle or not? The test was where the attitudes and sympathies and loyalties lay. I also wanted to know what the reaction was to the North Vietnamese, who were talking about unification. That was the great holy crusade. The NLF was partial to it, and the true believers were completely loyal to it. But the NLF's first objective was political power—or the opposite, which was opposition to the present political power, Ngo Dinh Diem. That's why, when Diem died, there was a mass defection from the Viet Cong. The name of the revolution for them was "Get Diem." Once Diem was gotten, it was over. The true believers, who believed that the name of the revolution was political power for the Front, tended to stay. And for the northerners, the name of the revolution was reunification, so it didn't even begin to be over.

The thrust of our research was, What is it you really want and need out of life? And if you had these, or if you had a government that was clearly trying to deliver them, could it make a legitimate claim on your loyalty? We got a whole raft of answers, but they shook down into four categories. One was what we called security, or peace, or absence of anxiety. Physical security. Everybody wants to live in a secure neighborhood. So that had to do with the whole business of war and peace.

The second was local self-determination. There was a very strong desire to pick the guy who runs the village council. And very little interest in electing a national assembly. We asked, "Why do you vote in these national assembly elections, since it doesn't make any difference to you?" "Well, I vote because my son says good citizens vote." "I vote because it's considered correct to vote." Civics textbooks reasons. Not "I vote because I want to get that SOB out and this SOB in." Because they didn't see any payoff. This was particularly true in traditional villages.

The third one was economic opportunity, the so-called revolution of rising expectations. They didn't ask for things. That's a welfare-state mentality. [Laughs.] They asked for the opportunity to get things. It'd come in the form of complaints. "We don't like to walk a mile to get water. We'd like a well here." But they wouldn't dream of saying, "We want you to dig us a well." Only an idiot would think you'd do that. They would expect some kind of tradeoff—the government might say, "We'll dig a well here if you'll do some work on repairing that road, or you pay some money." The first time American AID teams just came in and dug a well and left, the villagers were often reluctant to use it. They felt there was some catch, that we'd come back and say "Aha, now you've taken all that water out, start paying up." It didn't dawn on them that this was free, no strings attached.

The fourth one was a catchall we called rule of law. Which was absence of corruption—that is, corruption in the sense of government

by whim. That's what bothered them. They wanted a codified, sys-
tematized way of doing business with the government. This again is
very traditional. One guy told me about going into a district office to
get a manifest to ship charcoal to Saigon. If he had to pay a bribe
under the table, he didn't care too much. He just tacked that onto
the price of the charcoal. What he wanted was a sign on the wall
saying, "Do these five things and you get the manifest." And he
wanted it to apply to everybody. But he'd never know. This one time,
he was told, "No, we're not issuing any more manifests." No explanation. So he walked out of the office, and on the steps he met the
brother-in-law of the district chief, saying, "I understand you have
some charcoal for sale." [Laughs.] Obviously, this drove him up the
wall. He was practically subject to blackmail.

Our findings were that if the government was delivering these four—
or was just trying honestly and moving in that direction—there would
be a legitimate claim to the villagers' loyalty. The Viet Cong tended
not to make promises of what they could do for you. There was much
more of "You need to do this for us." They didn't promise a lot of
material rewards. They were trying to appeal to nationalism and xenophobia, which is a fairly weak appeal, actually, up against material
gains. And we concluded that there was widespread opposition to
unification—that is, more northerners down here running things. There
was considerable opposition to the Viet Cong, who were seen as simply
another power group, of which Vietnam had lots. There was no po-
larization between good guys and bad guys. You had a society that
was potentially viable. What the South Vietnamese government rep-
resented in a general way—and it had some bad people in it—was
widely accepted. As governments go, it stood a pretty good chance if
it could get organized.

There was this slogan about hearts and minds—the idea that we
were trying to sell the war to the Vietnamese, who were reluctant to
buy it. But our assumption was that we had their hearts and minds—
that we were there because they wanted us to be there. We weren't
trying to create a mission for ourselves. We simply assumed that these
people did not want to be taken over by the North Vietnamese. And
I think that was the case. I mean, after all, most of the fighting and
dying in Vietnam was done by South Vietnamese. It wasn't done by
the Americans. Our casualties were a mere flyspeck compared to
theirs. And South Vietnam had been seeded by a million Catholics
who came down from the North and were militantly anti-Communist.
There was growing awareness, probably because of propaganda, of
the disparity between North and South, particularly in economic terms.

So it was not true that people didn't care who won. You heard this, but it doesn't even make common sense. Obviously they had a vested interest in who won. It would affect their lives. The notion that it didn't make any difference was absurd.

Of course, you're never sure of attitudes. Everybody you ask has got a vested interest in lying to you if he needs to. And there was a kind of distrust and suspicion. Eighty-five percent of the population of Vietnam in those years was in the villages. And the villagers are very suspicious. It's a cultural thing, and it's historically induced. Dean Thuc, the wisest Vietnamese I ever knew, head of the Faculty of Letters at the university in Saigon, told me, "You could write the history of Vietnam in terms of the double-cross. Everybody betrays us. Sooner or later, you Americans will betray us." He said this in '63 or '64. And it's true—you look at their history, and everybody has sold them out. Or they've sold people out. It's endemic in the whole society. There's great loyalty at the level of the *ho*, the clan. But above that, and across national barriers, extraordinary duplicity.

The Vietnamese have never had a successful relationship with anybody, y'know. Not with China. Not with the fifteenth-century Burmese. Not the Thais. Not the French or the Americans. Not the Chams, whom they emasculated, or the Montagnards, whom they drove into the forests. Nobody. They've never had a single, enduring, successful relationship with anybody. Now the Russians say they can beat this. I say, "The hell you will." Then they say, "Well, who are you to tell us how to deal with the Vietnamese?" I say, "Yeah, that's what I used to say to the French. I should have listened to them, and you should listen to us." [Laughs.]

Vietnamese history is written in terms of how they have always been picked on. "Everybody has always invaded us. The Chinese fifteen times, the Thais four times." It's a national syndrome—they're being bullied by everybody in the neighborhood. Of course, that's not the other guys' view. They say the Vietnamese are a very martial society, always have been. Their earliest figures of worship in the villages, 4,000 years ago, were generals, not gods. The first military academy in Asia was built in Hanoi. They had an army and a navy at the time of Christ that was astronomically big compared to other armies around. Prince Souvanouvong of Laos called them the Prussians of Asia. Yet they see themselves as defensive, as victims of constant aggression. And they really believe it. I'd say to 'em, "What you're saying is that for 2,000 years everybody's picked on you, and you've never picked on anybody." "Right." "They've invaded you, you've never invaded them." "Right." "Why do you suppose this is, that everybody hates you? You don't have a single friend." [Laughs.] "Well . . . maybe they're jealous of us?"

It comes down to an inability to trust—and it comes out in a hundred different ways. One thing we found in our minimal-needs research was a very low premium placed on education. In most societies, education per se is considered a value, because it's a way out and up. In Vietnam, what we got was that you have to be educated, in effect, so you can read the fine print on the insurance contract—otherwise they'll cheat you. You have to know how to count, because if you don't, when you go to the market you'll get cheated.

I had a Vietnamese friend who worked for the Asia Foundation in the early years. His name was Do Linh Thong. Once I said to him, "I've got an idea for a book. I think we can make some money. The Americans are coming in here by the hundreds, and there aren't many guidebooks. One thing Americans like are proverbs and pithy folk sayings. So what I suggest we do is make a comparative study. We'll have three columns in it. You'll have the original in Vietnamese, then a literal translation of it, then the American equivalent." He came over with some Vietnamese books of proverbs. I'd gotten some English ones. And we started writing them out on strips of paper and trying to match them.

At the end of the morning we had a big pile here and a big pile there, and we had about four or five that matched. So I started going through the Vietnamese ones. What struck me was how they were all very negative:

"In the sunlight all governments are the same."

"When the water goes up, the fish eat the ants. When the water goes down, the ants eat the fish."

I couldn't find a lot of ours like that. We have some, but not many. I said, "Don't you have any upbeat ones, like 'Every cloud has a silver lining,' or 'Laugh and the world laughs with you'?" He said, "No, come to think of it, we don't." Well, proverbs are the education of traditional people. They're the knowledge, the distillation of wisdom. And they're indicative of the pattern of thought. This is a negative, pessimistic, untrusting kind of society.

So we abandoned the project. Then I was sort of sorry we didn't just publish the Vietnamese proverbs. One of my favorites is, "The neck of the bottle is at the top," meaning it's leadership that screws things up. If you're in government, you feel this surely is true. And there were a couple that matched. One Vietnamese one was, "Don't measure the area for the stable after the cow has wandered away." Ours: "Don't lock the barn door after the horse is gone." Perfect match. But I couldn't find many of them. I mean, we don't have a proverb, "In the sunlight all governments are the same," do we?

Politics was totally different, too. It was the politics of the clandestine—the way you deal with the occupier. The Chinese had ruled Vietnam for a thousand years. Then the French. So a political group would have a figure who is the ostensible leader. If you're clever you can get around him, and you find behind him a second figure, who's the real power-holder. Only years later do you realize that the guy was put there for you to find, and there was a third one behind him. It's like peeling an onion. The Vietnamese seem to like that.

But it made things difficult for Americans, because it wasn't open decisions, openly arrived at. It was a big problem in the National Assembly. The constitution called for open debate. But you could tell these people didn't like to do it that way. They liked the smoky backroom wheeling and dealing. Tammany Hall–type politics, they just loved that. There was never a democratic, republican tradition.

The result was a whole different style. The leaders the system throws up are different. They have to be sly, paternalistic. Ho Chi Minh is a classic example. He traveled under at least forty different aliases. The official biographies, published in Hanoi, will vary on names, dates, everything. When a foreigner would point this out to him, he would just say, "Well, you must allow an old man a little mystery." He was behaving exactly the way a good clandestine political leader behaves. Throw sand in the face of the world. Nobody knows quite where he stands.

In the South, you often weren't sure whose side someone was on. We used to call it *attentisme*, the French for "fence-sitting." There's a Vietnamese term that means "to go down two roads at the same time." I've read that in the American Revolution, about a third of the colonists were for Washington, a third were Tories, and a third were on the fence. I always thought that meant they weren't sure. But it's a more dynamic thing. It's a person waiting to jump. They have very strong opinions, but . . . And that's what you have with the Vietnamese. A lot of people in the struggle between the GVN and the NLF were playing both sides. They were trying to figure out which side was going to win.

An "April 30 revolutionary" is a pejorative term in Vietnam today, meaning a person who joined the cause the day the war was over. Yet they tend to be accepted. There's some stigma, but there isn't a strong stigma about turncoats and desertion. I remember driving with Vietnamese in the early days out to Thu Duc, the big recruitment and basic training camp. We'd go through a village and there'd be some young men sitting drinking tea. Then another village, some young men drinking tea. I'd say, "Who the hell are these guys, and why aren't they in the army?" They'd say, "Well, they're probably deserters from Thu Duc." I'd say, "Really? Why don't you pick 'em up and take 'em back?" "Well, they'd just desert again." "You mean you don't really care?" "Well, yes, we care, but what can you do?"

You'd find the same with the Viet Cong. Tremendous defection. It was French leave, mostly, not defection in the sense that you join the other side. People just opted out. It wasn't a political act. The Viet Cong would run these guys down and bring them back, rather gently, talk to 'em, try to persuade 'em, and they'd desert again, and the VC would go after 'em. Not even punish 'em. If they betrayed them, yeah. If they joined the other side, maybe. If they came in under Chieu Hoi, the Viet Cong might be more stringent, especially after the program was tightened up and you had to bring in a gun or documents or information. That's betrayal, and the people you betrayed might get hurt, so they're gonna come after you. What used to get me was, first, how patient the VC were to keep going back and getting these guys. And second, how dumb the guys were to keep going back to their villages. The VC knew right where they were.

Another important thing was regionalism. You can't understand Vietnamese politics without it. Now, every country has geographic regionalism. We have it in this country. Even the Swiss talk about the South Tyrolese as if they were some breed apart. In Vietnam, of course, it couldn't be just two regions. It had to be more complicated: three. So you got the northerners, who are seen by the other two as overly sharp, money-hungry, crooks, liars. The centerites are seen as a bunch of blue-nosed snobs. And the southerners—the others say they're lazy, dirty, antimechanical.

On the other hand, the northerners consider themselves to be modern, progressive, rational. The centerites consider themselves to be educated, the inheritors and guarantors of Vietnamese culture, the only Vietnamese who really understand art and music. And the southerners consider themselves to be pacifistic, in harmony with nature. I came into the office one day with a group of Vietnamese, one a northerner. I said good morning to my secretary, who was a southerner. And I said, "What did you do over the weekend?" "Oh, I went out and sat on a hillside and thought about nature." We went into the office, and my friend closes the door and says, "Just like a southerner. Sat on a hillside thinking about nature." And yet I knew a southern woman who worked in Ky's office who would tell you in moments of pique, "All of this trouble we've had here in Vietnam is due to these hotheaded northerners. If they had a little more patience, like we southerners do, the French would have left just like the British left India. There would never have been a Viet Minh war. It's all their fault. They're the ones that had to push." Maybe she had a point.

All politics in Vietnam works within this. You can exaggerate it, and the Communists try to downplay it. They rage about it. I've heard them: "Bourgeois sentimentality, this regionalism—and the southerners are the worst of all!"

So you live in an ambiguous world where nothing is quite as it seems. There's six interpretations to explain anything. As we used to say: "Anybody who isn't thoroughly confused just doesn't know what's going on." And sometimes you felt that it didn't make that much difference—the people were so conniving and full of duplicity that it all canceled out in the end. Particularly the plotting and subplotting and counterplotting. It all just came to nothing.

Over three years, I watched Diem alienate one element of the society after another. He had lost the liberals and the left wing, including the non-Communist left wing, very early, before I got there. He had lost most of the intellectuals and the professional political types. He had alienated all the heads of the political entourages. With the strategic hamlet program, he was in the process of alienating the villagers. Then in the spring of '63 came the Buddhists. Even people in the embassy who knew nothing about politics were saying, "Well, he's gotta settle with the Buddhists. He can't alienate the Buddhists." The ambassador was telling him, "You've gotta settle with the Buddhists. You can't fight a two-front war." To me it was about a five-front war. But brother Nhu and Madame Nhu were saying, "That's what the Americans said with the sects in '55, you've gotta settle. Well, we didn't. We smashed 'em. The Americans were wrong then, and they're wrong today. We've got to smash the Buddhists."

That just generated more and more dissent. Then you got the young into it for the first time, and the Buddhist rank-and-file, who'd never been there before. I remember in about July, an ARVN major, a friend of mine, came to me very upset, saying, "I just don't know what to do. They've arrested my sister. Anti-Diem. She's twelve years old." I said to myself, Now they are alienating the officer corps. And when that begins to go, what have you got left? At the end we estimated that even 40 percent of the Catholics were against Diem.

So when the end finally came—there's so much bullshit about us conniving a coup, and Kennedy ordering it. It wasn't a coup in the usual sense. It was a collapse. Big Minh and his plotters said, "We're not gonna stage a coup here unless every general officer in the country okays it." So they sent their runners out. Obviously this got back to Diem, or Nhu, who was too smart by half. They said, "All right, let 'em stage a coup, and then we'll stage a countercoup." That's why at four o'clock in the afternoon, when Ambassador Lodge talked to Diem on the phone and said it's all over, Diem was saying to himself, It's just begun. We didn't know about their plan for a countercoup. We just thought he'd lost touch with reality. Then Diem was on the radio appealing to loyal troops to come and save him. The station was being run off power mains that came into the palace. All the rebels had to do was pull a switch. Somebody called Big Minh and said, "Should we pull the switch?" He said, "Never mind, who cares, let him talk. Nobody's gonna come." The point is there was a collapse, and the notion that there was a sizable element in that country who were still pro-Diem simply isn't true.

Everybody knew it was coming. We used to have bets on it. The wonder is that Diem lasted as long as he did. It was simply an inability to cope the way he should. I'm not sure anybody else could—obviously, we got a whole parade of clowns after him. We went through a government by coup d'état for two or three years until we got Thieu and Ky—who, believe me, really looked good compared to what we'd had in the past.

Early on, I wrote that victory in Vietnam in the long run will go to the side that gets the best organized, stays the best organized, and can most successfully disorganize the other side. I kept thinking, What they need is a Ho Chi Minh. Ho was an organizational genius. That was the one ability he did have—to create organizations, drown little ones in big ones, and use one to slay another. He would have just chopped up the NLF. He would have had people at each other's throats. But Diem polarized things. He just didn't have the skills.

When I first got to Vietnam, I was of the Kennedy generation: "Let every country know we will pay any price, go anywhere, do anything"—whatever the hell he said, that was what I felt. That was my spirit in Vietnam: I'm going to help set things right. Then the Diem government began to collapse. After the coup you figured, Now we've got that behind us, we've got a new government, things are gonna get better. Well, my wife and I were on leave and we went to Tokyo. Had lunch at the hotel, came out on the steps, and there was a newspaper box with *Stars & Stripes*. Myrna's standing where she can see it. I'm talking, and suddenly tears start coming out of her eyes. She's looking down. So I look down and here's *Stars & Stripes*: "COUP D'ÉTAT IN SAIGON." I had the same feeling—Oh, Jesus, not again. It just swept over me. And almost instantly there was another feeling: Why should

I feel that strongly? I'm on leave, I'm in Tokyo, it's not my country, why the hell do I care? And then a third feeling—Well, I really do care. But I wonder if I'm doing them any good, me any good, my job any good, by getting this emotionally committed. It was instantaneous, a white-light kind of thing that came to me. I kept thinking about it on the plane going back to Vietnam: What does this coup mean to me? [Laughs.] And one thing I concluded was that I should not get emotionally involved. It was a wise decision, because when Vietnam went down the tubes years later, it destroyed some people. One of my friends is living in Paraguay. Another is living in the desert in Utah. Graham Martin is just a hulk of his former self. It rocked me pretty badly in '75, but nothing like if I had not been steeling myself against it for years.

ANONYMOUS

He is a civilian who spent five years working in the American mission, beginning in 1960.

Saigon in the early '60s was one of the most delightful places to live in Southeast Asia. The streets were swept every day. There was order, no chaos. The French town planners had completely redone the city after the fall of the Citadel in 1861. They designed two-lane boulevards, spacious buildings, the Opera House, the Hotel de Ville, the mayor's office. They established the Grands Jardins and the zoo and the museum and very elaborate, nineteenth-century, almost baronial palaces for the governor general of Cochin China. The tamarind trees were very tall, and they gave effective shade on the sidewalks. The war was something that was happening to other people somewhere else.

The siesta hour arrived at twelve. Everybody went home and slept or did whatever, and went back to work at three o'clock. The Americans did the same thing. We knocked off at twelve-thirty and went back at two-thirty.

Foodstuffs were plentiful. We had access to the post exchange and to the commissary. We used the commissary for some basic things, but otherwise we bought most of what we ate on the local market—with the exception of chickens. The chickens were rather scrawny. We bought frozen, U.S.-produced chickens at the commissary. But we bought ducks locally. The beef was largely buffalo, and it was extremely tender. Delicious beef. Lean. The pork is the leanest in the world. Even Craig Claiborne, in one of his books, says that he never tasted better pork than what he had in Saigon. Seafood was plentiful and cheap. For example, we used to buy a kilo of these large shrimp from the South China Sea for fifty cents. You'd get fresh vegetables. Of course, everything had to be cleaned. Public health was always a concern.

There were plenty of little French *épiceries* where you could buy specialty vegetables. We had French bread delivered daily, still warm in the morning. Croissants, the whole shebang.

When we first got there, we had a Vietnamese cook who'd been trained by the French. He was with us for six or seven months. He left because we were always going out on official dinners—here, there, and everywhere. But a friend of mine had the best cook in town, and when my friend left, his cook became my cook. He was Chinese. A fantastic human being. He spoke Cantonese. He spoke Mandarin with me. He spoke French, and he spoke Vietnamese, and he also spoke very good English. And he was an amazing cook. From 1962, when he came to work for us, until I left in August of 1965, we used to eat Chinese food five or six times a week. He would also cook French dishes and American dishes. He used to make things like cakes and pies and little cupcakes for the kids on their birthdays. He introduced us to Hunan and Szechuan cuisine when nobody else knew what it was. He had credit at all the local grocery stores, and he'd go off on his little Vespa motorbike, wearing his Frank Buck pith helmet. People used to approach my wife or myself, even people who hardly knew us: "I understand you have a marvelous Chinese cook. His dinners are the toast of Saigon." And my wife would say, "When would you like to come over?"

We had the Cercle Sportif, which was 500 yards away from us. That was a marvelous place to escape at any time for swimming. You'd have your lunch beside the pool. If you felt like playing tennis, you could. And there was a Club Nautique, which had some of the best *tournedos Rossini* in town. The restaurants in Saigon in those days were superb. I think one or two of them could easily have been two-star restaurants in France. La Muraille, certainly, and another one was the Guillaume Tell.

Besides the cook, we had an amah to take care of the kids—but she needed a lot of direction, she was kind of a dim bulb. And a young woman who was the boyesse, she did things like the laundry, served at table, cleaned up. So we had two live-ins and the cook. We had comfortable housing—not fancy, but comfortable. It was a small villa. We had a car, a 1957 Plymouth.

The one thing we couldn't do—after June of '61, when the Viet Cong started to blow up the railroad—was take the train up to Nha Trang and the South China Sea. But you could fly there. It was magnificent. Seventh-century archeological site, white sand beaches, clear water for scuba diving, great restaurants, an oceanographic institute. In summer we used to rent a villa with other couples who had kids the same age, and right after school was out, the wives would go up to Nha Trang. The husbands used to go up about every third weekend. You couldn't drive up to Dalat, the mountain resort, up about 5,000 feet, nor could you take the train there. But again, you could fly. You weren't even supposed to drive long distances out of Saigon. So everybody got cabin fever after a while.

On Sundays, after church, we'd usually amble down the main street, Tu Do, a quiet little street. We'd maybe have coffee at the Continental Hotel, on the terrace, or we'd go shopping at the *épicerie* for something special. Or we'd go to the central market and buy fresh fruits and vegetables. And we did a lot of antique buying. The antique sellers came to your house. They'd show up with large wicker baskets and all of these treasures wrapped up in newspaper.

Then there were the other types of amusements—the nightlife. I was introduced to it by a friend of mine. He had been in Saigon maybe three and a half years when we got there. He spoke the language, and he was a hail-fellow-well-met. He loved a good time. He enjoyed going out to the bars and practicing his Vietnamese. So one evening, three or four months after I got there, he said, "Let's you and I go down and have a few beers, and I'll introduce you to the nightlife in Saigon." We went to one of the bars on Tu Do.

At that time, the total number of Americans was less than 1,000, and that included dependents. So there weren't that many bars, and many of the girls who worked in them spoke French. As time passed, the ones who spoke French declined, and the ones who spoke English in one form or another increased. But those were the days when we could sit around and chat in French.

The name of the game was always the same: "Buy me some Saigon tea." Saigon tea was very weak tea in a thimble-size container, and you paid something like sixty piasters, which at the official rate would have been about eighty cents. Beer at that time was only about thirty piasters, which would be less than fifty cents. The easiest way to do it was on a wager basis. There was a dice game called 69. When someone first asked you if you wanted to play 69, you did a double-take. The game involved five dice. The single dot counted for ten points. You got one throw of the dice. If you got one or more singles, you counted those and went on. But if you threw and you got none, then it was the other person's turn. When you got up to 60, the single dot then counted for one point—61, 62, 63, and so on. When you got to 65 you discarded one die, and you had four. When you got to 66 you discarded another, then another at 67 and 68. The best games were when you were evenly matched and you got to the end and everybody in the bar was watching to see who was going to win, with both sides down to one die trying to throw a one. It caught on. Every bar had it, even some homes had it. I think it was a French thing. By the time the real buildup of Americans came, in '65, it disappeared. Nobody bothered with it anymore. But in those quiet, somewhat halcyon days, when you could go into a bar and there weren't a thousand people milling around, life was a lot simpler and it was more fun.

So this was a very pleasant diversion. At first it was more of a fun thing—we were all married, and it was a night with the boys. Nobody ended up in bed with these beautiful young ladies. But as time went on. . . . Because the other name of the game was, "Hey, mister, you want to take me home and go to bed with me?" It was the big assignation game. And besides the bars, it went on in two of the big dance halls, the Dai Nam, which was run by a woman named Madame Marie, and the Dai Kim Do—the Great Golden World. The Dai Kim Do was the dance hall in Cholon. It was located on the property that had once been the Grande Monde—the Great World—which was French-authorized and run by the underworld of Corsican pimps and gangsters and Chinese criminal elements. At one time it had the famous Hall of 1,000 Mirrors—it was a first-class house of prostitution, and gambling was permitted. But all that was bulldozed after 1956, when Diem crushed the Binh Xuyen gangsters. A short time later all those places were closed up. But the dance hall was left, and it was something else. The dance floor itself was circular. There were raised platforms on which there were banks of tables. And on the bandstand, in the early days, there was a local Chinese band called Freddie Phuc and his All-Stars. They could never play on key, and they barely got their ensemble together to make music. But when you've got a gorgeous Chinese or Vietnamese girl in your arms, and you're dancing with her, you don't care too much what the music sounds like.

The girls would go from table to table, spending fifteen minutes with each party, dancing and talking, and you paid for their time. That's how they made their money. The woman in charge of the stable, as it were, would come by and hand the girl a little ticket. The girls would count up their tickets at the end of the evening, and that was how many tables they had been to. Their income depended on that. The more tables you sat at, the more popular you were, and the more money you made. If a girl wasn't reasonably popular, she didn't last, because they wanted the girls out there. So some of the best-looking girls of Saigon and Cholon were there. Most of them spoke at least one language besides their own. These girls were specially recruited, and young—most of them in the late teens or early twenties.

For some people, the point of going to the Dai Kim Do was just to be in the presence of an attractive young woman. The exoticness. They'd write home and say, "Dear Uncle Harry, last night I sat between two of the most beautiful women I ever saw in my life." But these girls were available. That was where their other money came from. The usual price was a fixed rate like 1,000 P, which in the early '60s at the official market rate was about fourteen dollars, fifteen dollars. At the black market rate it was half that. If you wanted to tip them for something extra, that was always there. Most of these assignations, except for the bachelors, were quickies. They had to be. Of course, in the early '60s you didn't have a curfew.

I guess it was in May or June of '62 that Madame Nhu's infamous dance ban took effect. I don't know the exact wording, but what she said was that to preserve the purity or the honor of Vietnamese womanhood, public dancing and private dancing are hereby prohibited. The nightclubs and dance halls could remain open, but no dancing would be permitted. Music might still be performed—but no dancing. And looking back on that time, which lasted a little more than a year, it took some of the hassle out of going to these bars. One friend of mine didn't dance very well, and he was always ashamed to go, because the girls were marvelous dancers. Now you could go and just talk to somebody. It was quite pleasant. But during that time the name of the game even more was, "Let's go out somewhere and screw."

I remember November 1, 1963, the morning after the coup had been successful and Diem and his brother had been killed. I was walking down Tu Do, and as I passed the Tu Do nightclub, the workmen were hammering back the dance floor, which opened that evening. They had probably taken it up in sections and hidden it somewhere, and they were just putting it back.

In general, there was an atmosphere of license. It goes with the territory. It exists in Thailand, and it had existed in Vietnam since the time of the French, and probably before. Sex was a commodity, and it was for sale. There was never a question, as you find in a singles bar here, of "Will she or won't she?" It was always a question of where, when, and how much. And there wasn't very much guilt about it. It was open. The Vietnamese didn't have the hang-ups about sex that we have—unless they were Catholic. So your partners could range anywhere from a streetwalker, if you took the chance, to the girls in the bars to the girls in the dance halls to the occasional European woman who might be available for a price or just because she was lonely.

There were a small number of beautiful French women. Some of them had been born there. They'd be at the Cercle Sportif in the skimpiest bikinis you've ever seen. But for an American to have a liaison with one of them was rare, because by and large the French didn't like Americans. Then there were the very, very beautiful upper-class Vietnamese girls who traded sex as a means of escaping the boredom of their lives. I knew some of them. These girls had their own cars, many of them had European educations, and they did their thing. Sometimes they were married, but not necessarily. And some Americans had relationships with the local girls who worked at the embassy or the AID mission or whatever. But the chance of being found out was much higher.

And of course, when all else failed, there was always the little boyesse, who according to tradition for more than 100 years helped the cook, helped the amah, usually did the cleaning, did the laundry, served at table, and screwed the master. That tradition carried on during the time I was there. How did you reimburse them? Little gifts from the post exchange, maybe some extra money in the pay envelope. It was like incest; it was convenient, familial, and cheap. [Laughs.] As long as they didn't get pregnant. Although I had a neighbor with a boyesse who had the habit at cocktail parties of grabbing American men by the crotch to indicate her interest.

It was a wonder world. I remember a colleague of mine who came out in 1964—good Ivy League upbringing, proper prep schools, the whole thing. He wasn't married, and when he got to Saigon and saw all these women, he went wild. Within three months he had contracted gonorrhea, so he had to get himself cured. From then on he got himself a steady girl, but he got her pregnant, so she had to have an abortion—which was difficult in Madame Nhu's day. Abortion was a real no-no, but the doctors did it anyhow. You could do it for about seventy-five dollars.

There was another fellow I knew with the USIS. He was in Vietnam for about two years. Good-looking guy. I remember going to his place one time, after all the dependents had left, and he showed us card files of all the women he had screwed during the more than two years he had been in Saigon. On individual three-by-five cards he had the name of the girl, her basic measurements, and then his comments. And he took Kodachrome slides of all these girls. All of them. He had more than 800 women catalogued. Two or three a day was no problem for him. He was insatiable. Another friend and I sat through about three hours of all the slides he had taken of these girls, in the nude, or with clothes on, posing. Including a few girlfriends of mine.

After 1965, when all the dependents went home, all bets were off. I remember we had a meeting and they said, "Look, people are human. Obviously the time will come, if you've got another year to go, when you'll want a little. Just remember that if you get yourself involved with a Vietnamese girl, ask yourself if you'd be ashamed to introduce her to your American friends and your foreign friends, including your Vietnamese friends." This was an older guy who said this, very wise and capable. And I remembered it, because that way you'd feel less guilt about it, which was always a problem. There were some girls you wouldn't even want to invite to come home with you, much less introduce to your friends. But a lot of the holier-than-thou Americans, after the families were gone, were seen at eleven-thirty getting out of a taxi or their own cars in front of their houses with Vietnamese girls. It was shack-up time for everybody. You didn't have your wife, so you had to have some kind of loved one, and these girls were eager. But the idea was: Don't flaunt it. Never flaunt it.

As for my wife, when she was still there—it reminds me of a story I once heard from a friend in Saigon who was a lawyer. In his final year of law school, back in the States, he had to put in some time with the Legal Aid Society. He was taking a case that involved a simple tort, and during the questioning of his client so he could advise her what to do, it developed that her husband was committing incest with their sixteen- or seventeen-year-old daughter, and it had been going on for quite some time. My friend was kind of appalled by the whole thing. He said, "Madam, don't you know that incest is not only a crime, a felony, but also it's forbidden by custom in almost every society in the world?" She said, "Well, I don't know too much about that. All I know is it sure do take a load off of me." I think maybe that's the way my spouse felt, too.

Early in the game, I think it was in 1961, I met a Vietnamese girl, and we were attracted to each other. Ultimately we became lovers and we had a nice affair, which lasted a long time, at least until 1962. At that point she met someone else, another American, and ended up marrying him. After that, I probably had no more than three or four steady girlfriends, and one of them lasted the final fifteen months I was there. There's a funny story about that. This girl, Suzy Wu, was gorgeous. She was part owner of a bar. And we initiated our relationship in the summer, which was when your loved ones—meaning your wife and children—would go up to Nha Trang. That was wonderful for them, and for the husbands at home: "I've got to get out of going up to Nha Trang this weekend, I've got a date Saturday night. I'll come up with something. I'll get malaria, maybe. . . ."

The families usually came back right after Labor Day. So I met my wife and kids at the airport, came back home, had lunch together, had our siesta, and then I came back from work about six-thirty. My wife said to me, "Want something to drink?" I said, "Yeah, I could use a nice cold beer or a gin-and-tonic." We started talking about what the summer had been like, and she said, "You want another gin-and-tonic?" I said, "Yeah, why not?" She brought it on a tray— a tray with a gin-and-tonic and a case of Helena Rubinstein lipstick. And she said, "Next time you see your girlfriend, tell her this isn't my shade." That was all that was ever said about it.

Not all American women were as understanding as my wife. There was one fellow, nice fellow, who had married an Italian girl at the end of World War II and had a number of children with her. She was rather ponderous. I remember on more than one occasion running up the back stairs where I worked, and finding him and his secretary, a very lovely Vietnamese girl—there must have been fifteen or twenty years' difference in age—holding hands and talking together. On the back stairwell. His wife, being the good Italian mother that she was, suspected that there was some hanky-panky going on. I guess the girl lived in her own house or used someone else's house for an assignation place, because the wife followed him there and took a walking stick with her. She surprised them in the room in the act, and beat the hell out of him with the stick. She bruised him. She cut him. She would have killed him. The girl just picked up her clothes and took off. Then the wife hauled him back home, and as I recall the story, she took all his clothes away from him, locked him in one of the rooms, and would go in periodically just to vent her outrage. By this time he needed medical attention. She broke his wrist. He was a mess. I remember seeing him all black and blue. He was finally sent home—I don't know if they fired him or not.

And there were some tragedies, some real tragedies. There was one girl I knew at the Phoenix Bar whose name was Phuong. She wore glasses, which was strange because not many Vietnamese wore glasses. She had a nice body. And she spoke very good English. She had more intellectual potential than most. She and I had been friendly periodically, nothing on a regular basis. Then I lost track of her. She'd been working in a couple of bars in another neighborhood. In late '64, I was in the post exchange and I saw this girl wearing a gray ao dai over white pants. I looked at her, and there was something familiar about her. I looked again, and it was Phuong. She had had her nose sharpened—because they have flat noses—and she looked quite different. She had on an engagement ring and a wedding ring. She told me she had met this American sergeant, and she married him. He was going back to the States in the spring of '65, and she was going back with him. I congratulated her, I was very happy for her. She had a child out of wedlock, too, and he was going to adopt the child. In fact, the child was living with them. They had an apartment in downtown Saigon. And that was the last I ever saw of her.

Then, shortly after all the American dependents went home in February of '65, there was a brief article on the back of the *Saigon Post* about a woman who was found dead by her own hand in the apartment of an American lieutenant colonel. She had used his service pistol, a .45-caliber, and she had blown her head off. I didn't realize that this was Phuong until later, when I was having dinner in Cholon with three friends, and we were talking girls as we usually did. One of them said, "Y'know, there's a real tragedy, a gal named Phuong who worked at the so-and-so bar, she killed herself about a month ago." I said, "I know Phuong, the last time I saw her she was at the PX, and she was married." It turned out the sergeant's commanding officer took a shine to Phuong, had the sergeant transferred out early, and she moved in with him. It didn't work out, and one day when he was off working, she killed herself. And he was sent home.

But there were some good things that happened, too. A lot of girls ended up with very lonely American GIs who suddenly found themselves the idol of someone else's attention—and these were just plain folks from the farms or the slums. How these things resolved themselves once they got back to the States, I don't know. But ninety percent or more of the relationships ended when the plane left with the American on it going home.

By 1965 it had changed. It got sleazier. I remember *Paris Match* had an article on Saigon, comparing it then with the period from '46 to '54. The headline was "*Saigon est devenue poubelle, bordel, et garnison au même temps*"—"Saigon has become a dustbin, bordello, and garrison all in one." It was true. I remember, after the buildup started, meeting a girl in a bar who had had smallpox. She was covered with scars. And I remember thinking, Well, God, even a former smallpox victim has a right to make a living.

LIEUTENANT GENERAL JOHN H. CUSHMAN

At the train station in Bronxville, New York, he is waiting for me in a modest car—a stocky man looking younger than his sixty-odd years, with iron-gray hair cut short and brown eyes, dressed casually. We drive to a big old wooden house in a leafy neighborhood. As we settle in the living room, his wife brings coffee and a plate of sweet rolls. On the wall above us is a portrait of a white-haired man in military uniform.

"My father was a career army officer. He was stationed in China in the early '20s—the 15th Infantry Regiment in Tientsin, China. I was born there. The oldest child. It seems as if I always wanted to go to West Point and be an officer myself. I finally enlisted in the army in 1940, after a year of college and a couple of years working. In those days you enlisted for a year and then took the examinations for West Point, which I did in July 1941. The war broke out in December, and our curriculum was reduced from four to three years, so I graduated in 1944. I was commissioned as an engineer officer and went into the Corps of Engineers. During the war we built airfields and ports in the Pacific. In 1951 I transferred to the infantry."

He retired from the army in 1978 and now has a busy schedule of military writing and consulting.

I didn't know what to expect in Vietnam, and I didn't foresee what was going to come. I can't say I ever foresaw what was going to come. That would have been asking a lot. But I knew the situation was not good. I had done some reading when I was in the Pentagon. And back in the mid-'50s, I had worked for Major General Lionel McGarr, who then was the commandant at the Command and General Staff College. In 1960 McGarr went to Vietnam as chief of MAAG. I was in the Pentagon in '61 when they were making studies of Vietnam, and McGarr was called in to give his views. I remember going to visit him in his quarters in Wainwright Hall at Fort Myer, where they put up visiting senior officers. He was getting his story together. He showed me what he was saying, and I read it, and it was bad. He referred to the "porous border," something like 800 or 1,000 miles of border with Laos and Cambodia that allowed the North Vietnamese cadres and supplies to flow in without restriction. And a coastline that long. So I knew things were not so good.

My first tour in Vietnam started in 1963. I went there from the Pentagon, where I was working in the office of the secretary of the army. I put in a couple of months in Saigon in an organization called ACTIV, Army Concept Team in Vietnam. We were testing matériel and doctrine. Helicopter tactics, that sort of thing. But I really wanted to be an adviser. I let that be known. And one day I got a telephone call from General Richard Stilwell, who was a brigadier general then and MACV J-3. He wanted me to go down and take over the 21st Infantry Division advisory team in the delta at Bac Lieu when Colonel Fred Ladd left.

At the time, there was a little contest between the press and the authorities as to how the situation was in the countryside. David Halberstam, Malcolm Browne, and a coterie of reporters like that were there in late '62 and early '63. They took a liking to some of the advisers in the provinces—John Vann, Fred Ladd, Wilbur Wilson. The reporters would go out and get straight answers from the advisers and come back and write them up in *The New York Times* or *Time* magazine, telling how bad things were. The people in Saigon were saying, "It's not nearly that bad, you're getting the wrong information, here's what it really is."

So when I got to Vietnam, I traveled a lot, because I was studying the army's use of an airplane called the Caribou. The Caribous would take off from Tan Son Nhut and go down through the delta, for example, stopping at all these little airfields. It gave me a chance to see the countryside. One day I went out to Tan Son Nhut and who should be on the same Caribou but David Halberstam. He wanted to go down into the delta. We blew a tire in Ca Mau, way down at the tip of South Vietnam. We sat there for two or three hours while somebody brought in a tire. I had a chance to talk to Halberstam— mostly listen, because I was new. He was talking about how bad things were, and I remember one thing he said, that we were in Ca Mau, "the southernmost province of North Vietnam."

This was also the time of what they called the strategic hamlet program. Sir Robert Thompson, the British guerrilla expert who straightened out Malaya, was an adviser to Diem, and in reality to the Americans, too. He sold the idea of strategic hamlets—rounding people up into fortified villages. When I was named an adviser, Dick Stilwell told me, "All right, now remember, we're emphasizing strategic hamlets. Strategic hamlets are the name of the game." I went over to the part of MAAG that was handling strategic hamlets. I wanted to get a picture of the program and what it was designed to do. That visit satisfied me that it was terribly important to do it well.

I had already visited people whose judgment I respected. Wilbur Wilson, for example, and Fred Ladd. Fred was very straightforward, very honest, very outspoken, an intelligent and perceptive guy. Talking to him, I got the picture that the strategic hamlet program was very badly managed. There were false reports of progress. Fred was saying, "This is a disaster. They're doing it too fast. They're coming in here with grandiose schemes and massive enterprises, and nothing's happening. They don't even do a good whitewash job." Others said it, too.

I went out on one of his operations. I never will forget it. In Saigon I was staying at the Majestic Hotel and having my meals at the Rex. That morning I was sitting on the roof of the Rex there, in a sweet kind of sunrise. Then going down to Bac Lieu, getting on an H-21, which is a rattletrap of a helicopter, and going into a rice paddy landing zone. Getting out and cruising around in the bush with a U.S. sergeant and some Vietnamese. Then getting picked up after a day in the paddies, and ending up that night on the roof of the Rex.

When I went to Bac Lieu, after a while I didn't completely agree with the official position coming out of Saigon. But I didn't consider the people in Saigon idiots, or unpatriotic, or deliberately deceptive. I could see that it was just a different view. It's not unpatriotic to be optimistic. It may be unrealistic to be optimistic, it may even be blind to be optimistic, but it's not dishonest to be optimistic.

We had a very small advisory team in those days. We didn't have any advisers at the district level. Only at the province level. And we had majors there, not very senior people. You might have had a province advisory team of ten people, maybe twelve at the most. The idea was that these guys would assist the province chiefs in making an honest judgment as to the reality of the situation. An objective picture. I wanted it to be accurate.

The 21st Division's tactical zone was the southern tip of the country, the provinces of Phong Dinh, Ba Xuyen, Chuong Thien, and An Xuyen. I had advisers in each province, and I said, "I want each one of you to draw a picture of your province. The area under government control, we'll color that blue. The area under enemy control, we'll color that red. The area that's contested, we'll color that yellow. And where the provinces meet, I want you guys to agree on these areas. In other words, if you say the line is here, I want the province adviser next to you to say it's there, too, in his province." I don't think this had ever been done before. Fred Ladd, I think, instinctively knew, but the idea of putting numbers and criteria on it had not been done before.

I've got this map in my mind's eye. This great big map—red, blue, and yellow. We wanted to have simple criteria. We eventually arrived at two criteria for blue: that officials could move around at night without an escort, and that there was no open Viet Cong taxation. There might be extortion, but the tax collector did not come around openly. We'd have our advisers go out and check these areas. They'd say, "Hey, we've got this blue here, I want to go out and see it." The Vietnamese would say, "You can't go out there, you'll get shot at." "Then let's don't make it blue, it's contested. Make it yellow."

In red areas there was not even a symbol of our control. Not even an outpost. The only thing that would happen in that sort of area was an operation that would pass through like a ship going through water. I remember going into one of those areas. I'll never forget it. I went on an operation in a VC village and saw its school. This was very interesting for me, to see the schoolbooks. And we saw money, VC money. Now, if you've got money you've really got a government. If you've got schools, you've got a structure. There was nobody in this village except women and children. We couldn't do anything about any of that, so we just left. I'm sure school was in session the next day and the men were back in the village.

Now, in the yellow areas you had symbols. You had your outposts. But the village chiefs slept only in the outposts. It was contested.

Well, it turned out that when you looked at the blue, it was just around the cities and towns. Very small areas. The blue areas had more population, but I forget the figures. We had maybe 10 percent of the area and 30 percent of the population. The other side had 60 percent of the area and 30 percent of the population, and contested was maybe 30 percent of the area and 40 percent of the population. The biggest area was red, the yellow was next biggest, the blue was smallest. That wasn't surprising. It was graphic, it was vivid, but it wasn't surprising. It was expected. It was interesting verification of what I had been led to believe.

One thing I learned from working on this map was that there were two governments in South Vietnam. This was such a fundamental reality, but it was not really understood. David Halberstam was right. There was a province of Ca Mau, and it was the southernmost province of North Vietnam. There was a province chief down there. There was a tax-collecting apparatus. There were district chiefs. And it didn't necessarily have the same boundaries as the South Vietnamese province. Sometimes the provinces didn't even have the same name. In fact, the province that Ca Mau city is in was called Ca Mau by the North Vietnamese and An Xuyen by the South Vietnamese. And it had slightly different boundaries. But there was a province chief. He was living in some cave underground or some shack. He wasn't surrounded by a lot of servants and gracious living like the province chief of An Xuyen, but he was running that province. He was probably collecting more taxes in those days than the South Vietnamese. And he controlled more area. Both governments had their schools, they both had their courts—they had everything.

I'd say the light turned on for me when I went through that little mud-encrusted village with grass huts and saw those textbooks. Saw the people, saw the looks on their faces. People who resented your being there but didn't want to show it. A certain fear and hostility. I suppose it's the look of somebody who sees an enemy but doesn't want to provoke him. Withdrawn. Clearly people of the other side. But that wasn't what really made the impression—it was the evidence of a structure, a very detailed structure. I would look at the enemy order of battle, up to the province chief, and I'd ask questions: "Tell me who that guy is." The Vietnamese intelligence guy would pull out his briefing charts—they had great briefing charts, wonderful charts, prepared in very meticulous detail. They really learned how to brief over there. They had been trained by the French to keep records of all kinds. They'd say, "We think the province chief's name is such-and-such. It may be an alias. And this is their province, it's called by a different name."

Now, about a month or two after I got to Bac Lieu, Bob Montague showed up. He had worked with me in the Office of the Chief of Staff in '59 and '60. He was a very fine officer. Brilliant, first in his class at West Point. He was coming to Vietnam, and was a lieutenant colonel. In my position as senior adviser—I was a lieutenant colonel holding down a colonel's position—I was authorized two deputy senior advisers, one for managing the advisory team, and one strategic hamlets adviser. I fought to get Bob Montague as my strategic hamlets adviser. And when he got there, we put together a concept of pacification for the 21st Division.

Yes, I could have chosen to focus on purely military matters, and lots of people did that. I did want to have the military operations, but I thought they should all be in support of the primary concern, which we called province rehabilitation. It was a bone of contention whether the division should have a mission in pacification. A division is a fighting unit. And it turned out they were not given any responsibility for pacification. I was very much against that, because it took the division commander—who had ARVN forces—out of the planning for pacification. He became just a fighter, going out and chasing the VC. Which is an aimless, pointless way to function. When I was an adviser, I insisted to my division commander, "You have to have an interest in pacification. That's got to be your mission." The key problem in Vietnam was the contest between these two governments, and you had to defeat that other government and its structure. You had to win back the loyalties of the population, the hearts and minds, one heart and one mind at a time. You couldn't just go out there and run a lot of operations and try to kill a lot of so-called Viet Cong. You had to go at it much more systematically, much more subtly, much more basically than that. I insisted on it in my division, but this was not the way it went everywhere.

Bob and I built a new kind of operation with a new kind of doctrine and organization. We built it as we went along. It was a political-military operation, a combination of military security and political improvement. One of the first things we did was suggest that the Vietnamese stop building new strategic hamlets. I think they were willing. They had already built 700 so-called hamlets in that area, and I think it was so goddamn evident that they were going too fast that they probably figured it was about time they got some advice like that. Then we found a major, a Vietnamese major at division headquarters who had been involved in pacification years before, working for the French. A grizzled old guy. Spoke good French. He told us about a concept the French had used: the oil-spot technique. So we called ours the oil-spot technique. The idea was to go into a district and stick with what you controlled and work outward, like an expanding oil spot.

We set up a pilot model and we chose the district of Vinh Loi, where Bac Lieu was, and the division headquarters. After testing it there we'd pass it on to other districts. The first thing you had to do was establish what you controlled. I called this the "moment of truth" for the district chief. We'd go into a district and we'd ask him what he controlled. The district chief would probably be a captain, and he'd take us over to a map and say, "I control all of this." I'd say to him, "Well, let's go over to this place." He'd say, "Wait just a minute, I'd better get the civil guard company for an escort." All of a sudden he knew he didn't control what he thought. Then I'd say, "Where can we go without an escort?" Because that was our definition of a blue area.

When I got back from my first tour, I wrote an article for *Army* magazine. [He reads from the draft of his article.]

> Measured against these criteria, the oil spot in Vinh Loi
> district did not extend much beyond the city limits at Bac
> Lieu. . . . It was a healthy experience for our young district

chief to arrive at this truth. No longer did he have to delude himself and his superiors. Now he could face his problem like a man. More important, he could begin to take the concrete, pragmatic steps necessary to cope with the problem. Division had presented him with a simple recipe. Our district chief thought it just might succeed. The personality of the district chief began to change. He began to have hope.

I can remember that. Before, he hadn't been honest with himself. Now he recognized reality. I think it may have been the first time anyone had encouraged him not to live in a dream world. When he had the strategic hamlets program, he was just a funnel of money and advisers, he was part of the machinery that wasn't producing anything. We said, "Let's not pretend to do the impossible. Let's do what we can." One of our key points was to take it more slowly, to be satisfied with years of work, and not keep pushing these guys to report results.

Then the notion was to start at the edge and go out. You'd go into a hamlet that was contested, and you had to pacify this hamlet. First thing you had to do was give them some security. This would be the military, or "clear" side of things. [Reading again.]

The pacification group would be the basic unit. . . . First, it would have one "hamlet action team" for each hamlet undergoing pacification. This would be the "civil" or "hold" side of the organization. Second, it would have platoons of paramilitary forces—normally for the immediate protection of the hamlets undergoing pacification. This would be the "military" or "clear" side. . . . The hamlet action team would contain from four to five civilians. These men were to be selected from the local area, specially trained, and indoctrinated. Theirs would be a political, psychological, civic action, economic, organizational, intelligence, and military function.

I remember our training charts, all in Vietnamese, training these people to do this kind of work. I remember sitting in Bac Lieu with Bob Montague and Dick Holbrooke and my people and the Vietnamese, writing the lesson plans for training these people, spelling out what's expected of them. And this was not an American invention. We got a lot of it from this old major. It was a Vietnamese and an American thing. Our approach was to provide the structure and the system for doing it. We couldn't step into the shoes and skins of the

Vietnamese. They had to do it. Later on, the Americans started taking things over.

Remember, this was 1963. Up to that point I don't think that at the district level there had been anything systematic like this, at least in my area. Things were haphazard. Go out and conduct some more operations, shoot off some artillery, pass out some bulgur wheat, which was the famous USOM stuff they used to pass out—and which the Vietnamese used to feed pigs. It was hit-and-miss. Everyone had his project up in Saigon, right down through the stovepipe, but it wasn't pulled together. And with the strategic hamlets, the diagnosis of the problem was correct but not the treatment. It was as if I said to you, "You're overweight, so you're going to starve for a month." Or, "You've got to get yourself in shape, so I want you to do 100 push-ups tomorrow." It wasn't until '66 or '67 that they put our kind of pacification in effect throughout the country, and Bob Montague had a lot to do with that. By that time it was called CORDS. Two and a half years later it was all in place, with big money behind it. It was a terrific program. It was working. The thing is that it was turned on too late.

How did the pilot program in Vinh Loi turn out?

Well, I left Vietnam in April 1964, a few days after the first pacification group finished training. It took a long time to set up. And there was a big hiccup on the first of November, 1963, when the coup against Diem took place. They replaced just about every province and district chief in the whole country in the next few weeks. It was disastrous. We were waiting for a couple of months before things really got rolling again. Meanwhile we were developing our thinking, but it took us until December or so to get the new division commander's support. So when it came right down to it, Bob Montague and I had only a few months to get all this together and get the cadres going. I think after I left, the program probably suffered from the lack of my obsession. It was more than a conviction with me, it was an absolute driving determination to make this thing succeed. And then other programs got started, other ways of going about it, different ideas. Bob also went home after his year was up. Frankly, I think if I'd gone back there a year later I probably would have been disappointed.

By the time I left, I knew what the problem was. I knew it so goddamn well it was painful. And I knew the answer: It was pacification. I thought that we could win the war with the thirteen right men, four corps senior advisers and nine division senior advisers. They could make pacification work. But we needed the right people, and we needed to keep them here. Make it possible for them to see their families. Move their families to the Philippines. Two or three years later they started doing something like that.

When I got home, I couldn't forget Vietnam. I was obsessed with it. I made a pest of myself at the National War College. I could see us heading to disaster in '65, when we started to put American troop units in there. I wrote my thesis on the proposition that U.S. units should not go into the countryside. The ARVN should do that, and the U.S. troops should be used to cut the Ho Chi Minh Trail. I brought back this fantastic set of briefing charts, and I lectured all over. And I wrote my article sometime in '65. I couldn't get it cleared. There was nothing classified about it, but it was sensitive. It was bad news. The Office of the Secretary of Defense wouldn't clear it. They allowed it to be sent to the war colleges and put in the libraries there, but it couldn't be published. Finally, in 1967, it was cleared and published in *Army* magazine. With certain changes. For example, my article started out, "The central problem in South Vietnam is that the Viet Cong insurgents are in control of vital areas of the countryside." They changed it to, "A thorny problem in South Vietnam is the Viet Cong control over parts of the countryside." From their way of phrasing, it sounds like a nagging little itch you've got there. You're dying of cancer, and they say you've got hemorrhoids. I wrote, "When I arrived in July of 1963 and when I left in April of 1964, the Viet Cong government was the dominant force in the majority of the countryside." They said, ". . . the Viet Cong government appeared to have control in large areas of the countryside." Appeared!

OGDEN WILLIAMS

My first tour ended in 1957, and I didn't go back until 1962. Kennedy was making a big push in Laos and Vietnam. As part of that, they greatly beefed the AID mission and MAAG. I resigned from the CIA in early '62 because I got a better offer from AID, and I went back as a special assistant to the AID mission director.

In 1962 the Americans still had the same enthusiasm and spirit as in the '50s, but Vietnam had changed. The second Indochina War, starting in 1960, was going full blast. The Communists had realized the elections were not going to take place, so they had better start the war up. And the war they started—which was very effective— was a war of sabotage. They began with political assassinations at the village level. And they told people, "This is a lesson. Don't get out of line." They'd kill the very good officials and the very bad ones. They'd leave the mediocre ones and say, "Okay, you just play along, but report to us."

So our idea was to get in there, try to strengthen Diem, and prevail. Those were the days of counterinsurgency. The theory was that the guerrilla is somebody swimming in the sea of the people. You try to win the support of the people. Therefore we had all kinds of projects designed to improve rural life. Hundreds, if not thousands, of schools were set up and furnished. Roads, bridges, medical facilities, agricultural projects, better seeds, better fertilizer, hog programs, corn programs, all designed to improve the lot of the local guy. And in many ways they did.

Now we come to a crucial point. One thing I learned—and it can be applied to El Salvador or anywhere else—is that you can take a country under siege like that, and you can first help it to install the most representative government in the world, and everybody has a nice school to go to, and they have social justice, agrarian reform, all the good things that are supposed to solve these problems—but it won't do any bloody good as long as that little guy can come out of the jungle at night and put a gun in the ear of the local official and say, "Listen, all this do-gooding stuff from the government, forget it. We represent the revolution, and unless you agree, something awful is going to happen to your wife and kids, not to mention you. Don't ever forget that. Don't ever think this government can protect you day and night, because we will get you if we want to. Go on doing your job, just don't do it too well. And keep us informed of what you're doing so we can take countermeasures."

That's exactly what happened in Vietnam. All the good government in the world was not going to take the place of security. It takes years and millions of dollars to build a bridge, and it takes fifteen minutes to blow it up. Any idiot can blow up a bridge if he just knows a little about explosives. But building one is really difficult. That's true in every aspect of building a nation. So the poor South Vietnamese were constantly trying to build their institutions, train their people, and constantly getting sabotaged.

I suppose in the last analysis, unless everything had been in their favor, the South Vietnamese just didn't have what it would take to hold off the North. I had a friend named Henri Mege, an old Frenchman pushing seventy who'd been a French cavalry officer in Vietnam for twenty or thirty years. Now he was making his living as an artist. He said, "Monsieur Williams, you know, these Vietnamese will be very grateful if the Americans can win this war for them. They don't want to be taken over by the Communists. But they won't make quite enough effort to do it for themselves. They don't have the *élan vital*, the energy. The dynamism is on the other side. The fanaticism iṣ on the other side." He said this in '64.

South Vietnam, God knows, was war-weary, and world-weary to a certain extent. Particularly the ruling class—not necessarily the young. It had been a quiet colonial backwater for a long time. Great permissiveness. When a society finds itself in that position, it deteriorates. And the North Vietnamese were a tougher breed anyway. The North Vietnamese were the hard Cromwellians against the Cavaliers. Dour types. Scots. And the southerners looked more like Italians. More fun, nicer. Even within South Vietnam, the farther south you went the nicer people got. If you were a South Vietnamese officer and you retired, you might want to go live in the delta, because the people were nicer down there.

I never had any ideological qualms about giving everything I could to the cause of the South Vietnamese. Because generally speaking, they were laissez-faire people who simply liked to live and be left alone. They weren't mad at anybody and had no desire to conquer the world. When they got violent or vicious, nine times out of ten it was out of hysteria and stress. Whereas the Communists were just the opposite. They always did things for a purpose. They would come into a village and round up all the people, grab the village chief and denounce him for working with this "fascist government" or some damn thing. Whatever their ideology said. Then they'd commit the most God-awful atrocities. Kill the children one by one and disembowel the wife and then put the guy's eyes out and leave him alive. All in cold blood, not out of any hysteria at all, not even out of any ill feeling. Just to drive home a political lesson. Very effective stuff.

People often said that the most efficient, least corrupt guy in any given province was likely to be the local VC leader. And it may have been true. But that doesn't mean the cause they were representing was more humane at all. Quite the opposite. Let's take France in 1940, at the beginning of World War II. France was a paradise for the American tourist. Everybody loved the place. Charm, everything wide open. Lots of corruption. No patriotic fervor. It was in a state of decadence. And into this came the Germans. Not just the Germans, but the Nazis—and not just the Nazis, but the SS. A bunch of guys clean and disciplined to the core. Every cell in their body in perfect fighting fitness. Polite when they're told to be polite. Well dressed.

Correct. And fanatical. They went through the French like butter.

The moral is that fanaticism can be built around bad causes as well as good. Lots of people in the '30s said, "The Nazis are great guys, look how efficient they are." Just like in the '60s, people who didn't know them said the Viet Cong are great guys, look how dedicated they are. The best advocates in these causes, the best cadre, the best foot soldiers, may very easily be on the wrong side. Some of the Communists were undoubtedly imbued with a holy fire. But in North Vietnam, information was totally controlled. They actually thought they were coming down to help the southerners drive out the colonialists—us. That's why they were willing to fight, and that's why they were willing to die.

What does the West, including South Vietnam in those days, really want? What does it believe in? Well, what the South Vietnamese believed in, and probably what the United States believes in, except for some firebrands, is comfort and reasonableness. We want to be comfortable and reasonable. Comfort is a good thing, and reasonableness is a very good thing. But neither of them are fighting faiths. South Vietnam in 1960 had a political vacuum to fill, and basically they wanted to be left alone to enjoy one of the most lovely and pleasurable environments I have ever known. But no fighting faiths to speak of. These people had to try to preserve something far better than what the North was offering, and in the end it cost them 200,000 battlefield dead. It was Sparta attacking Athens. Sparta finally defeated Athens, but today who remembers Sparta?

JIM VINCENT

A short, barrel-chested man in his fifties, with a red bandanna around his forehead holding back a shock of graying hair. He offers a beer; we sit by a small pool in back of his ranch-style house in Lafayette, California. He sells real estate. But one room in the house is filled with memorabilia from a twenty-three-year career in the navy: swords, medals, a Viet Cong flag with Sat Cong scrawled on it, and a plaque given to him by the men of the Vietnamese 3rd Coastal District—the so-called junk force.

He enlisted in the navy in 1948, spent eleven years as an enlisted man, and was commissioned as an ensign. "In early '64, I received orders—I didn't volunteer—to Vietnam. I was to report as a dry-docking adviser to the navy shipyard in Saigon. I had done two and a half years in Cuba as an instructor, so I wasn't afraid of going to a foreign country.

I knew there was gonna be culture shock. What I was worried about was people killing you over there. [Laughs.] What did I know about combat? I did some hunting with a shotgun, but that's about it. Maybe I had seen some combat on TV."

Much of the fault for how the war ended, he feels, lies with the press. "I remember thinking on my way home about the reporting being done on Vietnam. I didn't like it. For me, the war was over. But for my junk crews . . . God only knows. Reporters, what a con game. Some of them really could do a job objectively, but they were outnumbered by people who would do anything to come up with 'good copy.' The pen is mightier than the sword. Goddamn those who could care less if their pens teamed up with the Viet Cong's sword."

After I'd been working two weeks in the shipyard, the senior navy adviser called three of us recent arrivals into his office. We're supposed to meet the old man, get acquainted. He's wearing tropical whites. One of the things he said was he likes to take his new arrivals and put 'em in the field for a while. Expose 'em, see what their colleagues are doing. He said, "No one's gonna be able to fight this war sitting in an air-conditioned office like this one. You've got to know what's going on out there. Now, I have an opening on Phu Quoc Island, down at An Thoi, the headquarters of the 4th Coastal District. I'd like one of you to go down there for a couple of weeks." I'll tell you, I said to myself, Oh, God, not me. NOT ME. I looked at this one officer, and he was looking at the pictures on the wall. I looked at the guy next to me, and he's smoking a cigar and looking at it. So I looked up at the captain, and just then his eyes caught mine. He says, "Okay, Vincent, you'll go." When he said that, my heart sank. This is it. This is what it feels like when they send you off on a suicide mission.

The captain said, "Stop and see the personnel officer, he'll arrange transportation for you." My legs were weak when I left his office. I was detached from my body. My mouth was dry. It's comical now, but that's how it was. I went up to this lieutenant and said, "Captain Hardcastle told me to see you about transportation to Phu Quoc." He said, "Oh, you're the lucky son of a bitch, huh?" I said, "What do you mean?" He said, "That fucking place is just teeming with Viet Cong." And he's grinning. My first instinct was to go across that desk and hit him. I'm about to die, and he's laughing.

I had to get up early in the morning, so I was gonna turn in and try to get a good night's sleep. But I wrote the Last Letter Home. When my wife got news that something had happened to me, she'd pull that letter out, and all of a sudden she'd see the hidden meaning. "Tell the kids that it's important for me to be serving my country." That day I had gone over and drawn a .45, because now that I'm going into the field I'm eligible for a weapon. The army sergeant had me count the rounds of ammunition. He gave me twenty-one, three clips. And he told me that when I came back, I'm gonna have to account for 'em. I'm thinking, I hope I don't have to use 'em. And how'm I gonna account for 'em if I have to use 'em?

When we landed, it was a dirt airfield. This red dust was everywhere. The crew chief said, "This is it, Lieutenant." I got out of the plane and said, "Where do I go?" He pointed to this little building. "Just go over there, somebody'll pick you up." The place is deserted except for a few Vietnamese. He took the plane down the runway to turn it around. Sweat's oozing out of me. I don't know what to do. I'm saying to myself, I don't want that plane to leave. If nobody meets me, when that plane comes back I'm gonna flag him down. Just then there's a burst of laughter and American voices. I look up and here comes this navy officer, Wes Hoch.

We go down and get into this junk. God, it was a dirty, smelly thing. I knew it was gonna sink. Pretty soon the Vietnamese junkmen came aboard. They approach with weapons, and I'm thinking, Hey, are these Viet Cong? But I'm eyeing Wes, and he isn't excited, so I'm playing it cool. As we sail down, he points out a couple places on the beach. "We've taken sniper fire from here, and from there." Even before he told me, I noticed the junkmen: One rolled over and woke another guy up. One cocked his rifle. One or two were in a prone position. My adrenaline was really flowing.

But we got down to An Thoi okay. Wes had a nice shack there. It was strictly Jungle Jim. By that I mean rattan furniture, the fan, the cooler, warm bottles of beer lined up, and his bourbon or gin or whatever. Really tropical, really lush. The kind of thing that if you ever got in a nice inn in Hawaii, you'd want your room to look like this.

The Vietnamese were wearing black pajamas. This is no particular uniform. It's just a peasant garb that's inexpensive, anybody can buy it, and very easy to take care of. Everybody wore it in the countryside. The junk force wore it, too. Wes Hoch wore it, and the enlisted man there had a pair. He took me into this little village and said, "If you want some, now's the time." I said, "Well, I'll get a souvenir." I went in and the guy measured me. "Okay, two hours, you come back and I'll give it to you."

After a couple of weeks down there, my mind is turning. I'm thinking, Hey, I can handle the chopsticks and the food. I'm learning to speak some Vietnamese. I can count. I can say, "I'm sick." I can say, "I'm hungry," and "I'm not hungry." I can say, "Hot coffee." I can say "No." I can say "Yes." And the flies are no longer bothering me. At the dinner table, there's this one big bowl of rice in the middle. Just before you scoop some out, you wave your hand and the flies leave.

So at the end of two weeks, I said to Wes Hoch, "Y'know, this might surprise you, but I think I'd like to be a junk force adviser." He said, "I was hoping you'd say that." When I got back to Saigon and saw the commander, he said, "Yeah, Hoch says you're a pretty good guy, and we could use you." Except the unit they assigned me to was in the Mekong delta, the 3rd Coastal District. Oh, God, the fears came back. I was already comfortable in this other place. Now the Mekong, the swamp, the jungle. I had heard about the Mekong. It was bad.

I went down and reported. The navy lieutenant there was Jim Dyer. He was gung-ho. Always wearing marine fatigues. He gave me a briefing. We had eight junk divisions. Six in the greater Mekong delta area, and two farther north. The idea behind the junk force was that a lot of the Viet Cong infiltration and contraband came from the sea. The Viet Cong tax people and cadre often traveled by sea. If they can do it in a nice easy junk ride, why go through the snakes and the jungle? Why do it in four days if you can do it in two?

Our area was right along the coast. Shallow water, where the fishing craft were. Well, who's gonna check the fishing craft? They never went out far enough for the navy. So the coastal force was formed, using indigenous junks. The Viet Cong wouldn't know the difference. The junks would be just like any other ones out there. They'd get local fishermen and pay 'em to report any suspicious activities. But when they started building the junks, they found out the fishermen didn't want to expose themselves as informers and then become disemboweled during the night.

So they didn't know how to man this force. Of course, they had officers. Many of them were infantry, but as long as they were with the junk force, they were Vietnamese Navy. Then somebody got the idea to supplement the fishermen with paramilitary junkmen—and a lot of them came off the streets of Saigon. More than one of 'em were told by a judge, "It's jail or the junk force." These were the cowboys. And that was a good thing. Because you could make their day. [Laughs.] Give 'em a Thompson .45, put 'em on ambush: "Wow, yeah, man, we're gonna do some good." That's why we called 'em "squirrels" every now and then—because they were squirrelly, nutty, and nothing scared them. That was an affectionate term, by the way. Usually we called 'em "junkies." They were nonconformists, but very fierce fighters—and loyal.

These were our junkmen. I came to work with 'em, and I came to love 'em very much. There was a kinship that formed between me and these people. The men didn't have a uniform—they were entitled to wear the navy's black beret, that was it. They wore black pajamas. At this one base in Tiem Ton, I had maybe a total of forty-five people. There were supposed to be maybe sixty-five, but people were always sick or on liberty and what have you. They lived in this little triangular mud-walled fort. And they had their families there, wives and kids. They had about four to six command junks, the big ones, and some motor-sailer junks, built to go by sail or by motor. But they didn't use sail at all. The VC taught 'em a long time ago that you go faster with a motor, and you don't depend on the wind.

The base was on a river, so we patrolled from the mouth of the river outward, and along the coast. I went out often. We'd go with a command junk and maybe two motor-sailers. Whenever we'd see junks or sampans—and we saw 'em all the time—we'd have to wing it: Which ones do we search? Which ones do we challenge? Well, the junks over there have eyes painted on the bow. Different areas, different-shaped eyes. The junkies weren't world travelers, but they could recognize a junk that wasn't from their area. And the fishing junks are only licensed to bring in their catch at a certain place, right? What are they doing fishing here, when they're so many miles from their port and they don't have refrigeration? That made 'em suspect, and you'd go for 'em. Maybe they're just ferrying people or supplies. Maybe they've got fish, and they're drying it. You pick and choose your junks by instinct. Which junk looks like it's trying to get away from us? Which one is making for the shoreline? Which one is leaving the pack? And when you get a junk, you don't just come up on it. We used to hail 'em. We'd fire a round. It didn't take 'em long to see what the command junk looked like. We used to put a .30-caliber machine gun right on the bow, so it was prominent. They knew us. The covert feature never really materialized.

If they'd heave to, we'd go alongside and search 'em. Little things you learn: When you go alongside, always keep them between you and the nearest shoreline. Because if you don't, and there's an ambush waiting, they have you in a crossfire. You keep a little way on. Whenever you board 'em, the junkmen are right there with the guns pointed down at 'em. If they don't have papers, we take 'em in or take the junk in, take it back to wherever they said they were from.

The patrols I was on, we got maybe a total of six Viet Cong. When

I say six Viet Cong, I mean people that were highly suspicious. Things to look for: We stopped one junk and asked the junkmaster, "Are all your men fishermen?" "Yes, they're all fishermen." We went down to look at 'em. The skipper saw one guy and said, "Look at his hands." I looked at 'em. They were as smooth as mine. The skipper says, "Stick out your hands." The guy doesn't respond. The skipper pulls out a .45, puts it against his forehead and says, "Stick out your hands." So he put his hands out. The skipper says, "You do a lot of work with your hands as a fisherman, no?" The guy started to say yes. The skipper took the .45 and I thought he was gonna knock his head open. The guy jumped back. The skipper told the junkies, "Take 'im."

The other thing we had to worry about was base defense. We'd have land patrols around our perimeter. I learned about punji stakes and booby traps. You had to be a presence. You had to have credibility with the local villages. Otherwise, the village in effect becomes a Viet Cong village. If you're a presence and they know you're there to protect them, they start swinging the other way. When the base at Tiem Ton was set up, the village was hostile. They wouldn't even sell 'em anything in the market. The VC told 'em all these horrible things would happen if they did. By the time I left, we had even put up a volleyball court. We'd challenge the villagers. In one year, hey, we're into sports. We're pacifying this village.

You learn about the Viet Cong. The big lie, the propaganda. On one patrol we came across this old iron bridge. Obviously put there by the French. It was destroyed and lying in the water. Rusted, graffiti all over it. And the graffiti said, "Look what the government did to your bridge, so you can't get your rice to market." Several months later, we went down there and the bridge was clean. They repainted it. Here's a dirty ol' bridge, and somebody very crudely repainted it. I mentioned it to the skipper. He says, "Yeah, maybe they want to paint it a pretty red color." We laughed about it. Then the next time I went down there, new graffiti. Now it's: "Look what we did to the bridge to stop the government's tax collectors from coming in to get your money." I turned to my counterpart and said, "Everybody knows they claimed the government did it. Why did they change?" And he said, not knowing he was giving me some good advice on Communism—it was just common sense to him—he said, "Yeah, but the little three-year-old doesn't know. And when he gets to be four and five he can read for himself." I said. "But his parents will tell him." He said, "Yes, but when he sees it that way year in, year out, he starts to suspect his parents are lying."

Or they'd leave signs for the junkmen: "Cowards. The American must lead you." They'd put the signs around the perimeter. They'd dig little positions out there, we'd come under attack, and then we'd get a patrol and go out. The next time we went out, the skipper says to me, "Maybe we'll stay in the back now." I always went where the skipper was, and he was usually right behind the point man. I said, "It's because of the signs, isn't it?" He said, "Maybe, but the petty officers asked me if they could go first." Sure enough, the signs are there. "The American must lead you by the hand." The junkies are laughing, kicking the signs over—"Number ten, Number ten!" A couple of days later, we had another patrol out. New signs. "The American is afraid. Force him to go first. We want to kill him first." I said to the skipper, "Where do you want me to go now?" He laughed. "Go wherever you want."

During a firefight, we'd yell at each other. We'd scream, curse each other out. "You cowards," that sort of thing. I remember one night we were under attack in the base. The French had taught 'em how to build these bases—very primitive and very good. An equilateral triangle. You put an automatic weapon at each corner, and you can bring a crossfire on any point. Not only that, but if one of 'em is knocked out, the other two can still cover 360 degrees. The walls were mud. At the base they could be as much as eight feet thick. Then it tapered to the top, and there would be little firing ports. And at each corner was a round position where you could maneuver a heavy weapon.

I didn't have a station. I went where I went. I was firing from this one position on the wall. And this junkie was firing his BAR. Every now and then he'd quit firing, run around, jump up on the wall, and he'd yell. Then he'd jump back, laugh, shoulder the gun, lean into it and open fire. He did it once or twice. My mind wasn't on it. But one time that he yelled, I heard him say, "*Co van my*"—*co van* is adviser, and *my* is American. I'm the only American adviser there. This guy is talking about me to the VC. So I ease up real close to him, and sure enough, he's telling the VC, "Hey, come in here, I've got an American adviser here, you can have him. C'mon, right this way." Then he'd jump around behind his gun and open up. At the time, it wasn't a bit comical to me. I slapped him on the arm to get his attention. He looked at me, startled. I said in Vietnamese, "What the hell you saying that for?" He looked very surprised. "Oh, you understand Vietnamese?" I said yeah. So he says, very seriously now, "Why don't you stand on the wall and yell, and then I don't have to quit shooting?"

During my time over there, I said: When I leave this country, I want to be able to say that my troops are better off because I was here. I wanted 'em to be more aggressive. I wanted the villagers to know we were there. I wanted 'em to be good to the villagers. I didn't want to see any pilfering going on. And I wanted the junks on patrol. I knew our junks were recognized, just like you recognize the silhouette of a police officer. So I wanted the VC to see more of us out there. And when I left the country, I said to myself, I know they're better off now than when I came. I saw the men getting more pride. I saw more of 'em wearing a uniform rather than the black pajamas. And we were effective. I think we cut infiltration from the sea, just by our presence. Maybe we diverted the VC to other areas. Maybe they still got the same stuff by sea, but they moved thirty or forty klicks down the coast. But not in my area.

Maybe I made it fun. Breathed some excitement into it. They enjoyed my company, I enjoyed theirs. They loved to hear you talk Vietnamese. They'd just sit with their mouths open when I quoted Vietnamese proverbs. It gave a lift to their morale by me trying to sing a song with 'em around a lamp at night, while one of 'em's picking a guitar. Teaching me the words. I knew a lot about knots, and I could do tricks with line. I used to show 'em, and it'd boggle their minds. I taught the skipper how to do the twist. He taught me how to play Chinese chess. They couldn't believe I knew these things. And wherever I was, if it was evening, there'd be a crowd. If I went to eat with a junkie and his family, there'd be a bunch of 'em hanging in the windows, kibitzing. If I said, "Anybody got a cigarette?" two or three would pop up. I just fit in with 'em. The English have a saying: "He went bush." Well, I went bush. It was mutual respect.

I used to do crazy things to help morale. I knew this medical officer in Saigon. We got to be buddy-buddy. He got me a whole stack of towels. Just plain white towels. I took 'em down to my bases and gave 'em to the wives. Boy, they thought it was great. Their towels were thin. Our towels were good cotton thick plush. Luxurious. I used to bring magazines for 'em. They couldn't read, but they loved the pictures. They'd cut 'em out and put 'em on the walls. You'd go into a mud hut and there's a picture from *National Geographic*. Whenever my mother or my wife sent me candy or boxes of cookies, I'd pass it out to the junkmen's kids.

I also wanted to know everything I could about my counterpart. I wanted to know what made him tick. What upset him. Was he afraid of his immediate superior? Was he there with political connections? If he's got connections and he's going back to a fat job in Saigon, you know he's not gonna stick his neck out too far, because he's not a fighter. In which case you get the XO and get him to be the fighter. But the worst thing you can do is make the skipper lose face. So you let him know how important it is for him to man the radio in the command post while you and the XO go out on patrol.

Once I got ahold of some trip flares. I wanted 'em for our perimeter. I got a chopper to take me into Tiem Ton. I headed for the skipper's shack, which was my shack, too, when I was there. Tai—he was the skipper—was reading the paper. He said, "How are you?" But I could see he was depressed. I said, "Tai, I've got trip flares, let's put 'em out." He says, "Oh, maybe tomorrow." This wasn't like him. Well, I knew that Tai wanted to marry Co Mai in the village. *Co* means "Miss," and her name was Mai. He knew he couldn't marry her there, because if he did, the VC would do her family in. So he wanted a more secure area. He'd been out there a long time. He'd already requested a transfer twice and was turned down. I knew he had put another request in, so I said, "How did your request turn out?" He said, "The commander disapproved it."

So I'm thinking to myself, Okay, Vincent, how do you handle this one? I said, "Y'know, Tai, I can see the future, when you and Co Mai get married." He looked at me and said, "Yeah? When?" I just said, "I bet she brings you at least three strong sons." That got his attention. Paper came down. He says, "Yeah, I want three sons. Three is a lucky number." We talked about playing with the kids, this and that. Then I said, "It's very sad, because I think when your sons grow up, they must learn to speak Chinese." The Vietnamese and the Chinese have never loved each other. Boy, you'd have thought I pole-axed him. He threw the paper down and said, "Never! I'll kill 'em first." I said, "Yeah, but isn't it a shame? Wouldn't it be killing the wrong people at the wrong time?" He looked at me, and he smiled. He said, "*Dai-uy*, let's put out the trip flares."

One time we ran into an ambush coming out of the Co Chien River. I was with Junk Division 37. We were leaving Junk Division 35 and heading north on the China Sea toward our home base. We started out at five o'clock in the morning, so I was crapped out. I was sleeping in the deck house, because it was chilly. All of a sudden I heard this loud crack, like a tree snapping. Our coxswain is on the tiller, and he's crouched down between two fifty-five-gallon drums of water. That's his protection. Also our water. I roll over and say, "What was that?" He points and says, "*Viet Cong bung*"—they're shooting. We go in closer to shore and all hell breaks loose. They're firing at us from ten or fifteen positions. The two end positions were automatic weapons. You could hear the shots, *zing-zing-zing*. I'll never forget the sound. And the dull *thuck* as it hits the junk. It goes right through. So there's no place to hide.

We make a firing run and turn around. I figure, Well, that's over, we're free. But sure enough, we turn around and come in again. Then we come around for a third run. This time we're not paralleling the bank any more, we're coming in. I say to the skipper, "What are your intentions?" He says, "We're gonna land." I says, "Why?" He says, "They've got automatic weapons. I'm gonna take 'em." We're almost bottoming now. By the time we bottom we probably had a good twenty-five yards of surf to run through, and at least another twenty-five yards of sand to get up to their position. And they're still firing. I'm thinking, We have four guys aboard the command junk, including me, and three guys on the other. I look at the skipper and I shake my head. And I say, as calmly as I can—you don't want to panic—I say, "It's very difficult to take a machine gun away from somebody who's shooting at you." He looked at me and said, "You don't think we oughta do it?" I wanted to scream, "Hell, no!" but I said, "No, not a good idea." He said okay and gave the order. We're already bottoming. I just knew, This is it, boy. But we turned. And as we turned to leave, this skipper, Lieutenant Bong, takes an M-1 rifle. There was a sampan anchored in this little cove. He stands up on that junk, and with cool and deliberate aim, squeezes off eight single rounds, slowly, at that sampan. Bullets are still flying all around, but he was so angry—and that sampan was something he could damage. I betcha he put half the rounds in it. *Bang. Bang. Bang.* He was a hell of a man.

It wasn't long after I came back from Vietnam, I was an instructor at Coronado.* I got a call one night from Jim Dyer. He was in the States. He was drunk. And he was crying. He said, "Didja hear the news?" I said, "What news?" He said, "Lieutenant Bong and his men were wiped out." I said, "What the hell are you talking about?" He said, "Yeah, it just happened today. His base was attacked. He counterattacked but the Viet Cong were waiting in ambush."

They were very brave people. They trusted us. And we let 'em down. I think of people I knew over there, and I wonder what camp they were killed in. What mass grave they're buried in. Our junkmen had a motto. The motto was *Sat Cong. Cong* means Communist. *Sat* means to kill. *Sat Cong*—Kill the Communists. We had it on our patch. The junkmen had it tattooed over their hearts. At one time I was told it was a requirement for 'em, so they didn't go over the hill. But I found out that wasn't true. It was just a macho thing. Jim Dyer got that tattoo. And I know what happened when my people were captured when I was there. That tattoo was usually carved off before they were killed.

*A navy base near San Diego.

When I left and I was debriefed, I had to fill out a form. This is what I put down. Number one was for advisers to be stationed at the junk bases permanently. If the Vietnamese can live that sort of life, the Americans should be able to. And it was important for the Americans to live with the Vietnamese—to share the same quarters if possible, or the same type of housing. The same insect repellent. Not only that, but I went a step further. I felt the American should be paid maybe 25 percent more than his counterpart, no more. If you're a lieutenant making $100 a month, and I'm your adviser making $2,000 a month, where's the empathy? There is none. But how about if I'm making $125 a month while I'm in your country, and the rest of my money is put in trust somewhere. That's all I'm allowed. Now I'm gonna have to live just like you. When you're in the market haggling over a belt or a pair of bathing trunks, I'm there haggling, too. No division between the haves and the have-nots. If you can't get batteries for your little AM-FM radio, and I come along with a big stereo, where's that feeling of sharing? Of becoming a blood brother, so to speak?

But sometimes it seems like nobody's listening out there. I don't think anybody read what I had to say. I remember that debriefing form—it was about eight or ten pages. Starts off with name and rank and title and what you did there. Then it starts asking a bunch of questions. "What accomplishments have you had in your sector?" I got to about the third page and it dawned on me, This is garbage, this questionnaire. Whoever came up with it, I don't think they've ever been in-country. On the third page I came to the question: "How easy was it for you to get your counterpart to think like an American? Easy? Very easy? Difficult? Very difficult?" I answered, "I didn't get him to think like an American." Then I asked a rhetorical question: "How easy was it for your counterpart to get you to think like a Vietnamese?" And right across the page—you talk about frustration—I wrote, "The person who came up with this questionnaire should be court-martialed." And I turned it in. I just knew that before I left the country, some bird colonel was gonna call me in and chew me out. But I never heard another thing about it.

I was there when we lost the advisory war. The first U.S. combat troops showed up a month after I left. So obviously the war was not going well. It reminds me of an analogy that I liked. I think I heard it in Vietnam, and I think it was Roger Hilsman who said it. He said that when you've got a mean tomcat terrorizing the other cats in the alley, and you want to destroy the tomcat, one approach is to bring in a bulldog. The bulldog can obviously tear up the tomcat if he can catch it. So the bulldog will chase this tomcat all over until it trees.

In which case the bulldog will run around the tree, bark like hell, and eventually get tired and go home. Then the tomcat comes down and continues. Another thing wrong with the bulldog approach is that he doesn't know the difference between good tomcats and bad tomcats, and he has a tendency to chase all cats.

The way to get that tomcat is to find a loyal but meaner one. Not only will he chase him, not only does he know the difference, but he'll go up that tree after him, and he'll keep going 'til he gets him. That's what my philosophy was. Train the Vietnamese to do it, and do it better. When I heard that story, I thought, My God, that's it. But we were getting ready to send the bulldogs.

BOOK TWO

DIGGING IN

★

CHRONOLOGY
1965–1970

1965

March 8: The first American combat units arrive in Vietnam: two marine battalions whose mission is theoretically to guard the Danang airbase. A rapid buildup begins.

June 11: After yet another government shuffle, General Nguyen Van Thieu is named chief of state and Air Vice Marshal Nguyen Cao Ky becomes prime minister.

October: The first large demonstrations protesting the Vietnam War take place in the U.S.

October: The 1st Cavalry Division mauls three enemy regiments in the battle of the Ia Drang valley.

December 25: President Johnson orders a pause in the bombing in an attempt to get negotiations started. The pause lasts thirty-seven days.

December 27: Herbert Aptheker, Tom Hayden, and Staughton Lynd arrive in Hanoi, the first delegation of antiwar activists to visit.

1966

March: U.S. troop strength in Vietnam is now 215,000.

April 12: For the first time, B-52s take part in the bombing of North Vietnam.

June: U.S. bombers hit the outskirts of Hanoi and Haiphong.

July 6: U.S. POWs are paraded through the streets of Hanoi and attacked by angry mobs.

October: Defense Secretary Robert McNamara returns from Vietnam with a pessimistic report.

December: *New York Times* journalist Harrison Salisbury visits North Vietnam and reports extensive damage to towns and cities from the American bombing. By year's end, 389,000 American troops are in Vietnam.

1967

April: General William Westmoreland, commander of U.S. troops in Vietnam, returns to Washington for consultations. At President Johnson's urging, his public statements are optimistic. Privately, he reports that he can see no way of ending the war without stopping the infiltration of troops from North Vietnam.

April 25: Ellsworth Bunker succeeds Henry Cabot Lodge as ambassador to South Vietnam.

August 3: President Johnson increases the limit on the number of U.S. troops in Vietnam to 525,000.

September 3: In nationwide elections, South Vietnam votes in Nguyen Van Thieu as president and Nguyen Cao Ky as vice president.

October 21: Large antiwar demonstration in Washington.

November 30: Johnson ousts the increasingly gloomy McNamara by nominating him to become head of the World Bank.

1968

January: The siege of Khe Sanh begins.

January 31: The Tet offensive begins. Heavy fighting continues for almost a month.

February 28: General Earle Wheeler, chairman of the Joint Chiefs of Staff, makes a pessimistic report to President Johnson and relays Westmoreland's request for 206,000 more troops. An intense debate begins within the administration. The new secretary of defense, Clark Clifford, is charged with preparing a major policy review.

March 12: Senator Eugene McCarthy nearly defeats Johnson in the New Hampshire Democratic primary.

March 16: Senator Robert Kennedy enters the presidential race. On the same day, troops from the Americal Division massacre hundreds of civilians in the hamlet of My Lai.

March 22: Johnson announces that Westmoreland will leave Vietnam by June to become army chief of staff. His replacement is General Creighton Abrams.

March 25: Johnson meets with his top advisers, the "wise men." Most of them tell him to look for a way to end the war.

March 31: Johnson stuns the country by announcing that he will not run for reelection. He also slows the bombing of North Vietnam and calls for unconditional negotiations.

April 4: Martin Luther King, Jr., assassinated.

May 10: Talks between the U.S. and North Vietnam begin in Paris.

June 5: Robert Kennedy shot; dies on June 6.

August: Richard Nixon and Hubert Humphrey are nominated for President by the Republican and Democratic parties, respectively. Antiwar demonstrations outside the Democratic convention in Chicago erupt in violence as police attack the demonstrators.

November 1: Johnson halts the bombing of North Vietnam.

November 6: Nixon elected U.S. President.

During the year, more than 14,500 Americans die in Vietnam, the highest annual toll.

1969

January 25: The first substantive session of the Paris peace talks is held. Representatives from the South Vietnamese government and the National Liberation Front are included.

March 18: The secret bombing of Communist bases in Cambodia is initiated.

June: U.S. troop strength peaks at 543,000. President Nixon announces the withdrawal of 25,000 men, marking the start of "Vietnamization."

August 4: Kissinger meets in secret for the first time with a North Vietnamese negotiator, Xuan Thuy.

September 3: Ho Chi Minh dies.

September 16: Nixon says he will bring home 35,000 more troops.

October 15, November 15: Enormous antiwar demonstrations in Washington and across the country.

December 15: Nixon pledges that an additional 50,000 troops will be withdrawn from Vietnam by April 1970.

1970

February 21: In Paris, Kissinger meets secretly with Le Duc Tho, the man who is to become his negotiating opponent.

March 18: Prince Norodom Sihanouk, the ruler of Cambodia, is overthrown in a military coup. General Lon Nol takes power.

April 13: 429,000 U.S. troops remain in Vietnam.

April 20: Nixon says that 150,000 more troops will be withdrawn over the next year.

4

TWO SOLDIERS

On March 8, 1965, a battalion of U.S. Marines—about 3,500 men—waded ashore near Danang, the first official American combat troops in Vietnam. They were not the first to fight there, of course. "Advisers" had been doing that for some time. But the adviser war had failed. South Vietnam's government was more flimsy and its army more vulnerable than ever before. While the South was stumbling through seven changes of government in 1964, the North had begun to infiltrate regular army units and to deliver heavy weapons to the Viet Cong.

The week before the marines arrived, President Johnson triggered Rolling Thunder, the sustained bombing raids of the North. One launching point was the Danang airbase, and General Westmoreland wanted more men to protect it. Ambassador Taylor objected, foreseeing that the first troops would not be the last. Johnson rejected the advice. The Vietnamese were informed on the day of the landing.

At first, the marines stayed inside their perimeter. Then they took to patrolling nearby paddies. Soon they were on the offensive. But in May the Viet Cong struck throughout the South, battering the best ARVN units. McNamara privately told Johnson that South Vietnam's chances of lasting another year were "less than even." Westmoreland pleaded for more men. He got them. By the end of 1965 there were 200,000 Americans in Vietnam.

The two soldiers in this chapter, an army general and a marine "grunt," were part of that first flood. The general's orders were to block the North Vietnamese in the central highlands—the South's weak spot, from which a quick attack could slice to the coast, splitting the country. The grunt's orders were to kill Viet Cong. Both men succeeded.

In the process, they learned something about the war's elusive nature. The general saw it from above—literally, since he commanded the lst Cavalry, a helicopter division. He saw a sweep of mountains and jungle that could hide armies, and a long border that his enemy could cross at will, while he could not. The grunt saw it from below. He saw bushes and treelines and spider holes and caves and hootches: places of ambush. He saw rotted feet and splattered brains.

What they accomplished made a difference. American troops rescued South Vietnam from collapse, and the North soon recognized a formidable new obstacle. At the battle of the Ia Drang valley, the general's choppers whisked in the troops that battered an NVA regiment. The very success may have backfired, for it helped convince Westmoreland and Washington that the enemy could be worn down quickly. But the South got a crucial gift: time. And slowly, as Americans poured in, parts of the countryside were reclaimed.

Still, the general and the grunt returned home troubled. The general's great love, the helicopter, had proved itself. He had learned tactical lessons that could be passed on. But he said publicly that all was well in Vietnam, when he knew it was not. Looking back, he has his regrets.

The grunt simply found Vietnam hard to forget.

LIEUTENANT GENERAL HARRY W. O. KINNARD

He is a small man with a husky voice and the matter-of-fact pride one might expect from a general. We talk in the living room of his house in Arlington, Virginia. Behind us is a glass-doored cabinet displaying a set of antique Japanese porcelain. A calendar hanging in the kitchen comes from one of the companies he has consulted for since retiring from the army in 1969. The calendar's theme: helicopters.

Born into an army family in 1915, he graduated from West Point in 1939. After fighting in Normandy and Holland he emerged from the World War as a full colonel at the age of twenty-nine, "rather young for an army type. I came back to the U.S. and took over the airborne test section at Fort Bragg. I had a history of being interested in helicopters, and in 1962 I was tagged by General Buzz Wheeler to head up a new experimental division to try out what was called the airmobility concept, the idea of using helicopters in lieu of ground vehicles and ground weapons systems. I took over what came to be known as the 11th Air Assault Division. It was activated at Fort Benning. On the first day I was the only name on the morning report. The division literally grew from zero.

"In 1965 the army chief of staff, H. K. Johnson, came and told me that President Johnson was going to go on national TV to make three announcements. One, he was going to declare a state of emergency. Two, he was going to announce that the 11th Air Assault Division would become the 1st Cavalry Division, Airmobile. And three—guess what? We were going to Vietnam."

I was regarded as a zealot for helicopters.

One reason the helicopter didn't come of age in World War II was simply that it wasn't capable at the time. It was a crude bird that required unending maintenance and could carry very little. But the helicopter has evolved. For the first time in history, you have a machine that can carry people and things; that can fly while it's motionless with respect to the ground; that can even fly backwards or sideways. People can get on and off while it's flying if necessary, and sometimes it is. In Vietnam, often we'd have to hover at five or six feet so people could jump off into elephant grass, or jump off on top of a mountain where there's no place to land. It also gives you the ability to negate terrain. Before, when a soldier was fighting on the ground, he had to fight the enemy, fight the weather, and fight terrain. Now he still has to fight the weather and the enemy, but the helicopter—and I use a high-blown phrase—the helicopter does away with the tyranny of terrain. Bridges, rivers, minefields, you name it—they become totally meaningless. You don't have to worry about whether that road is muddy. You go right for the enemy.

The helicopter is different, and it's not just different in degree. It's different in kind. That's why I say it's revolutionary. Something like the helicopter comes along only rarely in history, every few hundred years. In Vietnam it was the main reason that American forces were able, with a force ratio of about four and a half to one, to contain a basically guerrilla force. Whereas if you read guerrilla warfare experts, they say you need fifteen to one. That's a big difference. The helicopter allowed you to react very, very quickly, and you could be indifferent to any ground ambushes that might be in place, because you simply didn't use the roads. Under the French, when a village would be attacked by the bad guys, you would arrive to find the bodies and the smoking ruins of the fort. But we could get there and could change the balance of firepower and forces in minutes. Not hours, minutes. We could catch them in the act.

The marines were the first division in-country, but the Cav was the first whole army division. We got there in July of '65. My mission was to keep North Vietnam from cutting the country in two. That's why we came to be stationed at An Khe, in the highlands about halfway between Pleiku and Qui Nhon.

I had an enormous division area, 100 miles by 100 miles. It covered three provinces: Pleiku, Kontum, and Binh Dinh. I put one brigade in each province. I told them I wanted them to learn the terrain, the geography, the enemy, and the friendly forces. I wanted them to get to know the ARVN commanders and their hang-ups and how good they were and what we could do to help. I told them to plan some operations where we would put some of our guys with the Vietnamese, provide helicopter lift, intelligence, whatever they needed. Furthermore, to tell them we'd be there if they got in trouble, and explain how quick we could get there. In other words, begin to make the ARVN feel like they had somebody who was really going to be there when they needed it. Get them to feel good about themselves and start carrying the fight to the enemy.

Up to that point, the ARVN hadn't had that kind of support. There was one tiny little fort with a rudimentary airstrip, and that was the law west of the Pecos anywhere near An Khe. It was Indian country. The ARVN were just huddled in there hoping to hell the enemy wouldn't take them on. Patrolling was nominal, and morale was not good. It took a full-fledged operation to run a convoy from Qui Nhon up to Plei Me. And outside the forts, the Viet Cong were totally free at night to go where they wanted.

The fighting was usually the set-piece thing where the enemy would decide they wanted to take out some hamlet or some post. They would carefully reconnoiter it. Prepare the battlefield, which they did extremely well. They'd have everything picked out. Where their aid stations were going to be. Where their stocks of ammo and food would be. They even knew where they were going to drag their wounded and dead. We captured one guy who had a chart of a CIDG camp they were going to attack. It was incredible, the minute detail. They had all the barbed wire and emplacements, everything about that camp. Then, with great surprise and superiority of force, they would strike, usually at night. It was a hit-and-run type of thing. They didn't feel it incumbent upon them to stay and fight. What was incumbent on them was to live and fight another day.

We did a few unusual things when we first got there. The first was to build thirty-five kilometers of heavily reinforced barrier around the base camp. We made a large, tough base. We made it that way so we could defend it with a minimum number of guys and the maximum number could be out chasing the bad guys. And I wouldn't let any Vietnamese inside the barrier. I remember visiting the marines once. I went through the officers' billet, and there were Vietnamese cleaning women asleep under the beds of the officers. Well, at the 1st Cav I wouldn't let any Vietnamese of any description inside the barrier. For all I knew they were in cahoots with the VC. No cooks, no laundry women, no geisha girls, nothing. You have to make it black and white. If you start saying, Only when this or that, pretty soon they're in all the time. So I just said, Nobody. Ever. And because of that, we were never accurately mortared.

Another thing. Before I went over there, I saw a picture of an American unit with all their white underwear hanging out on the lines. I was raised in World War II, where you didn't have white underwear, because if you hung it out, airplanes could spot it. So I had all my guys dye their underwear olive drab. I even took our yellow shoulder patch and dyed it OD. When I got to Vietnam and had my first press conference, some smart-ass newspaper guy said, "Well, General, I hear you had all your soldiers dye their underwear." "Yes, I did." "Well, I bet you don't have on OD." I said, "How much you want to bet?" I opened my shirt and there it was. That's a small thing, but I figure it makes a psychological impression. You make the troops think, Boy, we're not letting anybody in the base, we've got all our underwear dyed—I'd better keep my ears up.

For a few months we ran small-scale operations, getting our feet wet. We were the new boys on the block. Then the North Vietnamese made their first effort to cut the country in two. Their plan was to capture the camp that was the outer protection to Pleiku. Then they were going to capture Pleiku and head south. There were three regiments operating as a division: the 32nd, the 33rd, and the 65th. From radio intercepts we knew the 65th was coming down the trail from the north, and when they converged with the 33rd, that was a good sign: Katie, bar the door.

We had a few minor things going on when we got word that the Special Forces camp at Plei Me had been jumped. As it developed, it had been jumped by the 32nd, which was a Viet Cong–type regiment. But these regiments weren't your normal black-pajama guys. They had heavy weapons—rockets and heavy mortars and heavy machine guns, including some that could fire at helicopters. They were being reinforced with even heavier weapons. The NVA, on the other hand, had regular uniforms and more crew-served weapons. They had helmets and other equipment. They tended to be a lot more aggressive.

Their doctrine was the so-called close embrace—they wanted to get right up against our guys as quickly as possible so we couldn't use our firepower against them. Hard to say which one was the better fighter. The VC in many ways were tougher, because they wanted to live to fight another day, and they were skillful at getting in and out.

The VC regiment surrounded the camp at Plei Me. That began the battle of the Ia Drang, which was really a campaign that lasted for a month. When it began, we didn't know that another regiment, the 33rd, had taken up an ambush position on a piece of high ground along the road from Pleiku to Plei Me. It's a distance of thirty, maybe thirty-five kilometers. This was the typical thing they used so well against the French. Their game plan was that the ARVN, who were stationed in some strength in Pleiku, would come out the road to break the siege of the camp, and—guess what? But the ARVN, who knew this game as well as anybody, were reluctant to move. They were gandy-dancing around. The first thing we did was move up and take over the defense of Pleiku so they wouldn't have the excuse that they had to defend it. Then they put one foot out of the foxhole, but they still weren't moving out. I think maybe their intelligence was better than they let us know. They might have known about the ambush. In any case, they were a real reluctant dragon. So we put some of our forward observers with them and brought in artillery to a position where it could provide support.

Meanwhile, at Plei Me the siege was very close. There were a lot of guys in the camp, maybe 300 or 400 Montagnards. They were tough cookies, and they had a strong position. They were being supported by our air force. I think the VC game plan was not to overrun the camp quickly. They wanted the bait out there.

The ARVN finally got up against this ambush. They moved the tanks up and the ambush took them on. But this time our artillery made it a different ball game. The VC were used to being fired at by rifles and machine guns. Now they've got 105s coming in. That's different. Our observers were right there in the lead vehicles, and they knew where to put the artillery. So the ARVN were able to pull back. They didn't drive off the ambush, but they were able to disengage and regroup.

We brought in more artillery. Now these ARVN guys were feeling pretty good, so they moved out. They went through the ambush and broke out to the camp. The 32nd broke off the fight and birded off into the bush, as did the 33rd, which was on the hill. When we got to the camp, we found an awful lot of dead VC around.

Then there was this hiatus while they were deciding what to do next. I asked Westmoreland to give me a mission-type order. Before that, he'd have some intuition about some hill and say, "They're in there. I want you to go in and stay twenty-four hours." Or maybe forty-eight hours. We'd go in, and it'd be a dry hole. He'd been in Vietnam a long time, and he had a lot of knowledge, but month-old intelligence didn't work. I told General Larsen, who was my immediate boss, "I don't know how to do what Westy's telling me to do, to go someplace for twenty-four hours. But if you give me a mission to go find the enemy and fight him, I know how to do that." They said, "You've been asking for this. Now we're telling you: Go find these guys and fight 'em."

I took my cavalry squadrons and started sweeping over a large area with them. What we'd do is find an area where we thought they'd be, or we'd get some clue from the cavalry. Then we'd put at least a battery of artillery down. That was a brand-new lesson I learned: Get your tube artillery in position before you go into a hot spot. Even if that means making a separate landing to seize the place for the artillery. My dad was an artilleryman. I like artillery. I thought it was wrong to fight a guy rifle to rifle if you can use artillery. I taught that to my guys: Use the biggest thing you can. The Marquis of Queensberry does not apply. There's nothing unfair, if he shoots at you with a rifle, to hit him with a mortar or artillery or even the air force. So when we were searching out there, we'd put the artillery in so it could cover the area of search. If we hit something, *boom*, the big guns were ready.

Another thing we learned was that the best intelligence came from one of our choppers being shot at. That was proof positive you had a hostile. You knew where he was, and he was there then—not yesterday or today, but right now. I really beat hard on my guys about contact being the name of the game. It wasn't necessarily the favorite method of the pilots, but it worked.

Another lesson learned was that a helicopter unit not in contact with the enemy is de facto in reserve. I didn't need a designated reserve. The old idea of one up and three back—forget it. If a unit wasn't in contact, we could pick them up so quickly and move them that they were all the reserve I needed. That was a tremendous discovery, because every army has always thought in terms of having a reserve that's only committed in an emergency. The idea that we could move so fast, it was like somebody cut the tether for me. We could play cat-and-mouse with the VC. If you're tramping through the brush with a battalion, he's not going to attack you. You're too big and too tough. You've gotta put something out there he thinks he can take—

a platoon, a company. Now you look vulnerable. He doesn't know about Big Brother who's waiting.

This went on for a month. Lots of fights. But the biggest was in the Ia Drang valley. This was the 1st Battalion of the 7th Cavalry, the lineal descendant of Custer's outfit. Commanded by a fine soldier named Harold Moore. They went into this landing zone called X-Ray. It was right in the shadow of the Chu Pong massif, a large mountain, about 7,000 feet. The part near X-Ray was in South Vietnam, and the mountain spilled over into Cambodia. It was a favorite place for the bad guys to refit. They owned it. Nobody had ever been in there. It turned out that this new regiment, the 65th, had come down the trail and were in there doing their final refitting and collecting guys and resting up before they began this big deal of cutting the country in two. They were spoiling for a fight. Hal Moore lands at their doorstep. Fortunately we had the tube artillery in place. Fortunately also, our gunships with rockets could get there in a hurry. Because these guys came boiling out of the hills like a bunch of mad bees. Even though Hal had his whole battalion, this is a battalion versus a regiment, a three-to-one ratio in their favor.

We immediately began picking up guys who were moving through the bush, flying them in there and building it up. The fighting lasted for about five days. It was very heavy for the first three days, then maybe sporadic on the fourth day. Very tough fighting. And the NVA guys were cocky. They did some wild things. We had one platoon that was entirely cut off from the main body, and they said these guys would pop up and laugh like hell, make some wild remarks, and then pop down again. They kept trying to get into hand-to-hand combat to avoid our firepower. Which was smart on their part. We used mortars, we used artillery, we used ARA, we used air force A-7s dropping 500- and 1,000-pound bombs. I violated a lot of principles about how hard you work your guys and how many hours you fly your helicopters. I almost literally flew the blades off the choppers.

While the fighting was heavy I requested a B-52 strike on the Chu Pong, which I figured was full of these guys. But we didn't get one until it was too late. The process was horribly slow. The request came all the way back to this country for approval. By that time it was five days later or something, and we had chased the bad guys out. Since we'd been at such pains to get the damn strike, we went ahead with it. But whether we killed anybody or not we'll never know.

We didn't chase after these guys into the Chu Pong. I probably should have. But it had been such a hell of a fight, I didn't do it right then. By the time we got ourselves ready and chased them with the

ARVN, they had gone out of the X-Ray area. We pushed them the final distance over the border. I requested permission to follow in hot pursuit because I wanted to put them totally out of the war. I didn't want to just rough them up. There was no big territorial obstacle. It looked to me like we could go right across the Cambodian border. We had contact. I wanted to keep a hand on 'em. Westy approved it, Ambassador Lodge approved it, but it went to Washington and was disapproved. I was told no. So guess what? Five or six months later, these guys had regrouped and here they came again.

I had grave misgivings about not being able to go into Cambodia or Laos or North Vietnam even in hot pursuit. Short of that, I didn't see how it was going to be possible to keep the guerrillas from being reinforced at will. It was pretty clear that if you can't quarantine the area where the guerrillas are, it's very unlikely you're really going to pressure them. You might be able to hold them if the people behind you don't get tired first. But as far as being able to put them out of business, there's no way. So you kept butting your head against the reality of a war where you have a fifty-yard line and you're told to play your game on one side of it. The other guy's able to play where you are, but you can't go where he is. At best that's a long-term stalemate, and our people aren't good at that. Democracies are not good at protracted conflict. The Communists have known that for a long time. They write it in their books, and they believe it, and they're right, unfortunately.

I didn't feel we were going to bleed the enemy to the point where they'd give up. In the first place, they were so fanatical that it didn't occur to me that even very heavy losses would make them quit. And I never particularly liked the idea of the body count. I think there were other commanders who felt it was a macabre and dumb sort of thing to do. But Westy always argued that there wasn't any other way of telling anybody what you were doing or how big a bite you'd taken out of the hostiles. I always thought, and I can't prove this, that he did it because the ARVN were making preposterous claims about what they were doing against the enemy. He finally said, "Show me the bodies, show me the weapons you've captured, and I'll believe you." That spilled over to the American forces.

The idea of attrition was important. But it was only important if you were fighting an enemy that had less staying power than you did. Given the attitudes in North Vietnam versus the attitudes in the U.S., and given the fact that they had no news media to battle, it never looked to me like attrition was going to hurt them. Besides that, it seemed kind of dumb to me to fight their kind of war, to allow them to fight as guerrillas, when by going into North Vietnam we would have forced them to fight conventionally. We needed the kind of attrition that you could get by heading straight for Hanoi and saying, If you don't want to surrender, then get in my way. Then we would have been talking about big-time attrition. We would have been capturing their equipment. We would have been overrunning their towns. Finally there would have been pressure from their people, because we would have been in their backyard.

Unlike the French, we could have won that kind of war, assuming our people were supportive. The French weren't supportive toward the end. But they also had relatively few troops there, and they never had helicopters. In my opinion, the helicopter didn't make just a small difference. It made THE difference. But if you ever started talking about this kind of thing with your superiors, people would say, "Oh, you're just beating your gums. The ground rules are . . ." And I already knew what they were. I guess people felt I was just squirming around in my straitjacket.

The top military men, General Abrams and others, thought we should never fight a land war in Southeast Asia. They didn't think we should have been there at all. But once there, I think almost any soldier would have wanted to carry the war to the enemy. The idea of a limited war that goes on for some indefinite period, where you're just holding the guy at bay, that was never a military concept. That was a civilian concept.

My guess would be that generals didn't make nearly enough noise. My guess would be that sometimes soldiers are too-good soldiers. They take what's given them and try to do the best they can. They're not as vociferous and forceful as they should be. What probably should have been done was a few guys at the Westmoreland level should have said, "There's only one way to win this war. If you won't let me fight it that way, I'm turning in my soldier suit." Now, that gets people's attention.

But nobody did anything like that. Including me. I never got to that point. I got very frustrated, but I never got to that point. Another thing you have to remember is that at the time my division was there, it was early in the war. We were giving them a shit-kicking. We were beating hell out of them. Nor was there that much hue and cry in the press. I think also, in fairness to myself, I felt it was incumbent on me to prove the airmobile concept. I had to bring a brand-new way of fighting into the field and try to make it work. That was a hell of a job. I was convinced that air mobility worked like gangbusters. That was a tremendous thrill. So I didn't have quite the same perspective as somebody who had a straight-legged division and came in, let's say, in 1970. I'm not trying to be too easy on myself, but I'm trying to make an argument. [Laughs.]

I never told anybody I was going to quit because I didn't like what was going on. Sometimes in retrospect I thought maybe I should have. I wished I had. But I didn't. And when I came back from Vietnam, I tried to put the best face on what we were doing, in interviews and all. That was probably wrong, too. I guess I did it because I felt it was important for us to hang in there, and I thought if I said we were losing, it would be more ammunition for people who wanted us to fold up. I had made my decision to stay on in the army. I wanted to have my shot at being promoted. So I went along with the party line— light at the end of the tunnel, that sort of thing. To some extent I even believed my own press, because when I was there it was going pretty well.

Once I was denied permission to go into Cambodia, I never again requested permission to go. But I did make other proposals. I said, If we can't go into North Vietnam, let's at least make a strong position across the DMZ and extend that across Laos so they can't outflank it. I felt it was critical that we keep the guerrillas from being reinforced. Fighting that war was like trying to fill a bucket with a hole in the bottom.

When the idea of a northern border cutoff wasn't agreed to by anybody, I suggested a kind of last-ditch one that I didn't think anybody could object to but that would have been a tremendous effort. This was toward the end of my tour, in the spring of '66. The idea was to build a barrier all up and down the border of South Vietnam, exactly like we had done at my division base at An Khe. I had some good statistics to go on. What I had in mind was a 100-meter swath, sort of like the Russians have along their borders to keep people from leaving. The swath would be skinned right down to the ground. You would have had multiple lines of barbed wire, concertina, trip wires, and antipersonnel mines. You would have had watchtowers with searchlights, and strong points, pillboxes with machine guns, with artillery backing that up. You could fly up and down the trace with helicopters and fixed-wing aircraft so anything that got across would be a trickle, not a flood.

I thought it would take a year to build, maybe eighteen months. I asked my engineer battalion commander to put pencil to paper on the numbers to come up with some approximation of what would be involved. I suggested that we get the Japanese or somebody to come in and cut down the forest to speed up the process. I thought the

Japanese would think it was a damn good way to get a lot of free lumber. They cut timber up in Alaska and the Pacific Northwest and take it all the way back to process in Japan. They're almost devoid of wood, and it's an important item to them. They're eager-beaver workers, so I felt we could get in hundreds of Japanese with bulldozers and power saws. And every time you finished a strip, you would start to guard it and then worry about the rest. You could thin your forces in the rest of the country—put light forces where you've completed the barrier. The enemy could have tried to mass against it and come through at any one point, but I felt our surveillance was better than anything he had. We could pick him up before he could do much about it.

Well, that was turned down, too. I made an oral presentation to either Westy or Larsen or both. They just thought it was nutty. Nobody got enthusiastic about it. Nobody said, I'd like to see your numbers. Nobody even tried to test the assumptions, which kind of made me unhappy. It wouldn't have cost a nickel to go proposition the Japanese and say, What do some of your lumbering people think about this? I had no doubt the South Vietnamese would have approved it. But it was just one of 10,000 things going on, so you don't fall on your sword.

WARREN WOOTEN

Cousineau and I scored the first big hit for the battalion. The first body.

It was a funny thing, too. We were cherries. It was my third day in-country. They were breakin' us in, so they took us from the main base and put us in this firebase. We had perimeter security. As the sun was setting, I remember sitting in my fighting hole. There was a kid on a water buffalo. I watched him. He started at the far end of the line. We were facing this rice paddy, and a hamlet maybe 1,000 meters out to the front of us. This kid on the buffalo came down, and he'd stop, turn the buffalo, and point it toward the lines. He was marking things. It didn't really sink in, I just happened to notice it. But it gave me a clue.

And there was something else. I'm a country boy. I'm used to the night sounds. When the frogs and the crickets are going, everything's all right. When they stop, that's when I wonder. That night, when the sun finally set, it was dead still. There was not a sound in the air. So I was already a little jittery.

Three of us were going out on a listening post. On the way out,

Cousineau and I saw something suspicious. We just backed up and held for a second. The area wasn't jungle, it was more sand dunes and tropical desert. We were going around the side of the paddy, and there were dunes above us. Shrubbery along the way. What we saw was a man huddled behind a bush with his rifle sticking straight up in the air. You could just make out his outline.

I moved back to Krause. He had a Bren Starcluster that fired flares. I told him to fire when we opened up. A flare was our signal that we were coming back into the lines. Then I went back to Cousineau and we both emptied twenty-round clips into that bush. When Krause shot his burst off, it lit up enough that I could see this man jerking all over the place. I trained in that much more intense with my rifle. After our clips were empty, we started running like hell back toward the line.

We hit their point element, I think, because for the rest of the night we had light to medium contact. They'd run in, try to put a hit on us, and back out. It may have been a platoon or a company of VC.

Krause got killed there with another unit. I found his name on the Wall. Bless his soul, he was a quart low but he was still a good kid. I wonder what happened to Cousineau.

He is a dark-haired man of slight build who looks like he has been somewhere and back. His face seems tired. He is an auto mechanic. We talk in his apartment near Golden Gate Park in San Francisco.

At seventeen he dropped out of high school and joined the marines. It was March 1965, the same month the first marine units landed at Danang. In September, he shipped out for Vietnam. Thirteen months later he came back, not exactly a happy-go-lucky nineteen-year-old. After two more years in the marines came a tough decade: marriage, divorce, motorcycle gangs, too many drugs, too many jobs. In 1980, "I was all fucked up one night on drugs, too fucked up to get up and turn the TV off. It was about 3:00 A.M., and this commercial came on. It couldn't have been better timing. They had this guy walking around through a deserted park, saying: 'Have you had drug problems? Do the people around you not understand you?' I was sitting there thinking: Yeah, man, you got me. What really hit me was: 'You don't even know where the people are that you fought with.' Yeah, man, yeah. They flashed a number on the screen. After a bunch of phone calls, I got in touch with the Mission Street Veterans Outreach Center."

We made a tactical assault on one of the beaches around Danang harbor. After I was there about a month, they broke up the battalion and sent about three-quarters of us off to other battalions. I wound up in Bravo Company, 1st Battalion, 4th Marines.

Bravo 1/4 was on an island near Chu Lai. It wasn't a big island, maybe half a mile long. There was a village at one end and a village at the other. And an island across from us that you could walk to at low tide. It was known as Snaggletooth. It was a mean motherfucker. Totally VC-patrolled. We never made any kind of contact with 'em. They might snipe one of us off. And guaranteed we were gonna walk through a gang of land mines. We lost one whole squad, but that was because they just flat fucked up. They kept going over there and setting up ambushes in exactly the same spot. Hell, everybody on that island was a VC sympathizer if not actually carrying a weapon. They picked up on the pattern, and one night they walked up and blew away the whole squad.

But there may have been a little more to it. The sergeant in control of that squad was a machine-gunner. He went across with 'em that night. A few days earlier, our company commander had ordered him to shoot up a sampan with his M-60 machine gun. There was maybe one guy on there, along with a few women and some children. You could see he didn't want to do it. But he wiped the whole fucking thing out, killed 'em all. I don't remember why. What I do remember is that he turned around and looked at the CO and said, "Y'know something? I just killed myself."

Around January they shipped us to Phu Bai, and as time progressed we moved farther and farther north. We started to get a mix of VC and NVA. Then they moved us out to a place that's infamous in my memory, the Rockpile. From about April or May, I spent all the rest of my time near there: Dong Ha, Quang Tri, Con Thien, back over to the Laotian border and into Laos. Just trying to spook up the NVA and see what the hell was out there.

After we got up north it was a completely different war. Night and day. With the VC, we'd hit our share of booby traps and mines, take a few sniper rounds. Get frustrated and sweaty. With the NVA, we could hunt and look and dig and go for weeks and not find a thing. And all of a sudden, *Bang!* We're in the midst of a big motherfucking blowout.

There was one ambush I clearly remember. They loaded Bravo Company and Delta Company on choppers before sunrise. These were the old shudder-and-shitboxes, the CH-34s. Looked like old tadpoles. They were scary enough. When we hit the LZ, both companies lined up in a long line. We were going across rice paddies to treelines, and across more paddies to treelines. We had a good 2,000 meters of rice paddy with a treeline ahead of us. And we had ARVN boots along with us to train. These boots were fifteen- and sixteen-year-old kids.

They took a squad from each platoon and put 'em out front. They were fifty, maybe seventy-five meters ahead of us. Crossing open rice paddies with dikes in between. If we had been half smart we would have reconned that first treeline by fire, but we didn't. We had been told it was just gonna be a sweep, and we probably wouldn't run into anything.

Our point elements were right up at that treeline, and man, all at once the whole fucking world exploded. Everybody up there was dead [snaps fingers] like this. Delta Company made a flank and tried to come in from the other side, and the same thing happened to them at another treeline. I mean, they just got their shit blown away.

So here we were—one squad dead out of each platoon. We were out in the open. The shit was bustin' all around us. We started to make an advance, and it was like a second explosion of the world. How the fuck people walked out of that, I don't know. I shouldn't say walked, because we dropped down into the paddies and hustled our asses like snakes through that water and rice and back over the first dike we could get to. Which put us about 150 meters off that treeline.

We tried to move over the dike a few times, but we finally gave that up because every time it was like the world would explode again. So we called in naval support fire. I was up on one end of the line, and they dropped a Willie Peter round right on top of the other end. I don't know how many people got fucked up from that one. I know I saw 'em carrying ponchos for quite a while—. [Cries.]

Anyway, they finally corrected the fire. They brought in all these little Hueys with .60-calibers on, and rockets. The gooks were trying to blow the birds out of the air. Then the Phantoms came in. They were dropping 250- and 500-pound bombs in there. They'd rake the hell out of it, and we'd start to go over again. We'd take more shit and call in more air and artillery. Trying to make a move. All the time this is happening, we've got the ARVN boots throwing their gear down and hightailing it out the other way, because they don't want nothin' to do with this. I remember people shooting at them.

It went back and forth like this all goddamn day and night. You have to remember we had people up there that died in the initial burst. If there was any of them alive, they died during the night, because we didn't get to 'em 'til the next morning. The Phantoms didn't use napalm until it was just coming down sunset. Then they put napalm all over that son of a bitch. Napalmed the holy fuck out of it. We spent a restless night on the dike. No more shooting.

The first thing we did when we moved up the next morning was recon the treeline by fire. Then we moved in. We had specific orders not to fire if we came across anything. We were supposed to use frags. Everybody was spooky as hell, and the idea was that if any rifles were being fired, it wasn't us. I got in trouble over that one. Because the first thing I found was—you learn to see things over there. It was all brush and tree limbs, everything blown to shit. Right up through the bushes I saw some little fine black hairs. I looked for a second, and they moved. There was no way I was gonna drop a grenade and run. So I stuck my rifle down there and I blew that son of a bitch's head completely off. It comes flying up out of there, blood going all over the place. The CO chewed my ass out but good for shooting the gook instead of fragging him. Because the whole operation broke up— people came running over, "Hey, man, we got one." The CO put me out in the rice paddies again. I had to start grabbing the bodies of the kids from Delta Company, dragging 'em out of the paddy, putting 'em up on a trail.

Then they rounded us all up, put us on choppers, and we didn't see a base camp for sixty days.

First they moved us to the A Shau valley, and then up around Dong Ha and the Rockpile. It's a hilly area with large valleys that flow between the ridgelines. The Rockpile was this one big hill that looked like a pyramid, where you could get a view of all the ridges and valleys. We chased the NVA all around there, through these incredible tunnels they had in the ridgelines.

After a while we were way under operating strength. We had maybe five or six people to a squad, and a full marine squad is twelve people. We had been chewed up in the ambush. We got some replacements, but then we got chewed up in the A Shau, chewed up around the Rockpile. Booby traps, snipers, heat exhaustion, disease. When I came back from sixty days in the field, I didn't have hardly any bottoms of my feet left. Immersion foot. Our feet were wet all the time. You carry extra socks in the field, but hell, you take off a dirty pair of wet socks and put on a clean pair of wet socks. You never have time to pull your boots off and let your feet air and dry. You'd set in at night, but it was goddamn cold up north, especially in the rainy season. Even if it wasn't the rainy season, that jungle was still dripping water on you. And if you were in an open area where it was hot, you were wading through rivers or paddies or something. Constantly wet.

It seemed like the whole country was an enemy. The animals, the reptiles, the insects, the plants. And the people—you just couldn't respect 'em anymore. You knew they were going, "Eh, GI Number One," during the day, but at night they were trying to kill you. And it rains so much you just don't understand why that country doesn't sink. Your whole immune system starts breaking down. You get these ungodly cuts all over your hands and arms from the vegetation. Seems like everything's got a point on it. The cuts get infected. They turn into big open sores. It took me months after I got home for my feet to really heal, and for the sores to close up. I've got scars all up and down my legs from leech bites.

The NVA were chewing us up, and we were chewing them up. But we weren't chewing them up the same way. We might find a cache of weapons. We might score on some of the snipers. In a day we'd usually get at least one body. But sometimes we'd go for four or five days before we'd get a shot off. Slushing through mud, sweating. I got malaria and blackwater fever and collapsed with a 106-degree fever. That got me out of the field. But 104 wouldn't get you out. Immersion foot wouldn't get you out, because we were short of men. You literally had to be dying.

One thing that starts driving you is the rage. Seeing people hit, not knowing if you're going to make it through the next minute or not, and not having any contact. I've seen footage from World War II of kamikazes coming in on ships. There's this one segment of a man on an antiaircraft gun. There's a kamikaze coming right at him. The guy's pumping away on this gun, just pouring lead out there. You can see that the plane's hit and it's starting to wheel over and go into the drink, way out there. But the guy doesn't stop shooting. He's following it all the way down into the water, and it's in the water, and he's still at it. That's exactly how the American kids were in the war, with that rage, man. We'd see one gook, and he might dart behind a wall or a building, and the whole company would open up with every goddamn thing we had. You'd just see this wall start disintegrating. We wouldn't even hit the gook, but we just couldn't stop.

You have to understand that for sixty days we were running eighteen-hour days. That's another reason your immune system breaks down. You might cop off a half-hour's sleep during the day while you're on the move, because you stop for chow. You just forget about the chow and fall asleep. Then you move on and try to have a bite. Crackers and peanut butter to keep yourself plugged up, because you've got the shits. So you don't think straight. You lose a certain capacity. You try not to think, but your mind's chattering at you. I don't know how to explain it. It's a numbness. It's a sadness. It's pain. It strips you raw. It takes you down to a real animal mentality. The rage becomes a kind of life force. You use it to make it through.

This happened outside of Phu Bai. We were going in on a company sweep through a village. It wasn't a search and destroy, just a search mission. We took sniper fire going in. Got into the village. Typical scenario—you had old men and women and kids. No young men. We go through it. Don't turn up a goddamn thing. Go out the other end and we take sniper fire. So, fuck it. We turn around, back through it again. Don't find a goddamn thing. On the way out, we take sniper fire. No casualties. Now, the day's getting hotter and hotter. We're searching and searching, taking sniper fire. Toward the afternoon, we're pissed. We're hot. No water. Hungry. Just burnt out and pissed off. And finally one of the snipers hits somebody. A sergeant. He got his third Purple Heart out of it. It was a minor wound. But the lieutenant turned around and said, "I'll be a son of a bitch. This is the last fucking round we'll take out of there." He called a Phantom in. The Phantom dropped napalm on the fucking village with the inhabitants still in it, and we walked away. It had just come down to, "Hey, fuck you sons of bitches." Even though that was a sympathizing village, and every swinging dick and split in the place was a VC, that was an atrocity. It really was. But who gave a fuck? That's the last we had to deal with them.

There was times when we'd work at night in five-man teams to try to pick up intelligence. We weren't looking to make contact. We didn't want them to know we were there. We'd move down a trail and hope we could snatch somebody. We didn't take prisoners. When I say snatch, we were hoping we might pick up a carrier or an officer and get papers off him. He usually wound up with his throat slit. In my team I would not allow prisoners to be taken. I let that be clearly known. I'd bring back any papers, but I just felt too exposed trying to haul somebody back.

That was a rage thing, too. It was like: Die, you motherfucker, die. It was one of the few times you got to look one of these motherfuckers in the eye. And I didn't fuck around about it. I pulled that one off as quickly and cleanly as possible. But I still got a charge out of watching their eyes. Some of 'em—one of the things that really got to me—their eyes. There was a defiance in their eyes. It was like: You got me, but fuck you anyway.

I hated them. They weren't even people. They were filth. They were animals. That's a mentality that gets pushed on you in 'Nam, and even in boot camp. It's them and us.

I was gung-ho until the time I went on R&R. It was July. I went to Japan. Just being there blew my mind. I hid out in the hotel room. I ate my meals there. I got laid once. I ventured out a little bit at night, but not a lot. For one thing, I was naked—I didn't have my weapon with me. And I had a lot of sores on me. It was just too weird being back with all these people running around in three-piece suits.

When I came back I started having some questions about it. I still did my job, but not as well as before. I tended to fuck off more. I knew by this time we weren't gonna win the war in this fashion. It felt like a hopeless cause. And I was coming to an awakening that, hey, I wanted to live. I was thinking less and less about my duty and more and more about, goddamn it, I've gotta survive this thing. Plus by that time I had committed enough mayhem over there that it was getting pretty disgusting. And I had seen enough mayhem that I was sick.

After R&R I spent two or three weeks at Phu Bai training new people. I did feel a sense of responsibility to those cherries, to try and teach 'em that it was a life-or-death situation. Then one day we were out on patrol. I had a twelve-gauge shotgun. Ninety percent of the time I carried my M-14, but I had my twelve-gauge that day because it was a pretty secure area. I was breakin' in a squad of cherries. I was tail-end Charlie, drag man. Watchin' 'em go down this trail. Every goddamn one of these people walked past this old man sitting about ten feet away behind a bush. I spotted him and I just went on automatic. Laid the son of a bitch out. Half decapitated him. Killed him instantly. With not a fucking thing there to prove he was VC.

I wound up standing with locked heels in front of the battalion commander over it. He said, "Well, you're already in the infantry. You're already on point most of the time. So we'll just let fate take its course. I'm gonna send you back to the company, and we're gonna give you some rear-area punishment here." I had to stand for three days with a pack on my back filled with sand. It probably weighed 150 pounds. I stood in 100-degree sun. The rest of the time they had me filling sandbags, me and some other fuckups.

That was another thing that broke me in my attitude about the war. Because I had just come down off the DMZ. If you see somebody in the goddamn bush, and the son of a bitch has let seven marines walk by and hasn't raised his hand up, what the fuck's going on? Actually, he was taking a shit. But he could have waved and let us know: Hey, don't shoot me, I'm just taking a shit. But that didn't happen. I saw somebody huddled up in the bushes, and I didn't stop to see if he had a weapon. They said I should have slowed down and identified the man. But if you're in a hostile area and you try to identify somebody, you're gonna get your shit blown away, it's that simple. On the DMZ, if somebody's hiding in the bush, you kill the motherfucker. I learned that day one.

So yeah, I did overreact. But what the fuck did they expect? I've done sixty days out in the goddamn bush. I had seven cherries there, and I was gonna teach those kids what the fuck to do to stay alive. I had charge of those people's lives. I was just turning nineteen. I spent my nineteenth birthday filling those sandbags. July 28, 1966. That was my birthday present from Vietnam. The troops would walk up and say, "Hey, man, don't feel bad about it. You did the right thing." But it didn't change the facts, at least for me, being a kid and wanting to be the ideal marine.

So they sent me back to the bush. After a while, I pulled a little trick to get out of the field. We were patrolling, and I fell over a ledge. It wasn't very far—twenty-five, thirty feet. I bounced and rolled on the way down. I was shocked that I wasn't hurt when I got to the bottom, other than a couple of bruises. So I faked an arm injury. The corpsman knew I was faking. He and I were real close. He said, "Do you really want to do this?" I said, "Yeah, Doc, I can't stand this shit anymore." He said, "We really need you out here, but okay. I'll send you back." And I went back.

A few days later they walked into an ambush and Doc got killed. He was going down to try to save some dead marines who got killed by a machine gun. The machine gun got him. When I heard that, it tore me to my very soul. It was my duty to have been with those people, and I wasn't there. I was fucking off. I had committed a court-martial offense, malingering like that. I really let those people down. And I owe Doc a hell of a lot. I've only recently gotten to the point where I can go to the Wall and say thanks.

That happened in September. From then on, it's a fog. I totally unplugged. Pretty soon, I knew I was past my time to leave. I still hadn't received orders. We had a new platoon sergeant. We were back in Dong Ha. I walked up to him and said, "Y'know, Sarge, I'm here past my tour date. I feel like I'm pretty lucky I made it through. What I'd like, if you'll okay it, is for you to put me back in the rear. I don't care if I have to burn shitters. I don't think I can do you people any good out there any more." It shocked me, because he looked at me and said, "Y'know, you're probably right. I have no problems with that at all." And I wound up in the mess hall.

I finally got my orders. I remember hustling my butt over to the airstrip and getting on a C-130. I think there was four or five other kids going down south for whatever reason. A C-130 will carry about 230 or 240 combat marines. I climbed onto this bird and it had a full load. The full load was bodies stacked like cardboard along the sides. Three or four bodies high, both sides of the plane. There was just a small walkway in the center aisle. There was no place to sit when we got on this plane, because they had all these bodies. That's what was happening in October of 1966 in 'Nam.

One of the nightmares that bothered me for years—I haven't had it for about three years now—is I'm out in the jungle. I've got my fireteam there. We're in a kind of swamp, with triple-canopy jungle. It's a real muddy, swampy, filthy, slimy, bad area. We make contact with these gooks. They're advancing on us. We're all shooting 'em. And they don't die. They just keep coming. They're killing my team. Finally it's just me. I'm still retreating, firing at these people. Finally— and this is another thing. Toward the end of my tour I started getting a little nastier about how I killed. I shot more for the head, instead of trying to hit the torso. In my dream, after my team is killed, I'm finding that the only way I can kill these motherfuckers is to shoot 'em in the face. There's a half dozen, and I kill off all but one. This motherfucker is still advancing on me. The reason he's still alive is I've run out of ammunition. I've got a pistol, a .45. I'm hunting for it, because I know it's there. I'm searching through the mud, and he's coming at me, firing and firing and firing. I never finish the dream, because just as he's up there and I'm finding the pistol, I'm screaming. And I've screamed myself awake.

5

GRUNTS AND REMFS

T hen all hell broke loose."

The phrase is almost a throwaway. Every Vietnam combat vet uses it to describe the firefight most fresh in his memory. Yet the power of the image is strong: One thinks of a weak spot in the earth's crust, a cracking, and a sudden eruption of everything hell has to offer, all the rage and hatred and blood lust and pain and noise and flame boiling into the world. After 1965 all hell did break loose in Vietnam, and for the next ten years it seared the country from one end to the other. Hell also broke loose in the lives of millions of soldiers—Americans and Vietnamese—who were the instruments and victims of the war's fire.

Usually it came without warning. *BRRRAAAAATTTT*, the small arms opening up from a treeline or a village or a bunker hidden in foliage. A minute, or ten minutes, of deafening confusion—hit the ground, hunt for cover, shoot back, run, shoot some more. Then silence, as the enemy faded away. Then a cry: "Medic!" And a pause as the unit regrouped and waited for the helicopters. Most firefights were short and decided nothing—except for the dead and maimed. A battle that lasted for hours was memorable; one that lasted overnight was a major engagement; one that lasted for days was an epic. The grunts played an endless game of hide-and-seek. Vietnam's metaphor is not the trench of World War I or the sweeping campaigns and beach landings of World War II. It is the ambush.

There was a science to combat, of course. It could be learned. But 'Nam was a cruel university that dealt out the severest of punishments for mistakes. And nothing, certainly not Advanced Infantry Training, could prepare you for Vietnam. The first lessons a cherry absorbed were mundane, such as how to keep his pack light. Carry a pair of dry socks, toss out the underwear and shaving equipment—you won't need them. Many men died in their first few weeks, before they had time to learn other simple matters, such as diving for cover fast enough. Those who survived moved on to higher levels of education: How to move through a jungle—avoiding the trails, which might be booby-trapped—without making noise. How to spot a nearly invisible trip-wire. The true experts finally developed a sixth sense that whispered to them when death was hiding in the next treeline. Yet all the learning, all the experience, could slip away in a moment of surprise or fatigue. "One of my pet peeves is that a large percentage of the people who were wounded and killed were hurt because of mistakes," says Walter Mack, the marine company commander who opens this chapter.

Some grunts so mastered the art of combat that they still talk proudly of being "professionals." Most were content to get passing grades, to survive. Some discovered a special talent and carved out their own lonely territory. Men with sharp vision and steady hands took to the night with Starlight scopes as snipers. Small, wiry, crazy-brave grunts became tunnel rats, pursuing the enemy into underground mazes. GIs who yearned to fly wangled their way into helicopter units and became virtuosi with machine guns swivel-mounted in a chopper's door. Each soldier's taste was different. Some loved walking point; others loathed it. Some feared Bouncing Bettys, others mortars. More than a few, once they had walked into the valley of the shadow of death, found they were quite at home there. The hunt and the kill became a plea-sure, or a compulsion. Every unit had a few men who were viewed by the rest with awe and disgust. These were the volunteers for killer teams and night ambushes, the ones who cut ears and carved insignia into foreheads. The war's darker currents were seductive, and most grunts dipped into them at some point before climbing back out, shaken. Combat could grab you and hold you in thrall. Jurate Ka-zickas, a reporter and the only civilian in this chapter, saw the war as a horrible waste, yet for two years she went into the field over and over, looking to put herself where the fighting was heaviest. Even today she says she is not sure why.

As in all wars, 90 percent of the time a foot soldier's life amounted to exhausting work and stupefying boredom. Patrols, patrols, patrols, endless walking in 100-degree heat under a seventy-pound pack. Rain that seemed to fall for weeks at a time. Mud, dust, mosquitoes, leeches, sweat, sores, bad food, no sleep. In such conditions, a firefight could come as a crazy relief, a blast of sound and speed, with time stretched out and the mind soaring on adrenaline to levels of keenness never before touched. For pure thrill, say the grunts, nothing matches shooting and being shot at. And for a pure sense of power, few things match an angry young man with an automatic weapon. Weeks of filth and exhaustion might tell him that he had sunk to something less than human, yet a squeeze of the trigger made him an avenging god.

The other two constants were love and fear. In armyspeak the term is *camaraderie*, but the feeling between men in combat goes much deeper than that. In a realm where little heroisms occur daily, where risking one's life for a comrade is just part of going to work, emotions swell to appropriate size. Again there is a paradox, because as Angel Quintana puts it: "After six or seven months you get hard. You almost don't feel your own feelings." But by that time the bonds are already forged. True, the grunts saw, with eyes first astonished and then jaded, the worst of what human beings can do to one another. But they also saw what people will do *for* one another. The certainty that "I would cover their backs, and they would cover mine" gave birth to a kind of respect and trust that left a hollow once a vet was back in civilian life.

Fear was like your skin: It enveloped you always. Even GIs in the base camps, known to the grunts as REMFs, for "rear-echelon motherfuckers," felt a steady low-grade fear, for who knew where and when the next rocket would come crashing in? Out in the boonies, the fear was simply cranked up higher. Sometimes it was so bad that it kept you from sleeping. Or maybe you could smother it beneath a hard-won armor of indifference. Either way, it was there, an electrical current through the gut. Some grunts gave themselves over to it, adopted fear as their flag. They were called "shitbirds." Out of fright, incompetence, or plain cussedness, they shirked duty or always did things wrong. Larry Thetford and Duane Cornella, two army draftees in this chapter, took their distaste for combat to unusual lengths—and escaped. Other vets might feel contempt for them. But in the 'Nam, with sane and insane turned topsy-turvy, who can say what was honorable? Did it make sense to keep fighting when hardly a GI believed in the cause?

John Catterson, a marine rifleman, talks of a shitbird in his fireteam who got out of the field: "They made him a cashier at the PX in Danang. When they sent him back to the rear, we were all a little pissed off about it, because he pulled it off. We felt a bit cheated. But the truth is, nobody wanted him to be with us anyway." The same mixed feelings applied to REMFs in general. Grunts were proud of doing the dirty, dangerous work. They often resisted taking R&R if their buddies were staying out in the field. They lorded it over the clerks and cooks and deskbound lifers. But they longed for those same jobs and were rewarded with them when they got short. As for the REMFs, they felt guilty and somewhat unmanned about having it easy—but rarely guilty enough to request combat duty. Anyway, there was comfort in numbers: Support troops outnumbered combat troops in Vietnam by about ten to one.

And the rear presented its own problems. Boredom was a plague that sometimes killed: Witness the story about the three scout-dog handlers who poured gunpowder on the ground in the shape of a big peace sign and then were burned to death when they set it off. Alcohol, the age-old antidote to an army's woes, was joined in Vietnam by a candy-store array of drugs. The mamasan who cleaned your room would sell you marijuana and heroin, and a medic with imagination could provide almost any pill or ampule he dreamed up a reason for ordering. Life passed in a haze of highs and heat and Jimi Hendrix. But the war's rot still penetrated. "Everything was corruption," remembers one REMF. Racial hatred flared. Fragging became an occupational hazard for officers and NCOs. Today, a kind of romance still attaches to fragging—the notion that soldiers took righteous revenge on their persecutors. For a view from the other side, it is worth listening to Sergeant Woody Wanamaker's account of flying back to Vermont with his best friend—that is, what was left of him.

For Harry Behret, an army meteorologist, the turning point came when his housegirl and eleven other Vietnamese workers were killed in an accident because a GI known to be a drunk was given the job of driving them to the base. "After that," says Behret, "I just got drunker and alienated from everybody. . . . I didn't even see myself as a human being." Jim Duffy, a helicopter door gunner who watched a five-year-old boy get run over by a truck: "We laughed it off. One less gook, forget it." The dehumanization spread from the enemy to the civilians to oneself. And having become, for whatever time, "an animal," it was doubly hard to come home. The GIs had much of value to report about human savagery and tenderness, but few people back in the World wanted to hear. Families preferred not to know what their little boys had been up to. Strangers, stoned on moral fervor, used 'Nam vets as an easy target. And many ex-grunts, with their baggage of guilt and memory, found it easy to think as badly of themselves as others obviously did.

In other words, all hell broke loose again—only this time the incoming was emotional. So the GIs did what came naturally: They dove for cover. Some now say the battle is ending, as the country slowly gets over its shame. But some haven't climbed out of those foxholes yet.

WALTER MACK

It is hard to imagine him ever in repose. When we talk, he is head of the Organized Crime Division of the U.S. Attorney's Office for the Southern District of New York—a tall, lean, sandy-haired man, younger looking than his thirty-eight years and bristling with energy. He cancels several appointments before we finally meet in his office. The walls are lined with books, the desks and tables cluttered with papers and tape cassettes. A set of barbells sits in a corner, and he flexes isometric hand grips while we talk. Every half hour, phone calls come in about an operation the office is running that night. He is disappointed when the target fails to show up for a rendezvous with the undercover agent.

He is the son of a wealthy and prominent businessman. He attended private schools and Harvard. "I decided when I first went to college that it would be good for me to spend some time in the military. Having lived a spoiled life, I thought the discipline would be good for me. Plus the Marine Corps has that male-ethic lure. I figured it would toughen me up. And there's a service orientation in my family, the idea that public service is something that should be part of your life.

"Then there's the fact that combat is a challenge. It's very exciting work, and you can even delude yourself into thinking you're doing something of value. I need that. My friends would say I'm an adrenaline freak, and I am to some extent. I could not have been in the military and been a logistics or supply officer. I don't think I could be a trusts-and-estates lawyer or a corporate lawyer. I'd get bored to tears. I definitely have a death-wish side. I ride a motorcycle. I like to fly, I have a pilot's license. I make decisions around here that are chancey. And combat is a turn-on if you do it right."

After ROTC at Harvard, he became a second lieutenant in the marines in 1965. In May 1967, he was sent with a military police battalion to Danang, where he helped guard the airfield. Then he requested transfer to combat duty, and in late 1967 he was given command of a rifle company in I Corps, near the DMZ.

I was scared to death when I took over that company. One side of me was saying, "You've got to do this. You're not going to Vietnam and come back and say you lived in Danang in a hut and had your laundry done and never really got shot at." The other side of me was saying, "You've got to be nuts, you're not going to be a military hero, you're not going to be a military person. You don't need this." I remember what it was like flying into the camp at Cam Lo, with a lot of battle-hardened marines and a company commander who was very well respected. He was being pulled to go somewhere else, and here's some little schmuck coming in from Danang, without combat experience.

I took over the company and started to organize it the way I wanted. I had been reading a lot of the manuals, and I had some ideas. But I'm not one of those people that come in and change everything right away. It was slow. Little stupid things. Like the 60mm mortar, which is a weapon that few people in the Marine Corps understood. I don't know why. It was used frequently as a direct-fire weapon in combat, which is not what it's made for. It's an indirect-fire weapon. I don't think it's a great weapon, but if I had it I used it. I sure as hell wasn't going to carry the damn thing around if we didn't know how to use it. Well, when I got to Cam Lo these three 60mm mortars were sitting somewhere in the mud. They weren't even being used in the perimeter defense. I got the mortarmen out on the range the second day, and we starting firing all sorts of practice rounds. I told them I didn't want to depend on the 81mm mortars, which were in a different location. I wanted them to be active and alert at night. I plotted places where I wanted them to fire. After a while they got very accurate with the damn thing, and they developed some esprit de corps. So it had its value. You could fire it rapidly, and it was an effective antisniper weapon. And right there under your thumb. You don't have to call in with the radio and clear the fire mission and then get the call-back saying, "What was that grid? Can I have that number again?"

My basic idea was to use firepower rather than human power to get results, so I tried to get every damn weapon I could. I wanted tanks in my perimeter, so I screamed and yelled and got tanks brought down. I did that for three reasons. One, it was a good place for them. Two, I knew they were all sitting around not doing a goddamn thing where they were. And three, there's no better thing to have if you're going to be attacked or overrun than some tanks. They have good radios, so you can communicate with them. They have a variety of rounds that can be effective if you're overrun, fleshettes or shrapnel. And they're a security blanket for the troops. I also stole M-60 machine guns whenever I could find them. I think we had more M-60s than any other company in the battalion, because I knew automatic fire was so important in a firefight. You have to get as much lead in the air as possible right away. I used to get my supply people hyped up to go find M-60s. They'd disappear into Dong Ha and come back with M-60 parts hidden all over. We had about fifteen machine guns, when there are only about six allowed in a rifle company.

I was also one of those guys who believed in aggressive patrolling. I thought we were too static in our defensive positions. There was no reason to cede the area outside your perimeter to the North Vietnamese at night. That gave them more access and power, and you were bound to take more casualties because they could pick and choose their opportunities to hurt you. My feeling was they should not count on all those areas being entirely free. As time went by, I started sending volunteer patrols way the hell out in the boonies. They'd be gone four or five days, like real recon types. That's one of the reasons we rarely got hit. We had a pretty good idea of what was going on around us.

It paid off during the Tet offensive. One of my platoon commanders came back from a long patrol and he said that things were too quiet. He had the feeling there were a lot of troops in the area. Our job at the time was to secure a perimeter and provide security for a district headquarters down the road and guard a bridge. We had invented a method of preparing small charges of TNT that we would throw into the water at intervals to keep divers away. It was so much fun to set these huge firecrackers off, making these fantastic waterspouts, that it kept the troops interested. And that night we were alerted because of the patrol. So about two in the morning, somebody spotted three or four sappers who were floating down the river to blow the bridge. This guy killed all the sappers with a TNT charge, and he started firing. That woke up the people who presumably were on post, and they spotted the security team for the sappers on the riverbank, and killed all of them. As a result, we suffered no casualties during Tet. If the sapper unit had blown the bridge, that would have prevented the reaction team from getting into the district headquarters when it was attacked, and it would have left my forces divided on either side of the bridge. I imagine we were supposed to get an attack. But because we got them going in, I think the assault team just skipped us and went around to join the attack on the district headquarters, which was hit very badly and almost overrun.

Of course, early on I had some people who were supposed to go out on patrol, and they didn't, and I found out about it and got madder than shit. Their favorite tactic was to say, "Okay, skipper, we're going out to grid so-and-so." They'd go about ten feet in front of the lines and go to sleep for the rest of the night. One night I was patrolling the lines and I saw two or three cigarettes sitting out about twenty or thirty yards in front. I asked the topper, "What the hell's going on, who's smoking out there?" He was covering for them. That was early in my stay, and I'm sure they thought, This green skipper doesn't know what's happening. He said, "Well, it must be a farmer or something." I said, "Jesus, no farmers are supposed to be out in that area this time of night. Maybe we'll call in some mortar fire on those cigarettes." "Well, you better not, you better check with sergeant so-and-so"—who was leading the patrol that night. That was my first inkling. One other time I found out because one of the people on patrol was a gung-ho type, and he was disgusted. Afterward he came back and asked to speak to me and said, "I want you to know we never went out to that place. I just thought you ought to know." The first time, I just talked to the guys and said that if it ever happened again in the company I was going to reduce the person in rank. The second time, I did.

Little by little you learned how to fight the war. The test is the small-unit leader—the sergeants, corporals, lieutenants, captains. Can they learn the lessons and train their troops so they'll survive? Because it's not the popular thing to do. Americans are lazy, unless they have somebody kicking their ass one way or the other. They don't like to put greasy paint all over themselves in the hot sweaty daytime. They don't like to wear flak jackets. They don't like to wear helmets. They don't like to take care of their rifles enough to keep them working. They don't like to use fire discipline, which is essential. They don't like to take care of their feet.

It's a lot of very small things. One of my pet peeves is that a large percentage of the people who were wounded and killed in Vietnam were hurt because of mistakes made by small-unit leaders—an unwillingness to think out what's going on, or a loss of control or professionalism. Which is precisely what the North Vietnamese expected the Americans to do: to hurry, not to think, to be lazy. The sloppiness varied from unit to unit, squad to squad, fireteam to fireteam. But based on what I saw, we were much sloppier than we should have been. And there was usually a relationship between casualties and attention to discipline. I'm not talking about everybody having to shave every morning. I'm talking about learning how to fight that war, how to utilize the advantages the Americans had—because we had a lot of advantages, in firepower and medical care—and minimize the disadvantages, which were lack of knowledge of the terrain and the people, being easily spotted, and having fixed positions, not being able to blend in and use the land.

Maybe I'm a very linear person, but any time I set out to do something, my feeling is you can learn how to do it and minimize the risks. I'm talking about professionalism, the willingness to stay up that extra hour the night before the patrol to do your homework. Like taking the time when you're extremely tired to do your map study and plot out where you're likely to be ambushed. To have the discipline not to walk along a treeline, or a trail, or a road, at a time when you're likely to get ambushed. To check with your intelligence officer to find out the latest reports. To check with the person responsible the next day for air operations to find out what is available and when, so you can get air support a little quicker. To know what the weather is going to be. It's not anything earth-shattering. I don't want to give the image of me sitting in my bunker every night with a candle. But combat is susceptible to analysis. It can be rationalized the way anything else can. I'm not saying I was the only one who did it. I knew some marine officers there who were much tougher than me. They ran terrific companies. They weren't ogres, but they did insist on discipline, and they had enough energy to ensure that their standards didn't get worn down by combat and the heat and the cold and the rain.

I made my troops wear camouflage on patrol and made them wear helmets and told them I didn't want them smoking. I know they smoked, but I was tough on that because I believed if we were going to stay safe we had to move in the boonies and not be typical Americans, smoking and listening to radios. I remember having a demonstration where I put a helmet out on a flat area, and then I put another helmet out there with branches and stuff on it. It was easy to pick out the helmet without anything on it. I asked, "Which one would you shoot at?" I also did it with people. I put camouflage paint on one guy and all kinds of bushes on his helmet. I put another guy out there, a white guy with no paint and nothing on the helmet. At about 150 meters you couldn't even see the guy with the camouflage paint. The other guy stood out loud and clear. I said, "Where would you be shooting?" Right for that white face. A lot of people were getting shot in the head. That was a pretty graphic demonstration that you stood a much better chance of getting blown away if you didn't do what you were supposed to do.

The greatest enemy was habit. Always eating at the same time. Always sending out patrols at the same time. Always having them come back the same way. Having them unload their M-16s just as they came in. Always having them come in at the same place in the perimeter wire. Always moving your company at the same time every day, or in the same formation. Always having your medevacs done the same way. Anything that could be predicted was bad, because you were constantly under observation. You had to keep the enemy on the defensive, keep them wondering what you're doing.

Another problem was fire discipline. Part of teaching fire discipline is logic, and part of it is having experienced people who've been in firefights. They recognize that well-aimed fire is much more important than firing all around in the air, because the whole idea is to get the enemy's head down so he does not have an accurate shot at you. And you have to *learn* that. You can tell them time and time again, but until they've been fired at and the rounds are zipping over their heads, they don't recognize that it's important. You have to rely on your experienced NCOs to pass it on. You tell the troops, "You've got 700 rounds with you. You may not get any more. You may be sitting out there with ten or fifteen North Vietnamese around you, and if you fire all your rounds and we can't get any more to you, you're the one who's going to suffer. Make every round count." It's a salesmanship job, and like everything else, the secret is leadership. You have to get through to these eighteen- or nineteen-year-old marine riflemen that it's not how fast you can get the rounds off, it's where those rounds go. If you're firing properly, the chances of your buddy surviving are better as well. But if you fire all over the place, that's just what the North Vietnamese want to hear. They want to know where you are, and when they hear so many rapid-fire rounds they can fix your location quickly. If it's in a dusty area, the muzzle blast can be seen. They know exactly where it's coming from, and they can get well-aimed fire back at you. And they're probably in a camouflaged position while you're out on patrol somewhere. So you have a much greater chance of getting killed.

If I were to say one thing I was most proud of when I was there, it was that my unit took very few casualties. But there were few of those that did not result from something that could have been avoided. There was one guy who had a new M-33 grenade, and he pulled the pin and held the grenade too long and it went off and killed him. The person who was with him said that somehow he had gotten the wrong information and thought that the grenade wouldn't go off until it hit something. He was testing it. He was stoned at the time, but there was this rumor going around, so he might have tested it out even if he wasn't smoking marijuana. You can't help saying to yourself that maybe you should have had a better education program on the grenade so that a rumor like that couldn't have occurred.

Another stupid thing was when you'd dig a big foxhole in a position where you're going to get mortared. Anywhere you stayed for more than a week, you were very likely to get mortared. Which was fine.

But marines were very seldom in the habit of putting rooves over their foxholes because it was a lot of work. You had to fill up sandbags and get steel girders or something like that and pile them up high enough. Well, the first few days we were on this one hill, we must have taken two or three casualties simply because I was too slow to say, "Hey, let's get some rooves up." We took a couple of casualties and everybody put rooves up and we never had another one that way. After that we started carrying sandbags if we were going to be in a position where we might take artillery or mortar fire, and we always put rooves up if we were going to be there three days. Those are mistakes. You learn from those, but human beings suffer because of them.

After a while, the company got a reputation, and we stopped getting hit. The other companies would get hit, but we were very seldom attacked by a North Vietnamese unit. They couldn't find us in a situation where it was to their advantage, so they stayed away. And the radio traffic intelligence was that our company was singled out as one you just didn't mess with. We had so much firepower and we'd get it in so fast, whether air support or artillery or just the automatic weapons we carried, that we seemed more efficient. I think that's the greatest indication of our success, that we were left alone. The battalion commander thought we were the best company in the unit. We were the reaction company. He used us for dangerous missions, and we usually did a good job. Morale was good, and casualties were low.

Then I went on R&R. And while I was away, the XO walked the company into an ambush and they took 50 percent or 60 percent casualties. There were thirty or forty dead and fifty or sixty wounded in a company of 180 people. That's the one searing recollection I have of the entire Vietnam experience.

It happened like this. I was in my eleventh month, and I hadn't taken an R&R the whole time I was there. I was one of the few officers there that long who hadn't. I had been in Danang, so I was no hardship case, but they had some policy that everybody had to go on at least one R&R. The colonel was saying, "You have to go, it's a policy, you have to go once." I said, "I'm not going while my company is in the field. I don't give a shit." Finally they brought the company into Camp Carroll for a week inside the perimeter. We had been patrolling hard. It was going to be like R&R for the whole company. So a bunch of my platoon leaders got together and sort of insisted that I go on R&R because it was my last chance. They said, "You've got to go, skipper. We're not going to be doing anything. We'll be sitting in Carroll and you'll only be gone five days. It's a good time to go." So I went to Hong Kong.

During that time a convoy got ambushed in the Landing Zone Stud area, in the northwest. They needed a rifle company to react, to be pulled up by choppers and go to the scene and get the convoy out. Because of its reputation, my company was taken from Carroll. And the XO, who was in command, made some mistakes. He sent a platoon down the road to find out what was going on and try to get to the convoy. The platoon was pinned down, and the rest of the company went in and it was a huge ambush. It was exactly what the North Vietnamese were hoping for. The whole place was a killing zone. It was on a steep hill where the NVA were dug in with a lot of supporting automatic weapons fire. The first people were hit trying to go up the hill. They were locked into the killing zone. They couldn't go up the hill because there were all kinds of nests. Then the North Vietnamese just waited for the other units to come in piecemeal, and when they did they locked them into the killing zone. To be fair, it happened to a lot of people in Vietnam. There were a lot of units ambushed. But you should *never* be ambushed. To the military professional it's apparent that being ambushed is always the result of not thinking or being rushed. And the experienced person recognizes that the North Vietnamese ambush everybody that way. They pin down one unit and chop up everybody who comes in to help them. So you can't come down the road, because that's where they expect you. You've got to do something crazy, and it may take another hour or two to get in there. Go around, come in a different place, do something funny they don't expect.

I started hearing about it as I came into Dong Ha. I was getting bits and pieces, and I couldn't believe it. Then I found the colonel and he told me. I was devastated. If I cried in Vietnam, it was then. A lot of the people who were killed were good friends of mine. We had lived together for four months, shared the same tents. And I was outraged. I was looking for the guy who walked them into that ambush. I wasn't going to beat the shit out of him, that isn't my style. I just wanted to make sure he never got close to my company again, and I wanted to dress him down, to insult him. The colonel had to spend an hour cooling me off, saying, "Leave him alone. Stay away." He realized the guy knew he had blown it. There was no way to bring back the dead and wounded, and it wouldn't have done him any good psychologically. And he was already gone, relieved of his duties. I never saw him again. But I'll never forgive that. And oh, I felt a lot of guilt. That was the most serious action the company faced while I was there, and I wasn't around.

That was when I was most terrified of getting hurt, when I came back from R&R. There were these heavy casualties in my company, so it was more obvious that death could happen to anybody. And I had lost the shell that I had built up over the months. When you're out in the field, you can't think about home, you can't think about being relaxed. I used to religiously put out of my mind thoughts of home, because boy, you really set yourself up. If you start worrying about yourself, you lose the aggressiveness and the ability to act quickly, like an animal. I did not read mail when I was out on an operation. I didn't even want mail delivered to me. That was the worst thing, because if you read a letter from your mother or your girlfriend or sister and they're telling you what's going on at home, and how they can hardly wait until you get back, it really undercuts the ability to do the job.

When I went on R&R, all that toughness dissipated in five days. I was eating well and sleeping well. I called home and talked to the people I was close to. We talked about when I'd get home, what we'd do together, where I'd live. I bought some suits, spent some money on presents for people. To top it all off, I was short, I only had about thirty days left. I started to think, "Hey, I'm going to live." But on my way back, all of a sudden I realized I still might never go home. I might never see those people again. I might never get a chance to enjoy those suits. I was saying, "Hey, I'm scared. I've done all these things and I want to get home. I want to do a lot of other things. I could get killed here, and I don't want to die. Is it worth it to me? What am I doing over here?" Because I'm not one of these great save-the-world-from-Communism types. I was there mainly for the experience, to learn. And I had lost the hardness necessary to say, "Hey, I may not survive, but so what? If I lose my leg, I'll still keep going. If I'm dead, who's going to care?" You delude yourself into not caring that much. It took about two weeks to get that back.

But in some ways, coming back and finding the company decimated helped me. I was so outraged and upset by what happened that I realized I had to get in there and take over and mend what wounds I could. In that situation you don't have the luxury to sit around and say, "Oh, how awful." It was a practical matter of trying to put the company back together. Writing the letters home to the families of the people who were killed. Trying to find out what happened to your wounded, how they were, if they're getting better, whether they're coming back. I went around and talked to everybody in little groups. I apologized for not being there. And I tried to take the lesson.

So I'm not of the school that Vietnam was absolute chaos, no one knew what the hell was going on, there was nothing you could do to avoid disaster, and you were lucky to get out alive. That seems to be the current vogue in analyzing Vietnam—that it was something no one could ever understand or fathom. Americans ran around, and what happened to them was going to happen no matter what. You're much more likely to find that attitude among the field troops, not in the officer class, especially in the Marine Corps. A lot of people had questions about whether what they were doing was of value, but I'm talking about the day-to-day tactical conduct of the war. It could be solved, and if it was solved with discipline and judgment and professionalism, the chances of success were increased. That's why a Calley* incident is so outrageous. Most professional military men are more critical of Calley than any civilian would be, because it's such an insult to a professional's ability to handle the combat situation. It's a travesty. With adequate leadership, those things don't happen. They're not part of war, and they don't have to be.

I'm one of those masochists who feel that Vietnam was very good for them. It was a training ground. I don't think I would be here today without it. I think I'd be in a Wall Street firm, or I might not even be a lawyer. Small-unit leadership in a combat role asks more of a human being than almost anything else—as much thought, intelligence, and ability as any other job you can think of. If there were more combat of significance involving the United States, I'd probably go back into the marines.

ANGEL QUINTANA

An infantryman almost never sleeps. Even if you have time to sleep, you can't, because you have all these memories in your head. If you're near a fire-support base, then you sleep even less with the noise of the cannons—the 155s, the 105s, the 4.2s, all firing at the same time. It's like an earthquake. And when you're in the jungle, you're afraid. As macho as you may be, you feel it. You know that death is behind you. You don't know whose turn it is. There are times when you lose the fear because something happens, like they kill a friend of yours. For five or six days it goes away because you're so shook up from losing your friend that life means nothing to you. Then it passes, and you start to be interested in life again. You start to be careful. But during that week, you could get killed, because you take risks. You're

---

*Lieutenant William Calley, Jr., was convicted of murdering twenty-two civilians in the 1968 massacre in the village of My Lai.

in a trance, thinking of how close you were with that person. It's like they killed your brother.

We talk in Spanish—his English is shaky. We are in the Veterans Outreach Center in Newark, New Jersey, where he works as a counselor. During the afternoon his clients drop in with their problems: drugs, marital battles, disputes with the VA. He has had his share. When he came home to Puerto Rico from Vietnam in 1967, he started drinking. Now, at age forty, he has been married four times and has children from all four marriages. His current wife has lasted the longest: five years. They left Puerto Rico for New Jersey in 1982, and he finally stopped drinking with the help of a VA psychologist. He gets a 40 percent disability check because of his wounds and post-traumatic stress. He is a husky man with curly black hair, a classic Latin mustache, and a wide-open face that manages to be sweet and mischievous at the same time.

After high school he won a scholarship to college, but "I was young and I had so much energy exploding inside. I didn't pay any attention to my classes. I just went to independentista *political meetings. So I flunked out, and they drafted me into the army. I said, 'Here I am,' like a sheep they send to the slaughterhouse when it's fat. I thought there wasn't a chance of my getting out of Vietnam alive. The first problem was that I didn't know English."*

My first contact with Americans was in the army. Even though people told me that white Americans were racist, I had never had the experience. But I started to learn. For a Puerto Rican, basic training is nothing like what it is for a white American. We didn't speak English, so we had trouble understanding orders. For that, they'd kick us around. They called us "spics" and "fuckin' Puerto Ricans." They called us all kinds of stupid names. Every time they heard us speaking Spanish, they'd punish us. They'd say, "You are now in the American army. You have to speak English." Then they'd put us on overduty, doing KP or standing guard, even if it wasn't our turn.

It wasn't only the whites who were racist against us—the blacks were, too. We had problems with both. The blacks took out on us what the whites did to them. We got kicked by both sides. We were the ham in the sandwich. The only way to fight back was to stick together—and we did, the Puerto Ricans. Unfortunately, we aren't like that outside the army, either here or on the island. In the army, yes, we were united.

One time during basic I was downtown in the city of Augusta,

Georgia. I was with a friend of mine, a black Puerto Rican. His name is Hector Joubert. We went to Vietnam together. We were buddies. We were about to go into a bar, and I saw a sign. It said, "No niggers, no dogs, no Puerto Ricans." That got me to thinking that in this country, a dog is worth more than a Puerto Rican. And neither of us could go into the bar. He was really screwed, because he was a black *and* a Puerto Rican. [Laughs.]

It was a trauma. It was like I went to Vietnam in basic training, without having been to Vietnam. When I finally went, I was already traumatized. I had such an attitude that when they gave me my rifle, the first people I wanted to shoot weren't the Vietnamese but the people who gave it to me.

Almost all the Puerto Ricans went into the infantry. We weren't like the "Newyoricans" who grew up here and spoke English. They could get jobs as clerks or cooks or other jobs in the rear. Those of us who came from the island went for infantry, because we couldn't speak the language. What we could do was pull a trigger. Anyway, the Puerto Rican brought up on the island has that machismo, which says that being a clerk or a cook is something shameful. So we volunteered for infantry. What we wanted to do was fight.

As soon as you get to Vietnam, things change. You don't see as much racism. And you don't have to salute. In the States, if you didn't salute they'd give you twenty push-ups. But no lieutenant was going to pull that in combat. I remember we got one of those rookies out of West Point who started that shit. Right away the sergeant told him, "Don't you try that here, because it won't be long before somebody messes you up." Even so, I had some trouble with a racist lieutenant from Miami. He called me a "fucking Puerto Rican." I got in a fight with him and he gave me an Article 15. I told him—when there weren't any witnesses—"Don't ever think about putting yourself in front of me in a firefight, because I'll blow your head off." After that he never turned his back to me. In combat you can kill anyone. A lot of people died that way.

I got to Vietnam on December 14, 1966. I was in Saigon for five or six days, and then I got sent to Pleiku. I was in the 4th Division, the 1st of the 22nd. They gave me my M-16. I still didn't know much English. Sometimes I couldn't understand what they were telling me. But I knew more than I did six months before. And if they swore at me, I understood that. I could say those words, too. That was the first thing I learned, to say "motherfucker" or "kiss my ass" or "fuck you."

When I got out to the field, the first thing I did was look for Hispanic faces so I wouldn't be alone. I was lucky. Nuñez, who was in training with me, was there. So were Hector Joubert and Cedeño and Riberito. Flor was in the same battalion, but not in my unit. These are just the Puerto Ricans. About four Newyoricans were there, too. A lot of Hispanics were in that unit.

Joubert got wounded. I got wounded. Riberito got wounded. Nuñez is 100 percent service-connected for malaria and stress. And Flor . . .

Every time there was a firefight, we'd look for each other when it ended. If someone was missing, we'd search. One time, after a firefight, Nuñez disappeared. For two days we were going crazy looking for him. We organized patrols. Crying and crying. But we never found the man. One day he showed up, laughing. It turned out he had a problem in the fire-support base in Pleiku, and he had gone back without telling anybody. We almost jumped on him and beat him to death, because we had been crying for two days.

We operated around the Ho Chi Minh Trail. Our unit was a reaction force, so we'd move around the whole area: Quang Tri, Qui Nhon, Dak To. The point man when I got there was an Italian. I liked him, and he liked me. There's not much difference between Spanish and Italian, so he understood me pretty well. He started to teach me the point man's job—reading the map, using the compass. When he was relieved, they put me on as point man. I did that for seven months. The only times I got out of the field were when I got malaria and when I got wounded in a place called VC Valley. After that I was short, and when you're short they don't let you be point man. They try to increase the chances of your staying alive.

A reaction force moves every day. You walk all day. You stop in the late afternoon, and you build the perimeter. You start to dig, fill the sandbags, cut branches. You make your bunker with the sandbags and the branches on top. You put out your trip flares. You put out your Claymores. Each platoon puts out an observation post with two people. The others take turns on guard. In the morning you have to empty the sandbags, break up the bunker, and walk some more. Every day. Until the mission is over and you go into the fire-support base, which is up in the hills, too. You stay there three days. They give you hot food, because when you're in the jungle you're eating C-rations, and there's no time to be heating up food.

The first few months in combat are difficult. You're adjusting to a new life. You suffer a lot. The only thing you know about war is what you've seen on TV. I never imagined it would be so violent. Everything's so easy in the movies. The hero always wins, the bad guy loses. But in Vietnam we didn't know if we were the good guys or the bad guys. We were stuck in a country that wasn't ours. If you asked an eighteen- or nineteen-year-old why he was fighting there, he'd say, "I'm here because I was drafted. But I don't know who the hell the Vietnamese are or what they've ever done to me."

I saw a lot of battles. I can't even remember my first firefight, there were so many. After a while, you get used to it. They attack you, and people die, and it's a normal thing. You fight and kill people and wound people, and it seems normal. After a while, the people who've been with you for a month, two months—suddenly they're getting killed or messed up. But the worst thing is the fear that grabs you. A horrible fear that won't let you sleep. You can't concentrate. The slightest noise, and you open fire. And since you can't sleep, you don't do anything but think. You have daydreams about your family, your house, your friends. The people you left back home. And you cry at night when you're on guard and nobody can see you. You cry for the suffering, the pain, and for the fear that invades you because you don't know when you're going to die. By now you have it in your head that they're going to kill you. You just don't know when. You see other people die, and you think you're going to die, too. The terror goes with you all the time.

I almost never wrote home, because what was I going to say to my mother, unless I lied? I could tell her that I was fine and not to worry, but how could she not worry, knowing I'm in a war? When the mail arrived, and they started to pass out letters, and nothing arrived for you, that was the worst thing that could happen. Everybody reading their letters, and you don't have anything to read. So here's what we did: If you got two letters and I didn't get any, before reading your two, you'd give me one. I would read it. Then we'd trade. If I saw somebody going off by himself and sitting under a tree because he hadn't gotten any mail, I understood the message. And I said, "Brother, do you want to read my letter?"

When you got a letter you were supposed to burn it. You weren't allowed to have it with you, because it might get lost and the enemy could write to your family as part of psychological warfare. But nobody burned them. You didn't get mail very often, so you kept the letter inside your helmet. And if you didn't get any mail the next time, you took it out and read it again. When it was falling to pieces, then you'd throw it out.

In the monsoon season, you couldn't save anything. You'd get a little plastic bag and try, but everything was so wet that the paper would stick together. The monsoon is three months of rain in torrents. It's like living in a swamp. You go into a rice paddy, and the water's up to your neck. You make a hootch, and the rain knocks it down. You have to collect branches and sleep on top of them so the rain will go underneath you. You're so wet all the time that you get jungle rot and sores. And the temperature—I got heat exhaustion two or three times. I was the point man, so I had to go in front. I carried all my combat gear, I was checking the maps and the compass, and I had my rifle. Plus a machete, because the point man cuts a path through the jungle. And the effort of cutting a path in the heat. . . .

That was the only time I could sleep—when my body was so tired that I couldn't go on. If I had to stand guard, I'd be falling down asleep. We had a trick we did with our bayonets. You put the bayonet right under your chin, touching the skin. When you'd fall asleep, the bayonet would stick you and wake you up again. I remember one time when I had done guard duty for three nights running. We were short of people, because when they kill a few of your squad, the replacements don't get there right away. Sometimes my fireteam would have only three people, when it was supposed to have seven or eight. We would have to divide guard duty. You'd get woken up every two hours. I had gone three days without sleeping well. And Charlie attacked with mortars. I was sleeping under a lean-to. Hector Joubert came and said, "Quintana, they're hitting us with mortars. Let's move." I said, "Those are our mortars." He said, "No, no, they're Charlie's mortars, and the rounds are falling inside the perimeter. Let's head for the bunkers." I said, "Look, I've been three days without sleeping. I don't give a damn if those mortars are Charlie's, ours, or the devil's. I'm going back to sleep. Fuck it, *chico*." Finally he had to grab me by the legs and drag me to the bunker, with the mortars falling all around.

At first you think a lot about combat and the people who died, but after six or seven months you get hard. You almost don't feel your own feelings. You learn to live in that world. And you watch the cherries come in, the replacements. Instead of carrying a combat pack, they have huge rucksacks. They're carrying shaving cream, aftershave, razors. They have undershirts, underwear, notebooks, pens, a ton of stupid stuff. You see them on patrol trying to climb a hill, and they're sliding backward. Then you grab them and say, "Look. You can throw out the undershirts. You won't need them here. The underpants, too. And the clean socks. You don't take off your boots in combat." A few crazies did take them off at night, but I never took mine off until I was given new ones. If there's an attack, how are you going to operate without boots in a jungle full of spines and pungi sticks?

And you'd say, "Throw out that fucking notebook. When we get to the fire-support base, they'll give you some paper and a pen. In the jungle, forget it, you ain't got no time for that. And the shaving cream—get rid of it. You won't be shaving." We used to cut each other's hair. You could cut it however you wanted—a Cherokee, or Kojak style. There wasn't any reveille formation.

A lot of people got malaria because they didn't take their pills. It was one way to get out of the jungle. There were people who took risks so they'd get wounded. I saw one soldier shoot himself in the leg. He destroyed his own leg to get out. I remember one Indian kid— but he wasn't trying to get out. He left a girlfriend behind in the States. One day he got a magazine that his people sent him, and it said that his girlfriend married some other guy. He went nuts. He was a gunner—he carried the M-60. He told me what had happened and we tried to protect him. But he was looking for death. He took a lot of risks. He would open fire without hiding behind a rock or a tree. He fired like a crazy person. But they didn't kill him. He left Vietnam before I did.

Sometimes we'd get wounded prisoners, and we'd have to carry them to the medevac. The helicopters would take them away, but by that time they'd be dead, because we'd kill them first. If there was a firefight and some of us died, there'd be a lot of pain and hatred. Someone would shout, "VC wounded, we need some medicine." Whoever was pissed off that day—maybe they killed his friend— would say, "I've got the medicine for him." *Psshow*. It was difficult to protect a wounded prisoner. Sometimes we'd get them to the helicopters and the crew would throw them out. You'd see them flying down, like birds.

One day we were going to help another company that had been attacked. We got ambushed. The NVA were giving it to this other company, and giving it to us as well. First, our captain was killed. He had gotten there a month or two before from Germany. A young man, blond, very white. A sniper shot him. Then we called for artillery, and it landed on us. I don't know what happened—the FO was an idiot or somebody made a mistake at the battery. The rounds fell right on us and killed a lot of people.

That day, I thought we had no chance. I was there hugging the ground, saying, We're all going to get it. Our own artillery was bombarding us. That was the moment I was closest to death. But nothing happened to me. Apart from the terror, I wasn't wounded. Finally the artillery and the air force made the NVA retreat. I think twenty-two of us died, and there were a lot of horrible wounds. I carried bodies that day. We were down in a gully. We cut branches and put the bodies in ponchos and slung them from the branches and carried them just like dead pigs. I remember climbing out of that gully and going to the LZ over and over.

In VC Valley, Hector Joubert and Riberito got wounded. Their bunker was blown up by a grenade. The VC got into the perimeter with a suicide attack. Joubert got hit with seven grenade fragments. But the worst was when Flor got killed. That's what hurts me the most inside, the death of that kid. I see his face in my sleep. A grenade blew him to pieces. And I was there. I saw it.

I was wounded by a mine. It was one of ours, a Claymore. The Claymore is curved on one side, and it explodes in that direction. But the VC had turned it around so it was facing in toward our perimeter. We were under attack. Somebody heard a noise and detonated the firing device. The Claymore went off right in our faces and wounded three of us. I was hit mostly in the arm. I was in the hospital two months. When I got out I went back to Pleiku, but I was very short, so they kept me in the rear.

When I came home, I was practically an alcoholic. In Vietnam, no. There was nowhere to drink, except when you got to the fire-support base and the Red Cross gave you two or three beers. Nobody can say he came out of the jungle drunk. There's no beer stand in the jungle. [Laughs.] I started getting drunk when I got out of there. I needed medicine, and I prescribed it for myself. Looking for a way to forget. It's stupid, because you're never going to forget. The past is a sickness you can't cure.

HARRY BEHRET

He was born in Brooklyn in 1947 and raised in Queens. His father worked for United Parcel Service. He is a heavyset, dark-haired man with a mustache and a quick, nervous pattern of speech, as though he were biting on his words before they were completely spoken.

"When I was a teenager I became a strong right-winger. Head of the College Conservative Club at Queens College. Vice president of the Young Republicans, head of the Strom Thurmond Teenage Republicans. I think it replaced my religion. I saw the first peace marches, and I couldn't buy that. I had a gut reaction they were wrong, so I decided to do some research. Limited research: right-wing literature on the subject. For me it was simple, black and white. The good guys, Americans and democracy, in the white hats, against the black hats, the Commies and strange Oriental people.

"When I got into my junior year I was so busy running eighteen different conservative movements that I had no time to go to class. I wasn't particularly interested in class anyway. Queens College took a dim view of me not taking finals, so I basically flunked out. I had already written the draft board telling them I no longer wanted my student deferment. I had this conviction that if I was going to support the war I might as well do it. Also I was not real happy with the way my personal life was going. So I got myself drafted and wound up in basic training.

"During basic I managed to enlist for a third year instead of the normal two, because it was obvious that anybody who didn't go for special training was going into the infantry. By this time I had realized that I did not object to being in Vietnam and fighting for my country, but damn it, I wasn't going to commit suicide. I had this image of being in the rice paddies with one of these drill instructors, and it just didn't appeal to me. So I signed up for meteorology school at the cost of another year. And I went to Fort Sill, Oklahoma. The first day, they told us we were all going to Vietnam. I had requested Vietnam anyhow, so I was happy with that. I just wanted to see what it was. I wanted to test my beliefs, this thing I had built my life around for three, four years. Conservatism, America, democracy, freedom. Was I right, or were they right—the leftists, the pinkos?"

The base was at Dau Tieng, right by the Michelin rubber plantation in Tay Ninh province, about twenty miles from the Cambodian border. That wasn't a bad place. It was a base for the 25th Infantry Division, but we were assigned to the artillery. If you're a meteorologist in Vietnam, what you do is send up weather balloons four to six times a day. You track these balloons and you get information as to the air temperature, air density, humidity, and wind speed and direction, which would all affect the flight of a shell. That information is fed into computers, and the computers lay out the coordinates for the guns, the elevation, the azimuth. Supposedly this has a big effect on the accuracy of the guns. I had my doubts.

The balloons were filled with hydrogen gas. Now, because hydrogen gas was considered an explosive—which it definitely is—we were stationed right behind the ammunition dump. For around ten months I lived about twenty yards from tons of explosives. We were surrounded by 155mm batteries, by eight-inch batteries. The artillery was constantly firing. At least once a week you'd have a mad minute, where everything on base would open up. They'd shoot the antiaircraft, the .50-calibers, the .30-calibers, the 105s, the quad-.50s, just blasting away at the surrounding countryside. You had the artillery going and the guys in their bunkers shooting off their M-16s. It was supposed to be harassment and interdiction fire, but it was known as the mad minute. And it was really a spectacular display. All this ordnance, just opening up and going to town. It was fun to watch, especially if you were stoned.

The base got shelled anywhere from one to five times a day. It was almost a constant siege. You could get mortared or rocketed in the morning, once around lunchtime, once in the evening. After a while it was like a game. Most of the attacks were very short-lived, any-where from four to twelve rounds. And unlike the John Wayne mov-ies, you never run through a mortar barrage. What you do is just lie down. If the rounds are landing far enough away, you run to your bunker. But if they're too close, you just lie down. Because with mortar rounds, the only ones that can kill you if you're lying down are the ones that land right next to you or on top of you and blow you all to shit. The odds of that are slim. The other thing that can get you is shrapnel flying through the air, and if you're lying down you're fairly safe.

If it's a rocket, you hear it coming. Those rockets used to scare the shit out of me. That screech—it's like a train coming at you, but a little more high-pitched and rumbly. You have a few seconds once you hear it. You get to be able to judge by the sound if it's coming real close to you. If not, you can run to a bunker. Of course, there's always that margin of error. With mortars, you might hear a pop as it leaves the tube, and then the explosion. You have the artillery going off all the time, twenty-four hours a day, and when you first get there, incoming sounds like just another explosion. But after a while you can tell which is incoming and which is outgoing. There's no way of describing it, you just know. Two different sounds, two different kinds of explosions.

The only time it really got to me was when I was filling a balloon. The balloons were about eight feet high and six feet wide, so you had this big cloth that was filling full of hydrogen. You had to be real careful. You'd wear ground wires so the static electricity wouldn't set it off. There were a few incidents where guys were incinerated by static electricity setting off the hydrogen in the balloon. It ain't a real stable substance. So you had this monstrous balloon full of hydrogen gas and you're in this tent blowing it up and incoming starts flying in on you. The shrapnel was red-hot. One piece of it going through that balloon, and you had a fireball.

The worst time was with me and this other guy, Les. He was from Texas. He'd been a defensive tackle on the college football team, weighed about 250 pounds. We're in there with the balloon, we just tied it off, inflated to its maximum, and we hear the ground shaking from incoming mortar rounds. So we hit the dirt. Then rockets started coming in on us. They were hitting our area. I had this big metal box next to me, and I told Les to come over. I said it would be safer, the box would protect him. I was no fool. I had a metal box on one side and a 250-pound Texan on the other. But the ground was shaking and the rockets were coming in. I had this knife that I used to cut the cord, and I started trying to stab the balloon so the gas would go out. And I kept missing that damn balloon with that knife. This balloon was as big as the tent, and I was three feet away from it, but every time I tried to stab it, an explosion would come and the balloon would shake and I'd miss. I could hear the shrapnel hitting the tent—it might have been shrapnel, or it might have been pebbles thrown up by the rockets. I really thought I had had it. At the end we just looked at each other and knew we were fucking lucky to be alive. The tent had shrapnel holes in it, but none of the shrapnel hit the goddamn balloon.

One scene I remember vividly. Some VC mortar team lobbed three mortar rounds on us. Only three rounds—that means they're out there with one mortar tube. And one mortar tube—that means two Viet Cong, each maybe five feet two in height, 110 pounds, between sixteen and eighty years of age. With a rusty piece of metal, popping three rounds on the base. *Pop-pop-pop*. The helicopter gunships go off and strafe the area, the jets come in and napalm, the eight-inchers and the 175s and the 105s go off, and the .50-calibers are strafing. Then everything dies down. And you hear *pop-pop-pop*—they fire three more rounds at us. At that point I knew there was no way we could win that fucking war. You had these two guys in sandals with a rusty piece of metal, and they take on these gunships and these batteries and all this technology. We've just blasted the surrounding countryside all to hell, and what do they do? They shoot back. I was awed. It was one of those incredible moments when a human being does something you think is just impossible. I was kind of proud. I said, "There's no way we're going to beat them." I could see them firing the first three rounds and *di-di mau*-ing, which means getting the hell out of there. But to stay there, take it, and then shoot *back*! Forget it. They've got more than we've got.

(After refusing an order to leave his bunker during a mortar attack to inflate a weather balloon, Behret was threatened with a court-martial. He decided to extend his tour in Vietnam, which would allow him to take an "early out" when he got back to the States.)

• • •

I came to the conclusion that Vietnam wasn't that bad, it was just that the army had messed it up. And being in the army would be just as bad if I was in Texas or Germany. Vietnam had some advantages, because you did get R&R to Bangkok or Tokyo or Hong Kong. You got more money. Cigarettes were fifteen cents a pack, booze was cheap, the pot was plentiful, and it was less Mickey Mouse than it was Stateside. Shining your boots, clean uniforms, trimming your mustache—you could forget about all that. It was being in Vietnam *in the army* that was bad.

So I put in for a six-month extension of my time. When you extend, you can ask for reassignment. I did a study and found the safest place in Vietnam. I asked guys who had been there a long time, "Where would you go if you had the choice?" They said, "I'd go to Nha Trang." There was no metro unit in Nha Trang, but there was one ten miles away in a place called Ninh Hua. All right, that's where I want to go. I put in for it. The transfer came through before the court-martial was processed, so they said, "We're rid of that. Let somebody else worry about him. It ain't worthwhile to court-martial him."

In Ninh Hua, instead of being on this big infantry base, you're on this small hill, surrounded by barbed wire as usual, living in holes in the ground, basically. No PX. No infantry around. Unlike the other base camp, this was in a pacified area. They hadn't seen a Cong in ages. But it was the same old military bullshit. Fill up sandbags, send up those big old balloons. There was nothing but an artillery battery there. God knows what they were firing at. The interesting thing about artillery was that in order to be a good battery commander, you had to fire your rounds. So they would do H&I fire—that's what it's called when you shoot into an area where there's a chance the enemy might be passing through. If you didn't fire enough rounds, they'd cut back on your ammunition ration. When this battery fired off its 100,000th round in Vietnam, they had a celebration. It was a big to-do. They flew down some colonel, some muckety-muck from battalion head-quarters, and he fired off the 100,000th round, and *Stars & Stripes* took pictures. And unlike Dau Tieng, you would occasionally learn the results of what your shells did. Like once we blew up a school-house. Fortunately school wasn't in session then—no thanks to us. Another time some new lieutenant gave the wrong firing mission, so instead of firing north they fired south. The shells landed a few yards away from a freighter in Nha Trang harbor. He left real soon after that.

The drugs were heavier than ever there. It was like a drug supermarket. We had booze and pot and booze and speed and pot. I was drinking much, much heavier. I would start off the day with a can of beer, hit the hard stuff and smoke the dope, and by the time I got to bed I was reeling. I was coming as close to alcoholism as you could possibly come. It was out of just plain boredom and repugnance for the military existence. It was very rare that I was straight, even on guard duty, because there was no danger. There were no mortars and rockets. No one in that place had ever heard a shot fired in anger. We were put on guard duty at night, and no one really cared about it. You went to guard duty in dungarees and sandals, with your rifle slung over your shoulder, with joints in your pocket, and someone would sneak down a radio and some wine and beer, and you were ready for a good party. You're in a stupor, and you're lying back, and the sergeant of the guard comes around. He says, "Somebody has to be awake," and he shines a flashlight in your face. And you say, "Get that fucking flashlight out of my face or I'm going to blow you away." That was the basic attitude. So it wasn't really a war. You were getting combat pay, and the guns were going off and blowing up monkeys and trees and whatever they were blowing up. But it was meaningless. The psychological toll on you was incredible. For me it was worse than Dau Tieng. At least there you were getting shot at, there was some rationale behind the insanity. This was just plain insanity.

Being ten miles from Nha Trang, this wide-open town, your basic purpose in life was to get off that little hill and into the flesh pots. Now, Nha Trang was fun initially but it grew old fast. Eventually the reality hits you. At that point I started a little bit of reading about Vietnam, the culture and whatnot. You usually weren't there long enough. Most people did their twelve months. I'm working on eighteen at this point. The joke was that Behret's been here so long he has his own voting card. I read some things by Bernard Fall, I don't remember what else. And I had respect for the people, okay? I mean, I was no shining example of Western man, but in comparison with some of the other guys I was great. The guys would get dumped on by the military constantly, so they had to have somebody to dump on.

You'd hit Nha Trang, and you'd see the Vietnamese, a people with some history and some pride. And what you see is armless and legless people begging in the street. You have kids selling dope. You have prostitutes. The whole town, the whole fucking area—it was a rural population, they used to live off the rice paddies, the rubber industry, the fishing industry. Now there was nothing but a bunch of service industries serving the Americans. If you weren't a whore, you worked in a massage parlor. Or you were hustling drugs, or working as a waitress in a restaurant serving Americans. Or you sold trinkets to the Americans. Or you worked on a base and you burnt their shit, or you dug their sandbags. The whole thing had turned around to where they were serving us. The total degradation got me. It slapped me in the face.

One of our guys was called the Round-Man because he was short and fat. He was an alcoholic. The only thing he was known for was the time he came down with clap in the mouth, probably his shining moment in the military. His job was to drive our rations truck down to Nha Trang and pick up perishables that we couldn't store at the base. He kept running the truck into buildings and trees on the roadside, so they felt he wasn't good enough to drive the food around. What job did they give him? Driving a truck into the village and picking up Vietnamese workers every day. It was a real joke for a while until he had an accident and killed twelve people. One of them was my housegirl, who I kind of liked. This guy was driving the workers and he was playing a game of chicken with some guy on a bridge that would only take one vehicle at a time. The truck went over, skidded, and threw the people out into the road, head-first. I was selected to ride shotgun for the medics down at the accident site. The first thing I saw is somebody's brains lying in the roadside. Bits and pieces of people all over the place. When I got back to the base, somebody was upset because there was a big inspection that day and we didn't have the Vietnamese to clean up for us. It was a real inconvenience.

After that I just got drunker and alienated from everybody. Nobody I had come in-country with was left, and I wasn't making any new friends. I was furious. My tolerance for the military was less and less, and I was more of a fuckup. In rifle inspection, they would pick up my rifle and find cobwebs in it. When I had guard duty it would take three guys to drag me down to the bunker in the dust and prop me up in a chair where I could sleep it off. I was selling drugs. I was winning $400 a month playing poker, and from my winnings I was shylocking, so I was making more money than anybody else around. I would walk around with $1,000 in my pocket. I never shot smack, but anything I could smoke or swallow I would do. I just wouldn't shoot up. I knew a lot of guys who were doing it, but I wouldn't stick a needle in my arm. If I could have gotten over that phobia I would have.

It seemed to me that everything was corruption. The first sergeant's girlfriend ran the enlisted men's club on base. The guy who was handling the garbage would drive it down and feed the sergeant's pigs with it. The mess sergeant was taking our food and selling it to construction crews for booze because he was an alkie. Everybody was doing something, everybody was selling something. I was selling drugs, cheating at poker, and shylocking. I would lend five, get six back at payday. I was unhappy as shit but crazy as a motherfucker. It was lunacy. Surrealistic. We had the highest VD rate in the country. I caught the clap three times at least. It was nothing. You had the clap, it was like having a cold. One time I really got sick and they helicoptered me down to the hospital. I was delirious, lying there totally out of it, and they brought in a Vietnamese kid with a broken arm. The bone was sticking out. And they said, "You've got to take him five miles down the road. No Vietnamese allowed in here." It was perfectly natural.

At that point the military were after my ass. I cursed at my warrant officer, so I got busted again. I had three Article 15s on my record, and they knew if they could get me one more time they could send me to Long Binh jail with a bad discharge home. They hated me and I hated them. So they started putting pressure on me. One little thing stands out in my mind. I'm an animal lover, so I always had a monkey or a dog around me. They said, "We have too many dogs on the base, we've got to get rid of some. Behret, we're gonna get rid of your dog." I was supposed to take it out and shoot it. What they wanted me to do was refuse to shoot the dog, so they could bust me and send me to jail. I shot the dog. And I felt absolutely demeaned by it. I started hating more. Five or six of us got together, and each of us had a man among the lifers that we were going to kill if the base ever got hit. And I would have killed him. There's no doubt in my mind that I would have blown him away. But the opportunity never came.

Eventually my time ran out and they shipped me home. I just pulled in and toughed them out. But the last three months were hell. I was a time bomb. And when I finally got my orders to go home, why, I cried. I was sorry to leave. How the fuck was I supposed to go back to the States to civilian life? No college education, no skills, and in 'Nam I was the richest man on post. There was no way in hell I was gonna fit in back home. At that point I didn't even see myself as a human being. You spend three days in a row up on speed. . . . One time I was on guard duty and when I woke up the next day, I had put out my cigarette on my stomach. I had two navels. So I knew I was not in good shape. I was close to breakdown. But at that point it was the only thing I knew.

So I came home. I had around six hours processing out at Fort

Lewis. I waited an hour at the airport, where I tried to get a beer and they wouldn't serve me because I didn't have ID. Flew home to my parents, and I was a civilian again.

The thing that hurt me the most was that I put myself to the test and I failed. I felt responsible for the things that were done and the people who were killed. I never protested that this alcoholic was put in charge of driving people. I laughed on the sidelines like everybody else. I saw twelve people die, just out of a racist mentality. And it was something I subscribed to, or at least I went along with it. You always have an image of what you would do in a situation like that. You think you won't let it happen. And you let it happen. Then you know that if you had been with Lieutenant Calley, you would have been shooting people, too. You realize you're a human being. And in the proper place, and the proper time, with a gun in your hand, you will act like the animal a human being can be. It took me a long time to accept that I was a shylocker, that I dealt drugs, that I saw people as gooks. That I let myself be put in a position where I shot a dog. Every test I had to face, I didn't do what I should have done. I went along with the military. I resisted to the point where they were going to chop my neck off, and then I went along.

The only thing I got out of it is that I have a five-year-old son, and he ain't gonna do what I did. My experience will help in that respect. I think there's been a Behret in every fucking war in this country's history, but there ain't gonna be no more Behrets in no more wars.

LARRY THETFORD

He is thirty-four but looks much younger: slim, blond, with his hair cut in a kind of shag, shoulder-length in the back. He is wearing a dark blue turtleneck, an odd transparent plastic jacket with a high Edwardian collar, stovepipe blue jeans, and dark, snakeskin, pointy-toed cowboy boots. He is edgy with energy, extroverted, a performer. During the interview he does impressions of the other people he talks about, complete with their accents. Whenever we take a break he paces around, shimmying shoulders and hips to music in his head.

His father was a jet pilot, then an official in the Federal Aviation Administration. Larry—who changed his name to Chris DeMarco in 1972—is a rock-and-roll musician and recording engineer. He brings along a demo tape he has just cut, featuring a song he wrote called "Cherry Boy." This was his nickname in Vietnam; a "cherry" was someone new in-country, or someone young and innocent. The lyrics:

He was as tough as nails,
He was mean as hell.
No one knew for sure
Where he came from.
Some said he came from the war
But no one knew for sure.
One look in his eyes,
You could see his victims die.

(Chorus):
He's ready for a firefight,
Future killer in the night.
He's ready for a firefight,
He thinks he's all right.
His mama told him so.

He was the boy wonder,
Captain of the team.
Traded his football
For an M-16.
Now the daily body count
Has replaced the score.
His sweetheart's face
Is the face of a whore.

(Chorus)
Cherry Boy—
He learned his lessons well.
He knew he was right.
He knew God was on his side.
Come on, Cherry Boy, shoot shoot.
Cherry Boy—
He loves to love to love to love that war.

In 1966 he dropped out of college and enlisted in the army "because my dad wanted me to be in the navy so I said fuck him, I'm gonna join the army."

Here I am in Vietnam, right? Ready to go to fucking war, ready to do whatever I'm called upon to do. And I'm typing all day long. Twelve hours a day. They made me spit-shine my boots, you had to have ironed fatigues and everything. I lasted about one week. There was a sergeant there, the master sergeant, and this guy was a real creep. He nagged me and nagged me, had everybody doing extra work after duty. It was really a drag. I couldn't handle it. Then I saw they wanted volunteers for long-range reconnaissance patrols. And I saw a couple of Lurps. They got to wear tiger fatigues and red berets and everything, and I thought they were really cool. They wore the Vietnamese camouflage, black stripes across green. The army had camouflage fatigues, but they were creepy. They were not stylish at all. And in 'Nam, you had to have your clothes cut right. Otherwise you were a goon. Especially in Lurps. Everybody had their fatigues cut by a Vietnamese tailor.

One day I just flipped out and picked up the typewriter and threw it against a wall. I had already decided I was going to join Lurps. I was procrastinating, and then I freaked out and dumped the typewriter. The master sergeant started to come down and I said, "Forget it, man, because I'm volunteering for Lurps." He said, "It's a good thing, otherwise you'd be in fucking jail, Jack." He figured there's not a lot of guys who make it through Lurps. I didn't know that then.

What I did know was that nobody fucked with you. You didn't have to shine your shoes. You went out for a week and when you came back you got a week off. And nobody told you nothing. You could carry your weapon in base camp, you could wear a beret, and I thought this was great. It's just like in high school, you find out who the basketball team is. "Oh, those are the hotshots over there, right?" I was into sports, and I always wanted to be one of the stars of whatever I was doing. There was no way I was gonna be a typist.

The worst thing you could do was recon platoon. That was a group of maybe 150 men and they were always short, because they were always getting wiped out. The recon platoon was filled with guys who were fuckups, discipline problems. The officers would put them in recon platoon and get them bumped off first. I had a couple of friends there, and one of them got shot in the heart. His name was Pencilneck. He got shot right here, man, a bullet went into his chest. But he didn't get sent home. When he was better he got sent right back to recon platoon. He flipped out: "Oh, wow, man, I can't believe this." So he joined Lurps. Got into Lurps to escape dying—he thought. I got into Lurps to escape typing.

Recon platoon would go out in a big group. Lurps was more exciting because there was only five of you on a team. You're not looking for contact. Your mission was to avoid contact. You just sneaked around. That was how I viewed it: scouts, Kit Carson. You go out there and as long as you're cool and you don't get busted, everything's great.

We had to go through Lurp school. You wake up at four o'clock. You've got five minutes to be outside with your weapon, pistol belt, twenty-one magazines—one in your weapon—twenty-pound sandbag in your pack, four filled canteens, eight grenades, including smoke. And then you have to run eight miles in an hour and fifteen minutes. Otherwise you're immediately out. Every day, seven days a week. If you make it, you have to climb over a big obstacle thing with ropes. Then straight into class, where they teach you how not to get killed. How to avoid contact. And we did drills. Like we walked in intervals of about five yards, in a line. And if you got into contact in the front, this man would go down first and open up. The next guy would go to his right, the next guy to his left. I was the fourth man back, I was the map carrier, I could go either way. And the last guy would turn around so we would have 360 degrees covered. We would just put out firepower, *brrrrrrrrrrrr*, all the way around to try to break contact, and then, *bap!*, cut out. It didn't really work, though. In general, the guys that got into contact got killed.

Most of the guys dropped out. It was difficult to get through Lurp school. I liked it because it was so hard. It was a crazy thing but it really got my juices going. I didn't even think about what was going to happen when I got out into the field.

So I finish Lurp school. I graduate, I get my red beret and everything. Feeling great. We didn't have to salute people. We didn't wear any insignia. No patches, no rank, nothing. We were Lurps, that's all. I mean nobody hassled us. They were afraid of us. They thought we were crazy. We *had* to be crazy to do that job. So they said, "Let 'em alone, they might kill you or something." We even lived by ourselves. Segregated.

Nothing much happened on my first few missions. Then I got transferred to another team in Duc Pho, which is south of Chu Lai. I got on a new team, and they took us to the battalion LZ. We got into the TOC and they started telling us our mission. The fucking battalion commander was drunk. And he tells us—this is daylight, now—he tells us he wants us to walk from the battalion LZ for maybe ten or twelve klicks across rice paddies and abandoned villages to these three mountains. We were supposed to set up on one and move the next night to another, and then move the next night. The team leader says, "Uh, we're not supposed to walk in low ground, first off; we're not supposed to go anywhere in daylight, second; so this mission is not kosher at all." The major says, "You're gonna fucking do it. That's all there is to it. Get going."

My best friend, Pencilneck, was the point man. Then there was the team leader. I forget his name, but he was a college graduate and he was going home in a week. The next guy was this asshole, a real gung-ho jerk. He carried the radio. Then there was me. Then the guy behind me. He was a really nice guy. Okay. We started walking in the daylight. It was getting toward the end of the day, but it was definitely daylight. And this was in a hot area.

We had been going about half an hour when we found a 60mm mortar emplacement that the marines had left. The team leader calls in that he found this thing, and they say check it out. So everybody is standing around. The team leader starts walking through the emplacement. And there's an explosion.

I was picked up into the air and dropped on my back. It seemed like before I even hit the ground I heard somebody screaming, "Oh my Gooooood! Oh, my Goooooooood!" I crawled up to the radio operator and his bicep was hanging off his arm. His forearm was really fucked up and there was blood all over his face. We didn't know whether we were in contact or not, so we had to put firepower out. I'm crawling and firing at nothing, just so if somebody's out there, they're not gonna run over and cut our throats. The guy behind me is firing. And this radio operator is crying. This is the guy who's always pushing everybody around, a great big overweight guy. He was crying like a baby. Me and the guy behind me said, "Fucking fire or we'll kill you, man!" So he starts to shoot. I got on the radio but then he grabbed it, because he was the radio man. And all the time, the people on the base were *watching* us, man. The other Lurp team had nothing better to do, so they were sitting there with their binoculars watching us.

I crawl up to the team leader. He's sitting up, completely covered in blood, and he's trying to put his leg back on. Which had been severed just below the knee. He was delirious, out of it. We couldn't get him to lie down. All this time—this happened in about fifteen seconds—we didn't know if we were going to be in contact. I had to knock the kid down. I shot him up with morphine and hooked him up with an IV, which is like a blood expander, because he was bleeding like you wouldn't believe. I had never seen anything like that. But you don't think. You just take care of whatever's got to be done. Some guys flip out, and some guys flip in. I reacted by going inside and becoming almost super-calm.

We looked up at Pencilneck, and he was just lying there spread-eagled, flat on his face, and *completely* red. I thought, "Oh, he's fucking dead." And I had to deal with the team leader. I mean, I didn't know what to do with his leg. There was just a little piece of meat keeping it hanging, and he'd been trying to put it back on. We weren't prepared to deal with that kind of stuff. You get a little first aid, but *God*. It's another thing when a guy's leg is blown off and his eye is—I mean, he was really fucked up. The booby trap went off right underneath him. His face was completely bloody, and his eyes, you couldn't see them, there was blood everywhere. I couldn't tell whether he had eyes in his head or not. And his arms were all blown up, his stomach had big holes in it. He was just sitting there repeating, "Oh, my God." As soon as I shot him up with the morphine, he went out.

So the choppers came blowing in, right? *Rrrrrrrrw, ssssshrow.* The creeps. They wouldn't come down to pick us up for about ten minutes because they didn't know whether we were in contact or not and a chopper at that time cost half a million dollars. They'd rather lose all of you than lose a chopper. We're going, "Come on, man!" I was freaking out. I was on the radio saying, "Come on down." But the radio had been hit so we were transmitting but not receiving, and after a while I gave up. Finally they came down and got everybody on. Pencilneck by this time was sitting up. He wasn't hurt too bad, got some shrapnel through him. Little pieces all over his back. It was a hand grenade, I think. Somebody hooked it up there. It could've been a marine booby trap to get *them*.

I didn't know I was hit. By that time all I could think about was that fucking battalion commander who's responsible. I got off the chopper and I was heading for the TOC. I was really going for him, man. I was really pissed. I didn't know whether I was gonna kill him, or just say a few words to him. But I had to go confront this guy. Because it really broke my heart that the team leader was going home in a week. This was his last mission, and it was bogus from the get-go. We should never have been there. It was this drunk bastard's fucking fault. So I was heading for him and some lieutenant grabbed me just before I went into the TOC and said, "You're hit, get on that chopper." I got on the chopper and got to brigade hospital. I see the team leader and they've got his leg all wrapped with gauze to try and save it. They patched me up a little bit and I was just going back to the Lurp headquarters, and they wouldn't let me go. I was saying, "Fuck you, I'm not going to the evac hospital. Fuck all of you, man, I'm going back out there." I was crazed, out of my mind. I was enraged by the fact that this had all happened. I didn't want to go to that hospital. I didn't have my leg blown off. I just had a hole in my arm, big fucking deal. Piece of shrapnel went through my arm. You don't feel it. I didn't know what I was going to do but I wasn't going to the hospital, and I was definitely going to have something to say to this head guy. I was ready to kill some gooks by then, too. Then it passed.

We got to Qui Nhon, the hospital. The people all came running out, taking everybody off the chopper. They wouldn't let me walk. They took me on a fucking stretcher. I'm going, "GET OUT OF HERE, MAN!" I could walk, I was okay, but they make you lie down, they put a tag on you like a fucking piece of meat. Finaly some nurse comes over and starts talking to me. She asks me, "What's your mother's maiden name?" I'm going, "GET THE FUCK AWAY FROM ME, MAN! I'm not telling you shit! My name and rank and serial number and that's it. I don't want you calling my mother and getting her all fucked up."

Then they come and cut all your clothes off. These are my fatigues that I spent a lot of money to get them fixed up. And I'm saying, "Wait a minute, I can take 'em off." But no, snip snip snip. I'm going, "You bastards, how can you do this?"

Pencilneck was there and he had a lot of wounds. So they were washing him down, this nurse, and he gets a hard-on, right? She grabs ahold of his dick and says, "Eh, what's going on here?" And starts washing all around it. He's going, "Oh, God, wow." The funniest thing I've ever seen. He was happy. He was happy as shit he got hit again.

I was sent back to base camp. The first thing I hear is about the team that went out after us. My team got wiped out, so they were short on men and they sent out four-man teams. The first one that went out had two ex-cooks on it, real tough sergeants, cool guys. They were friends of mine, went through Lurp training with me. They go out with two other guys. They're set up on a hill at night and they call in to say they see flashlights coming up the hill. They need artillery. The battalion commander says, "Fuck off." That was the last they ever heard from them. They found the two cooks. One of them was buried alive with his hands tied up. The other was shot in the head. They never found the other two guys. Just their boots. They were taken prisoner. The VC make you take off your boots when you walk. When I heard that, man, I said there's no fucking way I'm going back out there. No way in hell.

I had to figure out how to get back to the hospital. Somebody told me—you know those pills you take to not get malaria? Well, somebody told me you could get malaria if you took like twenty weekly pills at a time. I was supposed to go out the next day. I had to do something fast. So I . . . *pow*. I almost died. Real sick. Passed out and everything. It was the worst sick you can imagine. So I end up back in the hospital in the psych ward. Which is no big thing. They think you're crazy because you don't want to die. And they knew I wasn't crazy. They just put you there because that's their rule. It was a bunch of normal guys. I got passes every day. I talked to the psychiatrist and told him the truth. I said, "I don't want to die, I don't want to get blown up, and I'm not going to. There's no fucking way I'm going back out there, man. So if you think I'm crazy, send me back home."

Then I got an idea. I went and told them I was having trouble with my ears. I said, "I can't hear out of this ear." I just decided that they couldn't prove I could hear, if I was real good at it. And you can't be in a Lurp team if you can't hear too good. You'd endanger everybody. So they tested me. They test you with sounds like *mmm, mmmm, MMMM*, and you're supposed to lift your finger when you hear something. I said I could hear in my left ear but not in my right. I just psyched myself up that I wasn't gonna hear fuck-all in this ear. And I got certified as having a bad ear.

They sent me back to base camp to the same Lurp unit. The lieutenant was a Ranger and a West Point graduate, and all he did was suntan himself. He didn't go out on any missions, he just sent us out. He wore a bathing suit all the time and hung around listening to the portable radio and getting suntanned. This was our leader. We're dying and he's tanning. He decided to send me out on a mission, even when I showed him my profile. I said, "I can't go out, man. Look, it says, 'Not to be placed anywhere near loud noises.' What if I get in a firefight? That's a loud noise. I can't do that." He says, "You're going out anyway." I says, "Yeah?" I had another friend, a sergeant who worked for the brigade commander. All of a sudden I'm before the colonel with this lieutenant because I told the sergeant that the lieutenant was going to send me out even though I had a profile. We're there standing at attention and the colonel says to the lieutenant, "You're a West Point graduate, aren't you?" "Yes, sir." "Ranger, right?" "Yes, sir." "What is your mission? What are you trained to do?" "I'm trained to be a platoon leader, sir." And the colonel said, "That's what you're going to be." He put him in the field, man. The guy lasted four days and got his head blown off. He walked into a fucking tunnel. "Hey, anybody in there?" *BA-BOOM!* He died, man.

I got put on a unit with two other guys to go out into Montagnard villages. This was great. We'd go out and do inoculations, give 'em candy. Public relations stuff. And every two weeks they had to send me to Qui Nhon for a few days to have my ears checked. So I had it great. A good job, and going into Qui Nhon all the time.

The only bad part was the testing. They would put me in a booth, and they'd put a headset on me. The doctor sits out there in this glass thing and starts talking to me. After a while they started trying to trick me. They would speak in my left ear with part of a sentence and end it in my right ear. If I responded, they'd know I was malingering. But I did not respond. Not once. The doctor would say, "I know you're lying. I know you're shamming. I know you are." And I would go, "Huh?" He would say these things about my mother, that my mother sucks dick or my mother fucks animals. Really, really horrible stuff. He'd curse and yell. Call me a coward.

It was always the same doctor. After a while we had a kind of relationship, but I had to be really cool. In the first place, I had to act like I was real dumb. I couldn't let them know I had any intellect at all, because then they could play with me even more. I acted like the poor dumb soldier who was a lost sheep. To convince them that I couldn't be smart enough to conceive of this scam. That really pissed me off because I have a large ego. And the doctor hated me. He really believed that he ought to bust my ass. It amazed me. Especially a doctor. Doesn't he know it's not cool to kill people? Or to die for no reason? They're supposed to have compassion for people. And I'd already been hit, y'know? C'mon, gimme a break.

I'll never top that performance. I created this character who was slow-minded, who was a victim, who was really meek, who couldn't do anything even if you did send him back to duty—a blown-out character. When they'd say I was lying, I'd just sit there. I would see his mouth moving, and I'd look at it, and I would act like—huh? Just blank.

They knew I was lying. It made me feel a little creepy. I wasn't too proud of myself in one way. But I wasn't gonna die either. I had done my work, I had spilled my blood, and I wasn't gonna do any more. I certainly didn't want to see anybody else get fucked up. I could not handle that one. I mean, c'mon. It has to change somehow, somebody's got to say, "Fuck you, man. I'm not doing it." And that was my moment. I was already in Vietnam, so I had very little to work with. I mean, I couldn't go to Canada. I was stuck.

Finally I got sent to the Philippines. They tested me there. Then I got sent to Japan for two weeks. They tested me and told me, "We know you've been lying." But they couldn't prove it. So they sent me back to Walter Reed Hospital, where God came one night and cured me. It was miraculous. It was a real religious experience, let me tell you. One day they were testing me and I went "Ah! Ah! Ah! I think I hear something! Oh, my God!" Started crying and everything. Over a couple of days I started hearing a little more and a little more, and this doctor was so cool. He knew what was happening, but he never spoke about it. He was happy to let me go. See, when I got back to Walter Reed, I wanted out of the army. But they won't let you, if something's wrong with you, because it's too expensive for them to take care of you. If they let you out, they have to pay you money. So they keep you in. I had to get better to get out. So I got my hearing back and they assigned me to Fort Dix in New Jersey as a drill sergeant. Six months later I was out.

JOHN CATTERSON

A small, spare office in a mid-Manhattan law firm. Papers piled in the corners of the room. On the desk, pictures of a handsome woman and towheaded children. Behind the desk, a balding, rumpled man wearing a white shirt, a tie, and pin-striped pants. He is an activist: New York State coordinator of Vietnam Veterans of America, and a member of the group's national board of directors. He often appears on TV to talk about veterans' issues, something he boasts about a little. At the time we talk, he is heading a lobbying campaign for a bill that would grant free tuition to Vietnam vets in the New York State university system— a bill that eventually passes.

"I was born in Rego Park, Queens. Went to Catholic grade school, Catholic high school. Spent a year in college at St. John's, but I didn't want to be in college. I wanted to find out what life was about." He enlisted in the marines in 1965 and got to Vietnam in early 1966. "Second battalion, 4th Marines. They called us the Magnificent Bastards."

After six months in the field he was shot twice through the leg. The bullets shattered his femur, so he was sent home.

I started out near Danang. Eventually we moved up to Dong Ha. We were the first American ground units there. That's when things really changed. Suddenly you started to see people with uniforms, organized units, Russian weapons. They had some heavy artillery and mortars. I can remember seeing 20mm cannon on wheels. There were no booby traps because they used the trails as much as we did. But there was serious resistance, and more traditional-type military operations. Sending whole regiments out into the hills. Of course, we'd take the territory, then we'd pack up and go home. Two weeks later we could be fighting the same group on the same hill. It never particularly made sense.

But you sure kept learning new stuff. One night we were sitting in a defensive position. We had dug in, with sandbags, and there was a tank about ten meters down from us. And I hear, *clank!* Then another clank. I said, "What in hell's that? Who's making the noise?" Pretty soon the word comes down that there's somebody out there throwing rocks at the tank, trying to draw fire. Now, that's crazy to me. This was way up north. We were either inside the DMZ or right below it. So there was no such thing as friendlies—no friendly villagers, no friendly anything up there. We had a starlight scope, one of those night scopes, and we were scanning the position. But we could hear the clanks. Rocks were hitting all around the tank. Somebody said, "Get the hell in your holes and stay down, because I'm telling you, one of those rocks isn't going to be a rock. It's going to be a grenade." Bigger than shit, all of a sudden there comes a thump on the ground, and *boom!* A concussion grenade. They were trying to catch us off-guard. It would have worked, too, because by that time I was getting used to the rocks and I probably would have ignored it.

Two hours later, *clank, clank.* Rocks again. This time I could hear the tank's turret scanning. It was like an electric hum. I heard that turret start to move, and I knew they were either sighting in or bringing the barrel down. I think they figured out where the rocks were coming from based on where they were landing. So there was a thump on the ground and then a *boom!* from the tank, and the next day there was a guy out there cut off at the waist. The rest of him was in the trees, blown away.

You got to the point where you could smell and feel people around. All your senses were a lot keener. Like your sense of hearing at night. You'd sit out there and it'd be absolutely quiet. You could put a battalion on a hill and hear a pin drop. And as soon as darkness fell, your whole instinct was outside the perimeter. You're depending on the guys on the other side to protect your rear or your flank, and your whole sense of being is out there. You were like living radar.

You also learned to move through dense jungle without making any noise. You move slowly. Stop. Listen. Watch where you put your foot. Usually you had a guy on point and two guys a little behind him on the flanks. It was like a diamond formation moving into the bush. And when our platoon walked point, it was always the same three guys—well, depending on the situation. If it was just a hot walk in the sun, I'd let some other guy walk point. But if I had a feeling we were going to hit shit, it was always us three. I'd walk point. Over here was a guy named Corn. He was stealthy like a snake. The guy could sneak up and bite your ear off and you wouldn't even know it. And the guy on the other side had been an E-5 and was busted down. His name was Little Bear. He was an Indian. Every time he went back to the rear he got drunk and shot the place up. They had to put the guy in a straitjacket one night because he went after the whole battalion. We'd go back into the area and they'd show movies. You know what movies they'd show? Vic Morrow in combat. No shit. World War II. We're sitting there watching one night, and *b-r-r-r-r-r*, somebody puts a burst of automatic rifle fire across the screen. It was Little Bear, really drunk. They took him away. I heard they sent him to jail. But out in the field, he was the guy you wanted. Big hulk of a guy, and you could never hear him coming.

I remember a day when we had a B-52 strike, and then my squad walked point for the whole battalion on a sweep of the valley. Boy, I'm telling you—I couldn't imagine such quiet. We were terrified that there were battalions of NVA up there. We found all these tunnel complexes. We found food, hospitals. I was thinking, Oh, shit, all we've done is scared 'em up to the end of this valley, and when we get there we're going to be in some shit. There were a lot of bodies around, and you could see there'd been a lot of people there a couple of days before. We never did make contact, but we were quiet. You could hear the damn radio crackling fifty meters behind. You'd pass the word—turn the radio down. You'd move. You'd stop and listen. There were a lot of hand and arm signals. Nobody talked. If you had to say something, you wouldn't shout. It was hushed, even when you'd take a break. When you moved out, you'd pass the word very quietly. I can remember, in training, shouting, "All right, we're moving out! Saddle up, we're moving out!" But in-country, everybody just stood up. You didn't have to yell. Everybody got up and started to move. You knew where you were going and how to do it. One step at a time.

You'd listen for grenades hitting the ground. Or when you heard a mortar tube, somebody would yell, "Incoming!" That was a word that stung you right in the heart. You'd move quick and get under a rock or behind a tree or something. And if you were in a perimeter at night and there was a gunshot, you'd hear, "Accidental discharge!" Because as soon as you hear a shot, everybody's up, everybody's awake. Later, when I was in St. Albans Hospital, I can remember lying in bed and a truck went by on Linden Boulevard and backfired. All the grunts sat up and sort of smiled at each other.

Another thing you did was try not to stand out. The VC and NVA would look for somebody who stood out in the crowd. Officers and platoon commanders and radio men and corpsmen were targets. Corpsmen were supposed to carry a B-1, a medical bag, and a pistol. Some of them carried rifles instead, so they wouldn't stand out, and some even carried packs, like grunts, instead of their B-1s. And when somebody got hit, we didn't yell, "Corpsman!" We'd yell, "Lame duck!" There were other code words—"Cadillac" was a killed-in-action, "Ford" was a wounded -in-action, and there was another car for a prisoner. Instead of yelling, "Wounded man, send me a corpsman," you'd yell, "Lame duck in my position." *Lam duc* means something in Vietnamese, that's why we adopted it. I don't even know what it means.

I can remember the first time our platoon got assigned a second lieutenant. For the most part, we had these two sergeants who acted as platoon commander and assistant platoon commander. One day we got a second lieutenant, and we were going to show this guy how we operated. He showed up in freshly pressed fatigues, wearing a chin strap and shiny gold bars. I can remember the little titter of laughter that went through all of us. When somebody was new, we said they smelled of Cash Sales. That was where you went to buy new fatigues, which had a smell to them, like new blue jeans or a new shirt. One of the guys went, "Oho, I can smell Cash Sales from a mile away." We were going to sweep out a village we had swept a hundred times before, just to show the lieutenant how we operate. And this sergeant, Sergeant Williams, said, "Possibly the lieutenant does not want to wear his gold bars into the field today." He'd speak circularly, not telling him what to do, but recommending. "Possibly the lieutenant doesn't want to wear those gold bars because possibly the lieutenant will get identified as a lieutenant." This guy also had one of the new chin straps with a little cup. Nobody else wore a chin strap. That way, if there was an explosion and your helmet came off, your head wouldn't come off with it. Williams says, "You don't see anybody with a chin strap on. And the lieutenant might want to think about dirtying up that uniform before we go out into the field." Well, he wasn't going to go that far. But he took off the chin strap and his bars. He said he was going to do that anyway. Boy, they were just gleaming in the sun. Make a nice target.

The sergeant used to say, "When we get out in the field, we know who our leaders are. We know who the officers are and we know who the leaders are. We don't need gold bars to identify rank in this outfit." We knew just what he was talking about. If the shit hits the fan, and there's a four-star general over here and an E-5 over here, you're going to do what the E-5 tells you, and fuck the general. He ain't gonna get you out of there alive. The same with the lieutenant. He tried very hard. I can remember being out on a night patrol. You could look off across the field and see our tents two miles away. The lieutenant is there with a map and compass, orienting us, trying to get us back home. Everybody's just standing around. From the back of the squad comes Sergeant Williams, shotgun over his shoulder. "What the fuck is going on now?" The lieutenant: "Well, I'm orienting the map, shooting the azimuth—" "Fuck the azimuth, that's the tents over there, let's just walk in that direction, *Lieutenant*." Another time on a night patrol, the lieutenant was talking to somebody on the radio and the sergeant came up and said, "Hey, Lieutenant?" The lieutenant said, "Yes, sir!" The sergeant used a line that I still use today. He said, "You don't have to 'sir' me, Lieutenant, I'm one of the enlisted men."

There was a lot of dope, a lot of booze, a lot of beer, a lot of drinking and partying—back in the area. But we had a guy who once brought two cans of beer out into the field, and I thought they were going to lynch the guy. We just didn't drink in the field. Didn't smoke dope in the field. You had to depend on everybody. You get a guy who sits down at ten in the morning and takes a beer out of his pack, you're gonna shoot this guy. Nobody needs a guy who's even the slightest bit off, who's not paying attention.

We did have some shitbirds, though. There was a black guy on my fireteam named Smitty. He used to say all these spooky things. One night we were in a foxhole and he was on guard duty. The sun was just rising, and I had woken up. He was lying flat on his back looking up at the sky. I said, "C'mon, what the fuck you doing?" He said, "I have to stay low, 'cause at this hour every day thirteen birds fly over me." And he used to talk to himself. I think it was an act, almost like a Klinger. He got himself to believe he was crazy after a while, with this "thirteen birds fly over me" shit. And he'd talk about how he was going to die in Vietnam. He'd say, "I had a premonition last night. I shouldn't go on this operation." My fireteam leader would say to him, "If you're gonna die in Vietnam, what the fuck are you worried about? It's over for you. The rest of us have the uncertainty. You have certainty. You can come to terms with that."

He would play mind games with you. When we'd go out on an operation, he'd stand around talking shit like, "We're all gonna die today. They're out there. They're gonna get us today. Why the fuck we going out there?" Nobody wanted to hear that. You're headed out and this guy in the back is saying, "Oh, there's some fucking gooks out there today, man. And they got mortars. And they got helicopters. Look at them helicopters over there. They ours?" Back in the area, in a secure area, he'd be a struttin' dude, a tough guy. But as soon as you came near the wire and loaded up, he'd get real solemn and start talking. On an ambush, he'd talk to himself all fucking night. Somebody would say, "I'm gonna kill that motherfucker if they don't get rid of him." And he'd always have something wrong with him. He'd have an equipment problem. A rifle jam. Little things. Right before the squad was moving out, he'd have a reason to go back and get something. And when you're moving, you're moving. You're gonna leave this guy behind. He got left a couple of times and was written up for it. Eventually they pulled him out of the field and made him a cashier at the PX in Danang. When they sent him back to the rear, we were all a little pissed off about it, because he pulled it off, he got out of the field. We felt a bit cheated. But the truth is, nobody wanted him to be with us anyway.

Then there were the ARVN. We did a lot of sweeping through villages, and we'd go out with a company of ARVN. We used to call it a "county fair." We'd take a blocking position outside the village and the ARVNs would sweep through. You could tell if there was going to be any shit because the ARVN wouldn't sweep the village. If there were VC in there, they'd find a way to make us do it. They'd be the blocking force, and we'd be the sweep team. Every time that happened, we knew we would find suspects. We'd just walk into houses and start sifting through their stuff, looking through their closets, turning up their beds. We called ourselves the Zippo squad, because you were told that if you took fire from a village you could level it. Or if we found something, we just burned houses. I remember we found a box of white phosphorus grenades in a house, and the woman was kneeling outside. The fireteam leader went out, saying, "You VC, you VC," and torched the house.

Every platoon was assigned two Popular Forces guys. We had two little guys we called Victor and Charlie. One night we were going out on a listening post, and I was going to take one of these guys with me. But he disappeared. I went back to my sergeant and said, "Victor's over there with his lieutenant and he's supposed to be out on the LP." My sergeant said, "Well, walk over there and get him." I dragged him off and made him come out. He kept saying to me, "No go, no go, no, no LP, no go, *beaucoup* VC, *beaucoup* VC." I said, "*Beaucoup* VC, motherfucker, if I'm going out there, you're going out there." So we went out. We set up under a couple of trees and spent the night. The next morning I wake up, and here's Victor, walking around with a stick in his hand, poking the ground, poking out all these little pungi-stake pits. When you'd poke, they'd cave in. There was a thin cover of earth, and underneath are the stakes. He knew right where to look, right where to find everything. Right in front of us. I said to the guy next to me, "He probably dug them last week, that's why he knows where they are."

The VC guys were relentless. Once we were out on an operation on the Street Without Joy. Victor and Charlie were with us. We stopped in the morning and one of them disappeared. I found him back in a little hootch filling his canteen. I said, "C'mon." "No, no go, *beaucoup* VC. *Beaucoup* VC, no go." I just pointed a rifle at him. I made him go. I had the feeling, it's your country, brother, and if I'm gonna defend it, you're gonna help. But then we stopped for lunch, and afterward they were gone. Completely gone. Then things started to happen, and we never saw them until about three days later.

Our platoon had been on patrol all morning. After lunch another platoon moved through to take the point. There were these three guys—Valeran, Zimmerman, and Strehle, who had been on my fire-team but had moved to this other platoon. I stood there and watched them move through with their fireteams. Then I started to move out with my squad, and bullets came zinging down and everybody ducked. We were sitting out in a field, and ahead of us was a dike. Beyond that was another field, and a treeline and then a village. Valeran, Zimmerman and Strehle were already out in the next field, and they were all killed, along with three or four other guys. Valeran had turned around and yelled, "Uniformed men in the treeline!" and he stuck his head up long enough to take a bullet right in the face, through his cheek.

We moved up and dug into the dike. For the whole night we watched them bombing the treeline and the village, shelling them, and a navy destroyer off the coast dropping five-inchers on them. It went on all night. I'm down here behind the dike. It's about 100 yards to the treeline. I've got a guy from the Associated Press with me. We're in this foxhole, and we're dug in pretty deep. I look out, and here comes a VC right in front of the treeline. Just walking along, up and down, looking around. He's got a Thompson submachine gun, like a grease gun. And just down the way we've got two snipers, guys that have specially equipped rifles with scopes. I drop down and I'm whistling to this sniper. I'm going, "Look out there, let's shoot this guy." Then the VC takes his gun and shoots it up in the air. Tracers. And the reporter wheels around and says, "The guy's trying to draw fire." This reporter had been in the bush longer than I had. He had more savvy than most marines in the company. So he says, "He's trying to draw fire." And another guy, Parker, says, "Well, he just drew some." So Parker and I shot him. We squeezed off about five rounds and found out the next morning that we got him. As soon as we did that, mortar rounds starting dropping right behind us. The VC were walking them right to us. I said, "Holy shit, he came out to draw fire for the mortars." But with that, the helicopter gunships came in and took care of the mortars.

We stayed there for two days behind this dike. And it was the same thing: Every so often you'd hear *pop-pop-pop!* The VC would jump up, *pop-pop-pop*, and then drop down again. The next morning we wake up and it's a bright sunny day. Beautiful. They tell us we're going to assault the treeline. I said, "You gotta be kidding. We've been out in the bush ten days, nobody shaved or washed, nobody had a decent meal last night." But they say, "Load your weapons and get ready, we're going to assault." We started out and I looked down the line. There were 100 guys strung out on this line, walking to the treeline. The sniper jumps out, *pop-pop-pop-pop*. I don't see anybody fall, but everybody starts screaming, running, yelling, like you saw in boot camp. We assaulted this treeline in an open line. I never saw anything like it. We ran right past the guy we shot the night before, and right into the treeline.

Now we're snooping and pooping into the treeline. We had maybe fifty yards of bush to go through, and you could start to see little hootches up there. We're trying to figure out where this sniper is. We're standing by this trail, and all of a sudden we hear *pop-pop-pop-pop*. I look back and here's this dude standing and shooting back the way we just came. He had a little spider trap, and he was down in there when we passed over him.

We sneak up. Here come about six other people who had seen him, too. This Mexican sergeant says, "Wait for him to pop up again. We'll get him when he pops up." We're waiting about twenty minutes, and the guy wasn't coming up. We weren't exactly sure where he was. Suddenly he leaps out of the ground, takes his rifle, looks over his shoulder, and here we all are. It was like, "Hello." Somebody shot him real fast, on full automatic, gave him a full burst. Caught him right in the face and down the front. The guy just fell right back, holding his rifle, his eyes open. And one of our guys said to me—it was a saying we had—"There's always that 10 percent that doesn't get the word."

JIM DUFFY

He is a wiry man in his early forties, with a sharp, sad face and an abrupt manner. We talk in his small Brooklyn apartment while his eight-year-old daughter plays nearby. He works for AT&T and is in charge of safety issues for his union local. He was an early member of Vietnam Veterans Against the War.

"I'm a Bronx Catholic working-class kid from the streets. Both my parents worked for the city. We were pretty poor. My father retired on half-disability in the early '50s, and the money he was getting from the city was garbage. So in '65, when I graduated from high school, it was a matter of do or die. College was out of the question, it wasn't on my agenda. I had to get out of the Bronx. I figured I'd enlist in the army and join the Signal Corps, learn a trade. I fell for the recruiter's rap, hook, line, and sinker. I did basic at Fort Dix, and then they sent me to Fort Gordon, Georgia, for communications school. What they neglected to tell me was that you needed security clearance to go to communications school. They sent me through the first half and kept me as a holdover for about four months waiting for my clearance. It never came, so they shipped me to 'Nam. I got there on St. Patrick's Day, 1966."

He spent ten months in-country with the Signal Corps. Then he agreed to stay for another year.

I extended my tour for a couple of reasons. Had I come back from 'Nam, the rest of my time in the army would have been in the States or Europe, and I knew that I would wind up in jail. Before 'Nam, I liked Stateside duty. But 'Nam changed me, so there was no way in hell I would be able to take that kind of pettiness. A lot of guys extended their tours for that reason. The early-out program was one of the smartest things the government ever did. "Hey, man, we've gotcha. So you want to get out early? You hate the army, huh? Well, we'll let you out three months early. All you've gotta do is stay in 'Nam. You're already bent out of shape from the place, so you might as well stay. And you know what's gonna happen if you go back Stateside."

The other reason was to fly. I already had a passionate love for flying. Before going to 'Nam, I tried to go to flight school, but I didn't make that. I was envious of the guys flying. So first I started putting in for transfer to an aviation company. And they just kept saying to me, "No, no, no, no, no, nononononononono." After about nine months I said, "Okay, fine, I'll take another year over here." Well, that opened up their eyeballs a little bit. I said, "I'll stay if I fly." They said okay. About a month later I got orders, which meant I had an additional fourteen months to do. They sent me over to an aviation company with the Cav. They gave me a ship, introduced me to the

crew, asked me if I knew anything about the M-60 machine gun—
which I did, I had spent a lot of hours behind it—and I just started
flying. On-the-job training.

Flying helicopters in Vietnam was one of the purest things. It's not
like flying in the States. First of all, in a chopper you're more open.
More exposed to the air. It's not like you're in a commercial plane
where you're strapped in. Also, there's no FAA regulations. There's
some military regulations, but you didn't bother with that crap. So it
was like—I don't know. Take the Indianapolis 500 and elevate it. The
thrill that a racecar driver must get—and now you're free from the
tyranny of terrain, as they say. Hey, man, I can do anything I want,
go anyplace I want, up, down, backward, sideways, shoot between
the trees—unbelievable. That's the first thing that hit me, the sense
of freedom. You've conquered a force of nature—gravity. And your
perception of the world is radically different. You're up above, and
you see. You're not bound by roads. Every time I got in a Chinook
it was the same feeling. No matter how many missions I flew, every
time we'd lift off it was an emotional thing. Every time. I'm getting
it right now, thinking about it.

Chinooks—they were great. Hueys were fun, but the shithooks were
great because they were faster than a Huey, more maneuverable. It's
like the difference between a small car and a station wagon, but
because you've got tandem rotors, you can twist right around on a
central axis, and you're a little bit faster. Great to fly. Two pilots and
three crew. The pilots would rotate around to different ships, but the
crew—that was our ship.

The Cav used helicopters for everything. We used Chinooks on
combat assaults, which is not that common. When I saw *Apocalypse
Now*, it blew my mind to see that Cav unit in attack formation, because
I was flashing on assaulting a village from the sea. This was south of
Quang Tri, right near the coastline. We'd take six gunships, six slicks—
nongunship Hueys—and three Chinooks, load 'em with grunts, and
go in. We took off at dawn and went out to sea a mile or two and
started circling. Got the entire flight into formation. Meanwhile, we
could watch the artillery tubes popping. And we could see where the
artillery was hitting the village. We waited our turn. The artillery
would prep the area, and the last round they'd fire would be white
phosphorus, Willie Peter, and that was the signal. Once you saw the
Willie Peter round go off, you knew the artillery barrage was over,
and everybody would swing down and go into formation, drop down
to about ten feet above the water, and go in.

You'd fly your three gunships on point, and then you'd fly a sort of wedge. Gunships on the outside, and one on the ass end, and all the ships carrying infantry in the middle. The three in the front would go in first, make a pass, and then start circling around. You'd come in, drop off your troops, lift off, and get out. In a prolonged battle we'd make ammunition supply runs. Go back, load up with ammo, go back in, drop off the ammo. If anybody needs to be taken out or bodies need to be taken out, you swap—throw the ammo off, put the bodies on, take them back, take the bodies off, put the ammo on. Back and forth, back and forth.

The pilots like to go in low because of detection. But I also think they got their nuts off that way. It adds to the thrill of the chase. Flying above the treetops and above the water was a beautiful thing. An immense sense of speed. Your indicated air speed would be 120 knots, which is about 130 miles an hour. You're hanging out over the gun and the wind is pushing your face to the side. Think about doing fifty miles an hour in a car and putting your hand out the window. Then think about doubling that speed.

You're cradled over the gun, which is mounted on a bar with a pivot. It has an aviation mount on the ass end—two handles with twin triggers. You hang out over the side of the gun with the trigger handles back by your waist, and you hold onto the carrying handle on the top of the gun. You hold that so you can lean out over the gun and get a better-angle shot at what's below you. Then, depending on what you've got to fire at, you can spin the gun any way you want. If you're flying the left side and firing to your rear, you just spin the gun out with your right hand. And then if you've got to fire forward or walk your tracers into a position, you can spin the gun on the pivot and catch it with your other hand, and you've got a handle with a trigger there. You get extremely intimate with that gun. It's like your baby. A lot of times I would have gone out of the ship if I wasn't holding on to the damn gun. You hit a sudden pitch or roll, the pilot has to bank real sharp for one reason or another, and if you're not holding on, the centrifugal force isn't going to help you on that one.

Most of the missions blend together, almost like one mission. Base camp was An Khe, and depending on where the area of operations was, you'd set up a forward LZ and operate out of there. Return to base camp for major inspections. Sometimes you'd get in a firefight every day, sometimes you wouldn't be shot at for a week. Sometimes just one or two rounds, somebody's plunking at you with an old bolt-action job left over from the French. Other times you run into North Vietnamese regulars and they've got AKs, or they've set up an ambush in a mountain pass with 12.75 antiaircraft guns, the Russian version of a .50-caliber machine gun. Getting shot at with those is an experience, especially at night. You're watching the tracer come up at you. It looks like this tiny little pinpoint, and it just floats until it reaches you, and all of a sudden it's about this big, like a football, and *psssssssshhhhhhwww*, it's right by you. That'll blow your mind.

They just loved to fire at us. Here's this big thing coming in and sitting down loaded with all this fuel and ammunition. If you can take us out, you take out a lot of stuff. Lots of people, too, if there's grunts aboard. It's funny—you wonder why they don't hit you more often, with all the shit they throw at you. Sometimes one well-placed round would take a ship down. Other times they'd stitch us bad, but all it would be is sheet-metal work, because they didn't hit any fundamental components, hydraulics or fuel lines. Sometimes you'd have to hover over a downed aircraft or an LZ that's under fire, being overrun, trying to figure out how to get in there and drop off fresh troops or ammo and pick up bodies and stuff, and the lead is being slung at you, the lead is being slung by everybody in every which direction, and you just wonder. . . . But you only pick up a round here and there. It's weird.

The first time I got shot down was a Mickey Mouse job. But the second time—it was on January 3, 1968. Two 1st Cav LZs had been opened up in the Que Son valley north-northwest of Chu Lai, slightly south of Danang. The idea was to block one of the main routes of the Ho Chi Minh Trail. These two LZs were almost back to back in a lowland next to a river. The 3rd Brigade of the division was concentrated there. The LZs were good-size, with large contingents of infantry, armor, and all three levels of artillery: 105s, 155s, and big howitzers, 175s and eight-inchers. When you had those big boys, you weren't fucking around.

We had been flying into this one LZ to help set it up. We heard it had been getting hotter and hotter. When it got really hot, we flew one mission in at night. On the morning of the next day, January 1, we were flying in and a North Vietnamese division literally came out of the mountains in broad daylight, blowing bugles and carrying flags, with fixed bayonets. They did the old human-wave trick. It was awesome to see—like, Wait a minute, this isn't according to the script. We're supposed to be fighting a handful of rebels running around in black pajamas. What's going on here? Didn't these guys read the papers?

All I did for the next three days, with the exception of a few hours' sleep, was fly ammunition in and fly bodies out. We flew around the clock, as much as we were capable of doing. We'd go to Danang, pick up ammo, fly out to the coast, down the coast, come inland, drop off the ammo, pick up the bodies, fly back out to the coast, up the coast to Danang, drop off the bodies, pick up the ammo. Over and over again. And close to the LZ, the fucking place was unbelievable. We had everything in there—jet fighters and what we called Guns à Go-Go, which were gunship Chinooks, armed to the teeth. We had already brought in a shitload of beehive rounds for the 105s. When the LZ is under assault, you take the 105 and drop it down to zero elevation. A beehive round is like a shotgun shell for the howitzer, loaded with ball bearings or nails or something. They were popping them off.

On the second night, you could see big explosions, and I figured they were on the perimeter. The LZs weren't that big, maybe the size of a football field, and shit was blowing up all over the place. The next morning, when dawn broke, we realized they had hit the tanks and APCs with RPG rounds. Blew the shit out of them. All the armor was destroyed, and they'd come through the wire. It was like chaos. It's just frames in my head—one frame is when we first went in, another is seeing the waves of Vietnamese coming out of the mountains, another frame is the explosions, another frame is the next morning with the wreckage of the burning tanks and the bodies all over the place.

We'd pick up heavy automatic weapons fire from the hills around the LZ as we came flying down into the valley. And on the third day, January 3, we were making another run. We dropped off ammo, picked up some bodies, and headed out to the coast. And the pilot fucked up. He was flying at 100 feet. Bad news. In that area, once you leave the mountains, there's a real flat open sandy stretch several miles wide, just shrubbery and bushes, not much good for anything. We flew right into a North Vietnamese patrol. We were so low that they stitched the shit out of us. Blew both our hydraulic systems out. The ship burst into flames. We had two gunships with us trying to keep up, but they were a ways behind. I remember firing all the way down. The pilots just got off "Mayday" twice. As the ground started coming up, I said to myself, "Oh, shit, twenty years old, what a fucking waste. Here. In this shithole." I grabbed on to the bar the gun is mounted on, crouched down as best I could, and there was the impact.

When I came to, part of the ass end of the ship was upright, and part of the frame was over on its side so that the left gun was sticking up. I couldn't move my legs. There was stuff all over me, junk, the tool chest. The ship was on fire and the ammunition was cooking off, and you could hear the North Vietnamese assaulting us. The gunner on the other side nailed a couple of them, but there were some left.

The gunships hadn't caught up yet. There was dust everywhere inside and I couldn't see a fucking thing. I remember I took whatever it was on top of me and threw it off, and very calm and cool, I said, Okay, you can't move your legs, try to move your toes. I moved my toes and said, Okay, my spine's not broken. Now I just gotta get out of here. We had an infantry captain on board. We picked him up at the LZ. I tried to pull myself up and the captain was there so I grabbed him and sort of pushed him out over the left gun. Then I pulled myself up over the gun. I'm grimacing now—I can still remember, it was so fucking painful. I slid down the ship and he dragged me away. I couldn't walk. That's when we saw the gunships come in and assault the rest of the NVA. They blew them the fuck away. Then we lay there waiting for a medevac to pick us up, and we watched what was left of the ship burning all over the place.

Later on I tried to figure out what happened. The paint on the back of my helmet was gone, so something had hit me on the head. Cold-cocked me. And it looked like one of the rotor blades cut the ship in half and hit me in the back. When you take a chopper and blow out its hydraulic system, it's like a giant kite. You have absolutely no control over it. So she went in, flipped ass first, the rear rotors touched first, and as soon as one rotor blade snaps then you get your imbalance, the heads start to go crazy, and the rotor will cut the ship in half. So I think I got hit in the back with a rotor. Anyway, it did massive amounts of nerve and muscle damage. It hit me right in the small of the back, at the beginning of the lower spine. It was weird, it didn't break the skin. But it caused a monstrous black-and-blue mark that lasted for months.

I got medevacked to Chu Lai. They put us in the Second Surgical Hospital and kept me there about two days. The hospital was overflowing. We were in the halls, on the shelves, lying on top of one another. I said, I'm getting the fuck out of here, man. So after two days they put me in a Jeep and drove me back to my company. What a ride that was, holy shit. I think I passed out three times.

They put me on a board. And I slowly forced myself to begin to walk again. It took me two weeks before I could go fifteen feet. Then I got to the point where I could fly again. There were different official levels of disability and I got up on this permanent level where I was authorized to get painkillers. We used to have good old Darvons. It was a capsule. You pulled it apart and there was a little opium ball in the center and white aspirin or something on the outside. You threw the aspirin away, popped a couple of those, washed it down with a warm beer, and you could fly for a week. Who needs a helicopter?

So the guys got me another ship. They took two five-gallon water cans, put a thing like a pillow on top, and strapped it all to the floor right in front of the gun. I could get into the ship slowly, and they'd help me mount the guns, because I really couldn't pick anything up, and I'd sit there and hold myself as well as I could and fly.

After a while, you develop this attitude that dangerous things don't mean anything. You become fearless. I carried that over into my first year or two back in the States. I could not comprehend what the civilian population thought was dangerous. I try to explain to people sometimes what it was like to be on an LZ, which is a fairly secure place, and go to the bathroom at night. The shitter is over by the concertina wire. You take your rifle or your pistol and a flashlight. You keep the flashlight off. And you sneak up on the fucking john. You try to check and listen real carefully, because the back of the john is right on the wire, and once they come through, they're there. Then you start checking it for tripwires. And when you do turn on the flashlight, you always hold it away from you, in case someone fires at the light.

We used to watch the air force and navy fighters, and you could tell how much time a pilot had in-country by the way he dropped his load. You'd watch them making runs on a village. All right, this pilot here, see him way up high there? He's a double-digit midget, he's got ninety-nine days or less to go. And that guy all the way down on the deck, who's coming in and dropping his bombs from about 150 feet, he's been in-country about six months. He don't give a shit. He could care less if he lives or dies. He's gonna come in at 150 feet and let it roll, and then do little flips over the goddamn village as he pulls out. And the guy in the middle just got in-country. He doesn't have the feel yet, so he's down halfway. He's still nervous, still scared, still cherry. But the guy who's a double-digit midget, he's dropping his bombs from about 5,000 feet. He thinks he's a B-52. He ain't goin' nowhere down there, man. There's small-arms fire down there.

We'd shoot the living piss out of the civilian population every chance we got. We always sprayed anything and everything that looked like it might be inhabited. Winning hearts and minds, right? It got to that point. I degenerated to that point, and I wasn't the only person who did. It started out with a policy that if you took a single round from a village, spray the village. A general punishment. And you degenerate to where you're just looking for kicks. I don't know whether it's to get back at the Vietnamese, to punish them. . . . A combination of our arrogance and also frustration, a lot of hatred and bitterness.

I remember one incident where we were hovering near a road. We were picking up blivets of fuel. Our rotor wash blew a kid into the rear wheels of a five-ton truck. He got squooshed. I watched this, and my gut reaction was one of horror. I looked toward the ass end of the ship, and my flight engineer had been watching the same thing. We looked at each other in the same way, and then all of a sudden we both changed and started to laugh about it. Ah, we got another gook. We saw a certain humaneness in each other, and in ourselves, and quickly squashed it, because that was dangerous. To open up, to have that kind of crack in the armor, was a one-way ticket to either insanity or death or something. In order to get through, you built this shell and you existed in it. It had certain rules that you obeyed, and one of them was an indifference and arrogance toward the population. No words were said, but both of us knew exactly what the other one was thinking. You could just tell, it was there. And we laughed it off. One less gook, forget it.

The standard procedure when you'd take fire from a village was to spray it as much as possible while you were still in range. Usually you had a mission to fly, so you couldn't be making U-turns and coming back on some village. We did that once, but that was after a ship went down and our medic was killed. He went to An Khe for something and hitched a ride on his way back and got shot down. Went down in flames. Everybody on the ship was wasted. We marked the area, and we peppered it real good. We paid special attention and shot it up as much as possible. I know of other villages where our gunships went back in and took care to level every hootch. I saw that happen from our ship. And I remember making a conscious effort during the dry season to use straight tracer rounds to burn villages. Your normal belts of machine-gun rounds have one tracer in every five rounds. We would try to get the straight tracers, nothing but tracers. You could get belts like that. The object was to start fires.

I can remember shooting one old woman in the back. The second time we got shot down, I just kept my hand on the trigger up until impact. Most of the fire was coming from the other side of the ship. But we had almost a macho glory thing, that the correct procedure for being terminated was to go down in flames, firing all the way. If you're going to go down, put out some rounds. That's exactly what I did. I saw this old lady out in the field, far out. I just swung the barrel around, laid a burst into her, swung the barrel back around and kept on shooting up anything and everything in sight, didn't matter what.

There was rotor wash, which was almost like a weapon sometimes. You could really fuck people over with rotor wash, just by going in and ducking the chopper. It was sadistic. The Vietnamese had these big flat pans that they filled with rice and put out to dry. You'd watch guys come in, and they'd flare the ship, lift the nose, and the rotor wash would come and blow everything away. Hit 'em with a 100-mile-an-hour wind. Because if you've got a full load on the shithook, you'd generate 100 miles per hour on the rotor wash. You'd be sitting there laughing at all these peasants running around, trying to pick up each individual grain of rice. You'd do that for fun, or out of total ambivalence. Fuck them, I'm going to set down here, that's my mission. I remember blowing a water buffalo through concertina wire. Blowing concertina wire through a village. Blowing hootches down.

One mission sticks in my mind. It's like a whole bunch of stories in one. We headed out toward the Laotian border, in the mountains northwest of Danang. We got to a village that was probably the closest place to paradise I've ever seen in my life. There were no young men in the village, all old people and women and kids. It was obviously an NLF village. But the sky was beautiful, and the terrain had been sculpted for this terraced farming. There was a gentle stream running through the village. It was like somebody had taken something totally in balance with nature and set it aside from the rest of the world.

We took about six choppers in there and we went in with grunts. We met no resistance at all. We dropped off the grunts, took all the villagers and put them on the choppers. The grunts burnt the village to the ground, killed all the livestock, destroyed everything they could destroy. This was nothing extraordinary. The reason it sticks in my head so clearly was the beauty of the village.

Then we flew out with the villagers. I think we packed about sixty or seventy Vietnamese in the Chinook, literally one on top of the other. And we took them to a concentration camp. Not like the Nazi version in World War II, where you had ovens and stuff. It was an area with row upon row of these tin shacks. They were packed together, with tin rooves and corrugated aluminum siding. Surrounded by a moat and high fences with concertina wire. At each corner was a watchtower. I could imagine what the temperature must have been inside those metal houses.

On the way there, we were flying at maybe 1,000 feet. I can remember having such mixed feelings for these people. The first thing I did was look around, and I took a big knife away from some old man. He didn't like that idea too much, but I didn't like the idea of him having it. Then I called one of the kids up to the gun. At first he didn't want to come. I gestured to him, come on up, and he did. He looked out of the chopper and his eyes got real big. I realized it was his first view of Vietnam from my perspective. So I said to him, "Where VC?" He looked at me—this kid was only nine or ten years old—and he said, "VC everywhere." He said it in English. As isolated as he was, this kid spoke enough English to understand what I was saying and answer me. "VC everywhere." I agreed with him, too.

WILLIE BOOTH

He is a dapper man, sporting a John Lennon cap, dark shirt, and gray slacks. He has an Afro haircut, sideburns, and neatly trimmed mustache. He lives in the Bedford-Stuyvesant section of Brooklyn and works at Alexander's department store as a security guard, patrolling at night with an attack dog.

He was born in 1933 and joined the army in 1952. "I always wanted to be a soldier. I guess because I used to see the guys come home from World War II. They were all dressed in their fancy uniforms, and they looked good." In 1957 he left the army but stayed in the reserves. Then, in 1965, "Something personal happened with my wife, and I just said, I gotta go back in the army. I had to get away. The army wasn't an escapist thing, but it was on my mind all the time. I had a good job, but military life was part of me. What I like about it is this: Number one, I like efficiency. I like doing a job to the best of my ability, and I like to see other people do a job the same way. And I like appearance. I like people to look good. If you look good to me, then I think you can do anything. That's what the army stresses all the time, appearance and efficiency. In civilian life it's not like that. You can go to a job and look like I don't know what, man, and your boss doesn't care. Plus, I learned a lot in the army, things that have helped me in civilian life. To me, it's one of the great experiences that a young man could ever have. I think all young men should have a taste of it, because it really makes you a man. I still like it. Actually, I still love it. With all the hardships I went through, I'm still military-minded."

I went back to active duty in '65. I had no idea I'd ever see Vietnam. In '66 I went to Korea. I made two stripes that year, E-4 and E-5. Beautiful tour. Then I came back and was stationed at Fort Hood, Texas. I was assigned to a training unit, teaching NCOs. In December of '66 I made another stripe, E-6. Staff sergeant. And life was so boring! Here I am, a big staff sergeant, sitting in a barracks with nothing to do. So I went to the recruiting office and talked about reenlisting. The guy said, "Okay, you're an E-6 over 10, that's good.

But the only place we have to send you is Vietnam." Now, I was going to get $6,000 for reenlisting. And I was so bored. So I said, "Good, I'll take Vietnam." And that was it.

I got there in April of '67. I had this MOS, 11-B-4-H. That *H* on the end means "instructor," so I figured I was going as an instructor. I said, "Hey, I know I'm gonna have it made." But there's a catch to an MOS. If you can teach a subject, you can damn sure do it yourself. [Laughs.] So they sent me down to the Mekong delta, man. Ninth Division. Never forget it. I stayed there about ten months.

The name of the first base was Dong Tam. We had two dredges on the Mekong River. And those dredges—oh, man, you should see the pipes, they were about twenty-five inches in diameter. They'd dredge the sand out of the river, and they made the base camp with it. Man-made. Sand from the Mekong. It was big, beautiful. All tents, nothing permanent. No Quonsets. But it was nice. I knew right away I wasn't gonna be teaching. I was assigned to a platoon. I was an E-6 but I was a squad leader, not a platoon sergeant. I was briefed by my company commander. Then I was introduced to my platoon leader. It sounded kind of hairy. I was kind of disappointed. I thought I'd be back at division, wearing those starched fatigues, spit-shined boots. But I'm a soldier, man. I didn't like what I was doing but I knew it had to be done.

Our general mission was to secure the Mekong River. We were supposed to secure both sides, all the way down to the South China Sea. For what reason I don't know. I guess because the Viet Cong could bring supplies in, but I really don't know. All I know is we had to keep that river secure. And we did that by patrolling on each side. We'd patrol with one battalion on one side and one on the other side, and we'd just go up and down, or fan out to the right or the left. Sometimes we'd go in by helicopter, sometimes by those ATCs. Mostly we operated off ships because you know what a delta is—it's water. And I couldn't swim, that made it even worse.

We couldn't stay out more than five days because our skin would be like a washboard. We'd stay wet for five days. Sometimes at night we'd have to climb a tree to get some sleep. From my feet to where I hung my pistol belt was nothing but sores. I had jungle rot. I was all fucked up. My feet would turn white from the water, and that water was nasty. In Vietnam they don't have bathrooms like they have here, they just do what they gotta do over these little streams, and it all comes back in the water. So five days was the maximum. When you got back with your feet like that, the only thing you could do was air 'em out. Don't wear any shoes for days, 'til they're completely dried out. It itches, man. When you take a shower you start scratching—scratch, scratch, scratch, scratch.

We stayed on this base camp about three months. Then we moved. The navy was attached to us, and we started operating off ATCs. Each company had five ATCs, and headquarters company had six. An ATC is like a small ship. It's got a motor and everything, and when it gets to the land it drops a ramp. There's a navy crew aboard, about five men. It can take forty or forty-five infantrymen. It's armed and armor-plated. A lot of times when we were patrolling the river, we didn't get off the boats until something happened. We'd always have two or three ahead of us with things that looked like real big chains with claws on them, sweeping for mines. Sometimes they'd miss those damn mines, and the third or fourth ship would blow sky high. Luckily I was never aboard one when that happened. But I've seen a lot of 'em get blown and everybody get killed. The VC could build mines out of anything—truck tires, fifty-gallon drums, anything. They'd submerge 'em, and the damn boat's rudder would hit 'em, and that's it. Blow the son of a bitch out of the water.

Another thing that would happen—we'd have young men who'd just gotten out of high school or college, they'd come over there, go out on a night mission, and walk off the boat. Because they just got there and they didn't know. The boat would be tied up to the pier. When you come up from below, you walk up a flight of stairs and make a right, then walk up on the pier. But if you're not familiar with it and it's dark, you can make a mistake and go off the stern. You just walk off into the water. I saw it happen. Young men, with all that equipment on, they'd walk to the stern and go off into the water, and the current would carry 'em under the pier and we couldn't find 'em. Find 'em three or four days later, all puffed up.

When I first got to Dong Tam everything was good. We'd go out on missions maybe four, five times a week, nothing ever happened. I told a guy one day, "Man, I'm sick and tired of this. Nothing ever happens around here." So I went out one day and got my taste. Paradise Island, never forget it. It was a beautiful island, man. All the flowers, the fruits, the pineapples, the mangos, the whole bit. Hootches, the little thatched houses. I mean, it was beautiful. You've never seen such beautiful flowers. All hell broke loose one day on that island. That's when I really got my first taste of Vietnam. It seems like the Viet Cong had gotten tired of us coming out there and bullshitting around. So they ambushed our whole battalion. We lost about fifteen KIAs. In my company we had about three, and maybe ten WIAs. One of my best friends, man, I seen him with his guts all hanging out, his face all messed up. I said, "Well, this is it." That kind of changed my attitude. [Laughs.] From then on it seemed like every time we went out, all hell broke loose.

It got so you couldn't get real close to a guy. I mean—look. You'd get closer to 'em than a brother. A guy you've never seen before, you just meet him today, and he'd tell you about what's happening at home with his family, and we'd talk about my family and we'd get drunk or high together, and we'd get just like *this* [presses two fingers together]. Then I'd never see the guy no more. Never see him. We'd go on missions, and I'd hear them call his number on the radio. All of us had line numbers. It would come over: "Line number so-and-so, Kilo India." Goddamn. Then sometimes I'd have the "pleasure" of going down and identifying him. Tough, man. Bitch. I think the first sergeant used to keep that shit for me. He'd say, "Okay, Sergeant Booth, you've got a mission this morning." "What've I gotta do, Top?" They'd be wrapped up in these bags, and you'd have to go down there and look at the guy who was your partner. I'd just say, "God*damn*."

I'll never forget this one guy. I don't know where the hell he was from. Me and him got real close. He was a quiet-type dude. I can see him right now. He had long hair, blue eyes, and we used to smoke marijuana together. We got to be so close, man. We were in the same company, Charlie Company. I was in the third platoon, he was in the second. And the second had to lead that day. It was the point platoon. Well, the night before, we got high, we sat up there bullshitting, but there was something funny about it. Like he wasn't really himself. I could feel it. So I said, "Well, I'll see you when we get back, man." "Okay, be cool now." He was much younger than I was. I was the old dude, man. I knew all about his life, he knew all about mine. That morning we left the ship about four in the morning. We planned to hit our beach about eight. About nine-thirty all hell broke loose. I heard his number called out. And I said, "Ain't this a bitch, I ain't gonna see him no more." Got zapped right through the head. Those were the things that really hurt you. I can't say I really got used to that. What I did was I didn't make so many friends.

I only lost one KIA in my platoon. And I was trying to get this dude—oh, man, this guy was a real religious guy. I forget his name. We were pinned down behind a big old berm—a berm is made out of mud and debris and whatever. We were all down there behind this thing. And Charles was tearing our ass up in front. We were all shooting, putting our weapons up on top. I couldn't see what I was shooting at, but I was putting it up there and shooting. This guy gets up there so he can look around and see. He really gets up. I'm trying to tell him, "Get down! Get down!" Before he heard me, man, he was hit right in the forehead with a .50-caliber shell. The whole half of his head just went off. Split, like that. I was sick for days. You talking about a sick dude—to see his head, his whole head, just go *wwwsssssshhhht!* And it seemed like I couldn't even hear the round when it hit him. It just went *wwwwssssshhhht!* And that guy was good, he didn't give anybody no problems. He just had a little too much courage, I guess.

After you've been out in the woods so long—well, what happened to me was, I was out there for about six months. And I was so damn scared that I went to division headquarters to see a psychiatrist, and I tried my damnedest to get out. I don't know if you've ever felt fear, but fear is a bitch. It's a feeling that is something else. I can't describe it, being scared twenty-four hours a day. I just wanted to get the hell out of there. I had seen so many people get zapped that I figured my time was mighty damn short. I could still do my job, but I was really scared and sick and tired of it. It was after that dude got his head shot off. That took a lot out of me. So I tried to convince myself I couldn't do it anymore. I figured I'd go to the psych and tell him, "Hey, man, I think I'm nuts or something."

I told him the truth. Well, actually, I was lying to him a little bit. I told him I just didn't think I could do it anymore. I said, "Man, I've seen this and I've seen that, and I just *can't do it*." I said, "Look, I can't swim, and we're surrounded by water." But he saw through it. He said, "Ain't nothing wrong with you. You just stop trying to play games on me, because they ain't a damn thing wrong with you." [Laughs.] I said, "Damn. You mean to tell me I gotta go back?" He said, "Hell, yeah! What the hell you think about other people? If everybody talked like you, then shit, we'd lose this war tomorrow." And he said, "The only way you will really overcome your fear is to get into it. I could get you off the line and put you up here in headquarters, but you'd be scared the rest of your life. You've gotta go back there and get in the foreground, get out there and forget what you've seen." So I said to myself, Well, the hell with it then, here I go. I didn't agree with him but I had to go back, because he knew what I was doing. He didn't give me no medication or nothing.

It took me all day to get back in the delta. He must have called ahead by land line or something, because on my next mission, I was point man. [Laughs.] They put me on the point. So I wasn't scared no more. I don't know why. Well, I was scared, don't get me wrong, I was leery, but I wasn't really scared like I used to be. I was on point and I had things to do. I had to watch for this, watch for that, do this, do that, because I had all these men behind me. I couldn't just crack up. So I overcame that fear. He was right. Had he taken me off the line, I would've been scared the rest of my life. But since he sent me back and I had to do it, I was aware of the danger but I wasn't as scared. I just needed someone to talk to, and he made me feel so damn bad, like I was looking for an escape, that I said, "No, no," and I went back and everything was okay. I stayed about three months, and then my lucky day came and I did go back to division as a teacher. But had I given up, I would probably be in a funny house today.

ANONYMOUS

He is a tall man with curly blond hair, deep blue eyes, chiseled features, and a quarterback's physique, so the soft voice comes as something of a surprise. He lives in New Jersey and works at a museum in New York. He is gay. In early 1968, having dropped out of the University of Wisconsin, he was living with his parents in Chicago, working at a boring job and suffering from an unhappy love affair. "I caught Michael in the clinch with my best friend. Oh, please.

"On April 20, 1968, I came home from work. My mother had my favorite dinner waiting for me. Everything was strange. My household is very Germanic, and things would always be thrashed out at the dinner table. Dinner was never a pleasant experience. But this one was very nice: 'Ah, son, do you like the meat? How are the potatoes? Is everything good?' I had the feeling something was wrong, but I didn't know what. After dinner my mother lifted up my plate, and there was the letter underneath from the draft board. 'Greetings.' Aha! That was it. They had gone through the same thing with my brother in 1958, when he was drafted. So I gulped, and they said, 'What are you going to do?' I said, 'Well, the first thing I'm going to do is quit my job and take a vacation, and then I'm going into the army.' I just felt that was an answer."

After several weeks in Vietnam with a line company, he sprained his ankle badly and was sent to the rear. While there, he wangled a job as a clerk in Duc Pho.

I was R&R clerk first, then I became casualty clerk for six months. When you're the casualty clerk, you've got to work the dog shift, from five in the afternoon till six in the morning. Originally my job was to go down and make sure the right body got in the right bag. All my

218 | STRANGE GROUND

predecessors had done these daily trips to the morgue. I said, "Fuck that, man. Leave that to the mortuary workers. I'm not going to do that. I'll stick to record-keeping."

I handled it all by telephone. You'd sit there in the hootch and the phone would ring. One of our guys would pick it up. Somebody at the other end would say, "Casualty." The guy on this end would yell, "Casualty!" I'd pick up the line and say, "Okay." "This is the 6th of the 11th Artillery. We just had a shell come in and three people got hurt." "All right, what are the names?" You'd take down the names and numbers and ranks. "How badly were they hurt?" It was either a GSW, gunshot wound, or a frag, or a broken bone in an accident. They were either treated in the field and released, or sent to a med station, or they were going farther than that—they needed hospitalization. I had to fill out the form. It wasn't much of a form, just basic info. And I had a tally. There was a big chart with an acetate overlay, and with a grease pencil I'd keep a tally of casualties in every battalion.

There was something very nice about it. If I tallied six to eight casualties a week, that was average. So it wasn't like masses of data. And I had my time to myself. I had to be there during certain hours, but at least there was nobody around, nobody to report to. You could sleep if you wanted. You just had to be there to answer the phone. And at five in the morning, just before dawn, I would take my Jeep and drive it up to the top of the hill that overlooked the South China Sea, and I would watch the sun coming up over the sea and get high. Then go down and have breakfast and go to sleep. That was my day.

It didn't take me long to realize what insanity was going on there. The casualties were always the stupidest kind. I remember three examples of real insanity. One was with my old unit, the 1st of the 20th. They were short on space, so people were sleeping in the munitions bunker. A shell landed right in it. Blew it out. Three or four guys who I knew were completely wasted. They shouldn't have been there in the first place.

Then there was an incident on guard duty. The people who were in the rear, especially at Headquarters Company, were low caliber in terms of soldiering. I mean, they shouldn't have been given rifles. Well, there were always three men in a guard bunker. One was supposed to be awake at all times during the night. The bunkers were these big sandbagged things with beams running across, looking out on the perimeter. With an entrance in the back. It would get so hot that some people would go up and sleep on top of the bunker where it was cooler. So one guy was up on top of the bunker, one guy was asleep inside the bunker, and one guy was on guard duty looking out the hole. The guy on top woke up and came around to the back to go in the bunker. The guy on guard was new, very nervous, and apparently his fantasies had just run wild. He heard this noise behind him, turned around, and shot the guy who was coming in. The guy who was sleeping thought there was an attack, and he shot the guy who was on guard duty. So here these two guys were killed, both dead as can be, and we had to take their bodies back.

The third insane instance was at brigade headquarters. Every brigade had a scout-dog team. German shepherds. The scout-dog team was commanded by a lieutenant who was a very attractive man. I suppose I remember him for that reason. He and a couple of friends had taken artillery shells apart and had poured the gunpowder out in the scout-dog yard into a big peace sign. Then they lit it. All three of them were killed by the burns. They just weren't careful enough, they didn't expect as big a flash as they got.

I lived in a little hootch with plywood walls and floors and a canvas top that looked like a tent roof. About halfway through my tour the canvas was all rotting so they put up corrugated tin rooves. And we took empty fuel-oil barrels, five-gallon drums, filled them with sand, and stacked them on top of one another around the building to shield against mortar or rocket fragments. Inside the little room each person had their space. Mine was cordoned off with a plywood wall. I built a frame for my bed, elevated it maybe three feet high. And the three of us would get stoned with one another every day of the week. Since there were no weekends, it was every day. We'd sit around and bullshit, tell lies and stories. And listen to music, because we had electricity there. Boy, those ten or eleven tapes are engraved in my memory. The Doors, *Soft Parade*. Cream, *Wheels of Fire*. Simon and Garfunkel, *Bookends*. The Moody Blues.

Pot was a funny thing there. Not everybody smoked it. I've heard all sorts of reports of the time I was there . . . 20 percent, 80 percent. . . . I would say in my area, maybe 40 percent of the people were smoking pot, another 40 percent were getting drunk. There were 20 percent who just wrote letters home. And listened to Barbra Streisand. Most people smoked their pot in a pipe, because cigarette papers were always getting sticky and soggy. You couldn't keep them dry in the humidity. Finally I came up with an invention. I cut a hole in the bottom of my locker and put a light bulb on an extension cord in there, so the light bulb was on all the time to keep things dry. American ingenuity.

One night the authorities decided to bust us. They knew we were some of the hard-core pot smokers. So they staged a raid. It was the most incredible raid. They came in both ends of the hootch with machine guns and MPs and CID men and the company commander. There were literally twenty people who burst in on this hootch. Of course in the army, in order to be arrested for illegal possession of anything you had to really possess it. It had to be on your body or in your locked locker. So the rule of the game was: Don't be holding. If you're traveling, keep it handy to throw away. And if you're at home, leave it out, but not on your body. They walked in and confiscated something in the neighborhood of four pounds of prime marijuana. It was all over the place. They lifted up the pillow of my bed and there were ten neatly rolled joints laid out there. They said, "Whose are those?" I said, "I don't know." They said, "Isn't that your bed?" I said, "No, that's the army's bed. I just sleep there." They checked in my locker, and here was this light bulb with all these Zig-Zags. But there was no law against Zig-Zags. They found other stuff that I had brought back from Australia. Some brightly colored silk underwear that I had picked up in Sydney, a skimpy men's-clothes catalogue. And they got the idea that they were really getting involved in more than they could handle. Ooooh-kay. They pushed that back and concentrated on the pot search. Which they couldn't find on us, so they couldn't bust us.

Oh, they were mad. They were so mad. My sergeant, Sergeant Walker, who was a lifer clerk—what a combination—he was very disappointed. *Very* disappointed. He said, "You know, you could be an outstanding soldier. Why don't you just come down and have a beer with me every night instead of this stuff?" I said, "Why, Sergeant Walker, how can you talk about drinking beer and getting yourself all fucked up in the middle of this hostile place?" So they just threw up their hands. After that we were always warned, because one of the MPs would come over and smoke with us, and he told us when there was going to be a crackdown.

We were always trying to find new ways to get fucked up. It was so terrible there, so boring. That was the worst part—every day was just like the one before. The only difference was maybe today would be wetter than yesterday. So it was a search for how you could possibly smoke more than you had smoked last night. It was a kind of challenge. We'd take a gas mask and take the filters out and tape over them, and just make a hole in one of the filters. We'd stick a joint in the gas mask and puff like mad, just keep breathing until you either dropped or it burned through. Sometimes you would drop, and sometimes it would burn through. Then there was Jimbo, the supply sergeant. He had a thousand pilot's emergency flight packs. Little plastic boxes that every helicopter pilot was supposed to have with him all the time. Inside the box was everything you needed—waterproof matches, a Swedish saw that you could straighten out and cut down a tree with—all these crazy things, including eight methamphetamine tabs of the purest government-issued meth you could buy. Well, that kept us going for a couple of months. We would just sit around and talk and talk.

This helicopter medic was stationed on the base, and he was in charge of keeping all the supplies. He got ahold of a PDR, a *Physicians' Desk Reference*, that tells you what the effects of all the drugs are. So he knew just which ones to order. Ritalin! Oh, my God, Ritalin! That's a drug they use for hyperactive children. They give them Ritalin and it cools them out. But in adults it has the opposite effect, it's a speed. Very mild, but if you take enough of them. . . . They were tiny little tabs, and if you took eight or ten you'd be up all night.

This medic could order anything as long as he could find a way of justifying it and disposing of it legally. He found out that certain drugs require constant refrigeration to be good. If there's no refrigeration, like in a power outage, they had to be destroyed. Well, if there was one thing you could count on, it was a power outage at least three times a week. So he ordered cases of amyl nitrate poppers, the real thing. I mean, there was one hell of a case of angina going around that season. He dropped into the hootch one night: "Well, I got 'em in case we needed 'em, but the power went out so I had to write 'em off." In New York in the '80s you'd have used them for sex or disco. In Vietnam it was just one of the bag of highs. People were snorting rubber cement, it was so bad. I remember being on guard duty with these poppers. We were standing on top of the bunker overlooking the perimeter, getting high as a kite, smoking a lot of pot. We popped the poppers, and the next think I knew, we were doing a Fred Astaire–Ginger Rogers number on top of the bunker. *Tap-tap-tap, da-da-da-da-da*.

One day the adjutant came to me and said, "Look, I'm trusting you with this because I think you're a person who can get around." He gave me a lot of money—$150, $200—and wrote up orders for me to go to Saigon. I was supposed to find someone to make a pair of lacquered wooden bookcases with the 11th Brigade insignia on them, to use as a going-away present for the commander. So I found myself going down to Saigon and staying in the bachelor enlisted quarters, which was in this old hotel. It was all very nice. I found somebody to make the stuff for me. It would take about ten days, and that was just fine. My orders were to come back in a couple of weeks with the goods.

One night I went to the Astor Bar and met this guy with whom I had a torrid affair. Paul was—oh, he was special. He had enlisted because he found out he was gay. He had been seduced in Grand Central Station in the men's room, and he was all shaken up about it. He felt that he had to reaffirm his masculinity somehow, so he had gone into the air force. Since he was stationed at Tan Son Nhut, he knew a lot of the Saigon locals. Pretty soon I was into the whole gay scene in Saigon. Which was overseen by civilians, Americans or third-national civilians who were stationed there permanently. They were the ones who had the homes and apartments and penthouses. The next thing you know, there were parties with bartenders and strobe lights, with thirty or forty people. But I had eyes only for Paul those days.

I got back to Duc Pho, and Paul and I started corresponding daily. I always had mail coming in, always in the same envelope and hand-writing, in-country. People said, "Gee, who's writing you every day?" But they didn't catch on, and I was always careful to burn every letter after I read it. It would just be newsy stuff: This is what happened today, so-and-so says hello, this one's no longer here, there's some new bar or some party.

I was R&R clerk again—you'd switch these assignments back and forth—and I arranged an in-country R&R for Paul and myself. That was a thing everybody heard about but nobody got. It was at a place called Vung Tau. A beautiful little French colonial city on the South China Sea. I went to Saigon, picked up Paul, we took a chopper down to Vung Tau and had ourselves three or four days of absolute bliss. Three days that are like a jewel in my memory. When we weren't in bed we were out taking pony rides or swimming at the beach. Eating French food every night. Oh, we had a good time. We kept saying to the maids, "No, no, come back, change sheets later."

After that we kept writing to each other, and then another com-mander was leaving and I had to go to Saigon again to have something made for him. So Paul and I had another couple of weeks. I got to meet more of the people in Saigon, who were such wonderful guys. I don't know why any of these people were in the armed forces, because they were all gay. There were probably a dozen of us who were very close. God, there were some gorgeous men there. This one guy from Boston, he and I had a little affair. Bill shared this apart-ment—a huge, three- or four-bedroom apartment, brand-new, with a balcony that looked over General Goodpaster's villa—he shared this apartment with a sergeant major who was known as the first mother of the army. A fifty-year-old gay guy who had a family and eighteen children back in Texas, and all these young boys running around in Vietnam. He wanted me to join his staff, but there was some quid pro quo connected with it. I turned him down. He said, "Don't you realize the kind of life you'd have here? The MACV swimming pool . . ." I said, "No, it's all right. I'll go back to my unit."

It was wonderful, my love affair with Paul. It certainly kept me going while I was there. Sex for most of the men meant prostitutes. This was some kind of deeper connection. I remember thinking at the time, "Oh, my God, we're going to remember this all of our lives." Wrapped in this midday sex heat in steamy Saigon. In the middle of war. With bombs bursting around us.

DUANE CORNELLA

A small studio apartment on East Fourteenth Street in Manhattan, a seedy neighborhood. There is a kitchenette, a loft bed, a mattress-couch, two or three chairs, and not much other furniture, but the place is overflowing with books: They fill several large bookcases and are piled on most other surfaces. Many of them are about Oriental religions or other forms of spirituality. On the walls are posters in a psychedelic style, and a large picture of Janis Joplin, nude except for a bunch of long bead necklaces. Duane clipped it out of Rolling Stone. *"It shows her vulnerability. That's what I like, because it's the way she really was, even though she came off as this hard person."*

He is a slightly built man of thirty-two, with shoulder-length black hair, granny glasses, and a little goatee. He works as a photographer for the Customs Bureau. "There were two things that led me to Vietnam. One is that I'm a foster child. My foster family never gave me much encouragement to do anything with my life. The other is that I was raised in Brooklyn in a blue-collar community where you're expected to finish high school and start working. College was never an option. I graduated from high school in 1967 and worked until 1969, when I got drafted. I was left to my own devices. There was no one there to say, 'Oh, God, Duane, you've been drafted, let's get you out of this.'

"At the time I was against all killing, all waste, all violence. I was against that even before I was aware of Vietnam. It's something I either brought into this life or it developed during my childhood. A certain respect for life, a certain gentleness. I never could stand any kind of cruelty I would see in my friends. I had this thing about not wanting to kill or maim anything. And I was definitely against the war. I was part of what was called the counterculture or the hippie movement. I *rebelled against everything. I had long hair and I wore the clothes of . . . Gypsies, you might call it. I was into music and drugs and hanging out. In 1969 I went to Woodstock. Philosophically I felt I was born that weekend. Half a million people there, peacefully. I could see I wasn't alone in my beliefs. That was in August of '69. In September I got the notice that I had been drafted.*

"Friends of mine suggested ways to fail the physical. The day before I was supposed to go, a friend had gone and he loaded himself up on downs. He said he was so out of it that he was nearly foaming at the mouth, and they still took him. So I said okay, so much for that. Another friend said, 'Why don't you punch holes in your arms? You'll probably fail the physical because they'll think you're a junkie.' But I felt it wouldn't look realistic to put holes in my arms the night before. I mean, the doctors aren't fools. And I guess I didn't want to stoop that low, even though I felt strongly about not going into the army, and of course not going to Vietnam. The only other thing to do was run away to Canada. People always ask me why I didn't do that, and I say, 'I wasn't brave enough.' I felt I'd be losing a lot. I don't agree with everything this country does, but it's still a nice place to be. I didn't want to give it up. So I decided to take my chances and go."

I got to the base camp in the afternoon. I had been in Vietnam two days. In the middle of the night they woke us up and said, "The company got hit. Get your gear and get out to the chopper pad, because you're going out as soon as it's light." The next morning we're on the choppers, flying out. No one's talking. It's like, "Huh? What?"

We're flying in. It's quiet. All of a sudden the gunners open up. They do that as a safety precaution. The helicopter comes in but it doesn't land. It hovers a couple feet above the ground. There's this tall grass, elephant grass. I had no training in jumping three feet with a full pack on, but they said, "Now you've got to jump off." I did, and I didn't break anything. You move away from the chopper because they've told you that much, and you just stay in the grass. The chopper takes off. There you are in the middle of this grass and you can't see anywhere around you. You can't see any of the guys you're with. Oh, my God, here I am, what do I do now? Then you hear someone coming toward you through the grass. You don't know what the hell's going on. It turns out to be one of the guys who knew their way around. He watches everyone get off the chopper, and he goes around and picks them up. Then they march us all in to where the company got hit the night before. The area's kind of barren and decimated. A lot of foxholes where they dug in. I remember walking in there, and the first thing I get hit with is the smell. The smell is like from a cold sweat, if you're around somebody and they've been sweating. It reminded me of Woodstock.

We went walking around from place to place for two or three days. In the middle of the third night, I got woken up by an explosion. We weren't dug in, I don't know why. We just slept in a circle and took turns being on guard with the radio. This explosion was a satchel charge that went off maybe twenty feet away. There must have been enough ground cover that all I felt was the impact. Nothing hit me. Within three to five seconds we were returning fire. I was scared, but I didn't freeze. I was scared enough to think about whether I wanted to fire my weapon. I noticed my field of fire was being covered. You're supposed to overlap with your buddy's field of fire, and mine was being covered by other guys. So I didn't fire. I'm laying there trying to hide inside my helmet, because I had no cover, not even a stick of bamboo. Near the end of the firefight I fired a couple of rounds into the ground. I didn't want to hit anybody. I just wanted to let them know I was there. "Hey, you guys, don't come over here because I'm shooting and you might get hurt." I wanted to get that message across, but I didn't want to hurt anyone. Both sides were firing, and grenades and satchel charges were going off. It was a short time, but it seemed longer. I could see our orange tracers going out and their green tracers coming in. That's how you can tell where they are, because you can't aim at night, you just have to move your fire according to where the tracers go. I remember seeing that display of fireworks and white flashes. Within a few minutes it was all over.

The next morning you find out who's hurt. This guy Duane Columbus got shot, so he gets medevacked back. I said, "Wow, that could have been me. A bullet with my name but somebody scribbled the last name wrong. Got him instead of me." One of the guys who had been there awhile said, "Listen, this is what you do. You ought to play deaf, and if enough guys play deaf the company will go back." A lot of times in this kind of firefight, when there's been explosions, people get temporarily deaf. I said, "Okay, I'll do that." I figured everyone is going to be doing it. He said, "They're going to come around and check." I saw the guy coming. I was still frightened, but I made myself even more frightened, and I just lay on my stomach looking out, watching. I knew nothing was there. The guy comes up behind me. He says, "Cornella, everything okay?" I don't answer. "Cornella, everything okay with your ears?" I don't answer. He says, "Cornella, can you hear me?" I still don't turn around. Finally he kicks my foot and I turn around real quick, like I'm scared, like all of a sudden he's there. I says, "What do you want? What? What?" He says, "Anything wrong with your hearing?" I says, "What?" He says, "One more time, Cornella," and he starts yelling, "ANYTHING WRONG WITH YOUR HEARING?" I look at him, give him a quizzical look, and I turn toward my friends and say, "What's he trying to say?" He writes down my name, and "Deaf." I get medevacked back. Here I'm expecting five or six guys going with me and no one's going back. I guess I was a better actor than the rest of them.

I knew that firefight was just the tip of the iceberg. I wasn't going to go through my entire tour with just one little firefight. I knew there was more to come. Okay, we didn't get hit hard tonight. That's no guarantee for the next time. Yes, this is real, this is happening. It wasn't that I was so scared that night, but I knew, hey, the odds are against me. So when I got back to the base I said to myself, I ain't going back in the field. That was too scary.

I go to the first sergeant. A real lifer. I says, "Look, I want to apply for conscientious objector." I just sat and rapped to him for an hour and a half. I told him my philosophy. I must have convinced him. He says, "Okay, you got three weeks to present your case to the major in charge." I started writing letters. But I had no grounds for it. The three weeks went by and I had to see the major. He says, "Well, you've got no case for CO." I says, "Yeah, I know, I realize that. I tried." He says, "Okay, so I'm going to have to order you back out in the field." I says, "Well, what happens if I don't go?" He says, "I'll throw your ass in jail." Then I said, "What happens if I go and don't fire my weapon?" He says, "Okay, go out and be a target." I felt this was not a person to be reasoned with, so I'd better just salute and leave.

They sent me out to a firebase they were working on, building it up. I stayed a couple of weeks. Then I got a bad fever from an infected cut and got sent back to base camp again. Someone must have been watching over me, because while I was having my finger taken care of, they gave the radio to another guy in my unit named Redman. The company went back out in the field and got attacked heavily. It turned out this guy was on guard duty, and he fell asleep. The North Vietnamese snuck up and cut his throat. Then they broke through the circle and cut five or six throats before anyone realized they were inside the perimeter. Then all hell broke loose and there were heavy casualties. A lot of the guys I knew got killed. The lieutenant got killed. So I felt I was being protected somehow, because the infected finger took me back to the base and the guy carrying my radio. . . . I'm thinking these things.

So they sent me back to the firebase. Once again I'm hooked up with everyone. I'm having a great old time. Everybody's hanging out in their little hootches, telling stories, listening to music, lots of good rock 'n' roll. At this point I've taken to not wearing my helmet, going without a shirt, and wearing a headband with a peace symbol I sewed on it. Finally, the captain comes over and says, "Look, I understand how you feel, but the major and colonel are getting on my back. Do me a favor and don't wear that peace sign, and be in uniform." I respected him so much for saying it that way that I did it.

But meanwhile I'm hearing reports that other companies are getting hit, and hit hard. High casualties. From nearby firebases. We're going out in about a week, and I'd be a fool to think all the other companies are getting hit and we're not going to. We're going out into a hot zone. I think we were the first firebase between the DMZ and the other firebases. It was just the DMZ, the jungle, and then us. For sure we're going to get hit. So I decided, Okay, my luck is just about running out. There's no reason for me not to go out with the company when they go back out. So I start devising this plan to get myself out of Vietnam. What it entails is "accidentally" shooting myself. With witnesses.

The plan was to shoot myself with my M-16 in my left foot. I wanted the bullet to hit the soft fleshy part of the foot and go right through. I had learned a lot in the classes on the M-16 about muzzle velocity and what happens to the round when it hits, how it tends to tumble. But if you get it right from the muzzle and you have the least amount of resistance, it won't even give it enough time to start its turn. I was looking for a clean hole right through. I picked the foot because I was a grunt and you've got to walk. And I figured the least amount of damage is going to happen to the foot. I had heard stories about guys who shot themselves with .45s, and that's insane. The round of a .45 is like the size of a dime when it enters. And when it exits! It's incredible. I heard of this guy with a .45 who really screwed himself up by shooting himself in the thigh and having it hit the front of the thigh, the back of the thigh, go through the calf and hit the foot. Really not doing it intelligently, if there is an intelligence to this. But the round of an M-16 is smaller than a dime, real small. I wanted to keep the damage as minor as possible. I was insane, but I wasn't stupid.

It had to look like an accident. I was breaking the law. I had to find the best time to do it. I marked my boot exactly where I was going to put the muzzle. I was looking for an opportunity for two days. Then the situation presented itself. I was on an observation post.

It was me and another guy, me holding the rifle and him the radio. We were standing on top of a slope watching the jungle during the day. There were soldiers out there, unarmed, clearing brush or something. We were there to watch them and observe the jungle. I figured this was the time.

So here I am, sitting in a crouch. My knees are up and the weapon is between my legs with the muzzle pointing down toward my left foot. I take the weapon off safety and put it on semi, the nonmachine-gun mode. Now I'm just waiting to pull the trigger. I've got it right on the mark on my boot and all I have to do is pull the trigger. I can do it any time I want. My heart's starting to pound. It's pounding harder and harder and I'm starting to sweat. I'm saying to myself, If I don't pull the trigger I'm not going to do it. I'm going to get too scared. At this point the guy on the radio says, "Cornella, they're giving religious services back in the compound, do you want to go?" I says, "Yeah, I'll go, and I'll mail your letters for you." To me that was another message. At that point I turned and made it look like I was getting up because I was going to run back for services. I made it look like one foot slipped out from under me. When it did that I pulled the trigger. And I fell back down again, because I wasn't really standing yet, I was in a half-crouch.

The first thing I did was put the weapon back on safety and throw it away from me. I looked to see if I had missed, because I felt no pain, nothing, not even a numbness. I looked at my boot and it looked like there was a hole there. It's soft material, the boot, so it closes back up. But it looked like it. Then I couldn't feel my toes. While this is happening the guy on the radio is saying, "A weapon went off, Cornella's been shot." That's basically all he said, he didn't say it was an accident. He saw the weapon go off and he saw me fall back down. I immediately turned myself around so my legs were higher than my head, to prevent shock. And it was hot, so I put my T-shirt over my head because the sun was in my eyes. I'm just lying there and I expect the medics to come and take care of me. The other guy is talking on the radio, and at this point I hear him saying, "It was an accident, his weapon went off by accident."

Then everyone runs over and right away they grab the shirt, thinking I'm hit in the head. I felt embarrassed, I had to say, "No, I got hit in the foot." This guy who'd been there a long time, he's like an E-4, he slowly takes off my boot. There's my sock, my green sock with red blood. Now he starts taking off the sock. I'm saying "Okay, prepare yourself not to see a toe or two toes. Prepare yourself for that, prepare yourself." He takes the sock off. All five toes are there, and a little dinky hole in my foot. A little bit of blood coming out. I've had worse cuts from playing when I was a kid. They're all taking care of me, and the captain who told me about the headband comes over and says, "Okay, you'll be all right, Cornella, we're getting a medevac, everything will be fine." Everybody's giving me encouragement.

I'm on the chopper pad, and the captain and sergeant and the E-4 come over to me. They start asking me stuff like, "Did you do it on purpose? Was this an accident or did you shoot yourself?" I've got to play it straight. I says, "No, I slipped, the weapon went off. I don't know what happened." The captain is not believing me. Out of nowhere, the E-4 says, "By the way, yesterday when Cornella was in the chow line waiting to eat, his weapon accidentally discharged." Which it did. What happened was that every time you go to get your food, you're supposed to have your helmet and weapon with you. Generally you sling the weapon over your shoulder with the muzzle pointing up toward the sky. You're on line and you're talking and playing around, and the day before I accidentally pulled the trigger while I was waiting. The gun went off straight up in the air. It's an embarrassing thing to have happen, because everybody knows you fucked up. They kid you, they don't get down on you. And you look around like, "Oh, I didn't do anything." They know you did, and it's forgotten. I had even forgotten about it. So here's this E-4 who's been in Vietnam for eight months or so, he has a lot of respect, and he says this to the captain. He acts as my witness and he doesn't even know what he's doing. So they thought something was wrong with the weapon because when they picked it up after I shot myself, it was on safety. I made sure of that for two reasons. I didn't want it to go off again, and I wanted it to be found that way.

The captain didn't say anything else. He and the E-4 left and I talked to the sergeant for a while. He knew for sure it wasn't an accident. No matter what the captain and the E-4 thought, he knew for sure I did it. He kept on saying, "You did it, didn't you?" And with my best Italian eyes I was telling him "Yes" but I was saying "No" the whole time. Had I known what type of person he was and how we got along, I might have said, "Yeah, sure I did." But I wasn't sure he wouldn't turn around and tell the captain. So I tried to communicate with my eyes.

That's how I got out. What happened was that when I made believe I was falling, the muzzle went off the mark on my boot. It was supposed to hit the fleshy part and what it did was hit the bone of my second-smallest toe, and completely fractured it. They had to do surgery and take out the bone chips. That was to my advantage because they had to put me in a cast and it took six weeks to mend. Finally they sent me to Japan, but they needed the space in Japan so they couldn't keep me there. Hospital beds were too valuable. So they had to send me home to convalesce. I knew that once I got home there was no way I was going back to Vietnam. No way. But they didn't even try to send me back.

It was on the hospital ship that I felt the most pain. Two types of pain. One was physical: Every time I lowered my leg I would break out in a cold sweat. I'd have to get up and hobble to the bathroom and come back and put my leg up and breathe heavy for a few minutes. I'd be gasping, and I had to cool off from the pain. The other thing was that I was in a ward and I saw the guys who had been through a lot of shit. I saw the shape their bodies were in, and it made me feel ashamed. That was hard, to see them. It was my first time seeing armless and legless people. But I'd rather do what I did than wind up like they did. At one point this guy came around asking me where I wanted my Purple Heart sent. But I felt really ashamed and there's no way I could have taken a Purple Heart after seeing all these other guys. I thought, These guys might have really believed in what they were doing, and here they are with serious injuries. They deserve the decorations, not me. So I said, "No, I don't want it." This guy was shocked. I kept on telling him, "It was an accident. It was an accident."

JURATE KAZICKAS

She is a tall, blond, handsome woman who lives in a big building with a uniformed doorman near the East River in Manhattan. The apartment is decorated in shades of beige and is curiously bare, with almost nothing on the walls. When I arrive, she has just come back from jogging nine miles. She is sunny, enthusiastic, emotional. She works as a filmmaker; her husband works on Wall Street.

She was born in Lithuania in 1943. Her father was an activist in the anti-Communist underground, and in 1944 the family fled before the advancing Russian armies to a refugee camp in Germany. Three years later they came to the United States. Her father started a small business that eventually made the family rich. "It's the classic success story, the immigrant who came to America and became very, very successful. So there was this immense feeling of patriotism toward the United States. We were safe in America, and war would never touch us here."

She had sixteen years of Catholic education. After graduating from

*Trinity College in Washington she volunteered to work in a Catholic
mission in Kenya, 100 miles from Nairobi, in the bush. She spent two
years there. "I wanted to stay in Africa all my life. My parents begged
me to come home for a year. They said, 'After that, if you want to go
back to Africa, you can go.' On my way back from Kenya I took a
trip around the world, and one of my stops was Saigon."*

I was overwhelmed. I was in Saigon for two days, and I remember
spending the whole time in bars talking to GIs. They were telling me
war stories, talking about bombing runs and artillery barrages, and
the VC, and the gooks, and how it's really heating up, and boy, it's
tough, and the Vietnamese army is so lazy. Kind of bragging about
it all. I didn't understand anything. I just listened. I was confused,
and yet something grabbed me. I swore I'd be back in a year. And I
made it. It took me the whole year, but I came back and got accredited
as a freelance reporter. This was February 1967. I was twenty-four.
    I don't even remember the first time I was in a firefight. I really
should, but when you're there for two years it all blends together.
Pretty soon I was in firefights all the time, and I know I saw more
combat than most GIs did. In the average company you'd have a very
bad firefight and then six weeks of nothing. But reporters who covered
combat just went from one to the other. Where is it happening? [Claps
her hands sharply.] Okay, let's go there. Spend four days with a
company, fly back to Saigon, hand in your pictures, write your story,
and get on another helicopter, there's big action up in Quang Tri,
Pleiku, Danang, down in the delta. Firefight after firefight after firefight. The stories were all the same: We were out on patrol and then
we were attacked. There were six men killed and twenty-four wounded,
and so on. Just the story of this firefight, what it felt like, what it
sounded like, the shouting that went on. The horror.
    One of my favorite stories was called "Just Another Patrol." I wrote
about what it's like with nothing happening, not a shot fired, the
boredom, the depression, the heat, the filth, the confusion. But you
can only write that story once.
    At first I was fascinated by the notion of why men would kill for
something they didn't believe in. Then, as one guy explained to me,
"Well, it's simple. They're trying to kill me. Somebody's shooting at
you, you shoot back." And I thought, Well, of course. [Laughs.] Those
soldiers were drafted, they were sent out there, they were handed a
gun and told to shoot, and they shot. Even the men who kind of
believed in the war when they went over got disillusioned when they
saw it wasn't working. The more VC we killed, the more they sent,

always more, coming in droves. We knew that South Vietnam would be Communist one day. It looked inevitable, we sensed it. So the anger in me started to build about the craziness, and I just wanted to write about how horrible it was, how truly horrible. How crazy and stupid.

You can't imagine some of the things I saw. Before one of my first firefights I had interviewed this guy, spent three days with him, gotten to know him. He showed me pictures of his wife and kids, and he had two weeks left, and he'd been wounded twice, and he didn't believe in the war but he thought it was his duty and he was sent there. The next thing I knew, I looked over and he didn't have a head anymore. When I say horror, I mean *you just don't know* what it's like to see somebody's guts spilling out, and arms and legs blown off. To pick up the arms and the legs and throw them in the stretcher, the shouts and the screams of agony and the bombs falling, the explosions, day after day after day. At the tempo I was going, I was surrounded by people dying. I can still smell it somehow. At the battle of Dac Tho I first saw a hill devastated by napalm. Our own bodies, the flesh just dripping, arms like wax hanging over trees, dripping, just melting away. The legs and heads and feet and boots and clothes. You're walking along and you step on something and it's an arm, and this was a guy you lit a cigarette with yesterday. Or I'd be with a general, with his shiny shoes and starched uniform, drinking French wine and eating ice cream, with candles on the table, and he'd be talking about his men and their souls, his boys and how they'd become men. The next day I'd go out and see that carnage, and they were all so young, so young. The North Vietnamese were sending down twelve-year-olds, we'd capture them or see them dead afterward, and they were little children.

When I got wounded at Khe Sanh, one colonel said. "Well, she finally got what she came to Vietnam for." They sensed something a little insane in me to always want to go back out, and quite frankly, I have not explained why I was so obsessed with being in combat. It seems amazing that I didn't get killed. I was shoulder to shoulder with men who were killed, and if you look at some of the pictures I took you know that the only way I got them was if I was standing on some hill as the Americans are charging up toward the Vietnamese on the top. I thought I was invincible as a reporter. I wasn't a GI. I wasn't fighting. I felt protected, I just knew nothing would ever happen to me. And I was never afraid. For all the horror, I kept on shooting pictures, I kept on taking notes, kept on writing about it. It was like I was just watching, listening, but never touching it. I didn't crack up at the things I saw, and I never cried. I heard them cry and watched them cry and talk through their tears about their buddies, but it wasn't my job to feel.

My mother thinks I had some unconscious desire to go back to what had been suppressed when I was a little girl in World War II. All this *boom-boom* was going on when I was two and three years old, and I don't remember it. She tells me stories of being in Dresden and I'm hidden in bloody bandages and she hands me to a German soldier and the train pulls out and Dresden is bombed. The blackouts, the air-raid sirens, the buildings shaking. At my christening party in Lithuania I slept through all the bombing. I don't know, I think it's bullshit, but some psychologist out there might say [mimics low portentous voice], "All these things were in you, and you had to reexperience them." I don't know. Yet all I wanted to see was the fighting. Of course, I knew that when I had enough, I could say, "Uh, helicopter please, I've got to go back and file my copy. Thank you very much, gentlemen, it's been great." I would turn back and see them standing there thinking, We've got to stay here. They didn't realize that in two days I'd be off in some other area.

It was confusing, because I'd go back to Saigon, take a bath, put on a miniskirt and some lipstick, and walk down the street seeing the flowers in the market and the guys sitting in bars drinking. I'd get something to drink and it was hard to think where I'd been twelve hours before. Sometimes I'd hang around with Sean Flynn and Dana Stone.* "Light My Fire" was big, and we'd go up to their apartment and play "Light My Fire" and drink and wonder, What the hell is this war all about? What is life all about? The worst part was that the guys you had left that day were still there. So I couldn't stay in Saigon very long. I'd get insecure after a couple of days. I felt I was getting sloppy, lazy, so I'd get on a plane and go up-country again. Sitting in Saigon I wasn't working, and that bothered me. I had to justify what I was doing there.

It was hard to do the kind of stories that I wanted, simply because I was a woman. The first reaction always was, "Why do *you* want to be here?" I'd say, "For the same reason as any male reporter. This is the biggest story in the world today. Anybody who's a journalist, this is where he wants to be." "But you're a girl, why aren't you writing about the orphans and refugees?" I had to go through that song and dance every time. I had expected that, I knew there would be a lot of resistance, because none of the agencies were sending

---

*Sean Flynn and Dana Stone: combat photographers missing in Cambodia since April 1970.

women to cover the war at that point. Some of the best female reporters had to pay their way over there, and there were less than a dozen of us covering combat regularly. Some of them were legends, like Kathy Leroy, the French photographer, and Dicky Chappelle, who had been killed the year before. We kept out of each other's way, we really didn't like each other. And of course, I was low woman because I was freelance. When you're identified with a paper you instantly have much more status and respect. The Vietnam War was filled with these weirdo freelancers, hippie guys who came in and said they were working for some paper and never wrote anything.

The longer I stayed the more I was accepted. I got a nickname, Sam. One guy called me Sam and it spread, and everyone would say, "Oh, are you the girl they call Sam?" Needless to say, the stories that went out about me, and about any woman there, were ridiculous. That I was lobbing grenades during firefights, stuff like that. And some that were just vulgar. Very upsetting. It was one of those things a woman had to put up with. There was a lot of speculation about what you were really doing there. Were you a USO showgirl? Were you entertaining the troops? Were you using your sex with generals to get stories and information? To be honest, some of that did happen, and it made things difficult for all of us female reporters. Some people thought I was with the CIA, particularly my male colleagues in Saigon. My credentials were with publications so obscure that they thought it was just a cover. Then when I was in combat so long, they couldn't figure it out. If I was CIA I should have been dining with the Vietnamese politicians.

I never knew how the grunts would take to my presence. Men at war are very superstitious. They have all their little rituals—you always carry a certain handkerchief, or you don't go out on patrol on Friday because the last time you did, everybody got wiped out. A lot of them thought a woman was a jinx. They'd go six or seven months without ever seeing an American woman, and along comes one, and she's not supposed to be there, so sometimes there'd be real hostility. It seemed to me that the career soldiers were the most hostile. Most of the grunts thought it was great. "Hey, you didn't have to be here? You paid your own way? Wow, you're crazier than I am."

There were guys there who liked to kill. Who really dug it. They were just getting it on. They scared me, they did. They couldn't wait to get out there. We'd be on patrol and we'd come under rifle fire, and they'd stand up with their M-16 or their machine gun and fire it from the hip, and I'd look at their faces and see how they were getting off on it. Screaming out, like "*Aaaaaaaaaaarrrrrrrr*, come and get me."

Loving it, loving it. I did stories about guys who liked to kill. They'd tell me, "It just makes me mad, those guys, we're gonna get them, we've gotta get them, I don't care, they're gonna kill me and I'm gonna kill them, it makes me feel good when I get another one, another Commie bastard, I feel *good*, eliminate one, I'm going to save America—." [Laughs.] They would talk that way. I remember one guy, a real macho type. Everybody said he was going to get it. I have a whole series of pictures of him standing up when everybody is crouched down, he's standing up firing into the bushes. He got it while we were on patrol. And for all his macho, his swagger, his bravado, there was this scared little child. I think with a woman there they put on the act even more. Remember, I'm six feet tall. I'm not a frail-looking little thing. I'm a strong woman, I carried my own pack. So they felt they had to be even more macho because here was this Amazon coming out on patrol.

Then with the generals and colonels there were always objections to my going out. The big thing was the latrine. Where is she going to go to the bathroom? Americans have this incredible obsession. Usually once you got out on patrol nobody cared. You'd disappear for ten seconds, and you had to be careful that you didn't set off a booby trap or something. But sometimes they would send three men to guard me when I went off to the bushes. Can you imagine being a GI doing detail duty for a girl pulling down her pants in the bushes? Humiliating. And I have one of the toughest bladders in the world. I can go for hours, hours, hours.

The other big objection was that "These guys have a job to do, and you're going to be a distraction. A firefight begins, and everybody's going to fall on you to protect you." That wasn't really true. When the crap starts coming in, everybody takes care of themselves. There were a few people who said, "Hey, how's she doing, let me hurl my body onto her body." Once I was almost knocked in the head by somebody who was scrambling for cover; he could care less what happened to me. And after a while I knew what to do when the action started.

The marines were the most difficult, because of their whole macho thing. The army grunts, they were going to go home and forget it. But a marine, his whole masculine identity is being reinforced, and when I showed up it was a little more threatening than to the army guys. Because if a girl can do it, it can't be all that tough, right? The marines insisted on having an escort for female reporters. One time they assigned a guy who was thirty pounds overweight and had been used to sitting at his desk in Danang. All of a sudden he's sent out on patrol with me in the hills around Con Thien. The captain of the company was about fifty-three years old. He wore a white parachute scarf around his neck and carried a shillelagh, and he led all his charges. He was a legend. He was distant and hostile to me. He was told to take me on patrol, and he could have said no. I guess while he still resented me, it was press coverage, and anybody who led a charge and was six feet six with a shillelagh and a white scarf had a flair for the dramatic.

We were dropped in by helicopter and took off for five days. No supplies would be brought in. It was supposed to be a very secret mission. Well, it was very hot and we were going through bamboo that had to be cut down. We were carrying heavy loads in this sweltering heat. It was a difficult patrol. There were signs of a lot of enemy activity. And after three days, my escort pulled a groin muscle. He can't walk, and he has to be evacuated. Now, whose fault is it? Mine, of course. I was going great, I was plugging away. I was miserable, but I did my interviews and kept quiet. But they had to call in a helicopter to evacuate this guy, and the captain was very, very bitter toward me because he felt we had given away our position by calling in the helicopter. The other guys said, "Lady, they know we're here. Believe me, they have known from day one we're here." So the helicopter came in, and I said, "I'm staying." I had been promised the patrol. But the captain said, "No, you are with your escort, pack your shit, you've got to leave." I was angry, and needless to say, my escort was humiliated. Two days later the company walked right into a huge contingent of North Vietnamese, and the captain led a charge and was killed. Something like half the company was wiped out. To this day I wonder if our chopper coming in . . . Of course, the chopper also brought in food and water and ammunition, so it wasn't a wasted trip. But I wonder if they said, "If she hadn't been here, it wouldn't have happened."

I was wounded at Khe Sanh during the siege. It was hard for reporters to get in there. Everybody wanted to go, it was the hot story. And one thing about being a female is that if there are five male reporters and you, and the chopper has seats for three, you're going to be one of the three. If they only have space for one and it's *The New York Times* versus a female freelancer, the female isn't going to get it. But a woman stood out. I never had to parlay sexual favors, but the American male with his chivalry, no matter if the bombs are falling, he'll say, "Okay, miss, why don't you come along, I'll see if I can get you in." So even though it was hard to get to Khe Sanh, I ran around, found a helicopter whose blades were whirring, and he brought me in, much to the distress of the official machine at Danang, which had a roster of people going in and out. Twenty-four hours later I was wounded.

I was interviewing some New Yorkers for WOR Radio. The tape was going. It had been quiet for two or three days. The sun was shining. It was a beautiful day. We had our flak jackets open. I didn't have a helmet on. It seemed like everything was going to be okay, like the siege was maybe over. People were hanging out their laundry. There was hope. And all of a sudden the rounds started dropping. Now, the cardinal rule with incoming is, when you hear it, fall flat on the ground. For some reason everybody panicked and we started to run for the bunker. In that time another round fell and wounded about six of us. I had it all on tape, it was interesting. "*Aaaaaaah*, I'm hit, I'm hit, *aaaaahhh*." Strange sounds, horrible sounds around me, but I just said, "Oh, I'm hit. I've been hit," and that was the end of that. I knew I was hit in my legs, because I had to drag myself to the bunker. My first thought was, "I'm still alive but I'm going to be paralyzed for life." I knew it. No easy thing, clean, dead, it's all over, picture in the paper. No. Paralyzed for life. And what for, what for? Plus I was hit in the face. I felt my face and there were bumps all over the place. Huge bumps, just as if you had lots of pimples. Shrapnel in my face. Well, can't worry about that.

We were brought into Charlie Med, which was famous for the work they did with traumatic injuries there. I insisted that everybody else be treated before me. I was self-conscious about that, and I said, "No, I'm not hurting, please take care of everybody else." I was in shock anyway. Fortunately there were only about ten or twelve wounded, and nobody really seriously, no head wounds. The funny thing was that one of my wounds was in the ass. A huge hunk, just short of my spine. It was a big wound, and this caused all sorts of consternation. When somebody gets wounded, the first thing you do is take all their clothes off, because little pieces of shrapnel might have hit them and you have to do a total inspection of the body. I thought, I can't believe this, it would only happen to me. So they set up this elaborate screen, nobody else but the chief surgeon and two assistants, no orderlies, no aides, and there was this big ceremony of pulling down my pants to check the wound. There stand these three men, and I'm lying on my stomach with my pants down. They're all looking somberly and I say, "Okay, is it below my bikini mark?" They say, "Yes, it's below your bikini mark." Okay.

I had to evacuate to Dong Ha at the end of the day. The only plastic surgeon in all Vietnam happened to be in Dong Ha and he operated very carefully on my face. Basically he took out every little piece and sewed it up. He said, "If you were a marine I'd just take a Brillo pad and scrub all this stuff out," because it was near the surface and he'd just rip open the face and the junk would fall out. But he took out all the little pieces one by one. I'm lying there, and along comes a helicopter pilot who looks down at me and says, "Well, your days in showbiz are over." I hadn't cried the whole day, hadn't cried ever in Vietnam. It was the first time. A little tear came trickling down.

Of course, the story that came out after my wounding was that they rolled me over and took off my clothes, and there were these knockers as big as watermelons. You should see her! I'd run into people who'd say, "Oh, yeah, you're the one, we heard about you."

After that I couldn't walk for a couple of weeks because of the shrapnel in my legs, but I felt it was important to get back to Khe Sanh. Kind of like falling off a horse, you have to get back on. By then the siege was over and the 1st Cav was going in to help evacuate the whole thing. I went back with the Cav on patrol, with George Wilson of the *Washington Post*. We had settled in for the night and there was a rocket attack. I completely flipped out. I was terrified. I'm lying on the ground, we hadn't had time to dig in, and they were falling and expoding, with that sound—*nneeeeeeeeyow—PCHOW!* Over and over, and it was at night. I said, "This is it, I know the next one is going to get me." Because now I knew I was vulnerable. George Wilson, bless his heart, put his arm around me, and he held me, and he had only been in-country three days. I was shaking. I said, "I've got to get out of this place, I've got to." Once you're afraid, you can't work anymore. It's no good. It's not that I was brave before, I was just stupid. I'd go anywhere. But once I was hit I was really, really afraid. I stayed in-country six months and I kept going on patrols, I kept pushing myself into it, but I couldn't work anymore. Just couldn't. I was tired. I was tired of writing the same combat stories. The sameness of it, the futility of it. It wasn't making a difference. My stories didn't matter. They weren't pulling the heartstrings.

When I came back to the States I talked to a couple of publishers. The only book anybody wanted from me was, "Gee, a girl at war, what was it like, a girl with all those men? What was it like jumping off a helicopter and the men saw you, and they hadn't seen a round-eye for seven months? Hey." It probably would have sold a million copies and they would have made it into a movie and I would have been rich and famous. But I couldn't do it. I kept thinking of what it was really like between me and those men. Very often I would put down my camera and help with the wounded, for which I was severely criticized by some of my colleagues. "We heard you played Florence Nightingale on that patrol." But there was a point where I could not continue taking pictures. There were too many men dying. You just threw down your camera and wrapped bandages, and you hauled the wounded, and you cradled dying men in your arms, so that their last moments were somehow . . . But not always, because I was sensitive that sometimes for men, this moment, maybe when your balls have been shot off, you don't want a woman to hold you. I was sensitive to a man's shame and humiliation in the act of dying. There were moments when I did not look, I did not go near. I'm not sure I was ever correct in—I don't want to call it the protocol of war. Being a woman, they don't think you belong there, and part of you doesn't think you belong there, and yet you're a journalist with a job to do so you do belong there. All of this is happening very fast: Do I reach out? Do I stand back? Do I watch? Do I take this picture? Do I bandage? Do I try to talk to him? Because what a story, his last words, this person that you got to know!

I remember one soldier said to me, "I don't want a woman seeing me die. I don't want it. That's why you shouldn't be here. It's not something women should be seeing. War is a man's business." That's the whole idea. What they were saying was, We're here to protect our country and defend our women and children. We've got to stop the Commies here because otherwise they'll be in Hawaii. We're here so our women and children will never have to see war on their own shores. But they were also saying, I don't want you to see me scared. I don't want you to see me cry the way I cry. I don't want you to see me bleed the way I bleed. And I don't want you to see me kill the way I like to kill.

WOODY WANAMAKER

"I was born in 1947, in South Carolina. My parents moved to New York, and I moved up when I was nine years old. My mom was a housewife. My dad worked in the glass business. In 1961 or '62 we moved to Jersey City, and my dad ran a bar and a small grocery store. As far as my childhood, I don't think there were any events of a traumatic nature. I wasn't involved with street gangs, I wasn't involved with drugs, I wasn't involved with alcohol. But it was getting nasty in Jersey City. The neighborhood was changing from white to black, but it was also deteriorating. It was crowded. There was a lot more street violence. When we first moved to Jersey City, there was no drugs. Maybe you'd

see a kid smoking a cigarette, and you thought that was a little wild. Then all of a sudden these guys were smoking reefer. Not like now, but it was getting bad for that time. We're talking about the early '60s, when people were really square. So I joined the army to get away from Jersey City. That and to continue my education. That was the fallacy I used."

He is a small, thin, black man with a raspy voice and a formal manner, slow to relax with the tape recorder. It is easy to imagine him as Sergeant Wanamaker, the hard-bitten lifer. Between 1966 and 1973 he did five tours of duty in Vietnam—a total of fifty-four months. In 1985–86 he spent seven months in the post-traumatic stress program at the VA Hospital in Menlo Park, California. Now he works at the Veterans Outreach Center in Newark. On the day we talk, his left foot is bandaged and swollen, causing him to limp. "There was some shrapnel in there left over from Vietnam. One piece was right next to a nerve. The doctors decided they would wait until it moved before they took it out. It moved about a month ago, and they got it out two weeks ago—fourteen years after I got hit. It's one of the souvenirs of war."

I arrived in Vietnam on June 10, 1966, and did my first tour in Phu Loi, near Ben Suc. My unit was the 1st Aviation Brigade. Most of the time I was in helicopter flight operations—we worked with flight records, maintenance schedules, crew briefings. At that time, the general mood I saw in Vietnam was really up. There wasn't any bickering, no "fuck the war." And there was a lot of—I guess, pride. Even though troops were dying and I hated to see it, I still had a sense of duty. I liked the army. I enjoyed it. And I made rank pretty fast. By the time I got home from my first tour, I was already an E-6. I was nineteen and a half years old, and I thought my shit didn't stink. I thought I had the world by the balls, and I was unstoppable.

I came back to the States in June of '67. I was assigned to Fort Stewart, Georgia. Back to Stateside duties, with spit-shined boots and starched fatigues. No more bugs in the bread, no more murky water. Electric lights and running plumbing. Good times again. But I hated Fort Stewart. It was in the middle of the boondocks. Speed trap. I wasn't at peace. It was very strange being back in the States. So eventually I reenlisted and went back to Vietnam.

This time I was with the 269th Aviation Battalion up at Cu Chi. I got in-country in November of 1967, and everything went well up until Tet of '68. That was the turning point in Vietnam, as I saw it. Tet was hairy. We didn't have actual ground assaults on the base camp, but we did get small-arms fire on the perimeter and heavy mortar attacks for six or seven nights. It was also the first time they used the 122mm rocket within III Corps, and that scared the living shit out of me.

In February of '68 another significant incident happened in my life: I lost my mother. I had emergency leave for thirty days and got back to the company at the end of March. Then I saw a real change in Vietnam. After Tet, the army went into a defensive mode, and so did the troops. The attitude, the drugs—there was marijuana use up the wing-wang. Every place you went, somebody had something going. Mostly the lower-ranking enlisted men. I didn't know much about officers and NCOs using drugs. Later on, I knew that some did, but at that point I thought we were above reproach, like the old NCO manual said.

Also at that point you could feel the racial tension begin to tighten. There was a lot of suspicion on everybody's part. Because of my young age, and because of my rank, I was accused of being CID I don't know how many times. I didn't hang around with all blacks, and I didn't hang around with all whites. My lifestyle was different. They couldn't understand that. Also at that time were the assassinations of Robert Kennedy and Martin Luther King. That made a change. Martin Luther King mostly because it made the black soldier see . . . I guess that things wasn't the way they were supposed to be. When we left for Vietnam, the States was on the road to integration and job opportunity. By '68 the war had gone on long enough that some people had already gotten out of the service and were back home trying to get their life together. There wasn't any jobs, and people didn't want to have anything to do with you if they knew you'd been in Vietnam. I felt that when I was home on leave, especially in my black neighborhood. "So you were in Vietnam? You gonna go back? You damn fool, you're fighting a white man's war."

Sometime during the summer of '68, there was a full-scale race riot at Cu Chi. It wasn't public in the States, but it was something I witnessed eye to eye. I don't know how it started. We were on the other side of the base camp. This infantry unit came in on standdown for two or three days, and there was some incident involving a black and a white at one of the EM clubs. It spread into their company area—blacks against whites, whites against Puerto Ricans, blacks against Puerto Ricans. I don't think there was any shooting, but they sure was going at it.

The racial issue was always there. It put me in a curious position. I wanted to be fair. I didn't want to hurt anybody's feelings. But I thought we had to survive together if we was going to survive at all.

And I had this one buddy named Al. He was an E-7, a very good friend of mine. We went through basic together, and we went through AIT together. We spent part of my first year in Vietnam together. We'd tell each other everything. He was a white guy from a little town in Vermont. It was kind of strange for me, being from a big-city ghetto and being friends with him. The S-3 office called us Salt and Pepper. We covered each other's backs. He was supportive of me when my mom died. It's hard to describe the comradeness that we had. Later on, I could say it was brotherly love.

Al and I set up a race relations group within our company. The aviation group picked up on what we were doing and decided to try it group-wide. I thought there was a need, especially after King's death, for everybody to get together and know what everybody else was about, because there was such a cultural difference. So we went to the old man, the company commander, and requested that we set up some training classes on race relations. We were going to start it as a volunteer group. The old man said, "We can't have it volunteer, let's make it mandatory." It was built on the idea of a cultural exchange. Let the guy from the Midwest know what the guy from the South felt. Because sometimes there's different slang words that would be misinterpreted. Or take someone who grew up in the inner city versus someone who grew up on the farm. You're going to have friction. We thought education was the key. If you educate somebody to their feelings, they can be more sensitive. That's what we felt.

Al and I were the co-leaders of the group. We would switch off, because one of us had to be in the office. Or we'd schedule the class at night after duty hours. That would get the troops really pissed off, because we closed the club. The classes worked for a while, but they deteriorated. Later on I thought it was mistake, because it only made them more aware of each other. It caused more friction. Instead of having a class on race relations, we had an argument on race relations. In one class we started out discussing black history. One of the guys pointed out that the textbooks in school had a very small amount of black history. And one of the whites said in essence that blacks hadn't made much contribution. Which was completely wrong, but he made the statement. That angered a lot of the blacks. We didn't have enough material and training to pull the two sides together. We was flying by the seat of our pants. And we was placing our values on their lives. We would say, "This is how we are, can't you guys get along the way we do?" That was a mistake.

That class put more suspicions on Al and me. People said we were CID. We were together most of the time. We didn't associate with the other NCOs that much. We didn't go to the NCO club. Neither one of us drank. People said, My God, these are two strange ones. He was in S-2, intelligence, which laid even more suspicion on us.

Then one night we had a drug shakedown. The NCOs along with the first sergeant would get together with some of the officers, and we'd go room to room looking for any drugs or drug paraphernalia. We found some marijuana. The next day, there was threats. Verbal threats. You'd be walking by, and people would say. "We're gonna get you motherfuckers." Stuff like that. You didn't pay any attention to it.

The night after the shakedown, myself and Al were sitting in his room bullshitting. The hootches had individual cubicles for NCOs. They weren't anything elaborate. The walls were screen, just a regular screen covering a few boards from the floor to the ceiling. There was an opening between the walls and the roof, about six to eight inches wide. And of course you had the sandbags around the outside of the building about four feet high. So if you'd stand on the sandbags, you could easily toss things into this opening if you wanted to.

I was sitting next to the door with my feet propped up. Al was sitting on his bunk in the other corner, lying down with his hand behind his head, talking about his wife or some shit. All of a sudden, out of the side of my eye I saw this shadow on the screen on the opposite side of the room. And I heard the spoon pop from a grenade. They probably had the pin pulled already. They tossed it exactly on his bed. By the time he picked it up, he just doubled over on it. Where was he going to put it? You don't have that much time. You only have so many seconds before the grenade explodes. So I guess—I can only guess—that he was saving my life by taking the full blast.

He wasn't actually blown to bits, but there wasn't too much left of a human being. I took some shrapnel. But the way he took the grenade, his body absorbed most of the exploding metal. He took 99 percent of everything that concussion grenade had. There's no way you can survive that.

The date was August 21, 1968. I can't give him the Congressional Medal of Honor. I don't have the power. But if I did, he would have it.

I probably went into shock. I say "probably" because a lot of the things that followed, I don't remember to this day. Maybe I don't want to remember. I can remember going to the dispensary and the medics looking at me. I can remember getting very angry. But angry at whom? I didn't know who it was.

The hardest part for me was coming home with the remains. I asked for and received permission to be the escort. [He is crying.] Facing his wife. How do you explain a life . . . ? How do you explain to a three-year-old kid . . . ? I couldn't explain to his son, at age three, "Your father wasn't killed in combat. Your father got killed by another American over stupidity." That's the hardest thing—you can't ever begin to explain it. Not to a three-year-old, and not to a twenty-three-year-old wife. And not to a forty-year-old mother or a forty-five-year-old father. You can't explain it away.

I didn't want to lie to them. But yet and still, I didn't want to tell them the truth. So I said it was a mortar round, that Al was hit by incoming fire. I couldn't bring myself to tell them. I'll always remember the day he was buried, and his mom at the graveside. The look she gave me. It wasn't a look of hate. She was looking for an answer. The answer the army had given her was not satisfactory. The answer I gave was not satisfactory. So she was looking for an answer with that look: Why? She had this question mark on her face.

The military told them basically the same thing I did, that Al was killed by enemy fire. They send you this officer who notifies you that your son has been blown to bits and there's only a little pile to be scraped off the floor and put in this little bag. Here's the remains of your son, whoop-de-doo, and here's $3.98, go buy yourself a Popsicle. But I saw that lady in all of her grief, I saw Al's young wife in all of her grief. And I saw his son, too young to understand, but with a feeling of loss already at three.

It hurt me. It did a lasting thing on me. It destroyed me, in a way. It was very hard for me to accept, that this guy was dead just because some asshole didn't like the way he parted his hair. I don't know who was responsible. I don't want to know. And I can't blame the individuals who did it, because it was a product of the times. Whoever did it, if they're still alive they're carrying a heavier burden than me. I can still remember a lot of good times with Al. But that one individual or individuals who killed him have to live with something bigger. If that guy would walk in this door right now, I'd probably shake his hand and say, "I understand how you feel. I might feel bad, but you feel a hell of a lot worse."

I went back to Vietnam and finished my tour. But I was very hard and callous. They used to call me "the bastard of Headquarters Company." I didn't get involved personally with anyone. It was strictly on a military basis. I looked at those guys and said, Is this the way you want to play? Then you'll get me at my worst. I became what the army wanted me to be: a hardass, not-caring NCO. It was easy for me to slip into that role, thanks to hatred. With the E-5s and below, any lower-ranking person, I felt: You did this to me. You took my buddy's life. You motherfuckers are gonna pay. It wasn't directed at one person, it was directed at everybody. I hated without malice. [Laughs.]

At first I didn't really want to know who did it. I had a feeling who it was, and at one point I thought I knew. I honestly thought it was a black person, which would make the situation more explosive. After I got back to the company, the first sergeant unofficially made sure he had an eye on me wherever I went. I guess he was afraid of what I might do. I asked some questions, but people were suspicious of me. I was so fucked up, I didn't really think of revenge. Maybe I was afraid to think of it, because I didn't want to see any more death.

After a month they transferred me out of the unit. I went down to the 187th in Tay Ninh. Later on, when I got my thoughts together, I wanted to find out who did it. But by then it was too late. I was in one area and they were in another. And by that time the person could have rotated back to the States. I found out there were transfers out of the company after I left. Whether those transfers came out of what happened, I don't know.

For the rest of that tour I went through the motions of being an NCO. I don't remember too much what happened. I was full of hate and revenge. And I have a bad habit: I can become a workaholic in a second. That's what I did over there. I worked. We was always short of people, so it was no hard task to find work. Most NCOs didn't do much typing. I did all the typing. After the incident I never let anyone touch an aviator flight record but me. I didn't trust no one. At times I worked eighteen, twenty hours a day. I would leave Operations long enough to take a shower, change clothes, and come right back. It was a survival mechanism. It didn't give me time to think. I had trouble sleeping. Finally I rotated back to the States, and that's when I started to drink heavily. I couldn't lose myself in work because I was on a set schedule. I had all this free time. To fill it, I drank.

I went back for my third tour in January of '70. I had been in the States five months. And I went back on a witch-hunt. I found out that one of the individuals who was transferred, and who I strongly suspected, was back in-country. This was a guy who couldn't stand my guts. It was no secret. He came up to me one day—this was long before the incident—and said, "Sergeant Wanamaker, if you wasn't an NCO I would kick your ass." He was a black guy. He felt I was an Uncle Tom. This was when the Afros were first coming out, and I stayed on my people's asses to get haircuts. It was a personal thing— I wasn't black enough for him, and he was too black for me. [Laughs.]

I went to see if I could find him. I was on my own individual crusade. A buddy of mine told me what unit he was in. I got myself assigned to the same battalion. But they probably got word that I was on my way back, because he wasn't in the unit by the time I got there. I called all over the country trying to find him. I was just going to follow him around and look at him. That would be worse than any torture I could come up with. Can you imagine that you've killed someone, and here's this ghost looking at you? I didn't want to kill him physically. Just seeing me every day was going to be enough to drive him crazy, or maybe make him want to end his own life.

But I couldn't find the guy, and I gave up the search. Once I was in-country and started back to work, the revenge became a secondary thing. I was just trying to survive myself. I drank heavily. I was a good NCO, but I drank off-duty. Any time after six at night, you could find me at the watering hole. If you wanted Sergeant Wanamaker, you knew where he was at. Matter of fact, one of the Vietnamese bar girls had my name embroidered on the barstool. At closing time I'd stumble home, go to sleep, wake up, and go to work. That's what I did for twelve months. And I continued for about six years after that.

I even did a fourth tour. I couldn't bear the thought of staying in the States, so I went back to Vietnam. I watched it change. And the more it changed, the worse I felt. When I was there in '68–'69, it was one thing. When I went back in '70–'71, it was another thing. When I went back in '72–'73, it was completely different. It was almost Stateside in Vietnam. You had inspections, change-of-command parades. Instead of devoting time to the war effort, we was devoting time to ceremonies. And as Vietnamization happened, you could see the losses. Areas that at one time was secure was no longer secure. Areas that American troops had fought and died for was just as bad or worse than before.

My last tour was at Bien Hoa. We was strictly flying ARVNS, working with VNAF. By then I was an E-7. I continued to make rank. I was always getting good evaluation reports, because the officers like you to be a hardass. Especially the older officers. The younger ones were a bid standoffish. There I was, an old seasoned salt. I had been on the other side of the hill for so long that I felt like I owned it. And nobody's gonna tell me how to run my side of this hill. I had a lot of young captains say, "Ease up, ease up." Ease up, shit. There's no easy way out. I just could not let go of that hurt. I couldn't let down my guard. And I didn't.

I used to fly a lot. NCOs didn't have to fly, but I did it just to occupy time. And I was on a self-destruct mission. Let somebody else kill me. If I get shot down, I have no more worries. I wanted to die, but I was too chickenshit to do it myself.

On January 21, 1973, we were on a recon mission. I was flying observation in the C&C aircraft. We were taking fire. The ARVNs was in heavy contact. We were directing aircraft into this one little LZ. We were at about 1,000 feet. The choppers was coming in, dropping off troops, and going right out. And there was a VC .50-caliber sitting up in the bushes someplace. Our aircraft got hit with an airburst, and I took a piece of .50-caliber in my foot. I got some of the Plexiglas from the cockpit in my arms. The helicopter crashed, *poom!* The crew chief and the co-pilot got killed, but me and the pilot were alive. I was still awake during the crash. I remember the gunship above us giving cover. I was on the ground for two or three hours. It was a night mission, and the medevacs were busy. Finally I remember the medevac coming in. I must have passed out, because I woke up in a hospital with a tube in my throat.

I left on January 23, 1973. I don't know when the peace accords was signed. I didn't follow that portion of the war. I was in Japan for a while, and from there I went to Letterman Hospital. I stayed there for a month or two. They was trying to reconstruct the bone in my foot and see what this other piece of metal was going to do. They made a few attempts to take it out. But every time, it still hadn't moved away from this one nerve. So they decided to wait until it moved.

After I got out of the military I was a very secretive person. I didn't trust no one. And I felt a lot of guilt over Al, a lot of shouldn't-haves. I shouldn't have been such a hardass. I shouldn't have gone by the book all the time. Maybe I shouldn't have been around Al as much as I was. I shouldn't have had him for my friend. If I didn't have him for my friend, he would still be alive.

And I was angry all the time. I don't even know why I was so angry. Sure, I lost my buddy. But there has to be a deeper reason than that. It's still a question in my mind today. I fucked up a lot of things since then, supposedly off this one anger. I've let a lot of good people go by who could have been my friends. I carried around that anger like a fifty-pound bag of shit on my back. I used it as a reason for drinking, as a reason for my marriage breaking up. I was just as guilty as the individual who killed Al, because I used it in order to survive.

I finally ended up in Reno, Nevada. I was divorced about two years. Very isolated. Full of self-anger and blame. A life without direction. I was working in a counseling field, but I was messed up myself. I wasn't drinking all that heavy, but I was getting thoughts like, "I'd be better off dead." My day consisted of getting up, going to work, going back home, and watching TV six hours a night. That was it. I spent all my time alone. I stopped talking to my family for two years straight. I didn't talk to anyone about Vietnam, but I thought about it constantly. It was like a preoccupation. I never got violent or anything, but it was there. I knew it was only a matter of time before it came out. And when I woke up in the morning, I'd start thinking about how it would feel not to wake up. That would scare the hell out of me.

That's when my basic survival instinct took over. I starting talking to this one person who told me about the Vet Center in Reno. One of the counselors there recommended that I try the program in Menlo Park. He said, "It'll do you a world of good. You need it." Thanks to him, I did. I took a leave of absence from work. It was supposed to be three months but it stretched into almost seven. I still had a job when I got out of the hospital, but I decided that being alone in Reno was no good for me. So I came back here.

That program saved my life.

While I was in Menlo Park, I called Al's wife and told her what had happened. That was a painful conversation. It was hard for me to do it. My focus group encouraged me, so I did. Cathy said she had her suspicions, but she never wanted to broach the subject. She said she knew that in my own way, and in my own time, I would probably get around to talking with her. She was just waiting.

6

BANDAGES AND
BODY BAGS

War demands healing as well as killing—and in Vietnam, thanks to the helicopter, healers worked wonders. Men with terrible wounds could be plucked from the jungle and whisked at 100 miles an hour to a field hospital. Once there, nearly all survived. In some cases, the healers wondered whether that was such a good thing.

In the first line of healers were the medics, a breed of soldier viewed by the grunts with a kind of awe, like a shaman. They were almost all known as "Doc." Along with the ranking officers, they were the spiritual heart of a platoon. On patrol, they tried to be inconspicuous, because the enemy shot at officers and medics first. Yet they routinely crossed ground under fire to help the wounded. Then, with their battle dressings and plasma bags and morphine Syrettes, they wove the thin thread that kept a dying man alive until the medevac got there. They often had to decide in an instant—these medics little older than the average grunt—whom to treat and who was past treatment. As Jack McCloskey remembers in this chapter, mercy killings were not unknown.

Maybe the hospital staffs saw the worst: day after day, the metal birds *whap-whap-whap*ping in, heavy with the bloody results of bullets, bombs, grenades, mortars, mines, shells, booby traps, rockets, friendly fire, crashes, accidents, disease. James Hagenzeiker, a surgical technician, says his operating room was like "a butcher shop." He also talks about the giddy confidence he had for a time: "I thought that once somebody got to the OR, we could save him." Then a man died, shot through the aorta and the vena cava. James cried, even though "it wasn't cool."

The psychiatrists saw wounds of another kind. The war produced relatively few psychiatric casualties in-country: for many vets, the payback came years later, at home. But John Talbott, fervently anti-war even before he went to Vietnam, found himself in the odd position of telling troubled soldiers that it was best for their mental health to go back to the killing.

And there were the nurses, young women in a madman's world, who spent their working hours on wards of shattered bodies, and their off-hours—if they wanted—at an endless round of parties. Here the dangers were not Bouncing Bettys and RPGs, but burnout and married men. Jane Piper remembers the good times, as well as the kid who bled to death, his eyes big as saucers, during her first week. And taking the wounded to the back of the hospital after surgery, to wash the mud out of their hair.

JACK McCLOSKEY

"I was born in south Philly in 1942. Grew up in southwest Philly, mostly in the projects. My father spent his life in the merchant marine. When I was fourteen, my mother died and he kind of abandoned us. I went into an orphanage for four years. In Pennsylvania the law says that if you're in an institution like that when you turn eighteen, you can sign yourself out. So I did. I kicked around for a year and a half and joined the navy in 1963. I had never heard of Vietnam. It was peace-time."

He is a short man who looks older than his forty-three years: gray hair, a bushy mustache, deep lines in his face. His skin is cratered from a chronic rash that has affected him since he came home from Vietnam. It is Sunday morning, and he is nursing a hangover with coffee and cigarettes. We talk in the kitchen of his San Francisco apartment. He is something of a legend among veterans: an early member of Vietnam Veterans Against the War, one of the first to run rap groups, and an architect of the Vietnam Veterans Outreach Center program. For four and a half years he headed the center on Waller Street. Recently he quit, being, he says, "burnt out." He is looking for work that does not involve Vietnam.

During his first hitch as a marine corpsman, he saw combat in Santo Domingo in 1965. He was discharged the next year but stayed on active reserve to help pay for college. "On July 4, 1967, I got a telegram saying: 'You have been reactivated. Please report to Philadelphia Naval Shipyard.' I'll never forget that. July 4.

"By this time I had gone through some changes. When they sent me

*to Camp Lejeune for retraining, and it came to picking up the rifle—
because navy medics go through a lot of weapons training—I refused.
So I got called a coward and everything else. They kicked me out of
the Field Service Corps School and cut me orders for 'Nam.*

*"I wanted to go. I just didn't want to shoot. I liked being a medic.
It was my generation's war, and in a way I was excited. I wanted to
see. I think every male has that part of him: How am I going to do in
combat?"*

From the time I got over there to the day I left, my outfit was always
in combat. I was in Golf Company, 2nd Battalion, 7th Marines. It
was a grunt outfit. Our first assignment was on top of this hill, watching
infiltration. We'd do night patrols and ambushes. Later on they made
us a helicopter assault battalion. We were aboard a ship called the
Tripoli. They'd take us by helicopter and drop us in for anything from
three days to thirty days. We never knew where we were going. Then
they'd pull us out again. We'd maybe go back to the ship for a day
to clean up, and they'd drop us back in. We were everywhere from
Danang up to the DMZ.

I remember my first time under fire, actually seeing the bullets
hitting people and feeling them come by me. I was scared shitless,
but when the shit hit the fan I was calm. I could operate. I didn't
freeze. I could patch up people under fire. It was: Hey, Jack, you're
not a coward. It felt good.

I remember the first guy I treated. A young guy, about eighteen or
nineteen. He had stepped on a Bouncing Betty, and it literally blew
him apart. I remember running up and him saying, "Doc, Doc, I'm
going to live, ain't I?" And me saying, "Sure, babe," and then he
died. I held his hand, and he died. I remember crying. I cried at the
next one and cried at the next one and cried at the next one. But it
got to the point where I stopped crying, because I thought I'd either
kill myself or go crazy if I felt for these guys. I started thinking, I'm
going to stand up next time in a firefight and expose myself and end
it. So I started shutting down. Not having emotions. Steeling myself:
You've gotta make it, therefore you can't cry anymore. I put myself
in a cage. It worked enough that I could function.

I was twenty-four, older than most of the kids there. They gave me
a nickname: the Hippie Doc. And they called me Plasticman, because
I was skinny. They said I could slither in and out of things. I was
Plasticman, the Hippie Doc.

I was always caught in a dichotomy—if I don't treat these kids,
they're gonna die. But if I do treat 'em, they're gonna perpetuate

something I no longer believe in. I always felt uneasy about that. I made it a point never to carry a weapon. I had a holster, and I carried battle dressings in it. When I first got there, they issued me a .45 and I put it in my footlocker for the rest of my tour. I was afraid of saying to them right up front, I'm not gonna carry that. I was afraid someone would shoot me. I found out that was bullshit. There were other medics who didn't carry a weapon, and the marines treated them very well.

I felt I was a good medic. The guys told me I was good. I did everything from tracheotomies right in the bush to patching guys up to treating villagers and kids. When I came back to the States I was really pissed, because the only thing they would let me do was empty a bedpan. A lot of guys feel pissed about that. A kid from Harlem may have been a good machine gunner or a good rifleman or a good medic. For the first time in his life, he has some responsibility. Then he comes home and he's just another nigger again.

I not only had to deal with the physical, I had to deal with the emotional. Guys seeing their buddies get wasted. Guys wasting people themselves. Guys getting Dear John letters. I remember one guy whose wife just had a baby. He had about five months to go, but he felt he wasn't gonna make it. People get intuitions. The guy got killed a month and a half later. He never saw his kid. I remember him saying, "I'm scared, and I know I'm not gonna make it." I tried to encourage him: "Yes, you are, just keep your head down. You made it this far, you can make it another five months."

Most of the wounds I treated my first few months were sniper rounds or booby traps. The worst wounds were the mortars. What shrapnel can do to a person is worse than bullets. Like slaughtered cattle. Literally meat. You saw guys that were gonna be fucked up for the rest of their lives. You knew that, just looking at their injuries. Foot off. Arm off. Sucking chest wound. You knew these guys were fucked up, but you had to treat 'em.

I've always wondered about some of the guys—whether they made it or not. Because you never know. If they're hurt bad enough, you're never gonna see 'em again. And you don't know how well you did. Some of them I knew were maimed for life. Or they had head wounds, and they'd be vegetables. You can't do much for a head wound. You stop the bleeding, patch it up as much as you can, start an IV, and that's it. Send him out. Maybe his memory will be gone, or he'll be paralyzed. What happened to those guys? Some of them will die from their wounds twenty years later. I think about that. Do they know they're walking dead? Infection will set in. Or the guys who became paraplegics, it's very common that their kidneys will fail after a while.

There was a part of you that was like God. You had to make life-

and-death decisions. Especially if you got a lot of casualties at one time. You treated those you felt would make it, knowing there were probably some others that you could save, but if you treated them, some of the others would die. Your objective was to save as many as possible. Say you saw a guy and you knew you'd have to spend a long time with him. If you did that, two or three others would die in the meantime. You'd say, Okay, he's my last priority. He's so fucked up that I may do something for him and I may not. But these other guys, if I do something they'll make it. You could give life or you could take it away.

I don't know if it was killing or what it was, but there were times when we had guys really hit bad, and I'd O.D. them on morphine. Gut wounds. That's one of the most painful wounds there is. If a guy steps on a mine or gets hit with shrapnel in the limbs, usually it cauterizes. You have to stop the bleeding, but the wound itself will cauterize the nerve endings. You give these guys morphine, and they're not in so much pain. But a guy who's got his guts half hanging out, those were the worst. We'd have guys wounded at night, and we couldn't get in a medevac until the next day, and they're screaming— that used to bother me. At least three or four times I actually killed guys with morphine. I've talked to other medics since then who did it, too, but I didn't know it at the time. It was just something I did.

I remember the first time I did it. We were on an operation up in mountainous terrain. Very heavy jungle canopy. We had been out for a couple of days, up by Charlie Ridge. We got hit right at dusk. One guy caught it in the gut. We couldn't get him out. Too much fire, and we'd have to clear an LZ. So I did it. That night. I could see him suffering, so I O.D.'d him. And then I did it a couple more times. Nobody knew I did it. I think some of the guys knew I was going to. I had some guys beg me to do it: "Doc, don't let me suffer like this." I did it. And there's always that thing that sticks in the back of my head—whether they would have made it or not. I don't think any of them would've. But it still doesn't sit good with me.

I went on R&R to Hawaii and saw Lydia. I married her when I got home. She flew over from Vassar to meet me. I remember we got into arguments. She could have arranged for me to go to Sweden or Canada. But I felt I had to go back to 'Nam. Although I was very against the war when I took my R&R, I felt I had to go back. These guys were my family. I would be abandoning them. Part of that's my orphan background. But I had to go back. I had to go back. I think she understands now, but at that point she couldn't. She couldn't fathom why I'd want to put myself back into that thing.

In March, I was made senior corpsman. This is how it happened.

The company was going down a mountainous trail. One of the marines saw a mine. He called up the engineer attached to us. As the engineer moved up to the mine, the VC or the NVA command-detonated it. The engineer got hit and called a corpsman up. I was the closest one. He was about twenty meters away. I ran up in a crouch. As I ran, they opened fire and caught us. The senior corpsman got hit and lost half of his hand.

I got out there and started treating the engineer. You always put the guy you're treating in front of you, between you and the fire. That's what probably saved my life. I was behind him, and I was skinny. He was hit in the leg. He had a cut artery, and I stayed there to stop the bleeding. They were firing. I remember the rounds—shit, I saw the rounds coming in. Mortars and bullets. They were hitting beside me, hitting him. The guy was still conscious. I could feel the hit of the rounds.

Finally the company laid down a base of fire and the NVA fire slacked off. I started dragging the guy back. That's when I noticed he got it in the stomach, in the shoulder, in the back of the neck. He got hit five more times. And I got shrapnel in my face and my arms. But I pulled him back, and he made it. He lived. They gave me the Silver Star for that. I didn't feel that brave or anything. What the fuck was I gonna do? I'm treating him, so I can't jump up and go back.

The senior corpsman was watching me treat the guy under all that fire. When he got back, he said, "If McCloskey isn't hurt that bad, I want him to take over as senior corpsman." So for the next six months I did that. My job was to stay by the commanding officer and negotiate with the rest of the corpsmen.

After a while it became a job. It became like factory work. Okay, he's hurt—treat him. Go to the next, treat him. Don't feel—move. Don't feel—move. One thing I started doing was not asking guys their names when they came into the company. Eventually I'd learn them, but I didn't want to know. They were humans, but I didn't want them to be humans I knew. I didn't want to hear about their families. I didn't want to know where they were from. I didn't want them to use me as a counselor anymore. If I had to, I did it. And I didn't let them know, because that wouldn't have been good for them. But my attitude was: You get hurt, I'll treat you. That's it. Don't talk to me. Just don't talk to me.

I started doing something I was really ashamed of. I used morphine. I did it to deal with some of the shit that I saw. It helped me. This started happening about three months before I left 'Nam. We had gone on this one operation, Allenbrook, where my company got wiped out. One of my best friends—there were three of us that used to hang around together. A white guy named Casey from a small town in New Jersey. This black guy named Allen from Birmingham. And me. All of us were medics.

On Allenbrook, we were going through a village. I was back in the middle of the company with the captain and the RO, and the platoon that was on point got hit. The NVA let part of that platoon get through and opened up with machine guns and mortars. Classic ambush. The village was fortified with bunkers all around, and these people let us get through and opened up. We were pinned down. Then another company tried to get up to help us, and they got it bad. Casualties, casualties, casualties. I don't know how many casualties. At least twenty-five killed and 100 wounded. I'll never forget that as long as I live. We had wounded all over. I was treating them so fast, but they were all around me. No matter which way I turned, there were more wounded, and more calls: "Medic! Medic! Medic!" I didn't have enough pans, I didn't have enough time, I didn't have enough people. When we ran out of battle dressings, we started taking them off bodies. I didn't give a fuck about infection. I just wanted to stop the bleeding and get these guys medevacked out. Using shirts, fatigues, anything. I thought I'd go crazy. And still rounds coming in. When's it gonna stop? You just treat people, treat people, treat people. That's what you do.

Then there were all these bodies. We literally stacked 'em. Put 'em in body bags. I was numb. I became a mechanic. Put this one in a body bag. Put another one in. Put another one in. The stares. These guys were dead, but their eyes were still open. After a while I couldn't look in their faces. So I'd pack 'em in and try not to look— [He is crying.]

Casey got killed that day. He got hit once and got another call for a medic. He went out again. He got hit five times before they killed him. His nickname was Mike the Mongoose. That's how they broke it to me. Allen came up and said, "Mike got it." They never let me see his body.

A week and a half later, we came back into the field. I was working in medical supply, but still doing ambushes. Allen came in one time. There was an ambush set for that night. He had wrenched his knee. It wasn't bad. We were real short of corpsmen. It was either him go out or me. I said, "Okay, you go out tonight, and tomorrow I'll send you back and we'll get your knee checked out." I put an Ace bandage on it.

Allen got killed that night. The platoon walked into an ambush.

They weren't all killed, just Allen and a couple of other guys. I remember it was by a graveyard. The next day I had to go to the morgue. I identified his body. He got it in the back of the head.

That hurt me. I was tight with the guy, and he was a damn good medic. I think he was nineteen or twenty. Gregarious. Made everybody laugh. Real tall guy, well built. An athlete. And sensitive.

When Allen got killed, the black medics asked me over to their hootch. I felt honored. In the bush there was no racism, but in the rear there was a lot. They were playing rock and smoking and dancing. They partied for their guys. There was sadness, but it was like a religious ceremony. Passing a joint around: "This toke's for Doc Allen." They told me, "This is because Doc liked you. He said you were okay for a honky."

Then I started using morphine. We were in base camp, getting ready to move out to the Philippines. I kept thinking and thinking and thinking of Allen and Casey. I just took a morphine Syrette and put it in my leg. There was a euphoria. Whoa, okay. I continued to do it—sometimes in the bush at night, but most of the time I did it in the rear, on what they called sitdown. In the field, I was too busy. But aboard ship, I'd lie there thinking and thinking. I got to a point where I'd start shaking, there was so much shit going on in my head. When I wanted to scream, I'd do a Syrette. It would calm me down. I would lose the edge of all this horror. I didn't like the bad memories. If I got high, I could think of Allen and Casey and remember the conversations and good times we had. I'd do two or three quarter-grain Syrettes a day. As a corpsman, I had my own unlimited supply. I never mainlined it. Always in my leg or my ass cheek or my arm.

Another thing that got to me: Right before I left, we had gone through a ville and some civilians got hit. I had about two weeks to go. There was a lot of fire. We were sweeping the ville, and we were getting rounds at us, so we started shooting back. Some women and children got hit. But I stayed behind a rock. I wouldn't move into the area, because I had two weeks to go. I knew this was my last op. No way was I going to risk it anymore. I have a lot of guilt for staying behind that rock and not going over to help 'em.

When I left 'Nam I had a bit of a morphine habit. I sneaked fifty-six Syrettes back with me. I got stationed here in San Francisco, at Hunters Point Naval Shipyard. Less than two weeks after I got back, they had a big antiwar march. October 15, 1968. I remember joining that. And I remember walking and hearing people speaking from the podium. All I heard was "Killers! Killers! Killers!" At that moment the peace movement turned me off. Bitterly off. It wasn't until Kent State and Cambodia that I decided I had to do something.

After that march I went and threw the Syrettes in the ocean. I never did morphine again. But I had incredible nightmares. There's one that always comes back when I get really depressed. I'm in combat. I reach in my medic bag to pull out a battle dressing. And as I open the battle dressing, it starts to turn into a body bag.

JAMES HAGENZEIKER

He was born in 1947 and grew up in New Jersey. His Dutch-boy good looks—blond hair and mustache, muscular arms, trim frame—come from his father, an immigrant who worked for Holland America Line. He lives on Manhattan's East Side, where he works as a technician in a medical research lab. The apartment has little furniture or decoration—a TV and a stereo, lots of records, and a big fish tank crowded with plants and rocks but almost no fish, "because my biochemist roommate kills them by giving them too much food."

In 1967, "the draft board was hot on my case. I started looking at this army enlistment program where they would guarantee you whatever you wanted to do. When I finally got my draft notice I went down to the army recruiter. They showed me a big book with all these jobs. You could be a land-mine deactivator. There was a two-week course for being a nuclear-warhead disarmer. I wanted to pick something safe. I figured they'd never send a surgeon into a combat zone, so I thought the next best thing was to be a surgical assistant. I enlisted for that. I got to Vietnam in '68, about a month after they had that great big Tet offensive."

They assigned me temporarily to the Eighth Field Hospital in Nha Trang, the 44th Medical Brigade. Oh, God, I liked that place. It was very secure. I was working an eight-hour shift, and in the afternoon, everybody would go to the beach. You lay on the beach and the mamasans came around and sold pineapples and bananas and Coca-Cola. The army issued you a field mattress that was perfect for surfing. There were permanent wooden hootches with electricity, so guys had fans and refrigerators. There was a PX and an NCO club. One guy there would get drunk in his hootch on martinis every night. He had his own little refrigerator with the mixers, and he had the olives and the martini glasses and everything.

I was there about a week. They put me on a surgical ward, a big sixty-bed ward. I was working at night. It was me and a nurse. While I was on that ward I had a guy die on me. It was my first emotional shock. He was an ARVN soldier. He had frag wounds or something in the leg. He had surgery that day and he came back and got sick on the anesthesia. He had vomited and aspirated it, but I didn't know that. I went back there and the guy was making all kinds of commotion. I couldn't figure out what was wrong with him so I went to get the nurse. She was reading a book so she didn't want to come. She kept telling me to go back and take the guy's vital signs. I tried to, but the guy kept jumping all around while I was trying to take his blood pressure. He was talking but I couldn't understand him. The whole wing was full of Vietnamese soldiers, and they were all trying to tell me what was wrong with him. He was going, "*Uhhhhh, uhhhhh, uhhhhh,*" and motioning to his throat, but I couldn't really tell. The only way you can tell what's wrong with somebody is if they're lying there and you count the respirations or you take the pulse, but the guy was flipping all around and I couldn't.

So I went back and told the nurse, "You better come look at this guy, he's acting really weird." She says, "Oh, okay." Now the guy is standing on his bed and he's holding his dick like he's going to pee on the floor. I said, "Oh, that's what's going on, he's got to go." I ran to get a basin so he wouldn't urinate over the side of the bedstand. When I got back the guy was flat out on the bed. I still don't know why he was holding his dick, I never could figure that out. So now the nurse is getting upset. She says, "Go find the doctor." I ran the equivalent of about three city blocks to find the doctor, who's over in intensive care in a separate building. By the time we came back the guy was in respiratory arrest. The doctor's going, "Holy shit, go get the respirator." I get it and the respirator doesn't have a mask. Now the doctor is pissed off and he says, "Go find me another one." I have to run across the street to the other ward to get their respiratory equipment, and by the time I get back the doctor is giving mouth-to-mouth resuscitation to this guy. And they're doing cardiac massage. My eyes are like—I'm saying, "Holy shit, what's going on, this guy didn't have anything wrong with him." The next thing I know the doctor turns around and says, "Well, this fucking guy's dead." He was pissed off and he walked out. He was mostly pissed off at the nurse, because she was responsible for the equipment, and overall she was responsible. He asked her what took her so long to come and find out what was wrong with the guy, and she said, "Well, I didn't think it was anything serious." He felt she was negligent. But I felt that we both screwed up. I felt stupid. Here's a guy who goes just like that, and it was something pretty basic.

Then I had to put him in a shroud. You tie the hands together, tie the feet together, take the penis and tie a piece of cord around it real tight. Because everything goes, they lose their muscle control, and if there's urine there he'll urinate all over everything. So you tie it off like it was a hose. You take cotton and stuff it down his throat. Take cotton and stuff it up the nose. Stuff cotton in the anus, because immediately they start to ferment, to bloat out. Then you put them in a sheet, and you have to wrap them up real tight so they can't flop around. There's a certain way of putting it all together. That was my first really big traumatic thing. That wasn't funny at all.

We had this other guy in the recovery room who had a frag wound in his stomach. One of my jobs was to go and clean it out. You'd pour peroxide in there and let it fizz, then you'd squirt it out with water to get all the peroxide out and wash it a little bit. Then you'd put a new bandage on it and tape it up. I went through this for a couple of days, and one day after I got finished I caught the guy sticking his finger in there. This is when I was still naive about the whole thing. I said, "What are you doing? This is stupid. If you keep sticking your finger in there, you'll get an infection." He says to me, "Yeah, I know. I've been in this hospital with this infection for a month and they can't cure it. If I stay in here another couple of weeks, I'll be excused from combat duty." His company had a policy where they wouldn't send you back into combat if you were really short. Every day I'd finish doing all this stuff and I'd say, "Okay, go ahead." He'd stick his finger in there and then I'd put the bandage on and tape it up. It was absurd, the whole procedure. I shouldn't even have bothered. But I did my job and he satisfied himself.

Then I was sent to the 22nd Surg, a MUST unit—Medical Unit, Self-Transportable. This was in Phu Bai. There was a big cemetery there. The Vietnamese cemeteries were much different from ours. They made these big round plots and they'd bury families in there. It turned out that the tent me and these other guys were living in was right next door to one of these things, and we actually dug our bunker in a grave. We didn't know it was a grave when we dug the bunker there. We didn't dig up anybody.

The surgical part of a MUST unit was these collapsible metal boxes. The sides folded out and up and the ceiling folded down. They opened up into a tiny little room. They were made out of some kind of light metal so they were easily transportable. They weren't any protection from bullets or anything. So essentially you were standing in the open when you were operating, and sometimes you didn't know what was going on outside, whether the explosions you heard were incoming or outgoing. And you couldn't say, "Well, screw the guy on the table, I'll get down on the floor until this is over." I remember one night we were doing this guy who had multiple frag wounds of the intestines. We started this laparotomy on the guy and we wound up having a mortar attack. I was scrub on the case and I had on a flak jacket and a helmet and a surgical gown and gloves and mask. The surgeon, too. Everybody was crawling around on the floor, including the anesthesiologist. He was sitting on a stool on the floor, squeezing the bag. Every time a mortar would come, the little bottles would bounce off the shelf. Me and the surgeon were shitting bullets. It was weird, you're in this little aluminum box and you don't know if the whole place is being blown away outside or if the shells are falling 200 yards away. We fixed all these little holes in the guy, sewed him up, and I thought it was a pretty admirable job under the circumstances.

I was a surgical technician. It was very different from what we had done in the States. There we more or less followed the protocol of a civilian hospital, just pass a lot of instruments to the surgeon, hold the clamps, stuff like that. In Phu Bai the first case I scrubbed on was a guy who got fragged in the leg and the back. When somebody has a traumatic injury, where the projectile goes through, it kills tissue around the entrance and exit wounds. So you do a procedure called debridement to cut away all the dead tissue so the rest of the stuff can heal up. We had these debridement kits. They had three clamps and a pair of forceps and a scissors, and that was it. I had been used to working with a surgeon with 200 different instruments.

The surgeon was starting the debridement. I handed him the forceps and the scissors and he handed them back to me. He says, "Here, you do the ass and I'll do the leg." I just looked at him—like, what are you talking about, I'm not a surgeon. I said, "I don't know how to do this," and he said, "What's the matter, don't they send you guys to a dog lab or something?" I said no. He said, "Well, this is as good as a dog lab here. Here's what you do. You take the forceps and you pull on the tissue. If it moves, you leave it alone. If it doesn't move, cut it off. Go ahead, you do the ass and I'll do the leg. Try not to cut anything that looks like a nerve or an artery. Pull on the stuff, and if it snaps back it's probably an artery. The nerves are these white-looking things. Don't cut them if you can help it." He knew that the ass is mostly a giant muscle, so there's not too many nerves or arteries that you can get yourself in serious trouble with. That was my first case.

We did that kind of stuff 90 percent of the time, all day, all night, these debridements. Most of the wounds that we saw were mortar wounds. We wouldn't even sew them back up. We'd debride out all the dead tissue, pack the wound with dressings, and send them down someplace south in a day or two. We'd never see these guys again and we wouldn't know the outcome of the injury. We'd debride an arm or a leg and we'd never know whether they'd eventually lose the arm or have reconstructive surgery or whatever. We did whatever was necessary to save life and limb and tissue. Real primitive stuff. We did laparotomies and bowel dissections. We did no head work, no eyeballs. Anything in the head we'd ship right out in a helicopter to one of those hospital ships where they had a special setup for doing neurosurgery.

The technicians did a lot of surgery. Of course we didn't do any bowel work. They wouldn't let us go into a joint. But we would do all the superficial debridement, the muscles. And of course we'd do a lot of amputations. You can't screw that up because the thing is gone. You just put the tourniquet around the limb, take a knife and cut through the skin and muscle until you get to the bone, and you take a bone saw and just saw it off. It's like working in a butcher shop. After the limb is sawed off, you clamp off the major arteries that are left in the stump, put a suture through them, and tie them off. It's a very simple procedure that takes about ten minutes. We hadn't been trained to do anything on this scale, so the orthopedic surgeons would teach us as they did things. If we were working on a leg, they'd say, "Okay, this is such-and-such a muscle, and this is such-and-such, and usually the main artery runs underneath the bone through here and behind this muscle." I learned a tremendous amount of anatomy and physiology. They'd teach us how to watch out so we didn't cut veins and arteries. The body is pretty ingeniously designed so all that stuff is in an area where it's protected. Like in the leg the arteries usually run very close to the bone and deep inside, so you really have to be doing extensive work to cut any of that stuff.

One time I cut a nerve on this one guy from the 101st Airborne. This is funny, because at the time I felt really upset about it. The surgeon said to me, "Don't worry about it, it's just a superficial nerve." I met the guy later on when I went back to Nha Trang, and he told me that from the surgical procedure he wound up with his toe and part of his foot being numb. So he got out of being in combat. He was very grateful that I cut his nerve. It was lucky for him that it wasn't anything serious. I'm sure he collected disability, too, though it didn't really disable him. He was happy about the whole thing, so I felt no more guilt.

Another thing we did was a lot of circumcisions. The guys would get a couple of weeks off from duty for that, so when we didn't have a lot of casualties we'd have a whole row of guys who'd just had circumcisions. I guess they benefited from it. It's cleaner, and some doctors say that statistically your wife is less susceptible to cancer if you're circumcised. They'd come in and say, "I want a circumcision," and even if they didn't need it the surgeon would say, "Oh, yeah, you need a circumcision for sure," and put down whatever the technical name is for an inflamed foreskin. The surgeon didn't care, he knew what the score was. And then if the other guys in the combat unit noticed that Fred went and got a circumcision and he's been gone two weeks, they would say, "I'll go, too." The only guys that didn't luck out were the ones that were already circumcised.

It sounds really weird, but I kind of enjoyed being there. At the time I was very into medicine, and I loved the surgery. The camaraderie was great. And somehow or other all of us managed to remove ourselves from the reality of the situation. I had some guilt or anxiety as I realized what the whole ordeal was like, that people were really getting chewed up. I felt grateful that I wasn't out there with the guys. And one of the things that helped buffer the shock was that we didn't see these guys after we finished with them. Depending on how seriously injured they were, they were shipped out the same night or the next day. As far as we knew, we saved almost everybody's life, or saved their limbs. We didn't see a guy two years down the road with the arthritic knee, or the guy that wound up losing his arm. I was so naive that I thought we did a great job and these guys lived happily ever after. It didn't occur to me that most of these guys were in for lifelong disabilities, complication upon complication.

For example, a blast impaction. If you got very close to a mortar round that went off, besides the fragments from the mortar itself the explosion picks up all the dirt and dust and sticks and stones in the area and blows it right through the skin. What you have to do is take a knife and cut the whole length of the leg, cut open the fascia, and dig in there with your finger to get out the globs of mud. The fascia is the layer that covers the muscle, it's a real strong connective tissue. But a lot of the stuff you couldn't even get out. These guys would have gravel embedded right through the skin, and most of the time it would wind up under the fascia. You'd try to get out the biggest chunks. I'm sure that for years the body's going to be rejecting that crap through the skin. Some of it probably won't go through and would cause all kinds of adhesions. God knows what kind of complications you'd get from that.

The guy who sticks in my mind the most, he got hit with an RPG round, a rocket-propelled grenade. I think he was in a Jeep. It blew off one leg at the thigh and one leg at the ankle. It took off his left arm at the shoulder, took off the tips of all his fingers on the other hand, and half of his penis. He was what you'd call a real basket case. When he came in we were all going crazy because he was bleeding all over the place and nobody thought he was going to live. Somebody put pneumatic tourniquets on both his legs, the kind you inflate, and I was trying to hold him up while they put a clean sheet on the operating table because it was all blood-soaked. Well, somebody else turned the tourniquets on before the guy was asleep. The guy reached up with his only hand that had the fingers blown off and he grabbed me by the face, because he was in so much pain that he was grabbing out for something. He was screaming bloody murder and I was screaming bloody murder because his finger bones were sticking right in my skin. Everybody was yelling and screaming, trying to get this guy intubated and put to sleep. But there was no place to stick IVs in him. Every place that you'd normally put an IV in was gone. And he was bleeding to death. The only thing they could do was vein cutdowns on his neck to stick the blood right into his neck. Later on I had to do the leg that was blown off at the thigh. I can remember grabbing those big muscles of the leg and pulling them back, and there were rocks in there and tree branches. I thought, "Holy Christ, no wonder the guy went crazy when they turned on that tourniquet." I'd pick up one great big muscle and pull it back and try to dig out as much of the dirt as I could. Everybody was expecting the guy to die and half-figuring it would be for the better. Sure as hell, the guy lived through it. The next day I saw him over in the recovery room, and he was real happy about it. "Oh boy, I'm alive."

Another case I remember was a guy that died. He came in and he was shot right through the aorta and the vena cava, the main artery and the main vein of the heart. That he was still alive was pretty phenomenal. This guy came in fully conscious, and he was freaking out. I didn't think he was going to die. By that time I thought that once somebody got to the OR, we could save him. I thought we were miracle workers. He was thrashing all around going, "Oh, my God, I'm going to die! Holy shit! This is it!" We couldn't get the IVs in him for a while. I said to him, "Listen, man, you've got to calm down, you're okay, you won't die, we're going to take care of everything here, don't worry about it." The incredible thing is that I believed this myself. When the guy finally died—I think it was the first guy I ever saw die on the table—I was so totally shocked that it shook my confidence tremendously. I think I even cried. But I tried to fight it back because it wasn't cool to cry.

After that I saw more. You don't normally see people die on the operating table, but in Vietnam they did. They died from shock, mostly. They'd bleed so much that all of a sudden the shock would make the capillaries start to bleed, and the blood would coagulate and they'd lose pressure. I remember one guy who came in after some kind of mortar fragment went into his armpit area. He was in the pre-op ward and he was really happy because he figured he'd have this thing fixed and then he'd be out of it because he'd be going home. He was real short. He even wrote his wife a letter, told her what happened, that he was in the hospital and they were going to operate and he'd probably be home in a month or two. He gave the letter to an orderly to mail, went into the OR, and he died. I don't even know if they figured out what he died from. I guess it was from shock. They couldn't control the bleeding. They went all over the place trying to find out what the hell he was bleeding from, but it was a real complicated area and the more they went looking around the more he would bleed.

Another guy was shot in the femoral artery in the leg. We saw a lot of those, and they didn't normally die. I started off on the case and I went to get something for supper. When I came back to the OR they had his stomach open, these great big clamps were on the aorta where it bifurcates into the leg, and they couldn't control his bleeding. That guy bled to death, too. Other guys would come in and there wasn't too much hope of saving them. Guys with multiple vascular wounds would die. Sometimes the bullets would bounce all around inside, pick up a couple of major arteries, and if enough arteries are severed, then no matter how good or how fast you are, the guy would bleed to death.

The most upsetting night was when we got this bunch of guys who had been out on a search-and-destroy mission. They ambushed a bunch of Viet Cong coming down a trail and wiped them out. They had a new guy along, and this guy was dying to throw a hand grenade. He'd never thrown one in combat, so he kept whining to the lieutenant to let him do it. So the lieutenant says, "Okay, what the fuck, we've already given away our position, it can't hurt to chuck one out there. If there's anybody still alive it'll kill them." The new guy pulls the pin on the grenade and drops it in the dark. It went off and messed up about six guys really bad. On top of that we got a couple of other guys from some big offensive in the A Shau valley. That was one of the nights when we were working frantically. We had garden hoses in the OR, and when we'd finish a case we'd just wash everything down with garden hoses, hose it all right out the door. Blood and meat and dirt and sand, right out the door.

Toward the morning we had this great big plastic bag full of arms and legs and stuff. We always had a big hassle about who would have to bury the arms and legs, because Graves Registration would take the bodies but they wouldn't take parts of bodies. Nobody wanted to bury the stuff because it was manual labor, you had to go out with a shovel and dig a deep enough hole to bury it. When you got off after working all night you didn't want to go out and work for another hour in the heat digging holes. So there was this big hassle when we got done at night about who would bury the stuff, the day crew or the night crew. Well, I was running through one of the other ORs, and I said to my friend Rich, "Listen, man, just save all your arms and legs for the day crew." He turned around and said to me, "Y'know, we're really getting fucked up with this shit. Just think of what you're saying." I started to think about it, and I realized, Holy shit, yeah, this is really strange. Here I'm thinking nothing of it and I've got this great big plastic bag full of arms and legs and hands and fingers.

Later I went out to bury it myself. It was morning and I was sitting around on a log. I had a shovel and this bag of stuff. The mailman, this hippy-dippy mailman, was sitting out there smoking a joint. He said to me, "What do you have in the bag?" I said, "Arms and legs." He didn't believe me. He said, "Oh, bullshit." I said, "Here, look." He looked in the bag and it flipped him right out. He took off. He couldn't believe that there I was, bullshitting about the weather, and there was this horror story in the bag.

The marines used to pick up our laundry. In surgery you drape everything with sheets and towels and stuff. Sometimes it would get so busy that we'd pick up a big wad of sheets and throw it in the laundry hamper and it would have something in it like a finger or an arm or a hand. It wasn't because we were morbid, it was just a hectic situation. The marines used to get really pissed off when we'd leave this stuff in the laundry. They had all these Vietnamese that they hired to do the wash and the ironing. One time a marine guy comes and says, "This Vietnamese woman quit on us because she's sitting there watching the dryer and there's a hand flipping around past the window." Or else they'd get these towels and flip them out and a finger would fall out, washed and everything. Another time a guy came to pick up the linen for the marines and he backed the truck up to the door with the tailgate open. He went in, and in the meantime a guy came out with a leg he had to bury. He put the leg on the tailgate of the truck and went to find a shovel. The marine came out and saw the leg sitting there on his tailgate, and he thought the guy tried to throw it in the truck. He got so pissed off that he opened the door of the OR and threw the leg in at us, and he said, "You guys think you're fucking funny with this leg, shove this up your ass." Then we had a big hassle with the marines to get them to do our laundry anymore.

DR. DENNIS GREENBAUM

When we talk, he is in charge of the emergency room at St. Vincent's Hospital in New York City. We meet in a small examining room near his office. He is wearing a white hospital smock over a shirt and tie. For a year, starting in August 1970, he worked in the small medical station at LZ English, the headquarters of the 173rd Airborne in Vietnam. While there he wrote hundreds of letters, took thousands of photographs, and kept a kind of diary about things that bothered him in the army medical apparatus. "I've probably got two thousand slides. I tried to document everything. I'm very compulsive that way. Even the way the slides would fit into a letter; you could fit three rows of two slides each very nicely in the envelope. I wrote to my fiancée every day, and I'd send six slides in every letter. There was nothing else to do there."

The hospitals were in pretty remote areas—remote from the war, that is. And we gathered that the NVA and VC pretty much respected hospitals. Either that, or the hospitals were so well protected that they were rarely hit. So a doctor's life over there was pretty good. The salary was certainly competitive with training salaries. I understand that one doctor was killed while I was there or soon after I left. But during that same time I knew of two doctors who had been in my class who were killed in the States. So the mortality rate was higher outside the military. [Laughs.]

We had seven professionals in my unit, five physicians and two dentists. There was no need for seven of us to be there. No need at all. We did a lot of pacification work with the civilians. And the dentists, if one-quarter of their time was devoted to GIs, that was a lot. Most of their time was spent with the Vietnamese. And of the remaining five of us, they could have easily gotten along with three. The bulk of what we did was sick call and nonwar-type injuries—car accidents, overdoses, VD. We had sick call every day twice a day, in the morning and in the afternoon. One of us was officially on call to handle all the casualties that came in at night. But where was everybody else going to go? I mean, nobody was going out to the movies. So in fact everybody was available if there was any trouble.

To tell the truth, there might be twenty people on sick call all day, and one guy was really all that was needed. In the morning, sick call was a little heavier, and two of us would be there. In the afternoon just one of us. You'd work two days out of every five, and on one of those you'd just help the other guy. It was a tremendous waste of people.

Our hospital was a twenty-six-bed clearing station. Now, military medicine in a war zone is put together on the basis of a FEBA, the forward edge of the battle area. That's where the guys get shot. The two forward edges of the opposing FEBAs go toward each other until they get very close, and then the guy with more guns and troops knocks the other guy out and the other guy falls back. The first medical interventions occur right on the FEBA, usually by medics. But in a guerrilla war there is no FEBA. We were built for a FEBA, and there wasn't one. So in some cases, all the clearing station did was delay definitive treatment. The helicopter would go out to pick up a casualty, and their protocol was to bring that casualty to the clearing station. The mistake was that sometimes they did that instead of taking the casualty to the evacuation hospital, which was only thirty minutes away. Most of the time these guys were smart enough to know which casualties could be taken straight back. The only guys they would bring to us were the ones that were dying and couldn't make it through that thirty minutes. We would do basic resuscitation, and the chopper would wait on the pad until we finished. We'd stabilize the patient and generally go with him on the chopper back to the hospital. So in most cases the only casualties we'd see were guys who happened to get hit right around us, and hit too badly to make the trip. That's why we didn't have much to do.

The problem was they hadn't changed the Table of Organization and Equipment since the Korean War. That meant the equipment we had wasn't up-to-date either. Not long after I got to Vietnam I got a letter from the director of medicine at St. Vincent's, where I had been doing my internship. The people at St. Vincent's are a close-knit group, so this guy wrote to say hello and see how I was. I wrote back describing the situation, that we were the primary group responsible for resuscitation of some major casualties, and that our equipment was terribly outmoded, terribly. If you compare our capabilities with the Yom Kippur War in Israel, the difference is unbelievable. In Israel the physicians went up to the front lines. They would intubate patients, they would support respiration, and they would give transfusions within thirty seconds of the guy being hit by a bullet. They carried bottles of plasma and they had laryngoscopes and endotracheal tubes and manual resuscitation bags. In our clearing station we didn't have proper endotracheal tubes. We didn't even have monitoring equipment—no EKG machine. I mentioned that to the St. Vincent's director, and he wrote to me, "I read your letter to the hospital staff, and we were appalled at the conditions under which you're expected to work. Therefore we have arranged with the Lumiscope Co. in Tokyo to send you monitoring equipment." So we got the equipment that way: The hospital made the contact and the manufacturer donated it. Well, the machine arrived and our company commander went down to Tan Son Nhut to pick it up, and the Vietnamese asked him for a thirty-dollar import tax. Can you imagine?

I was also disturbed by the capabilities of the physicians there. In the evac hospitals most of them were very well trained, and you had a full spectrum of doctors the way you do in a civilian hospital. There were a few GMOs, general medical officers, and a few people on the junior resident level, and then a number of people at higher levels—fully trained neurosurgeons, general surgeons, and people with experience in trauma. But very often the doctors at clearing stations were only GMOs. There might be one senior person who was assigned to handle more serious problems. This would generally be an internist. But to give you an idea of how things were: We were a medical company in support of a brigade. In addition to us, there was a brigade medical commander with the rank of major. His function was to supervise all the medical activities at the brigade. Well, after three months this major was kicked out for marijuana use. That's irrelevant, because we can assume that was pretty unusual. The thing that was characteristic of the military was how he got his job. I don't know what kind of military experience he had. Maybe a lot, but I doubt it. And before that, this guy was running a fat farm. He was pushing diet pills to fat people. So the highest-ranking medical officer in our brigade was this major whose entire experience was running a fat farm. That was not the appropriate choice. And the next-highest rank was a captain who had the same training I did, which was a year of straight medical internship and one year of residency. He was two years out of medical school. And we were handling all these casualties. We were taking care of our own GIs, and they deserved better than that.

I remember the chest wounds. Here was I, with no surgical experience, operating on some guy's chest, which in civilian practice is done by the most senior of surgeons. With no experience and no time to prepare a scrub for operating, I'd have to go in and isolate where the bleeding was, put in chest tubes, and actually do the operation, because there was nobody at the clearing station more qualified than me. There were people at the evacuation hospital, but that was sixty miles away.

We did some interesting stuff that was tricky, even though we tried not to get in over our heads. I remember one guy who was shot in the femoral artery and had a huge bleed. What we did was isolate the artery and tie a big suture-ligature around it, and brought the ligature out to the skin, and just ligated it enough to prevent further bleeding. Then we went back to the evacuation hospital with him, notifying them by radio that this guy needed to go right to the operating room. That was one case where the clearing station was probably life-saving, because by stopping the bleeding we gave him the chance to make that sixty-mile trip.

The ARVN troops had the lowest priority for treatment on the list of all the casualties you could get. The highest was any U.S. person. The second-highest was a U.S. dog from the canine corps. The third was NVA. The fourth was VC. And the fifth was ARVN, because they had no particular value. The only thing below them was the civilians. I gathered that these were standard military priorities. Except I wasn't really told about the dogs until we started getting them. That was kind of an afterthought. The first dog came in and I said, "What the hell are we supposed to do with this?" Somebody said, "Oh, yeah, the dogs, they're top priority, just like U.S." My reaction was, Okay, who cares? I mean, nobody else was coming in at the same time, and it wasn't like choosing the dog versus an ARVN. And the dogs, as we were reminded many times by our dog colleagues, were there to do their job in the American military. There was a very strong relationship between dog and man. These dogs could not be retrained to a new master. If the master is killed or goes home, the dog is shot, and that's about $10,000 worth of training. It wasn't really fair, because they didn't shoot the master if the dog died. [Laughs.]

I remember one guy brought in a dog that had been fragged by a grenade. He had one small injury, but it had lacerated his renal artery and he was bleeding internally. We had no real means of operating, so we sent the dog down to the 77th Evac in Qui Nhon, where there was a veterinary section. But we told this guy the dog needed blood, and he said, "Well, you're going to have to give him human blood." We said, "That's ridiculous, you don't give a dog human blood." So he reported us because we were not maintaining the dog's proper priority, since the dog had the same priority as a U.S. troop. What he didn't understand is that the dog would have a reaction if you gave it human blood. Nothing came of him reporting us, but he was upset that we wouldn't give blood to his dog. What they did in Qui Nhon was pull in a dog off the street and transfuse the dog right away from the useless one.

The NVA, of course, had important information. The IGs would be called if we got wounded NVA, and we'd be asked to treat them very carefully and properly. The same was true but to a lesser extent for the VC. They weren't as highly organized, so you couldn't get any important information from them. But you could get some local information, and they were always questioned, so we did our best to keep them going. I had a friend who was in one of the smaller outlying landing zones, and he went out on a chopper to an area where some American soldiers had wounded a number of NVA. They asked him to maintain the NVA while they were being questioned, since these guys were too sick to be brought into the clearing station. He did that, and when it was over and he had all these IVs going and he had resuscitated them, the GIs said to him, "Okay, that's all we need, thanks very much. Take the IVs out now." He said, "C'mon, how can we do that? These guys are still alive." "Well, they're NVA, and we got all the information we needed." And he stopped the IVs. I haven't spoken to him very often in the last ten years, but I can tell you he talks about it every time. It's bothering him. But what was he going to do? He was brought there by helicopter in the middle of the night, he had no idea where he was, and they were all going back in the helicopter. Is he going to say, "No, I'm staying here with them. Send out Florence Nightingale"?

Actually, the priorities made military sense. You're not really there in a civilian ethic. Your function is not to be a doctor in the sense that you're providing care to humanity. And this case with the NVA was an exception. I'm sure they would have died anyway, and if they had been in better shape they would have been taken back. Usually, the NVA received humane treatment medically. And in a situation where you have limited resources, and you're told that American colleagues come first, and then the enemy, for the following reasons, I think that makes sense. They don't say that if you have an ARVN who might survive versus an NVA who absolutely won't, that you have to treat the NVA first. But within the general realm of things those were the priorities. And it affected everything. If the weather was bad and the choppers shouldn't fly, they would certainly go out and pick up a GI. They might go out and pick up an NVA. But they wouldn't go out in bad weather to pick up an ARVN. And they shouldn't. But I don't think the medical priority list ever affected anybody's chances of survival. Yes, there were times when we would choose, but you were always going to do the GI first. That was obvious. You didn't need to be told about that. I mean, those guys were talking to us in English.

DR. JOHN TALBOTT

He is a psychiatrist and professor in New York City. We talk in his pleasantly messy office—piles of papers tucked in corners, graph paper taped to the wall—with him behind his desk, eating lunch: yogurt and a peach. He is tall, thin, forty-seven, with brown hair streaked with gray, and a beard. He is wearing a white shirt, striped tie, khaki slacks, and Wallabees.

In 1966, a year after finishing his residency in psychiatry, he was drafted. "I worked very hard not to get drafted, and I was against the war from the start. I've always been pretty left-wing. So I tried to use as much influence as I could. I wrote letters. I tried to get people at the university to say that I was teaching in a particularly critical area. Didn't work.

"Then I tried to get posted where I would not be vulnerable to going to Vietnam. Rather than taking a cushy job in California or someplace, I went to Fort Bragg, North Carolina, where I figured I was moderately safe. Often the payoff for a cushy job was that you spent one year there and one year in Vietnam. If it was that versus two years in the swamps of North Carolina, I would rather spend two years in the swamps.

"But after a year at Fort Bragg I got my orders for Vietnam. They came out of the blue. My wife and I didn't expect it. I don't know why we were so naive, but it just blew us away. We considered moving to Canada but decided not to. What I did was plunge into learning Vietnamese. Also, I got scared. I had never taken my rifle training, and I thought I should learn how to fire an M-16. I was the only psychiatrist on the base doing a lot of work with units out in the field, so it was easy: I picked a unit and said, 'Listen, I want to come out and practice on the rifle range every day at lunchtime.' I got pretty good."

I can remember arriving like it was yesterday. Setting down at Bien Hoa and feeling that rush of hot air as the plane filled. We came in during a period when they were afraid there'd be shelling. There was a line of guys underneath protective buildings, and as we got off, they ran on. No refueling, no nothing. And off the plane went again.

The whole procedure took twenty, thirty minutes. This was in April of '67.

I remember going through the streets of Saigon in a bus with chicken wire on the outside. I was overwhelmed by the heat and the stench and the people all over. A lot of people. And I remember being struck by the disparity between people at the front and in the rear. There was a rear not because of distance, but because of attitudes and levels of command and amenities. Guys a mile away could be living in ditches, versus having a golf course and a swimming pool and a refrigerator full of ice cream. It was bizarre to see guys coming out of the field with flak jackets and grenades and bandoliers and powder burns, next to guys with their golf clubs. You'd go to the PX and see guys straight in from the field alongside guys picking up their steaks.

And the poverty of the Vietnamese. I don't mean just economic poverty; there was a sense of impoverishment, emotional drain, resentment, a combination of anger and depression and apathy and "Screw you, Charlie." The Americans seemed well equipped and moderately okay. They'd be leaving in a year, maybe dead but maybe alive. The Vietnamese seemed mired in it. I had done some research before I went over, and I realized that the line between North and South Vietnam was drawn for the first time in something like 1355. Bizarre. It's 1967, and we're dealing with the same DMZ they had in the fourteenth century. The line drawn back in those times was something like a mile from the new one. And the issues were the same: the rice bowl in the South and the industry in the North, along with different sets of values. Crazy.

When I arrived I was depressed. It was a shock, even though I'd prepared for it. The first thing that happened was that I found my commanding officer in his bed. He was depressed, too. This was the head of psychiatry. I arrived and a kid from Brooklyn picked me up. Not a kid, a guy. He was very nice. He took me around showing me various things—the hootch where I'd be staying, the clinic—and then he said, "Let's go meet the CO." I said okay. So we went around the corner and here's this guy lying in bed, blanket up over his head. It was ten or eleven in the morning, maybe noon. I said, "Hello, sir, Captain Talbott reporting for duty, sir." He just rolled over. I don't think I saw him more than a day or two after that. He probably had a month or two left on his tour, but he was a basket case. He was a casualty. This was my boss, lying in bed. I thought, Shit, I'm going to wind up like that. And the funny thing was that no one treated him. They just protected him. They were marvelous in protecting people. I think the feeling was, Well, what the fuck, he's going to get out anyway, and we'll just hold the fort. Once he gets back to the States he'll straighten out. I think he had found out his wife was fooling around with somebody. That was the crowning blow, but that was just one of many.

Nobody there liked the war much. Not necessarily for political reasons, but for personal and economic ones. We didn't want to be there. But the doctors were mostly antiwar. I remember antiwar posters on people's lockers, like pinups. Of course, our unit wasn't typical of the U.S. Army in Vietnam. Even the enlisted men we had in the psychiatric group tended to be very smart, college dropouts with psychology and sociology majors. We talked about the war incessantly and passed around books. People were reading Bernard Fall. One guy was very right-wing. He believed it was a just war, and we should win it, bomb the shit out of them. I couldn't believe that. There were some others who were at least laissez-faire about the war. When I got there I expected to get into arguments, but the amazing thing was you could say in the mess hall, "Jesus Christ, Lyndon Johnson is an asshole," and you wouldn't get an argument. I remember listening to Johnson's speech when he said he wouldn't run again. I heard it on Armed Forces Radio up in my office. He said, "I will not seek election or the nomination of my party," and in the hospital this cheer went up. I went out the door and there were corpsmen and doctors yelling their lungs out. They thought the war was over, that Johnson had admitted he was wrong. That was a tremendous moment.

In the army training, they start off the lectures by saying, "The purpose of the Army Medical Corps is to maintain the fighting force." So you learn from the start that your purpose is not to help people grow or feel better about themselves, your purpose is to allow them to fight the best they can. In the beginning I thought, "Shit, I'm going to be sending poor slobs back in to fight." Well, that didn't happen. What I found myself doing was much the same thing as in the army back in the States. The same marital troubles that were present at Fort Bragg were present in Vietnam. The amazing thing was that even though these guys were separated from their wives and families, I'm not convinced there was a higher rate of marital problems. Guys living with their wives had problems back at Fort Bragg, and guys separated from their wives had problems with their wives fooling around. Yes, I saw some combat reactions, but the day-to-day clinic activity tended not to be people cracking under the strain of war. If anything, the psychiatric casualty rate in Vietnam was very, very low, the lowest of any war ever. I expected I was going to see a whole new world of psychiatry when I went to Vietnam, but I didn't. I had a couple of guys come in saying, "If you don't send me back home I'm going to go crazy." They'd usually be threatening. And you'd say, "Okay, go crazy." They were not really crazy. They were Klingers. They wanted to get out. But for the most part, the boring, stupid thing about being a psychiatrist in Vietnam was that you weren't really doing combat psychiatry. If there was a way to do your work by telephone, you could have gone back to your wife and kids.

One interesting thing I did work on was problems that affected whole units. Oftentimes they would come to our attention through a dispensary doctor in the field, usually a guy just out of medical school with a year of internship. He'd call up and say, "It's funny, everyone over here is developing high blood pressure. Can you come take a look and tell me what the hell's going on?"

You'd have the dispensary doctor talk to the commanding officer first. Then you'd go to the CO yourself and tell him he's got a medical problem. Would it be okay to poke around a little bit? He'd say, "Sure." And then you start talking to people. We had one case with a transportation unit where the guys were getting shot. Why was this one company getting shot up and not other ones? We found out they had a gung-ho sergeant who would do chickenshit stuff. These guys would drive at night all the way to Duc Tho and come back down with vegetables in refrigerated trucks. Well, they got short-staffed for some reason. They used to drive with a man riding shotgun, so first they took the shotgun guy away. The drivers reacted a little bit to that, but not a hell of a lot. Remember, these guys are driving all night. Then the sergeant came in and said, "You've gotta clean up your areas during the daytime, you've gotta get out and march." It was bullshit. They began to develop symptoms. I don't remember whether it was headaches or ulcers or what. I went next door to another transportation company that wasn't having this problem and I said, "How do you do it?" "Well, we make sure there's a shotgun on at least the first and last truck in the convoy. We put a heavy gun on there. And when these guys get done with four days of driving, they get thirty-six hours to sleep." They didn't harass the guys during the day and make them do calisthenics. So I went back to the CO and I said, "Look, I examined two of your units. They've got the same staffing problems. You've got an uptight sergeant here who's causing the men trouble and it's not working. You've got a choice of either having these guys crack up and be in the dispensary all the time, or getting rid of that sergeant." He got rid of the sergeant.

It wasn't always so clear-cut. We had another situation where guys refused to take their malaria pills. They thought they could get out of combat that way. In that area of the north, malaria was rampant. Their officers' first reaction was to say, "Okay, if you don't take your pills, we'll court-martial you." These guys were saying, "Forget it, we're gonna get killed anyway. That's no threat. Put us in the brig? Terrific, we love it." So we went up there and talked about some of the consequences of malaria that aren't so nice. Cerebral malaria—being delirious and losing part of your brain is something that scares the piss out of people. It's okay to threaten your liver a little bit or have some bugs floating around in your blood, but talking about going nutso for a long period of time is something else. I don't think we used scare tactics, but we said, "Look, you should know if you do this, there could be consequences."

I also ran into some really weird civilians. I kept seeing guys who were working for these construction companies. I'd see them for alcoholism, sometimes for drug abuse. They'd be shooting up or they'd run a bulldozer into an officer's house, and the police would take them off to the pokey. They'd call me up and I'd go see the guy and take a history on him. Now, after a while I'm beginning to get a composite. I'm beginning to get a sense that there's a whole bunch of people over there who haven't been home for twenty years. Some of them are married. Their wives live in Indiana, California. They have kids, maybe. I'd say, "Why are you here?" "Big money. No taxes, get double time for all the stuff we do, overruns." "What do you do?" "Drink." "When were you home last?" "For Christmas." "How long?" "One day." "Didn't the company give you more time off?" "Oh, yeah, but when I get time off I go to Singapore." Some of them I'd run into in bars, or at the officers' club. In Saigon you had a lot of them—some of the career diplomats, some CIA people. All sorts of them.

I gradually developed the sense that there was this whole fringe or frontier population out there, people who couldn't make it in mainstream America pushing a bulldozer. But they could push that same bulldozer abroad. You took a history: "Where were you before Vietnam?" "Indonesia." "Where were you before Indonesia?" "Malaya." "Where were you before that?" "Korea." You could trace the trouble spots of the world, and they were there. Working for one construction company or another, on government contracts, all highly paid, highly skilled. They were more comfortable living these isolated lives away from their wives and families, drinking a lot. They weren't patriotic. They weren't there because we were going to win the war and they were supporting our boys. The reason they gave was usually money. But when you got underneath that, what you found was a strong need to stay away. Probably the frontiersmen were like these guys. They didn't like Kansas City, and that's why they went out to where the Indians were shooting. When they ran out of Indians, where did they go? They went to Indonesia, Korea. . . .

Then there were the combat reactions. Every four or five days you'd work in the emergency room. We saw only the psychiatric stuff. And there wasn't much. Occasionally it'd be the emergency-room stuff you see here: Somebody who has headaches, it's two in the morning, they're depressed and they can't sleep. But the war-related stuff tended to be combat reactions. I remember one kid came in completely blown away. He was mute, wild-eyed. What had happened was that he was out on patrol and he was on point. He had lit a cigarette. Then he dropped his lighter. He stooped down to pick up the lighter, and just at that moment a sniper shot at the light and hit the guy right in back of him. So his stupidity had caused this guy to be killed, and he was a basket case, in terrible shape.

You'd deal with kids like that in the time-honored way. There are three principles of combat psychiatry, and they go back to 1918. A doctor named Thomas Salmon, who was head of army psychiatry, went over to France and saw the difference between the French and English treatment of psychiatric casualties. The French were having no casualties and the English were having tremendous numbers. So Salmon looked at what was happening. With the English, the moment somebody was psychiatrically ill, they'd ship them back home, where they would develop war neuroses that would last for years and years. The French would keep them near the front and say, "Look, take a break, pull yourself together, and in two or three days we'll send you back to the front lines." So they had none of the guilt of bugging out. They got a rest, but it wasn't a complete reprieve. From looking at that, Salmon said there were three principles of preventive psychiatry in the army. One was immediacy: You've got to treat everything right off the bat. The second is proximity: You've got to treat it right near where it occurred. You don't evacuate people hundreds of miles away. And the third is expectancy. You say, "You will get better, and you will go back to work."

I'll give you a couple of other cases. One guy was out with a patrol and they came under fire. He froze. His lieutenant was hit. He felt he could have saved the lieutenant if he hadn't frozen and was able to fire, and also if he had been physically able to go over and bind the lieutenant's wounds. But he didn't, and the lieutenant died. Another guy was out on patrol, and he was supposed to be skilled in sweeping for booby traps. That was his job. On some unconscious level he sensed there was a booby trap, but at another level he didn't, and the thing went off. For some reason it did less damage to him than to another guy, even though the guy who tripped it should be the one who gets hurt the worst. So he had a double feeling, of having endangered himself when he knew subliminally that something was wrong, and then of having his friend hurt. He didn't know whether the friend lived or died, but he assumed he died.

Both of these patients were in bad shape when they came in. The first guy was trembling, almost inarticulate, sweating, fearful, moaning, almost like a dog. The second guy had terrible nightmares, all sorts of guilt, anxiety, panic attacks in the middle of the day. He drank to calm down.

Frequently what we'd do with these guys is just provide them some rest, good food, and two days in a reasonably secure setting, away from the stress, with the expectation that they'd go back. Sometimes I'd give them drugs—tranquilizers, Amytal. Sometimes I'd just talk to them, and I'd be able to send them back right away. Others I sent back a couple of days later. There were some we even put on a light sleep treatment—give them a sedative and have them sleep a couple of days. These guys had often been out long hours, up all night without any breaks. But the major part remains having them tell the story and connect with whatever feelings they had—being scared out of their minds, or guilty, or whatever. Sometimes we'd use hypnotic techniques, or even chemical hypnosis like pentobarbital. With the kid who came in mute—he had what's called a hysterical mutism—I was able to sit down and say, "Okay, you're going to tell me." A suggestive technique, not a real hypnotic technique. "Why don't you tell me what happened? You were out in the field. . . . " He wouldn't talk to begin with, but you could usually get the mute people to talk by a series of exercises. Get them to say "*Aaaaaaahhh*," stuff like that, and eventually talk.

The old catharsis principle is still true. I might even go so far as to play sounds of machine guns or bombs to bring the person back to it. Even if they can't remember, you try to get them to re-create the time. "First I did this, then I did this, then I did this." The principle being that burying the stuff causes symptoms, and when you unbury it and get the person to repeat it and air it, then it's no longer frightening.

The treatment was almost always effective. You tended not to ever have to evacuate those sorts of people. Sure, there were people who cracked under pressure. But those people probably had disorders that might have made them crack in this country, too. The war could be the trigger, but it would be hard to prove it was the only trigger, or that the incidence of breakdown with schizophrenia or manic-depressive disease was any higher than in the civilian population. So we didn't evacuate a heck of a lot of people, and the guys we did evacuate tended to have serious conditions like schizophrenia.

In some ways it got harder to do the work the longer I was there. In the middle of my tour I had an illness that had a profound effect on me. I got a bellyache. It turned out to be my appendix, but it was a long story because no one believed I had appendicitis. Everyone assumed that it was either psychosomatic because I was upset, or it was just the flora and fauna changing in my gut. I had diarrhea and then I had cramps, and the pain was classical, right where the appendix is. But with the appendix you're never sure. It was worse and worse and finally one day it went boom. I was operated on, and then I developed every complication in the books. I had peritonitis, and I had an abscess, and I was in bad shape. Finally I wound up being air-evacuated out.

I was in the intensive care unit for a while, with kids all around me dying. It was horrible lying in that ward. When you lie there for twenty-four hours, immobile, while all around you eighteen- and nineteen-year-old kids are screaming, moaning, blown apart . . . Awful. *Awful*. There wasn't much left of some of these guys. And the thing that made it worse for me, I don't know why, is that they were politically so naive. They didn't know what the hell they were doing. It seemed a shame. I knew what I was doing there. I had made a decision, and whether it was right or wrong, I had decided to go rather than get the hell out of the country. I was a consenting adult, and I knew what the hell I was into. These kids were nonconsenting minors for the most part. They really didn't understand.

Then I was in the hospital in Japan for a while, and I learned a lot there from guys on my ward. I met people who'd been in Cambodia, who'd been in China. I learned that all the stories I had sort of thought were true were really true. Throwing guys out of helicopters when you're interrogating them—all the terrible stories. The guy in the bed next to me was a lunatic. He was a mercenary. I think originally he was Scottish, or maybe Scottish-Canadian. Tough bastard. He loved killing. He was in one of those Ranger things where they were all over the place, training Montagnards, Laotians, all that shit. They were never in Vietnam. The guy was nuts. This was about the fourth time he'd gotten shot up. I don't think he'd been home in five years, and when that war was over he'd go find another one. So I know that sort of person.

It was hard for me to go back to Vietnam after being in Japan. I came back much more cynical about the war. I'd really seen it rip people apart, and it wasn't nice. I was much more cynical about what the army said it was doing and what it was really doing. The lies about body counts, about where troops really were, about atrocities. That made it harder to do my job. These soldiers would come in, and I knew that even though I didn't believe in the war, it was better for the person's psyche to send him back to it. You might think, "Well, let's get all these guys out of Vietnam," but you'd leave a nation of cripples. To send the men back might not be better for Patient X, because out of 100 guys, some are going to get killed—but for the rest, the result is that psychiatrically, they end up better.

It's a paradox. The doctors talked about it all the time. We'd joke about it. Some people said they'd tell patients, "Look, I'm not getting out, and you're not going to get out either." One guy, when someone would come in and say, "I want to get out of the war, I can't stand it, I'm gonna go crazy," would say, "Well, I'll tell you how to get out." He'd take out a map of Vietnam and show the guy how to walk to Cambodia and then China.

JANE PIPER

She picks me up at a suburban train station in New Jersey—a handsome woman, about forty, with short brown hair and blue eyes, dressed in a businesslike blouse, jacket, and skirt. We talk in her office at a nearby hospital, where she is an administrator. For years she worked as a nurse, though she is now somewhat disillusioned with the profession.

But in high school in Connecticut, to be a nurse was a dream—since she was too short to be an airline stewardess. The army paid her way through college in return for a three-year enlistment. "I graduated, took my boards, and went to basic training in August of 1969. Six weeks of partying half the night and sleeping through classes. Then they took us out to the country someplace near San Antonio. We had three days in fatigues and combat boots. They put up a tent hospital and we did a mass-casualty drill. We learned what an M-16 and a .45 could do. They put some cans of sauerkraut out in a field. Some major fired at them. He said, 'This is kind of like what the body does.' There'd be a little hole in the front, and the back of the can would be wide open, with the sauerkraut dripping out."

She had been told that only volunteers went to Vietnam. Most of her class volunteered. She wanted to go to Japan. But one Friday morning in February of 1970, the phone rang. "It was the chief nurse. As soon as she told me who she was, I figured some patient had died and it was my fault. She said, 'I want you to be the first to know. Your orders have been changed.' I said, 'Oh?' She said, 'Yeah. You're still going overseas. But the hospital in Japan that you were assigned to is closing down. You're going to Vietnam.'"

During the first couple of days I watched a guy watch himself bleed to death. A real young kid, probably nineteen. I'm not sure what all his injuries were, because I didn't take care of him. He had a tracheostomy and he had developed pseudomonas, which was one of the most rampant infections over there. It had eaten away the tissue, so you could see the trachea where the tube was going in. He wasn't going to make it, but he didn't know that. His tracheostomy tube had a rubber cuff that you inflate. Actually, there's two cuffs that you alternate so you get a good seal around the trachea. You can't keep the same cuff inflated all the time because it can erode into the tissue. So every half hour or so you take the air out of one and put it into the other.

Well, a nurse pulled the air out of one of the cuffs, and it had eroded into an artery. The kid was sitting up. His eyes were already larger than normal. You have to picture this skinny kid, very white, with blond or reddish hair, and lots of infectious process. You could see his ribs and sternum. Then suddenly all this blood was gushing. His eyes got like saucers. People started running in. They pulled the curtains, the nurse rolled down the bed, and they started suctioning. But they couldn't do anything. He bled out within forty-five seconds. That was my first week.

I got there in March. Around July, I started to cry myself to sleep at night. My older sister died in August, so I went home on emergency leave. I didn't realize until I got home that I had been crying for a long time. It was just the despair of the injuries on the unit and having to go back the next morning. I didn't want to change units, but it was getting to me. Taking guys on a stretcher to the back of the hospital, under the canopy, to wash the mud out of their hair. Scraping the mud off all these young bodies that would never be whole again. I didn't even notice I was crying every night.

I was at Cu Chi. The 12th Evacuation Hospital, semi-mobile. Quonset huts with sandbags. Maybe 200 or 250 beds. I was assigned to thoracic and abdominal intensive care. Twelve-hour shifts, six-day weeks. We used to party at night when we weren't working. Shifts were from seven to seven. We'd sit at report at seven in the morning and pass around these huge juice cans. We'd be so dehydrated that we'd go through four cans during report. Then if things were really quiet, sometimes we got to take two-hour breaks. We'd decide who got to go back to bed first.

With the guys on the ward, we'd talk about home. Where they lived, what they were going to do, where they went to school, what kind of car they had. They'd talk families and dreams—what they had wanted to do, how they got there, how they'd done in basic or flight school. On the wards you were in view all the time. They called you "Ma'am." Or "Captain" or "Lieutenant." We'd try to find them books or magazines if they were able to read. If they could eat, we'd try to get them whatever they wanted. Not many of them ate. They had tubes into their stomachs. One of the nurses had an electric fry pan. You can make pizza in an electric fry pan if you've got the mix. I think it was Chef Boyardee pizza. Everything comes in the package. These poor guys would wake up in the middle of the night and we'd be cooking pizza in the back room. The smell would go through. "I smell pizza." "No you don't, go back to sleep." I'm surprised we were so callous. It amazes me now that we let them smell it.

They didn't stay long. All we did was stabilize them. Then they got shipped home—unless they were so unstable they were probably going to die, and that was rare. The Vietnamese died more often. It was almost as if they gave up. Nothing worked for them. We did all the same things that we did for the GIs, and it just didn't work. They didn't heal, or they broke down. But most of my guys were shipped out to Japan or Okinawa. I don't know names. Didn't write any of them down. I've gone to the Wall and stood there at the right year and read names, but none of them click.

I worked nights more than days. Time went a lot faster because I could sleep most of the day. Get up at noontime and spend an hour in the sun, and then go back and sleep the rest of the day. Get up for supper and go to work.

The first week I was there, a general came in to give Purple Hearts to some of the wounded. There was a kid who was maybe twenty. I doubt it, though—probably nineteen. As black a person as I have ever seen. Just ebony. He was lying on those olive-drab sheets. They couldn't save one leg, so he was an above-the-knee amputee on one side. Then they tried to save the other, and couldn't. That morning he had gone back and had the other leg amputated. I stood there while that general gave this kid a Purple Heart for his legs. That's when I started to think, What is going on here?

I had some rough patients. I remember a guy named Glenn. He

had tried to commit suicide and didn't quite manage to do it. He did blow his legs off, but he survived the grenade. I don't know how we knew that, because he never said it. He had a colostomy. He was being shipped out to Japan. From our area, the real sick guys would be helicoptered out in the middle of the night to Saigon in time to catch the plane out. The choppers usually came in at two or three in the morning. About nine that night, I had changed his colostomy bag, and I said, "I don't want you to use this again. When you leave, you're going to be clean. So don't use it." Of course, he had no control over it at all. "Gotcha. Won't use it, ma'am. No problem." Then we got in a sixteen-year-old Vietnamese kid who was in congestive heart failure. The emergency room didn't tell me, but they didn't expect him to live. We were watching him. I had him sitting up in bed. I allowed his father to stay, which is something we never did. His father was lying on the mat on the floor next to his bed. I was doing half-hour walk-throughs down the unit. At one point I looked up and he was gone. So I was rolling down the bed, the corpsman was calling for the crash cart. Call the ER, get the doctor! My bandage scissors slammed against the bed, which was metal. That made a noise. There was a flurry of activity. We lost the kid. We got the dad and the body out of there. And the corpsman said, "Glenn wants to talk to you." I went over and said, "What's the matter?" He said, "I am sorry. I really am sorry." He was being so serious. He said, "I tried, but when the lights went on and people started yelling, I thought we were being attacked." He pulled down the sheet and he had just filled that co-lostomy bag. We got to laughing until we heard the helicopter coming in. I never found out what happened to Glenn.

I had another guy who was a triple amputee. He wouldn't let us do anything for him. One arm was gone, the other arm was injured, and both legs were gone. One night we found him—with the stump of his arm, he was trying—the IVs were hanging from a wire that was strung down the Quonset hut. He started to rock the IV bottle with his stump. Trying to get it to crash. We grabbed it just in time. He thought he'd bleed to death if he dropped the bottle and it pulled out.

We took care of one kid—I had fun with this guy. He got to us with a bullet in his heart. They got him in so rapidly from the field that we saved him. I had him that first night and the next morning. He woke up, and I said, "You're going home." Of course, that was all they needed. Their eyes would light up. I said, "You are one lucky dude. Do you know what happened?" He didn't. I said, "Do you know where you got hit?" He started feeling around. I said, "You had a bullet in your heart, and you are still here."

There were other guys with the million-dollar wound. Maybe they got shot in the belly and they had a colostomy that would be closed later. It didn't hurt, and they had their arms, they had their legs, they had their eyes. They were going to walk and be okay. They'd just lie there and smile.

Little kids were rough. If they weren't very sick, we had some fun times with them. Turn them into pets. But the ones that died were pathetic. The little ones that would be wandering around with their older brothers or sisters while they were setting mines for the VC, and the mines would go off. We had cases of plague and malaria. I've got pictures of a kid who came in and had been treated by a Vietnamese doctor for a growth on his thigh. It was a sarcoma. He was six or seven years old. His only hope would be to take the leg off at the hip. We couldn't find his parents, and we told the interpreter we were setting him up for surgery on such-and-such a date, so the interpreter should try to get his parents before then or we would take his leg without them. We were trying to teach him how to walk on crutches. I've got a picture of him at Christmastime with a tear right on his cheek. He's standing there with his crutches, saying, "Don't cut off my leg."

His mother came after he had gotten his pre-op medication. We had started an IV. It was that close. He went to sleep and the mother came in and talked to the surgeon. We all sat there and cried. She decided. . . . [She is crying.]

She asked the doctor if he could guarantee that the cancer would be gone. He said no. He said that if it was his son he would do the same thing, but he couldn't guarantee it. So she decided not to let them do the surgery. She sat around until he woke up. We took the IV out. Then she took him home.

That's one I always cry about.

There was a lot of support there. A bunch of nurses would sit around in some room, talking about what had happened that day. There was a lot of camaraderie with the doctors, too. You partied together and you cried together and you worked together. Guys would talk about their families and their wives and being homesick.

There was a party every night. Basically I partied with the helicopter pilots. I don't know how I got started with them. Maybe they partied the most. A couple of nights after I got to Cu Chi, some guys came up and said there was a party. They wanted to come over with a Jeep and pick up whoever could go. That happened every night. You had to remind yourself that it wasn't going to be like that when you came home. There were so many more men than women, and it felt really good. As long as you didn't get carried away. [Laughs.] Women who were not being called up every day Stateside, it was quite a turn-on to be so wanted. Even if you never went to the same place twice, there was always a party. There was always somebody calling: "We've got a group doing such-and-such, won't you come over? How many of you can come?" We had a softball team called the Bunker Bunnies. We would play anybody with our rules, which were that the men had to bat from the opposite side of the plate that they were used to. And they couldn't catch fly balls. We generally won. There was always a barbecue afterward. They'd fly in shrimp from the coast. And there was always steak. I found that incredible. Once a week at the officers' club we'd have a cookout with real hamburgers and hot dogs.

There was also a movie every night. We saw *M*A*S*H** there. At first they banned it. They wouldn't let it into the country. Then they relaxed the ban. The enlisted guys were watching it the same night we were. They started earlier, so as soon as they'd finish a reel, they'd run it over to the officers' club. We'd run it and wait for the next one. As we were watching it, we'd identify who each character was at the 12th Evac. "Oh, yeah, that's so-and-so." The spit-and-polish guys that always looked so starched you couldn't imagine them ever sitting down, and the other guys who were laid-back. They never went around in bathrobes, but they were never quite put together.

If you worked well and you partied well and you didn't use your rank and you were sincere and you pitched in, you had no trouble. But God help you if you tried to pretend you were better than anybody else.

Days off, we used to fly around. We'd go out to the airfield and find a helicopter that was taking supplies someplace and was coming back the same day. We'd ask if there was room, and if there was, we'd hop on and fly around the countryside.

It was a hard-drinking life, for someone who didn't drink much before she got there. I don't remember ever being drunk, but I always had a drink in my hand. We drank Gwinks—gin and Wink. There was a lot of gin, and you couldn't get tonic, but you could get Wink. People drank an awful lot. It was the one escape, and people used it. There were people who drank severely, even among the nurses. The pilots drank heavily. And I'm sure a lot of people were into marijuana. You could buy the cigarettes right off the streets from the mamasans, already rolled. It got so you'd just sit around listening to music, on the floor in these tiny little rooms with your feet pointed toward the middle. Every half hour or so somebody would change the tape. You'd blast the music.

Some relationships that started over there are still going on, but not many. There were a lot of geographical bachelors. Of the three guys I dated, two were married. One I found out about, and when he was ready to leave, I said, "You could have told me. It didn't make any difference, but you could have told me." He gave me the old line. It went various ways: I'm going to get a divorce when I get back anyway. I didn't want to hurt you. It just happened, and I didn't know what to say.

My second guy was named Lee. I didn't know he was married. I got back to the States and connected with him again, because we were at the same duty station. Then I found out he was married, and I broke up with him. I was the one who found out—he certainly didn't tell me. He was my first real love. He was a twerp. [Laughs.]

Some of the men were right up-front, but most of them weren't. I don't know if it was the times or the geography or what. They'd take off their rings as soon as they got on the plane, and about three weeks before they went home they'd put them back on so they'd have a tan line. The chances were real good that the guy you were dating was married. The way you found out was to go to the Red Cross director. She was in the room next to me. We used to call her Mom. Big black gal. You'd say, "Hey, Mom, you've got to find out about so-and-so." She'd come back the next day and say, "Uh-uh-uh, this guy's got three kids. Be careful." She'd do the whole rundown, and you'd go back with enough ammunition that you could keep yourself under control if you continued.

A lot of it was just good fun, but sometimes it would get more serious. Whoever left first, that was usually it. There were a lot of people left behind. I watched nurses who connected with doctors. The doctor would go home, and the whole thing would end right there. He'd leave saying, "I'm going to divorce my wife." Letters would come, and then they'd come farther apart, and then they wouldn't come at all.

I'm sure some of it was not knowing whether they were going to be alive the next day. Deciding that it's one thing to be married and another to be monogamous. Although there were some guys who were very straight. They'd write home every night, come out and have a good time at a party, and go home. They managed to survive real well.

You tried not to think about the guys going out. You'd wait for the phone to ring when they were supposed to be back. They didn't talk about what happened when they were out there, for the most part. One friend got his legs broken in a crash, and he was disgusted because they gave him a Purple Heart and it had nothing to do with being fired at. He was embarrassed. I said, "To hell with the embarrassment. You're going home. So what you've got two legs in a cast? You're going home." But when you were at a party, you'd always wonder how many of the people there wouldn't be at the next one.

We had one Chinook that crashed and burned. It was stupid. They got into a pattern of landing about the same time every day. Finally they got shot down. There were nineteen or twenty guys on board, some of whom were leaving. We lost most of them. That was a bad one. Sometimes you'd go in in the morning, and guys you had partied with the night before were in there.

In Cu Chi a Doughnut Dolly was murdered while I was there. I'm not sure if they ever caught the guy. A GI got into her quarters and stabbed her. We never knew if it was somebody she knew, or if he was trying to steal something or what. After that, they put rolls of concertina wire all around the women's hootches, and they had a guard, a corpsman. At that point we could no longer get the men inside. [Laughs.] We used to have to bribe the guards. "We'll be right out. Five minutes, just five minutes." "Nope." "Oh, man, please, please. The next batch of cookies that comes, I'll give them all to you."

I don't mind fences, but if I see concertina or fences with barbed wire on top, I just get cold. I'll never get over that stuff. It was like being in a prison.

I remember the guys watching me for two days while I pumped seventy or eighty units of blood into a North Vietnamese guy who later died. They'd ask me why I was bothering. This guy was behind a moving curtain, but they knew who was there and what I was doing. For two twelve-hour periods, he just lay there and watched me until he died.

We had a VC who was shot through the neck. That was his only problem. He was a short, stocky, muscular guy. He scared me because he had his legs and arms, and he could move. But his neck was sore. He would follow you with his eyes but his head wouldn't turn much. So he looked shifty. We had him next to a little guy of about four who had swallowed a fishhook with the line attached. His mother had brought him to the hospital. They took out the fishhook and put a feeding tube into his stomach to rest the esophagus for a couple of days. To keep him from pulling out the tube, we had arm guards so he couldn't bend his elbows. At one point this kid was supposed to be taking a nap, and he started crawling over the side of the crib. Nobody saw him. We had concrete floors. The VC prisoner yelled to us to try and let us know. The kid hit the floor anyway. But the prisoner didn't scare me anymore after he tried to warn us. He just seemed like a normal guy who was on the other side.

We had one Vietnamese who'd been injured by an empty bazooka. The VC had put it against his abdomen and fired it. Just the shock waves tore him apart inside. Then there was an old man who had been burned. He had systematic cuts on his arms and legs. They had stroked slashes all the way up and down. Then he had been burned from head to foot. He had no hair. He looked like a little wax doll. I don't think he lived.

There was a lady my wardmaster had taken care of. The VC had taken a bayonet and shoved it up her vagina. I'm not sure why. Her husband was there while she was in the hospital, and that was the story he told. On the other hand, our guys used to drop people out of helicopters. The pilots told me about it once. They were bringing a prisoner back and interrogating him. I guess he wasn't talking. I don't know if it was ARVN or Americans, but they just pushed him out.

When I first came back, I was in a bar with some friends and I heard some college jock spouting off about the horrors of the M-16 and what it did to the body. I finally couldn't stand it any longer. I went up to him and said, "You obviously have never seen what an AK-47 does to the body." I turned around and started to walk away. The place was so packed that I couldn't get away fast enough. He grabbed me and said, "You sound as though you know." I said, "Yes, I do. And it bothers me when I hear people who obviously haven't been there telling only one side of it. Yes, our people are doing things, but I've taken care of the remains of what the VC have done to their own people. Don't tell me we're the only ones being brutal over there."

These days, I basically stay quiet about it. I learned that it's not something to talk about. I didn't get right out of the army when I came home. I still had two and a half years. That gave me enough time to be with people who had been there, so it was okay. I could talk about it when I needed to. I think that helped me avoid delayed stress. Once I got out of the military in '73, people would introduce me and say, "She was in Vietnam." I'd just say, "Yeah, but that was a long time ago." Someone might say, "Oh, what was it like?" But they didn't want to know, because when you started to tell them they turned green. So you gave little banalities and let it be.

There were more bad times than good times, but we had a lot of good times. I grew up there. I learned to be a nurse there. I jelled a lot of my thinking. It was sobering. There seemed to be so little reason.

I couldn't understand why we were there. I have never understood how people can hurt each other so.

I got very old there. I don't feel old now, but I felt old then. Life became so special. The little things became so important. I've lost a portion of that, but every once in a while I remind myself that I promised I would never ever forget to appreciate grass. An open space without a fence. Being able to walk where I want to walk. The basic freedoms that people take for granted. Bathtubs with bubblebath. And not having sandbags and concertina and death all around.

7

HEARTS AND MINDS

It was called "pacification." The idea was as old as the French war in the Red River delta—in fact, the word itself was originally French. The problem, too, dated back to those years: how to win the war in the countryside, where, as the litany had it, the villages belonged to the government by day and to the guerrillas at night.

Pacification became akin to a faith for some Americans. It had its prophets, men like Edward Lansdale, John Vann, and Robert Komer. They preached, correctly, that if South Vietnam and its American backers ignored the political contest in the villages, the war could not be won. The message was not widely heeded in 1965 and 1966, as American troops rushed in to shore up a tottering government. But by 1967 the prophets were no longer crying in the wilderness. The top military and civilian leaders embraced pacification, and the troop buildup was matched by an explosion of programs aimed at making loyal South Vietnamese citizens out of the peasants. A super-agency was created to tie the effort together: Civil Operations and Rural Development Support, or CORDS. And a new man was brought in to run it: Bob Komer, Harvard MBA, ex-CIA man, nicknamed "Blowtorch" for the style in which he tended to express his passions. He was given ambassador's rank and was number three on the country team, just below Ambassador Bunker and Westmoreland.

The theory of pacification was simple: The peasants lived under two governments, Saigon and the Viet Cong. Only a few were enthusiastic about either one. The Viet Cong's arguments—for land reform, for example, and against the foreign invaders—were often persuasive. So was the fact that their cadres tended to be local men and women. So was their tactic of killing anyone who worked too well for the Saigon

side. But the peasants could be won over—said the theory—by the
right mix of security and prosperity. Once they no longer feared visits
by armed bands in the night, and once they had tasted the fruits of a
lavish American aid program, they would refuse the Viet Cong the
support that a guerrilla army lives on: taxes, recruits, food, shelter,
labor, information. Gradually, the insurgency would wither away.

It was a solid enough theory. To put it into effect, CORDS had
hundreds of workers in every province by 1969. They came from AID,
the CIA, the State Department, the military. And they ran a range
of programs rivaled only by the War on Poverty back home. Farming,
medicine, public health, education, administration, finance, and civil
engineering got injections of American know-how and cash. Schools,
roads, markets, ports, bridges, and refugee camps were built. Local
militias were armed and trained to keep the Viet Cong out of the
villages. A centralized intelligence apparatus called Phoenix was set
up to identify and capture Viet Cong cadre. The Chieu Hoi, or "open
arms," program invited unhappy guerrillas to defect. Private American relief agencies, religious groups, and quasi-Peace Corps organizations such as International Voluntary Services sent volunteers and
money. Some of these nonofficial Americans saw themselves as working in tandem with CORDS, others tried to keep a distance.

Komer was well aware of failed pacification plans in the past—the
French "agrovilles" and Diem's "strategic hamlets," both of which
involved moving peasants into fortified villages. Those bids had crumbled partly because the peasants so deeply resented being torn from
their ancestral lands. This time it would be different: Fifty-nine-man
teams of young Vietnamese, known as Rural Development Cadre,
were sent to live in hamlets. Some members of each team were trained
in military tactics, some in community work.

But like many American theories in Vietnam, pacification slammed
into a reality more complicated than it had appeared. First, and most
obvious, there was little point in building schools and clinics that the
enemy could blow up. The same applied to personnel: During one
seven-month period in 1966, 3,015 Rural Development workers were
either killed or kidnapped. Corruption at every level soaked up American aid. Medical supplies found their way to the enemy. And the
subtleties of Vietnamese society often stymied American pacification
workers—who, as Bob Boettcher makes clear in this chapter, were
not necessarily America's *crème de la crème*. Because the Vietnamese
countryside was stripped of eligible young men, many RD cadre were
recruited in the cities and had little in common with the peasants.
Village elections run by Saigon officials and American advisers often

failed to produce real leaders. Doug Hostetter, a Mennonite who worked in Quang Tin province in the north, says that the CORDS people in his town never recognized that there were "two civilizations" there: the townspeople, who were poor, Buddhist, and often pro-NLF, and a superstructure of government officials from the big cities, who were Catholic and contemptuous of the locals.

Pacification also took on a brutal face in unreceptive regions. Viet Cong villages often were simply obliterated, as Doug Hostetter describes. Usually this meant bombing and then bulldozing, a technique the Vietnamese called "ironing" a village. The idea was that if hearts and minds could not be won, better to drive the people off their lands than have them growing food for the guerrillas. Such territory was often sprayed with Agent Orange and declared a free-fire zone, where anything that moved was assumed to be an enemy. After a time, the villagers might be allowed to return, under proper Saigon supervision. This kind of pacification, of course, produced millions of refugees who crowded the cities and towns, providing more work for the pacifiers.

Then there was the problem of how to measure progress. Under Defense Secretary Robert McNamara and his "whiz kids," the military bureaucracy fell in love with cost-benefit analysis and "quantitative measurement." In Vietnam, the result was a mania for reports that could be analyzed by computer and summed up in tidy graphs. John Peterkin, a district senior adviser, remembers filling out twenty to thirty reports every month. He also says that such gauges as the Hamlet Evaluation System were notoriously skewed by human factors, especially the desire to get ahead by painting a pretty picture. Bob Boettcher goes further: He says the HES was "a fraud."

Nevertheless, progress was made—in some areas, great progress. After the Tet offensive, as Americans at home started to turn against the war, Komer decided to focus on security goals, where speedy gains could be made, rather than social welfare, where results were more elusive. As Dick Burnham, a province senior adviser, points out, local militias were now given first-rate weapons, including the M-16. That could make a big difference at the hamlet level, where the Viet Cong suddenly found their maneuvers met with formidable force. The guerrillas, in any case, had been devastated by Tet. Heavy fighting through 1968 and 1969 bled them further, driving them from many strongholds. Chieu Hoi and Phoenix "neutralized" tens of thousands of cadre by one means or another. And Burnham adds that such measures as raising the price of rice helped win over the peasants, who saw their earnings tripled. As time went by, more and more of South Vietnam was "pacified"—notably the rich Mekong delta. Americans and Saigon officials could travel when and where they wanted. Roads were open. Viet Cong activity dropped to near zero.

But it had come too late. By the time the Americans and the South Vietnamese started pouring resources into the village war, public opinion in the U.S. wouldn't wait. Our boys were coming home, and South Vietnam was not yet ready to face the North alone. As Bob Boettcher says, "We wanted to accomplish a hell of a lot in a short time. Build representative government. Effective administration. Economic development. And military security. All at the same time, and while the country was under attack day and night. That's a large order, it really is. And it was just too much."

ROBERT BOETTCHER

When we meet, he is a tall, trim, boyishly handsome man of forty-one, clean-shaven, with silver-gray hair. Dressed in a gray pin-striped suit, he speaks with a southern drawl, the result of an upbringing in Texas and college in Alabama. We talk in his office in midtown Manhattan: he is a grant officer at the United States–Japan Foundation, which gives grants to projects promoting better relations between the two countries. In the 1960s he was a Foreign Service officer and then a congressional aide. As staff director to the House Subcommittee on International Relations, he headed the investigation of the Koreagate scandal, which led to a book, Gifts of Deceit: Sun Myung Moon, Tongsun Park and the Korean Scandal. *When talking about Vietnam, he favors a kind of folksy, cynical humor, but one feels that in many ways he remains the bright, ambitious idealist who arrived in-country in 1968.*

"I graduated from college in 1964. If I had been three years younger, I could say that I was part of the sixties campus political movement. I was not. I was a little before that. I was from the civil rights era, really. But I was a liberal, sure. And I was a liberal in the Deep South, not only on the race issue but on other things. I was a Kennedy-Johnson liberal."

After college he got an MS in international relations at Georgetown, spent a year in Japan to learn Japanese, passed the Foreign Service exam, and was eventually posted to Sapporo.

While I was in Sapporo a good friend of mine who was an FSO stationed in Vietnam came to visit me on his way to the States. He told me that the work being done by the civilian provincial representatives, young FSOs, was fascinating, important, challenging, something I would find stimulating. And it was constructive. He said he thought I ought to go down there, and he wanted to know if he could write a letter to Bob Komer, who was in charge of the pacification program, and tell him about me.

I thought about it and said okay, despite the fact that I was in the country I was most interested in, Japan. I thought the experience I would get in Vietnam was something I should take advantage of. And I had confidence in my friend. If he thought the work was worthwhile and good for one's career, I was interested. That was quite aside from any doubts I might have had about the whole rationale for the United States being in Vietnam. I had reservations, but I wasn't really sure. And I thought the way for me to know was to go there.

Pretty soon Komer sent a cable asking for my transfer. I was sent back to Washington for training. Everybody who was going out to work in the pacification program, including military people who were going to do noncombat things, passed through the State Department Training Center. The pacification program was a great mix of agency personnel, one of the greatest mixes in the history of the U.S. government. Well, if anything, I left the training with more doubts than before. After listening to these lectures, being in discussion groups and talking to my colleagues, I wasn't sure we were going about this the right way, or that the people running it knew what they were doing.

But I didn't know. I hadn't been to Vietnam. So I went. And within a month I decided that this was a futile crusade.

My friends had urged me to get into the area where John Vann was, because Vann was the best guy out there. He was the head of CORDS in III Corps. But I was sent to IV Corps, which was the Mekong delta. I was in Vinh Binh province, which was a troublesome province. I was at the provincial headquarters for a little and then was sent down to district level—Tra Cu district. This is farther in the boonies. I got there in the fall of '68, about six months after the Tet offensive. An enormous amount of territory had been lost to the Viet Cong and was still nominally under Viet Cong control. So in the fall of '68 Saigon decided that they were going to have an Accelerated Pacification Program. The APP, it was called. During a certain period, in several stages, the South Vietnamese were going to regain control over large areas that had come under the sway of the VC. The military was supposed to go in and reoccupy the areas. Then civilians, both Americans and Vietnamese, were to follow with self-help programs.

My job was to go around to the villages and hamlets with Vietnamese officials and take measures. I was also supposed to listen to what the local leaders were saying about the security situation. The barometer for all of this was a report that you sent in each week or two, grading the hamlet on how pro–Viet Cong or how pro-government it was. These reports were designed so they could be graded by computer. There were all sorts of different categories, maybe thirty or forty. Overall security. Local government. Whether or not there's a health facility. Whether or not the Rural Development Cadre had moved in and ensconced themselves. Whether or not taxes were being collected. Whether or not the land-reform representative was there. For each one of these indices you'd have five little squares, and you'd blacken one with a pencil so a computer could read it. Just like the SAT test. An *E* was the worst: *A* was the best. You had to get up to a *C* at least.

Well, this was a fraud. It was a paper exercise. In the first place, everyone knew that the higher-ups at the regional and Saigon levels wanted positive reports. We had been told that, not in a memorandum or lecture, but the word gets down to you. In many instances, reporting that a village or hamlet was now under government control reflected nothing more than the local Vietnamese commander and a couple of American advisers driving into the hamlet in the middle of the day, meeting the people, shaking their hands, and asking them how things were. "Oh, very good." "Well, you're with the government, aren't you?" "Oh, yes." Then you could give the hamlet a big *C*. But everybody knew, and every writer about Vietnam since the 1950s had said it, that the countryside was under the government's control during the daytime and under Viet Cong control at night. People were having to pay taxes to both, and some people had double loyalties. Some were simply dyed-in-the-wool supporters of the Viet Cong who masqueraded as government supporters in the daytime. I've been to a hamlet with military officers, and we'd look at each other and say, "Gee, it sure is a good thing it's twelve noon instead of twelve midnight, because if it was midnight we'd have bullet holes in our heads."

There were all sorts of ways of putting the thing in a favorable light, and that's what people did. Say you had one Rural Development Cadre unit serving four or five hamlets. That's spreading them very, very thin. Ideally there should be one for each hamlet. But if there was an RDC unit in this hamlet here, then you'd say there was one in all four or five around there, even though the RDC might never have been to those hamlets. Then there was the question of whether or not the roads were open to the hamlet. It was pretty hard to get around that one, but you could say the road was open if you went all the way around the province, skirting all the Viet Cong territory, and came in from behind. Or say you had government troops in a village. That was good, you could mark that down. But the quality of the troops varied. The training they had was sometimes negligible, and so was their willingness to defend the village.

It was bad enough on the local level. Then, six or eight months along, I talked to a guy in Saigon who was one of the main computer programmers for the whole CORDS system. I told him how the villages and hamlets were upgraded on the basis of very, very shaky reasons. He said, "Oh, that's nothing. In Saigon they average the numbers out and they take them up a couple more points." They'd just increase the grades. For example, if this hamlet is a *C* and the next one is a *B*, they would figure there was no reason for a *C* hamlet to be right next to a *B* hamlet, so they'd make them both *B*'s. As a result, Washington and the American people were told that things were getting *much better*. Much better! In one fell swoop, we've gone back and recouped all our losses from the Tet offensive. Now anything more we get from the enemy is a gain. Well, that was a fraud.

What disillusioned me so fast was the APP, the Vietnamese government people, and, for that matter, many of the American advisers. These people were not the best and the brightest by any means. You had Americans from all over the country, from all walks of life, whose careers were not going well in the States—broken-down ex–civil servants from the Detroit Board of Education, people from various federal agencies, people who had been riffed out of the army at the rank of major and who came back to government as civilians. They volunteered for Vietnam because it was interesting, exciting, and profitable, and it could get them away from the old lady who's been driving them crazy for the last eight years, and the kids screaming. They all got on the Vietnam gravy train, because you made damn good money in Vietnam. You got the standard government salary plus this enormous amount for hardship because it was a war zone. You could go out there and live for practically nothing and put a lot of money in the bank. Well, these were not the kind of people who would be expected to work effectively with peasants in an underdeveloped country with an entirely different culture.

And they were describing the situation out there as more favorable than it was, I guess because they were supposed to be making progress. They had tasks and they wanted to report that they were carrying out those tasks. It's natural in a bureaucracy, you always try and make things look good to the next level up. You can say, "Look, the situation is hopeless," but the next level up has got the *next* level to report to, and the highest level, in Washington, had decided that this was *not* hopeless, that it was very hopeful, and that we were going to win, by God. So that position had to be accommodated. But I did not see these people working very hard. I saw them having a damn good time. It was more visible at the province level than at the district. There were more Americans, more of an establishment, more opportunity to set up your country club.

The CIA people were the worst. I was appalled at the kind of people the CIA had out in the provinces. The career CIA people at the embassy were very smart, high-quality professionals, good at political analysis and I suppose at running intelligence operations. But the typical spook in the provinces was an ex-cop. And if you didn't know that he used to be on the San Diego or Baltimore police force, you could guess it. These guys loved to ride through the streets and down the country roads in their Jeeps with all manner of weapons strapped to them, gunbelts and helmets and all of it. They had lots of booze, lots of women, the best furniture, and the nicest places to live. They had their own private airline, Air America, to take them anywhere they wanted to go on a moment's notice. They played a Terry-and-the-Pirates game, swashbuckling, lots of bravado. Some killing, too. They were after the VCI, the Viet Cong infrastructure. This is where you get your assassination squads. These guys would go out with some Vietnamese and try to catch Viet Cong or kill them. Then they'd boast about it the next day. There's nothing wrong with that, actually. But they really didn't grasp the gravity of the situation they were dealing with, or its complexity.

On the other hand, you had John Vann. If there is an authentic hero of the Vietnam War, it's him. If anybody understood the way it should be fought, he did. He understood it as early as '63 or '64. And by the late '60s he was famous. Every civilian in Vietnam knew about John Vann. He had been out there early on as a lieutenant colonel in the army, and had a big falling out because he disagreed with the way it was being done. He thought there had to be a more comprehensive and committed pacification program, which would win the loyalty of the people in the countryside. Eventually he resigned from the army and went back to Vietnam as a civilian, working for AID. Wherever he went, he put his ideas into action. Eventually what he thought should be done became policy all the way up to Washington.

But by the time Vann was transferred to the delta, I had heard a lot of negative things about him. Opinion about Vann was not unanimous. I heard he was nasty, kind of a martinet, that he liked to chop heads off, and that he wouldn't listen to anything that went against his preconceived notions. When he first came down to Vinh Binh province, all the American advisers were gathered together, because the great John Vann was going to deliver his inaugural address, as it were. He went on and on about the way he wanted things done, and ended with, "Failure to carry out my orders, gentlemen, means only one thing: immediate dismissal."

When he came down to Tra Cu, I had some discussions with him, and I didn't see anybody else who seemed like such a worthwhile person to work for. So I told him that if he had a job he thought would be right for me at regional headquarters or even in Saigon, to let me know. He said, "Oh, you don't want to work in Saigon, those guys don't know what's going on at all. But I'll see what I can do at regional headquarters." A month or two later comes word that there's a job. I became deputy director of the Field Operations Division, handling a number of things: local elections, training of local officials, the RD cadre, the People's Self-Defense Forces. I was on the regional staff, and that got me around to all sixteen provinces in the delta. I worked with Vann for a little more than a year.

Vann liked to hop about by helicopter every day. He didn't spend very much time in the office. Next door to his office was an apartment building where American civilians lived. As soon as Vann came to Can Tho he wanted to have his helicopter land on the roof of this building, because it was convenient. It created an uproar among the people living there. They didn't want that kind of disturbance, and besides, some of them liked to lie around up there in the sun. But in one fell swoop, Vann had somebody go up and paint the circle where the helicopter should land, and that was his heliport. One time I was coming out of the building at the same time he was coming down the stairs. I said, "How you doing, John, did you have a good day?" He said, "No, nothing special, just twelve provinces today." That was not unusual for Vann.

One of the things I was responsible for was the RD cadre. They dated from '65 or '66. Originally they were called the Revolutionary Development Cadre. It was a name conjured up by the Americans, but the Vietnamese thought it sounded too much like the Communists. So they decided to call themselves Rural Development Cadre. The notion was that we wanted our side to appear to be progressive. The other side should not have exclusive use of that concept. Our side was going to have peace and freedom and economic development and widening of popular participation, as opposed to the side that was terrorist, destructive, oppressive, and aggressive. So the RDC were a bunch of young guys in VC-type black pajamas.

They would be assigned to a village or a hamlet. They were supposed to work directly with the people in defending the hamlet, because they were armed, and in providing all kinds of services: digging trenches, installing a sewage system, helping build a new marketplace, medical help, first aid, agricultural projects, gathering intelligence. And political education, or indoctrination if you will. Because they were young, they were packaged as something dynamic, something really progressive, symbolic of the vigor of the government side. They were like an armed Peace Corps.

Well, the RD cadre had a mixed record. In some cases they were wonderful, and their overall reputation was pretty good. But there were lots of reports of guys sitting around doing nothing.

In each province there was an American adviser for the RDC, and they varied a lot, too. Language was a huge barrier. By and large, the Vietnamese spoke more English than the Americans spoke Vietnamese. So the advisers would talk in English, and a lot of the Vietnamese didn't understand half of what the advisers were telling them, but the advisers thought they did. Of course, these Vietnamese had all been through a lot of advisers. And if the Vietnamese guy speaks pretty good English and has been through a few American advisers, chances are he's learned to handle them. He knows pretty much what the Americans are going to say, and what they're going to push for, and he will assure the American that certain things have been done, when they might or might not be. I would guess that no more than one-fourth of American advisers really knew what was going on in their province.

The People's Self-Defense Forces was another example. They got started in '68 or '69. You had the regular ARVN forces operating in a large area and doing the major combat stuff. Then you had lower-level forces such as the Ruff-Puffs. They were more puff than rough, actually. And beyond that the farmers in the hamlets and villages were going to become a militia. They were going to have weapons, not to keep all the time like soldiers, but to be stored someplace and taken out when needed. First they got the oldest leftover weapons, which could be M-1s, World War II model. Then they moved up to M-14s. Then we had this crash program: The PSDF is going to have M-16s all over the country. The Americans brought thousands and thousands of M-16s into the country and started distributing them. That shows a steady improvement of defensive capability, doesn't it? No, it really doesn't. It's a metaphor for the whole thing. Because these people weren't trained very well if at all. But the most important thing, from the American point of view, was that you could say that in X number of provinces there were X number of people in the PSDF, and they all had their M-16s, and therefore the government was in a much stronger position. And with these figures, Americans at various levels, and Vietnamese, too, could hold impressive briefings for their superiors—be they military or civilian, in Vietnam or Washington, or in the Oval Office.

Another thing I was supposed to do was oversee local elections. There were several waves of them at different levels. But the schedules were set in Saigon in the typical way. By such-and-such a date, X number of provinces will have had elections in such-and-such a percent of villages and hamlets. X number of officials will be elected. X number of officials will be trained. That's the mentality you had to deal with. So we went through this election business. I was going around with a guy named Colonel Dong. He was the province chief of Vinh Binh province. He was a buffoon. It wasn't that he was so tyrannical; he was just autocratic and liked to show his authority. We were having one of our big election pushes. I would go around in a helicopter with the province chief and some other people to a district or two, dropping down in a few villages to have meetings. We were trying to show that the government was serious about the elections, explain what elections were, who they were going to elect—village chief, administrative chief—and that elections were really a good thing. The province chief would make a big pitch. Part of it was to urge people to run for office. We were in one village and Colonel Dong said, "I want people to run for village chief. Who's going to run for village chief?" No hands. "Who's going to run for village chief?" No hands at all. "Somebody's got to run for village chief! What about you?" He'd just point to people. "All right, you, you, and you run for village chief." That was that.

The day was set aside for the election, the polling booths were assigned, ballots were printed, polling places were secured by military personnel. Everything was in order. The day before the election I was talking to Dong and I said, "How are things?" "It's all set." I said, "You think there's going to be a big turnout?" He goes, "I *know* we're going to have 95 percent. I made sure."

So the elections were artificial, because they were just a part of the numbers game. Back home, the antiwar movement was saying that we were supporting a dictatorial government. So the policymakers in Washington wanted democracy. The way they did it was to hold local elections under the military with voters herded to the polling places, sometimes with candidates picked at random.

Corruption was another constant problem. For example, sports and recreation were something we were encouraging. So the district chief in Tra Cu, the local Vietnamese military man, wanted to get some basketballs and baskets, rackets, nets for volleyball. Could we get any stuff for him so he could give it to the people? We got a lot of stuff, gave it to him, and he was so happy. And we were pleased. We found out later he had sold it and pocketed the money. The guy who was the local health man for the government used to do the same thing with medicines, bandages, and medical equipment. He would sell it to people who could afford it.

There was one notorious guy who was a member of the national legislature. The Americans at the province level knew he was just as crooked as can be. But I used to have arguments with Americans in the embassy who were covering the national political scene. We would almost come to blows over this guy. They'd say, "No, no, look, you can't say that, this guy is a progressive force." See, one of the problems in Saigon was that we were always trying to promote negotiations between the South Vietnamese and the Communists, but Thieu wouldn't cooperate. So the embassy was interested in people who were anti-Communist but who favored negotiation. This guy was one of them. He owned a couple of newspapers, too, and he would criticize the government for corruption [laughs], and for heavy-handedness in dealing with the people. These are things Americans like to see in newspapers. The embassy political officials would say, "He's one of the great liberal leaders of this country. We *need* more men like him." And I'd say, "But he's a crook!"

So I was skeptical about our chances for success. And then in the middle of 1969 I went to An Giang province. An Giang was the exception to all the justified pessimism. It was controlled by the Hoa Hao sect. And it was totally secure. By and large, Americans like me didn't go to An Giang because there were no problems there. But I made a point of going because I had heard so much about it. I went there three times, I think. You didn't fly to An Giang unless you were in a hurry. You could drive, because it was so safe.

An Giang was in the middle of the delta, surrounded by other provinces that were half Viet Cong or even three-quarters Viet Cong. It was so secure that the Viet Cong made a point of never going there. We would get reports every once in a while of some Viet Cong who happened to cross into An Giang province. They'd be annihilated. Why? Because the Hoa Hao, which is a social, political, economic, and religious sect, is also very anti-Communist, and these guys co-operate with each other. If some VC slip over into the neighborhood, someone is going to let the local commander know about it immediately, and the local commander, who is probably a Hoa Hao too, is going to go out and zap them. That kind of thing was lacking everywhere else in Vietnam.

An Giang was also highly developed economically. There's no big sign on the road when you go from one province to another, but all of a sudden you'd notice that the houses were much neater and finer. The people were better dressed. There were electric lines running all over the place. The sampans along the canals had motors. There were Hondas and tractors. Many more houses had a car or a truck or a van. The city of An Giang had a bigger commercial section than any I'd seen. There were cattle everywhere. And people had a very positive attitude, they felt like life was okay. I was excited by all this. I had always felt that the Vietnamese were pretty capable, and in An Giang I saw it.

An Giang was a big realization for me. I knew how bad it was in all the other places, but until I went to An Giang I didn't realize how different it could be. In An Giang there was a point of loyalty around which everyone could organize. It was the Hoa Hao. Then I looked at the Catholic villages I had visited. Sure enough, there on a village scale were some of the signs of An Giang. Higher level of development. More commerce. Better education. Better facilities. And better security.

I started going around telling people in a hopeful way, "Look, there's got to be some kind of rallying point different from what the government is presenting. Look at An Giang." I was thinking, What we've got to find is how to introduce the secret of An Giang to the rest of the country. But I didn't know what it was they could do, what it was they could say, that would make 20 million Vietnamese as loyal to their government as the people in the Hoa Hao were to their elders.

In the long run, An Giang made the futility of the task come home even more. There was not enough time. All these crash programs had been done too late and too fast, and they were shaky. Still, I thought it was better to have them than not to have them. I was glad those hundreds of village officials were being trained, and I hoped some good would come out of it. I thought the elections were a good thing, even under those circumstances. I don't want to leave the impression that everything we were doing was bad. We wanted to accomplish a hell of a lot in a short time. Build representative government. Effective administration. Economic development. And military security. All at the same time, and while the country was under attack day and night. That's a large order, it really is. And it was just too much.

While I was there, I felt that hardly an American would be able to go home and say, "I accomplished this. From my being there, this,

this, this, and this was done. I made this contribution to saving Vietnam from Communism." I don't think that anybody who said that could back it up.

Bob Boettcher died in 1984.

DICK BURNHAM

We meet at his office in Washington, where he manages syndications for the International Finance Corporation, a private-sector affiliate of the World Bank. The walls of his office are decorated with framed announcements of loans for development projects in third-world countries. He is tall, thin, graying, in his fifties, dressed in a conservative blue suit befitting a banker. He has come equipped for our talk with notes and papers from his Vietnam service.

"I grew up in upstate New York. I went to Amherst College, where I got a bachelor's degree in history with honors. Then I studied at Harvard Law School and received a degree in 1961. After Harvard I went into the Foreign Service. I took the basic course with intensive study of French. I was posted in Paris for a couple of years, and in Bordeaux for about ten months. Then I came back to Washington and didn't have any interesting jobs to do, so I volunteered for the Vietnam program.

"They were choosing men who were bachelors, most of whom already spoke French, and giving them a ten-month program in Vietnamese language, history, culture, and counterinsurgency training. This started in the fall of 1964 and ended in June of '65. Then we were assigned to the AID advisory effort. I did it because I wanted something more exciting to do than hanging around the State Department in Washington. The building is hateful, and as a junior officer, most of the jobs are boring. Also, Vietnam seemed to be where the action was. Of course, I signed up before we had sent in American troops. There were only advisers, but there were a lot. By '68 and '69, there was far too much action."

I spent a few days in Saigon and then went down to the delta, to Kien Hoa province. If you drive from Saigon to My Tho and then cross the river on a ferry, you're in Kien Hoa. It's almost due south of Saigon. Basically the population was Buddhist and traditionalist, with some Catholics. We didn't have any Hoa Hao there at all. A few Cao Dai, of a different variety from the ones in Tay Ninh. The southern part of Vietnam is very rich country, and not overpopulated. The farmers had forty or fifty acres each. Beautiful flat delta farmland. Nobody was hungry down there. When I went up north, I saw people who looked quite hungry, but not in my area. There were coconuts falling off the trees. There was food everywhere. Lots of people were poor and probably didn't have all the rice they wanted all the time because it was taxed away from them by both sides. But nobody was starving. It was a very, very rich area in terms of potential, if not in terms of production at the time.

Ben Tre, the province capital, had maybe 30,000 people. It was a pretty secure place. You could wander around at night without much fear. But you couldn't drive along country roads. If you were someplace at night, you stayed there. The people who were not in the province capital or district towns were in villages and had to deal with both sides—the government in the daytime and the Viet Cong at night, or sometimes the Viet Cong day and night. The government might only come through on operations. The Viet Cong was very strong in the province. But there was a lot less fighting than you would have thought. First of all, nobody bothered anybody's dependents. You didn't treat the family badly because a young man was in the VC, or the other way around. It was an unspoken rule. Most of the small operations carried out at the province level didn't bump into anybody. And the Viet Cong didn't seem to kill many people either. Both sides recognized that warfare has a political objective and only a political objective. You don't accomplish anything by just killing people. So there wasn't that much killing.

The VC might make an effort, say, to close a road. Just before I arrived, they closed a road to one of the districts. They closed it by killing anybody who came down it. Then nobody comes down it and you don't have to kill anybody else. You control the road. You don't have to kill many people to exert that power. But the farmers were able to bring crops into market without much intimidation. The government controlled most of the waterways, which was pretty easy to do.

The Viet Cong side was hoping that the government would just collapse. When I'd been there about a year, they shelled the province capital for the first time. They killed maybe 200 people, because nobody was ready for it. Nobody had a bomb shelter or anything. Shells would come right down through the roof and land in somebody's bedroom and kill everybody. A really nasty situation. After that, people built shelters, so the next time, few people were killed. But it's interesting the VC didn't do it before. I think they wanted to discredit the province chief. And I think it was a sign of weakness. If they could have the control they wanted without doing that, they wouldn't do it. But if the government's getting stronger, shelling the city is a way of showing that it isn't as strong as it thinks it is.

The experience I had was probably different from what people were having in the northern part of South Vietnam, where there was a huge American presence. When I got to the delta, there were no American combat units at all. Security was provided by Vietnamese soldiers only. Up north, propaganda against Americans would be effective: "Those nasty people are coming and killing you and ruining your country." But I don't think it had much effect where we were, because there weren't many Americans. I don't think the notion of a war of independence against the Americans meant anything in the south. Half the population of the country was south of Saigon. Obviously, most of the American military liked to go north. That's where it was exciting. Most of the action was there. But it was a different war from the one we were fighting in the delta.

The province chief was Tran Ngoc Chau, who was quite well known because he was extremely dynamic. He had been a member of the Viet Minh coalition fighting the French, and then after the partition he had left the Viet Minh in opposition to the Communists and had gone south. His brother was an officer in the NVA. So here was a man who felt strongly that the government of the South should be preserved. To show you what kind of guy he was, he was elected to the National Assembly from that province after he left there as province chief and moved to Saigon. Thieu wanted his own man in there, but Chau won. He had a feeling for those people and their needs and desires. I remember being in Saigon with him one time, and we passed by the Cercle Sportif. He said to me, "Y'know, if we could just take all the Vietnamese who are in that building right now up in an airplane and drop them out, we'd be better off." He was a real nationalist, but also a strong anti-Communist. I think that combination probably came closest to what people in South Vietnam wanted.

My first job was to be his civilian adviser. He also had a CIA adviser for intelligence. At first, there were only two or three AID people in the province. We had a couple of Vietnamese working for us, and a few Filipinos. I would try to get men and material flowing from Saigon into the projects we had. I was also supposed to learn as much as I could and report to Saigon, so they would have it at the embassy. Like everybody, after I'd been there about three months I thought I knew everything. The normal TV journalist never stayed longer than that. Then you began to realize there were deeper and deeper levels. I got to know the town and the countryside very well, and I had many friends among the Vietnamese. Again, this is different from somebody in uniform up north. Everybody treated us normally. We weren't freaks. There were no nasty massage parlors and bathhouses in the province.

In June 1967, Ambassador Komer appointed me province senior adviser in Kien Hoa, which meant that I was the top adviser to the province chief. By that time I had over 200 military officers on my staff, plus several AID people, a couple of USIA people, and some CIA people on the overt side. My deputy was a lieutenant colonel in the U.S. Army. I was in a position to know more of what was going on in that province than any other American, not only because everybody reported to me but because I'd been there longer. I spoke Vietnamese—not terribly well, but I could get along. And I spoke French fluently.

Normally my day consisted of getting in a Jeep or helicopter and going to look at something. I might accompany the province chief. Go to a hospital or a fort, or go see something being built. A bridge, a road, an irrigation canal, a school. We had an education adviser. We'd budget funds to build schools and buy textbooks. That was an interesting program. I can't remember the precise statistics, but we had something like 40,000 grade-school students in a province of 600,000. It was one of the largest provinces in Vietnam. But there was only one high school when I got there. One high school in the whole province. It was on the French system, so it offered the baccalaureate degree. It conferred about 100 baccalaureates each year. So you had an enormous pyramid—a huge number of schools at the lower level, which we added to, and one high school. In order to rise in the government or become a doctor or a lawyer, you had to have a baccalaureate. Which meant that this system was choking off opportunity. I think one of the causes of the war was that people with ambition couldn't rise in that system. We meddled a little bit with it by building a few high schools, but obviously we didn't change it. We also meddled with it by helping to open up the job market and by improving the economy.

I remember once we persuaded the deputy chief of the Viet Cong's medical corps to defect under the Chieu Hoi program. Here was a man from the South. He worked as a surgeon on the Viet Cong side. But he had not gone through medical school. He had gone to Hanoi and gotten some kind of training. He had done a decent job for the VC, but there was no job he could get on the government side, at least at the beginning. Exactly why he left the VC we couldn't be sure. I think he probably had arguments with the administrators there. Anyway, when he came in we tried to get him a job at the government provincial hospital. They turned him down because he didn't have the right training. On one level, that's understandable. But from another point of view, you've cut off his opportunity. Well, we had to work very hard. We gave him jobs working with our medics. We were able to keep him going, but in an artificial way, through the American presence. The Vietnamese weren't going to accept him. Yet he told me, and I believed him, that if we had been able to assure his VC colleagues that they would be satisfied from a career point of view, they would have defected bag and baggage and come to our side. But we couldn't do that.

We had a big medical program and a refugee program. We'd build shelters and feed the refugees. Thousands of people came out of the VC areas to the shelters. Now, they came out for two reasons: Life was pretty miserable where they were, and they were hoping it would be better. On the negative side, they wouldn't get bombed by us if they were on our side.

Agriculture was another of the programs. There wasn't much for the agricultural adviser to do at first. As we've learned at the World Bank, the principal stimulus for economic development in the countryside is agriculture. And the principal stimulus for agricultural development is price, or demand. Technique is secondary. If you have demand, technique follows. We can help with technique, but if there's no demand, all the technique in the world is useless. When I arrived, the price of rice—and these numbers aren't exact—was maybe seven cents a kilo. And there was a food shortage. People were poor. Naturally you feel poor if you grow rice and only get seven cents a kilo out of it. How can you be anything but poor? The Viet Cong says the government is treating you badly, and you think, Of course they're treating me badly. I can't make a living. Besides, they've got nasty administrators.

Finally the economic section of the U.S. Embassy convinced the embassy and then the South Vietnamese that they should triple the price of rice, to twenty-some cents. In order to soften the blow to the urban population, they had a rationing system, or special stores where you could buy it at a subsidized price. Anyway, the problem in the Vietnam War was never the urban population. Most of them were in favor of the government. It was just a minority in the countryside that favored the revolution. So all of a sudden rice was three times as expensive. A farmer could make three times as much money on the same field. That just transformed South Vietnam.

There was one district that we started pacifying before I became province senior adviser, and I stepped it up. It was called Ba Tri. We picked it because it was fairly easy to defend. It's at the bottom of the central peninsula in Kien Hoa. Also it's an area that had been devastated by the Viet Cong, but was theoretically very rich. We persuaded the ARVN to keep one or two battalions in place in the district to keep the VC out. And all of a sudden we saw it transformed. Vastly more rice was being grown, and other kinds of food. Then we saw other things happening. People in rags were buying new clothes, bicycles, Singer sewing machines, outboard motors. What they did with the motors was reverse the prop, put a tin shaft around it, and make a pump that could raise water out of the canals. They started buying these Lambretta taxis, basically a Lambretta with a platform on the back, a three-wheeled jobby where you can seat ten or fifteen people. In one of the reports I've got here, it says the number of pigs brought to market increased from 300 to 650 over six months. That's a change. Part of it was the better security. Part of it was the higher price of rice. And part of it was encouraging people with the right markets and technology.

We also helped by bringing in some of the new rice strains, so they could increase the yield on a field of rice by three or four times. All of a sudden the country was prosperous. So who needs the VC? The only way the VC can rule in that situation is through intimidation, which of course was their main tactic all along. You get somebody cooperating with the government, and you kill him. The next guy that tries to cooperate, you kill him, too. Finally nobody wants to cooperate with the government. It's pretty easy. Or you fire at passing airplanes from the center of a populated area and hope the planes shoot back. Everybody knows about that. What's more important was this economic revolution going on.

The other revolution was the change in weaponry and training given to the provincial and local forces. When the Viet Cong hit us at Tet, their provincial and local forces had much better weapons than the South Vietnamese. Instead of arming our ally, we had left them for years with hand-me-down World War II weapons. But after Tet, the army command decided to make serious changes, and the weaponry was vastly upgraded. We started to get adviser teams to come in and train provincial and local forces. I think we even started to pay them a little better. Give them more respect, more position. By "we" I mean the government of South Vietnam. This was very, very important. It's what they should have done in the beginning. That sounds like hindsight, but those of us on the ground at the time all felt that way. There were no American forces protecting me. If I lived or died, it was because of the local forces. So when I saw them with worse weapons than the Viet Cong had, I knew something was wrong. Nobody wanted to listen at first. I don't know why—maybe just inertia. It's probably easier to send troops from the United States than to get a financial allocation from the U.S. government to arm somebody else. But if there's any lesson from Vietnam, that's one. If you want to help somebody, give him enough. Don't string him along until the only way to help is to send U.S. troops.

I have an interesting story about Tet. After the battle was over, a television reporter called me from Saigon and said he'd like to come down and interview me. I said, "Sure, come ahead." He arrived with his camera crew. We were at province headquarters. He started chatting with me while his crew was setting up. He said, "Now, Burnham, this has really been a disaster, hasn't it? All this destruction. This is horrendous for the United States and South Vietnam, isn't it?" I said, "Well, it's a mixed bag. There's a lot of destruction and a lot of people killed. On the other hand, all the Viet Cong agents surfaced and started marching through the streets saying, 'We've taken over,' and gave it everything they had. But in the end, we kicked them out of town, killed lots of them, and got all their agents identified. I think this is a turnaround." At that point he cut me off and said, "You sound just like Ambassador Bunker. I don't want to talk to you, you're lying to me." And he stomped off with his crew. He could talk to anyone he wanted, there was no censorship. So he walked around talking to everybody on my team until he could find the person who told him exactly what he wanted to hear. And that guy was on the evening news for ten minutes a couple of days later. Somebody from the States told me about it.

It's hard to say that when I left in '68, pacification was progressing; 1967 and 1968 was a very troubled time in Vietnam. We had the Ba Tri area, but the rest of the province was on hold, because the level of violence had gone up dramatically. The government side introduced more weapons and better troops. Also more Americans, not in my province but elsewhere in Vietnam. And more American air power. On the VC side, you started to get main-force units coming in from the North. Then you began to see something I hadn't seen before: big battles going on, with lots more soldiers dying. But those kinds of battles were good for our side. If one VC guy is killed and one government guy is killed, the government is going to win, because it's got a lot more people. Even if it's two to one or three to one. If they're out there slugging it out, the government is going to win.

In fact, after I left, almost all of Kien Hoa was pacified like Ba Tri. Once you get the core pacified, there's less and less area for the VC and the main-force enemy troops to maneuver in. There were nine districts in the province. When I came in, we could drive from the capital district to one district without any difficulty, and to two other districts if we mounted a kind of convoy. The rest you couldn't drive to at all. You had to go by helicopter. When I left, you could travel without a convoy to the two where you needed a convoy before. It still wasn't safe to go to the other five. But within a couple of years, that was all resolved. Before the fall of South Vietnam, you could travel everywhere in the province. It was pacified. And this was the province where the Viet Cong started up in the South.

The fact is that the political equation was already on the government side. First of all, when the country was divided in two, you had almost a million Catholics come down from North Vietnam. So you have a million people who hated the Communists—hated them so much that they brought all their families to the South. Secondly, you had people like the Hoa Hao and the Cao Dai in the South, who hated the Communists. Anyone who had strong religious feeling wouldn't feel comfortable with the Communists, and that meant a great number of people in the South. And the government, whatever its failings, didn't govern very much, if you will. It governed a pluralistic society, and a consumer society. A person was free. Whether he was able to vote for the prime minister of South Vietnam is relatively irrelevant. How many people care that much about that? He was able to grow what he wanted on his land, he was able to buy and sell and live where he wanted to, go to any church he wanted to, marry when he wanted to, and do whatever he wanted to do within his economic ability. He was a free man. There was a court system that was probably corrupt, but it worked. Government officials were often corrupt, and taxes weren't always fair, but based on my three years there, my feeling was that the vast majority of the people would rather have kept the government they had. The people in the countryside were obviously the most discontented. The price of rice is an example. Once that problem was solved, it took away a lot of their complaints.

So when I say the government was doing pretty well, I say it because eventually we won the war in the South. Almost all the populated areas of the South were controlled by the government, before the North invaded. Kien Hoa province never fell to the Viet Cong—it was invaded from the North. Pure and simple: It was conquered.

JOHN PETERKIN

The apartment is immaculate, everything perfectly in place, lots of chrome and glass and black and white. Shag rugs, a piano gleaming in the small living room, folded paper hand towels in the bathroom for visitors. The building is a new high-rise in a middle-class neighborhood in Queens, New York.

The man of the house is black, burly, in his fifties, with a big Afro and a mustache. He spent most of his life in the police or the army, and now works for the post office. There is something of the parade ground in his bearing, and of military bureaucracy in his speech. On his second tour in Vietnam he married a woman named Anh. Her relatives are trickling out of the country, and two have just come to live here: a teenage girl and a boy of about twelve. So the apartment is too crowded: The family is looking for a house.

He served in Korea, then spent fifteen years in the reserves. In 1968 he was recalled to active duty for six months and decided to sign up for a full eighteen-month tour.

I was at Fort Benning for about six months, when I got orders that I was being reassigned to Vietnam. Then they said, "We've got something you may like. We're going to start training district senior advisers."

I got in-country in June 1969. I was assigned to Phong Phu district in Phong Dinh province, in the Mekong delta. South Vietnam had forty-some provinces and about 1,800 districts. Each province had a province chief who answered directly to the president. He was normally a military man. On the American side there was a province senior adviser. The PSA was supposed to advise the province chief on military operations, police operations, medical operations, economic development—every aspect of what it would take to run a state in the United States. And in each district of every province we had a district senior adviser. He was responsible for the same things as the PSA, but just in one district.

Phong Phu was a classic district. Well organized, fairly secure; you could go just about anywhere in it. There were seven villages, and each one of them had several hamlets. I lived in the district chief's headquarters, which was a military compound about 100 yards outside the town of Phong Phu. The DSA team consisted of eight men including myself. I had a weapons sergeant who was responsible for teaching the Vietnamese about the use and care of weapons. I had a medic sergeant to check on the medical situation in the hamlets. I also had an engineer sergeant who was giving advice on the building of a water purification system for the district town. I had a civilian who didn't live with the team, but was assigned to give support for economic development projects. And I had a Phoenix adviser, a lieutenant. The Phoenix program was supposed to gather intelligence on the Viet Cong. The guy on my team was trying to chart who they were, where they were, and how they operated in the district.

I remember one time an American came by my headquarters to tell me they were going out on a Phoenix operation. Any operations in my district were supposed to be reported to me first. This guy was with one of the teams that would go out to apprehend the Viet Cong. He came in and I said, "Look, you don't have to report here. Just let me know you're in the area, but I don't want you reporting here." I didn't want to get involved with that. I wasn't trying to be under-handed, but I didn't want to be involved in something that may at a later date be found not to be acceptable. I had been a police officer for a long time, so I was well aware of what was legal and what was illegal. I'm not saying Phoenix was legal or illegal, I don't know. But what's interpreted as being legal one day can be illegal the next, depending on who's doing the interpreting. These teams were sup-posed to go and apprehend. That could mean taking somebody into custody, or elimination. If there's resistance, it becomes an elimina-tion.

Maybe I was being unfair, because there were many things reported about the Americans and South Vietnamese that were never reported about the VC and NVA. The NVA would attack small hamlets at night. They'd just kill, wantonly kill. One example really hit me be-cause I was there on the day before the attack. I was playing with a couple of little children, about three or four years old. I used to practice my Vietnamese with them because they wouldn't laugh at me. I was in the habit of staying overnight in the hamlets, which I didn't have to do. But that night I went back to my headquarters. And the VC attacked the hamlet. I got there the next morning at eight o'clock, and the very same little kids I was playing with were dead. A hand here, a leg there. Mothers shot up. It was like a mas-sacre. They killed everyone in the hamlet, except a few who escaped. They did it because there was an outpost there.

These outposts were small, reinforced-mud strong points. Normally they'd house platoon-sized reinforced units of the popular forces—guys who were full-time military but not part of the active army. Similar to the reserves here, but full-time. They were paid a salary and lived in these strong points around the district. They were like the forts we had in the West—your whole family stayed there with you. That's why the families got killed when the VC would overrun the place.

I'd go and spend nights with them, and so did other people on my team. Different posts every night. Some posts were good, some were bad. It depended on the commander, on the experience he had, and on how burned out he was. If you fight a war for a long time, I don't care how good you are, you get burned out. I'm surprised the Vietnamese were able to fight as long as they did—they'd been at it since the 1940s against one occupier or another. So some of the outposts weren't so good. But if you didn't go and visit them, they'd all become bad eventually.

Our economic projects could be either urban or rural. In the towns, we'd help set up markets or stores. In the rural areas, it might be buying a tractor or a water buffalo, upgrading the breeding stock, digging a fish pond. All this came from funds voted by Congress. Now, this one portion of the pacification program led to a lot of graft and corruption on the part of Vietnamese officials. If you didn't closely supervise, there was room for corruption. And the only way to find out what was going on was to get out and around. You couldn't do it from headquarters, and you couldn't rely on reports. Then again, many DSAs didn't know the language. You can't supervise a project if everyone's speaking a language you can't understand.

An example. I went out to look at a couple of agricultural projects. One was a fish pond. On paper, the pond had been dug, and the fish were in it. This was in an area where the DSA didn't usually go, because security wasn't that good. I insisted on going. The district chief came along. The hole wasn't even dug. I said, "Where's the fish pond? Where's the water? Where are my fish?" [Laughs.]

Then they made the fatal mistake of speaking in Vietnamese. The district chief couldn't tell them that I knew enough Vietnamese to understand, because I was right there. So the village chief told the farmer, "Keep your mouth shut. Don't tell the adviser anything." I understood him. I looked at the district chief, and he knew I understood. Now, normally an American would have answered right away. But you don't with the Vietnamese. They have this thing called "face." You know something, and they know you know, but you don't make an issue of it there and then. You take it up later. That was part of my training. I went back with the district chief that night, and we started an investigation. That was one of my fortes. Being a police officer, I knew how to conduct an investigation. It turned out that the village chief had kept the money for the pond. He gave the farmer a little bit and said, "Don't worry about it, this is for you. You don't need a fish pond anyway." He thought he'd get away with it because normally nobody went out to see. And my civilian adviser hadn't gone out because he was scared of that area. All his reports were based on what he was told.

I also had to check on allocation of public funds. Villages and hamlets would get money based upon population and the number of officials they had. As part of pacification, we were trying to occupy more and more of the villages that had been under VC control. We gave them money to build houses and village offices. One day I was taking a trip down a canal in my boat. In this one little hamlet there were about ten houses. So, ten houses, and families averaging about five children. The men are away in the army, but maybe there's an old man or woman around. So maybe sixty or seventy people live in that hamlet.

Then I looked at the report on that hamlet and it says 800 people live there. I said, "That's impossible, I counted the number of houses. Even if I figure ten to a house, that's only 100 people." I went to the district chief and said, "Chief, look, if they stack bodies ten high they couldn't have that many people in the hamlet. I've been there. It's impossible. I don't mind you adding on a few bodies here and there, because I know you don't get enough money, but gimme a break."

The village officials were another problem. For a village to qualify for money, the officials had to live there to prove it was a functioning village. Now, the minute you become an official, you become a target for the VC. No one wanted to be a target, so they wouldn't stay in the village. Even the village chief wouldn't stay at night. Sometimes the whole village government would go to a more secure village, spend the night there, and go back during the day. They might only go there when they expected me to visit. I knew it was going on, but I couldn't catch them. I'd say, "If you're a village chief, you've gotta take chances. If I'm going to stay in these places at night, you've gotta stay, too."

One morning I figured I'd catch 'em, so I got up early. Usually you can't leave the district town until somebody clears the road for you. They'd minesweep it every morning. That morning a Vietnamese convoy came down and cleared the road, and by sheer accident they were going to the village where I wanted to go. I hopped in my trusty Jeep, took my four VC with me—they were my bodyguards from the Chieu Hoi program. [Laughs.] I inherited four VC. They were good, you gotta give them credit. Never take a South Vietnamese bodyguard if you want to live. They don't pay attention to the job. But the VC did. So I got my four VC and my interpreter and told the district chief I was going. He hopped in his Jeep with his people, and off we went. We had a four-Jeep convoy. And on the way we passed the village staff carrying their typewriters down to the village office. They probably got word by radio that I was on the way down, but they didn't have Jeeps, and I did. I beat them there. When I got to the office, it was bone-dry. Nobody there. I waited for them. So I said, "Look, you gotta make up your minds. If this is going to be a functioning village, someone has to stay here. Otherwise I'm gonna have to downgrade it." Which is what I did.

But that got me in trouble. One of the big things in the pacification program was the Hamlet Evaluation System. It was important. It also had an effect on your efficiency rating. How much you increased the level of security in your district was going to influence how you were graded, and that means favorable assignments in the future and also possible promotion. So if I decide that my district doesn't merit the rating that the previous DSA has given it, and I decide to downgrade it, I'm not only going to make myself look bad, but also the province senior adviser. And he's not going to like that too much.

When I got there, I noticed that there were a few areas in the district that we weren't getting any information from. I said to the district chief, "Look, why don't we visit this area?" He'd say, "VC, VC." Finally we went. I saw nothing but palm trees blown down and vegetation all burned where they'd used defoliants. Nothing could grow. I saw a few water buffalo or the remains of water buffalo, but no rice paddies, no houses, no people. The hamlet was deserted. It didn't exist except on paper.

I downgraded a few hamlets like that. I think I changed them from a *B* to a *D*. I should have given them an *E*. But my boss, this colonel, was up in arms about it. I had a real run-in with him. He was pissed. It takes years to upgrade, and in one stroke of the pen I downgraded. That means one of two things—or both. Either that the hamlets never were *B* hamlets, or that enemy activity has picked up in that area. So it looks like the province chief either isn't doing anything to counter the new enemy activity, or the VC were always there and he never did anything. It reflects badly on him and on the PSA, because he should have been telling the province chief to do something.

But the hamlets stayed downgraded. I wasn't going to stay in the military, so my future didn't depend on my efficiency reports. I could afford to take a chance that other officers couldn't. I told my boss, "I know what the other DSA said, but I can tell you for a fact that the only way you can get into this village is with a reinforced rifle platoon. Now, if you don't believe me, come with me." I called his bluff. See, he knew what was going on. Nice fellow, too, but he wanted to make general.

JOHN AMEROSO

*He is a small, rapid-fire, edgy man who works in the Federal Agri-
cultural Extension Program in—of all places—the New York City area.
There is something almost spiritual in his love of farming, so perhaps
he is the right man for such unlikely territory. He was born in 1945
near Buffalo, the son of a factory worker. In 1968 he graduated from
college with a degree in agriculture. "I was all set to get drafted, and I
was thinking how I was going to get out of it. It wasn't that I was a
chicken or coward, it was more that there was the peace movement and
I was all involved with it. In high school and the first two years of
college, I was a strict conservative. Then I switched to liberal or left.
Now I can say I'm going right back to where I started from. It was the
time period, the '60s, the Movement time. I couldn't see myself going
to Vietnam to shoot when I didn't even know what was going on. So
I'm saying, 'What the hell am I going to do? Should I go to Canada?'*

*"In the meantime I had applied to the Peace Corps. They were
dragging their ass. But another group popped up. I was taking a course
in pastures, and the professor goes, 'I've got this thing here from International Voluntary Services. They're looking for people to work
overseas, in Laos, Vietnam, Cambodia, or Morocco.' Everybody went
'Ha ha ha, Laos and Vietnam.' I said, 'Really? Let me see that.' I sent
in an application and by April I was all signed up."*

I was in An Giang province, basically a peaceful area in the Mekong
delta, by the Cambodian border. My role there was to work with small
peasant farmers. They usually farmed five to ten acres of land. It
wasn't their land—they were sharecroppers. They would grow floating rice during the rainy season, and during the dry season they
would grow vegetables on some of the land, as long as it was next to
water so they could irrigate it. My original plan was to help them put
more of the land that usually lay fallow into vegetable production. That
way they'd have a little extra money, and they could advance themselves.

I lived in a little village called Cho My Lung. *Cho* means market,
and My Lung was the name of the market. There were about 2,000
people there, and it was right on the Mekong River. It was a little
crossroads with two-story concrete buildings for a couple of blocks,
and then as you went down the dirt roads, you had little thatched huts
and behind that, farmland. I lived above a store. It was beautiful.

You looked out my porch, and there was the river. On the other side was a Viet Cong province, right across the river, but they never came across because my province was controlled by the Hoa Hao. And behind the concrete buildings in the center of town were more thatched huts. Little alleyways and hundreds of people in little huts back there. Huts half the size of this room, nearly touching each other. They were raised a bit on stilts because of the flood waters. You'd walk across a board to somebody's house, then go out and walk across another board and be in somebody else's.

Oh, it was great at night when I used to go visiting. I loved it. I'd walk back there and go past some guy's hut—"Oh, John, c'mere, c'mere." I'd sit there awhile, and then a voice would come from somewhere else. Okay, I'd walk on the boards to another hut and sit there awhile. It was a friendly town, I knew everybody. And it was out of the way. When you got off the main road you had to get on a ferry and travel a good distance, and then drive a good ten miles around the side of this island to get there. I was the only American for miles around. The closest MACV station was maybe fifty miles away.

But you couldn't get away from being American. First of all, if you're American you're taken to be rich. Here you are, just out of college, you ain't got no money, you've never been in the work force to make any money. You're a volunteer, getting paid eighty dollars a month. But how do you tell this guy, "I'm not really a rich American"? Because when you think about it, you're still rich. Compared to the way they live, eighty dollars a month made you a millionaire. So they always saw you as being rich, and it was very hard to convince them you weren't. At the beginning they thought you must be CIA. They knew that word real well, it was like saying "G-men" back in the 1930s. A lot of them didn't know what the hell the CIA was, but they knew the CIA didn't wear army clothes, and everybody else did. And they thought it was funny that I spoke Vietnamese. I'd say, "I speak Vietnamese better than the CIA guys. They speak it like they're reading a book. I speak it like off the street. That's how I learned it." After a while they stopped saying, "CIA, CIA." But they were still a bit suspicious, especially the young people. The farmers didn't seem to care. They'd say, "What's your real motive?" I'd say, "Hey, we're here trying to help you. Hopefully you'll beat the Communists this way." And I'd explain my story, tell them I didn't want to be a soldier, I'd rather work in agriculture somehow, but still fighting the Communists. Some of them did believe that there are people in this world who would do that, come and work with great hopes and ideals. The term *tinh nguyen*, which means volunteer, is very much in their vocabulary. So they accepted me.

In my own mind I made an effort to eliminate both the Communists and the Americans. Who knows why they're fighting? Is it the theory about American imperialists? Or the Communists—what's their real interest in taking South Vietnam? Is it for the people, or some other reason? I eliminated that. I just said to myself, Well, with a good agricultural policy here, or a good land reform, you don't have to worry about either one of them. Why would they want the Communists in here if they had good land reform? And if the Communists went away, the Americans would go away. They'd leave an army base or two, but an army base is always a benefit to a country. So I just didn't think about the war. I never went near places where there were soldiers. I'd never go to MACV things, and I never went to the bars. I didn't like to talk to Americans. I hated it, because they'd always say the same things: "Where you from? Blah blah blah." Don't bother me, I've got other things to talk about. Farming, real things.

Basically what I did was just visit farmers and talk to them. Try to find out what they're doing, and give them basic training. I'd get up in the morning and go down to the market. It opened about four or five in the morning. It'd be dark out, and you could hear little market sounds, Vietnamese women talking away. It was a pleasant sound while you're half asleep. I'd get up about six-thirty, seven-thirty, whenever daylight came. I'd wash up downstairs and go to a couple of stalls I liked where they'd give you rice noodles with a little soybean cake, maybe little shrimps in it, or some fish sauce with hot peppers. That was breakfast. I used to love that. Then hot coffee. The coffee was delicious. They're big coffee drinkers, and the coffee was like espresso. Then I'd go out. I knew that the farmers get out early, about five o'clock, and they work in the fields and come home at eight or nine for breakfast. I'd visit them while they were back in the house. We'd talk and drink tea. Then we'd go out looking at fields. By twelve they're ready to relax, it's siesta time. After two they're out in the fields again. So my schedule was to visit a couple of farmers in one village in the morning, have lunch with them, and then go visit another farmer later in the afternoon.

Sometimes we'd walk out to look at the fields, but a lot of times we'd take a boat because there's a lot of irrigation canals. If it was rice, we'd look at the stage that it's in, see if it's all standing straight or if it's falling over, see if there's any insects. Then we'd sit around and talk about it. The guy would say, "Look at that stem. That stem is really nice compared to this other variety." Or, "Look at that stem compared to last year. It's probably because I used this fertilizer, or planted it at the right time, or planted it every twelve inches instead of every fourteen inches." Things you talk about when you talk about agriculture.

All I could do was make suggestions for new methods, because they knew their land better than I did. Mostly the problems they had were about diseases and insects, and sometimes I could tell them where they were going wrong. I could tell them about fertilizers. The best thing was to plug in on something to increase their yields, maybe by different varieties, maybe by fertilizer. Instead of one type of fertilizer, I'd buy another and say, "Hey, you don't have to use so much of this one." Or, "Okay, you've got watermelons growing? How about if you went out there and gave them a spray when you saw this little fly flying around, instead of waiting for its children to be chewing on the thing?"

I did it by a method I always liked, demonstration. Get one farmer interested and bring another one over to look at his fields. Say you wanted to do cabbage. I'd make sure you get a better variety of cabbage, higher-yielding. I'd get it from the Philippines or Taiwan. The Taiwanese had a little experimental station outside Saigon. They would give me seeds and I'd start a farmer off. Once he grew this cabbage, I'd invite other farmers from another village to see it. They'd go, "Look at that cabbage, wow, we want to do it, too." I'd show them how. These farmers are very progressive, they'll try anything new. They'd say, "Hey, you got some seed from Taiwan? We hear those guys are good farmers." There were a lot of Chinese publications in Saigon, and they'd work their way out to the villages, so they'd see nice pictures of Taiwanese farms.

I tried some completely foreign crops on them. I tried to push corn, right? There's two types of corn: field corn and sweet corn. All they grew there was sweet corn. There was a market for sweet corn, but it was always cheap. It wasn't that cost-effective. They should have been growing something else, but corn was so popular they knew they could always sell it. So I brought in some field corn seed from the Philippines. I thought I explained clearly to one farmer. I said, "See this corn here? Well, plant it, and we'll take the corn and use it for the pigs." This was a farmer I had known for a long time, but I guess he wasn't as bright as my other farmers. We planted an area four times the size of this room to field corn. He was amazed, because field corn outproduces sweet corn. It's much bigger, and you get two or three ears per plant where on sweet corn you get one. Then I came back later, and he said, "That corn was terrific! Did you see the size of those ears? The only problem with it—terrible to eat! Real terrible!" I said, "That's because we were going to feed it to the pigs." He immediately sold it and got a good price for it, and somebody somewhere ended up eating field corn. He sold it as eating corn. But he saved some of the seed, because he was going to plant it again. I couldn't get it through his head that this was hybrid corn. So the next year he planted it and got some big plants and some small plants with no ears. They didn't completely understand the theory of hybrid. I told him not to do it, but he still did it. He *sold* the corn, see, he *knows* he can sell it. He's not going to listen to me.

As soon as I got there, it was obvious that the farmers were interested in the new varieties of rice, the miracle rices. The floating rice, the hard red rice they had been growing for centuries, you could just let it grow, and you didn't have to do anything with it. The new rices you had to fertilize more, and you had to spray. And the new ones had to be irrigated because they were grown in the dry season. But the floating rice took seven months to mature, whereas the new ones were 120-day or in some cases ninety-day rice, so you might get two yields in one growing season. Plus the new rices are going to outyield the floating rice ten to one.

The big problem was capital to invest in irrigation, sprays, and fertilizer. How do you get it? I teamed up with another guy and we decided to get some co-ops going. We started with one farmer, Mr. Bao, and a couple of others who were his relatives. This guy was real good, real honest, and he was willing to try anything. Nothing but a peasant all his life, never owned any land, just getting by, but for an old guy he was a real good farmer. Well, we got a little loan, about 10,000 piasters, from the Save the Children Fund. With that we bought fertilizer, seed, and a pump. All they had to do was dig out trenches to get the water to the paddies, and they would all use that pump. One would use it one day, another the next, and they'd flood the fields. They did a total of maybe five hectares. They got two yields of rice, which put money in their pockets after the first harvest, and out of that money they paid back the loan.

They did so well that the next year everybody wanted to get involved. So we got a bigger loan from CARE. The idea was that we would buy a bunch of pumps at the same time, and at the end of each growing season they would pay back some money to an agricultural bank in the district capital. After the payment on the loan was made, whatever was left was put in an account, which would allow new groups of farmers to borrow that money to do the same thing. It would take each group maybe three or four seasons to pay off the loan.

When we got started I was out there myself, but then we brought in this guy Vic Savano. He had read a book on co-operatives, and he was sold on them. He was a fanatic. He would come in once every three weeks and we'd get together with the farmers. He was very good at speaking Vietnamese, and he'd tell them everything about co-ops, how to set them up, how it would work, who could borrow the money. And we'd have Mr. Bao come and say some encouraging words, like a religious talk. They were very enthused, they loved it. The thing they had going for them is that they all belonged to the same religion, the Hoa Hao. I don't think it would have worked that easily in any other area. Because, normally, Vietnamese peasants have a rough time getting along with each other unless they're in the same family.

I would deal with the technical parts. I'd go around and see how the pumps are working, what the next stage is in the ricefields. The farmers would fight over who was going to get the pump when, but they would usually work it out. My visits would keep the wheels going. "Uh-oh, here comes John. We'd better make sure we get along or they're going to take back our loan money." Each one got only half a hectare to a hectare, so there wouldn't be disputes about this guy getting more water because he's got a bigger field. And I'd be out there checking up. These were new varieties of rice, so they needed help. And I'd visit other farmers who wanted to get involved. I'd be the in-between man, and we'd give them the big selling job later on. I'd say, "Oh, you like that idea? Why don't we go over and look at this other guy's fields, and you can talk to him." I'd take the guy on my motorcycle and he'd talk to this other farmer. He'd get enthused, and when I'd go back to his village a week later he'd have a couple more farmers together to talk about it. Eventually we had five villages involved in co-ops, each with roughly five to fifteen families, so you had about fifty families. The co-ops covered about fifty hectares, roughly 100 acres. Which is pretty good for an area that never did that before.

And it worked. They made money. After the first year they were buying radios, and the next year they bought motorcycles, something they'd never had in their life. During the off season, the one or two months of heavy rains, they could use the motorcycles like gypsy cabs, transporting people from one ferry landing to another, so they could make some more money. And after I left it was still working, because they had their own organization, their own leaders. I remember once, during the last year I was there, driving down the road and saying, "Goddamn, look at that, look how green everything is here." All these fields, when generally during the dry season a lot of them just sat there doing nothing. All these fields into *rice*. That was something.

I said to myself: "Look at that, after two years, look at what was done here." That by itself was enough to make that whole area more independent, so they wouldn't think of going Communist or even taking any hogwash from Thieu's government. That was what my whole approach came down to. Agriculture was the way.

BEALE ROGERS

He is a smallish, white-haired man in his sixties, wearing a dark suit. We talk in his spacious Park Avenue office. He sits behind a big desk, as though I were consulting him about some ailment.

"I took training in general surgery, then went to Roosevelt Hospital in New York as an instructor in surgery. I ran the teaching and research programs there. It was during that time, about 1967, that I got interested in Vietnam. I heard about a program run by AID and administered by the AMA. They were recruiting physicians to go and work among the civilian population. I rather suspect they tried to recruit people for a year or two years but were unsuccessful. So they evolved a plan for volunteers on a two-month rotation. They paid your way out and back and gave you a per diem subsistence.

"Why did I go? It's a little hard to say. It was the prospect of a great adventure. A very useful kind of adventure. I was going to be working with people who even then, in 1967, were in great need."

I was assigned to a place in the Mekong delta called Phu Vinh, in Vinh Binh province, near Can Tho. Right away I was impressed by the dignity and beauty of the people. Certainly in Saigon and Can Tho, the way the women carried themselves, and the way they dressed, gave a sensation of elegance and flair. Even the countrywomen had that elegance of posture. And there was a demeanor about them, an identity, not of self, but of a national self.

Phu Vinh was a town of about 25,000, supplying probably another 60,000 in the environs. It was a beautiful place. There were canals. Not running water like in a bay or river, but tremendous amounts of water in rice paddies and dikes and trenches. There was evidence of war everywhere, but the people went on with what they were doing in a relaxed way. Children going off to school, laughing and playing. People marketing. Commerce on the canals, vegetables being brought to market. Yet war was all around. I was told before I went down that it was a secure area, but I quickly learned that wasn't so. There wasn't the intensity of the war in the north, but the possibility of injury and death and the tensions of war were there. I never saw anything happen. I only saw the results of it in the hospital.

In my short time there I was very attracted to the Vietnamese, but I didn't get a handle on them. The only way you could talk to people was through an interpreter. And they always told you what you wanted to hear. They weren't going to let their hair down. It was all very temporary. I wasn't there long enough to develop a friendship.

My position also isolated me. First of all, although I was only forty-four or forty-five, I had gray hair. And I was a *bac si*, that's a doctor. Therefore I was a person of some importance and position, and it didn't lead to intimacy. There's this respect for the elderly, and forty-four years old is elderly.

I was quartered outside the military compound, in a little well-constructed house, very comfortable, with another AID person. He was a lieutenant commander in the navy released for assignment there, and his job was propaganda, really. I've forgotten what the euphemistic term was for it. He was busy going about putting television sets into community houses throughout the province. Protection of those sets was his big thing. He had to keep them working and not let anybody bust them up, so they could televise from Saigon. "Gunsmoke" was the favorite program.

Next door there was another house occupied by AID people. AID was new to me, and it was impressive. There was an agricultural expert—he'd been not just a farmer but a farm agent. There was an ex-principal of a school in California. There was a police lieutenant from some major city. They were working with counterparts in the Vietnamese system. I was so impressed with these people who went out there eager to accomplish something. And with their frustration at being thwarted by the system. And being really impatient, not being able to slow down or take the nihilistic view, which was to say, "Oh, what the hell, I'm signed up for two years, let 'em do what they want and I'll go along with it." They fought, and they worked, and they got angry. When we'd get together, they had all these stories about the stupidity of it. For example, the schoolbooks that had been sent there. The teacher couldn't get the principal of the school to distribute them to the kids. The books were locked up, because somebody from Saigon might hold the local chief accountable. "We sent you 200 books, so where are they?" If he gave them to the kids he might not be able to account for them. Or the generating plant that was put in and wasn't operated unless there was a visiting dignitary. Because if it broke down, there was no way to repair it. They sent the generator and nothing else. No engineer, no one to run it.

The hospital was quite a shock. The French had built it. It was a pavilion-type hospital, about ten buildings that were in essence big rooms, all connected by verandahs. With an inner courtyard. The wards were great big rooms, open on both sides and airy, but open to every form of insect, animal, or human traffic. They were fairly comfortable in terms of ventilation, but crammed into a room with probably thirty or forty beds there would be at least 80 to 100 patients. Two, three to a bed. There would be one nurse during the day and a couple of dressers, who did the orderly-type chores. They'd change dressings. They were monks of some sort. There were even some Vietnamese Catholic sisters who brought the food around. But for the most part, nursing care and food and everything else was provided by the family. They brought their own cooking utensils and whatever food they could. The food that was provided was generally rice. Other than that, they brought their own supplies.

So there were great numbers of people coming and going. And you can imagine my surprise to see goats going through the open wards, and cattle right outside. The courtyards were grass, and the animals belonged to the gatekeeper, who was using the hospital grounds to graze his cattle. The fly problem was incredible. There was no screening. With all the animals on and about the property, you had every kind of dung. And there were no toilets as we know them. They just carried the patients out into the courtyard. Fortunately there was a heavy rain every day. I used to say, "They're flushing the toilets," because it would clean the courtyard out.

There was very little time to think about those problems, because about an hour after I got there, I was already in the operating room.

Here again, the United States was *trying*. The staff were on detached service from the military. There was a captain who was ten or twelve years my junior. Another captain had one year of internship out in the Midwest somewhere. There were about ten medics in the hospital, and about six out in little provincial aid stations. All on detached service. There were also some Vietnamese—ten or twelve nurses trained in Saigon, and supposedly three Vietnamese doctors. I only saw two of them. I don't know where the other one was. And relations with the Vietnamese head of the hospital were awkward and peculiar, because he was younger, poorly trained, insecure, and not very active. I was going to be there for two months, and then I would be gone. He'd been there for ten years and was going to be there for another ten, with the same overwhelming problems. I think he didn't know very much. So he didn't participate in the care of casualties. He avoided it. I remember one morning he walked in when we were overwhelmed with casualties and could have used ten other doctors. He came in just to tell us he'd be away for the day.

The U.S. government had put a surgical facility into the hospital. It was a concrete block building that had air conditioning when it worked. It had a receiving area and a small post-op ward and two operating rooms, and a central supply place where you could do sterilization and preparation of instruments. It was well conceived and nicely constructed, and had some nice equipment. Not so good as you would have in East Podunk, but better than a mobile hospital unit. Well, whoever was writing out the orders for supplies back in Washington had to be out of his crock. That was one of the crying idiocies you had to fight. The strongest pain medication that we'd have would be aspirin. We wouldn't have morphine. And we'd run out of the most fundamental things, like intravenous solutions, and yet in the operating room we'd have six of those silk vascular sutures that were difficult to come by even in Roosevelt Hospital.

One day, when we were just about down to no supplies at all, we got a call that five or ten tons of medical supplies were coming in by air. Everybody hopped on the truck and drove out to the airport and waited for the plane to come in. It turned out to be a shipment of Simmons mattresses. Now, that may strike you as ludicrous. To me it was appalling. It was worse than ludicrous, it was insanity. You had temperatures ranging anywhere from 96 to 110 degrees, and this was the cooler season. The humidity was usually about 95 percent. Practically every wound you had was infected. There was drainage and seepage, and there were no sheets or anything. The ideal way to treat bedsores or draining wounds was to have people on grass mats that could be picked up and taken out and burned. You put that same person on a mattress with the heat and moisture retained, and his back would break down in two days. Bedsores. So as far as I was concerned, they could chuck those mattresses in the river. They probably ended up in some province chief's warehouse, mildewed and gone to hell. I have no idea who ordered them, and I didn't ask. I didn't have time. I just remember the bitter frustration of it when they unloaded them off that damn plane.

There was also a tremendous amount of pilfering. There were rumors I couldn't confirm, but I do know that if I didn't have any antibiotics in the hospital, I could often give a patient a prescription and he could go down to the pharmacy in town and get it filled. Now, who owned the pharmacy? The brother-in-law of the head of the hospital. I make no inference. [Laughs.] I knew for a fact that in Saigon there were great mounds of medical supplies, but something happened between there and the provinces.

We had one case of a woman who'd been knocked down by a truck. Both legs were broken, the femurs. She was six months pregnant. There wasn't enough X-ray film to do a lot of X rays, so if you got one X ray per patient you were lucky. And I never could convince the Vietnamese technician not to take the X ray when they came in. I didn't need an X ray to tell me both legs were broken. What I needed was an X ray after I'd done the treatment to see if they were correctly aligned. Couldn't ever teach them that. So I was working blind. In this country she would have been operated on, and pins would have been put in both legs. But in a country without sterility you can't do that sort of thing. You have to treat them as I would have when I was a youngster, splinting them and putting them into traction. By the way, I'm not an orthopedist, so I'm having to do all kinds of surgery I haven't done before. Had to forget about malpractice, I'll tell you that.

I wanted to rig up a balanced suspension for this woman, so I sat down and diagramed it for this sergeant. He got the point of it. We drove pins through her tibia, and I had two frames built to hold the legs out so they would be in a relaxed state. These pins went out over the end, there was a pulley, and a weight on it. And there was another set of pulleys on top, counterbalanced by weights at the head of the bed, so that when she used a trapeze to pull herself up, all this would adjust to maintain the position of the legs. The sergeant had to build a whole frame, get the weights, get the pulleys, get the ropes, and he did all that. He was so proud of it. We put the woman up in this thing and she was the attraction for the whole community. People would come from the villages to see it.

I came in one morning and all the paraphernalia was down, and the patient was gone. I said to the nurse, "Where is she?" She said, "She elope." "Elope" was the term some Americans had tagged onto patients who got fed up being in the hospital. They'd just pull out and leave. I said, "My God, she can't, she's only been up in the thing for three weeks, and she has to stay there three months." The nurse said, "Oh, doesn't make any difference, she's a Cambodian." The racism between the Vietnamese and the Cambodians—you've never seen anything like it. To the Vietnamese, they weren't even human. So I said, "No, no, we have to get her back. Where does she live?" No records, nothing. "Let her go," she said. I said, "No, no, get the police." "What?" I said, "Get the police. She has stolen my pins, the ones I put through her legs. I want them back." Well, that was different. But later in the day the nurse came and said, "No, we didn't call the police. Here are the pins." The woman had pulled those steel pins out of her legs and left them under the bed.

The next day, there she is. Tears streaming from her eyes. I'm sure what happened in this case was that her husband, who's home with the kids and has no understanding of medicine, came and picked her up and took her out of there. Then when he got home he realized that she was in agony, so he brought her back. Well, later on, when I got home, the man who replaced me sent a picture of this woman standing on two legs, with her baby in her arms. That's a reward, a tremendous reward.

They were the most patient people. Stoical. Appreciative. You'd get there about eight in the morning and there would be half a dozen people sitting there with their babies, or injured children, or sitting beside somebody on a stretcher, just waiting for somebody to come. And then not rushing forward, not grabbing for you to come quick and do this, just waiting stoically and knowing that you'll come. Or you won't come. They just wait. I remember one cute little bright-eyed Cambodian kid who'd been shot through the lung. I operated on him and the dressings were painful. I had nothing for the pain, so I would talk to him. Mostly body language. I didn't know any Cambodian, and he didn't know any English. I knew I'd hurt him, I could see the tears in his eyes, but he would not call out. When I finished the dressing, I didn't happen to have a stethoscope, so I put my head down to listen to his chest to see if his lungs were expanding or anything. And this kid grabbed me around the neck and gave me a big hug and the biggest smile I've ever seen. This after I'd just hurt him.

I let it be known that I wasn't going to treat soldiers. That was the responsibility of the military. I was out there on a people-to-people program. I would help and consult and give my best opinions on casualties as they came in, but my main ward was for women and children and elderly civilians. On this ward, 25 percent of them had legs blown off. This was the great tragedy in Vietnam. It wasn't death, it was the maiming. The countryside was just covered with booby traps and land mines. They were of the simplest construction. Anybody could make them, and they did. You take a beer can, of which there were billions. You load the bottom with gunpowder, which you could get from unexploded 105 shells. You take a little paraffin, and then some shrapnel—glass, bits of stone, pieces of metal that you picked up. Some more gunpowder, and a lucifer match stuck through the edge of the can, and a piece of bamboo, right by that match, roughened and scored, so it wasn't smooth. That bamboo comes up through the top of the can, everything held in place by a little more paraffin. Then you plant those everywhere, so that a person coming along one of the paths hits the bamboo stick, which looks just like any other stick. The bamboo lights the match, and the whole thing explodes instantly, *boom*. The consequence was that many of the injuries I saw were feet that had been imploded. The force coming up through the ground just shatters the foot upward and drives dirt and shrapnel and everything right into the foot. It really implodes, with the foot kind of split apart.

Now, that might happen at four o'clock in the afternoon. By the time somebody got to the victim and they waited through the night, and then got the bus or walked or whatever to the hospital, I'd see them maybe twenty-four hours later. Under ideal conditions it would be the most difficult surgical procedure. Well, twenty-four hours later, and without any facilities, without any antibiotics to speak of, and no way to test for anything, the leg just had to come off. So I would have twenty-five percent amputees on my ward. I'd try to preserve as much of the leg as I could, hopefully always below the knee, to preserve as much length as possible and get a stump lower down.

Being a surgeon, most of what I would see would be injuries and surgical cases. I would say about sixty percent of what I saw related to the war. There were a good many direct casualties. Shrapnel, small-arms fire. Who fired the weapons? Government or Viet Cong? No one knows. You couldn't depend on what the patients told you, because it would reflect their sympathies. I saw gasoline burns that everyone said was the Americans dropping napalm. It served their purpose to say so, but all the paraphernalia of war lying about caused a lot of these casualties. There was high-octane gas that had been pilfered and used in the same way you'd use kerosene, with the result of an explosion and a burn.

All in all, the Americans worked much harder than anybody else. But even then, there were times when there just wasn't anything you could do. You couldn't start any earlier than the Vietnamese wanted to be there. There was always a break at twelve until two for siesta and lunch. And the hospital closed down promptly at five, as far as the Vietnamese were concerned. If you didn't get it all done today, there was tomorrow, and if not tomorrow. . . . All the Americans were there earlier than we expected to get started, and we all stayed until sundown. However, if there wasn't very much to be done, I did go home at lunchtime and take a little siesta if it was too hot. I came back one day, and there was this sergeant patiently sponging off a kid about three or four years old with a big tub of water. The child had a temperature of 105, and the sergeant was methodically sponging and sponging and sponging. The Vietnamese had just walked out. It

wasn't his job, he didn't have to do that, and he expected no credit.
I thought, He's an adviser? How can you teach somebody that?

The theory was that we were supposed to be teaching them. But
the Vietnamese doctors never came. I couldn't entice the one doctor
who had any kind of training to come to the operating room. After
all, I'm a professor of surgery, I could have taught him something. I
couldn't get him to come. After I got home I saw a picture of me
talking to the Vietnamese chief of medicine, and I realized that maybe
I was doing something wrong. Scrub suits don't have any pockets in
them, and Americans don't know what to do with their hands. This
picture shows me standing there with my hands on my hips. You and
I wouldn't think anything about it, but I wondered if it wasn't a position
of superiority and arrogance in the Orient. I don't know. Maybe the
director of the hospital would lose face if everybody saw me teaching
him. Maybe he'd lose authority.

One thing I thought I could do was just teach the fact that there
are germs. Now, the Vietnamese nurses knew that, but the dressers
didn't. It was obvious that they didn't, because they would go from
one bed to another using the same instruments to change dressings.
Obviously no knowledge of sterile principles. I would go with an
interpreter and talk to them, work with them, do the dressings with
them. I would say, "Now, when you've finished the dressing, you wash
your hands." I got them to use basins and soap and water, taught
them how to put the instruments into sterile solutions. "Don't touch
the dressing with your hand. Don't put your hands into the wound,
use the instrument. Discard the dressings into something that can be
thrown away or burnt. Then when you're through, wash your hands
and do the next one."

It took me two days to figure out that the patients were offended
that I washed my hands after I touched them. I then learned to wash
my hands first, before I saw the patient, so she didn't get the idea I
thought she was unclean. How many subtle things like that did I miss?
And never a one of these guys got the idea about germs. I never could
figure out why. Obstinacy? Maybe the language barrier? Whatever it
was, you're so inundated that finally you succumb to doing the work
yourself. You start out with a goal, but the overwhelming necessity
of getting the job done gives you no latitude for teaching. It's a luxury
you can't afford.

Of course, there were some conscientious, well-trained Vietnamese.
Most of them were in the operating room. There were two Vietnamese
anesthesiologists who weren't up to our standards but were good. And
a Mr. Lin, who was head of the half-dozen people who worked in the
operating room. Well, he taught me how to do some things. He wasn't

a physician, and he wouldn't have been able to explain the physiology to you, but he knew how to get in and out of a belly and take a piece of shrapnel out of an intestine. It's just that most of the Vietnamese were overwhelmed. So many injuries, never-ending, day in, day out, for years at a time. How much can you give and survive?

I never won that one about the germs. I never won anything. I came home having done I don't know how many operations, saved a few lives, comforted a few. But as to my doing anything lasting, I'm not even sure how my presence was received as far as doing my country any good. Did they think about it? Did they say, "That great United States did this for us?" Or did they say, "Why isn't it doing more?" Did they make any connection to the United States at all? I don't know.

I do know this: When I got there I was politically naive, and when I came back I was a militant dove. I came back so appalled—not finding fault with anyone, but just that this should be happening to such nice, simple people who didn't have any need of it and weren't going to gain anything from it. I wanted everybody out of there. I had no truck with the Viet Cong. That's about as despicable a way as you can fight a war, getting right down with the people and being sheltered by them and hiding behind them and using them. But I had no truck with the ARVN or the Vietnamese government, which was absolutely corrupt. And I thought the Americans were patsies. The best description I heard was from an air force major who flew a Piper Cub observation plane. About the first week I was there I said, "What's this all about? What are we doing?" He said, "Doc, it's like a giant marshmallow. Every time you push it trying to get it to go somewhere, you sink right in up to your armpits."

DOUG HOSTETTER

We talk at his office in the little American Friends Service Committee building in Cambridge, Massachusetts. Black-and-white photographs are piled on a table. He took the pictures during his three years in Vietnam, from 1966 to 1969. They show scenes of life in Quang Tin province, and each is captioned with a Vietnamese proverb or poem, including "We peasants are like banana leaves; the strong protect the weak ones," and "If upon your return you see the whole world has been destroyed, look for me in the recesses of your soul." The exhibit toured the country during the war; now it is headed for his twentieth reunion at Eastern Mennonite College.

He is a tall man in his early forties, with a full beard, brown hair, and an amused twinkle in his eye. He grew up in the Shenandoah valley of Virginia, his father a Mennonite minister. The Mennonites are a pacifist church. "Right after college, I was drafted. I got a CO, but I volunteered to go to Vietnam to do alternative service. I did it partly because I knew a lot of American young men were being sent to Vietnam. And it was a statement that my reasons for being a pacifist had nothing to do with being afraid of getting killed."

After two months of language training in Saigon, he was sent to work with refugees in Tam Ky. He was twenty-two.

Tam Ky was an insecure town. That is, the National Liberation Front was close to the edges. It's about 150 miles below the DMZ, about forty miles south of Danang, and five miles in from the coast, on Route 1. It's the capital of Quang Tin province. It has two hardtop roads, the one being Route 1 and the other being a kilometer and a half going out to a small airstrip. Two gas stations, a pool hall, and a small theater for traveling theater groups. If you include refugees, there were probably 30,000 people living in Tam Ky when I was there. I don't know how many before the war, but it had the feeling of a very small town. You could walk from one end to the other in a few minutes, and you got to know everybody. It was a market town in a fishing and farming area. Everything around was rice paddies.

The refugee camps were huge barren fields with rows and rows of little houses. Walls of mud and woven bamboo, and corrugated steel rooves, thanks to AID. In a room the size of my living room you would have fifteen people living—two families. There would be two or three outdoor privies for a camp of 1,000 people. No real sewage or garbage disposal, just open ditches running between the houses, full of foul-smelling gray water. And lots of sick kids, because with that many people packed in, the diseases are really bad. You'd see a lot of kids with scabies on their heads. Some malnutrition.

In camps that were close to American bases, a family would send a daughter off to be a prostitute to support the family. But the closest bases were twenty miles south, in Chu Lai. So the refugees would work as day laborers on any kind of job they could get. There was nothing for them to do. No land to cultivate. They were just living on whatever the government would give them.

I went in there very naive. I was supposed to be a community development worker. I had studied social work in college, and during orientation, I was told that a good community development worker gets the needs of the people together with the resources of the government. AID had given millions and millions of dollars to the Saigon government to help these refugees. But the refugees were hungry. A typical community organizer would say, There's a communication gap here. I've got to help the people to know what the government resources are, and help the government to know what the human needs are. Put them together. Real easy.

Week after week I went to the government offices, telling them: "Here are the needs. You've got the programs set up. The regulations say these refugees are supposed to get so much. I've been in the camps, and I find out they're getting a quarter, or a fifth, or a tenth that much. What seems to be the problem?" I would always be given tea and treated very kindly. And they'd say there was this or that problem, or somebody else was ripping them off, or the Americans just weren't giving them enough. So I'd go and talk to the AID folks. They'd say, "What do you mean, we're not giving them enough? I gave that refugee official thirty tons of rice last week."

So pretty soon you figured out what the problem was. The Saigon officials weren't interested in helping the local people. They were interested in helping themselves. And the Americans were in a difficult situation. Even if they knew these guys were corrupt, they had to work with them. If you got rid of one, he'd just be transferred. He'd never go to jail. This really pissed off the Americans. The CORDS person would tell me, "I built up a dossier on this guy and we went directly to the top people in Saigon. They just transferred him down to the delta. Now he's a province chief down there."

My disillusionment grew slowly. It probably took nine months. During that time I was teaching English in the high schools, so I was at least doing something. And I started to talk to the kids at school, or the other teachers, or the local pastors. Although most of the pastors didn't help much; in fact, two of the most corrupt people in town were the head Protestant pastor and the head Catholic priest. They had a whole variety of hustles. They'd get four or five different American units at Chu Lai to come up and support the same group of orphans, each one thinking they were the sole support. I'd often be at an orphanage when an American chaplain and a bunch of soldiers would come through. I would know that the pastor had just brought twenty or thirty kids from another orphanage so there'd be twice as many. The chaplain would come in and say, "For the last three months we've been supporting these sixty kids." Two weeks later there'd be another chaplain. "My boys and I have been collecting stuff from home, and we've been supporting these sixty kids. . . ."

The Americans never understood that there were two civilizations in Tam Ky. There were the local folk, who were basically Buddhist and Cao Dai, peasant farmers and fishermen. It was an area that had fought against the French. A lot of Viet Minh came from there. In 1954, when the French troops came south and the Viet Minh went north, a lot of local boys went north. And when the Americans came in and took over from the French, people didn't sympathize very much. The guerrillas were local folks who knew the area and often knew everybody in town. A lot of them were from the town. After I had been there long enough, I discovered that some of my students had other occupations at night. Even some of the North Vietnamese troops who came south were local people.

But all of the Saigon administrators in Tam Ky were Catholic. Most of them were from Hué, Danang, or Saigon. They didn't fit in. They were corrupt. The local people had no respect for the government and knew they were despised by these big-city Catholics. There were two completely different societies within the same town. I ended up having almost nothing to do with the Saigon people. I kept them informed about what I was doing, but I didn't rely on them for anything. I worked through the local hamlet representatives or through church people—the Buddhists or Cao Dai or Catholics from town.

I learned to speak Vietnamese fluently. It's a difficult language. It's tonal. If you say one word in six different tones, you've said six different words. *Ma, má, mà, mả, mã, mạ*—that's "ghost," "mother," "but," "grave," "to be false," and "rice seedling." You have to re-formulate the whole way you think and hear, which is hard. But if you have no other options, you learn it.

There were only two English-speaking Vietnamese in town—the principal of the high school and the Catholic priest. This is another part of the war most Americans didn't understand—the way culture and religion played in. It was an East-West war, but not in political terms. The Vietnamese have a saying that comes from the era of the French missionaries, which is *"Het gao, lay dao, nui con."* It means, "When your rice bag is empty, you adapt your religion to feed your kids." If you wanted to work with the French—if you were poor and hungry—you converted to Catholicism. Which was to become Western. You'd go to Catholic schools, where the whole intellectual tradition is Western.

The Americans fell into that trap. In Vietnam, less than 10 percent of the people are Catholic. Yet well over 50 percent of both houses of the Vietnamese congress were Catholic. Almost all the leaders were Catholic. Almost all the generals were Catholic. They were the West-ernized people who would work with us. They had converted not only their religion but their cultural allegiance. It was natural for a Catholic priest to learn English. To go down to Chu Lai and get all the chaplains to come up and give him aid for his orphanages, he had to.

It was so interesting to watch—it was as if there were two worlds. The Americans had power, but none of the knowledge. They were completely shut out of Vietnamese gossip circles. A classic example was when they built a new Chieu Hoi center in Tam Ky. The province adviser went to a local contractor and said, "How much would it cost to build this building?" The guy says, "The price of steel has been going up, and cement is impossible, and the road's been cut to Danang. Stuff is incredibly expensive. This is going to cost 150,000 piasters." The adviser says, "Impossible. Much too high." But there's only a handful of contractors in Tam Ky. He goes to the next one. The guy says, "Let me study it for a couple of days, and I'll come back with an estimate." He goes to the first contractor and says, "All right, what's your bid?" "I told him 150,000 piasters." "What's my cut?" "I'll give you 20 percent." In the end, the province adviser went to three or four different contractors. He paid three times what I could have built it for, and everybody he went to got a cut. The whole town knew, but there was no way he could break into the circle.

When I first got to Tam Ky, I moved in with a Protestant family. But after a while they felt uncomfortable. Every couple of months, the NLF would take over the town for a few hours. They didn't try to take it over completely, because it was the headquarters of the Vietnamese 6th Regiment. There was also a CIA house, an AID house, and a MACV headquarters, little barbed-wire compounds on the edge of town. The NLF would lob a few mortars or grenades toward the American compounds, but they were mostly into letting people know that they were the real government of the town.

This would usually happen between midnight and two in the morning. The NLF would come in and start fighting with the troops on the edges of town, mostly the civil defense folks. They'd fight for maybe an hour or so. You were soon able to tell the difference between an AK-47 and an M-16 or an M-1. A lot of the kids in the civil defense forces had little M-1 carbines, which are kind of like .22 rifles. Pretty soon the civil defense folks would throw their weapons down and take off. So you'd hear the end of the M-1s and the M-16s, and you'd still hear AK-47s, and you'd realize you're under new government. [Laughs.]

Then they start knocking on people's doors. Pretty soon, at a house nearby, you hear a very loud KNOCK KNOCK KNOCK. Everybody is lying low because of the shooting. Most of these houses are just mud walls or thick, crumbly concrete. So you're down on the floor. And you can hear: *"Mua cua, mua cua, mua cua len! Tap den, tap den, tap den len!"* That's "Open the door, open the door, open it fast! Turn on the light, turn on the light, turn it on fast!" Everything is absolutely quiet except for a baby crying somewhere and a few dogs barking. And here's a loud, confident, military voice, saying, "Open the door, turn on the light!" It goes right through you.

I remember sitting in my bedroom the first time and being absolutely terrified. I was the only American civilian living outside a military compound. There were very few Americans at all, just a couple of dozen MACV and a half-dozen CIA and a few AID folks. It was a small town. They knew where I was, and I knew they could pick me up anytime. I had to come to terms with that, and I did after the first or second time. It was a religious thing. I felt I was where God wanted me to be, and I was doing what I felt was right. So I just decided, it's in God's hands. If the NLF knock on the door and ask me to go out in the hills, I'll go.

They never knocked on my door. But they did on many of my neighbors'. It was close enough that you could hear the conversations. They'd ask if there were any soldiers living there. One time I heard them asking what people thought of the Catholic high school and the priest who ran it. Is he corrupt? Does he take money from the poor and build big schools to educate the sons and daughters of the rich? If people had said, "Yes, that's the kind of priest he is," the high school would have been blown up. But that priest was actually very good. So they said, "No, Father Tri is a good priest. He begs and steals stuff from the Americans, and he allows anybody to go to his school, even if they don't have money."

Because they gave a good report on that school, it was never touched. But the head of education for the province was a big-city man from Hué, very corrupt. He was taking 10 percent out of the salaries of all the grade-school teachers. I knew it, and everybody in town knew it. So they blew up his house. He wasn't there at the time, but he left the next day and never came back. A lot of people who were disliked in town never slept in their houses, because you never knew when the NLF would come in.

After the first time, the family I was living with got very nervous. So I moved into the Catholic high school compound. And as I got to know people, it turned out what they wanted most was education. Most of the rural schools had been destroyed. Tam Ky hadn't built any new schools. Classes had gotten bigger, but most of the kids in refugee camps weren't in school. And most of the people who had stayed in rural areas weren't in school. So I started organizing the high school students to teach grade-school kids how to read and write their own language. VNCS got the books and notebooks and pencils. Then we would give small scholarships to students who taught in the program. We started out doing it in the summer, when the government schools were empty. Later on, we developed schools throughout the rural area. The Saigon government didn't know all the places we had schools. Quite a number were in villages that were known as *xoi dao*, which literally means "rice and beans." It also means "black and white together": controlled by Saigon by day and the NLF by night. We'd work with the NLF social welfare cadre and the Saigon provincial education ministry. In the end, we even set up schools in hamlets with no Saigon presence.

The Saigon government had written off most of the rural areas, and even the refugee camps. After dark, the countryside belonged to the NLF, with the exception of the district capitals. There's a flat coastal plain ten to twenty kilometers wide. Then you've got mountainous areas with fertile valleys for another 100 kilometers or so. The Americans controlled maybe a kilometer west of Route 1, and that was it. So in 1965 and 1966 the Americans started bombing the areas they couldn't control. All the major structures that were outside the district and province capitals were bombed. Schools, marketplaces—anything built with concrete. It was all a part of pacification. If you can't control the allegiance of the people, they're going to continue farming, and they're going to help the guerrillas. So your other option is to depopulate the area. That's essentially where all the refugees came from.

The Americans would drop leaflets that had pictures of B-52s with bombs coming down. The leaflets would say, "Because the vicious Communists have come into this area, we will have to bomb it. Take your family and flee to areas controlled by the Saigon government, and we will give you protection." Usually the areas higher up in the mountains were bombed with B-52s. Most of the areas within five or ten kilometers of Tam Ky, the areas where I traveled, were bombed by Phantom jets. Then there was offshore shelling and artillery fire with 105mm and 155mm howitzers. H&I fire. You could hear it all night. That was to make sure people knew they couldn't live safely out there.

Even with all that, a lot of people had chosen to stay in the western areas of the province. The Americans were frustrated, because people were still growing rice and the NLF was getting supplied. I remember talking to soldiers who'd say, "We just can't figure it out. We moved everybody out of that valley two years ago, and the rice just keeps coming up." Well, people were living underground. Literally. They'd come up and farm at night, because it was the only safe way.

In late '68 or early '69 I started hearing from refugees about defoliation. At that point the Americans defoliated everything that was of agricultural importance. People who had just come into the camps said that large planes came over and dropped chemicals. They called it *thuoc dao*, which means poison. The poison would come out of the sky and everything would die. The farmers would dig up their sweet potatoes and peanuts—because the poison just killed the tops. They'd stay as long as they had food, and once it was gone they had to leave. That was the last phase of removing the people from the NLF. Total destruction of anything that could sustain life.

The *xoi dao* villages were areas the government thought it had pacified. Like Ky Phu. That was a fishing village spread out over maybe half a kilometer wide and two kilometers long. There was a small marketplace and a school and a little clinic. It had been an NLF village. The Americans attacked, and when the battle got to a certain point, the NLF told the villagers, "We're not going to defend this anymore. Those of you who want to stay and be captured by the Americans can stay. The rest can go farther north up the coast with us." I think it was about fifty-fifty. Of those that stayed, some were shot on sight, because the Americans assumed they were the people they'd been fighting. Some were arrested and put in prison.

Then the Americal Division wiped the village flat. Absolutely flat. Nothing visible stood. They even took bulldozers through, so if anybody was in bomb shelters or tunnels underneath, they were trapped. It's a sandy area, which is also tragic, because trees are valuable and hard to cultivate. If you destroy a tree, you've destroyed a lot. The Vietnamese had a word for it: They called it "ironing" a village. Ky Phu was "ironed."

I had a student named Buu, and I helped him rebuild his family home in Ky Phu after people were allowed back in. The area had been a free-fire zone for probably nine months. Anything that moved, anybody that went back and tried to get anything, was shot. Often people would have rice or gold buried. Buu lost some relatives who tried to go back and get stuff. After nine months of that, it was called "pacified." There's obviously nobody hiding out in tunnels anymore. Now people can go back. So the refugees went and rebuilt their houses.

I used to go fishing with Buu's father in Ky Phu. But late in '68 or '69, the Americans started tightening up on the coast, trying to keep vessels away, because guns and weapons were being smuggled. Now, these are fishing villages. They're on a part of the coast where it's impossible to farm. The earth is mostly sand. They make their living by bringing the fish in and trading it for other produce in Tam Ky. They've been doing it for generations, and they're good at it.

You get up at four in the morning and take out this twenty-foot bamboo boat. You string out a couple kilometers of fish net. Then you wait for the sun to come up. As it rises and the fish come to the surface, you pull in your nets. Before it gets to the heat of the day, which on the South China Sea is really unbearable, you've got your fish to market.

One time we went out fishing. There's a small kerosene lantern on the front of the boat. I was helping to row out beyond the waves to get the sail up. I heard a helicopter coming up the coast. Helicopters flew over Tam Ky all the time. Didn't faze me at all. Friendly Americans traveling to and fro. There were four or five boats going out together. All of a sudden, the kerosene lights went out and these guys started rowing like mad. I said, "What the hell's going on?" They said, "Do you hear that?" I said, "Of course, helicopters fly over all the time." They said, "No, you don't understand. Helicopters sink boats. That's what they're here for. Just last week, Om Hien's boat got sunk and he got killed." They told me that for the last couple of months, the helicopters had been sinking a lot of boats. The helicopter didn't find us. It was still dark.

When we went back in, I went to see the provincial head of CORDS, a marine colonel on loan to AID. I didn't tell him where I'd been, because they didn't like me running around in *xoi dao* villages. I said, "Y'know, I was down at the market the other day talking to some fishermen and they tell me the Americans have been shooting up their boats." He said, "Yeah, it's a new military regulation, number so-and-so. No craft are allowed within ten kilometers of shore between the hours of 1800 and 0600. Any vessel found within that area will be considered an enemy vessel." I said, "These fishermen have got to go out and fish. The only way they can do it is to go out while it's still dark and get their nets strung out and wait for the sun to come up."

This guy's response was: "Well, they're just gonna have to teach the fish to eat at other hours."

At one point there was an attempt to get me out of Tam Ky. I'm not sure of all the reasons for it. There could have been quite a few. This AID provincial rep was a little upset that I wouldn't cooperate with him totally. He wanted me to go to joint meetings with the CORDS people. I knew that there were CIA types in CORDS. I said, "I'm sorry, but I'm here with a church agency and I can't be part of the war effort." Then he asked me to meet with a guy from "the embassy"—that's what they called the CIA. He said, "This guy knows you're teaching down at the high school, and he'd like to know which of these kids come from rural areas and which come from Tam Ky."

I hadn't been there long, but I wasn't that dumb. The kids who came from Tam Ky, their parents lived in town. But the kids who came from rural areas, their parents lived out there. And most of the rural areas were controlled by the NLF. So it was a fairly safe bet that these kids' fathers or brothers were with the NLF. I said, "There's no way I can do that."

There were a couple of other things that made the Americans mad. So they started putting pressure on VNCS in Saigon to get rid of me. The embassy was saying, "You've gotta move this guy, we can't have him." It almost worked, but there was some publicity and it backfired on them. We ended up with regulations whereby voluntary agencies had complete authority over hiring and firing and disciplining their staff. So I went back to Tam Ky, and this colonel was furious.

The next thing may be a bit hard for some Americans to believe. One of my literacy teachers came to me and said, "My father would like to meet you and talk to you." This was months after the other episode. I said, "Sure, should I come to your house?" She said, "No, no, no, don't do that." She gave me an address clear off in a back part of town. I went there. Her father came in and said, "My daughter really likes you and appreciates the work that you're doing. I know you're not going to approve of this, but I've got a wife and family to keep, and my uncle was killed and I'm supporting his family." He had all these other problems. The end of the story was, "I'm working for the CIA." I said, "Oh? That's interesting." He said, "I've seen your file." "My file?" "Yes, there's a file. They've got pictures of you. They know you're not a Communist. They know you went to Eastern Mennonite College." Now, this is in a little thatched-roof house in Tam Ky, and a Vietnamese whom I've never met before is telling me I went to Eastern Mennonite College. He said, "They know you're a pacifist, but you're getting in their way. The work you're doing is playing into the Communists' hands." I said, "All right, all right, so what?" He said, "The CIA has decided to put out the word that you're a deep-cover agent. They're hoping the NLF will get the word."

I asked him what advice he had. He said, "I don't have any advice. But my daughter likes you, and I wanted to warn you." I didn't know what to do. Before I was there, an AID official had tried to live in Tam Ky as a civilian, and the NLF had blown up his house. He was lucky not to have been killed. But if I left just at the time this rumor was going out, it would almost be an admission that I was a CIA agent. That would not only compromise me anyplace else in Vietnam, but also VNCS and anybody who came after me. So I decided I couldn't leave.

A few months later this teacher set up another meeting with her father. Same house. He said, "I just want to tell you that I handed in my file report on this operation. It was unsuccessful. The word was put out, and nobody believed it."

By the end of my three years I felt like I knew too much. I was much more afraid of being killed by the Saigon political forces than by the NLF. I knew that the province chief's wife controlled the black market. I knew that his brother was involved with the agrarian reform scam that was ripping off the best land. I could have caused a whole lot of trouble for a whole lot of people.

But I made a decision early on not to be at all involved in Vietnamese corruption or politics. I spoke out and wrote about what American troops were doing. But I never said a thing about what was going on with the Vietnamese. It seemed to me that as an American, I was a guest in that country. Since I was an American citizen, I had a responsibility to speak about things that my country was doing. The things the Vietnamese were doing to themselves were sad, were tragic, but not something I should be involved with. That was also the advice of my Vietnamese friends.

I remember once I rented a room for our sewing class. It was half of a small building in Tam Ky. I went in one day and the other half was filled with AID goods, rice and powdered milk. My first intuition was to say, Well, here's all this stuff, why don't I run up to AID and say, "I know where you can pick up five tons of AID materials that's wandered off." But I talked to a couple of friends. They said, "Look, this is a Vietnamese problem. It's dangerous for you to get involved." One friend said, "Sure, tell AID. Go ahead. But don't open your door for the next few days. There'll probably be a hand grenade tied to it." So I went to the landlord and said, "I can't share space with this kind of activity. Either I'm going to move, or you have to move these supplies." He moved the stuff. I never knew what happened to it. I didn't want to know. It would have been sold on the open market somewhere.

When my three years were up, I left. The last week I was there, a group of teachers I'd worked with took me out to supper. They said, "Doug, we really appreciated your being here. You've loved our people, you've cared for us, you've tried to work hard, and you've tried to understand. But you've been like a man at the bottom of a waterfall with a small bucket, trying to throw water back up the waterfall. What we really need is for you to go home and build a dam across the top, to stop the water from coming down."

And that's what I tried to do.

8

NIGHT VISITORS

The dark side of winning hearts and minds was eliminating contestants of the other persuasion. The French had the efficient if brutal Sûreté. Diem and his security-obsessed brother Nhu had half a dozen police agencies that rounded up Viet Minh sympathizers and later Diem's political opponents. Those agencies, in one form or another, were passed on to the regimes that followed. The Americans, for their part, had SEALs and Green Berets, who took on various hush-hush missions, along with a panoply of mercenaries. But the most sweeping program for waging political war by force was a joint effort that became world-famous—much to the dismay of its organizers. That program was Phoenix.

The name was a bit misleading: It was the Western equivalent of a mythical Vietnamese bird with great powers called *phung hoang*. And as so often in Vietnam, the problem with Phoenix lay in carrying out what looked like an excellent idea on paper. The program was conceived by Bob Komer and run by the CIA. Its goal was to get the numerous American and South Vietnamese intelligence units to cooperate with each other. Through Phoenix offices set up in every district, information on the Viet Cong would be shared. Once identified, the enemy cadre could be arrested and interrogated, presumably leading to others. Little by little, the Viet Cong shadow government would be "rooted out." Phoenix's strike teams had a marvelously euphemistic name: Provincial Reconnaissance Units, or PRUs.

One obstacle for Phoenix planners was that the agencies participating were often competitive and suspicious of one another, and had little desire to share information. But even in districts where they cooperated, the program ran into trouble. Mere definition of a Viet

Cong "cadre" was a dilemma. As a safeguard against the use of Phoenix to settle personal grudges, the CIA required that before a target could be seized, he or she had to be identified by three different sources as a VC. But in the murky currents of Vietnamese politics, this bureaucratic imperative hardly offered ironclad protection. And then there was the problem of getting your man. Yoshia Chee, a Special Forces sergeant who worked with the PRUs, remembers that finding the right person in the right hootch in the darkness of 3:00 A.M. was no easy task.

During Phoenix's early days in 1968, its operatives tended to play by the rules. Thousands of suspects were arrested and questioned. But a change took place. As jails filled and interrogation schedules backed up, the PRUs grew impatient. More targets were simply assassinated—or were snatched, tortured, and then killed. The program varied crazily from district to district, depending on the quality of the Americans and Vietnamese running it. But as this new wave of terror washed over the villages, the black-pajama-clad PRU teams acquired the aura of the Gestapo in wartime France. "We had the sense that we were the law," says Chee.

William Colby, who ran Phoenix and went on to head the CIA, testified before Congress in 1971 that by the middle of that year, 28,000 suspects had been captured and 20,000 killed. Others believe the numbers were higher. How many of them were innocents falsely accused, mistakenly "hit," or gunned down as bystanders will never be known. Colby insists that Phoenix was not an assassination program, citing as proof his own orders to agents that it must not become one. The agents themselves knew better.

But despite its bloody imprecision, Phoenix worked to devastating effect. Ironically, it was one of the most successful American initiatives of the war. Stanley Karnow quotes Communist leaders as saying that Phoenix smashed the NLF apparatus in many areas and seriously strained their efforts to control the countryside. It also had corollary results. The PRUs gave villagers another reason to fear the Saigon government. And as word of Phoenix spread, it gave Americans another reason to feel disgust for the war.

FRANK SNEPP

He is the author of Decent Interval, *a book about the last years of the American presence in Vietnam. The book made him famous—or notorious—only partly on its own strength. As soon as it was published,*

*the CIA sued to silence him and to seize all his royalties on the grounds
that he had signed an agreement not to write anything about his service
without prior clearance. The landmark case went to the Supreme Court,
and Snepp lost. Now virtually every word he writes for publication must
be cleared by the agency.*

*He was born in 1943 into an old Southern family, and grew up in
North Carolina. As the Vietnam War heated up, "my draft board was
breathing down my neck. I was in the Columbia School of International
Affairs. I made it known to one of my professors that I didn't much
want to get drafted. It wasn't that I opposed the war, but I was adamantly
opposed to getting killed. The professor said, 'There's one way you can
beat it all—by working for the CIA.' That seemed like a good idea,
and with his help I was recruited into the agency. This was in 1968. I
was assigned to the NATO desk of the West Europe Branch. I loved
it. I worked around the clock. Then, one day, a colleague who found
my dedication to hard labor amusing decided to play a practical joke
on me. When a job application for Vietnam circulated through the
office, he put my name down without telling me. I was immediately
accepted because the agency was desperate for warm bodies. I protested,
but not too strenuously, because if you do that in the agency you don't
get another assignment overseas. So I was in Vietnam from '69 to '71,
mostly doing interrogation and analysis. After a few months in Washington, I did a second tour from '72 until the end."*

*He lives in Marina del Rey, a big apartment complex near the beach
in Los Angeles, and teaches journalism at California State University
at Long Beach. He also consults for ABC News. Not long ago, he
signed a development deal with a movie studio. The script outline was
cleared by the CIA.*

There were four species of CIA officer in Vietnam. One was the fellow
who had just been detached from the military, a march-in-lockstep
type who enjoyed the perks and status that came with being in the
agency. He never thought of questioning his orders. And generally
his job was so narrow that he was seldom exposed to the kind of
intelligence that might have kicked up his curiosity. He was wearing
blinders.

The second type was the kind of guy I was in the beginning: an
inexperienced, sometimes overly romantic youth who saw Vietnam as
a way of getting some seasoning and blue ribbons fast. Saigon was
the biggest CIA station anywhere, or just about. The agency had to
fill slots with anyone who came along, and I was one of those people.
Once there, we found that we could move our stars up in the galaxy

by playing along and getting along. We didn't ask the tough questions. Few of us had enough background in Vietnamese politics or history to know what the tough questions were. I had taken one academic course on Indochina. I shouldn't have been there at all. But I was, and so were a lot of others like me.

Then there was the third category, basically people who should have been selling insurance somewhere. They relished being in Vietnam not because it was patriotic, like the first category, but because it was fun. And they ran their operations that way.

In the fourth category were the technocrats—people who loved the CIA for the sheer beauty of the machinery. One of them was the station chief when I got there, Ted Shackley. He was the consummate technocrat, someone who seemed to have little patience for the moral issues surrounding the war.

It was in the second group, the frustrated artists and journalists and college professors, where you found the most turmoil—though in my case it took a long time to ferment. And no wonder: If you're working for the CIA, you're highly compartmentalized. Only people who were in the analytical branch saw more than a fraction of the big picture. Which meant that you could atomize your moral sense, reduce everything to what was just in front of your nose. You didn't have to think about the larger consequences of your actions or anyone else's.

For example, most of us were oblivious of the antiwar movement. I remember in '69 somebody asked me what I thought about it. I said, "I don't think about it. They don't have influence here." We were cordoned off from that kind of outside reality, and dismissive of it. I remember telling one of my embassy colleagues that protest back home was simply an expression of left-wing paranoia. Can you imagine that? I might as well have been living in some Orwellian society. Come to think of it, the embassy wasn't so far removed from Orwell. It was a controlled society, all right.

Apart from ignorance, another thing that made us skeptical of the antiwar movement was the intelligence we picked up. Radio intercepts and other reports established beyond any doubt that the North Vietnamese controlled the Communist movement in the South. But the antiwar movement was fixed on the idea that the National Liberation Front was an independent force. We dismissed them as knownothings. I can't tell you how contemptuous we were. All of us. I remember sitting in a session with the station chief one day and hearing him mock and belittle liberal senators or antiwar protesters. After a while, you'd find yourself chuckling along with him. Two or three sessions later, you'd be looking forward to the punch lines.

But it wasn't just a laughing matter. We didn't simply joke about the antiwar activists. We kept tabs on them, particularly when they traveled through Vietnam. I remember at one point we were monitoring the movements of Don Luce. This was just after he brought out the tiger cages story. The CIA was dogging him all over Vietnam, and I found myself having to scrounge through the files for something that would link him to Hanoi. We never found anything of the sort, but I came to think of Luce as the enemy. There was no incentive to step back and say, What are we doing? Why are we trying to prove guilt by association?

Nor did I ever ask myself, What's moral about this? Or even, What's legal? The legality was questionable, but it was arguable. The ethical question wasn't even arguable. But we never asked it. We assumed that we were right and righteous in keeping track of Don Luce. For a long time I persuaded myself that he had invented the tiger cages story—even though I used to go down to Con Son Island on weekends to swim and picnic within earshot of the cages. I didn't know they were there. The compartmentalization was complete. I don't say this by way of defense, simply by way of explanation.

Undoubtedly it was easier to develop some moral perspective back in the States, where you had some distance. In fact, when I went back to Washington in 1971 and began talking to some people outside the agency, I was shocked to discover the war was so unpopular. In hindsight I may seem like a Neanderthal. But you have to remember the times—the late '60s. Not just the years of rage, but the heyday of James Bond, before all the anti-CIA exposés, when spying was still seen as romantic. It was easy to believe that you were doing God's work by joining up and staying in.

Coupled with this was the excitement of the war itself. Don't forget: The agency protected its people well. Seldom were we thrust into free-fire zones. CIA people were not supposed to get killed. So you could sustain a Hemingway vision of the war without getting yourself in real hot water. Not that it was all fantasy. I remember one occasion: I was flying somewhere in a small CIA plane, a Porter, heading toward the foot of the delta. The plane had just gained altitude, and we started taking ground fire. I could hear the *pop-pop* of the rounds hitting the wings. Off in the distance I saw a curl of smoke, where a firefight was going on. Gunships were sweeping in, and I had this incredible exhilaration. I thought, By God, it's just as Hemingway says, the edge of life itself. And I started to look for it.

When I first got to Vietnam, I worked as an analyst and occasionally as an interrogator. Novice work. But I loved it. I spent considerable time in the prisons with Viet Cong cadre who had just come off the line, and I was tutored by a master CIA interrogator. The work made me so knowledgeable about the Viet Cong that I was given another job: helping to put together lists for the PRU teams, which were basically the action arm of the Phoenix program. I would go in with names culled from prisoners and captured documents and give them to the Americans running Phoenix. They were all very dedicated young men, all of them convinced that if we wiped out the Viet Cong infrastructure, the insurgency would collapse in on itself. I accepted this, too. I believed these guys when they told me they were going out to capture the VC and bring them in for questioning.

After a while, just handing over the names wasn't enough. I decided to try to go out with the teams. This was strictly forbidden. Officers in my position weren't supposed to be gallivanting around the countryside except on hard-and-fast orders. But I did it anyway, to see what it was like.

My first time out was sometime in mid-1970. This other CIA fellow and I drove to a little town outside of Bien Hoa and spent the afternoon with an American military type—a Green Beret, I think—who was in charge of four or five PRU cadre. We drank beer and Bloody Marys and worked up a chart on the hamlet where these guys were going that night. We pinpointed where the targets lived and handed over our dossiers on them. Then I said, "We'd like to go out on the mission." The team leader objected, but when I pointed out that we could help locate the targets, he said okay. It was that simple.

I remember this guy well, a real boozer. We sat around drinking and I thought, Jesus, I'm not sure I want to go out with a fellow who's all tanked up. But tanked or not, he was effective. He was a John Wayne character.

Sometime about four in the morning, we threw on some cammies, buckled up, got some M-16s and started out, first by Jeep, then by foot. Outside the hamlet, we stopped at a hedgerow to check the maps. Then the team went in. About half an hour later we heard shooting, and they came back breathless. I asked where the prisoners were, and the team leader said, "We got 'em." I said, "Why didn't you bring them out?" He just smiled and said, "Don't be naive."

End of episode. We went back to the safe house, everybody had breakfast, and I headed for Saigon. My reaction was: Well, naive or not, I've done my job.

I went out several more times during my first tour, always without authorization. And my naiveté began to drop away, particularly as I began looking at the numbers. We always kept two books on the VC, one on the size of the cadre network, the other on the Phoenix "neu-tralizations." The two should have matched up. But they didn't. You'd get reports of twenty VC killed in some district, but the estimate of the cadre structure wouldn't shrink by ten or even five. Obviously, somebody was getting killed, but it wasn't VC.

One reason for this awful discrepancy was that no one had a good fix on the target. Sure, we were after "VC cadre." But who fit that description? No one ever came up with a clear idea, although the bureaucrats at CORDS tried. They told us, "Category A is full-time cadre. Category B is part-time. . . ." But what kind of answer was that? Who's full-time? Who's part-time? A water carrier? A woman who plants a grenade in a pineapple and hands it to some poor sap on R&R at Vung Tau? We probably killed a lot of part-time hangers-on, but that didn't affect the core cadre structure.

So Phoenix was an imperfect concept, and in practice it became chaos. We did have good intelligence on who some of the primary cadre were. But I couldn't verify, from the times I went out, that we ever hit the right target. Sometimes people were brought back for questioning, but since my Vietnamese was nonexistent, I could only do an interrogation through the interpreter, and no doubt a lot was lost in translation, since the interpreter, being a Vietnamese on the government's payroll, had equities to protect, too. So who knows who got caught up in our net? It could have been Joe Schmo or Nguyen Van for all I knew.

Eventually I wrote up a memo to William Colby, who was running CORDS at the time. I said, "Ambassador Colby, there's a problem here. The figures don't match up." I put the memo in channels—by which I mean I gave it to my immediate superior. It disappeared. No response. So I wrote another memo. Put it in channels. Again, no response. At which point I became extremely concerned—number one, that we weren't killing Viet Cong. Number two, that the system didn't work. You could put something into the maw of the CIA bureaucracy in Vietnam, and nothing happened.

A short time later, Colby testified before Congress and I read about it. He said something to the effect that we had killed or captured 20,000 Viet Cong in the past several years, that the Phoenix program was effective. I pulled out our estimates of the size of the VC cadre network. It had not shrunk by 20,000 or by any measurable amount. And it wasn't that they were recruiting new cadres as fast as we were killing them, because we had other intelligence suggesting they were having trouble finding replacements for the tremendous number they had lost in the Tet offensive.

It was a bureaucrat's epiphany. Obviously something was wrong. We weren't achieving our goals. If there had been evidence that we were destroying the cadre structure, I might not have had so many second thoughts. But when things began to go awry in such an obvious way, you couldn't justify the mistakes or the carnage.

Or the cynicism of the men on high. Once they realized things weren't working—and there was plenty of evidence—they should have shifted gears. But they didn't. They held to their wishful thinking, at the expense of more and more lives. That's when the war became an obscenity.

Of course, I can scarcely cast the first stone. My only response to the screw-ups of the Phoenix program was to write those memos. And God knows, it troubles me in retrospect. I should have done more. But in those days I was a "quiet American," not so much opposed to the war as to the waste, the inefficiency, and the futility. I became horrified that we knew it wasn't working, that we were willing to fool ourselves, so that killing became meaningless. The Phoenix program was my introduction to the corruption of the intelligence process.

But a lot of other things happened to make me see the light. Take the My Lai episode. I was very friendly with the press in Vietnam, partly because the station chief urged me to be. I was young, many of the bureau chiefs were about my age, and I could move easily among them. I'd go to cocktail parties at the *Newsweek* villa and hobnob. One day I met a buddy of Ron Ridenhour, and he told me this story about My Lai. I said, "Wait a minute, that's not so. The U.S. military wouldn't blow a whole village away." It was incomprehensible to me. I went back to the embassy and talked to my immediate honcho. I said, "A story's circulating that we wiped out a village. It sounds like nonsense, but maybe we should check with headquarters, put something in channels." Well, nobody wanted to know anything about it or put anything on record. That's because once you put something in channels, you've got to deal with it. So long as you don't focus any cable traffic on it, then baby, it's not there. That's the way the analytical section reacted to that bit of information. It died.

Then there was the Sam Adams episode. Sam Adams was a CIA officer and a friend of mine who was back in Langley when I was in Saigon. He did a landmark study on how many Communist agents or sympathizers there were inside the Saigon government. From looking at captured documents, he came up with a huge number—something like 15,000 or 20,000. We got a drop copy to check for errors and comment on. I'd been culling through the same documents as Sam, and I said, "This guy is on to something. We should at least go with the ballpark estimate." But nobody wanted to do it, because nobody wanted to acknowledge that the Communists had riddled the government. Once you admit that, there's no room for Vietnamization, right? You can't go forward if your allies are Swiss cheese.

So the CIA decided to classify Sam's report out of sight. But in Washington, he leaked it to the press. People from *Newsweek* came to me in Saigon and said, "Are these figures right?" I knew they were closer to reality than any of the estimates we were fobbing off on the press, or even on Washington. So I was caught in a dilemma. Do I confirm this? Well, I did. It was the first time I stepped out of the traces. You may say, What a revolt. But for me it was. It took me out of the Good Soldier Schweik routine. I began to think, Maybe there's a reality here that's not getting to Washington. Maybe I can help.

On top of this, there was the famous Green Beret episode, in which the CIA was linked to the killing of a Viet Cong agent. This guy was a double agent, supposedly one of ours, but actually one of theirs. And some Green Berets who had gotten a tip from the CIA reportedly took him out and killed him. Allegations about CIA complicity seeped into the press, and Creighton Abrams went bananas. The CIA station found itself in hot water, because it looked as though Ted Shackley had misused the Green Berets and involved the agency in the murder of an agent. I was never sure whether he had or not. But anonymous CIA officers were quoted in the press as saying that it happened, and it was a "termination with extreme prejudice." I had never heard that term before. It was a devastating term, so deliciously sinister, and yet innocuous. It really rattled me—all the more after I went over to the *Newsweek* villa and they started asking how many people we had "terminated with extreme prejudice." The whole episode helped strip away the illusions shielding me from the consequences of our actions there. I was staring at the reality.

I wasn't the only one who reacted that way. There was a minirevolt in the CIA station. People were saying, "The CIA shouldn't be a party to cold-blooded murder. It's bad for our image, it's bad for our consciences." The vibrations got picked up at CIA headquarters, and the director tried to calm everybody by circulating a memo saying, "The CIA does not assassinate people or condone assassination. Don't do it." I've often thought about that memo. It was a lie, an outright, blatant lie from the director of Central Intelligence. Later on, when I came back from Vietnam in 1975 and walked right into the Church Committee investigations, I discovered that the lie was much larger than I had thought. In fact, we had sought to "terminate with extreme prejudice" Fidel Castro and a number of other people. So that memo from the director was the ultimate scam, a cynical bid to keep the Boy Scouts in the trenches from asking too many tough questions. It helped to jolt loose my own ties to the CIA. If you've never been on the inside, you can't appreciate how stunning it was to discover that the director had lied to us. Because you assumed that, even in a situation as morally ambiguous as Vietnam, there was still a solid sense of values at the center of the CIA. But there didn't seem to be. And for those of us down the line, that meant we were involved in a moral crapshoot, with no justification for our more extreme actions.

But you didn't need to know all that to become cynical. Just talking to the North Vietnamese could do it to you. We got very few defectors from the NVA, so when we did get one, we wrung him dry. In my own interrogations, I always bore in on motivation—why Uncle Ho's boys kept going. I started out thinking they were highly indoctrinated. That notion quickly gave way to a less flattering view. Basically, I think they were trapped. Their families were hostage up north. They couldn't defect to their home village because it was hundreds of miles away, and South Vietnam was alien turf to them. When they came down the Ho Chi Minh Trail, they were told they wouldn't come back alive, period. They would be bombed and shelled to oblivion, and if they fell into the hands of the enemy, they would be tortured to death. We captured letters and diaries full of moaning and groaning about impending death. And it's true, the casualties they took were unbelievable. So there wasn't much for NVA troops to hope for. Whatever they did—retreat, surrender, or advance—they were dead men. And they carried that fatalistic view with them right onto the barbed wire.

I'm not talking about the Viet Cong cadre. They usually had a strong ideological background. But the NVA were different. Try to engage an NVA soldier in a political discussion, and you'd find he didn't have much to say. He hated the Americans, and that was about it. The literacy level among the average NVA was nil. So it finally came down to one thing: They had convinced themselves, as perhaps only Vietnamese can do, that they were fated to die in the South and it was a worthy death if it got the Americans out. They figured: "My parents are under American bombing. My two brothers have already been killed. I've got no place to go." They'd also been told that the southerners all eat children and sleep with the Americans. So what would you do?

Some antiwar protesters used to talk about the NVA's superior "moral position," as if that's what kept them going. That's a lot of claptrap. The NVA's sense of morality was so outrageous and nonexistent that somehow morality became irrelevant. I kept thinking: What kind of commanders could put men into the field endlessly and see them mowed down? Christ, they were throwing 60,000 or more troops down the Ho Chi Minh Trail each year, and few were coming back. What could we have done if we were so indifferent to human life? That's why all the antiwar propaganda about atrocities became just noise. Atrocities? The atrocity is putting 60,000 men into a meat grinder every year.

Even so, there's no denying that the NVA were committed. Their morale, wherever it came from, was remarkable. In fact, that became a throwaway line in our intelligence estimates: "North Vietnamese morale isn't wavering. It remains as strong as ever." Sometimes I wonder if we really grasped the meaning of that. Because once you've concluded the enemy won't bend, the policy inference should be: We should get out, and fast. But none of the policymakers I dealt with ever drew that inference. All of which made me more cynical than ever, I suppose. Here was a situation where our intelligence was always pointing in one direction, and it had no impact on anyone. You had to become cynical about that. And once you realized that intelligence on this issue was irrelevant, you stopped wasting your time trying to get it. You just moved on to the next subject.

That's how you begin making compromises in the CIA. The logic runs something like this: If I hold my tongue today, I will pick up enough credit within the system to be able to tell the truth tomorrow. But tomorrow never comes. You keep postponing it. You make more and more compromises. And finally you lose sight of the truth. You forget where the ethical standards lie. That's because the agency is very good at blinkering you with euphemisms, like "termination with extreme prejudice." You don't often have to admit the worst to yourself.

I remember one time, at the beginning of my second tour, I discovered that a prisoner I was interrogating was being beaten by the South Vietnamese police. So I went to one of my superiors and protested strenuously. He said, "What do you want me to do? Go in and argue morality with the Vietnamese? Tell them that beating him up is wrong? I can't make that argument to a Vietnamese cop whose village is getting shelled by the VC every night. Give me a pragmatic reason for objecting." I said, "Well, I can't get any strategic information from him." He said, "With that I can argue." The end of the story is that I was taken off the case. But the point is, that's how you learned to deal with problems. You didn't argue morality. Morality was not part of the vocabulary. Pragmatism was.

Once you accepted that, it was hard to break out of the mindset. You kept retreating from the moral choices, and opting for another euphemism, another blinder. And you were rewarded for that—for adopting the language of the system.

It's often said that there were a lot of disenchanted young CIA officers in Vietnam who saw the light and wanted to blow the whistle. Well, there were. But like me, very few acted on their concerns. Maybe they wrote one memo and then sat around kvetching. It never went very far.

A lot of people now claim to have been opposed to the war, or at least to the compromises it entailed. They wring their hands and say, "Mea culpa." Well, why didn't they do that at the time, for chrissakes? I'm thinking in particular of the military guys who got up and blew the whistle on Westmoreland in the trial. General McChristian, all those guys. They're now suffering the torments of the damned. Well, screw that, a lot of American boys died because they didn't do it then. They didn't search their consciences and stand up when it could have made a difference. I think that was true of me and many other young officers. We made some gestures and some smoke, but very little fire.

YOSHIA CHEE

He is a muscular, barrel-chested man with shoulder-length black hair, mischievous eyes, and a scraggly mustache. We first meet at a party in San Francisco given by another Vietnam veteran. Yoshia is wearing jeans and a T-shirt emblazoned with the famous line from the movie Treasure of the Sierra Madre, *spoken by a Mexican bandido: "Badges? I don' have to show you any stinkin' badges!" It is a joke on himself, because his accent resembles the bandido's. It is also an eerie comment on his service in Vietnam. For several weeks he avoids my phone calls. Finally he agrees to talk, and we meet in his apartment, in a working-class area south of Golden Gate Park.*

He was born in 1946 in Hawaii, the son of a Chinese-American man and a Native American woman. His parents soon separated, and he was raised by his father in East Los Angeles. "At first I thought I was white—not white really, but like anybody else. Then I went to the first grade and found out it wasn't so. Being a half-breed, I wasn't Chinese, and I wasn't Indian either. Ever since I was young, that's one of the biggest wars I've been fighting. My father tried to raise me with the ideals and the principles of a Chinaman, but nobody is more prejudiced than the Chinese. They call the non-Chinese ghosts, so I was a half-

ghost. *Even my cousins called me names. But everybody else just thought I was Chinese.*

"When I was sixteen years old there was a big change in my life. In the Chinese way, when you're sixteen you're a man. You can smoke, drink, gamble. But you have to earn your own money. We lived in Santa Monica by this point. That was a big change, too. I realized I was totally different from anybody else. In Santa Monica it was the Beach Boys and Frankie and Annette. Parties on the beach. And I looked like I came out of West Side Story. *I was a greaseball. The only thing that made me popular was I had my own car. I worked three jobs to get my first seventy-five-dollar car. It was a '54 Chevy convertible. It had no windows and no backseats. You sat on milk crates.*

"By this time they were sending people to Vietnam. There were patriotic things on the media. There was even a tune, 'The Ballad of the Green Berets.' So in 1966 me and my best friend, this Samoan guy named Lulu, we joined the army. I wanted to prove something, because I was an Asian-American and an Indian to boot. I wanted to prove I was a first-class citizen. My father was always telling me, 'You're American.' But I had this accent. I haven't ever gotten rid of it. Now Cheech and Chong make money out of my accent."

Since coming back from Vietnam, his life has been troubled. He has worked as a bodyguard and as a roadie for rock-and-roll bands, among other jobs. *"I was taking a lot of speed. And I had a couple breakdowns. I would destroy everything in the house."*

In recent years, with help from the Veterans Outreach Centers, he has shaken himself loose from the past—to a degree.

To me, being in the Special Forces was something as romantic as being Beau Geste in the Foreign Legion. That's how innocent I was. I had those kinds of dreams. It was going to be just like in the movies, where only the extras die. I would come back with all these medals, and the women would faint when they saw me in this sharp uniform.

The army wouldn't let you join the Special Forces until you were twenty-one, so I had to wait. You were supposed to be a Spec 5. But I already had a specialty in hand-to-hand combat. I was a black belt in judo, and I knew Chinese boxing, because all the men in my family did that. I was five feet ten and in great physical shape. That's what they wanted. So I volunteered for Special Forces and started my training. I learned radios, weapons, medicine. I went to jungle survival school in Panama. From there we went to Okinawa, and then we graduated.

In Okinawa they were forming special groups called Peregrine Groups, made up of all Asian-Americans. Out of the 200 that started in my class, only twenty-five of us finished. All Asians. We got regular Special Forces training plus lots of endurance exercises. A lot more intelligence training. And more hand-to-hand combat. We spoke a lot of French. We were supposed to learn Vietnamese, so we could really live off the land. It would have been nice if we were fluent in the language, but we weren't. We didn't have enough time, and it's a hard language.

We were supposed to fight on the same principle as the peregrine falcon. It comes out of the sky at 200 miles an hour, gets its prey, and takes it back to the young ones. That was the whole idea: Come in fast, do your shit, and get out. The theory was that being Asians or half-Asians, we would look like the Viet Cong, live like the Viet Cong, and think like the Viet Cong. If you think like them, you can beat them at their own game. But that was a big mistake. How can you take somebody out of Chinatown in Seattle, and expect him to beat the Viet Cong when he doesn't even speak the language?

Of course, at that point you think you're one of the best fighters in the world. You're young and strong and full of come. You can do superhuman feats of strength and endurance. And you have a heart the size of San Francisco. You're just like a puppy, a pit bull puppy.

We got in-country in late '67, a little before Tet. We went to a stinking village up in the highlands where nothing was happening. Nothing. Dogs would bark at night, but the war was miles away. Once in a while you could hear a couple jet planes go by. We were going, Fuck, what is this? I came out here to kick ass, what is this shit?

We started working with the Montagnards. We had two teams, fourteen guys each, and we were training all these Montagnards. Teaching them how to set up mines, how to use plastic explosive. And we're still saying, This is war? This is chickenshit up here. All we do is run, drill, run, drill, run some more. But we started getting familiar with the country. Pretty soon we adapted to everyday village life. We discovered opium, too. It was great, so we started doing unmentionable quantities of the stuff. We found out the Montagnards had their own poppy fields. I decided, Wow, this is great, I want to live here for the rest of the war.

When Tet happened we were on rotation from the highlands, down in Danang. After it was over, we moved down by the Cambodian border, and they started sending us out on missions. The Peregrine Groups mostly worked in III Corps, near the border, or in the delta, or inside Cambodia. Our job was to look for sympathizers of the Cong. Also we looked for hospitals and supplies and arms caches.

But the main objective was to wipe out sympathizers or collaborators. Anybody who was under the slightest suspicion of working with the Cong was a marked person. We worked with the PRUs and the ARVN Special Forces and all kinds of other weird guys: Thais, Filipinos, Chinese born in Vietnam. There were even Abos; those guys were great for reconnaissance.

The idea was great on paper, like the Declaration of Independence or the Bill of Rights. We were supposed to grab the Cong suspects and send them back for interrogation. Not many made it back. It was interrogation on the spot. And I think we ended up settling a lot of disputes between villagers. If you owed some guy money, or he did something weird to you, you'd go out and snitch on him. You'd say he's collaborating with the Cong. Then the Phoenix people would call us and we'd get him in the middle of the night and torture him a little bit. Maybe he was collaborating, maybe he wasn't.

I remember my first mission. It was called "Randall." Remember Randall on TV? He was a bounty hunter. The mission was named after him. We were transported on trucks. Not big military trucks, just common trucks that went on and off the base. The trucks would drive down the road and we'd jump off in groups of three, roll into the brush, and disappear. That way the VC didn't know where people got off. When it was my turn to jump, I was so scared that I froze. I swear to God, I froze. After all that training and thinking I was superman. I was number five. Numbers seven and six jumped, but I froze. I was holding up the other guys. They were shouting, "Number five, jump! Number five, jump!" Then this guy comes over. Instead of pushing me, he pulls out his .45 and cocks it, and says, "Number five, jump." So *pppssssshew*, I went. But at that point I shit in my pants. I had to stay with shit in my pants for three days. At one point I turned my fatigues inside out. Then this guy comes around, a captain. He looks at me and says, "Goddamn, smells like shit around here." I thought, Oh, God. That was my first mission.

We had three targets that mission. We didn't get them. Plus a radio station, supposedly. It turned out to be a small transmitter with a coat-hanger antenna on it. That was their main transmitter for that area. It was hidden inside a five-gallon peanut-oil can. It didn't look like a radio, it was so primitive. It was probably French surplus from the '50s. But they used all that stuff. They were well organized. They had runners with codes, plus that radio. What we went through to get that little transmitter. . . . [Laughs.]

Most of our missions either turned out half-assed, or we weren't successful at all. And a lot of people got hit who didn't have anything to do with it. We'd be told that in such-and-such a village there's a collaborator. Usually we'd get photographs of the guy. They would drop us around twilight, maybe eight, ten miles away. Then we'd make our way there. By the time you get there, it's three o'clock in the morning, and that's perfect. Nobody is expecting you. That's one of the keys, shock.

Usually all fourteen of us would go in. Fourteen is a great number for a small force. It's fast and it's efficient. Some guys would go in the house, and some would stay outside. At that point we'd make a lot of noise. But we'd have a guy covering every single house. Anything that moves too fast, we shoot the shit out of it. Or we'd just throw a grenade in. Grenades are a bit shaky with those hootches, because they're made of bamboo. You can get hit by your own grenade. So mainly what we had for this kind of mission was shotguns. We used ten-gauge shotguns a lot, with double-ought buckshot.

If we found the guy in the house, we'd try to take him alive. Maybe he wouldn't be there, or it would be the wrong house, or somebody would fire at us. Then you just started shooting into the corners. Anything that moves, you shoot it. It's dark, and you don't give a fuck what it is anyway. We had a saying, "*Gomen nasai*," which means "Pardon me." It comes from the Japanese. Sometimes if there were four houses in a row, and we weren't sure which was the right one, we'd kill everybody in the four houses. It happened all the time.

If we caught the right guy and he was a head honcho, we'd take him back. If it was a head honcho they really wanted bad, he would go all the way to Saigon. Or somebody might come out from CID or MI or just somebody in plainclothes with a funny haircut and shades. Those guys—you never asked questions about who those guys were.

But if you grabbed a guy who wasn't going back to Saigon, you'd interrogate him and then kill him right there. You find out what you need to know and just kill him. Or you kill everybody in the place. Or just a couple of people. You had to leave your mark that you were there, to warn those guys. You'd throw aces. I used to throw the ace of spades. Or the jack of hearts, or the king of diamonds. I used the joker a lot, too.

We'd try to get all the information we could—supply dumps, meeting points, dates, times, hospitals, more collaborators' names. Most guys didn't tell us what we wanted, but some of them did. You were dealing with patriots, and patriots don't talk. We were just making martyrs out of them. It's pretty unpleasant to talk about this, but there were some ways of torturing people without really getting into the Dark Ages. You've got to always have shock on your side. One of the favorite things was popping one of their eyeballs out with a spoon. It won't kill the guy. The eye can be fixed. But it's awfully painful and shocking. Just imagine having one of your eyeballs hanging out. I would talk—if I had one of my eyeballs hanging out, I'd say I killed Kennedy. I'd agree to anything in the whole world.

We would do that, and they still wouldn't talk. You could do anything—like skinning the bottom of their feet and beating them with a bamboo rod. That won't kill you, either, but it's painful. Another favorite one was to carry the guy to a five-gallon drum of water. Then you hold his head under water until he's drowning, pull him out, and hold him under again. It won't kill you, but it's pretty scary.

The really drastic torture I saw was performed by the Vietnamese on their own people. They did all this weird shit. They'd use their K-bars to saw on people till they got down to the bone. One side of the K-bar is serrated, so they'd keep sawing till they got to the marrow. It's awfully painful. Useless, too, most of the time. Or chopping fingers off, that was very Vietnamese. Then there were beatings—you grab somebody and put a bag over his head, tie him up, and beat the shit out of him. Or dropping guys out of helicopters, that was a method of interrogation. I saw that all the time. Oh, he tripped and fell. Being handcuffed, it's easy to go right through the door.

But you rarely got anything out of them. Just more hatred. More reason to fight us back. There was no end to it.

The only way you could prove you got the target was to bring back his ID. The military ID had a photograph. But maybe he didn't have an ID, or you couldn't find it. Then you'd bring back his head. It was more efficient to bring a head back than a prisoner. They wanted these people exterminated anyway. And cutting heads is an Asian tradition. The Buddhists have been doing it for thousands of years. If you cut your enemy's head off, he's not going to be reincarnated as a human being. He'll come back as an object or an animal—something low, a dog or a cow. Do you know how many whacks it takes to chop a head off? It takes a lot of whacks. The vertebrae in the neck are one of the hardest things in the world to crack.

The ROKs used to chop a lot of heads. We did a few operations with them, too. Those were tough guys. They were the most inhuman motherfuckers I ever saw in my life. Their methods of interrogation— I once saw one of them kicking somebody's head. He kicked it until the head just exploded like a watermelon. So he kept kicking it until it was just goop. It was unreal. It's hard to describe these things. It was almost like a Fellini movie.

Another thing we did was look for Viet Cong hospitals. We'd get word that a hospital was operating in an area, and we'd try to find it. We got to a couple. Our duty was to wipe out the whole hospital. It wasn't just to go out there and say, "Okay, guys, gimme all your medical supplies, and we'll call it quits." The thing was to go in there and get the doctors. Get the nurses. Get the patients, too, fuck it. Ain't that shitty? It is shitty. Of course, our hospitals got hit, too. But we weren't supposed to be doing that.

Usually it'd be underground. In the middle of the night, we'd go in shooting. Anyone in white, you shoot first, any way you want to do it—separately, or lined up against the wall, whatever. Then you get the patients. Some of them even wanted to fight back. But it's hard in the confusion. Our whole force was Asian. We all had slanted eyes. We all dressed in black pajamas. A lot of times we had mercenaries with us. So the Cong couldn't tag it back to blond, blue-eyed guys with green uniforms and chewing gum.

The biggest stink I heard when I was there was over the My Lai stuff. That happened because the guys who went in there were wearing uniforms. They had on their nameplates. Plus someone took all those photographs and everybody was outraged. On a lot of operations we weren't even allowed to wear dogtags. The only way of recognition we had was a password.

We were high most of the time. Fourteen kids, fucked up on Methedrine. They gave it to us for endurance. You can walk for miles, and you don't fall asleep. It works a lot better than glucose does. When you're stoned on meth, you can do incredible feats. So most of the time we were stoned. We had to be stoned. I can't see anybody in their right mind doing the stuff I did. And we were allowed to go to Saigon a lot, to the bars and whorehouses. We said, Fuck the curfews. The MPs wouldn't fuck with us. Just wearing the PRU patch, it was like having a sheriff's badge. You don't ask no questions of the sheriff. People would buy us drinks. We had the sense that we were the law.

One of the things I didn't quite allow at that point was rapes. Anything else was fine—burn the house, kill the water buffalo and pigs, no problem. I did that, too. But no rapes. That part of being the conquering warrior, I didn't go for it. One time I was out with these Vietnamese Special Forces. I don't know why, but those guys did the most inhumane things to their own people, you wouldn't believe it. Two guys were ready to rape this woman, not with their dicks, but with a pop-up flare. A pop-up flare is when you pop the back and this flame comes out. They were about to stick it in this woman's twat. I'm lying against a mango tree, smoking a doobie and talking to my best friend. And out here are these other ARVN sitting around laughing. When the two guys were ready to do it, I took out my sidearm and shot from the hip and killed them both. I just went

Bam! Bam! Bam! Bam! Bam! Bam! The other guys started to jump on me. But my friend had one of our light machine guns, and he aimed it at them and said, "Get lost. Good-bye." He understood. Raping that woman was just pointless. Why make unnecessary pain? There was no gain in that. She didn't know anything. She was no use to them. Besides that, it was just fuckin' nasty. But what impressed me was my doing that. I felt like I was losing it. I was playing God, or playing executioner. If you sit down and consider it, and you consider yourself a human being, it doesn't quite fit, does it?

All my life, I've tried to keep things in order. I try to do things right, and I have this sense of order, that things should fall into place. It's like the old Chinese philosopher, Lao-tzu, trying to explain everything by these two forces. How the whole life cycle goes around, how the earth cleans itself up. It's all in this order of things. If you go against this order, then it's unreal, it's unstable, a bit like a hallucination. It's out of the order of things. And that's what Vietnam felt like after a while. My mind was like the Hoover Dam when they shut the escape valve. All that pressure from all that water, tons and tons of fucking water. But if they let it escape, it could wash out half of Nevada.

On April Fool's Day, 1969, I lost my whole team, everybody but my best friend. I had pretty much the same team the whole time. People got wounded, but nothing very serious. I lost a lot of mercenaries and South Vietnamese regulars, and a couple of guys in my team got transferred and started running their own squads, but I had never lost any.

Our mission that day was to get three guys in Cambodia. One was a sympathizer and two were NVA. They were going to be in this one village near a rubber plantation. Supposedly the whole war was going to be shortened by months if we got these guys. They were a must. We were offered R&R for days and all this extra money for doing it, just like a bribe. But we had to take three extra people with us. One was a captain. One was a second lieutenant, the captain's aide. And one was a major who was my immediate boss at that point, my CO. He was from Langley, Virginia. Old South, Confederate money. Went to West Point. He didn't know shit about war. He wasn't out there. I was. But he outranked me for miles.

The landing zone was about three miles from the village. There was jungle everywhere, swamp and muck. It wasn't regular mud, it was muck, like clay. It sticks to you. It oozes. You can't walk two miles a day in that shit. But there was a path from the LZ to the village that was pretty clear. Still kind of sluggish, but safe. The helicopter flew away. They were going to come back in four days to pick us up. In the meantime we were supposed to have the heads of these three dudes.

Now, this is the way I would have done it myself. I would have come in not three miles away, which tells everybody that we're there, but farther down, on the other side of the fuckin' mountain. Then I would wait until dark to go into the village. I'd wait till the middle of the night, between three and four o'clock, when everyone is sleeping the heaviest. Then all you gotta do is take out the sentries. But no, we had to go in during the day, just because this asshole major didn't know anything. He knew as much about guerrilla warfare as I knew about Vivaldi. Actually I knew a lot more about Vivaldi. [Laughs.]

We did everything wrong. We left them plenty of time to get everything underground. The three dudes were gone. I could tell this village was a bad place. It stank. There was nobody of military age, not even ten-year-old kids. It was toddlers, old-timers, and a couple of women. But there was all this rice. There was enough rice to feed a platoon of seventy people. Our platoons were forty people, but theirs were bigger. And there were only seventeen of us. We were looking for stuff like medical supplies, but there was nothing. Not even containers. The only thing they couldn't take away was the rice.

It felt very shaky to me, so I grabbed this baby. I held him by one of his ankles, I guess. Of course I made sure it was a baby boy. I put my sidearm along his head, and I told this woman I was going to kill the kid unless she told us where the soldiers were. The lady looked at me straight in the eye. It was like she was telling me, "Go ahead, I can always get another one. There's nothing you're going to get out of me." There was that hatred. I just thought, Fuck, what am I doing here? What the fuck am I here for? Then the major told me to shoot the kid. I would have done it, but the whole thing, something in the back of my mind—I saw this woman's face. And I said, "Fuck it, you shoot it. It's not going to be on my conscience." And the guy shot it. He shot the baby. I almost shot him. Then he wanted to round up everybody, shoot them, and burn the village. That was his intention. I refused, and I had witnesses. Plus my guys were more seasoned than he was. But I was in trouble. I had disobeyed a direct order from my CO. He said, "When we get back, you guys are gonna be in deep shit."

We left the village and started walking down a road. The captain took point. He outranked me, and he was an excellent jungle fighter. And he bought it first. A few miles down the road we got ambushed. They caught us right in the open. They had a recoilless rifle hidden in the plantation and heavy fire from the treeline. They were dug in, waiting for us. And the ground where we were was baked clay, the hardest shit in the world. It was like granite. We had no entrenching tools, so how in the fuck can you dig? The sharpest things we had were bayonets. So it wasn't pretty at all. It was terrible.

We were getting our asses kicked. The recoilless rifle was bugging the shit out of us. We had an emergency call sign, W-O-Q, that would alert any aircraft in the area to mark our position and call a chopper and get us out. I'm calling, "WOQ,WOQ, WOQ, WOQ." I also called in an air strike. The major had told me, "If we get hit, we'll just call in an air strike. No problem." But the strike never came. If we could have gotten a strike, we would have come out smelling like a rose. Another day in the life. But one by one, my guys were dying. The lieutenant was one of the last ones. He fought bravely, for a staff aide. He went down, and then my medic went down. I was hit in the leg and in the side. My best friend was wounded in the throat. He was wheezing and bleeding. But he still fought us out of there. I was in no shape for fighting. And he carried me back to the landing zone, which must have been ten miles. We snuck back, hiding in the bushes. We had one of those little radios, the battery-operated short-wave ones. Sometimes they worked, sometimes they didn't. We kept sending WOQ, WOQ, WOQ, WOQ. But when we got back to the landing zone we waited a day and a half for a chopper. Waiting out there was something else. We knew the NVA were looking for us.

Finally the choppers came, a medevac and two gunships for support, with a squad of men on each gunship. We flew out to look for the bodies. We found them in the village. The village was empty, but the bodies were there. They were naked, with no heads. The heads were piled up. And these were my friends. People I knew and loved dearly. People that I slept with, that I shit with, that I told all my fuckin' stories to. I knew their hometowns, their hamburger joints, their drive-ins. Their favorite football teams. What type of lady they liked. What they were gonna do with the GI Bill when they got home. So nowadays, April Fool's Day is a very bad day for me.

I stayed in the hospital for a month. I wasn't in good shape by that point. Jungle rot, malaria, some kind of weird bouts of fever. I felt drained. I felt like it was my fault. And I felt like a complete stranger. I was a stranger to myself. I was tired of the scene. The smell of death, the smell of fear. The blood. All the fucking blood we spilled for nothing.

After that they gave me the Silver Star. My best friend got it, too. And I stopped working with the PRUs. They assigned me a whole rifle company of Vietnamese draftees, people with six weeks' training. There were only five Americans, counting myself. We were supposed to give them advanced training. We were in the rear. I was no longer in black pajamas. I had a tiger suit, the same kind that the South Vietnamese Special Forces used to wear. I still wore my beanie all the time. We would go on patrol, but just night ambushes and that type of thing. Not too far outside the perimeter. Regular grunt shit.

Now let me tell you what happened on Christmas Day, 1969. I lost forty-two men, including five Americans. It wasn't really anybody's fault, we just got caught in an ambush. Actually, it was an ambush of an ambush. There was supposed to be a cease-fire, but we went out. We ambushed these people first, and we let everybody know where we were, and all hell broke loose. That's how I know that some of the ARVN were real fighters, because I saw them prove themselves there. Some people died real bad. I lost some people that believed in me.

When I came back from Christmas Day, I was a different person. I was no longer reliable. I was no longer fit for combat duty. That's what my chaplain said. He said I was unstable. I went to see him, and I said, "I don't think I believe in this. We're not going to win. They're right, we're wrong. This is worthless." And he started giving me all this shit. This is the battalion chaplain, and he's carrying a Colt .45. Supposedly this stuff I told him was confidential, but he reported it. They sent me back to my unit, but I wasn't into heavy combat anymore. I was into bunkers. [Laughs.] I did a lot of stationary duty, just sitting there waiting for my discharge. In the meantime I was being reviewed by this board. They had a doctor, an analyst. . . . They decided I was no longer reliable. There was no doubt about it.

You know something? I think it was fear. I felt fear for once in my life. And I mean fear, which is a different thing from being scared. When you feel fear—you ever hear the expression, "turning yellow"? I had that impression, that my skin was turning color. It wasn't fear of getting killed or maimed, any of that shit. But I had a fear of something. I can't describe it. It's like some people get in elevators. It was like a phobia. A phobia for the whole thing, the whole country.

What I decided to do was completely obliterate my brain the best way I knew how, which was opium. When I wanted to put away the war, opium was the best thing in the world. When you're tripping with opium, you can picture yourself in your father's tackle box. That's what I used to do. Like I was looking at my old man's tackle box, and I'd remember how he used to have his leaders on one side and his pliers on the other. Or maybe I'd remember how many drawers are in the kitchen cabinet of my father's house, and what stuff is in them. In one drawer you have paper sacks. In another one you have aluminum foil. In another one, knives and forks and spoons. That's what I used to think about. Or I used to dream about making love to white women. Or how many women I had fucked in my life, trying to remember their names. I used to think about playing Go, movements around the board. Or riding horses in Bishop, where my other relatives lived. Way the fuck away from the place I was in. Any place that had no tropical weather and no stinking gutters. Chinatowns smell like Chinatowns all over the world, a combination of trash, nutmeg, ginger, all these dry spices, plus human shit. All teeming in the heat of the night, with the bugs. And you're in some little opium den. You've got your faithful candle. You've got your pipe. If the house is kind of fancy, you've got someone to burn it for you. Otherwise you had to prep your own medicine. If you were too fucked up to prep one, you'd eat it instead.

Then I did some time in the stockade. This is how it happened. I was in a whorehouse in Cholon. It was off-limits, to start with. But there was some brass in there, a couple of full birds. There was one big room with all these partitions and little hallways between them. The partitions were the bamboo shoji type, with oil paper or flowery cloth screens. Between the partitions there's these little curtains hanging from a piece of string. That gives you some privacy—not much, but enough to make love with. Then you have these towel boys that come around with the drinks, if you want drinks. Either beer or cognac.

I smoked some opium that night, plus I had a shot of Methedrine. A speedball, we called it. Then the whorehouse got fragged. Someone threw two grenades in there. They were American grenades, the ones that have breakshot inside. Every single piece of breakshot becomes another little grenade itself. Me and this woman were almost in the middle of the big room. I had my head toward the wall and my feet toward the door—actually not the door, but the little curtain I'm talking about. The partition was on three sides of us. The lady was on top of me. All of a sudden her head disappeared. It was just gone. And there was this spray, like wet spray. My dick was still inside her. The only thing that saved me was I was lying flat on my back. The killing radius goes up and out. If you're down on the ground, it blinds you and you feel like the wind is knocked out of your lungs. Your ears ring for days. But I got a cut finger and that was it. Both people on one side of us died, and the people on the other side were badly wounded.

The MPs came. I was part of the walking wounded. I was in shock. I was dazed. I thought I was more seriously wounded, because I saw all this blood on me. All this spray, and pieces of—God, this is hard to describe. It's almost like a bowl of Jell-O that splatters in your face. It's that kind of texture. I didn't want to touch it. And everything was in slow motion. Speedballs do that to you. They make you rush, and then slow down, and then rush. Of course, we were all naked. You don't have any rank on your dogtags. They asked my rank. I said, "I'm a captain." "Well, Captain, would you kindly go with the sergeant out there? We're gonna take you to the hospital to examine you, sir."

In the hospital they figured out I was a first sergeant. But when my Purple Heart came down, I was written up as a captain. "Captain Yoshia K. Chee, the government of the United States . . ." How does it go? They have a little rap they tell you about the country being grateful. By this time I had various decorations. I had the Silver Star and a Bronze Star with *V* for valor. I had two Purple Hearts. I got the Gallantry Cross from the South Vietnamese Army—anybody that got a Silver Star got that one, too. I was recommended for the Distinguished Service Cross. So this colonel was going to give me another Purple Heart while I was in the hospital, and I refused it. I go, "Well, Colonel, sir, I don't want it. Thank you." He says, "How come you don't want it?" I says, "Well, I've got a couple of them." He says, "Then this is a ticket home," because if you got three Purple Hearts, it was automatic. I says, "I don't want it. So you can take it back and shove it up your ass, sir." The guy gave me an Article 15 and took two months of pay and gave me the medal anyway. I gave it to a nurse. And I ended up in LBJ for a little while, until they found out about all the brass that had been in the whorehouse.

Then I got out. I didn't have any orders. I don't know why, I guess because I wasn't reliable. I was constantly getting fucked up and getting into fights, getting drunk on duty, all this crap. Then I went AWOL for a month and a half. I was living with a mamasan in Saigon. They thought I was missing in action. I was losing my sense of time. I was losing a sense of who I was. My brain was shutting off, just from being there. The only thing that kept me there was a heroin habit. I had a habit worth $300 a day in Stateside prices.

I finally got arrested for being AWOL. They brought me back to LBJ, and from LBJ they took me under heavy guard to Japan. I left Vietnam on November 20, 1970. I was in Japan for—I don't know, it could have been two days or two weeks. Then they took me to Fort Lewis, Washington. Then down to Colorado. I had a board review me. Supposedly I was unstable. I was really hostile. So I got a medical discharge. In Colorado they made sure I boarded a plane to LA, and as soon as I got to LA I took a cab home, and that was it. I was out of the army.

Before I came home, some of us managed to get some heroin transported to Hawaii and from Hawaii into Oakland. Several kilos. We divided it among a bunch of people. And I smuggled home some opium about a year before I left. I sent a stereo to my father. It was one of those reel-to-reel things with two speakers. In the speakers there were two slabs of opium, probably half a kilo. And inside the stereo I had some more chunks.

I remember the night I came home. My house was dark. Then I saw my father in there. He had aged like ten years since 1968. This was only 1971. I saw that he wasn't superman. He looked fragile. A proud old man. I went in. He said, "You're home, huh? Good." Still playing the tough guy. But I knew he was jumping for joy inside that I was safe.

I went upstairs and flushed my ribbons down the toilet. All of them. My father says, "Do you want a drink?" He never used to drink. We went down and had a toast to my return home. I told him, "I'm not going to any American Legion meetings. I'm not going to parade in uniform for you and your friends." We sat there drinking. I never saw my father cry before in my whole life, and he was crying. I asked him, "Hey, did my stereo arrive?" "Yeah, it's in the garage." I went out, got one of them Phillips screwdrivers, and all the opium was there. I went back to my room that used to be my room when I was a kid.

I always slept with a sidearm in my hand. The next morning, when I woke up, I found out that in the middle of the night my father snuck in and took the clip out of the pistol, ejected the bullet in the chamber, and put the gun back in my hand.

That was the safest fucking place in America, and I was dreaming about being in 'Nam.

9

THOSE DARING YOUNG MEN

In modern warfare, control of the air gives an immense advantage—and to say that Americans controlled the air in Vietnam is an understatement. We overwhelmed it, especially in the South. Along with choppers of every size, a menagerie of fixed-wing aircraft crowded the skies. There were reconnaissance, transport, defoliation, and communications planes. "Puff the Magic Dragon" gunships. Phantom, Skyhawk, and Thunderchief fighter-bombers. And the B-52s, or "Buffs," for Big Ugly Fuckers. If a grunt humping the boonies heard a plane, he could take comfort: It was his. Air power was the ultimate technological fix, a major reason we would succeed where the French failed. In the South, planes would rain death on the enemy when he had friendly troops in trouble; in the North, bombers would throttle supply lines and so batter the society that Ho Chi Minh would tire of the punishment and sue for peace.

For President Johnson, this last goal was most seductive. Surely the North Vietnamese, like his old opponents in the Senate, would knuckle under in the face of superior power. Also, the air war was convenient because it could be turned up or down. From August 5, 1964, when the first planes hit the North, Johnson continually fine-tuned the level of bombing. He (and Nixon) used bombs to send messages: that America meant business; that the President was angry; that the President was VERY angry; or that he was in a mood to negotiate.

In the process, three times as many tons of bombs were dropped on North Vietnam as were dropped by Allied forces in World War II over Europe, Asia, and Africa combined. The figure is somewhat misleading, since many of the bombs in Vietnam fell on empty jungle. Still, 100,000 civilians were killed in the North. No one knows how many died in the South, but the toll was certainly higher. Against this, one can balance the large number of American and ARVN soldiers whose lives were saved by the air war.

The men who flew the planes were an elite, with jet fighter pilots at the top of the pyramid. They were the young men with the right stuff, cocky and gung-ho. They had been trained for combat as a game—and the reality did not prove horrifyingly different, as it did for soldiers on the ground. Strapped into a tiny cockpit, moving faster than sound, they were isolated from the war, literally above it. Competition was the thing. Says Pete Sillari, who flew backseat in a Phantom off the U.S.S. *Constellation*, "The credo for fighter pilots is: 'I can fly better than you can, fuck more women than you can, and drink harder than you can.' " This is not to say that combat missions were not dangerous, and that pilots were not afraid. But fear became part of the high—and the high was addictive.

Of course, a pilot tended not to think about certain things. These included what he was doing and what could happen to him doing it. Pilots love to talk about the technical prowess of their planes, or about the game—dodging the flak, outmaneuvering the SAMs. But most talk little about the destructive capabilities of what they carried: bombs, napalm, rockets, white phosphorus, CBUs. Once the ordnance hit the ground, it became abstract, bursts of smoke and light on a field of lines and colors. Pete Sillari again: "We never thought about who we dropped our bombs on. It wasn't an issue. . . . It's the drop of the bomb, not where it lands. It's the action, not the result." And John Buchanan, an A-4 pilot, adds: "Aviators are like doctors. . . . You have to cover up a lot. . . . It's so macabre . . . that you layer over things. Like when we talked about napalming people, the expression was 'making crispy critters.' Or when you had a crash, you 'bought the farm.' "

Did Americans intentionally bomb civilian targets in the North? With one exception—Dick Rutan—every flyer I talked with said no. Some spoke of the North Vietnamese putting guns on top of schools and houses, and nearly all said that dive-bombing, especially when one is under fire, is not a precise art. Misses, often by a mile, are inevitable. But one gets a very different picture from antiwar activists who visited North Vietnam (see Chapter 11)—so different that I often wondered how this could be the same war, the same bombing campaign.

And did the air war succeed? The debate still rages. In the South, tactical air strikes were devastating when the enemy was trapped or attacking en masse; and having air support made a world of difference to the grunts' morale. B-52 strikes were viewed with awe, and with derision, by the ground troops. One attack could blast a tract of jungle to twigs and splinters, but there was often no evidence that the enemy had been there. Many former Viet Cong say roughly the same thing: that the B-52s caused terror but not decisive damage. And of course, air strikes in the South epitomized the dilemma of American fire-power. By killing civilians who happened to be in the wrong place, they often sparked more sympathy for the other side.

In the North, the air war failed more clearly. It destroyed countless tons of supplies, slowed transport and industry, and cost the North dearly. But supplies kept coming south, and morale did not break. On the contrary, it may have been tempered—the London Blitz effect. As early as 1966, Johnson's top advisers had reports that the bombing was not working and would not work. Other reports disagreed—and Johnson kept escalating, until he called a halt in 1968 to get negoti-ations under way.

Many of the pilots who flew over the North knew, or sensed, that it was not working. They could physically see what the policymakers could only read: that in a peasant society there is little to bomb, and that the North Vietnamese, by sheer manpower and primitive trans-port, could keep supplies flowing. Here the pilots' experience was like the grunts'. They were dying and being captured, and for what? To bomb a bamboo bridge that could be replaced in a few hours? To move dirt "from one side of the road to the other"? There were a few targets that presented challenge and glory: the Doumer Bridge, the occasional MiG. But once they were downed, would anything change?

Also like the grunts, the pilots felt they were fighting a war in shackles. Targets couldn't be hit until far-off bureaucrats said so. Certain targets—mostly in or near Hanoi or Haiphong—were per-manently off-limits. MiGs couldn't be attacked if they were sitting on the ground at military airfields. The "Rules of Engagement" were a bitter joke. Squadron commanders and wing commanders were ob-sessed with the number of sorties flown, the tonnage of bombs dropped, the quality of bomb-damage reports. Careers were being made. Quo-tas had to be kept. The pilots themselves needed more missions so they could get air medals, or even a Distinguished Flying Cross.

Yet for all that, what comes across most in talking to pilots is how much they loved it. "I must confess I enjoyed the war part of it," says John Buchanan. "It's phenomenal, the sense of euphoria to have come back from a mission where people were shooting at you." They liked the camaraderie, the elitism, the competition—but most of all they loved flying. "I wasn't gonna feel any sense of pride if we won the war," says Pete Sillari. "It wasn't about beating the Vietnamese, or beating Communism. It wasn't *The Bridges at Toko-Ri*. It was a bunch of guys out flying, who got off on flying, and that was exactly what they were there for."

PETE SILLARI

He picked up his nickname, Squirrel, in the navy—"for socially aberrant behavior." He is forty-one when we talk, a smallish, wisecracking man who lives with his wife in a house complete with outdoor hot tub on a ridgeline in Stinson Beach, California. He works for ComputerLand.

After navy ROTC in college, he couldn't pass the eye test for pilot training. Instead he became a radar intercept officer, or RIO—the backseater on the F-4 Phantom.

The RIO's job is to look at the radar, find an enemy aircraft, and then essentially control the plane. With the radar you can see this other guy maybe thirty, forty miles out. The pilot can't see him, so you tell the pilot what to do. You keep the enemy on the scope and help the pilot to get behind him or at least in visual contact. You want to put yourself in a good tactical position. That was my job—that and backing up the pilot on flying the plane. I didn't have a gas gauge, so I always had to ask what the fuel was. I had no warning panels—they were all up front. So you're always second-guessing the pilot. You're a professional backseat driver. Pilots can have trouble with a thing called target fixation. When they roll in and start looking at the target, sometimes they'll concentrate so hard that they fly right into it. So you're also there to scream at the guy, and that's always what you did. At a certain point he's supposed to pickle the bombs off, and when you reach that point you yell "Pickle!" once and pull the stick until you start seeing the altimeter gaining numbers instead of losing.

I was on the *Constellation*. We got in-country in the spring of '68. It was right then that Johnson said we weren't going to bomb north of the demilitarized zone. That was good news, as far as I was concerned. I was not too eager to go over the beach. I felt prepared for engaging a MiG. It felt safer, more even. But going over dry land, that sounded a little too risky. There were too many unknowns. There were SAMs, there was ground fire. I just was not interested in those flights. I liked being at 20,000, 30,000 feet.

We did two cruises, separated by about six months. I stayed pretty bright about it until the second cruise, and then I got a little bitter. On the first cruise I kept thinking somebody actually did know what we were doing. I didn't understand what was going on, but I trusted my superior officers. I figured they were having some sort of discussion with people back in Washington, and the thing actually had a purpose, and it was what they were reporting in the papers. But the second cruise, all of a sudden I started asking a lot of questions.

It came out of the frustration of not being able to do what you think your job is. On two cruises I flew 200 missions, and maybe a third were bombing missions. We'd move the dirt from the north side of the road to the south side. The next day we'd move the dirt from the south side of the road to the north side. To no purpose that I could see. It looked to me like we were just dropping in the jungle. There weren't people around. There weren't trucks. We were bombing the Ho Chi Minh Trail, or we'd go down south of the DMZ and fly up the east side of Laos, right next to North Vietnam. We'd find the passes that the Ho Chi Minh Trail went into. We'd bomb the passes. We'd bomb ferry crossings on rivers. Or we'd bomb an interdiction point, which is the coming together of a couple of different roads. But I couldn't see them. From what I've read, they built them so you couldn't see them from the air. It was like going out and bombing a dump every day. The FAC would tell us we were on target, but I couldn't see it.

If you couldn't drop your bombs on target for some reason, or you ran into weather, they had these free zones where you could just drop. That didn't make sense to me either. It was like: Go to the state of Nevada, and anywhere in the state of Nevada, drop. We just kept pouring in more. And it wasn't just us. On the nights we went up, under the cloud cover you could see the lights from these arc-light strikes, the B-52s. On my second cruise, more than twelve months after I'd been there the first time, it was still going on and on, like this black hole.

On all those missions, I can remember bombing trucks once and people once. Maybe we were doing a great job and it really did make a lot of sense. But it didn't seem to be too purposeful. It wasn't that I wasn't gung-ho. I always wanted to do a good job. I wanted our squadron to be the best. But as for the whole thing, I just wanted to be done with it. I had no feeling of animosity toward the Vietnamese people. I wasn't gonna feel any sense of pride if we won the war. It just didn't register. The flights themselves were exciting, but it was about flying. It wasn't about beating the Vietnamese, or beating Communism. It wasn't *The Bridges at Toko-Ri*. It was a bunch of guys out flying, who got off on flying, and that was exactly what they were there for. One time I made that assertion—that everybody was there just to get their rocks off. They enjoyed flying. Only one guy said, "No, no, I'm here because I think our country—" and so on. And some guys were into getting medals. They had a whole attitude of, We better do good because this may be the only war we get for a while.

The thing that really did it for me was one hop when we missed the target by miles. The FAC dropped a flare and we lined up, and either we didn't understand his instructions or we didn't get lined up right. You have all these parameters based on an ideal glide slope at an ideal air speed and a particular altitude. If you do all that you get a bull's-eye. What always happens is you're steep or shallow, you're fast or slow, and the pilot is supposed to correct for that. Well, that's a pretty wild correction. You've got all this high-tech stuff, but you just gotta make this wild-ass guess. This time the pilot guessed wrong. Something screwed up.

I went to the debriefing and said that's what we had done. The guy put down some euphemism I didn't quite understand. There was always this jargon that the intelligence operators used. So I said, "Excuse me, Chuck, but what's that you wrote down?" The gist of it was that because of the debris that was stirred up and conditions at the target, we couldn't assess the battle damage. I said, "Oh. But that's not what happened." He said yeah. I said, "Well, don't write that down." He says, "I've got to write this down." I said, "What do you mean, 'I've got to write this down'? We were two miles from the target. We weren't even close. We fucked up." He said, "Well, I've got to write this. The word came down from the admiral that you won't miss your target." I said, "That's great. I didn't see the admiral with us." Then he tells me this story that we can't turn in bad stats, because if we do it goes up the line, and when finally the navy turns in its stats for the Route Pac—they had Vietnam split up in route packages—the air force guys will say, Hey, these navy guys have only got an 80 percent effectiveness rate. Look at us over here, we're 87 percent effective. You should give us that territory.

All of a sudden it had gone from a unified effort to an intra-team squabble. That just set me off. The target had no particular consequence. The empire would not stand or fall based on what we did that day. The whole point was that we couldn't tell the truth about it. I was so pissed and upset by that. It was probably the biggest thing in making me cynical—that and seeing day to day that nothing much was happening.

We never thought about who we dropped our bombs on. It wasn't an issue. That was the curious thing about the whole experience: There were people who were somehow impacted, but that part never came up. Let's agree that everybody was telling the truth, and most of the navy flyers actually knew that they were never dropping on people. Because that's what they told us. We were dropping on a road, or on trucks, or over a free-fire zone, which from the air was just wilderness. Let's say that's a given. But we were having an impact on people's lives. To have bombs dropped on you for a good portion of every day, it's got to really affect the way people live. But that never entered into it. It wasn't like, Aha! We'll wear down the Asian devils. [Laughs.] It wasn't, Hey, we're gonna beat these guys. *These guys* never existed, as far as I could see. There was only us. It was a very one-sided thing. It's the drop of the bomb, not where it lands. It's the action, not the result. Nobody saw farther than their nose—farther than their canopy, maybe.

The only time I thought about dropping the bombs was the time when there were people. The FAC said there were gooks in the trees. I don't remember the situation. They either had somebody pinned down or they had been chased to that position. All I can remember is I wasn't sure we should be doing that. But I didn't quite know what to do about it. It was like—Ooh, it's too late now, I guess I should have thought of this earlier. We dropped, and apparently there were nine people killed. The FAC was very cavalier, he was talking about how we nailed nine—I forget how he put it. I guess maybe "slopes." I can remember being real bothered by that.

But all the rest of the time it was very sterile and cool. I got in this little steel box that was as fast as the speed of sound. It was air-conditioned. I had all this high-tech equipment around me to get me back to my home steel box, where I had a hot shower and a hot meal, and then I'd get drunk every night. There was never any contact with people on the other side. SAMs connect you up with people on the ground, and MiGs connect you up with people. But for us, it was the war nobody showed up for—except us. And we said, We don't care if you don't show up, we're gonna have a war anyway, fuck you. [Laughs.]

JOHN BUCHANAN

"I'm forty-eight—obviously," he says, but it isn't. He looks ten years younger, a tall, lean, intense man who serves me bran flakes and tea when I arrive. The apartment outside Washington has a temporary feel:

*newspapers stacked three feet high, clippings covering the table, a row-
ing machine in the living room, weights scattered about. He relishes his
role as an odd bird, an ex-marine combat pilot who works with liberal
groups like the Center for Defense Information, trying to change American policy in Central America.*

"I was born in Daytona Beach, Florida. Went to military school and
then Columbia Military Academy in Tennessee. Graduated from there,
got an NROTC scholarship, and went to the University of Virginia for
three years. Flunked out because I drank my way out. Well, rather than
flunk out, I left. Question of honor. [Laughs.] I was gonna write the
great American novel. I stayed out a year doing research on the beach.

"In those days, everybody had to go to the military. I went down
and took the flight test for the marines and astounded 'em. Obviously
if I was smart enough to get into ROTC, they figured, 'Boy, here's one,
and he's healthy and everything.' They were ecstatic. I was in the flight
program before I knew it.

"I really didn't want a military career, but I wanted to be an aviator.
I just loved the thought of flying. I ended up in a squadron in El Toro,
flying A-4 Skyhawks. I wanted to go to Japan, so in 1962 I put in for
a regular commission in the Marine Corps, figuring that was a way to
impress the commanding officer that I was indeed a career-oriented
person. It was very hard to get into squadrons going to Japan. Believe
it or not, that year I think they only picked sixty-four people in all of
marine aviation for a regular, and I was one. I didn't intend to take it,
but by God, so many hundreds of guys had put in for it and not gotten
it, I figured they'd lynch me if I refused it. Besides, then I wouldn't get
to go to Japan."

*After a tour in Japan as a nuclear delivery pilot, he came back to
the States and was stationed at Quantico. By 1967 he was married, had
two sons, and had a degree in American diplomatic history from George
Washington University.* "I was doing very well. I was one of those go-
getters. And then my brother—he was a helicopter pilot in the Marine
Corps, a very brave and heroic young man—came back from Vietnam.
He was flying one day down at New River, and some deskbound lieutenant colonel with a load of troops in back of a CH-53 ran into him
as he was taking off. Cut him down. He crashed and burned on the
runway. That day I was taking my last flight in a refresher course before
I went to Vietnam. I happened to be flying over New River. I looked
down and saw this big ball of flame. I said, Well, looks like somebody
bought the farm down there. I came back into the parking lot and the
squadron CO and the operations officer came walking out. They said,
'Buck, we've got some terrible news for you.' So I didn't go to grad-

*uation. They just sent me my diploma, because I went to his funeral.
Settled my family in a new home and went to Vietnam."*

You have to remember that I was accultured. In the South, our entire
history had been of violence. First, we considered that our ancestors
weren't the effete sons who had the mansions in England. Under the
law of primogeniture, our ancestors had to get out. They came over
to make their way in this brutal country by force of arms. They trained
as soldiers rather than being the elite. We had the military schools in
the South—we didn't have Choate and Andover, nice preppy schools.
We had Virginia Military. The Citadel. We used slavery, that's a form
of violence. When that war was over, we figured we'd won the battles
but not the war. We pride ourselves on being better generals. I grew
up in that culture.

I got off the plane at Chu Lai. My friend Darrel Shelor came in a
Jeep to pick me up. We had flown together as boys, as lieutenants.
We went up to the O club and got into a conversation. I said, "I know
what's going on over here. We're bombing these villagers. I'm not
gonna bomb any villagers just because somebody calls me in on 'em."
I knew that was happening, because pilots talk to each other. My
brother had talked to me about it.

Well, my very first flight out of Chu Lai, I was flying wing on a guy
who graduated flight training the same day I did. We went down about
twelve miles south of Chu Lai. There was a beautiful little grove of
palm trees. In the middle was like a little white Southern Baptist
wooden clapboard church with a tin roof and a steeple. Some Koreans
from the Tiger Division were supposedly taking sniper fire from there.
Bill went in first. His napalm sailed over the church and went into the
trees and burned the village out there. I figured, Well, hell, do the
best I can. I dropped my napalm. *Whoom!* The church blew up. Then
we dropped our snake-eyes in the village and so on. Those are 250-
pound bombs with drag fins on the back. You come in low and drop
'em and the fins open up to retard the bomb.

When we came back, Bill was telling everybody: "Here's Buchanan,
who's not gonna bomb villages, and the first thing he does is blow up
a church." They were all razzing me. I went out to dinner that night
and had on my uniform. When I came back, they had taken my Nomex
flight suit and gotten a stencil made. They had stenciled on the back
CHURCH BURNER. Nomex flight suits were hard to come by in those
days. I had to wear that for about four months till I could get another
flight suit.

I later learned that what I had stood for was exactly right. Those

Koreans down there were running dope. They had a big dope trade and extortion racket going. They'd run up against somebody that gave them a little hard time, and they'd call in air strikes on 'em.

I flew A-4 Skyhawks most of my career. It's a tactical aircraft, a bomber. In my mind, it's one of the finest little airplanes in the world. It's so small that you have to kind of slither in and get down into the seat. When they put the cockpit down, your shoulders are wedged against the sides, so when you fly the airplane, you feel like it's part of your body. It's that intimate. The gun sight's a foot and a half from you. All the instruments are right there in front of you. It's so close that you have to have cutouts in the console for your legs to fit in.

It's a very simple plane. It had nothing but a practically straight control system. No radar, nothing. It was like a stork, set up very high on its landing gear because it was designed to take one big fat nuclear bomb under the belly. It was a very poor airplane on landing because a crosswind could almost flip it over. But gradually they began to develop it as a fighter-bomber. They widened the landing gear. They put brakes on the sides of the wings to keep it more stable on landing. It did a hell of a job in Vietnam. We carried a lot of bombs— twelve 250-pound bombs or perhaps six 500-pound bombs, plus two napalms or Zuni rockets. And you had 20mm cannons. Not that we won any wars, but it was a good bomber.

I loved the plane. You get in there and if you want to pull up, it feels as if you just lean your body back. You're actually pulling the stick back, but it's as if you just lean. If you want to roll, you just turn your shoulder and roll. It's part of you, and you become part of it.

In Vietnam, the main purpose of the A-4 was close air support. A typical day might begin around midnight. One of your crew members would come into your hootch. He'd shine a light in your eye and wake you up. You'd get up and do a TPQ, which is a radar-controlled bombing run. You go down, check your target, pre-flight your airplane in the dark. Launch off. You'd fly out somewhere in northwest South Vietnam. En route, you'd make radio contact with this radar unit. They'd lock onto you and direct you over this target—presumably. You were controlled automatically, and the bombs were released automatically, but it didn't always work, so we backed it up manually. You would fly at precisely 20,000 feet, at the right air speed, precisely level. Try to make your controls very smooth. They'd say, "You're one minute from target," or something like that. "Stand by—mark mark." You'd go *boom boom*, like that, and drop 3,000 or 4,000 pounds of bombs on the guys below. You had no idea what you were bombing. Turn around and come back.

You normally had two hops scheduled a day. If you were on an interdiction sort of thing, maybe early in the morning three or four of you would go up and bomb something in North Vietnam. Or you'd be in support of a mission like a helicopter assault. Those were like milk runs. You go up there, the spotter says, "We've got marines in contact." You go in and bomb, napalm, snake-eyes, do a little strafing. At the end of the flight you'd give your report on your plane status—up, down, having mechanical problems. You'd go up and debrief with the S-2. Go eat lunch. Come back and do it again. [Laughs.]

On alternate weeks, or every three or four days, you'd be in the alert squad. All day long you'd sit there in the ready room. We'd keep three two-plane sets ready to go. The infantry out in the field would get into a battle. They'd call Danang. Danang would call Chu Lai. All of this is very quick. We'd jump in the airplanes and launch off and go. Then you'd come back and do some more of your regular work. After supper I'd go out and sit by the beach and make a thirty-minute tape to my family.

Normally, I'd be going to bed about that time. Some guy might come staggering in who'd had a drink too many. He'd say, "Hey, Buck, can you take this mission for me?" So I'd sneak in another flight just before midnight or right after midnight. I think I was over-compensating a little bit after my brother's death. Another way I'd do it was to go down to the alert room on days I wasn't supposed to be there. I'd keep an eye on things. If all three sets of planes went out, I'd be accidentally standing around in my flight suit. I'd put on my harness, get another guy, and we'd be handy if a call came in before the other planes got back.

There was constant competition to get more missions. If you're a squadron commander, you want your squadron to fly all the missions they can. You want to drop the most tonnage you can. You want to push your guys for more ribbons and awards. The group commander has four or five squadrons, and he puts the pressure on his squadron commanders. He has a better chance for promotion if he can say his squadrons dropped more bombs and had more flight hours than the others, and got a better fitness report every six months.

It was the same with me. I wanted to have more air medals and ribbons than the other guys. I remember one hairy mission I was on because I had an argument with Darrel the day before. I was mad as the devil—not mad, but a competitive sort of thing. I said, "Darrel, you didn't give me a flight today. Give me one tomorrow up over the DMZ." Because you got two points toward your air medals for getting shot at, or for going north of the DMZ. You only got one if you didn't get shot at. Air medals aren't like the Distinguished Flying Cross, which is an individual award. You might get air medals for a heroic award, but usually they were nothing but ticking off the points. Every twenty points you got an air medal. So the faster you accumulated points, the more air medals you got. This might be the only thing you had over the other guy when you came before the promotions board.

I must confess I enjoyed the war part of it. It's phenomenal, the sense of euphoria to have come back from a mission where people were shooting at you. That's the ultimate gamble, your life versus theirs. Of course, you can't say it was real fair. [Laughs.] I was coming in on an A-4 with bombs and rockets and everything, and they generally had maybe a 14.5. But there's no way to describe the euphoria. If you took the guys coming into the locker room after the Super Bowl, even though they're getting a lot more money and they're greater heroes in front of 75,000 cheering people, that's probably 50 percent of what post-strike euphoria is like if they really shot at you.

Like at night, if you'd go up north and dive into someplace where there's tracer fire that looks like a damn fire hose of red balls coming at you. The red flashes are zipping past your cockpit. I'm not a religious man, but on missions like that I prayed like a son of a bitch going down. You drop your bombs and get the hell out of there and come back and, man, you can float. I could probably communicate with dope addicts pretty well. [Laughs.]

Aviators are like doctors. You have to become—I don't know what it is. You have to cover up a lot. When somebody in the squad gets killed, at first you're very efficient. You're getting the accident board together. But that night at the O club, you're all saying, Well, I wonder what the old so-and-so's doing now? Who's gonna volunteer to go home and spend the night with his wife? Ha ha ha ha. You have to laugh over it.

It's so macabre, a lot of it, that you layer over things. Like when we talked about napalming people, the expression was "making crispy critters." Or when you have a crash, you "bought the farm." That comes from the fact that everybody carries a lot of insurance, so when they get killed the wife and kiddies can go back to Arkansas or Texas or Oklahoma or wherever, buy the old farm they've always wanted, and settle down. It's bravado. You have to get past the fact that most aircraft accidents are fatal. One good thing about them for the pilot is that you don't usually crash and come away all maimed. You're usually dead, or you walk away from it. It's not too easy on the family, but you won't know too much about it.

I had all these damn noble ideals, but you get so used to it. You're flying these missions two or three times a day. Maybe it's a scramble alert. You're sitting there in your flight suit. The plane is loaded. The bombs are on it. You've pre-flighted it already. You're already strapped in your suit in the waiting room. All of a sudden the bell rings. You leap up. You run and jump in the airplane. You buckle yourself in. They're starting the air starter. The guy comes running up behind you with your knee board with the coordinates. While you're strapping in and putting your helmet on, the guy's starting the engine up. You give him the signal and start the plane. You roll out of the chocks and you're gone. *Zzzhhhoooooom.*

Your wingman joins up with you. You switch radios. About that time they hook you up with a spotter plane. He says, "Okay, this is so-and-so, your target is a platoon of Viet Cong overrunning a marine installation," or whatever. He says, "I'll mark the target with white smoke." "Roger, I have you in sight." *Zooom,* he drops the white smoke. He says, "Okay, that's about fifty meters short of the target. Move your bombs 50 meters at twelve o'clock from my smoke." You say, "Roger," and you go over, *boom, boom, boom,* and then you stop to realize that fifty meters from his smoke was that village you just blew away.

You go up there and you don't *know.* You don't know. Here's this spotter in an O-2, flying around at a speed where he can see things. The guys on the ground are calling him and talking to him on the radio. They're saying, "We're down here taking fire from 175 guys." It may be seventeen. These kids on the ground are very excited, and you would be too if you were being shot at. The enemy probably looks ten times bigger in number. "Jesus Christ, we're being trapped down here." They're talking to him, and he's looking, watching the fire. You're 10,000, 15,000 feet up there. You don't know. You can't say, "I'd like to debate this awhile. Can we analyze this a little better? What is the hypothesis you're working on?" You don't do that shit. You just say, "Put the smoke on it." And you bomb the hell out of it. You don't know.

It didn't bother me at the time. Well—maybe I'm a hypocrite, because I wrote about it to my diary and to my wife. I'd tell her, We did some pretty bad stuff today. It wasn't exactly My Lai or anything like that. But I would recognize some of the stupidity. I guess you just say, This is war. The innocents get killed in a war. You write it off that way. I don't know how you do it.

I remember one time when I was up in a helicopter. This was later, when I was with the infantry up at Phu Bai. We were looking for a zone to put in a battalion-sized landing. As we came back in the early dawn, we noticed about twenty guys going into this village. We saw they were Viet Cong rice-carriers. When we got back, I told the regimental commander and everybody what I'd seen. We sent our company up there and they got into a big firefight. Sent another company in, and another company. I think there must have been about thirty actual combatants that had sneaked back into that ville. They were trapped in there with whatever supporters they could get from the ville. They were trying to save their lives by then.

We surrounded them with a battalion and then we blew 'em away—along with the rest of the ville. We called in air strikes and artillery all day long. Well, after this great heroic battle was over, they went in and counted enough eyelids and toenails and kneecaps to claim there were something like 450 KIAs. You'd walk through the village and see how many shin bones were sticking out of the dirt. Hell, we bombarded that village all day. And you knew that whole damn village was not all VC. Some of them were just villagers.

I could recount several tales like that. It really got me. Didn't turn me against the war, exactly. I thought we were doing the right thing in the war. I thought we were there for the right reasons. I wasn't sure it was being prosecuted right, but I didn't get disillusioned. Maybe more cynical, though.

I didn't think much of the TPQ flights at night. They were just garbage runs, going up and dumping bombs. Then later I learned how they were set, because I worked as the assistant division air officer for about a month. My job was to stay right there on the desk for a solid twenty-four hours. Then I'd sleep for twenty-four hours and be on for twenty-four hours. Each of the regiments all over I Corps had to call in and give me so many targets for the night. I would locate the targets and put the pins on the board. I think we had about seven regiments, and they had to turn in about thirty-five targets a night.

Then, when I went from the division down to the regiment, I found out how they picked those targets. Each day I'd have to start haranguing my young captains who were with the battalions. I think I made each one turn in five targets a night. I'd keep calling. I'd say, "What are your targets? What are your targets?" "I don't have any targets." "Well, make up some targets." They would give me some coordinates. If they didn't do it, and I kept calling 'em and couldn't get 'em on the radio, then I would take the map. I would look and I'd say, Well, lessee, this map here shows a river coming down off this mountain like this. It shows a trail crossing it here, leading to this village. Okay, if I were them I'd have my camps in this ravine. I wouldn't be up on this spine here. I'd be along this ravine where the water is. So I'd pick out some targets along the ravine and call 'em in. In other words, we were just putting our finger up in the wind and saying, Ah, that's the direction. And we'd drop bombs, tons and tons of bombs. You couldn't help but see how stupid that was. And it's the sort of thing where everybody gets a lot of credit. The 1st Marine Air Wing has dropped so many tons of bombs this year on indicated targets, that sort of thing.

We had a valley. You may have heard of the A Shau valley. That was one of the main ingress routes for VC and NVA coming south. Well, somebody before my time had decided that we would bomb a ditch across the A Shau valley and flood it, so it'd be difficult to get across. They actually thought we could do that. There was a stream that ran through here, and we'd dig this ditch. So every time there was some mission we couldn't go to because of something, we'd contact TPQ and take our bombs over and drop 'em across this line in the A Shau valley. Later Darrel Shelor and I would go over and instead of just dropping our bombs, we'd fly up and down the valley. Slow down to about 350 knots and fly 150 feet or 200 feet off the ground. There were all these bomb craters. Thousands of bomb holes. Tons of bombs that we dropped there.

We'd fly along there and pretty soon some tracer fire would start coming out of the hills at us. We'd pull up, go in and bomb the fire out of 'em and feel we'd had a nice day. Rather than just throw the bombs in a mudhole. We'd provoke 'em, they'd shoot at us, and we'd fire back. We used to do that until an F-9 recon Cougar flew over at about 350 knots and got their butt shot down and bailed out and landed in the A Shau. Somehow they got rescued. But good God, can you imagine, that's like a tiny bee setting down in the middle of army ants. Holy Christ. I thought, Well, from now on I'll be a little more careful. Fly at 500 feet and 500 knots.

Another time we were in a valley near Hoi Anh. We'd been off bombing somewhere. This spotter plane called up and said, "Do you have any more ammunition?" We said, "We've got twenty mike-mike." He said, "Roger, I've got three VC out here on the road. Let's see if we can get 'em." So here are these two jets. I don't know how much an A-4 costs, a half-million dollars or whatever. Doing 500 knots in an air-conditioned, pressurized cockpit. With all your chow back home and a bed to sleep on. Here's this road. You fly over and see these three guys jogging along the road with their black pajamas and little hats and their AK-47s. Roger, you have them in sight.

Generally you strafe the length of the road instead of across the road. Well, we were making runs across that road, firing 20 mm cannon. One 20mm shell going off is like a grenade exploding. That's a lot of power. You could see the *pap, pap, pap*, the white water and dirt jumping up in the rice paddies and on the road. We made about three passes each at those three VC, standing on the road with AK-47s. And they stood and fired back at us. Stood there in the road firing back. We never hit 'em, thank God.

What kind of courage is that? Jesus, what ideology, what belief, what hatred drives a man to that? They stood there with those rifles and shot back at us in those two expensive airplanes until we ran out of ammunition. That's some kind of spirit you have to admire. I'd like to meet those men someday. I'd have to walk up and say, You're some of the bravest men on the face of the earth, mother.

I had 223 missions in six months to the day of flying. I would have shot for 500 missions, which would have been phenomenal, in thirteen months. But when you had six months in, they transferred you. Only the lucky few escaped. So I spent seven months with the infantry and went back home.

After a few more years of being a whiz kid, I went back for a tour in Thailand. By this time I was turned off to the whole theory of it. All we were doing was flying down to bomb Cambodian villages. After a while I told 'em I just didn't want to fly anymore. I was the airfield operations officer. I had more than enough to do to run that crummy airfield for twelve months. So I devoted myself to it as best I could. I could have kept flying if I wanted to. I had lost all desire.

It could have been other things, too. I was beginning to have psychological problems with it. I could get in the airplane and be flying, and the farther I'd fly from home base, the more tense I'd become. It was just living hell to fly. It probably had something to do with my brother. Not being a psychologist, I only have hints of this from reading, but they say when some member of your family dies like my brother had, it can hit you years later.

I certainly would have kept flying if I could. When I gave up flying, I gave up $300-a-month flight pay. I figured my career was ruined. I figured, this is it. I didn't like what was going on, but when you're in the military you're getting prestige and power and promotion and money. You don't just turn your back. It takes a brave man to say, The hell with that. Not many of us do. I guess if it hadn't been that I was getting more tense and more tense, I would have probably bulled on through and tried to go for bird colonel and on up until I got my retirement with the max money I could—and gone fishing.

DICK RUTAN

Hangar 77 at the Mojave, California, airport. Inside is a strange, spidery plane with a fuselage no larger than a glider's but gossamer wings as long as a Boeing 727's. It is the Voyager, *designed for an assault on the last great aviation record: flying around the world without refueling. The pilot who plans to keep it aloft for twelve days—along with his partner, Jeana Yeager—is a lanky man with craggy features and graying sideburns. He retired from the air force in 1978 after twenty years and has been a test pilot ever since. His military career included 325 missions in Vietnam. While there he won five Distinguished Flying Crosses and a Silver Star.*

He looks worried and weary; raising money for the Voyager *flight has taken years, and there still is not enough to make the attempt. But his eyes shine and his face fills with energy when he talks about Vietnam.*

I went right from gunnery school to Vietnam, in September 1967. I was there through the fall, winter, the Tet offensive, the Khe Sanh fiasco, and then left a year later. I flew out of Phu Cat. It was a new fighter base near Qui Nhon, a couple hundred miles south of Danang.

The F-100s were mainly ground support. That was the mission. After you got over the initial excitement, it became routine and boring. It was 3:00 A.M. scrambles out of the alert barn to fly through the clouds and drop bombs by a radar-directed delivery. Or we'd be called into an area and the FAC would be there, and he'd put a smoke on the ground and we'd bomb it and go home. Sometimes there was a little excitement going on, but it was always as I was leaving. A guy says, "I got troops in contact. They're overrun." We'd go and drop our bombs, and then he'd want to get rid of us and get the next flight in. So I'd always be leaving with the excitement of combat going on and never be able to hang around.

A strange thing seems to happen when you get into a combat situation. It was common with everybody in the fighter squadron. Everybody wanted more missions. They wanted the hard missions. Troops in contact? Man, they'd be throwing each other out of the cockpit to go. The guys would hang around and scrounge more flights. It was combat. It was exciting. It was an addiction to a drug you created within yourself, called adrenaline. All of us became adrenaline junkies. You'd pump a lot of adrenaline during the flight, and when you'd come down you'd be just as high as if you were on some wild drug.

Then you'd try to unwind and sleep, and if you didn't fly the next day, you'd say, "Where's my hit? Man, I need a hit. I've gotta go fly again. Get me on the schedule. Get me some troops in contact."

Well, I had this friend named Bud Day. He went over there about three months before I did. He and a couple other guys started an organization that was called Commando Saber. Their call sign was "Misty." They were the only F-100s that flew over North Vietnam. See, the problem in the North was that the targets were elusive. There were thousands of truck parks, thousands of gunsites, but they'd all move around. Very fluid. We'd take a photo-recon airplane and make a strip run up there someplace. It'd see all kinds of truck parks and transshipment points and maybe storage areas. The recon guys would come back, develop the film, and some intelligence two-striper would figure out where all the targets were. He'd give the photos to the pilots or frag 'em the next morning. Then they'd try to bomb. But during the night, all the trucks and storage areas would move. That was coupled with the fact that the pilots had never been there before, and they were going up in this hostile area to try to find this target and bomb it. The success rate was terrible.

So Bud Day says, "Hey, let's fly up there in F-100s, and we'll act as forward air controllers. We'll find the storage areas. We'll find the active truck parks. We'll mark 'em with a smoke rocket and put strikes on 'em right there. We won't let 'em get away at night, or worry about somebody else trying to find 'em." They started out with one airplane, one mission a day, and it looked pretty good, so they got permission to build it up. Before I left we were up to about six sorties a day.

I hadn't arrived in-country when this was going on. When I first checked in at Phu Cat, I heard that Bud Day was there, too. I went looking for him. I walked up to this little Misty outfit, this high-secret area on the base that nobody knew very much about. And they said, "Bud Day's just been shot down up there." I missed him that day. The guy that was with him in the airplane was rescued, but Bud wasn't.

So the three months that I was bombing trees in South Vietnam, Bud Day was lounging in a prison camp up in Hanoi. But I kept having this fascination about the Misties. I'd see 'em go out at dawn, and they wouldn't come back until mid-afternoon. In the bar at night I'd talk to 'em. I'd say, "What do you guys do up there?" It sounded really exciting. I thought, God, I'd like to be a Misty, too. [Laughs.] Can I be one? Could I go up there?

It was strictly volunteers. You had to be selected. And they only let you go up there for about 120 days. That was the tour. It was very high-risk. We lost five times more airplanes per sortie than the F-105s did. The bombers would come in at high altitude, see the target, dive out of 15,000 feet, pull off above 6,000, and go home. They'd be over the target a handful of minutes, they'd come in high and go out high, and they were in-country probably about twenty minutes at the max. Whereas the Misty, he'd go up there and spend four to five hours at very low altitude over North Vietnam. Getting continually shot at. Just tickling 'em.

I was begging to go up there. I needed some more excitement. So a friend of mine put in a word with the Ops officer to let me into this outfit. Then you were kind of in the inner sanctum. They took you away from all the other fighter pilots. You lived in your own compound area. And your job was to fly low-altitude recon over North Vietnam in a two-seat version of the F-100. Find targets of opportunity and mark 'em with white phosphorus smoke rockets. We had eighteen smoke rockets on board the airplane. No ordnance other than our 220 rounds of 20mm cannon shell.

I found out later that the North Vietnamese knew all about us. Especially the gunners. They called us "the deliverers of the white death." Because before, if they were found, they could move. They'd stand around and laugh the next day when all the fighters would come in and bomb an empty site. But we went in there and found 'em, and fifteen or twenty minutes later a flight of F-105s joined up and we killed 'em. That got their attention, see.

When a new pilot goes into the Misty outfit, he flies in the backseat for five or six missions, until he learns the ropes. He learns how to dodge ground fire. He learns how to see gunsites. So the first time I went up to North Vietnam, I was in the backseat. And I was useless. Normally the pilot in front was in command of the mission, and the guy in back was the bookkeeper. But this time the guy in front did everything, because I didn't know what was going on.

My first impression when we crossed the DMZ was that somebody had turned the goddamn place into the moon. I've never seen so many bomb craters in my whole life. I was appalled. And the thing that really got me was the city of Dong Hoi. It was the first major city north of the DMZ. It was a citadel city. You could see the citadel. They had a nice port there. You could see it was a fairly large town. But they had bombed that thing right into the Stone Age. All you could see was foundations. There was not a stick standing. Totally destroyed. Absolutely, completely destroyed. There wasn't a living soul there. And I thought—Why in the world? Why? Why did we do that?

Then the ground fire started. There were a lot of gunsites shooting at us. We put in some strikes. I think somebody got shot down and rescued during that flight. I thought, Wow, I've finally found the excitement.

You'd take off in the early morning mists of Vietnam. You'd climb up through the weather. Then you'd spend twenty minutes sitting there alone, reflecting on what was going to happen to you today. Kind of awesome. There was very little talk. You'd fly up past Danang, past the DMZ, and hit your tanker. Then you'd back off from the tanker with a full load of fuel, and you'd turn and head for the coast of North Vietnam. Very quiet. The air is just dead calm. Sun hasn't come up yet. It's about a five- or seven-minute run from the tanker to the coast. You strap in, check your .45 or .38. Tighten down your strap, get your oxygen mask tight, check the G-suit and make sure it's clamping down on you okay. Set the pipper down, make sure the rockets are armed. Turn off all your emitters. Then you just stretch, very quiet and calm and extremely peaceful. You get down real low. All of a sudden the coast is closer and closer, with a mist over the rice paddies. And you know that within a handful of seconds, the whole world's gonna break loose. It did every morning. [Laughs.] Because there's a lot of guns on the coast. They'd all shoot, and there were so many of them you could never shoot back. Mainly they were ZPUs and .50-cal's, which we didn't concern ourselves too much with. Just before you'd come in, three or four of those guns would open up with a lot of tracers and stuff. Then you'd pull and start your jink. *Boom*—back and forth, up, around. You'd pass that area and get down lower. Then you'd see what the morning was like. You'd go up and down the rivers. The adrenaline would start pumping, and the war was on.

Every hour we'd come back and hit our tanker again. The airplane would fly about three and a half hours if we just went cross-country and conserved our fuel. But when we're low altitude, in and out of burner, trying to keep a lot of speed on the airplane, doing jinks at six or seven Gs, we could only go fifty minutes to an hour. Then we'd have to go out and refuel. My G tolerance—God, I was fantastic. [Laughs.] A lot of times I'd make a pass and ease off to what I thought was one G, so the guy in the back could take a picture. I'd say, "You got the picture?" "No, I can't lift up the camera." I'd look at the G meter and I'm still at three. I'd ease off to one so he could pick the camera up. As soon as he took the picture, then it was back to six or seven Gs, reverse course, jink back out of the area.

At noon or one we'd go home, and there'd be another three-hour debrief where we'd regurgitate all the information about what we'd seen.

When we found a target, the backseater would call in a flight of fighters—say, Buick Flight, F-105s out of Takli, Thailand. He'd turn 'em over to the frontseater. Usually we'd climb up to a higher altitude and we'd see 'em coming in. We'd rendezvous. We'd get 'em in an orbit. And I'd say, "Okay, I've got a 57mm gunsite. It's really active. It's guarding a transshipment point right over there. It's on the edge of that river." Then I'd roll in and mark the target. Pull off and say, "Hit my smoke," or "Whoops, I missed, hit 100 meters north of it." Then the fighters would go in and drop their stuff and leave. I'd go down at low altitude and look real close and see what we hit. And I'd relay the bomb damage to the fighters going across the horizon.

Let me tell you about the guns. I had a fascination with guns. It's the sportsmanship of the whole thing: We're shooting at them, so they ought to have a chance to shoot back. After we spent a lot of time up in North Vietnam, we figured out the guns were very regimented and formalized. The sites were always round. In the middle they have the rangefinder and the guy who sets the computer and the guy who raises his flag and says, "Fire!" Then there'd be five or six guns spread around in a circle. There were thousands of gunsites, but very few of 'em were occupied at any one time. They'd move around. They'd stay in one place three or four days and then move. We found they'd move around in maybe a fifteen- or twenty-mile area.

It was a cat-and-mouse game with the guns. When we first started going up there, they shot at us all the time. Then they got smart. They knew that if they shot at you and you saw them, you were going to climb up, and about twenty minutes later a flight of F-105s with daisy-cutters would show up and blast their ass. So if they were protecting something, they'd shoot as soon as you'd come over the horizon. That would tip you off, and you'd climb up a bit to try and find out what the hell they were protecting. But a lot of times they only shot when you had your belly up to 'em and you weren't jinking very hard and they thought they had a good, clear shot. When they'd fire, golf-ball-size tracers would come by the airplane. Between the wings, every place. The tracers would come so close that you could see the golf balls and feel the shock waves. It's like rain on the side of the fuselage, or a guy with a baseball bat going *bam-bam-bam-bam-bam-bam* on the airplane. Not from shells hitting you, but from the shock waves. If one hits you, you're done. A 37mm shell is six or eight inches long. The back is a burning tracer, and the front has a contact shell. If it hits you, it goes off with shrapnel, and it just sieves the airplane, all the hydraulics and the fuel system.

We had a rapport with the gunners down there. They knew that when they shot and didn't get us, they were gonna get hit. Guaranteed. So now, when we went up there, we spent a lot of time but they didn't shoot a lot. We even got to know the gunsites after a while. Each Misty kind of adopted his own. Every day you'd find out where yours were, or you'd say, "Oh, that's P.K.'s site over there. How're they doing?" And when you got home you'd say, "Hey, P.K., I found your gunsite, they moved across the river on the side of Brown Route intersection." When he went up the next day he'd find these guys and play with 'em a little bit.

So we knew whose gun was whose, and whether they were good shooters or bad. If they shot real bad, we wouldn't mark 'em. There was one guy, we called him the Kid on the Karst. He was on a karst outcropping along a road in Laos. I don't know how in the world they ever got a .50-cal machine gun up there, but he was absolutely the worst gunner in the world. If we'd orbit around him, he'd always be shooting off on the other side of the orbit. I mean grossly wrong, like he was a friend of ours, just saying "Hi" and spraying the air with his tracers. Never even came close to us. And we protected him. We made sure that nobody ever hit him. We took care of the Kid on the Karst. But there was a guy up in another area who was very accurate. We'd go in, and if we had any extra ordnance, we'd have one of the fighters save a bomb and try to hit this kid. Because he was a real threat.

If a gunsite knew that you knew where they were, they'd have to move that night. So at the end of the mission, you'd go back down the trail on the way home, and you'd find all the sites, and if you were in a particularly good mood and nobody shot at you that well, you'd say, Well, I'll leave 'em there. Pretend I didn't see 'em. Then they wouldn't have to move. They could rest. But if they shot one of your guys down, or almost nailed you, or you had a bad letter from home, or the eggs weren't very good that morning, and you were pissed, on the way home at night you'd go down and put a smoke rocket on every one of those gunsites. *Ptchew! Ptchew! Ptchew!* That was good in a way, because they'd have to move. They'd clean all their stuff up and spend the entire night breaking down the guns, moving, cutting new camouflage, and you knew the next morning they were going to be tired. On the other hand, you might not be able to find 'em. If you didn't mark 'em, you knew where they were.

After a while it was easy to spot the occupied gunsites. Here's what happened. Say I'm a gunner, and this is my gun, boy. I don't want to get bombed, so I'm gonna really camouflage my gun. I cut all this brush and put it around the gun. Then I walk back ten feet and make sure I can't see any part of it. So how could anybody know there's a gun there? Well, the dumb guys, they didn't realize that the bottom sides of the leaves were a different color from the top sides. When you cut a tree and throw it up on your gun, half the leaves are gonna be upside down. And you don't put upside-down leaves in a six-position circular site unless it's a gunsite. They never figured that out. If they could have flown over and looked down, they'd have probably just shit their pants about how obvious they made their guns.

There were different passes, too, like the Mughia Pass, where there was kind of a funnel. All the roads had to go through there, and our planes were always bombing it. Very unsuccessful. In some of the areas in Laos, along the Ho Chi Minh Trail, they'd pick stranglehold areas like road intersections. When they'd start out, the road wasn't even visible from the air because it was down in deep jungle. They'd find where the road was and bomb an area two miles around there into nothing but dirt. Not a living thing. A wing of F-104s or F-105s would just go and bomb a point on the road. They'd bomb and bomb and bomb. Or on a mountainside, they'd try to make a slide come down to close the road. And I'll tell you—I spent three tours in Misty. I was a Misty FAC longer than anybody. And I never one time saw a road closed or cut. All that was a total waste of effort. Absolute total waste. The North Vietnamese had those roads open within a handful of minutes. I'd go up there and I'd see a major strike going in. Pulverize the road. Wouldn't even be a road left. I'd come back later and all of a sudden, out would come a little bulldozer going right over the bomb craters. Didn't hardly slow it down.

They were turning jungle into dust. For nothing. It did not work. But you had to be there to see that it didn't work. Until the Misties got up there, the bombers would go in, and their photo recon would say, "Oh, boy, the bombs are on target, a whole squadron of airplanes put all their bombs on this road and they all had good hits." But they'd bomb and leave. The Misties were up there all day, and we saw what happened. I'd come over in the morning, and the road would be just pristine. I'd call the AB Triple-C—that's the airborne command and control center, a C-130 that would orbit overhead. I'd say, "Hey, the road's not cut. There's trucks going by." That'd really upset 'em. Because they just relayed to Westmoreland, and I'm sure Westmoreland told his boss, "We just strangled the whole Ho Chi Minh Trail." It was a joke. It was the most gross waste of bombs I've ever seen in my life.

The other thing that bothered me was the night bombing. There were people who were totally night-dedicated. Those guys would go up fragged for some truck park at night, and if they couldn't find it, they'd invariably drop their ordnance on villages. We'd go in and check with the AB Triple-C at dawn. And the guys would say, "Oh, God, Misty, we had a fantastic truck kill last night." I'd say, "Where is it?" "Two klicks south of the intersection of Brown Route and Green Route." We'd go over there expecting to find truck hulks and stuff. Nothing. The road is clean. But we'd look four or five or eight miles away, and there'd be a village in flames. With all kinds of fresh bomb craters. I'd radio, "They just hit a village last night." They'd argue with me over the air. The night command post was called Moonbeam. He'd say, "No, no, no, you're wrong. They hit trucks." Well, I knew more about that area than they ever thought about. I knew every square inch of it. I'd just tell him, "Look, you son of a bitch, I'm right here looking at it. Don't give me this garbage. There's no trucks at all. There's nothing on Green Route, it's empty and clean. There's a village, and it's in flames." And I'd give him the coordinates.

It bothered me so much that I wouldn't give credit for a truck unless it was burning or I could go see it in pieces. I didn't give any estimated truck kills. That really irritated 'em, because they were getting a lot of kills before we got up there. All I know is I went up there and saw a lot of villages burning when they were claiming trucks on the road. I saw that over and over again. It was appalling. I thought it was irresponsible. Fraggin' villes, they called it. Really a shame.

I'd report it back, and nothing would happen. Remember, here I am a lowly captain. I don't frag the targets. I don't have the overall picture. I'd tell our commander, but he wasn't in the mainstream either. The report would get written up in a form and sent off on the wire. I don't know what they did with it. Maybe they didn't believe it. The problem is, in retrospect, that those crews—which might have been forty or fifty airplanes—come back and report this great big kill they had. The gunfight at night. The big story. All those things get fed into Saigon. All of a sudden this little Misty guy shows up and says, There weren't any trucks, there was a village burning. What do you do? Now you're in the Westmoreland atmosphere. And the Westmoreland atmosphere says, Hell, who's this Misty? I'd rather believe this big truck kill, so I can go to my President and tell him what a good job we're doing.

The Misty policy was, we never hit a village. We left the villages totally alone unless they shot at us out of there. We'd look them over real close. If they started to park trucks or other stuff that I could see, and they shot at us, then we hit them. But I must say my experience was that they did not hide a lot of stuff in villages. I personally only took out one village the whole time I was there. We were doing a rescue, and a .50-caliber gunner came so close to nailing me I couldn't believe it. The whole town was shooting at us. When the rescue forces came in, I thought that gunner presented a significant danger to them. It was a long, thin village. So we put a smoke rocket at each end of it. We were out of fuel when we did that, and I had some fighters overhead. I said, "Okay, put all your bombs between the two smokes." I went out to get some fuel. When we came back, between the two marks there was nothing but dust. Rubble. They totally obliterated the village. But that's the only time I ever did any village action.

I want to see that village someday. That was the only thing I ever did—well, it was a military target, and they had a really good gunner in there. The village was in the lower end of what we called Rutan Valley, because I caught some trucks in the open there once. Someday I'd just like to drive those roads and look at the karst formations, the little river valleys. I don't know why. To see if it's rebuilt.

Little by little, the number of Misties built up. It became more and more popular. We did find a lot of targets. I don't know if we developed a reputation, but I do know that when a Misty said we killed a truck, we killed a truck. Damn sure. Because of our tight criteria. We were appalled about how things were being exaggerated. The lies and deceits. Then I'd hear McNamara and his other pukes talking about how well we were doing. I'd think, Somebody's lying to 'em. They're not getting the right skinny. Maybe they're that stupid anyway, or that naive. And the military, as far as the stuff they were forwarding back to 'em, weren't helping things any. We wanted to win the war. We wanted big body counts. We wanted to be victorious. And we weren't. It bothered me because I was on the team. I was a military person sent over there to do a military activity.

That was another thing that bothered me. The politicians do all their work. When they fail, they send in the military. It's just another arm of our national power. Well, goddamn it, when the first GI goes over there and gets killed, then the outcome of that thing should be either we go out in total defeat, or Vietnam ought to be the fifty-first state. The politicians should say, Okay, here's the enemy, you're the military, go and do it. But when I've got some civilian in the Pentagon telling me how to do a mission, or telling me that there's gunsites that we can't even hit, you know who's down there kissing their ass? Ramsey "Dupe" Clark and Jane Fonda. Or the fact that we couldn't hit Haiphong harbor because it was full of allied ships. "Free world" shipping. The majority of it was British. You'd think that during the war, Haiphong would be full of Russian and Chinese ships hauling war matériel in to support their ally. But that wasn't the case at all. You ever wonder why we never hit Haiphong harbor? Because we might make the British mad.

Our bombing accuracy was very poor. Later on it got better because they had laser-guided bombs. But the air force depended on the "Hit my smoke" type of mentality. The majority of them couldn't pick out anything on the ground. Every once in a while you'd find somebody that was interested in what he was hitting. Like one navy guy came up. I had a bunch of trucks. Put a smoke rocket on 'em. "Boy, good smoke. Hit my smoke." The guy says, "Wait a minute." I says, "What for?" He says, "I'm waiting for your smoke to get out of the way so I can see what I'm bombing." I thought, "Well, goddamn, this is neat. Got somebody who's interested." He flew around and said, "Yeah, I see one there, there, there. Okay, I got it." He went in, *pow*. Couple of trucks burned, bunch of ammo exploded.

I almost shot down an F-4 one day, I was so mad at him. The flight came in, and I'd really hung myself out for a gunsite that was protecting a SAM site. Real lucrative target. We got shot at really bad. I marked it. The F-4s didn't seem like they were listening to what I was telling 'em. All they wanted was to get their bombs off and get the hell home. I gave 'em my typical bomb damage assessment: "No bombs fell within 100 meters of my target. No visible damage." "Okay, thank you. Boy, this is our champagne flight. We're going home, we've got 100 missions." I says, "Hey, that's great. At least you won't come up here and bother me anymore. Maybe your replacement can hit something." Didn't faze 'em. They were going home.

My attitude got worse and worse. I was getting into the area of combat fatigue. Short-tempered. Tired. Eighty percent physical fatigue, 20 percent frustration. I went through a major personality change. Really hard to get along with. By this time I was the old head, see, and the new guys got to fly with me. I'd be checking 'em out, doing pilot training in a combat situation. I had to take guys up there and show 'em how to jink, how to look for the sites. I'd let the guy go, and he'd start jinking. He isn't jinking hard enough. I'd be thinking, There's a gunsite. Doesn't he see it? God, he's gotta see that gunsite! Sure enough, he'd set us up and they'd shoot. *Bam!* They'd almost get us. I'd grab the stick—"You son of a bitch, don't you see the site? It's as plain as the nose on your face!" He says, "No, no, I don't see it." "Well, did you see the tracers?" "Yeah, yeah, I saw that." [Laughs.] "Well, that's it, you can't ever put your belly up to a site like that." He's new, y'know. Hell, when I was first up there I didn't see anything either.

The Misties had a problem with last missions. When somebody would fly their last mission, there was a big celebration. The fire trucks would meet the airplane and we'd hose the pilot down. He'd be hauled off to a big party, and we'd say good-bye. Everybody knew what their tour length was, when they were getting close. The commander would say, Okay, we're gonna fly you Tuesday, Thursday, and you get your last mission on Friday. But we lost a lot of people on their last mission. It's the last-mission mentality. You want to bring home the bacon.

We had a good-bye party for six people who were getting ready to leave the Misties. A good friend of mine named Chuck Shaheen was part of it. There were six guys at the party, and all but one of 'em got shot down on their last mission. From then on, nobody knew what their last mission was. When the guy rolled in and saw the fire trucks, that was his last mission. And it was a good thing.

Well, I was gonna fly in the backseat of Chuck's last mission. It was my 105th mission in Misty. I had about another week, maybe two weeks left on my tour. And that day was interesting, because we were trying something new. We were so frustrated with how bad the bombing accuracy was that we talked the powers that be into letting some in-country fighters come up to North Vietnam, the guys who were used to doing close air support. To test it, we'd go find a real secure target where there's not a lot of activity. These guys will come bomb it, and see if they do any better for accuracy. We'll show those Thailand guys that the F-100s are really good.

We found a real nice target in a river valley. Three or four trucks parked right on the edge of a karst. Big steep karst, trucks parked at the bottom. But once we got the fighters up there, a big thunderstorm moved in just opposite. We had to go around the storm, parallel to the karst, to bomb the trucks. So there was a real restricted run-in.

Okay, our great in-country bombers showed up. We briefed 'em on the target. And every one of 'em missed. They missed as bad as any of the F-4s did. One guy says, "Oh, shoot, I forgot to reset my altimeter." Another guy says, "Oh, no. I put my mil setting wrong." They were really feeling bad.

The trucks were still down there, so we said, "Okay, we'll do some high-angle strafe." At a high angle the guns aren't real accurate, but we thought maybe we'd torch something and bring home a couple of truck kills. Everybody had made about three runs around the circuit—past the thunderstorm and down the same run. Never saw any ground fire at all. So number one came around, shot from a high angle and pulled off. Real safe. But Shaheen, this is his last mission. He says, "Hey, let's get in the circle with you. We'll be number five, and we'll fire our own gun." He came in, and instead of high-angle strafe he brought it down flat to a low-angle strafe. This is when you pull off about fifty feet above the ground. There had been a lot of airplanes coming down the chute, and somebody had been just sitting there. He decided he was going to shoot on our pass.

We're supposed to be well above the top of the karst, but now we're coming lower and lower, and all of a sudden we're below the karst. Real low, man. I've never been this low. I thought, Well, okay, I'll ride with you this time, you SOB, but you're not gonna do it again. He came down, *P-R-R-R-R-R-R*, he fired, and just about the time he fired and started to pull we got hit right under the seat. I looked back and saw nothing but fire in the rearview mirror. The whole back end of the airplane is full of fire. He pulled up, and I saw where we had pulled up: the coastal plain. The F-100 would hold together for twenty seconds, no matter what happened to it. It'd fly for twenty seconds. That meant you could turn and get over the water or over the jungle and bail out. But as we pulled up and looked, we weren't within twenty seconds of any kind of safety. I could see hootches and people all over the place. I thought, Okay, Hanoi Hilton, here we come. Finally did it.

Shaheen was in burner. The intensity of the fire told me we maybe didn't even have twenty seconds. But just about the time we pulled up, he took it out of burner. When he did that, the fire turned white. It was fuel mist. We weren't burning internally. The tank was gutted, and all the fuel was coming out. As it foamed back across the afterburner plume, it caught fire, and it was a huge torch, something like 600 or 700 feet of fire behind the airplane.

Our F-100 teammates came in and said, "You're just torching, you aren't burning." Wow, maybe we can make it. We turned and started heading toward the water. It's about thirty-five miles out there. We dropped the drop tanks and all the rocket pods, so we were clean. Then I started looking at all the fuel we were losing. You could see the totalizer unwinding like the second hand on a watch. There was no damn way we were gonna make the coast. All the transfer tanks were pumping fuel into this feed tank, but it was gutted, so all the fuel was going overboard, with a little going in the engine. I says, "Shaheen, I think the only way we're gonna make it is to light the burner again and try to utilize more of the fuel in the thrust." That might get us going faster before we ran out. He said okay.

Everybody came in real close. I said, "Okay, we're gonna light it up." Lit the burner. *Boom*, big long fire started again. The guys said, "No sweat, you're just torching. It isn't burning inside." We're in a slow climb, but the Mach is increasing all the time although we're running out of fuel. I kept looking at the coast, thinking, Yes. No. It's gonna be close.

So we went burning out to the coast. By the time we got there, we were at about 18,000 feet, going about Warp 3. Right near the speed of sound. Because we're real light now, and in max burner. Then of course we're out of fuel, and the fire flamed out. There was a kind of parabolic curve as we went down. At about 10,000 feet we ejected, and we had a nice comfortable float in the Gulf of Tonkin until they came and picked us up.

When we were burning, heading for the coast, I kept remembering P.K. saying, "You've done too much. You've been flying too long. You oughta quit." I made myself a promise right there. I said, You let me get to that coastline and out of this plane, and I ain't never coming up here again. And I wasn't, either. As soon as I made the coast I felt very relaxed. I thought, Dick, all you've gotta do is eject and you're going home. Going home! So I ejected, and I was sitting in the raft thinking, The war's over. I could see the coastline over there, and I was never fuckin' going up there again.

10

IN MINE ENEMY'S HOUSE

On August 4, 1964, in the first bombing attack on North Vietnam after the Tonkin Gulf incident, two planes were shot down. One pilot was lost. The other pilot was Lieutenant (jg) Everett Alvarez, Jr., who attained the dubious honor of being the first American captured in the North. Over the eight and a half years he was a POW, nearly 600 other airmen would be captured, while some 2,000 were killed and 1,000 were declared missing. But flyers who fell to earth were not the only American POWs. Both soldiers and civilians were captured in South Vietnam. Most of them were held in jungle prison camps in Cambodia. Some were marched north. Many died in captivity.

North Vietnam had signed the 1949 Geneva Convention on treatment of prisoners but reserved itself an ingenious loophole: Perpetrators of "crimes against humanity" were not covered. The "genocidal" American bombing was considered such a crime. The pilots, therefore, were "war criminals" and "Yankee air pirates." They were also useful—not only as hostages in negotiations with the U.S. but as propaganda tools.

Mike Benge and Jerry Driscoll, the two POWs in this chapter, were small fry—an AID technician captured in the South, and a young air force lieutenant shot down near Hanoi. Their treatment was brutal enough. But it should be pointed out that the more senior POWs—especially the group known as the "diehards"—suffered physical and psychological assaults far worse than did Benge or Driscoll. Such high-ranking prisoners as Commander James Stockdale, Lieutenant Colonel Robinson Risner, Commander James Mulligan, Commander Jeremiah Denton, and Lieutenant Commander Richard Stratton were routinely tortured to get information or to force them to "cooperate"—for example, by making antiwar statements. Badly hurt men were not given medical aid. They were shut up alone in tiny, dark cells for months. They were painfully shackled. They were starved. They could neither write nor receive letters.

Jerry Driscoll is more typical of the bulk of prisoners, who had roommates and were left alone for long periods—particularly after 1969, when treatment improved. Mike Benge experienced the other pole of captivity: the long trek through South Vietnam on the way to a jungle camp in Cambodia.

Probably nothing could prepare someone for such an ordeal. The air force did its best, putting its aviators through POW training before they went to Vietnam. But as always happens, the pilots were trained to fight the previous war. The U.S. had been shocked when twenty-one American POWs refused to come home after the Korean War. Those who did return described the psychological techniques that came to be called "brainwashing." To set a standard for future POWs, President Eisenhower promulgated the Code of Conduct, whose key provision read: "When questioned . . . I am bound to give only name, rank, service number and date of birth. I will evade answering further questions to the utmost of my ability. I will make no oral or written statements disloyal to my country and its allies or harmful to their cause."

But backed by the Code of Conduct and forewarned about brainwashing, Americans shot down over Vietnam were not ready for physical torture that began almost the moment they reached Hanoi. Such torture is irresistible. Everyone "breaks" sooner or later. As Richard Mullen, a navy POW, puts it in the book *P.O.W.*, "I don't know of a case where an individual didn't give something. It may or may not have been the absolute truth, but I'd be almost willing to bet that everyone gave at least something through torture, and only through torture. [Even so,] it eats away at you and you are mortified. The feeling you betrayed your country, I think, was a common feeling amongst every one of the POWs."

And as the North Vietnamese kept torturing prisoners in pursuit of more "confessions," taped statements, and public appearances, a bitter debate grew in the camps over "resistance posture." The diehards insisted that POWs resist to the verge of death or permanent injury before giving in to any demand. Others adopted a wide range of stances. The few who cooperated with the North Vietnamese were kept away from the other POWs and given special treatment. Some agreed to be released to antiwar delegations; the rest called this the Fink Release Program. Such divisions produced their own pressures, as prisoners worried not only about preserving their lives and dignity in the face of the enemy, but also about their standing with fellow POWs—and what that might mean when they finally went home.

Americans, of course, were not the only ones to have nightmarish experiences as POWs. Civil wars are famous for inspiring ferocity, and this one was no exception; the Vietnamese were routinely brutal to one another. And Viet Cong or NVA who fell into American hands often did not fare well. Shooting of wounded prisoners was standard operating procedure in many units. GIs sometimes used torture to extract information on the battlefield. And the notorious "tiger cages" on the prison island of Con Son, where many Viet Cong cadre whiled away the war, were an ingenious product of American industrial design.

MIKE BENGE

He is a stocky man with a big head, sandy hair, pale blue eyes, and a stutter that comes and goes. He works as a forestry expert for AID in Washington, D.C., and lives in a high-rise apartment complex in the suburbs. We talk in a cramped room that does double duty as a study and a bedroom for his two-year-old daughter, who wanders in every few minutes to show off a toy or a drawing. She and Mike speak in a mixture of English and Khmer because his wife, Ne, is from Cambodia. She was in Phnom Penh when the Khmer Rouge marched in; after being driven from the city in the mass exodus, her family roamed the countryside for nine months, finally escaping to Vietnam and then to France. Mike met her when she was touring the United States with a Cambodian dance troupe.

He was born in 1935 and was raised on a ranch in eastern Oregon. After college at Oregon State, he applied to the CIA, "because it had to do with foreign travel. But the CIA told me to try AID. So I wrote and AID said, 'Well, if you're thirty-five years of age and have ten years of professional experience, we might be interested in you.' They told me to write to International Voluntary Services. I wrote and they said, 'Hey, you sound great.' "

After two years in Vietnam with IVS he transferred to AID. By the time of the Tet offensive of 1968 he had been in-country five years, working almost the whole time with the Montagnards in the highlands. He spoke fluent Vietnamese and several Montagnard dialects, and had developed a reputation for cantankerousness.

• • •

I was very close to the Montagnards, and I had been going through a whole series of initiations that they have for elevating you to a notable. And before the '68 Tet offensive, the only valid intel came from a Montagnard rebel group. A few days before Tet, they told me there was a very big buildup of North Vietnamese down toward what we called the Kilometer 14 area, between the Cambodian border and our provincial town, Ban Me Thuot. I took that information up to the American military and tried to check it out. They took it to the Vietnamese, who told them it was a bunch of horseshit from the Montagnards. The Vietnamese attitude was, No, there wasn't going to be any attack. So everybody was out celebrating.

On the night of January 27, Gerry Hickey and everybody who was working with the Montagnards came up to my place for a little Tet party. Gerry and I got together almost every Tet, it was a kind of ritual. Someone had brought a bottle of Courvoisier and Gerry and I were out on the balcony toasting each other. The Chinese firecrackers were going off, the tracers were flying. About that time an 81mm mortar landed out in front of my house. I said, "Oh, shit, Gerry, I think this is the real thing."

We were there all night long, drinking coffee royals, keeping everybody awake. Between the adrenaline of thinking you're going to get overrun and the coffee royals, we were pretty goddamn high. Nobody knew what in hell was going on. We were firing off and on, but mostly my job was to get people not to fire, because every time we'd fire, we'd take fire from the South Vietnamese. We were much more worried about them than the NVA.

The next morning when it got light, I hopped in my Jeep, told everybody to keep low, and went out to check and see what was going on. I drove down to provincial headquarters and saw a couple of APCs knocked out. Then I went to sector headquarters because they had an American military man who was supposed to prepare all the civilians for evacuation. Nobody knew where the hell he was. Evidently they found him later hiding under his bed. People were strung out. Nobody knew anything. Nobody had any fucking idea whether the NVA had retreated, withdrawn, what the hell was going on. I went around checking all my people.

Finally I went to get some IVS kids who were living down in a hamlet where there were three companies of Montagnard rebels. It turned out that the NVA had come right through there, and the Montagnards had done a hell of a lot of fighting. The IVS kids were very independent and didn't like to report or be responsible to us. They had an attitude. Well, they had left town three days before and hadn't told me. So I went down looking for them and got captured in the process.

There were also some missionaries down that way. After I went for the IVS kids I was going to drop in and get the missionaries out. But as it turned out, they really caught it the next night. The North Vietnamese had come in and set up a command post in their church. The missionaries were all in a bunker in their house, and the preacher got permission from the NVA to come out and negotiate. He came out with a white flag, but when he walked out they just gunned him down. Then they went over to the bunker and began gunning down everybody in it. Just blew them away. Kids and all. I think they killed about twelve people. Two ladies survived. Both of them were underneath all the bodies. But one of them died while they were taking her out. She had twenty-three wounds or something.

I was driving down to the village where I thought the IVS kids were, and I saw some troops crossing the road. I could see that they didn't have the right-colored uniforms, and some of them were wearing pith helmets. They were NVA. So I began backing up the road. I backed into the missionaries' compound—and from the other side of the road came about thirteen NVA. They had a B-40 rocket launcher pointed at me, and their AKs and SKs. So there I was, just looking at them. I was carrying a five-shot Police Positive that I always carried, but it was mainly for some of the strange altercations you ran into. And five into thirteen didn't divide out too well.

It was ironic: The squad I got captured by was a North Vietnamese propaganda squad. And their leader—you have to imagine a North Vietnamese who really didn't have command of English trying to say, "Surrender, we will give you humane and lenient treatment." This guy had a little Hitler mustache and his hair came down in his eyes about like Hitler. It was really weird, like out of a movie. Here's this little Hitlerite guy, telling me, "Sullendah, we give you humane and renient tleatment."

So they captured me and took me down to their battalion headquarters, which wasn't very far below, just out of this village over into a graveyard. They had their field headquarters there. They had telephones, comm wire strung all over. The troops took my watch—robbed me, more or less. Then one of the officers told them, "You're not supposed to do that," but of course I never got any of it back. They began questioning me there and I told them I didn't know anything, I was an agricultural adviser. There wasn't anybody there who knew me because they had used all the local Viet Cong as shock troops in the attack. So they just passed me back through the lines.

I was thinking, Oh, shit, what do I do now? Scared isn't the word. I was shocked, kind of numb. You don't realize that you're there. It seems not real. And they kept moving me. We walked all day and all night.

Initially they didn't touch me. But the next day we ended up down by the Ban Me Thuot leprosarium. A few years earlier, just before I came to Vietnam, they had captured three missionary doctors at that leprosarium. No one ever heard of them again. But mainly the lepers had been left alone. The South Vietnamese wouldn't have anything to do with lepers. They were out there in a compound, and missionaries took care of them. But the North Vietnamese had taken it over and set up a rear-echelon area. It was like a real weird dream. They had captured a bunch of these young Montagnard rebels. And they had rounded up all these lepers, maybe forty or sixty. All these goddamn lepers. Some of them had fingers and body parts missing. And the NVA were holding a kangaroo court on these young rebels, using the lepers as a jury. These were kids maybe twelve, thirteen, fourteen, fifteen, sixteen years old. They were accused of crimes against the people, very anonymous crimes. Fighting with the traitorous South Vietnamese government. Fighting against the people's liberation army. The NVA had a squad or more of their own people mixed in with the lepers, hollering, "Guilty! Guilty!" Psyching the lepers up. And of course, the lepers, what could they do? They were caught between a rock and a hard place. They got psyched up and shouted, "Guilty! Guilty! Guilty! Kill 'em! Kill 'em!" It took about fifteen or twenty minutes, and they ended up executing all of them. They hauled the rebels off in the bush to one side, you could hear the fire, and then the troops came back.

After letting me watch that, they began questioning me. Asking whether the province chief was there, what his name was, what the names of all the Americans were. I refused to answer. They had a North Vietnamese who spoke English—at that time I wasn't letting on that I knew either Vietnamese or Montagnard. The North Vietnamese took a pistol and put it up against my head. I told them I didn't know anything. I was an agricultural adviser. I had made up my mind that I wasn't going to give the names. Of course I knew all the people personally. We all drank together, played cards together. Everybody knew everybody else's name in town. But just prior to the time I got captured, they had rotated most of the people out and a new group came in. So I made up my mind that I was going to forget all the new guys and use all the old guys' names if I was pushed to that point. When I told them I didn't know anything, the guy cocked the pistol—it was a .32, probably a magnum—and showed me there was a round in it. He let the hammer off and put it up to my head. Again I told him I didn't know anything, and I could feel him tense his hand. I thought, Oh, shit, I bought the farm. Then he said, "I'm going to ask you one more time." He pulled back the hammer and I knew that was it. So I said, "Okay," and I told him. But I told him the names of all the old people, who were no longer there.

The whole thing was a game with the North Vietnamese, anyway. It was to push you to make you confess and give in to them, that was all it was. It didn't matter whether the information was right or wrong, just as long as you played the game. As long as you gave them some information, they eased off on you. If you gave them the wrong information—some of the pilots would tell them, "My commanding officer is Captain Midnight"—and they found out later that they were ridiculed, they would knock hell out of you. But they wouldn't kill you. You could push them to a point, and then you had to give them that psychological thing so they had domination over you.

They moved me for another day way on back into the bush. Then we got to a camp and they threw me into a little cage. In the cage with me were a couple of guys—one was a Vietnamese captain who was the company commander at the Ban Me Thuot radio station. The other was a guy who worked as the interpreter and boy Friday for a civilian contract group, some electronics outfit that repaired radios and things. I knew him real well, he was a good friend of mine. He was burnt pretty bad. His hands and face were burnt and his hands were partially blown off. He told me that he had personally killed about seventeen NVA. They took him out of the cage the next day and killed him. Evidently they had a summary trial. That was a very common practice.

They held us in that camp about a month. It was run by the VC, although they were under instructions from the NVA. We never had anything to eat but boiled manioc. We lived in this cage. It was made out of bamboo poles about two or three inches around, lashed together with rattan. It had a grass roof on it. It was about eight feet by nine feet, with three people in it, sometimes six. They kept us in chains all the time so we wouldn't run off. Chains around our ankles and around the logs, with padlocks.

They'd periodically interrogate us, but it was just a kind of game. They'd ask me the same things: what I did in the province, who was who, where I lived. I kept giving them the names of the people who had left. After a while the VC figured out I spoke Vietnamese and Montagnard. I was trying to talk to one of my guards. He was a

Montagnard who was VC but was really homesick. A lot of people working with the VC got caught up into it. The VC grabbed 'em, trained 'em, gave 'em a rifle, and maybe they ended up shooting at the South Vietnamese or maybe they shot up in the air. And when they had a chance to make it home they would run off. This was one of those kids. I kept trying to talk him into going home with me. Well, they caught me doing that and the guards got changed.

So I just made the best of the situation. The name of the game was survive. I'd talk to the Montagnards and get them to give me some of the jungle greens they normally ate. Trying to scrounge. Food was nearest and dearest to your heart. [Laughs.] You'd overconcentrate on hunger. That's one of the big things you can think about, apple pie, turkey. . . . You'd dream about a big meal.

After a while I found out that they had an American nurse and a missionary in another cage. They had been captured the day after I was. And after about a month, the VC moved us from that camp. There were about six of us at first, the three Americans and three Vietnamese, and maybe a dozen troops with us. We were down in the southwest part of the province, and they moved us around the bottom and into the southeast. I later found out that they moved us because word had gotten out where we were, and the Americans were trying to come in after us. One day an American plane flew over us as we were moving over a hill. It banked over me and I could see the pilot, see his face. He wagged his wings and went off.

We moved for months, hiking through the woods. For a while they moved us around near the first camp. Then they marched us into a camp in a malarial area. There were about ten cages, maybe thirty or forty prisoners. Up in the mountains. You could have seen these camps from the air because they always kept the camp areas swept very clean of leaves and everything. It was a health measure. The mosquitoes could hide in the leaves, so they always kept the camp very clean. They'd take us out and give us propaganda lectures every day. We were mainly living on manioc. At times we were given a little ration of tobacco or some salt. I would hoard it and trade it off to the Montagnards for greens or anything I could get.

I got cerebral malaria there and almost died. I was delirious for about three weeks. If it wasn't for the nurse I would have died. She kept me alive. She'd hit me and make me wake up enough to eat or drink a little water. She was able to get some water down me, and some rice soup. That's the Asian remedy for sick people, rice soup. The VC wouldn't give me any medicine, even though they had raided our provincial warehouses during Tet and took all the medicine out of them. Their attitude was that if we died of natural causes, or it would look like we died of natural causes, that was all right. But they couldn't outright kill us. They were under orders from the North Vietnamese. Even when I was with the North Vietnamese, they were afraid of their own bureaucracy. If we were killed, there might be great ramifications. Somebody might find out. The Communists are trained to tell on each other. I was always traveling with anywhere from three to a dozen guards, so somebody might get pissed off and end up telling. Of course, the North Vietnamese put down the political line that we were war criminals and we were going to be tried before a world tribunal and executed for war crimes. So the Viet Cong seemed . . . well, a little unconcerned. They were just doing their job, and they kind of liked doing a perfunctory job. If I died of malaria, they could wipe me off the books. If they killed me, no.

For about a month I was almost dead, but they moved us anyway. The next camp we got to was a political indoctrination camp for the Viet Cong. There were maybe twenty VC there. They had the Montagnards out in the fields cultivating manioc. They kept me and the missionaries caged up. Usually they'd let us talk to each other, sometimes they gave us hell about it. Then they moved us again, and pretty soon the missionary died. His name was Hank Blood, and he died sometime around July 4. This was in the rainy season. They left us out in the rain, and he got pneumonia, and it took him about three days to die. They took him out and built another lean-to and had him lying out there a couple of days. They'd let us go see him and talk to him, but we couldn't do anything for him. We gave him all the blankets we had. We begged them to give him some medicine, because they had a hospital camp nearby. But their attitude was, Let him die. So he did, and we buried him in a shallow grave. The girl—she belonged to the Christian Missionary Alliance—held services over him. And I decided I was going to survive even if he died.

So it was just the girl and me. Her name was Betty Olsen. She was a nurse, trained in working with lepers. She was a very nice girl, just a girl who had been brought up in that missionary atmosphere. Her parents were missionaries in Africa. The Ivory Coast, I think. She went to a religious school and a missionary college up in Nyack, New York. That had been her whole life. She was curious about how the other part of the world lived. Of course, the missionaries looked at me as being very hedonistic. I ran around with the natives and drank rice wine and slept with them and ate their food and went through their ceremonies. But she was very curious. She was twenty-nine or thirty years old, and she had her own grit. In a way she reminded you of a Katharine Hepburn type. She wasn't an all-the-way beaten-down missionary type. She had an extra bit of grit.

We spent a lot of time talking about food. Different recipes we could remember, things we'd eat. Of course, by this time we had lice and ulcers all over our bodies, and we were getting pyorrhea—teeth getting loose and our gums oozing putrefying crap. It's what you get with beri-beri. When you start getting malnourished, you spend a lot of time talking about meals that you ate at one time or the other, or good places you know to eat, or what you'll eat when you get out. It was mainly to lift each other's spirits. Even when you're talking about food, you don't do it in a depressing, depraved way. It was more about the great steak you'd eat when you got out. Hell, she'd never eaten out in a good restaurant. So I'd say, "When we get out of here, I'll take you out and we'll go to this great restaurant."

They moved us over to another camp. By this time I was pretty weak. It was hard for me to walk. Legs like a couple of rubber bands. I was using a bamboo cane. I found out later that the Montagnards were trying to recapture us. They followed us all the way through the mountains, so the VC kept moving us. During this one-month period they were moving us every two or three days. I didn't know why. And then they got orders to move us over into Cambodia. They marched us all the way down to Dalat, around Dalat, and almost down to Tay Ninh province. We were getting a handful of rice a day, and we were trying to eat anything else we could. There were little nuts, kind of like pistachio nuts, wild on the vine. I would grab them and poke them in my pockets and try to roast them up at night. Sometimes we caught some land crabs and we could throw them in the fire at night and eat them. The girl wasn't too much on eating this stuff, but I would eat anything. I knew I needed extra strength. If they caught us doing that, they might kick us and take away the nuts or the crabs, but it depended on what kind of mood they were in. They didn't want you eating anything other than what they gave you, the reason being that they didn't want you to get any stronger and run off.

The days were drudgery. You just moved. At that time I was walking barefoot. They'd move you for hours at a time. From sunup to sundown. Get you in with enough light to put up your hammock, and you'd lie down and go to sleep. The next day they'd move you again. Moving through jungle. We went through different areas. We went through seas of leeches, where the whole ground was up with these goddamn leeches. Just solid leeches. We went through miles of that in one place. These leeches were about two inches long or less, and they'd be sitting on the ground with their heads up in the air, just waving around. There'd be literally millions of them, millions. You'd walk through them and slide on the goddamn things. Leeches dropping on you off the leaves. Bleeding all over. You'd get them in the groin, they'd crawl up your ass or down your neck. You'd pull them off your groin, bleeding like hell, your pants stiff with goddamn blood from the leeches. You tried to tie up your clothes as much as you could to protect yourself. The girl and I would pull leeches off each other when we could. And if you had a little tobacco or a little soap that you saved, you'd try to smear that up and put it on your legs to keep the leeches off. Either tobacco or soap, they both worked. And there was a leaf that grows in the jungle, I don't know what in hell it is, but it's very effective. You'd run into it and take that leaf and rub it on and the leeches wouldn't get you.

We'd go through dry areas. Or it'd rain on us. We had a piece of plastic that we'd try to keep over us. And we'd move on. We went through areas where the mosquitoes were so goddamn bad that your hands and arms and face would be just black with them. You'd rub down your arm like this, and it'd be all mashed mosquitoes and blood. For about three days we went through a place where the mosquitoes were so bad you couldn't even sleep at night. You'd lie in your hammock, which was made of a light canvas, probably from old bulgur wheat bags that we used to give away. You'd be wearing black pajamas, was all. They'd sting through the hammock and the pajamas, so you'd just be alive with them, lying there alive with them. You'd reach under the hammock and try to get them off and you'd feel a million little tiny things getting you. Sometimes we got up in the middle of the night to move camp because they were so bad.

The girl began to get very weak. They'd kick her and drag her and raise hell with her. So I ended up telling them that she and I weren't going anymore, that we needed rest. They said, "Oh, no, you don't. We're going or we'll kill you." I said, "Fuck you, you can't kill me. You're under orders from the North Vietnamese." They got real angry and started beating me with rifle butts. They threatened to kill us, cocked their guns. I told them, "Fuck you, I'm not going anyplace. I'm sitting down here. You want to kill us? We're dead anyway, what the hell." They threatened us, punched us, kicked us, fired in the ground, and I said, "Go ahead, kill us. Go ahead, we're already dead, but you can't kill us." So they backed off.

They moved us almost to Tay Ninh, then back up over into Quang Duc province. Then I crossed the border into Cambodia. But before I got there, she got so she couldn't move anymore. I told 'em we had to rest again, so they camped at one of their rest houses. It was near a tributary to the Mekong River. They had fish there, and they had pigs and chickens and a garden with squash. They took me over to the psy-war officer and paraded me in front of the soldiers, saying, "This is the American, the supposedly great and invincible American. They brought all their airplanes and technology, and look at this guy. He's not invincible." I countered him in Vietnamese. I said, "Shit, I haven't had anything to eat, I get a handful of rice a day, I've never had any medicine, I've got malaria and beri-beri. You'd be in the same condition I am." They took me off and made up their minds not to try and use me as a propaganda tool again.

I told them we needed something nutritious to eat or the girl couldn't go on any longer. I said, "Hell, you've got a camp nearby with pigs and chickens. You can really give us something nutritious to eat." They conceded and said I could take her down to the river and wash, and we could get some bamboo shoots down there, and they'd cook us up a good meal. We brought back the bamboo shoots. They gave us corn and I think some mung beans and rice and bamboo shoots, but they only boiled the bamboo shoots once. Now, these people know bamboo. It has a very high concentration of something, I think it's prussic or cyanic acid. You have to boil it to boil off the poison, dump the water, and boil it again. That's when you can eat it. We were so hungry when they gave it to us that we just wolfed it down. It was the first corn we had seen and the first mung beans. The bamboo seemed to be extremely bitter, but it didn't register. So we gorged ourselves.

Within a half hour we both had stomach cramps and were immobile. Then we both got diarrhea. It was so bad we couldn't get out of our hammocks quick enough to go crap. And after a while you weren't crapping anything, you just had these cramps. I took some vines and tied 'em between the trees so at least we could have a little decency when we ran out to crap. It took her about a week to die. In three days she was in such a weakened condition that she was almost gone. She lay there so weak that she couldn't get out of her hammock to crap. She lay in her own goddamn shit, and they wouldn't help me wash her. I begged them to bring water so I could wash her, but the best I could do was cut a hole in the bottom of her hammock so she could crap out through the hammock. They just let her lie there. But I never died. I made up my mind I wasn't going to die. I had diarrhea for about three days and got over it. But they deliberately tried to poison us so it would look like natural causes.

I buried her, and I became very depressed after that for a while. Then they began moving me again. I became so weak I couldn't crawl over an eight-inch log. Couldn't raise my legs that high. I'd have to sit down on it, use my hands to lift one leg over, lift the other leg over, and pull myself over the log. Then find something to pull myself up with. I couldn't walk up stairs. They had steps cut out of hillsides with pieces of log to make stairs, and I'd have to crawl up on my hands and knees. Finally I got so I could hardly walk at all. We were over in Cambodia by that time. I knew as soon as we crossed into Cambodia. You could hear airplanes flying up along the border. In Vietnam, any time we heard aircraft, we hid. But as soon as we crossed the border, we walked right up the middle of the trail and didn't pay any attention. There was commo wire strung all the way north, and there was a steady stream of North Vietnamese coming down the trail in the other direction, one after the other, a hell of a lot of North Vietnamese.

After crossing the border I got turned over to some regular prison chasers. North Vietnamese guards, handlers. That's what their main job was, going down to the border and picking up prisoners. I could hardly make it, so they'd knock me down with rifle butts and hit me while I was down and tell me to get going. One day a North Vietnamese officer caught them knocking me around like that. I was trying to get up. He stopped and said, "Can't you see this guy's too weak to walk? This isn't the way you're supposed to treat prisoners." He was a warrant officer or a lieutenant aspirant, and he kept telling 'em, "No, that's not the way." So he turned around and walked north with me. He walked north with me three days, and then he said he couldn't go any farther. They would go through checkpoints, just like a valve gate. Once they went through a checkpoint and got their orders signed off, the only way they could go was south. They could loiter a certain amount of time without getting in too much trouble, a week or so. They were very, very strict with these checkpoints. That's evidently how they kept them going down. He told me all this. So he had to turn around and go back down or he'd get court-martialed. He was a halfway decent North Vietnamese guy. They're not all that bad, and they're not all Communists either.

They had rest camps about every four hours along this trail. One night they pushed me off in a camp and I was so goddamn weak I couldn't walk. I was just barely putting one foot in front of the other. They had a medic in camp and he looked at me and said, "Hell, this guy's so malnourished, he's not gonna make it." He gave me some vitamin shots. They were very big on that in Vietnam, vitamin shots. And he told me, "Just hang on, you're almost there, just three more days." I said, "Fuck you, I've been hearing that for the last month."

They called the camp where we were headed, at the end of the line, the "land of milk and honey." They propagandized about how well they treated the prisoners, how they let you listen to the radio and play around, exercise, do what you want. All you can eat. All that shit. That's what they were telling their own troops. The troops you'd run into, they'd say, "Oh, you're going to the prison camp, that's the land of milk and honey."

One time I was in a rest camp and I stole a green melon they were going to eat. I heard them talking about it, so I stole it and I ate it. The fucker was bitterer than hell, I damn near killed myself. It was something you have to cook a very particular way because it's so bitter. I had stomach cramps for three days after that. By that time I was already starving anyway. Mainly I was surviving on green frogs. Little green frogs that were hatching out. The damn things were everyplace. Whenever I could catch one I'd swallow it whole. If they caught me, they'd hit me and take it away from me. But a lot of times I could grab the goddamn things when the guards weren't looking. Then other times they'd allow me to take baths. I had ulcers all over my body. And I remembered something I read when I was a kid. It was a story about an old trapper, a mountain man named Hugh Glass. How a bear ripped up his back when he wasn't with anybody else, and how he survived after he got all these maggots in his back. What he'd do is lie down in the water and the fish would come and eat at the raw flesh. I remembered that. Whenever they'd let me take a bath, I'd go down and lie in the creek. They had these little fish, and I'd let them eat off all the dead flesh out of these ulcers that I had. It helped to heal the ulcers. And I always tried to catch them. I don't remember how many I ever caught, probably half a dozen or so. I'd eat them raw. It was harder than hell to catch them, but Jesus Christ, I'd get a whole swarm of 'em all over me. It kind of hurt a little, too, tugging away at you. The ulcers were sore anyway. But it was a way of getting the dead flesh off.

Then, about three days after I saw that medic, we made it up a hill into this camp. The hill was like a star, or like your hand, with about eight ridges radiating out down the mountain. They had a prison wing on each of these eight fingers. They moved me into one and there were two other Americans there. When I came in, my hair was white, what little I had. It all came out—I had almost no beard, and no body hair. I was hobbling on this cane. One of the other Americans estimated me to be over seventy years old. At the time, I was thirty-three.

They had a hospital camp there, so they brought over this medical doctor. He talked to me in both French and Vietnamese. He got a crowd around and told them how dehydrated I was, almost dead, so he was going to give me an intravenous feeding of sucrose. He got some sugar and made it up into a sucrose solution. He had a little bottle with a piece of rubber like an inner tube at the end of it. Probably all very goddamn sterile. And he's got a needle, and he's trying to get it into my vein. He can't find a vein. Finally we find a vein back behind my right elbow, and finally he got the needle in. Everybody's going *Ooooo* and *Aaaaah*, the great doctor showing how it's done. I'm lying there for about a half hour, and it's draining into me, but real slowly. Everybody's getting tired, the doctor's getting bored. I hear him ask the medic to go get a bowl. I can't figure out why he wants a bowl. But he gets it. The guy pulls the needle out of my arm, takes the rubber off the top, pours the sucrose in the bowl, hands it to me, and says, "Here, drink it."

Welcome to the land of milk and honey.

After a year in Cambodia, Mike Benge was marched north on the Ho Chi Minh Trail to Hanoi. He spent over three years in camps there, including a total of twenty-seven months in solitary confinement. When he was released in 1973, he immediately returned to Vietnam and worked with the Montagnards until the end of the war.

COLONEL JERRY DRISCOLL

When we talk, he is, of all things, head of air force ROTC at Berkeley. The program is popular and noncontroversial—though ironically, some fifteen years after the Vietnam storm swept the campus, the ROTC building was recently burned to the ground in an arson attack for unknown reasons. We talk in his temporary quarters. He is a lean man in a trim blue uniform, with dark hair and eyes and a jutting jaw. He is in his late forties, but at times a memory makes him look like an impish little Irish boy. Other times his jaw sets in anger, his eyes seem to recede, and he looks both baleful and sad.

He was a POW for almost seven years.

So here I am being interrogated in Hanoi. The first twenty minutes or so weren't too bad. They asked some questions—where I took off from, what my approach was, what the target was. I answered all those questions with name, rank, service number, and date of birth. It wasn't a very big room. There were two Vietnamese officers interrogating me. Speaking fairly good English, but with an obvious accent. Very serious.

They're asking these questions, and I'm just in a daze. After only twenty minutes, when they got zero answers to their questions, they started beating up on me. There were a couple of guards. They hit me with their fists all over. One of 'em hit me with his rifle. I was hurting. It didn't take a genius to realize that they meant business, and they'd just as soon kill you as look at you. And I had no defense. You could swing at 'em, I suppose, but common sense tells you that's just gonna make 'em madder.

So I realized one of two things was gonna happen. Either I'm gonna get beaten to death, or I'm gonna get so badly hurt that I'll tell them something I'll be sorry for later. Back in survival school, a year and a half before, the scenario was: You've been a POW for nine or ten months. You've been giving name, rank, and service number all this time. You do that one more time and you're gonna go out of your mind. Well, I had reached that point in the first twenty minutes. I wasn't going out of my mind, but I was looking at death right there. They were just beating on me. I had already made up my mind that if I was gonna say anything at all, I'd try and lie as much as I could. At survival school, they said you shouldn't do that. You can get yourself in a lot of trouble when they find out you're lying. But how would they know? I was gonna take that chance.

As soon as I started talking, they stopped beating up on me and dutifully started writing down everything I said. I tried to keep it simple. And I qualified everything I told 'em. I'd put my head in my hands, trying to look like I was deep in thought—which I was, thinking: What am I gonna tell 'em? It was half play-acting and half real. I'd say, "Well, I'm not really sure, but I think it's this way." I had enough wits about me to realize that, hey, if you do tell 'em something, at some future date they're gonna come back and ask you to repeat it.

They wanted some target information and some biographical information. Where I grew up. Who my friends were. Who the members of my squadron were. What my target was. I lied through my teeth. This went on for about three hours. Then they left the quiz room— "quiz" was our jargon for interrogation. I was by myself. I had on my flying suit and boots. No food or water. Just in a daze. I was all by myself for about two hours, and then they came back in for another three hours. This lasted about two days, I think: three hours' quiz followed by two hours alone. Sometime in the third day I saw the inside of my first cell, which was at Heartbreak Hotel.

I was a first lieutenant at the time. Twenty-six years old.

When I grew up, I never planned on a military career. I went to the Air Force Academy for two reasons. There was the draft, and it was a good way to fulfill that obligation—might as well do it as an officer. And it offered a chance to get an education I couldn't afford, coming from the family I did.

I graduated from the academy in 1963 and got my wings the next year. I was assigned to the F-105 Thunderchiefs. In 1965, I went to Thailand with the 469th Tac Fighter Squadron, based at Korat. I was a brand-new first lieutenant. We got there on the twelfth of November, and two days later I flew my first combat mission. I was flying daily missions, sometimes a couple of missions a day. And on the twenty-fourth of April of 1966, on my 112th total mission, my eighty-first over North Vietnam, I got shot down and was immediately captured.

The target was a highway-railroad bridge north of Hanoi. A vital link, with traffic coming down from China. We knew it was there. We'd been saying, Let's go get it. But they wouldn't let us hit it until the twenty-fourth of April. The military wasn't picking the targets. The White House and everybody else was. It was a politicians' war.

To this day I have no recollection of getting out of the airplane. I thought I was going about 450 knots. But when I came home and told my flight commander, he said, "No, Jerry. Not 450. Try 550." That's over 600 miles an hour. I was inbound to the target, about ten miles north. My squadron commander had just gotten shot down. He was the mission commander in the first flight of four. I was in the second flight of four. We could hear over the radio that he'd gotten hit by a SAM. He never made it. He got killed.

We'd gone right over a flak site, and they were firing point-blank. Just filled the sky. I guess something hit the tail end of the plane and probably split a hydraulic line. When that happens in the 105, the pressure just forces all the hydraulic fluid out. It burns, also. I was told when I got home that I was a flying blowtorch. There was a flame out the back twice as long as the airplane. I thought I was hit, because the airplane kind of jumped. But I had no cockpit indications. Then I got a call from my number-three man: "Pecan 4, you're on fire." Just about that time I got my first cockpit indication, a blinking over-heat light. A red light. Then some other lights lit up on the caution panel, and the aircraft started to roll. I hadn't moved the stick, so I realized I had no control. It was time to get out. I reached for the ejection handles, and the next thing I know I'm on the ground.

I didn't get hit on the head, but I was doing 550 knots, inverted, at 1,000 feet from the ground, with the zero delay connected. That means as soon as I separate from the seat, the chute opens. I got maybe two swings in the parachute. Then I'm on the ground, still in my seated position, confused, thinking I'm still in the airplane. I tried to get up and got pulled back by something. Turned around and saw my parachute coming down in a rice paddy.

I realized, My God, here I am. Hit the disconnects to the canopy. Stood up and took off my parachute harness. I was taking off my G-suit when I was captured. The people that captured me were mostly farmers and a few militiamen. They had some old rifles from Dien Bien Phu days.

I was pretty well beat up from the ejection. I had no broken bones, but my helmet was gone, my right glove was gone, the right sleeve of my flying suit was shredded all the way up to the seam on the shoulder. I had half a dozen cuts on my right arm, which eventually got infected because I didn't get any medical treatment for the first couple months. I had a whiplash injury, a twisted knee, a sprained ankle, and I was in a state of shock. I hurt like hell. What probably helped me was that I was unconscious when I went out of the plane, so I was limp. I wasn't tense. But it was enough to beat me up really bad. I certainly wasn't gonna resist.

For the next couple days, I still have blank spots. The next thing I remember, it's night, and I was in the back end of a military truck that wasn't covered. I was blindfolded, hands tied behind my back. I was cold and wet. There'd been some rain. And the next thing I know I'm in a room being interrogated.

Then I'm in this cell. That's where I had my first contact with another American. It was a small area with a few cells. We were all solo. Each cell opened to a little hallway, and you could look out through the cracks in the board to make sure there was nobody there. I heard a loud whisper: "Hey, Lieutenant." I had taken off my flight suit when they gave me my prison clothes, and one of the POWs—it turned out to be Jim Stockdale—had washed my flight suit. My rank was on it. They didn't know who it was, so they said, "Hey, Lieutenant." I said, "This is the lieutenant." The guy says, "This is Captain Charlie Boyd." "Hey, Charlie, it's Lieutenant Driscoll." Charlie was shot down two days before me. He was in the other squadron at Korat, so I knew him.

At Heartbreak they interrogated me every single day, twice a day, four or five hours at a crack. I kept lying to the end, qualifying everything I told 'em so that if they ever caught me—which they did. They told me to repeat something, and they said, "But last time you said it was this way." I was quick to remind them how unsure I was. And they said, "Well . . . okay." I breathed a sigh of relief and kept on going. At that point they weren't beating me up anymore because they had kind of broken me to the point where they realized it was useless. And I kind of had them hooked.

After two weeks at Heartbreak, Boyd, Al Brunstrom, and myself were taken out, blindfolded and handcuffed, put into a Jeep, and taken to the outskirts of Hanoi to another camp that we called the "Zoo." We were told it was an old French movie studio. I was put in one of the buildings called the Pool Hall. That's when I first found out about the tap code.

I heard this tapping on the wall. It was frustrating. There was obviously a man on the other side trying to send me some kind of a message. Then I noticed that the rhythm changed. Out of desperation I started counting off the alphabet, and lo and behold, I got the message, "Put your ear to the wall." Which I did, and I heard the voice of Jon Reynolds, who was shot down in November of '65.

Jon told me about the tap code. It's a five-by-five matrix, like a tic-tac-toe game but with five spaces on each side. You put the alphabet in there, using *C* for *K*. That takes care of the twenty-six letters. *ABCDE* across the top, and *AFLQV*—God, I still remember that— down the left-hand side. Then you fill in the rest of the blanks with the rest of the letters. The letter *M* would be three taps, meaning the third row, two taps, the second column. One, two, three, then a pause, then one, two. For a long time, if you couldn't talk through the wall, that was the prime means of communication.

After only three days at the Zoo, I got pulled out to the quiz room. Charlie was there. We were told that we were going to be roommates. As soon as the door closes on our new cell, it's like magic—tapping on the side wall. It's Quincy Collins, who was shot down in September of '65. Quincy told us a lot of things. What had been going on at that camp. The idiosyncrasies of the camp commander. The policies that had been handed down by Colonel Risner, who was the ranking American prisoner. And Quincy told us about the Sunday church service. The senior man in each building would make some kind of sound that we all could hear. Usually he'd thump on the back wall. We'd all stand up, go to the center of the room, bow our heads, and say the Lord's Prayer. A short time later he'd make another sound. We'd turn, face the east—because that was the shortest distance to the United States—put our hands over our hearts, and say the Pledge of Allegiance. We did that every single Sunday we were in North Vietnam, whether we were solo, dual, or in one case where I had fifty-five roommates. Every single Sunday.

About the last week of June, one of the guards comes by and asks for one of our sets of long prison clothes—a long-sleeved shirt and long pants that they'd given us. We each give him one. A couple days later he comes back and gives us our clothes, with one big difference: a large black number stenciled on the back of the shirt. We don't know what this is for until the night of July 6, '66, when we're told to put on that particular set of long clothes. A short time later the turnkey comes by. Charlie and I get taken out, handcuffed together and blindfolded. We find ourselves in the back seat of a military truck with other POWs. After a short truck ride we get taken off. I then get handcuffed to another American by the name of Tom Barrett. Eventually the blindfolds are taken off and we can see that there's about fifty of us, standing two by two in the middle of the street. In front of us is a large group of people standing on both sides of the curb, with a few individuals standing just into the street with megaphones. They're acting like cheerleaders. None of us understands Vietnamese, but it was obvious. Getting the crowd worked up.

At this time in the war, Ho Chi Minh was calling us war criminals. Every time we'd be called out for interrogation, they'd call us war criminals and say, "We're going to put you on trial." Now Ho was going to march the war criminals through the streets of Hanoi for the people to see. Big propaganda thing.

We start going down the street. Things are going along okay. There are guards on either side of us, one on one. They've got bayonets on the end of the rifles. The bayonets are pointed at us. They tell us to bow our heads. About halfway through the parade we turn down a street that isn't so well lit. And now the people with the megaphones have done their job. They've done it so well that the crowd has become a mob. Some people have broken through the cordon of guards with rocks and bottles and sticks. They're getting in some pretty good kicks on some of our guys. At one point somebody got through and got a good kick on Tom. He went down on one knee. I just pulled on the handcuffs and said, "Hey, c'mon, Tom, we've gotta keep going. We can't stop now." By this time the guards no longer have the bayonets pointed at us. They're pointed at their own people, to protect us. And the guards are scared.

We get to our destination, which is the Hanoi soccer stadium. It may have been their intention to let the people into the stadium, but by this time they aren't about to let those people in. It's a raging mob. So all the entrances are closed except for one. And the people are trying so hard to get at us around that entrance that one poor guy falls down, and like a domino effect, they all start falling on top of one another. Now there's this pile of humanity in the doorway between me and safety. And I mean a pile of people about four or five feet high. I'm wondering what's gonna happen next. Well, there's a North Vietnamese officer on the other side who sees our predicament. He sticks out his hand, which I lunge for and grab. And with his help I literally walk over this pile of people, pulling Tom behind me.

Eventually we all got in there. They closed the one door, brought in some trucks through the back entrance, and took us back to our respective camps. That was the end of that. I think that evening I was probably closer to dying than the day I was shot down. And I know exactly what it feels like to be the intended victim of a lynch mob.

As it turned out, that whole operation backfired on Ho Chi Minh. There were Japanese photographers there, and a lot of East Europeans. When it got back to the Western press, there was so much bad publicity about what almost happened that the war crimes trials never came off. World public opinion was totally against him.

Then we moved to Briarpatch. Actually, I got to see quite a few of the camps. From the Zoo I went to Briarpatch, and then I went up to Son Tay and came back to the Annex, which was right next to the Zoo. I was at Little Vegas, Dirty Bird, Camp Faith, Camp Unity, and Dogpatch, which was near the Chinese border.

The routine varied a little, but not all that much. They'd ring the gong at about five-thirty. They banged some angle iron over an old artillery shell hanging from a tree. A horrendous, raucous, grating sound. Sure as hell got you up. At six we had to listen to the Voice of Vietnam, or Hanoi Hannah, as we called her. It was the same broadcast we'd heard the night before at eight.

We'd exercise as soon as we got up. They made sure everybody got up. They had rules and regulations, almost like a military school. [Laughs.] You had to roll up your gear and fold it a certain way. We didn't want to follow that, but it was to our benefit because it kept things nice and neat. You put your bedroll at the foot of the bed— this is starting in '67. That's when we got into a regular thing. During the first year, this doesn't really apply, because we were in such poor health. We didn't get much food and there was a lot of torture, so we couldn't do much.

But we're now in mid-'67. I'm living with three other guys: Jon Reynolds, Bruce Seiber, who are air force, and Ray Alcorn, who's navy. These guys were shot down in '65, so they've got me beat. I'm the new kid on the block and the junior-ranking guy. But the four of us are together for the next two and a half years, from mid-'67 until about December of 1969. Twenty-four hours a day. We got to know each other very, very well.

Here we are in Little Vegas. In a room that measures about eight feet by eight feet. Two bunk beds. Things are pretty cramped. We can use the bunk beds to do push-ups. And the little floor space between the bunks, about eight feet long—it takes about half an hour to walk one mile, pacing back and forth. A certain number of laps is a mile. So each person, after you do your basic exercise—running in place, push-ups, sit-ups, what have you, then you get your turn on the track. One guy at a time. Once every two hours, you walk for half an hour. If you're not doing anything else, or talking with your roommates, you're out there pacing. Racking up the miles. It keeps your legs in shape, and it keeps you slim and trim. [Laughs.]

We usually didn't walk during the broadcast because the guards would come by to make sure you weren't. You were supposed to listen and pay attention to all the good things Hannah was coming across with. So that was a quiet half hour. Then after the broadcast they'd start taking individual rooms out for a bath. Once you were secure in the bath area, which was an enclosed stall, they'd lock the door and bring out another room. Until about 1969 they were paranoid about you seeing other Americans. They had about four or five bath stalls in Little Vegas, so four or five rooms at a time could be out. We'd do some communicating out there, but you had to be careful.

Then you go back to your room. You start on the track. Back and forth. At noontime they fed us our first meal. Most meals consisted of a large bowl of watery soup. There could be some greens in there, just leaves floating around. We sometimes called it weed soup. Or it might be potato soup, which was great because it stayed with you and was very healthful. Another staple seemed to be pumpkin soup. They'd just boil this gourd up. Believe me, there's only one way to have pumpkin, and that's in pie. I'm not a strong advocate of pumpkin soup.

Depending on what camp you were in and the time of the war, you'd either get a large plate of rice or a small loaf of bread. The rice is the equivalent of an eight-inch plate, heaped over. About the same amount you'd serve two couples for dinner. That's what each of us got for one meal. It seems like a lot, and once you get it down, you're full. But within two hours, you're hungry. The rice goes through you like water. For the next couple of hours, you're urinating quite a bit. But the bread, that fills you up much better and stays with you. That was especially good to see in the wintertime, when it got cold.

Once in a while, besides those two things, they'd give you a little side dish. A small bowl that might have a pumpkin paste, or meat. Put "meat" in quotation marks. It might be an old water buffalo that they slaughtered. Or guinea pig—there'd be small bones. We may have eaten monkey. The North Vietnamese themselves ate dog, it

416 | STRANGE GROUND

was just normal bill of fare. They'd raise the dogs, you'd see 'em around, and then all of a sudden they'd disappear. Sometimes we'd get dried fish, which was very good, high in protein. And sometimes the meat consisted of pork fat. How often you got meat really varied. It seemed to go in cycles. We'd get it for a few meals in a row, and then we wouldn't get it for some time. No rhyme or reason.

That would be the normal meal. You'd get two of those, one at noon and the other around six.

After the first meal we'd have our siesta. That's when we'd do a lot of our communicating. It was quieter. There were fewer guards around. Guards are guards, they'd slough off, just relax and daydream.

Hopefully you don't get called out for a quiz. Any time the door opened and it was outside the normal time, like naptime or dinnertime, you had this sinking feeling. Oh, God, what now? Especially if the guard opens the door and makes the sign to put on your long clothes. Which means you're going to quiz. You dress formally, long sleeves and long pants. Nine months out of the year it was warm enough that we could walk around in our shorts and T-shirts.

In the evening there was little if any communicating unless something extraordinary had happened. We'd just sit and talk, and at eight Hanoi Hannah would come on again. We'd go to bed at nine, nine-thirty. Of course the light didn't go out. It was the same light, a twenty-five-watt bulb that was hung in the room. They'd ring the gong and the whole camp went to bed. They'd come by and check you during the night.

Time didn't drag on as much as one might think. At times it did, but boy, before you knew it the day was over. After a while you'd realize, My God, I've been here a couple of years already. In 1970 I got moved out of Son Tay and back to Hanoi, and I realized I'd been there four years. My God, that long?

You'd think a lot about what you're going to do when you get out. You'd have all this money that the military was keeping for you. Some of us, especially the bachelors, had plans to go to Italy, buy a Ferrari, drive it across Europe to a port, put it on a boat and ship it back. I had plans to do that, but of course I never did. [Laughs.] You think about if you get married, what kind of house you might want to have. I learned about dairy farming because Charlie Boyd's dad was a dairy farmer. I lived with a couple of people who had been forestry majors, so I learned all about trees. From the navy guys I learned about carrier landings.

We all participated in the memory bank. We were each responsible for a list of prisoner names, an alphabetical list. The day I got to

Clark, in the Philippines, I rattled off all 200 names that I had, and this debriefer didn't have some of them on his list. I'd say, "This guy is coming home. I know he's alive, because I saw him this morning. He's gonna be home in two weeks, he's in the next group."

I'd go through those names at least once a day. The usual time was at night, when I was ready to go to sleep. Rather than counting sheep, you counted names. I knew exactly how many I had, and I'd count on my fingers as I'd go through 'em. All the *A*'s, all the *B*'s, all the *C*'s, and all the *D*'s. That would add up to my 200 names.

After I got to Briarpatch, I experienced what you could really call torture. The camp was kind of isolated, about thirty-five or forty miles west of Hanoi, in some little foothills. Small buildings with walls between them. The rooms were small, either one- or two-man rooms, measuring about six by ten. There were air-raid shelters dug underneath the bunks. No running water, no electricity. The bunks were wooden, set up on cement blocks. It's an old camp, probably from French times.

After only about a month there, a purge started. One by one they pulled out the guys, took 'em up to the quiz room, and tortured 'em to write a war-crimes confession. About the last week of September, Charlie got pulled out, and an hour or two later I got pulled out. I sat down with the interrogator. He asked me to write, and I refused. We sat and talked about it for a couple of hours. The conversation was the pros and cons of the war. Trying to convince me that I was doing the wrong thing. Communism is good, capitalism is bad. We sat and talked, and I sometimes nodded my head. After all that time he may have thought, My God, I haven't been able to convince anyone else, but I've got this one. So he asked me again to write. I refused. He said, "Okay, you go in the side room and sit on the stool and think about it."

The stool in this room is a stack of bricks a foot and a half or two feet high. Cemented over very smoothly. Very hard. For about the next eight hours I'm sitting there wondering what's going to happen. I can't get up and walk around or lie on the floor and get some sleep because there's a guard outside watching. Making sure I'm sitting there the whole time. I can't get up, and it hurts.

At the end of eight hours they call me back in and ask me to write. I refuse. At this point the interrogator got absolutely livid. He called in two of his guards. One of 'em had a pair of handcuffs. They took the narrow portion of the cuffs, put it across the wide part of my wrist, and tightened it down. Then they forced my hands behind my back and up around my shoulder blades, and they put on the other cuff.

Then they threw me on my stomach and one of the guards stood on the handcuffs to get the last possible ratchet. In this position, if you try to put your hands down, the cuffs cut into the sides of your wrist, causing excruciating pain. They said, "Okay, you go to the side room and sit on the stool and think about it."

Your hands are up around your back, and you have to try and hold 'em up there. If you relax just a little and try to bring 'em down— oh, forget it. At the end of the first day my hands had swollen up to about two or three times normal size. At the end of the second day, I couldn't wear my tire sandals because my feet had swollen so much. At the end of the fourth day, I found myself on the floor with blood coming from my forehead. I had obviously passed out. When the guard wasn't around, or when they closed the shutter because there was somebody passing by, I would get up and walk around. I'm gonna play it out as long as I can. There was a small table in there, just about the right height that if I leaned over, bending over at the waist, I could lay the upper part of my body across it, and if I laid my chest on it, my arms could rest on my back without pushing my hands down. I could get a minute or two of sleep. I'd actually drop off for a little bit. That's the only reason I was able to go four days, before I finally just couldn't stay awake. The guard had caught me standing up, and he said, "Sit down." I guess it was nighttime. That's when you'd usually drop off. It was kind of quiet. I was sitting there, and all of a sudden, *wham!* My head hurt, and I was on the floor, passed out.

At the end of the sixth day they called me back in and asked me to write. Up to then they just left me, figuring that when I'm ready I'd make it known to the guards. They'd take off one side of the cuff and feed me twice a day, but I could hardly eat. I tried to eat as much as I could, but I just couldn't.

When I refused to write at the end of the sixth day, there was a surprised look on this interrogator's face. I was kind of surprised myself. The guard took off the cuffs, but then he reapplied them, this time with my hands behind my buttocks. One of the guards came with a short length of rope, which he tied just above the elbow. Same thing on the other side. Then he tightened the rope so my elbows were together. Man. They said, "Okay, you go inside and think about it." Which I did. At the end of eight hours, I said I would write.

By that time you're bleary. You don't know what's going to happen next. You don't know how much longer you can keep going. You take it minute by minute, not day by day. Just try to keep going. I finally reached the point where if I held out any longer, I was afraid I'd go crazy. The pain affects your mind. You can't think. You become irrational. Plus I figured that I might have reached the point where I was going to lose the use of my hands permanently. That's one of the things that Colonel Risner had passed around early on: Don't let 'em do any permanent damage to you. I figured, Well, I've satisfied that requirement. I held out as long as I possibly could. For the longest time afterward, a couple years or so, I could hardly feel things on the palms of my hands. Even today, once in a while I'll doubt whether I'm getting the proper feeling, and I'll feel with the backs of my hands.

I wrote a statement that said I was sorry for the three missions I had flown over North Vietnam. I had told them I was only on my third mission. That was my war-crimes confession. I said I was sorry. I think the statement was a couple of pages. It was a real innocuous thing. Even when I was writing, I tried to put in some words and phrases that if they'd ever been published, it would have embarrassed them. So they didn't get exactly what they wanted from me. But I'm sure they felt like they had broken me. And I was feeling pretty low. I felt like I'd let myself and my fellow POWs and my country down. A couple of hours later, when they allowed me to go back to my room, I told the rest of the guys in my building what had happened. They were all senior to me, and they said that similar things had happened to everybody else. All of them had written some kind of statement after torture.

Everybody wrote eventually. You had to. It was either write or you're dead. There's no in-between. If they want something badly enough, they're gonna do whatever they have to to get it. But I was trying to make it go as long as I could. You wanted to show 'em that you don't just give in. What if they ask you to write and you just say okay? You can't do that. They'll keep coming back for more and more. So you make 'em work for it. You don't give 'em anything easy. I'm convinced that later on, when we had another purge, they said, "Oh, my God, here we go again." They knew what was gonna happen. It wasn't gonna take 'em two or three days to get a statement from the fifty guys that were at that camp—this was Son Tay. They knew it was gonna be twenty-four hours a day, seven days a week. That made us feel good. We were doing our job. Even though we were prisoners, we were still doing our job. We were still fighting 'em.

Here's where one could get into a discussion about the Code of Conduct. It says you're not supposed to give them any information or write any statements, all that stuff. But the code is just a guideline. In 1955, President Eisenhower signed this executive order—which is not law—that became the Code of Conduct. Well, for a while people said you've got to observe it absolutely, word for word. But in Vietnam, you quickly realized that you couldn't physically do it. Or you're dead. Some can take it more than others, but everybody's got a breaking point. Or else, you may not break, but you're also very dead. Because they're not going to stop. I guarantee you. They . . . will . . . not . . . stop, period.

There were some guys—one was Norm Schmidt. We were living in Little Vegas at the time. He was a major. He was taken out to quiz, and the quiz room was fairly close to the cellblock area. Some people heard a scuffle. He never came back. His remains have since come home, but he was killed. We felt pretty certain he was beaten to death. Either he resisted or he got into a fight with the guards. Another guy, Ed Atterbury. He was one of two who escaped in '69. They were recaptured after only twelve hours. Both of those guys got severe, severe beatings. One guy survived because he was in fantastic shape. Ed was beaten to death.

There was some controversy over so-called hardliners and softliners. The navy tended to be strictly, absolutely hardline. The Code of Conduct, word for word, no ifs, ands, or buts. If you mess up on one word of it, you're a traitor. There were some air force people like that. But what good are you if you get beaten to death? That's not the intent of the Code of Conduct. You're captured, and you have to maintain life in the most honorable way you can.

You found out very quickly, you don't want to piss the Vietnamese off. That's asking for trouble. Why make it worse on yourself? You go in there and resist as nicely as possible.

Some people disagreed with the idea of being civil to your interrogators. But by being civil, they won't put as much gusto into breaking you. When they finally get a statement, they'll be satisfied with less. For instance, my case. They tortured me, my hands swelled, I passed out, the whole bit. And every time they asked me, I just said, "No, I don't care to write." In a conversational tone of voice. So when they finally got me to write, I just said that I was sorry. If I had been surly, they probably would have beaten up on me more, and I wouldn't have lasted as long. It would have defeated the purpose of keeping them busy. And if they had really broken me, I would have said, "Yeah, I bombed women and children and hospitals." But I wrote a statement as mild as it could be. And they were satisfied. That's because I was civil.

They would always talk about their "humane and lenient treatment." Maybe they really felt that way, because they treated their own people as harshly as they treated us. That's the way it is in a lot of Asian societies. Human rights are almost unknown in that part of the world. For so many centuries, these people have led a hand-to-mouth existence. If somebody dies or gets killed, that's one less mouth to feed. That's the way they look at things. It doesn't bother them to put somebody in leg irons and beat 'em about the head and shoulders. They do that all the time. But they quickly learned from us that we don't do that, and we think that's inhumane treatment. And that's what we were going to tell our government.

They didn't like to hear that. I remember one interrogator who started out his military career as a guard. He was given a quick English course and a quick American history course and pressed into service. Just the look on his face—he'd shake his head in disbelief when I'd say that I was going to tell my government about the torture and show them the scar on my arm from the handcuffs. His answer was, "But you did not obey the camp rules. We had no choice." I said, "You had every choice. You didn't have to do that. It's known as torture. It's against the Geneva Convention." "But we're not signatories of the Geneva Convention." "That's okay, most people observe them anyway. And I'm going to tell my country that you tortured me and I had to write all these statements against my will."

In 1969 we had the good-treatment purge. I was at Son Tay. They started pulling us out one by one and torturing us to write a statement saying we'd been treated well. Can you believe that?

By this time most of us had been there for so long that we weren't in as good health as in '66. My weight was down, and my resistance wasn't as good. They put on the handcuffs, but not the way they did in '66 as far as causing the pain. They just cuffed my hands behind my back so I couldn't move 'em around. Then the prolonged sitting on the stool. It's hard on your bottom. It hurts. They put me in leg irons. I had somebody watching all the time. No beatings, but it's a real stress situation. I was uncomfortable and hurting, and I didn't have any padding on my tailbone. And they kept me awake. I got incoherent, almost. So it didn't take as long. You say, I can't take this anymore. People may say, Well, that's not torture. But when you're experiencing it after so many years, and your health isn't exactly sterling, and you're thirty or forty pounds lighter than when you were shot down, your resistance is lower. You even start questioning yourself. Is it worth it? Do I need the hassle for this statement they want?

I lasted about three days. In some ways I feel kind of bad about it. I just couldn't take it, but at times I feel maybe I gave up a bit too soon. It was more difficult after what I experienced in '66. I knew they would get it sooner or later. And for what—a good-treatment statement? They couldn't make a hell of a lot of hay out of that. But when I talk about it, there's a moment of guilt. Gee, I didn't do as well as I could. Then I have to go back and realize, Hey, I did what I did. I cost 'em a few days.

In October of '69, right in the middle of the good-treatment purge, the really bad treatment stopped. They hadn't gotten through the whole camp yet. One of the navy guys that lived next door to me had been in the quiz room for a couple of days on a stool. The morning of the third day, the interrogator comes in and tells the guy to write something, anything: "I don't care what it is." So the guy takes a pencil and just writes words on a piece of paper. Nothing. The interrogator walks out into the courtyard. There's half a dozen guards milling around. He starts waving the paper and yelling something in Vietnamese. We figure he said something like, "See, the Yankee air pirate has confessed his crimes." He comes back and tells this navy guy, "Go back to your room." And he was the last guy that got pulled out.

The next day, lo and behold, we get this Continental breakfast, loosely speaking. What it amounts to is old bread, maybe two or three days old. They've cut the loaf in half, so it's a broad piece of bread, and they've toasted it, maybe on a grill, and put like a cinnamon sugar on it. They gave each of us a piece of that. Well, that's okay, what's happening? It happened again the next day. And the next. And when the regular meals came around, we got a little bit more food. The quality started to improve. It was amazing. And by December, everybody was finally able to write letters home. Guys who'd been POWs for four and a half years wrote their first letter. We started getting packages from the States. I got my first letter a year later, on October 12, 1970. It was from my mother, and it had a March 1970 date. She was writing once a month, but I never got any until then.

We think there are a couple reasons for the torture stopping. Ho Chi Minh had just died the month before. We think the new leaders had a change of policy about the POWs. He was more harsh, absolutely. The guy was ruthless, absolutely ruthless. But the people who came afterward may have realized, Hey, we're not gonna win this war outright. Something's gotta give. And they knew we were more valuable alive than dead. So they probably thought, Well, we've got what propaganda value we can with harsh treatment. We may get more value now by keeping 'em healthier and making 'em feel better. And another reason, unknown to us, was that back in the States there was a big letter-writing campaign to the Vietnamese about the POWs. North Vietnam was very worried about world opinion, so we think that helped.

From '69 on, it was a day-to-day existence, combating boredom. By that time we were in large groups. Until the Son Tay raid, we had eight-man rooms. That was great, it was a field day. Then after Son Tay, we're talking huge rooms. It was old home week. All the bad jokes got told again. I finally got to shake hands with people who I'd been tapping through the wall with for years.

Being as junior as I was, I was among the masses. I never saw any of the people who cooperated with the Vietnamese. I was never asked to meet with antiwar visitors. Naturally, I would have refused. And I wasn't offered early release. I don't condone the people who went home early. They have to look at themselves in the mirror when they're shaving in the morning. I think the Vietnamese picked them at random, when they first got captured. They weren't mistreated, they weren't tortured. And they just elected to go along with it and come home. That violates a tenet of the Code of Conduct, which states: "I will not accept special favor or parole." Out of all those releases, only one had formal permission to go home. That was Seaman Doug Hegdahl, who fell off the cruiser *Canberra*. He was a curious situation, because he was a noncombatant. He fell off a damn boat, swam ashore, and got captured. There was international pressure on the North Vietnamese to release him. And he was the only one who got permission from the senior person in his camp to go home.

Since I came back, I've seen two guys who accepted early release. One was a very senior guy. I ended up getting assigned to the same place he was in 1978. Every time I'd go down a hall and he'd see me coming, he'd duck into the next office. He never, ever did meet me face-to-face. Ever. Another guy I met at a Red Flag exercise. I had the chance to go over and talk to him, and I met him face-to-face. He knew who I was. He just turned away.

In 1972 the bombing picks up, and about the fifteenth of May, I'm one of about 150 that get moved out of what's now called Camp Unity, a big portion of the Hilton. We get trucked up north to a camp called Dogpatch, five or ten miles south of the Chinese border. It's while we're there that we hear about the B-52s bombing Hanoi. It's curious—we're so far north that we neither see nor hear the B-52s or the bombs they're dropping. Yet the guards tell us it's happening. And nobody gets pulled out to receive a beating. There's no retaliation. The food doesn't change. So most of us are encouraged. Hey, maybe this is finally the end. Here their capital city's getting leveled, and our situation doesn't change one iota.

After December we don't hear anything else. The bombing stops. What's happening? We just go along. About the sixteenth of January,

Dogpatch is closed. They truck us back to Hanoi. We travel in broad daylight. The trip takes sixteen hours, instead of twenty-five when we went up. And the security is the least I've ever seen it. None of us are blindfolded. We're just handcuffed together. There's two guards in the back of the truck with us, and they couldn't care less. We can lift up the tarp of the truck and see the countryside.

Finally we get back to the Hilton. The old heads who stayed behind when we left in May start talking about the B-52 bombing. Their eyes light up, they talk about it in awe. They also tell us what's been happening in the States for the last two or three years, because they've been talking to all the new shootdowns. Pretty soon we begin hearing Hanoi Hannah talk about the Paris Peace Accords, which had been signed on the twenty-seventh of January. A short time after that we get our own personal copy of the protocol pertaining to POWs, wherein it states that no later than the twelfth of February of '73, a minimum of one-fourth of the POWs will be released. Knowing the Vietnamese as we do, we're pretty certain they'll wait 'til the last day and release no more than one-fourth. While we're waiting, Colonel Risner, who's then the ranking POW in Camp Unity, tells the camp commander how we want the releases to be done: sick and injured first, followed by shootdown order beginning with Alvarez, from August of '64. I think from my shootdown date I'll probably be in the first group.

The North Vietnamese start giving us large quantities of food. Fish, rice, bread, sugar, in an obvious attempt to fatten us up. We go along with it. They open up the rooms first thing in the morning, and they're open that way all day. Playing volleyball. Finally, after all these years, the twelfth of February arrives, and I am in the first group. I'm on the third of the first three airplanes.

It was a very emotional time. They brought us to the airport in six buses. Two buses per airplane. So here I am in bus five. When we first pulled up at Gia Lom airport, I could see the C-141. The first two buses went. The plane started taxiing out, and then it stopped because the second 141 came in and landed. It taxied in, and the first one took off. We're standing in the bus, and we started yelling. The guards were trying to keep us quiet, but we didn't care. It was real, it was really happening. Up to then we didn't believe it, even though we were in civilian clothes. They had given us these jackets and slacks and these tight, pointed Italian shoes.

The second airplane filled up, taxied out to the runway, and took off. We're looking. There's still two buses. I was thinking to myself, Oh, shit. It was deathly quiet for the longest time. Maybe twenty minutes, maybe five. Nothing. No sounds. Finally somebody said,

"Hey, look up there!" Sure enough, the third 141 came down the runway and landed.

We lined up in shootdown order. They called out my name. I stepped forward. There was a colonel. I saluted him and said, "Good to be back." He shook my hand and said, "Congratulations, glad to have you back." We stepped another twenty feet and there was another colonel. I saluted him. He turned me over to an air-crew member, who escorted me to the 141. He had to hold on very tight to my arm, because I was so emotional. As I began walking to the plane, I had reporters sticking microphones in my face and asking me questions, which I could not answer. I was all choked up, but it was too exciting to cry. As I got closer and closer to that 141, I looked up at the tail and saw a big red cross painted on it. On top of that red cross was a big, beautiful American flag.

11

AID AND COMFORT

In late December 1965, three Americans—Herbert Aptheker, Tom Hayden, and Staughton Lynd—arrived in Hanoi on what they called a private "peace mission." Aptheker was a historian and a member of the Communist party. Hayden was then a leader of Students for a Democratic Society. Lynd was a Yale professor of leftist persuasions. The three were traveling without passports validated for North Vietnam. They had been invited by the Hanoi government to study the damage done by U.S. bombers.

It was an unusual moment: citizens of a country at war visiting the capital of the enemy nation in open sympathy with its cause. But this first delegation was followed by a few in 1966 and 1967, then more and more as the war neared its end. One woman, Jane Fonda, came to symbolize all the visitors, because of both her fame and her extravagant gesture of posing for photographs at the controls of an antiaircraft gun. Many Americans have not forgiven her those pictures. But the bulk of the visitors, like the two in this chapter, were just foot soldiers in the antiwar army, unknown to the public except as traitors or as messengers of goodwill, depending on one's point of view.

Hanoi stood to gain much from these visits. Against the hail of bombs it had only one real weapon: propaganda. Guns and missiles could slow but never stop the air war, while public opinion, especially in the U.S., might force a halt. A year after the first antiwar group visited, Harrison Salisbury, the assistant managing editor of *The New York Times*, toured the North. Americans who had ignored or disbelieved the activists were shocked by his detailed reports of ruined cities and towns—this at a time when Washington claimed only military targets were being hit. But the bombing continued, and so did Hanoi's need for witnesses. Who better than Americans to publicize the claim that the campaign amounted to genocide?

In a sense, the visitors themselves were the mirror image of the bomber pilots. Most were young and full of fire—not for war or flying or the American cause, but for peace, or, in many cases, for revolution in Vietnam and at home. They went because they were curious; because they wanted to see how bad the bombing was, and how North Vietnam was faring; because they wanted guidance in their antiwar work. And they went looking for inspiration, which they found. The activists, like their opposite numbers in the military, tended to expect results in a year or two. In North Vietnam they met people who thought in terms of decades, and who seemed unshakably confident.

Another thing links these travelers to the soldiers: a certain naiveté. They briefly entered a culture they knew nothing about. In their dismay at the war and enthusiasm for the North, they were eager to believe what their hosts told them—even when, as Norm Fruchter relates, they struggled against that eagerness. They were on the other side of the looking-glass, trying to get some bearings. And all the while, there was a choking sense of responsibility. The bombs were American, and so were the visitors. They talk about seeing carnage that "we" caused, and about the eerie experience of being bombed by "our" planes.

After Hanoi conceived the tactic of releasing POWs to antiwar delegations, the visitors had to negotiate that thicket as well. Their feelings for the pilots could not have been more mixed. Many hated them as war criminals. Yet the POWs were fellow Americans—and simply men in a difficult spot. What could be said, and what was best left unspoken? How much could each side trust the other? Why had these particular men been chosen? Would the antiwar cause be helped or hurt by the releases?

How much influence the delegations had back home is debatable. Certainly the movement itself got a boost, since its leaders returned from Hanoi with fresh fighting spirit. As Norm Fruchter says, using "we" with typical ambiguity: "We came back and said, 'We're going to lose the war. No matter what we do, we're going to lose. No matter how hard we hit the North, we're going to lose. And no matter what we do in the South, we're going to lose.'

"That's how we saw our job."

CAROL BRIGHTMAN

She is in her early forties, a tall, thin woman with long blond hair and pale blue eyes, wearing jeans and a loose shirt. She is shy, serious. Her work in the antiwar movement made her a left-wing activist, and she has since labored for various causes, mostly in the women's movement. When we talk, she is an editor at the magazine Geo, *which has since folded. She lives in a cavernous loft in Brooklyn with her boyfriend, a Vietnam veteran, and his young son.*

In the summer of 1965 she began publishing a newsletter, Viet Report. *"It came out for three years, and there were a few issues where we printed 80,000 copies. They were used at teach-ins, for basic reading. At the height we had a paid circulation of about 12,000, but mostly it was 6,000 or 7,000. Even that was enormous, considering we didn't have any circulation department or any mailings. It was all word of mouth."*

The Bertrand Russell War Crimes Tribunal was organizing a series of teams to gather evidence of civilian bombardment in North Vietnam—bombardment of hospitals, fishing cooperatives, towns, churches, religious communities. The Vietnamese had let in very few people at that point, and I think my trip was as extensive as it was because it was crucial propaganda for them. As far as the American public was concerned, the bombing was still pretty much a sideshow to the war. And of course, part of the idea of those trips was to show over and over again that life in North Vietnam was going on. If a country can invite dignitaries from other countries and journalists from the enemy country and take them around, it's a statement in itself. So I was asked to go on this trip because I edited an antiwar magazine and it was assumed I would have a public to speak to. Why they didn't choose more Americans for this group, I don't know, but I was the only one.

The trip started in New York and went to London so we could meet the tribunal organizers and be briefed. Then we went to Cambodia. We left there on an International Control Commission plane to Vientiane. Then we caught another plane to Hanoi, which had to go up at precisely the right moment and fly at precisely the right level. If it was too high, it would be fired at by Vietnamese antiaircraft, and if it was too low it might get fired at from the ground. A plane had been lost in 1966.

There were five of us on the delegation. One was a guy from the

Dominican Republic who lived in Canada. There was a French doctor. There was the president of the Scottish mineworkers' union, who was a Scottish nationalist. And there was Tariq Ali, a wild-man Trotskyite who lived in London and was the son of a Pakistani pasha or something. It was a group of clowns, including me. The Scottish guy got very homesick and drank too much. He'd wander around at night in the hotel singing sad songs. And Tariq Ali made brilliant, militant speeches. He was always the one who spoke in response to the Vietnamese. I could never make the proper militant speech. He was always ribbing me about being compromised for being partly an imperialist.

We got to Hanoi in late January 1967. We spent the first three or four days there, getting our itinerary. I was always looking for something familiar, and the streets—I was pretty free to walk around—the streets of Hanoi reminded me a lot of Evanston, Illinois, which is a town between Chicago and the suburb I grew up in. There were a lot of big trees, not elm trees but they looked like elm trees. There were sounds of little radios going in the background, and people working on their cars, and a lot of low chatter on the streets at twilight. The scale of the buildings was very similar to Evanston, big houses that you're not sure whether they're houses or apartment buildings. I felt at home there. And it was quite an adventure. Endless rounds of meetings with officials and delegations, and cultural performances and visits to the war museum.

Our first exposure to war destruction was right around Hanoi. Before we started to travel, we went to workers' quarters on the outside of the city and saw a couple of temples that had been bombed. They gave us reports on how many had been killed and how many were injured. But for those first couple of days it was kind of abstract. We were taken out of our meetings, and we'd go out to see the damage, as if it was an illustration of what we were getting verbally. When we started to travel, that was reversed: The damage was so overwhelming and the explanations so insignificant.

Our group split into two. One group toured north of Hanoi, and my group went south. Most of the heavy industry was in the north, so I didn't see any major industrial areas. The main places I went were the provinces of Ninh Binh and Tan Hua. We would set out, always at night, traveling very slowly on the road. There was only one main highway, Route 1, and it was logjammed with traffic. We'd be in a group of three or four cars, a lot of us in each car. All the lights were off, but of course the American pilots knew where the highway was and knew that at night it was filled with traffic. It was very dark, and every few hundred yards there was a little station with some Vietnamese militia, girls or boys in their early teens. They had these lanterns that they used for signals. They would signal whether there was any sound of approaching aircraft and how far away they were. I remember getting out and getting in shelters a couple of times, but I don't remember any close shaves. The bombing was never so close that I could see it. I could hear it, and occasionally I could hear the planes, but I couldn't see the explosions.

During the day we would visit villages and towns and district capitals and provincial capitals. We would be welcomed, and there would be a standard presentation. Someone would start out with a report on conditions in the district or province before the French, after the French, and now during the war. Then someone else would report on the military conditions in the district or province. How many attacks, how many planes shot down. The third presentation would be about casualties and damage: schools, churches, towns, marketplaces. When we were in a small town, we would be introduced to survivors. Again, there was a kind of format—somebody would talk about the kind of planes that had hit, the kind of bombs. Then we'd be told how many were lost and how people were injured and what was happening to them now. Sometimes we'd be taken to a kind of shelter, where they'd have huge bomb casings. Some of them were enormous, from 2,000-pound bombs. More typical were the 1,000- and 500-pound bombs, then all these CBUs, canister bombs that throw out pellets. I would look at the serial numbers of the bombs and copy them down like a zombie. We'd be shown people with pellets still in them. This was day after day, over and over again.

Ninh Binh province was the base of the Catholic population that was left in North Vietnam. The towns, even the smaller district capitals, all have big cathedrals. We covered that province pretty thoroughly, including fishing cooperatives along the coast, the capital, which is called Ninh Binh City, and a large fishing town called Phat Diem. Most of these areas had been almost completely leveled by the bombing. In all the towns we visited, eight or nine of them, the church always stood out as having been leveled. Another thing we were shown was dikes. This was in Tan Hua province. They were dirt dikes, not cement, and they were constantly being shored up by human labor. These dikes had been bombed, whether it was deliberate or not. It was officially the policy of the U.S. not to bomb dikes, but it was not the policy to bomb Catholic churches or villages or fishing cooperatives either.

Every once in a while, when we were traveling, we'd see a SAM missile site. Two or three times I saw one moving on the road. It was the most obvious thing in the world, covered with a few trees stuck to it. People standing on it as if they were in a war memorial. They were distinct targets, obviously mobile, and the last place they were going to be housed was in the middle of a village. It was perfectly clear that the bombing wasn't reaching the military targets. It was simply demolishing the towns and villages. So all this touring was redundant. The carefully orchestrated assembling of the bombed villages wasn't necessary to convince us.

In the cities that I saw, there were different degrees of destruction. The areas around Haiphong that were industrial had been evacuated, but the buildings still stood, and they had jagged cracks down the side so you could tell they had been hit. You could see holes in the roof, but they weren't leveled. Ninh Binh was evacuated, too, rather than being leveled. The streets were densely packed. The housing was very close together. You'd see houses that were slightly damaged, and then there'd be a big gaping hole like a tooth had been pulled, where a missile or bomb had hit and there were no houses at all. But Tan Hua was just rubble, what I could see of it.

But when I think of the bombing in North Vietnam I think most of the villages. They seemed very fragile, little clusters of houses next to a canal. It seemed like you could wipe them out so easily, as if a giant foot had come down and ground them away. There would be a big crater where there had been a couple of houses, and you could see pieces of thatched roof in trees. That was something I saw quite often, a big hole and part of the house up in a tree. After a while we could recognize the difference between a rocket and a bomb from the kind of hole it made in the ground. A rocket made a deep, small hole, maybe twelve feet deep but only two or three feet in diameter. The bombs made holes ranging from maybe eight feet in diameter to sixty feet. It was always pointed out that as the craters filled up with water, fish would be put in them. The villagers would catch these huge catfish out of the craters. And a lot of kitchen utensils and other things would immediately be made out of the remains of a plane or the bomb casings. You could see that stuff in the peasants' houses, things that had been hammered out of aluminum or steel.

Before I went to Vietnam, I read the air force manuals that gave the in-house but not classified rationales for different levels of bombing. The definition of a target was anything whose destruction will measurably reduce the enemy's capacity to resist or to prosecute the war. That left anything open. In the case of North Vietnam, applying the definition literally would justify exactly what was being bombed.

If you bomb a capital and the whole place has to evacuate, you put enormous stresses and strains on social and political life. I had done a lot of homework on air force thinking, and I knew a lot about how air strategy was applied to counterinsurgency. There was an idea around that a totalitarian regime couldn't resist the strain of decentralization, and if you forced it to relocate its administrative headquarters and industrial headquarters and all the rest, you could easily make it collapse.

So I wasn't amazed when I got there to see that there was civilian destruction. I could never imagine the detail, but I knew that it was going on. In fact, they didn't really hit major industrial targets until after 1967. Haiphong had been bombed a little bit but not seriously. There were industrial areas right outside Hanoi that were decimated later but were intact when we were there. But they had certainly taken care of the churches and hospitals in the areas we saw. That was bizarre. It was weird and sick in a way, and the only way I could rationalize it from the Americans' point of view was that they thought it would put intolerable burdens on the society. For example, there were three major leprosariums that were bombed very early in the war. They were known to be leprosariums. The French were involved in two of them. Was it a macabre idea that you would try to force the lepers back into society, or force them to relocate in small units? Or did they think the hospitals were disguised military bases? I don't think so, not with the quality of aerial photography.

I also wondered about the churches. Often the church would be the largest building in town, and the town would be rather small compared with the church. Well, the churches would be bombed, and so would the surrounding areas. You couldn't say with certainty that the church was the target. But there were so many of them. In my notes, I must mention twenty or thirty that I saw.

I was surprised by the sophistication of the Vietnamese in the countryside. We would always have some Hanoi dignitaries and interpreters traveling with us, and we would get into a village and meet with the local administrative committee, which would be mostly women because the men weren't there. These committees struck me as an example of socialism in the best sense—that responsibility could be taken up by women, some of them with teeth blackened from chewing betel, whose ancestors traditionally would have had no power. And the way relations were handled was quite delicate. The Hanoi people dealt with the local people with a certain amount of respect and care, and there was not a great deal of foot-shuffling in response. These women would greet the officials, direct the meeting, and give reports on their village, and it was impressive. There was a standard quality to the speeches, but when it got down to questions or interviews with villagers, I had a sense of people who were forced to be conscious of their country's destiny, which was to fight to survive. It sort of en- nobled them and made them practical at the same time. It seemed to me that the organization of the country was too much ingrained in the people to be broken by an air war. Of course we were told all the time that Vietnam was going to win, but that isn't necessarily what you believe. We had all heard the Vietnamese statements of confi- dence. Sometimes they were disturbing because they were so militant and warlike. But being there, I got a different feeling when I heard Pham Van Dong say, "I will go to Saigon. I don't know when, but I will go to Saigon." Other people would say, "We are fighting for justice, and we cannot lose." Not "We will not lose," but "We cannot lose." There was only one way for them to fight the war, and that required enormous mutual support and singleness of purpose, and even more reliance on the party and the government, not less. So I latched on to that side of the reality and talked about it when I came home.

The Vietnamese would often say to me, "We know that the Amer- ican people aren't personally doing this to us. Maybe if you could let them know more about what we're like and how we live, they could have some influence on their government." This would come from peasants. Since I was the only American in the group I was the focus for these comments. I could understand why they were saying it, and yet I felt, "Oh, yeah, there's this great democratic American people back home who are asleep and couldn't care less, and won't care even when the chickens come home to roost." And here were these people who thought they might influence a society like the United States just by telling their stories. But as we traveled, my feeling grew that I was an emissary, and I was supposed to carry back this message and make everything all right. I didn't feel up to it. That made me feel embar- rassed and awkward, because I was presented with case after case of people who had lost their children, their husbands, their uncles, their aunts.

The thing I could never come to terms with was seeing so much physical mutilation. First of all, there were the reports of all the dead. Those are just reports, and those are people you've never seen. Some- times there would be survivors who would make it more real, or their houses, or where their houses used to be. But there would always be three or four people in every village who would be missing arms and legs and have very serious pellet wounds. Then we would visit hospitals and medical stations and we'd see people in really bad shape who were still under treatment. That was scary, especially the live wounds, the burns, the people who had been brought up from the South. We saw a lot of people who had been in North Vietnam for two or three years being treated for napalm and phosphorus, and their skin was still burning and falling off. Those kinds of wounds burn and burn. The tissue isn't reproduced, it's burning in deeper all the time. With the napalm burns you could smell burnt flesh. It was clear that some of those people were not going to survive, because blood poisoning sets in at a certain point. There were two or three people in hospitals who already had a leg amputated to the knee, which was from gangrene, not from having it blown off. All this was presented in such a clinical way. I can see the expression on my face in some of the photos I have, where I'm bent over my notebook, feeling very large and awkward and in the way.

At the end of the trip we met with the NLF people who had been brought up to the North because of severe wounds. These were mostly the napalm and phosphorus wounds, but we also heard stories of torture. It was undoubtedly deliberate on their part that this came at the end. These were stories of a level of barbarity that made the air war seem like something that would just pass, that wasn't so serious. Torture where breasts were cut off, fingers were cut off, horrible knife wounds. I was rereading my notes the other day, and I came across something interesting. Remember, this is after days and days of viewing the damage. It's an interview with a woman, thirty years old, and how she was arrested and tortured. How she was put in a tiny box and the box was beaten and it made her nose bleed from the concussion. She was starved. I'm writing this down very faithfully, "arrested, tortured," and then suddenly I wrote: "*This is a farce. Probably all happened, but it doesn't matter. Bestiality is not a war crime.* Put in night soil tank with old man and young man. . . ." And it goes on. I think the circuits jammed at that point. It isn't that I didn't believe her, but it was overkill, there was too much. What I was hearing about was bestiality. Was I supposed to say, "Oh, my, what a horrible thing, we must turn around and correct these gross war crimes"? It was just a farce. I didn't have any way to package it. I couldn't begin to comprehend the degree of barbarity that was involved in this, much less pass it on to others. Who would want to know? On an honest level, nobody wants to know these things. For a lot of people, it's enough to say, "I don't believe this, it must be a lie," because it's just too grotesque, it stretches your imagination. This was beyond what I ever imagined, and it was as if I couldn't hear any more.

I remember one incident where it all got very close. We were supposed to go visit a medical station that had been decentralized from the main hospital because the hospital had been bombed. We were going to see victims of a bombing that happened three or four days before. We bivouacked in this little camp outside of town in Tan Hua province. The next day, just as we were getting ready to set out, there was an air raid quite close. It turned out the planes had hit the suburb of Tan Hua City we were heading for. There was a lot of huddling and conferring, and they decided to let us go anyway. So we started driving to the spot. The traffic coming down the road got heavier and heavier, so we had to stop and get out of the car and walk. The town was being evacuated. There were hundreds and hundreds of people, carrying their belongings. There were people in litters and a lot of wounded people being carried out on other people's backs. Nobody was explaining anything. I, as usual, was not wearing socks, and when we got to the area the ground was still burning. I got a burn from it that I had for weeks and weeks. It got infected and wouldn't heal. My stigmata [laughs], my war wound.

We went farther on and we started to smell this smell of burning flesh. I've never smelled it since, but it's a smell that's just indescribable. It got very strong. There were a lot of wounded, and it was clear that phosphorus had been dropped as well as high explosive. Not huge bombs—500-pounders. But mostly phosphorus. CBUs had been used as well. Then we got into this village, and it was like a scene out of . . . I don't know. It was dark, and people had little flares. There was very little light, because you never knew when the planes were going to come back. You could see vague outlines of burnt structures. There wasn't much left. We went in one structure and the smell of burnt flesh was overwhelming, just nauseating. It turned out that it had been a butcher shop. I remember thinking, Oh, thank God, and gasping. It was like a crazy relief.

The medical facility had been bombed. We could see the twisted wrought-iron of the hospital, some of the ceramic stuff and a couple of beds. Someone from the local administrative committee had stayed to meet us. This woman made her report, told us about everyone who was supposed to have been there. I didn't get it down because we were just standing around, and it was drizzling, though there were these little fires going everywhere. She gave a quick summary and apologized that we couldn't meet the people we were supposed to see. And then in answer to questions it came out that they had not been able to save everybody there. They were victims of a previous bombing, and they had been brought there for our benefit. This bombing had happened and some of them had been killed. These people had been assembled in this place for us to see, and they had been killed. When I think about it now it makes me nervous—it makes me so nervous I want to laugh.

[She is crying.]

NORM FRUCHTER

He was born in Camden, New Jersey, in 1937. His father was a factory worker and his mother a bookkeeper. "I went to Rutgers and graduated with an English degree and not much sense of what I wanted to do. I got a Fulbright to study in England. It turned out to be incredibly stuffy. But in London there was a magazine called New Left Review *that was just starting. I gravitated toward it not out of a clear political instinct but out of a sense that little magazines were where the real action was. I went to work in London as a teacher, and I worked for this magazine. And I gradually became a socialist, or maybe even quickly became a socialist. This was between 1960 and 1962. Came back to the States in '62, married, and got involved with a magazine called* Studies on the Left. *Then I worked with the SDS community organizing project in Newark from '64 through '66.*

"In 1966 my wife and I went back to England. When the Vietnamese proposed a conference of American antiwar activists and Vietnamese in Czechoslovakia, Tom Hayden got in touch with me and asked if I wanted to go. This was in August of 1967. The conference lasted four or five days, and at the end of it the DRV issued an open invitation to the delegation to send seven people to North Vietnam. The people who wanted to go put themselves forward. There was some kind of shake-down, and seven of us who had asked to go were accepted by the Vietnamese." In 1969 he went again, this time as part of a crew making a documentary for the radical film collective Newsreel.

Now he lives with his wife and children in Brooklyn, in a townhouse they share with another family. He works as a consultant on education and has published two novels. We talk on the back terrace, with his cats jumping on and off our laps.

Besides museums and clinics and hospitals and the University of Hanoi and collective farms, most of the time was taken up with meetings and briefings. In the evenings there were more formal things, banquets and theatrical performances and concerts. We had a meeting and an interview with Pham Van Dong. And we met with representatives of the National Liberation Front.

One thing that struck me was the stress on the long domination of Vietnam by China. A lot of the history in museums was the history of the struggle against the Chinese. The refusal to be subordinate, and particular uprisings against the Chinese that were led by Vietnamese heroes and heroines. The Vietnamese were saying, "You have to understand that for most of our history we never thought about Americans. The Chinese are the colossus that we're worried about."

There was an immense amount of Soviet aid that we saw all the time. We saw missile launchers and cranes and trucks, and we knew that they were Soviet. We saw lots and lots of heavy machinery and equipment of all kinds. We saw East German and Czech and Polish railway engines and cars and hospital equipment. When we went to a factory that had been decentralized, we looked at the milling machines and they were Soviet. A lot of the antiaircraft stuff, especially the missile defenses, was Soviet. A lot of the light antiaircraft stuff and the machine guns and the rifles and the bicycles—an incredible amount of bicycles—were Chinese. So Vietnam was being supplied by both, but we knew there were problems. The Vietnamese would say that there were difficulties with overland transport, and that sometimes there were difficulties with the shipment of matériel from China. What was implied, or at least what we thought was implied, was that there were political problems. The Soviet Union was talked about only in terms of friendship and fraternal support. The Chinese were talked about both in terms of the current phase of support but also this enormous history of domination.

The Vietnamese were compiling evidence for the War Crimes Tribunal. They were meticulous about it. We would be taken to bomb sites in Hanoi and outside, and we'd be met by the local secretary of the tribunal, who would describe the bombing. When it happened, how many planes came over, how many bombs were dropped, the tonnage, how many square meters were destroyed, and then the list of everybody who was killed and wounded. They would read this off. They would read us the list of casualties by name and age. All this material was transmitted to the WCT office in Hanoi and then compiled into dossiers and shipped off to Stockholm. It was numbing for us to go through this. There didn't seem to be any way to say, "I don't want to hear any more of this," because how could you, right? You did what they wanted you to do.

On the second trip we went through all the major cities on the coast, all the way down. The farther south we got, the more destruction there was. These were B-52 raids for the most part. We saw a city called Vinh. It was pretty much destroyed. Then we got farther south to a city called Dong Hoi. Vinh was bigger. Dong Hoi was only about

40,000 or 50,000 people. There was nothing. There was literally nothing. We climbed a hill in the middle of the city, close to what was once the city hall, and everything we could see was wreckage. There was nothing standing but a couple of shells.

And the countryside had really been blasted. The cities were bad enough, but the countryside was literally cratered, especially when you were anywhere near a bridge. You could catalog the near-misses for a half mile. The craters were very deep. Lots of times the bottoms were filled with water, and there'd be all sorts of plants growing at the bottom. Cattle were grazed in the craters. You'd see a file of lean cattle going over this crater and down toward the bottom. It was lunar, absolutely lunar.

The Vietnamese said that they felt our bombing was very accurate— that everything we hit, we meant to hit. We had this photoreconnaissance, and while the photographers might misread particular structures, a lot of them were clearly marked. There was no mistaking churches. The Vietnamese didn't feel it was saturation bombing, Second World War–style. All right, B-52s bomb from high altitudes— and certainly in the southern provinces there was carpet bombing. That's why all the fields were bombed. But in the cities the jets made bombing runs. Even over villages the jets made bombing runs. They'd lock onto their targets with the coordinates that had been given to them. We were taken to hospitals in the middle of Hanoi that had been hit fairly badly. We saw churches that had been destroyed. We saw a hell of a lot of schools and technical colleges that had been destroyed. It's conceivable that the colleges had antiaircraft on the rooves, so maybe the pilots knew what they were and decided it was worth it to get the A-A. I don't know. Certainly some of the schools that had been hit didn't have any A-A. From what I saw, it would be hard to conclude that we hit those buildings accidentally.

I would have liked to believe that our bombing was accidental. But I came away with the notion that at first it was concentrated on knocking out the infrastructure, and then we had discovered that the infrastructure could be constantly replaced. So we went in for another kind of bombing. Now we were trying to intimidate the society to such an extent that we would break their morale, since we couldn't break their infrastructure. The Vietnamese charged that the bombing constituted an attempt at genocide. We repeated that when we got back home. I wasn't convinced of it, so I would simply say the Vietnamese made that charge.

Have you ever seen a cluster bomb? [Shows me a fragment he brought back.] The inside is filled with a soft explosive, and these are the pellets, embedded in the lead. When the explosive blows, this shatters, and the pellets come out at a high velocity and tear up whatever's around. There are about 400 little bombs in the mother bomb. And the only thing it's good for is personnel. It doesn't hurt anything else. We met people in hospitals who had been hit with pellets, and we talked to surgeons who showed us X rays. One surgeon said that the latest bombs were being filled with plastic pellets, because you couldn't trace plastic on the X rays. Once the pellet went in, there would be no way of knowing where it was and no possibility of removing it.

They reminded us all the time about Curtis LeMay's statement about bombing them back to the Stone Age. They used it as part of their propaganda: They turned it around and made the Americans the barbarians for trying to bomb them back into a barbarian state. So for us, it was a battle every day not to disappear into this mess of guilt and hopelessness about how the hell you were going to change that kind of policy. Given the scale of destruction, the antiwar movement looked much more feeble to me than it did back in the States. One of my friends who went later, in '68, described a similar feeling after seeing a bombed village. He was shaking his head and talking to one of the translators about how feeble he thought the movement was compared to the scale of the destruction he had seen. And the interpreter said something like, "Look, don't worry, George Washington didn't depend on the British peace movement to help him win the Revolutionary War."

They wanted us to understand that no matter how heavily the Americans bombed the North, they weren't going to be able to break the DRV. They also said that the war in the South was going against the Americans. This was in 1967. They said the NLF was growing stronger in the countryside and resistance was growing in the cities. They said, "The tide is going against you. We think that means you'll escalate the bombing in the North. Your idea is that the more you hurt the North, the more you force us to wind down the war in the South."

They wanted us to see that was wrong. The North was not going to decrease its support of the South. So what they showed us was the extent of the decentralization they had already achieved. They briefed us all the time on the evacuation of hamlets. How they got the children out and the small factories out. The way the antiaircraft and missile defenses worked. The way they minimized the bombing of the railheads and rail lines.

Secondly, they wanted us to understand that they were going to take an increasing toll of American planes. The more the escalation, the more planes coming over, the more they're going to shoot down. They were improving their antiaircraft defenses and getting more missiles from the Russians. They already had SAM-1s and 2s, and there were rumors that they had SAM-3s, which could hit B-52s.

It did seem that they knew what they were in for. That was the message we brought back. And that was the message they wanted us to bring back. General LeMay talked about bombing them back to the Stone Age—well, Vietnam was barely industrialized. It was a peasant society. For the most part, the Vietnamese had decentralized what industry they had. And they weren't decentralizing Ford Motor Company or United States Steel. The factories were small, anyway, and they were moved to places much harder to hit. You can't really knock out agrarian production when it's not agribusiness, which is feeding huge cities. Most of the production was feeding the local population. It's harder to starve a people that way.

What they did have to do was get matériel south. They did it on a road network that was constantly repaired by local crews in whatever place had been knocked out. Most of the roads were hard-packed dirt—only the main ones were asphalt. To reopen a dirt road that's been blown apart by bombs takes ten, twelve, however many hours, depending on the labor available. Most of the bridges were wooden. Even when the Americans knocked out some of the major structures, what the Vietnamese did was replace them with much smaller trestle bridges, or else with ferries. The ferries were just rafts that were shoved across the river by diesel launches. Very difficult to hit them.

Same thing with rail transport. It ran on single rail lines. When they were hit, the Vietnamese just rebuilt the tracks. We heard the trains running all the time, both in Hanoi and south of Hanoi. So given the level of stuff they were sending, which was never enormous, we thought they could keep the supplies going.

They presented themselves very fiercely as well. They said, "Our history is one of living with constant attacks and domination by foreigners. This is the latest one. We beat back all the rest, and we're going to beat this one. We know that in Western terms it looks silly to even imagine that a country whose GNP is such-and-such, and which has only 3,000 motorcars in the whole country, could withstand the industrial might of the U.S. But we're going to do it." Well, it was impossible not to be impressed by that kind of spirit. And of course, we were looking to be convinced they were going to make it, rather than that our country was going to destroy them.

So we wanted to believe what they were saying, but we also wanted at least to consider the possibility that it was only partially true. We'd sit down among ourselves and say, "Suppose this just isn't true. Suppose, in fact, they're taking an incredible pasting. The bombing is successful, the infrastructure is being destroyed, there's a level of poverty and disease and starvation. They're not going to make it. What would that look like?" Then we tried to figure it out. We were free to walk around Hanoi. We couldn't get out of the city, but in Hanoi we were free to walk wherever we wanted.

So I'm walking around, trying to figure out, Okay, if it's not true, then what am I seeing? What you see is a lot of purposeful activity. Whenever there's an air raid, people do what they're supposed to do. The antiaircraft batteries wheel into position. Nobody is hanging out in the streets looking like if they don't get something to eat that minute. . . . Nobody is stealing from stores. There's not a huge drifting population that's just hanging out. People don't look dissatisfied or underfed. There's rationing, but no petty thievery, because goods are left all over the place. Whenever there's an air raid, everybody piles into a shelter and leaves their bicycles in the street with whatever they have on them, all their shopping, and when they come out again they just pick up their bikes and go on. It didn't look like a society falling apart at the seams.

We knew that we were going back to play some kind of role at home, in a situation where we'd be met with skepticism. We would be talking to people whom we had to convince that the DRV was going to survive. So we thought that the more we could use our own skepticism to try to convince ourselves, the more effective we're going to be.

But the biggest problem was that none of us were prepared for the gap between Eastern and Western culture. None of us had ever traveled to non-Western societies, and we were in a culture that we didn't understand. We didn't know very much about the nature of families or the religions that buttressed them. We also didn't have the language. A few of us had French, but the Vietnamese in the DRV didn't use French even when they spoke it. All the officials we met spoke French, but they would never use it with us.

The best example of the cultural gap was the meetings with the American prisoners of war. I'm still not sure what those meetings were about. I wasn't very happy with them. I didn't see the point. I think it had to do with a Vietnamese notion of what you do with captured prisoners, which is different from ours. They had some notion of rehabilitation—trying to bring these prisoners to a sense of what they actually did, the reality of the two Vietnams and the one Vietnam, the history, the nature of the American intervention, all that stuff.

They said something like, "We have been working with each of these prisoners. But we're not Americans. We don't know the culture. We don't know how to evaluate them. These are your fellow countrymen. You will know much more about them. After you interview each of them, we are interested in your assessment." I thought to myself, of what? Of whether they were coming to see reality? I couldn't quite believe the Vietnamese thought these men would actually come to accept *the reality*—the one our group had come to accept and share with the Vietnamese. We could go back to the counterculture that we lived in. But if one of these guys had actually come to decide that the war was a crime, what would he do?

On my first trip, I think we saw three prisoners, and we wound up taking back two of the three. The meeting took place in no-man's-land. Our government was very keen on locating the POW camps. Because of that, we were blindfolded and driven God knows where in Jeeps. What's more, the place we were taken was not the camp. The Vietnamese said, "We're doing this to protect you as much as anybody else. You can't be put in a position where your government says to you, 'Look, it's a prisoner-of-war camp, you've got to tell us.'"

It was in a compound, with a desk, tea, and cigarettes, which there always were. We got there, and these Americans were brought in one at a time. We had a conversation with them. I found it a hall of mirrors. First of all, there's the problem of who they think we are. We're clearly American, right? But who are we? How can they place us? These guys have gone into the air force fairly young. They know there's some kind of opposition movement, but God knows what they believe it is.

There were some cookies and candy which the prisoners asked permission to eat, and when they got permission, they ate. Then we talked about who they were and how they got captured. We asked one guy where he was flying from, and he said he couldn't say. We asked him what his mission was, and he said he couldn't say. We asked him how many flights he had flown over Vietnam, and he said he couldn't say. We weren't going to push him. I wasn't even sure why we were asking. I didn't want to know. I thought it was a hopeless situation. They weren't going to give anything to us, because there was no way to trust us. If they were thinking anything along the lines of what the Vietnamese hoped they were thinking, they weren't going to reveal it to us anyway, because it could only get them in trouble when they got home. What they all said was, "We just hope the war ends. That's the only way we're going to get back. We're not going back unless the war ends, so what are the chances the war's going to end?" They asked about McCarthy, is the peace movement real, what's going to happen in the '68 election?

Some of them were prepared to say they weren't really sure the war was just—that they hadn't read a lot about it beforehand, that the stuff they'd read about it here was all one-sided, but if this stuff was true they weren't sure we had any right to be there. But mostly they asked a lot of questions about what was going on in the States—baseball, entertainment. They didn't ask questions directly about the war, how we're doing in the South, none of that. That would've been insensitive. And they were very careful.

I think we asked each one about their views of the war. There was a continuum from "I'm just not sure anymore" to "I'm a soldier, this is what my government decided." We also asked them about treatment. Everybody said, "Well, the food is not what we're used to, but we get as much to eat as the guards get. We're hungry sometimes, the diet is pretty thin, but we're reasonably healthy. We get exercise." All of them complained about isolation. They were pretty much kept alone. I think each of them told us that they'd seen only a roommate. They had no sense of how many other prisoners there were. We tried to ask about how much indoctrination there was. It was a delicate question, so we didn't ask it directly, but we tried to get a sense. What we picked up was that they were given a lot of stuff to read, and they were talked to, but that they weren't particularly pressured. They also asked us to take letters to their families, so we did that.

In general, we always assumed the Vietnamese knew what they were doing. This was one of the few times when I found myself thinking that they didn't. Not only did I not want to be there, but I also thought that it didn't make any sense, and it didn't make any sense from their perspective as well. Which was difficult. I mean, it's their war. It's not like I knew how to fight their war. But in this instance I thought, You've got this all wrong somehow.

Then we were told that two prisoners were going to be released to us, and we were going to take them back. If I had had a choice, I would have said, "No thanks, release them some other way." I understood why they were doing it: They were saying that it would help the antiwar movement if we were the vehicle for prisoner releases. They also hoped the prisoners would play a role once they were released. Not only would they say they hadn't been mistreated, but they would say, "We saw the extent of the bombing and destruction," or even, "We don't think the war is good." They had this notion that there's only one reality, and that these guys couldn't keep their own reality after having been exposed to *the reality*.

We wrote a paper in which we tried to counterpose our notions of

POW conduct to theirs. What we said was that the way POWs work in the West, the person's responsibility stops at the point they become a prisoner. You simply hold them. You're not concerned with their consciousness. They are hostages, if you will. The most you do with them is hold them and make clear to the other side that their treatment depends on reciprocal treatment from the other side. We said, Clearly you don't think about it that way. You're concerned with the consciousness of these men. You're concerned with their morality, with their integrity, with their souls. You want them to see the reality of the situation. You want them to see what they've done, and you want them to take responsibility. You even think that would be good for them, as well as for you.

So we put that paper out, but we didn't get a response. They took it, and who knows, maybe it went through channels and changed some policy. We did what we could, but we never saw the results.

12

BRASS

Two army generals, two epochs of the war. Bill De Puy arrived in April 1964, near the end of the advisory period. He was in-country when the first marines waded ashore, and he went on to command the 1st Division for a year. Bill Fulton got there just before De Puy left, when the massive American buildup was hitting its stride. As a colonel, he took a brigade of the 9th Division to Vietnam in early 1967, winning a promotion to brigadier during his tour.

Their different windows on Vietnam help account for what moves them now. De Puy, the counterinsurgency man, the soldier-intellectual, talks mostly about the wrong turns of American strategy. Fulton, commander of the innovative riverine forces as the war reached its boiling point, remembers specific battles and the problems of getting the ARVN to fight.

Both earned their spurs in World War II. Fulton fought again in Korea. They were men of experience. But in Vietnam, they were caught in the coils of a flawed policy. Traditional wisdom in the army cautioned against fighting another war on the mainland of Asia, but De Puy says that in Saigon there was little controversy; the choice was to intervene or watch South Vietnam collapse. "There may have been some astute military men who argued and worried about it, but I wasn't one of them. I really wanted to see whether by bringing in American troops we could turn it around."

Once troops were committed, their commanders found themselves handcuffed in ways that naturally galled professional warriors. In the first place, they couldn't give orders to the Vietnamese; instead, they had to "get cooperation," which could be exasperating. As Fulton spells out, the ARVN had a quicksilver quality—usually timid, occasionally fierce. Corrupt or incompetent officers often were shielded against American protests. And there was the basic strategy, anchored to the principle that Americans were fighting simply to defend South Vietnam. That meant no invasion of the North, not even a threat of one, and no major attacks on the Ho Chi Minh Trail or on NVA bases in Cambodia until late in the war. The commanders, of course, tried to make do with bombing and small-scale raids and "secret wars," such as the one conducted by the CIA in Laos. But generals in the field had to watch, time and time again, as battered enemy units slipped across the border, there to rest and refit and choose their time to attack again.

Most generals now argue that a different strategy could have changed the ending. The favorite retrospective plan is one put forward in General Bruce Palmer's book, *The 25-Year War*: a thrust across Laos that would have cut the Ho Chi Minh Trail. With American divisions blocking their way, the North Vietnamese would have been forced to fight full-scale battles—or extend their supply routes far to the west, no easy task. Bill De Puy reports that such a plan was proposed by Westmoreland and the Joint Chiefs in 1965 but was rejected in Washington. Westmoreland, in fact, kept pushing the idea until he left Vietnam in 1968.

By and large, the military blames Robert McNamara and his academics for the fatal strategy. But the top brass were not simply victims; they were also cheerleaders. Their optimistic pronouncements, so often contradicted by events, helped make the American public sour and mistrustful. If the generals' handcuffs were so painful, why was there not more protest? One answer is that soldiers are trained to follow orders. Another is that officers in line for promotion, no matter how unhappy with the rules of engagement, are leery of making a fuss. Often, too, their immediate tasks are consuming, leaving little time or inclination for cool-headed estimates of long-term prospects.

Most important, commanders in Vietnam were prone to the American afflictions underlying the whole war: hubris and ignorance of the enemy. Even given the North Vietnamese tactical advantages—the porous border, the inviolate bases, our pledge not to invade the North—the brass thought we would win anyway. Technology and sheer superiority would allow us to kill so many of them that they would give up. We did kill astonishing numbers. Then we gave up.

Bill De Puy concludes: "I don't think Americans can be expected to support a long, inconclusive war." He argues that GIs are ill-suited for counterinsurgency in far-off countries. Bill Fulton still believes that "unity of command"—that is, Americans commanding the Vietnamese—might have saved the situation. But the lessons learned give only small consolation. These two men and their generation fought the good fight against Hitler and battled to a tough stalemate in Korea. An agonizing loss was not the note on which they expected their careers to end.

GENERAL WILLIAM E. DE PUY

We meet at his pied-à-terre in Oldtown, Alexandria, a few blocks from the Potomac. The small brick building dates from Revolutionary War days; he is proud of this heritage, and of the flower garden he is tending when I arrive.

He is a small man with piercing eyes, dressed in a tweed jacket and tie. At first his manner is serious, businesslike, but as he warms to the subject a droll smile appears now and again. He was born in 1919 in North Dakota and entered the army as an ROTC graduate in 1941. He spent World War II with the 90th Division, landing in Normandy as a captain and ending the war as a lieutenant colonel. He then learned Russian, served as a military attaché in Hungary, worked in the Pentagon and the CIA, commanded troops in Germany, and became a counterinsurgency enthusiast. "In 1961 I took over the Special Warfare Directorate in the Department of the Army, which had to do with Special Forces and counterinsurgency. I was one of the guys on the counterinsurgency ground floor. I'm not necessarily the best at it, but there are few people who know more about counterinsurgency—both pro and con—than I do."

In 1963 he was promoted to brigadier general, and the following year he was sent to Saigon as the chief of operations for MACV. "When I arrived, Paul Harkins was still there, but Westmoreland had arrived as his deputy, and he took over during the summer of 1964. I worked for him for two years, and then in March of 1966 I took command of the 1st Division for a year. All in all, I was there almost three years."

When I first arrived it wasn't so grim, or if it was I didn't know it. In April of 1964, Vietnam seemed peaceful. On the surface, very little was going on. The country and the U.S. program were trying to recover from the coup against Diem. The government was a shambles, a comic-opera kind of government, with coup after coup. I traveled all over the country. In that kind of a war, most of the time nothing is happening. It's just like today—the sun is shining, the birds are singing, the flowers are in bloom. There were some intelligence reports that things were beginning to stir, but the countryside was quiet. No North Vietnamese units had yet gone into combat. We weren't even sure there were any in the South. It was a small war, a guerrilla war with an occasional strike.

But all that changed in December of 1964, when the North Vietnamese, as we now know, ordered an offensive. It was launched by an attack against the Catholic strategic hamlet of Binh Gia in Phuoc Tuy province, just east of Saigon. The town was attacked by the 9th VC Division. That was a milestone, because the 9th was the first division to be formed by the other side in South Vietnam. It was formed first from two regiments that had been around for quite a while, the 272nd and the 273rd. A general was appointed, and he took them down from War Zone C to the coast. In Phuoc Tuy province they rendezvoused with a trawler from North Vietnam and got AK-47s, 80mm mortars, RPG-2s, radios, and so on. The third regiment in the division was then forming near Song Be.

One of the two regiments attacked Binh Gia, and the other ambushed all the likely landing zones around there. It was a classic. There were no ARVN troops at Binh Gia. None. There were Catholic popular forces, the village militia. They were no match for a regular VC regiment, so the first part was easy. Then the VC held the town for a while, just to show they could do it. When the ARVN started sending in reinforcements, they were ambushed. In the course of the battle the VC destroyed a marine battalion, beat up an airborne battalion very badly, and knocked off a couple of battalions from the regiment up at Xuan Loc.

Well, this terrified the Vietnamese government, and shocked MACV. We were shocked to find there was a division, which we learned from interrogating prisoners. And we were shocked that they had switched from hit-and-run to what we saw as a more serious effort to take a place, hold it, and then destroy the ARVN forces. We saw that as the beginning of a new, higher level of war.

The same VC division then picked up its third regiment. In June of '65 they attacked the Special Forces camp at Dong Xouai. There again, although they didn't hold the camp, they destroyed it. They ambushed all around it and practically destroyed the 7th Regiment of the 5th ARVN Division. Two of its battalions were pretty much knocked out, plus an airborne battalion.

In between those two, there was another battle in Quang Ngai province, which was fought by the 1st and 2nd Viet Cong regiments. After taking the district town of Binh Ba, the two regiments ambushed all the routes that converged on it. They destroyed the 38th Ranger Battalion to the man and beat up a marine battalion badly, along with a couple of battalions from a regiment of the 2nd Division.

My job in those days was to allocate U.S. helicopters so the ARVN could use them for reinforcement. I went to the battles as a representative of General Westmoreland, so I know a lot about them. Matter of fact, the J-3 of the Vietnamese joint general staff and I found the 38th Ranger Battalion at Binh Ba. It went out of communication and nobody knew where it was. The VC had destroyed it and killed all the prisoners. There was a little circular mountain, a conical hill, that was terraced for rice paddies. As we flew over we looked down. They had arrayed all the bodies. They put the battalion commander and the American adviser at the very top, and laid the rest of the bodies out on each terrace all the way around like the spokes of a wheel. It was a vicious kind of thing.

I was in Vietnam during the whole controversy over whether to put in American troops. Out there it wasn't a controversy, because the Viet Cong were destroying ARVN battalions so fast. When I say destroyed, they weren't obliterated to the last man, but put out of action. They had to be rebuilt from the ground up. The VC got about four at Binh Gia. About four at Binh Ba in Quang Ngai. And three or four at Dong Xouai. Then there was Song Be, where they got about two, and Dau Tieng, the Michelin plantation, where they got two or three more. So the ARVN lost, let's say, fifteen or sixteen battalions in six months. That's big business.

In the spring, Westmoreland sent a message to Washington that said over the last few months we'd been losing almost a battalion a week, and a district town every month. He gave the government six months to live unless something was done. It was that opinion, and that sense of alarm, that underlay the deployment of U.S. combat troops.

From then on, there was escalation on both sides. The North Vietnamese Army was on the way south before we put the marines in, but we didn't really know that. Both sides were pursuing their own program. The North Vietnamese were going to send their armies south. It didn't make any difference whether we deployed or not—they were coming south. In Karnow's book there's a story about a North Vietnamese colonel who was sent south in 1964 to make a survey and see how the war was going. He reported back that they would never win the war in the South if they relied entirely on the Viet Cong. So they decided to send their troops south. And we were worried that South Vietnam would lose the war without us, so we sent in our troops.

Both sides were worried about "their" South Vietnamese. Both sides thought they might lose. So we both went in.

There was very little dissent within MACV over bringing in the troops. I would say General Maxwell Taylor, the ambassador, was the only leading figure who was reluctant. But he eventually agreed we had to come in. He was faced with a horrible dilemma in the early part of '65. He didn't want to fight a land war in Asia. But he was also the godfather of counterinsurgency. I'm just guessing, but I always felt he couldn't bear the thought that the whole counterinsurgency effort was going to be a failure in Vietnam without our doing everything we could to salvage it. I don't remember any discussions within MACV about the disadvantages of bringing in a Western army. It's an admission against interest, but I think we were affected by already having advisers in every unit and in every province. In other words, there were a lot of Americans already over there. It's sort of like being a little bit pregnant. There may have been some astute military men who argued and worried about it, but I wasn't one of them. I really wanted to see whether by bringing in American troops we could turn it around. We were totally preoccupied with the growing VC forces. From then on, pacification was secondary.

It seemed to me that we needed to get American forces in there and unshackle them so they could go to work against those VC main forces. That's an important point. In 1964, we had a project to strengthen the pacification effort in the city of Saigon and its immediate surrounds. It was called Hop Tac, which I think means "cooperation." I was involved in the planning. If you visualize a target with three rings, the center was downtown Saigon. That's the area where the Vietnamese police were supposed to be predominant. It was supposed to be mostly secure, with the police fighting problems of subversion and intelligence but not military actions. We called that process "securing." The next ring went to the fringes of Gia Dinh province and Long An province and so on. The idea was to use RF/PF and ARVN troops to get rid of Viet Cong district companies and village platoons. We called that "clearing." Then outside that, going as far as you want to go, was the area for search and destroy. I coined that term. It turned out to be infelicitous, because later when some marine was televised setting the roof of a native house on fire with his cigarette lighter, the commentator said, "Here's a marine company on search and destroy," and from then on a burning house was the "destroy" part of it.

But that had nothing to do with search and destroy. The idea at first was to take the better ARVN troops, like the airborne and the marines and the better battalions of the regular infantry, to search for and destroy the VC main forces. The VC would come in and try to take over a district town, kill all the local forces, and terrify everybody. They only had to do that once or twice a year, and it defeated any pacification effort. It convinced people that the government couldn't protect them and the VC were stronger. So this outer ring of Hop Tac was to be patrolled by the stronger ARVN units, to keep the VC troops out of the areas being cleared and secured.

When General Westmoreland asked for American troops, he intended for them to be involved in search and destroy. They would go after the VC main forces. In my area, when I commanded the 1st Division, it was the 9th Division, which operated in an arc north of Saigon. We were one-on-one with the 9th Division, so I got to know them quite well. My job was to keep them on the ropes and out of the populated areas. And we succeeded, by the way.

I have no apologies for that concept. It was right then, and it's right even in retrospect. Only the Vietnamese can handle the counterinsurgency job, and the American troops should defeat the main forces— keep them deep in the jungle so that pacification could proceed. The problem was that we didn't stick to fighting the enemy's main force.

We had some big victories over the main forces. That's what we did best, and what was needed most. As for having any luck against the guerrillas in my rear area, we weren't much better than anybody else, which was very poor indeed. I think the Phoenix program and the RF/PFs did a damn good job later, in the '70s. The problem was that it came too late. We were ready to pull out. And the North Vietnamese just kept coming.

It seems to me there were two driving circumstances in the war. The first was that the minute you bring in American troops, you concede to the other side a tremendous political advantage. And the Communists exploited that to the hilt. They were very clever at it. Along with that, we were slow in realizing that the North Vietnamese simply intended to win that war no matter what it cost. They'd send their whole army down if it was necessary, and as a matter of fact that's what they finally did. They sent seventeen divisions against Saigon in 1975. Whereas we went through a self-inflicted period of confusion, starting with counterinsurgency. We convinced ourselves that if we did that right, the war wouldn't get any bigger. Well, it did get bigger. We didn't know how to do counterinsurgency very well, and we had white faces. Plus the North Vietnamese looked at Indochina as a whole. They didn't hesitate to use Laos and Cambodia. They looked at the whole mountain chain and the Ho Chi Minh Trail and the Mekong River as a single theater of war. We tried to keep Laos as a separate problem, Cambodia as another separate problem—South Vietnam as one theater and North Vietnam as another. Disastrous.

When the 1st Cavalry Division was deployed to South Vietnam, General Westmoreland and General Stilwell proposed that we ought to block the Ho Chi Minh Trail as an extension of the DMZ along Route 9, which goes from Dong Ha on the China Sea to Savannakhet in Laos. The Joint Chiefs of Staff recommended it, too. One of the plans was to put the 1st Cav on the Bolovens Plateau in southern Laos. It would operate against the Ho Chi Minh Trail from the west, and the 3rd Marine Division would operate from the east. It would have been a big fight, no question about that. The North Vietnamese might have thrown in their entire army eventually, and we would have needed more divisions. But at least it would have been a clearly defined major confrontation. They would have had to fight.

That was rejected—first of all because the ambassador in Laos said it was not warranted, and an intrusion into Laos was a violation of the Geneva Accords. The people in the State Department in Washington didn't think the situation warranted it. The CIA people who were doing pacification didn't think it was that kind of war; they thought it was an insurgency. We in the military didn't have good evidence of an invasion from the North. Maybe a regiment was coming down, but not the whole NVA. McNamara had a study made by systems analysis, and I think it showed that the VC consumption of war matériel in the South was fifteen tons a day in 1965. Fifteen tons is so little that there's no way you're going to stop it. You might stop 15,000 tons a day, but not fifteen. So blocking the trail, which meant escalating the war, to stop fifteen tons a day just didn't make sense. Well, the real figure wasn't fifteen tons a day, it was a lot more than that. But for all those reasons, the decision was made not to cut the trail.

There was also considerable discussion of invading the North Vietnamese panhandle, from Vinh south. I don't remember any serious talk of going to Hanoi with ground forces. The reason people wanted to go up to Vinh was they wanted to take the entrance to the Mughia Pass. All the supplies that came from North Vietnam and went over into Laos and down the trail moved through that pass. People wanted to go up there and shut off the flow. But that would have meant invading North Vietnam, which might have brought in the Chinese. After Korea, Washington was nervous about that.

When you operate on the borders of the Soviet Union or China, you ought to expect to get the same treatment from them that we would probably give if we had Chinese or Russians in Mexico. We don't like to think the world is like that, but it is. That means anytime you're close to one of the Communist giants, there are a lot of constraints. If you do enough to win the war against North Vietnam, you're apt to bring in one of the superpowers. They don't want an American victory on their doorstep, just like we don't want a Communist one in Mexico. We don't even want one in Nicaragua. But if you scale back below the level of provocation that would bring in the Chinese, you have a hell of a time ending the war.

Why didn't we object at the time? We were good soldier Schweiks. In a military organization, you have two personalities. One is your own opinion as to what's best. The other is the team player, doing what you're told. That's a precondition to playing the game. We should have fought a lot harder for cutting the Ho Chi Minh Trail. We should have seen more clearly that a North Vietnam undefeated and a trail uncut would make it impossible to end the war. We should have been utterly frank about that.

However, we continued to hope that we could inflict such losses on the VC or the NVA that it would be more than they would be able to take. That's the alternative to cutting the trail. That's an attrition war. It's a dirty word now in military circles. I think the concept of attrition was an outgrowth of counterinsurgency—which, after all, is a form of attrition. So we fell into that trap. We thought, and I guess Mr. McNamara thought, and Mr. Rostow thought, and probably the President thought, and the JCS thought we were beating the hell out of 'em, and they couldn't take it forever. It turned out they controlled the tempo of the war better than we would admit. We beat the devil out of 'em time after time, and they just pulled off and waited and regained their strength until they could afford some more losses. Then they came back again. They took terrible losses at Tet, and even worse losses in the Easter offensive of 1972. It took them two years after that to gather together the forces they used at the end. But they controlled their own losses by the simple device of either fighting or not fighting. So we ended up with no operational plan that had the slightest chance of ending the war favorably.

We also didn't know about the redoubtable nature of the North Vietnamese regime. We didn't know what steadfast, stubborn, dedicated people they were. Their willingness to absorb losses compared with ours wasn't even in the same ball park. Way back at the beginning, when they attacked the destroyers in the Tonkin Gulf, we were doing what I call carefully controlled retaliation. Everybody thought, Oh, boy, we're sending American airplanes up and they'll bomb a couple of targets and the other side will be terrified. It was the notion of gradualism and retaliation, one more turn of the screw. I personally thought it would be a token of U.S. resolve, and a sample of what we could do. I really thought it would impress them. I now think it just infuriated them. And we just kept doing it. We did more and more and more and more, up until the Cambodia invasion and the mining of the harbors and the B-52s over Hanoi, and it was never enough. We never quite grasped the fact that the North Vietnamese intended to win. Regardless.

I figured out recently that if the North Vietnamese put up a memorial like the one we have on the Mall, and it was adjusted for the relative populations of our country and theirs, the one in Hanoi would have 7 million names on it. Just soldiers. Interesting, isn't it? The North Vietnamese lost about 500,000 dead, and the VC 300,000. That's 800,000. And we lost 58,000. Of course, the ARVN lost a lot, too. But the North Vietnamese main forces lost up to 40 percent of their troops every year. That's enormous. It's unbelievable. I didn't think they'd be able to keep their soldiers fighting, given the casualties we were inflicting. I should have known better. In World War II I fought in a unit with casualties like that. The 90th Division had 25,000 casualties in just eleven months, so I should have known.

When you're doing anything you think is important, there's a very high emotional content. It inhibits clear thinking—at least with me. When I was commanding the 1st Division, I was totally preoccupied with trying to find the 9th VC Division and the other main-force elements in my area. I was concerned about doing it better—more engagements, with more success and fewer casualties. It was a full-time job, learning how to do that. And you're very defensive. You only see the things you've been doing well, not the big mistakes you've made. We were all emotionally involved that way. We weren't as cool and detached as we should have been, and as we can be now. It's easy to be smart in retrospect. It's difficult to do it in the heat of the battle. I didn't do it too well. But I think I had a lot of company.

When you step back—and I didn't have these thoughts while I was there—you see the difference between a country that's fighting on its own terrain for its survival, and a country that's sending its forces halfway around the world to "contain" Communism. We asked a lot of sophistication from our public and our troops—maybe more than the country was able to give. I don't think Americans can be expected to support a long, inconclusive war.

The reason I think about these things is that I wonder what would happen if we went to war in Iran. There are a lot of parallels to Vietnam. It's a long way away. There's no threat to our homeland. In an expanded war, we'd have to go to the draft immediately. That would bring out all the opposition, bring the children into the streets again, polarize the Congress. No doubt about it, all those things would happen. That's a sobering set of consequences. And if it's close to the Soviet or Chinese border, it would probably be long and inconclusive.

Or take El Salvador. I think we have been pretty smart there. I'm impressed by the fact that we keep only fifty advisers in the country. I don't think there's anything wrong with giving them support with money and training and communications and intelligence and engineering and all that, as long as we don't Americanize the war. As long as we stay below that magic threshold. Nobody knows exactly where it is. The point is that it's very low. And it's easy to step over it in the eyes of the natives. If they look around and see Americans everywhere, it's an American war. If you have GIs going into villages or barrios and trying to sort out friend from foe, that's a disaster. It gives the other side a precious asset—call it patriotism, xenophobia, or nationalism. And once that happens, God help you.

LIEUTENANT GENERAL WILLIAM FULTON

In 1966 he trained one of the three brigades of the newly created 9th Infantry Division. The brigade had an unusual mission: It was to fight from navy boats patrolling the rivers and canals of the Mekong delta. Its formal name was a classic army acronym—MEDMAF, or the Mekong Delta Mobile Afloat Force. But it was known simply as the Mobile Riverine Force.

"Nobody in the U.S. had fought on rivers since Commodore Foote and General Ulysses S. Grant went down the Mississippi in 1862. That's the last time the U.S. Army and Navy teamed up in a riverine environment. But General Westmoreland wanted to get into the delta. Two-thirds of the people of South Vietnam live there. They produce 60 percent to 70 percent of the food. And it was felt, although never stated, that there was a kind of accommodation down there. The ARVN forces were not defeated, nor were they victorious. They never really tangled with the VC. It was a Mexican standoff."

Today he is retired after thirty-five years in the army, living in a big house in a pristine neighborhood of Arlington, Virginia. He is a tall, solidly built man, bald, with a gray mustache and a hearty, easygoing manner. During our talk, he takes down his book, Riverine Operations in Vietnam, *and guides me through the battles on the maps.*

Nobody in U.S. uniform ever really criticized the Vietnamese, but that was a bit of intellectual dishonesty, as far as I'm concerned. It was always: "Oh, well, they've been fighting for twenty-five years. They're tired. They don't fight on Saturdays and Sundays." Well, they really didn't fight until they were damn near forced to. I operated in the tactical areas of the ARVN 7th, 9th, and 25th divisions. They had regimental headquarters located within an hour or two's march of the VC main base areas. All you had to do was cross a few damn canals or maybe go over a river, and you'd find an enemy battalion. Those areas hadn't been broached for three or four or five years, and when the ARVN did go in, they got whipped and never went back again.

I was just a colonel, so I never really pushed the issue. I couldn't directly say, "These sons of bitches won't fight." But you couldn't help raising your eyebrows. The ARVN would just sit in their casernes. They went out on operations maybe once a week. They had lots of people in uniform, but they weren't out in the bush. When they did go, the way they fought was to come in on three sides and leave the fourth side open so the enemy had an escape route. They never cornered the rat. Whereas I was just beating my brains out seven days a week, trying to find the enemy. And the American commanders were not willing to acknowledge that the ARVN weren't holding up their part of the bargain.

When I first went into the delta, the American who had commanded the base at Dong Tam had just been relieved. He had gone there and announced to the ARVN, "Okay, you guys can sit back, because we're here now. We'll take over and run the war." Well, you couldn't do that either, because the Vietnamese were xenophobic as hell. They're very proud little guys. As a matter of fact, I don't think they were ever too happy about our being there. You had that feeling. There was great mistrust. They weren't very open, and sometimes there was an accommodation with the local Viet Cong. They didn't seem to want you to go in and kick the shit out of them. They figured, Live and let live, and we'll each have our honey. The ARVN held the district towns and provincial capitals, but you couldn't travel on the roads at night. The VC exercised full sway. They had their tax collectors, and they took their tribute on the rivers and the roads. They had their base areas. The ARVN could have gone in there every day of the week and fought, but they didn't. They didn't want to take the casualties.

I got in-country in January of 1967, and we didn't go afloat until the first of June. So for six months we operated out of Dong Tam. It was a base dredged out of the river. It required a battalion in itself just to set up the perimeter. At night the place could be overrun. My intelligence indicated that they could bring in five battalions against me. They could come overland and come across the river, and I would have been very hard-pressed to defend that ninety acres with about 3,000 troops on it—plus about 1,000 tons of ammunition, which fortunately they never hit. If they had dropped a mortar round on that ammo dump, we'd still be coming down.

So at first I had to defend Dong Tam and brush the enemy back. I had the division's ground surveillance radar, which picked up ground movement. It was on a tower about 200 feet high. I got down there, and the province chief—who I think was really a VC—refused to let me fire any artillery at targets picked up by radar, because we might hit the villagers. The U.S. colonel who had been on the base before me had accepted this. And that base had been attacked repeatedly with mortars and recoilless-rifle fire. The day before I took it over, we'd had something like fifteen killed and twenty-seven wounded from mortar attacks. Well, the good Lord helps those who help themselves. I had a friend who was the ARVN adviser. I told him, "Nobody can deny me the right to fire to protect my base. You tell the ARVN commander that I will not accept the denial to fire in defense of this base." Now, the first night I was in command I had over 675 radar sightings, and I shot artillery at every one of them. Whether it was a water buffalo or a farmer out there clinking around in the bush, I leveled it. After that I never had another mortar round land in Dong Tam as long as I was in command.

If you went airborne in the Mekong delta, you could immediately see what the political objectives of the Viet Cong were. They'd stake out an area. If there was a road that gave the ARVN access, the bridge would be blown. Sometimes they'd chase some of the people out. Then they'd let the vegetation get overgrown, and that became a base area. You could pick it out from a helicopter. The idea was, if they could get an area they controlled, or at least where they could base their main-force units, those units could circulate through an entire province. They did it almost on a scheduled basis. That way they could back up the local forces. Each Viet Cong district was a political entity that embraced certain villages and their hamlets. Each of those hamlets and villages had guerrilla squads. So what you had was an echelon. The village guerrilla squad, reinforced by the district company, reinforced by the local-force battalion, and on top were your main-force battalions that were components of a regiment.

Now, the Mekong delta is very much affected by tidal action. It's inundated for about four months of the rainy season. When the tide comes in, it backs the floodwaters of the Mekong up, and they just spread out over the countryside. So there's rice paddies and lots of streamlines and canals, and also lines of nipa palms and lots of coconut groves and some fruit cultivation—bananas, pineapples, and orchards. The first problem you had was to find the enemy, and you wanted to do it as early in the day as possible. If you had good intelligence, you could jump him and have him most of the day. But it was very hard to contain him. He didn't want to fight. The minute you had contact, you had to stake his lines of egress. That would usually be the streamlines, the water network. He'd want to avoid the rice paddies where he could be spotted from the air. I always kept a reserve force that could be airlifted. If I got contact, I would fly squads or platoons out to streamlines radiating from the point of contact. They'd get into defensive positions, and within thirty minutes you'd kill three or four scouts, who were looking to see if the routes were clear. If you could bump into those guys and shut them down, that little VC commander had to stay hunkered up, because he didn't know which way to get out.

I think the U.S. made one basic mistake, and that was our failure to fully integrate our operations with the Vietnamese. I'm told that at one point there was study given to having a combined command. I think it was rejected in Washington, but I've never been too sure. As a consequence—I mean, the ARVN sat back and watched us fight. As professionals, as American military men, we should have insisted that they conform to our battle plans. We were forbidden to do that. The only thing we had was "cooperation." [Laughs.] If the U.S., ARVN, and other free-world forces had been put under one command, the way we did it in Korea, the whole thing might have turned out differently. One of the principles of war is unity of command. In Vietnam it was violated, pure and simple.

For example, the first action I ever had was going into Nan Trach, the Rung Sat Special Zone south of Saigon. I went to the Bien Hoa province adviser, an American lieutenant colonel, and said, "I'm from the 9th Division. We're going into this area, and I'd like to get the ARVN to join us." This guy was just amazed. He said, "You want to go with the ARVN?" Well, I got two ARVN infantry battalions, two province boat companies, and a whole gaggle of RF/PF only too glad to go in once they knew we were going. It was the first time anybody had offered to take them in there. But when the U.S. commander of II Field Force came down, I said, "I have some Vietnamese units under my operational control." He proceeded to take me to task. "You . . . have . . . NO . . . authority to exercise operational control. General Westmoreland would be terribly upset if he heard you even intimate that you had them under your operational control." I was chastised. Cooperation, yes, but not operational control.

I had a very fine guy who was my counterpart in the delta, Brigadier General Tanh, who commanded the 7th Division. Now, he seemed to know where the enemy was every day of the week. He had his own intelligence network. The way it worked was that the little boy tending the water buffalo knew the VC were in Area A. He would pass that to the guy coming along the stream in the sampan, who would take it down to the bridge and give it to a guy on a Lambretta, and by nine or ten o'clock General Tanh or his G-2 would know. Maybe my troops would be close to Area A or A-1. I'd get a call at ten-thirty or eleven, and Tanh's U.S. adviser would give me an eight-digit map coordinate where the enemy was. Well, Jesus, I'd converge on it, and sure enough, I'd have a hell of a fight. But Tanh himself would avoid that enemy unit until I jumped on him. If I smashed him real well, Tanh generally knew where they'd leak out the next day, because they only had certain base areas they could go to. Then he'd pounce on 'em. It was sort of like a jackal attacking a wounded beast. He never would engage the enemy head-on if he could avoid it.

Tanh was a mandarin Vietnamese—a splendid-looking man, about six foot two and a half, rather a handsome guy. One time when we were airborne, he pointed out where he had been raised. His family had a large tract of land, a big farmhouse with a terra cotta roof. He was an aristocrat, educated. I was told that, before I got in-country, he had been a major and the province chief of Go Cong. The VC tried to eliminate him time and time again. They would attack his compound with his family in there, and he'd come charging out and fight 'em. Well, he became suspect because of this. The police actually arrested him, took him to Saigon, and put him in a hole for three weeks. They felt that because he hadn't been killed, and he'd fought the VC the way he had, that he was probably a VC. They suspected it was all a subterfuge. But he was fearless. Then he became a brigadier general and they gave him the division. He was one of the better commanders. But he still had to worry about excessive casualties, and he had to worry about politics. The 7th Division was the closest one to Saigon in the South, and it was the division that had moved against Diem. So Thieu's men used to keep watch on Route 4 to make sure Tanh's troops didn't cross that Ben Luc bridge going north. It seemed like those little guys were watching their flanks and their rears and playing all kinds of ball games that we never even knew about.

One time we were running an operation out west of Cai Lai and north of Cai Be. Tanh had a headquarters in Cai Be, and he had a number of battalions getting ready to go out the next day. I knew I had an enemy battalion spotted. All the earmarks: The friendlies had fled out of the area, the sampans were all clustered around the RF/PF forts. We knew the VC base areas. I flew over and saw banana fronds cut down—I suspected to cover their foxholes. I went to see Tanh and said, "General, I know where the enemy is. You've got units four or five klicks away. You've got airlift. I'd like you to give us a hand, come in and put in a blocking position." He wouldn't hear of it—but he would give me three airlift companies. He knew the enemy was there. He probably had reports a lot earlier than I did. But he wouldn't commit his forces. He didn't want to crunch with 'em. And you couldn't be too frank, because you'd insult him. So you danced around it. "General Tanh, we've got the enemy here." He'd give a blank look. No, he couldn't help today. He had a big plan tomorrow to go grab a cache of weapons or food. Or he'd just say no. And you had no recourse. I did get three lift companies from him, and we had a hell of a fight. But he wouldn't go. It was very disheartening.

In early May my brigade fought the 514th at a place called Ap Bac, where the VC beat the 7th ARVN in a famous battle in '63. I had three airlift companies all set to go. I had moved a battalion of 105s in the middle of the night. I had a mechanized company that I moved about 0100 hours. They were going real deep. I was going to put in one battalion high and another battalion low and move them toward each other, so that anything that leaked on me east or west could have been picked up by gunships. Beautiful plan.

We were all set to launch. I had moved my artillery out and put one battalion on the road when I got word from 9th Division headquarters that one of the airlift companies had been taken from me. Well, there goes your plan. We couldn't go deep without helicopters. So I told the S-3, "Well, tell the mech unit to go as far as they can into the Plain of Reeds." About ten minutes later the S-3 came back and said, "Division took another one of our lift companies." So I'm down to one. What can you do? Then they canceled the third one. Apparently they had some emergency someplace, so they just peeled 'em away from me. I told my S-3, "Call division and tell 'em they can just shove it. I'm not going to go fight today if they're going to play it that way." He said, "Jeez, Colonel, I have a feeling we're going to get something today. Why don't we just mount up and go out there by truck?"

Well, we did. I scrounged every truck I had on the base and we went out Route 4, up through My Tho and back west toward Cao Lai. We dismounted about ten-thirty and we started to get long-range sniper fire. As we moved along, we began to find tremendous caches of rice and weapons.

By this time I had the mech company pretty far north, and Lieutenant Colonel Skip Chamberlain was setting up his battalion in a firebase along Route 4 where he could put his mortars. Suddenly we got good contact. I had about five kids just chopped down right by a canal, and we knew that we'd run into a sizable enemy force. Well, we had the enemy's southern flank at that point. I told the mech company to move in and cut off the escape route to the north, which they did. The VC couldn't move east, where there was lots of water and rice, because they would have been exposed. There was one canal, but I happened to have a company right on that. I got Skip to move another company to the west. So we've got three companies on one flank, a battalion moving in, and here are the VC in an L-shaped position.

We took another company and put it across where the mech company was in the north. I moved the mech back down so I could assault from the west. Which we did, late in the afternoon. One thing with the VC—they fought like tigers, but when you closed with 'em and got close enough, they panicked. They'd stay in their holes and take everything that you could throw at 'em, but when you got ready to assault, they lost their cool. It's like a rabbit: He'll stay motionless and undetected, but when you get close enough he panics and takes off.

I don't know how many we killed, somewhere around 250. But the enemy responded. I had Skip Chamberlain on this firebase all alone down Route 4. He said he was being surrounded and probed. It was a technique the VC had. When they were in deep trouble, they would cause a diversion by trying to attack or feint at another point.

At that point I was at a regimental ARVN headquarters. The ARVN colonel had a cav troop right there. They could have gone down the road to reinforce Skip and help me out. All of a sudden, the colonel no speaka the English, and I had to go get clearance from the division. I called the U.S. liaison officer, but General Tanh was in Taiwan on leave. The assistant division commander wouldn't make a decision like that. Now, in this kind of situation we would have gone to the ARVN's rescue in a moment.

The U.S. forces had what they called TAC-Es, tactical emergencies. This is when you're in deep trouble. Only a general could declare one, but I didn't know that. So I declared one. I got a battalion from the 199th Brigade flown in to bail out Skip. But why didn't ARVN come to the rescue? All I was asking for was a cav troop, ten or twelve armored personnel carriers with machine guns and troops. Instead, I had an American battalion airlifted in from Nha Be, which is fifty or sixty kilometers away. The next day, Major General G. G. O'Connor, my immediate superior, showed up with the II Field Force commander. We'd had a hell of a kill, and they were sort of clapping their hands. But G. G. called me aside and said, "Bill, I want you to know that as a colonel you're not authorized to call a TAC-E." I said, "Well, I'm very sorry, but it was necessary and it worked." He said, "Granted."

Then there were the intelligence leaks. After I had been in the delta with the Mobile Riverine Force, I got promoted to brigadier general and I went up to the division headquarters to be the assistant division commander. I used to see the signal intelligence, all the radio intercepts. The VC would give instructions to their units and we would intercept the messages. They would give more or less the whole plan of the next day's operations for the RFs and PFs, and sometimes even for the ARVN division.

I had gotten to know Tanh quite well. I told him there was a leak. He said, "I know that. I have to wait as late as I can to issue orders, because I have enemy in my headquarters. If I issue an order at noon, the enemy will know it by seven or eight o'clock that night. But I can't wait much past five or six o'clock." So he would issue his orders to the regiments. All the spies had to do was go to the marketplace and pass the word along. By two or three in the morning, his plans would be coming back to us by signal intelligence. Tanh said, "I have many VC in my camp. I can only speak to my G-2 and my G-3." It seemed he didn't even trust his chief of staff.

One time while I was assistant division commander and Colonel Bert David was running the MRF, he was given a Vietnamese marine SEAL force of about thirty men under the supervision of the U.S. Marines. Down on the river toward Sa Dec there's a whole series of large islands. Bert decided he'd put the SEALs in there and give them a trial operation at night. They landed on an island, and as they were approaching a native hootch they saw a very bright light. The Vietnamese down in the delta use carbide lamps, little flickering things. This was a Coleman lantern, and it looked like a beacon. The SEALs spread out. Down the trail with a flashlight comes a guy carrying an AK-47. They scarfed him up and closed in on the hootch. It so happened that the guy they surprised inside was the S-2, the intelligence officer, of Viet Cong Military Region Five. He was on leave down there with all his papers and maps. He even had a diagram that had been taken from my brigade briefing tent in Dong Tam that showed the master plan for development of the base. Now, this tent was always under guard. How the hell he got it I don't know, but it had been traced on onionskin paper, and the printing was identical to the plan posted on the chartboards in the tent.

He was immediately turned over to the ARVN. I don't know what they did to this guy, but they obviously tortured him and squeezed every bit of information they could. Well, they found safehouses in My Tho and every city in the delta, and within the 7th ARVN Division they fingered twenty-nine officers who were VC. Hell, after that the ARVN thought we were the greatest thing since sliced bread, because we cleaned out the whole structure of VC informants and safehouses. So there was Tanh's leak—not one, but twenty-nine of them.

Another time we were operating in Bien Hoa province. There was a little town, Phuc Tho, on the edge of a mangrove swamp. Every time we made sweeps, if we attacked from the west through the jungle into Phuc Tho, the VC went into the swamp. If you came down the road, they faded into the jungle. Well, I launched an attack that came down the roads, through the jungle, and two boat companies and some ARVN came down the river. We totally sealed off this village, and we went in to have a search. The district chief was a little *dai-uy*, a captain, and we also had along the deputy security chief for the province, a Major Noan. Well, we started finding VC who were on the Bien Hoa province blacklist. We captured about thirty of these guys in two hours. But as we started to find these VC and identify them by picture and by name, Major Noan called off the search. There was a young State Department guy who was with the *dai-uy*, and I thought he and Major Noan were going to shoot each other. Noan just said, "No more," and that was it.

Well, Noan was later thought to be a VC. I think when he saw all his buddies being unearthed, he just ended the operation. The *dai-uy* was really upset, but there was nothing he could do about it. Noan was a curious character. He had his wife in the town of Bien Hoa, but he used to come down and visit a woman who lived in the Nan Trach. The VC could have fingered him any day of the week and killed him, but they didn't. Incidentally, almost a year later the *dai-uy* was having a big party at the district headquarters. Noan came to the party. He left about twenty minutes before the VC came out of the jungle and attacked. The *dai-uy*, his wife, and the State Department youngster were all killed.

But sometimes these little guys were so good they would just break your heart. I had one little ARVN commander down in Can Giuoc, Major Nguyen. He was a fighter. He was smart as hell, and he knew the enemy. Jesus, he'd been fighting for twenty-three years—first as a lieutenant for the French against the Viet Minh, and now against the Viet Cong. And he was still a major commanding a regiment. He had five battalion commanders under him, and some of them were lieutenant colonels. But he was still a major. You know why? Because he didn't have enough money to buy his promotion.

I began to cultivate him. I put a battalion into Can Giuoc, and I went to him and said, "Let's do an operation together." Yeah, he'd go. Hell, yes. It was a success, and after that he was fired up. Every time I went back into his area, I'd get two or three battalions from Nguyen. One day he got into a sizable fight, and I brought in air strikes and artillery for him. We decimated a VC unit. The next day he went in there and found a huge weapons cache. Machine guns, mortars, and rifles by the hundreds, and lots of ammunition. Under the Vietnamese system, he was given a certain number of piasters for each weapon captured by his troops. He had a gold mine there. He went up and bought his promotion the next day. Paid off whoever he had to and became a lieutenant colonel. After that, he would do anything I asked. I could go down there in the middle of the night and say, "Nguyen, I'm gonna fly in twenty-five lift choppers. Can you give me a battalion?" He'd never say, "Where are you going?" or "What are you going to do?" He'd just crank up his units and go.

But I had General Westmoreland tell me, "Never praise an ARVN commander to his superior." We were talking one day about some ARVN unit, it may have been Major Nguyen. And Westy said, "Don't ever let the higher command hear you say that. Because then the guy becomes suspect. They begin to think he's your man, and they'll relieve him." Again, this xenophobia. This tremendous pride. Very short-sighted. But understanding the psychology of other people—Americans don't do that very well. And I must confess, I happen to be a Californian and a Westerner. I miss some of the subtleties. The whole Oriental idea of face, the amenities.

You run into people who say, "The South Vietnamese are very noble, and they fought a hell of a battle." But they never really put it on the line with the United States. They did quite well in '72, when they beat the North Vietnamese up north. And they were probably very brave. But by God, the American policy should have been: Look, if we're going to stay here and fight, you're going to do what we say. After all, we were supplying them. We did it in Korea during the war and for years afterward. When I was there in '60, we controlled the ammunition and we controlled the gasoline, so that a division couldn't move against Seoul to support a coup. In Korea we exercised operational control over all forces. We didn't do that in Vietnam. We did everything with kid gloves. We didn't want to affront or insult the ARVN by forcing them to join our battles. The fact is that they were reluctant warriors. They were never willing to find the lion and beard him in his den. And we were unwilling to force them to do it. If you're going to pull it off, you have to destroy the enemy first. And I always felt in my heart that the ARVN were willing to sit in their little forts and protect what they had and hope that the enemy didn't come at 'em.

THE GOOD LIFE

For American civilians, South Vietnam was divided in two: You could either work "in the field" or in Saigon. Those in the field looked down a bit on the Saigon-bound, feeling that they had little idea of what was really going on. In turn, those who populated the embassy or MACV or USIS felt a certain pity for their cousins in the countryside. They might be closer to the ebb and flow of the war, but what they were missing!

Part of Saigon's allure was that of any old colonial capital in the tropics. It was beautiful and exotic, and the living was easy. The French had left their legacy of boulevards, villas, restaurants, the Cercle Sportif, the renowned Eurasian women. And long before the French arrived, the southern Vietnamese were an easygoing people who valued physical pleasures. Now the new Westerners had come, wielding the dollar. From stereos in the PX to black-market Courvoisier, from servants to nightclub beauties, nearly everything could be bought cheap. Robin Pell, an AID public-relations man, remembers strolling on Sunday among "the antique stores, the book vendors, a great pet market." Back in his villa, his cook would be preparing superb seafood. "It was a marvel," he says.

But Saigon, of course, was different from other third-world outposts: It was under siege. The war surrounded it, with enemy troops roaming just a few miles away. That lent a sense of urgency to life and helped make the city, as Pell remembers, "the hot place to be." Saigon drew the adventuresome, the ambitious, and the offbeat. The work was exciting. It seemed to matter. The pace was fierce; there was always too much to be done. Young men—rarely women—could win great responsibility.

And just as relentlessly as the Americans worked, they played. There was something unreal about Saigon, after all; while it was far removed from the 'Nam of the grunts, it was not "the World," either. If the rules were suspended in the boonies, so they were (for Americans, anyway) in the capital. Fantasies were acted out, new lives experimented with. "People were doing crazy things," says Julie Kayan, then a young secretary at JUSPAO. "Married men were reliving their adolescences, taking twenty years off their lives. . . . People's emotions were wild." There were dinner parties, cocktail parties, going-away parties, light-at-the-end-of-the-tunnel parties. And permeating it all, a touch of guilt—the knowledge that, nearby, soldiers were battling and dying—which may have only helped to fuel the fun.

The wife of a high embassy official had another view of Saigon. She describes it as a plush jail—not unlike other diplomatic posts, but with less to do because of the dangers. "It was like living in a country club," she says. The most enjoyable activity of the day? Menu-planning, which could take an hour in the morning. Otherwise, it was a round of barbecues and bridges and charity bazaars and excursions to pristine beaches on Con Son Island, a stone's throw from the prison that housed the tiger cages. Finally she fled, tired of the boredom, and of arguing with her husband about the war.

Besides the civilians in government service, another curious breed of Americans crowded Saigon—employees of the private construction companies working under contract. For most of these men, Vietnam was just another stop where the pay was good and the dollar powerful. Bill Crownover spent half his time maintaining telephone equipment and the other half in bars. His relations with the Vietnamese, he admits, were not exemplary. "There were times when I'd say, I know what I'm doing and I still don't care, by God. I *am* an Ugly American."

It may seem surprising that in Saigon, enjoying the good life, Americans grew disenchanted almost as surely as the grunts in the bush. The city's physical decline saddened those who stayed long enough to watch the changes: the choking traffic fumes, the chopping down of shade trees along the avenues, the spread of barbed wire like a cancer, the crush of refugees and maimed soldiers. A feeling of futility seeped in from the countryside despite the massive machinery hammering out good news. Americans who traveled widely, like Robin Pell, came back and shared skeptical reports. Those who rarely left the city, like Julie Kayan, saw the bitter faces of street children and drew their own conclusions.

So, like the soldiers, most Americans who spent their war in Saigon came home and tried to forget it. With the U.S. being torn apart over

Vietnam, it was hard to admit that you had fun there. A few incurables took a different route, of course. They fell in love with Saigon and never stopped believing or hoping that the war would have a happy ending. And they stayed around until the curtain fell.

ROBIN PELL

I was typical of a great many Americans who wound up in Saigon. If you were happily married, raising four children, living in Scarsdale, and dying to be head of the insurance company, you didn't end up in Saigon. If you were bored with your life, your wife, your job, and you couldn't wait for an excuse to get out, you ended up in Saigon. As a result of which, a lot of interesting, unusual people were there. During my four years, '65 through '69, it was the hot place to be. All the top people came through—the correspondents, the congressmen and senators. If the *Washington Post* had a reporter who just got a divorce and was miserable and wanted to get over it, they'd send him to Saigon. For some it worked brilliantly. For others it didn't work at all.

A duplex apartment in a small building on the East Side of New York. There is classical music on the radio. The Oriental sculpture and blue-and-white porcelain decorating the living room come from Vietnam, as do the shelves of books bound in green leather, with gold lettering.

He is a dapper man, about five feet nine, with short graying hair, fair skin, and striking green eyes, who was working at the Central Park Conservancy, a private group that raises money and lobbies for the welfare of the famous park. Before going to Saigon with AID in 1965, he had worked as a reporter, political organizer, Senate staff member, and State Department bureaucrat. As we talk, he guides me through big albums of photographs he took in-country: friends, girlfriends, street children, wizened peasants, landscapes.

The AID program in Vietnam was called USOM—the U.S. Operations Mission. USOM wanted material that they could use in the United States to publicize the work they were doing in Vietnam. So I was put on the payroll and sent out to Saigon. We would help out reporters, and I would visit projects to do feature stories and send them back to AID in Washington. I'd write the story and do the pictures. They were about people in the field and the work they were doing. Americans, of course. The idea was that you would highlight both the program and the personalities. Then AID would distribute the articles in the States, to hometown newspapers, sometimes a magazine.

I lived in a house, Number 16 Ngo Thoi Nhiem. I was told that the original French name for Ngo Thoi Nhiem was Capitaine Jaurigeberry. He was the Frenchman who led the final assault on the city of Saigon when the French captured it. I had a lovely villa, which I just adored. About two-thirds of the top floor was a screened living room with a tile floor and ceiling fans. It was a beautiful room. Downstairs was a dining room that I later turned into another bedroom. There were two bedrooms, a kitchen, and a bath. Then the owner decided he could make more money, and I got evicted. For a year I lived in a smaller villa farther down the street, across from the Lycée Marie Curie, the most chic girls' school. For my last year I was in downtown Saigon in an apartment.

When I first got there I had a marvelous neighbor named John Gilbert. John was with the AID mission. He taught me how to go around Saigon on Sundays. Sunday was when all the special markets were open. The antique stores, the book vendors, a great pet market. Around noon, when the stores would start closing down, you'd settle in a restaurant and have lunch. . . . [Sighs.] It was a special place. You lived well. I had to go to a developing nation in the middle of war to learn how to handle household servants. I always had a maid and a cook. When I met my cook she said, "What do you like to eat?" Well, seafood. "Do you like crab?" Yes, I liked crab. The first evening, *Monsieur* comes home from the office and she shows him what she's bought for dinner. She opens a brown bag and two live crabs go scuttling across the kitchen floor. David Halberstam describes exactly the same experience in *The Making of a Quagmire*.

It was a marvel, to have all this wonderful seafood to eat, and a cook. You'd have supper and go to a big bar, have a couple of drinks, maybe pick up a girl and bring her home. There was a famous band led by a guy named Joe Marcel. He did imitations, basically copying American tunes. His signature tune was "The Mashed Potato." And there were bad nightclub singers all over the place. Every one sang "I Left My Heart in San Francisco." They'd sing it with very mechanical gestures. I never liked that song much to begin with, and I learned to loathe it in Saigon.

In my work I focused on what was going on out in the provinces. The program was called Rural Development. AID was just starting to send these groups of Vietnamese-language-trained FSOs out to the provinces. As they went out, I followed them. I would go visit. I learned a lot that way. I had a network of friends in the field—what we called "good contacts at the primary level."

There was no aspect of that economy or civilian life that we didn't try to tamper with. In some places, very effectively. During the time I was in Saigon, we turned the rural economy around from a barter economy to a cash economy. Farmers in districts controlled by the Saigon government, with regular access to the market, could make a lot of money. We introduced the new miracle rices. We introduced fertilizer. We introduced a lot of small agricultural machines. In the delta, the Vietnamese developed a very good irrigation pump using an outboard motor and a kind of pipe sleeve with a propeller. So a lot of these programs worked, at one level. We built hamlet schools all over the place. We put a lot of money into hospitals. There was a public safety program, where we tried to upgrade the police. I always felt that one backfired. The most famous case was a program where we tried to deny resources to the enemy by controlling medicine and food, making sure they didn't leave the government-controlled areas and get smuggled out to the countryside. The problem was that you just created a whole new level of corruption, a mini-industry of corruption among the police. The peasant woman who's bringing her bread into the market would have to pay a little bribe to the policeman who is set up with U.S. encouragement to watch all the food and traffic coming in and out of the market.

As the AID mission built up, and as the whole rural development idea turned into pacification, and as USOM turned into CORDS, and the military took over, it affected the way news got to Saigon. John Negroponte used to say, "Everyone lies a little." He meant that everyone lies to make what they're doing look a little better than it is. If you're working in a school program, you emphasize the schools you're building, not the ones that were destroyed or the ones you've lost because the enemy now controls the area.

I used to read the monthly progress reports. I particularly remember one by a man named Ben Weaver. I never met him, but he was the senior AID man down in Vinh Long. I think he was gone before February of '66—before Tet, before the American troops were there in large numbers. His last report was very gloomy. He said he was trying to do X and Y and Z, and it wasn't working. The line that sticks in my mind is: "Meanwhile, the country bleeds and bleeds and bleeds." This was long before it really started to bleed. And it was a time when a province rep might have a staff of three or four. By the end, he'd have guys in all the districts and a sergeant outside his door who'd decide who could come in, and an enormous staff. He was a big deal.

As a bureaucracy becomes a big deal, it becomes much more self-interested. None of the later province reps ever wrote a report that said, "The country bleeds and bleeds." And if anyone did, Corps headquarters acted as a filter. They weren't about to let one of their boys send in a report like that. So I always felt that the biggest gap in information was not between Saigon and Washington but between Saigon and the provinces.

That all became vivid in the weeks before the Tet offensive. I went on a series of VIP trips around Vietnam. One was with Senator Joseph Clark of Pennsylvania. I knew Clark from Washington and asked if I could travel with him for a couple of days. He had been given the Westy-Bunker "things are going well, should be withdrawing troops in six months, light at the end of the tunnel" briefing in Saigon, and he'd made some noises to the press along those lines. He gave them some fairly optimistic quotes. The next day he started on his tour of the provinces. The first place he went was Ba Xuyen. I picked him up in Saigon afterward. When I met him, he was a very disillusioned man. He was finding out that the minute he walked out of Saigon, nothing was as he had been told it would be.

Our next stop was Quang Ngai. It's a large coastal province south of Danang and just north of Binh Dinh. Binh Dinh and Quang Ngai were the first strongholds of the Viet Minh in South Vietnam. It was always a real battle to make any progress against the enemy in Quang Ngai. But more important, it was a battle that had been going on for years and years, since the 1930s, long before the Americans got there. It was mountainous, perfect guerrilla territory, with a lush coastal plain. When I first went there in '65, they were trying to pacify the area between Quang Ngai City and the sea. Every time I went back they were having a variant of that same program. Again and again and again. Quang Ngai was a tough province.

So Joe Clark arrived in Quang Ngai, and the senior province rep was away. A major who was his deputy gave the briefing. It was a good, honest briefing. He didn't try to pull any rabbits out of hats. He didn't pretend that things were any different than they were. And he said, among other things, that the government had trouble finding good people to be on its side. That over years of conflict and war, both sides had made such demands for personnel that there wasn't much left, and if you went out to try and find leaders for cadre teams, you were looking at the bottom of the barrel.

We got to Danang and had lunch with the AID senior rep for I Corps and another guy from USIS, a hotshot. When Joe Clark repeated what the guy had said about Quang Ngai, they got very upset

472 | STRANGE GROUND

and insisted it wasn't true. They were obviously annoyed at the major for telling Clark this. I knew that major was going to catch it, and I later heard that he did.

Periodically the Americans would get a bee up their ass about some project. A classic example was this one district south of Saigon. It was in Long An province. The embassy always got pissy about Long An because it sat astride the highway to the delta. This famous pacification project came from Henry Cabot Lodge saying at a meeting, "Why can't we do anything about Long An province?" And one of the hotshots said, "I'll go down there, sir, and I'll do something about it." So they went pouring down. They picked a district and made it a model district. They poured in resources, and they poured in reporters. This hotshot did very good briefings. He was articulate and he spoke good Vietnamese. The press loved an articulate American who could make it all clear to them. But what happened is that if you focused on one part of the province, you pulled resources from the other parts. You got a temporary improvement in one area and the other areas went downhill. Then the moment you left the blue-chip area, it all collapsed.

There were a whole series of programs like that. Just prior to Tet the big number was a canal. It was a key communication line for taking rice and other supplies to the capital from the delta, which was the breadbasket of Vietnam. There was a big celebration when it opened and the first shipment went through. Anything like this was always accompanied by tons of press. People wanted positive stories to latch on to, and the mission wanted positive stories to sell. It was a marvelous little game. You had the reporters out there, the correspondents and the freelancers. Then the big editor would come in from Washington or New York. The big editor would get the big treatment: an interview with Ambassador Bunker and the VIP tour. Sometimes he would be sold on the idea that there were a lot of positive things going on that his reporters were missing. He'd get the reporters aside and say, "I want you to start covering some of that stuff." So these guys would descend on me and say, "What have you got here?" Rice. "Ah, shit, all right." Schools. "All right, I'll go down and look at some schools."

Then you had the showcase provinces. There were four of them: An Giang, Binh Dinh, and two others. Extra resources would go into them, and visitors would be shuttled to the showcase provinces. There was this constant search for the gimmick, the way to make good news vivid, to show people we're doing good things as well as fighting a war. I was aware of this constant pressure, from LBJ on down: Let's put those coonskins on the wall, try and make the war look good. The comedy in the end was that pacification could make progress and the country could go to hell in a handbasket at the same time. The French had the delta pacified at the time of Dien Bien Phu. We had the delta pretty much pacified as the country crumbled.

Tet was the turning point for me. Up until Tet I still enjoyed going around the country. But afterward, I took a trip out of Saigon, and starting at the end of the runway at Tan Son Nhut you followed a line of bomb craters all the way into the delta. There was much more physical damage. No matter where you went in the country, the wear and tear of the war was much more visible. And I had just had enough. I didn't enjoy it anymore. I had very few illusions about what was going on. When I first arrived, I could go out and meet people who were putting up schools, or go up to Quang Ngai and see villages being pacified, and it looked pretty good. You had to come back two years later and see them pacifying the same village to realize that it wasn't getting very far.

Among the civilians that I knew in Saigon, everyone talked about this being the great job of their lives. It was fantastic, what you were doing here, and how interesting it was, and all the freedom you had to get out and go around the country. But everyone left the country without so much as a second glance. I attribute it to the difference between what we wished and hoped was going on and what in fact was going on. You were working in these civilian programs where in theory you were improving life for the Vietnamese. But it wasn't the case, and a lot of people didn't even want to admit it to themselves. They just wanted to get out quietly.

This never came up in conversation. In Saigon you didn't sit around and talk about the big issues: Why are we in Vietnam? Should we really be here? To this day I feel that the Vietnamese didn't deserve what they got. Nothing they did would merit getting the North Vietnamese as their rulers. At the same time, you had to be awfully blind or dumb not to see what was going on. The Vietnamese also didn't deserve to have air strikes and napalm inflicted on them. It was impossible to use American power discriminately in a situation with villages and a civilian population. I knew that. But we didn't talk about it at dinner. We talked office chatter. Politics, AID programs, what's new in I Corps. "I was up in Hué the other day, and things are going better." "An RD team was overrun the other night in so-and-so district."

The closest we would come to real questioning was a comment I heard more than once: How come the best people are always on the other side? Why is it that when we go on a sweep and pick out the VC suspects, they always turn out to be the brightest guys in a village? I heard a wonderful anecdote from one reporter who worked for the *Philadelphia Inquirer*. He made a visit to a province in III Corps. The province chief was describing how he found a VC agent in his midst. He heard that one of his district chiefs was an agent. There were five district chiefs. He said, "I knew it wasn't X, because he's lazy and a drunk. I knew it wasn't Y, because he steals too much money." He went down the list and [snaps fingers]—"Him! He's bright, active, sharp—he's the man." And he was right. That guy was the VC agent.

That's as close as you came to questioning. But I knew a million stories like that.

The sex thing was only a by-product. With rare exceptions, there weren't women out there that you could communicate with and have a real relationship with. So you just tried to screw a lot, and you could do that in Saigon very easily. Mostly with bar girls, sometimes with girlfriends, sometimes with people who fell in between. No one has ever written much about the role of sex in the Vietnam War. It was best summarized by a reporter I bumped into once. He said, "Y'know, I have the theory that if the women in Vietnam had big copper spoons through their noses and looked like Ubangis, this war wouldn't have lasted half as long, and maybe wouldn't have even started." The French had a name for it: *le mal jaune*, the yellow fever. The great attraction of Indochina to the West. The beauty, the seductiveness, the opium, and, above all, the women. All those beautiful Vietnamese women in their ao dais. And the easy availability of bar girls.

The difference between skirt-chasing here and skirt-chasing there was the whole commercial aspect of it. You just went down to the bars and picked out a girl and took her home and it cost you a certain amount of money. In the early days, you would go to nightclubs and sometimes meet girls who'd come home with you for nothing. Later on it got to be more and more commercial. Then there were in-between areas, where a girl would be sort of your girlfriend but occasionally hit you up for money. And there was a small stratum of upper-class women, well educated, that you got to know as friends. But there weren't that many women you could talk to. At best, they might have gone to the local French high school. That was the top level of education. And it was very rare for a woman to have been outside of Vietnam.

I had one girlfriend, a marvelous, voluptuous creature who was passed on to me by a friend who already had a regular girlfriend. One day she presented an ultimatum. She said an old AID boyfriend was coming back and he wanted her to live with him. She said, "What do you want to do?" I just said, "I'm not going to offer you anything like that, so you'd better go with him." She vanished and I didn't see much of her. Then I started getting calls from her about once a month, at eight or eight-thirty in the morning. "Hey, Robin, you bee-zee?" She'd come bopping over for a quick screw and to hit me up for some dough. However, she got furious if I implied that the two went together. We'd have a screw and then she'd ask for a loan that I knew I would never see again. I don't know why she needed it. Maybe she just enjoyed me.

In the end, you got tired of it. And over time the GIs built up the bar scene, and commercial sex boomed, so it got less and less common to just meet someone at a nightclub and take them home. People would go to Cambodia and say it was like Saigon in the old days, casual. I stopped going to the nightclub where Joe Marcel played. Rather than a relaxed place to have a drink, it became very fancy, commercial, high-pressured.

Four years was too long. At the end it was just the constant grind of a wartime city. On my last Sunday in Saigon, I decided to do one last trip to all the markets I had learned to know and love with John Gilbert. I got out the door and walked two or three blocks. The traffic was so bad that I said, "Screw it," and went home.

JULIE KAYAN

She is a tall, slim woman in her forties, recently married, living in a smartly furnished apartment in a Manhattan high-rise. "I was born and grew up in New York. My father taught at Columbia. I went to Smith and graduated in '61. Then I got a job at Time Inc. *and finally went to Washington as the secretary to the* Time *bureau chief. This was in '64 and '65. Obviously,* Time *was very interested in the Vietnam War. Everybody was talking about it. And I had a good college friend, Edie Smith, who was in Saigon. While she was there, she met Johnny Apple of* The New York Times. *Before they got married she came back to Washington and stayed with me. I started thinking, Why not do something that I couldn't do if I were settled down?*

"I grew up in the '50s. It was a complacent decade. Very few of us had done anything that had any meaning. I was not an exception. But I did get idealistic over Vietnam. It seemed like a cause, something important. I thought I could contribute—I'm not sure how. And it was an adventure. So I wrote the Saigon bureau chief and said, 'I'm inter-

ested in coming out, and as you can imagine, Time's *not going to send me. What should I do?' He put in a word with Barry Zorthian at JUSPAO—the press center for the embassy. After a lot of delays, I got a job."*

I got there in May of '67. My arrival was tremendously gay. The airport was pandemonium, and I was met by eight people. A *Time* correspondent came. Edie came. Another college friend came. The JUSPAO welcoming committee was there. It was a whirlwind. It was Saigon. The city was very colorful. That first day, I went to dinner at the Apples' and was overwhelmed, because they never gave an idle dinner party. People sat down and talked about serious things. There were arguments and excitment. I was caught up in it.

The city dazzled me. It was very Oriental, even with all the Americans. It was much more beautiful than I had expected. I wasn't prepared for the physical layout, which was elegant. I wasn't prepared for the bales of barbed wire. I wasn't prepared for the Street of Flowers in the midst of it all—a street that's flower stall after flower stall. And I wasn't prepared for the traffic, which was insane most of the time and incredible at rush hour. It wasn't a city you wandered in, because it wasn't very pleasant. Motorbikes, motorbikes, motorbikes. And taxicabs—old Fiats that were rusted out, so in the rainy season the water would come through the bottom.

My first few months were happy and exciting. Work was fun, even though you worked tremendously hard. The hours were eight to six, with a break in the middle of the day, and half-days on Saturdays. I don't know if I've ever been so occupied in a job. I worked in what was called the "front office"—not directly for Zorthian, but for his deputy. There were three secretaries, and in fact we all worked for Zorthian. He was a bigger-than-life person, pure unleashed energy. People used to say, "Zorthian never sleeps." He'd play poker most of the night and then be up at six in the morning to go into the field. He knew the country well, and he loved it. I was lucky to work for someone that caring. He was not cynical, and an awful lot of people were.

Everybody was in overdrive constantly. That was the pace, fast-forward. There was nothing slow or lazy about Saigon. You couldn't make a plan or a list. Things just happened. Something as simple as going to the commissary—you went when somebody went. There was no other way to get there. You could go to the trouble of getting an embassy car, but normally if Zorthian's secretary was going for him, I went. There was a lot of jumping at the chance. Part of it was because people were there without their families, so they were filling their time to avoid getting depressed or lonely. I can count on the fingers of one hand the evenings I spent by myself. That doesn't mean there was a party every night. But it was not a place where you spent much time alone. Nobody had a telephone. Nobody had television. We read a good deal, but the entertainment of choice was other people.

At one point Edie told me, "This is a place where you need a very good friend, to remind yourself that you haven't gone mad." I understood immediately what she meant. You needed somebody to keep you stabilized, something familiar. There was nothing you could hang on to. There were no families, no children, no schools. Everything was immediate—coming and going. There wasn't a day when somebody didn't come or go. We constantly went to farewell parties. It was hard to get your bearings.

Part of it was the physical presence of Saigon—the traffic, all the people. But it also was the place. You'd wake up in the morning, have breakfast, and then lose control. You never knew what the day was going to bring—who was going to come in, what was going to happen, who was going to leave, what the news was going to be. People were doing crazy things. Married men were reliving their adolescences, taking twenty years off their lives. They were dancing. They were having fun. People's emotions were wild. You'd hear men say, "I haven't been happy for years, and I've found happiness at last." When I was interviewed by personnel before going out, I remember the people told me, "Your danger in Saigon isn't going to be mortars, it's going to be married men." And they were right. There was an awful lot of palaver. So I came out with my dukes up—No, siree, boy, I know you're married. Don't you tell me you're not, because I know you are. But I still had a couple of serious romances out there.

Being a woman was very different from being a man. We were in demand, and not necessarily for anything untoward. We were in demand as company, as dinner partners. I went to any number of occasions that I never would have been invited to if I was a man, just because people like to have a balanced party. It wasn't unusual to have dates for breakfast, lunch, cocktails, and dinner. Your dance card was packed.

You played hard, because that's all there was to do. Many people had good cooks, and they entertained a lot. I remember a massive bash on New Year's Eve about a month before Tet. It was billed the Light-at-the-End-of-the-Tunnel party. The list of people who were invited was extraordinary, and the party itself was extraordinary. High hilarity, everybody letting off steam. Another time there was a pig roast, which I remember because the pig had been somebody's pet. I was thinking, How could somebody do this to their pet pig? And there was a Hawaiian girl who worked at JUSPAO who staged a luau to end all luaus. It was the same thing: loud music, good fun. I heard there were drugs around, but I never saw any. We had old-fashioned booze, and a good deal of it. Liquor through the commissary was cheap and plentiful. If the party was at a place where I'd been before, I'd train the servants that if I said, "Gin-and-tonic," I meant tonic. I couldn't survive the gin and the tonic and the wine and the ninety-five-degree heat. It didn't feel good.

There was a lot of song. We had a group of people who got together to play guitars and sing. I remember one evening where we finger-painted. We had dinner, and then people said, "What do we do now?" Well, let's fingerpaint. The hostess happened to have some finger-paints. Just wacky fun. It's a difficult thing to admit: We were fiddling while Vietnam burned. We worked hard, too, nobody was goofing off, but it was not a black time, particularly at the beginning.

Of course you were very close to the war, and you did hear it. Everyone at one time or another went to the roof of the Caravelle and "watched the war." There were constant comments about the ludicrousness of having a well-made dinner with a French-trained cook, drinking elegant wines, in that kind of situation. There was something absurd about it. But it happened. The Cercle Sportif existed, and people joined it. Life does go on. You do adapt. You make it your home. My dog had puppies. It was all part of this craziness of being in a country at war in a city surrounded.

My happiest day in Vietnam was Thanksgiving of '67. The Apples were planning a big dinner, and they persuaded me—because I lived across the street—to have the cocktails at my apartment. Then we'd go to dinner at their house and come back to my place for brandy. It was one of those enormous gatherings, thirty people for a sitdown dinner. Then, that morning, Zorthian asked me if I wanted to go down to My Tho, a town in the delta. Of course I did. I hardly ever got to go out of Saigon, so when somebody would say, "Do you want to . . . ," I'd say yes and be in the backseat of their car. He was going to visit the province rep, but he was also going antiquing.

It was one of those days that just worked. It was Vietnam at its most enchanting, the Vietnam that was there but we never saw. Driving along and watching farmers with their water buffalo. Going to the market and the antique stores. My Tho at that point—it was hit hard during Tet—was a delightful little city. The children followed us as we wandered around the market. On the way back we stopped at a *nuoc maum* factory. Zorthian and I climbed up and peered down into the vats.

The Apples were frantic because I was away, and the dinner was supposed to begin at my apartment. But I was back in time, and everybody came. It was the usual mix, from high generals and congressmen and political officers to a friend of mine whom I hadn't seen in years and who just happened to turn up in Saigon. A perfect cross-section of life in Vietnam in those days. There were no social classes. People were people. For a civilian woman, it was a heady experience to be having dinner with people whose names you saw in the paper. That was a happy day.

But there was a certain amount of guilt, because at the same time, people were getting killed. That was hard for me to get comfortable with. A friend of mine dated a colonel who was stationed at Cu Chi. He would come in to see her and talk about the body count, what a great day they had, forty-five Cong wiped out. I never got used to the hate they had to muster up. I had to leave the room, because it wasn't something I was happy to hear. I wasn't unpatriotic, I just didn't like that part. And I didn't like the way he talked about it. But I understood that he had to talk about it that way.

When I was there about four months, I got sick and went into the 17th Field Hospital. While I was recovering, a really lovely young man there said, "What you need is some sun. I'm going to take you out to the river." There was a military recreation facility. So one day after I'd gotten out of the hospital, he picked me up. We were going to take a taxi. After much haggling with the driver, he agreed on a price. We got out there, got out of the taxi, and this lovely young man threw half of what he had agreed to at the taxi driver and said, "Go away." The taxi driver said, "No, we agreed. . . ." At which point the MP at the gate picked up his rifle and pointed it at this taxi driver and said, "Go." I was horrified. It ruined the day. I kept saying, "But you agreed!" And this young man, innocent and untouched, said, "But he's just a gook." And this was not even someone who'd seen combat. It was somebody working as an orderly in a hospital that had very little relation to the war. That was the sad part of what was happening. Halfway through my tour, I thought, This is not a good place. It's doing terrible things to people—to us and to them.

The children would stand outside the commissary and grab you as you went in and say, "Buy me Tide. Buy me Tide." It was for the black market—they certainly didn't have washing machines. Or they'd say, "Wash your car" or "Watch your car"—we never could understand what they were saying. But it was a threatening offer. It was sad to see that. The children were being corrupted because we were there with things they didn't have. We'd come out of the commissary with bags and bags of stuff. You'd buy what was there, just because it was there. If they happened to have Cheerios, you'd buy Cheerios, because you hadn't seen Cheerios for a while. Things I gagged on in the States, like Hostess Twinkies and cupcakes, would become divinely wonderful.

There were funny incidents, too. Malaria pills were a necessary evil. Everybody had to take them. The embassy had a dainty little pill. We ran out of those somewhere along the line. The army had these he-man pills. The first time I took one, I found myself deathly ill. I was walking back from paying a bill at the Cercle Sportif, and I was struck down. It was rush hour. I was walking past the gates of the presidential palace. All I could think of was, I'm going to be sick, and I can't be sick in front of all these people. So I went over to the fence of the palace and managed, as demurely as I could, to throw up all over, just inside the grounds.

And the bread—the bread in Vietnam is wonderful. But it was full of little bugs. After the first little bug you saw, you forgot about them. Well, you could always tell when somebody was new to Saigon. I remember sitting in a restaurant and hearing somebody say in a screaming voice, "Waiter! Waiter! There's a bug in my bread!" This poor man was practically having a conniption. And we were saying to each other, "That's not all you're gonna find, mister. Wait 'til you really start looking around."

I think of my tour as split in two. The first half was very gay, very jolly. Life was embarrassingly good. When the Tet offensive started and it was obvious that something serious was happening, I remember thinking, Well, at least this is what I came for. This is what I thought it was going to be like. And life changed radically at that point.

I lived about a block from the embassy, in a very elegant French apartment building with ceiling fans and few Americans. Lots of Vietnamese officials lived on my street. The American ambassador lived at the end of the street. For two or three nights before the offensive, it had been very noisy. Firecrackers, lots of running around. I had inherited a dog from the Apples—an unabashedly neurotic, suicidal dog. Around 3:00 A.M., you could tell the difference between what was happening and the firecrackers. The dog and I clung together. I got up and turned on the Armed Forces radio station. They were still saying, "When you go on vacation, remember to take your malaria pills." Not a break. Not a newsflash. Nothing. My housemate didn't wake up. After about an hour, a friend who lived in the building came down and said, "Something awful is happening. The lights in the embassy have gone out." So we got Carol out of bed and went up to the friend's apartment, which was the penthouse. I bravely said, "I'm going out on the terrace to see what's going on." At which point somebody shot at me from the street. The bullet went right through the wall and landed on the bed. I'm sure it was meant to be a warning shot. I bellied back in and said, "Things aren't going very well out there."

The first couple of nights were rough. There was a lot of incoming and outgoing. It was scary. Yet you ride it out, always with humor. Some people were quite reckless. It was eat, drink, and be merry, because we don't know about tomorrow. Well, tomorrow came and everybody felt lousy because they'd been working their way through the liquor cabinet the night before, saying, Dammit, they're not gonna get my wine.

I was the duty secretary for JUSPAO that week, so they sent for me the first morning. Zorthian was right in the middle of things. It was fascinating to see him get the reports from the provinces and coordinate press statements with the embassy. And we worked very hard. Obviously no Vietnamese were going to come to work. So people rallied. I have friends that I made during that time that I'd do anything for. A number of the women in the embassy lived in AID compounds near the airport. Those areas were pretty well shot up. So they evacuated most of the women, and we had about seven living with us for a week.

You do learn funny things about yourself. I learned that I'm terrific if people around me are crying and upset and scared. I'm fabulous. But put me in the same situation by myself and I'm a disaster. A little while after the Tet offensive, the VC blew up the ARVN radio station, which was fairly near where I lived. I did everything wrong. I went to windows. I went outside. I got hysterical. I whimpered. I cried. I did everything that I had protected other people from doing during Tet. I knew I wasn't supposed to go to the window, that was insane. But I wanted to see what was happening. The first two nights after Tet, I was astounded at how humorous and calm and collected I could be. But it was all show. It fell apart easily. Turns out I'm a real sissy.

Saigon was never the same after Tet. The mood changed. Nobody was cocky. There was a constant sense of anxiety and fear. For the next couple of months we were very restricted. Curfew came at six or seven at night. People gave sleep-in dinner parties—you'd go for dinner, and you couldn't leave. My building had a French concierge who had been there since the colonial days. He came over as a soldier and stayed. He was a madman, totally eccentric. He had seven pairs of identical blue swimming trunks, and he wore a different pair each day. After the Tet offensive he would sit outside his hut and philosophize. It was always the same thing: *"Vietnam, c'est fini."* I'd say, "It's not over." He'd say, *"Oui, c'est fini."* He lost his spunk. He'd mope around, and I'd try to cheer him up.

But I got very discouraged, too. I began to think, We shouldn't be here. I'm not so sure that we're in a position to tell another culture how they should do things. And I got tired of the cynicism. There was a refrain: "What are the Vietnamese people doing for themselves? What do they want?" Well, they wanted us to leave, that's what I thought they wanted.

Going out there as idealistic as I had been—I was going to win hearts and minds and save the world and help fight this important war—I wasn't ready for the corruption and all the people who would have liked very much to take me in some way. I was extremely fond of the Vietnamese I worked with, but frankly, most of the experience I had with Vietnamese was with people's maids. Which is a sad statement. And with the street people. The black market was bad, but we did buy things off of it. Most of the stuff still had the price tags on it from the commissary or the PX. It was all laid out in the street, probably stolen. I don't think it was helping the Vietnamese. It was helping the American reporters who weren't supposed to go to the PX, and who got their shaving cream and toothpaste off the black market. But it never ceased to offend me. And the children—you felt awfully sorry. Some of them were maimed on purpose, because Americans gave more money to crippled children. And some of them got rather nasty. I remember one of the few really ugly experiences I had, when a child asked me for money. I always tried to say no in a good-natured way, but I did say no. He spat at me. He was angry, because somebody else had given it to him and I didn't.

By the time I left, I was plenty ready. What I wasn't ready for was coming home. I left for Vietnam with people applauding, and I came back to people—not turning their backs, but they didn't know what to talk about. Lots of my friends protested against the war. So I couldn't really talk about it. And by that time I did think it was wrong. What troubled me was, I didn't know how we could get out. We had gotten into a mess. There was a tremendous buildup while I was there. Okay, so we should leave. Now what? Do we just withdraw and leave the mess we've created?

There was a real irony for me, too. I had good times there. I loved it for most of my tour. I got a huge kick out of it. How do you explain to somebody, when you're coming back from this horrible period of our history, that it was sometimes fun?

ANONYMOUS

She is the former wife of a Foreign Service officer who held a high-level post in the Saigon embassy from 1969 to 1972. "We got married in 1945, in Europe. I was OSS. He was air force. I'm an economist, and I suppose I would have been a person with a career. . . ."

Now, in her sixties, she has a career, in an organization that works for the betterment of women in the third world. She lives in an airy ranch-style house on a quiet street. She is uneasy talking about Vietnam, for that was where her marriage started to unravel seriously. "What I cannot answer is why the hell I went to Saigon. The more I think about it, the more it upsets me. I should have taken a stand at that point, and I didn't."

My husband's Foreign Service career started with various European posts. Then back to Washington. And then Asia for four years. I was one of the last real Foreign Service wives, the kind that pays a formal call on the ambassador's wife. By the late 1960s, we could see the changes coming. There was a restiveness among the wives. The younger ones didn't really care anymore about whether they were doing things properly. They just wanted to live their own lives, and I was all for that. I suppose it came about with women working. Wives started saying, "I don't want to go to that post." They had their own jobs in Washington, and to hell with it.

I had something to do with the change, because I worked to set up a wives' training program. Finally the Foreign Service stopped rating wives. That was what most of us were furious about. FSOs were rated on their professional skills—whether they could draft a cable well, that sort of thing. The wives were rated on their social skills. You were supposed to entertain well. You were supposed to be a hand-maiden to the ambassador's wife. Help at parties. Be gracious. Make calls. There was a whole ritual of making calls on your senior wives, taking your card around. That's why everyone had a little silver tray in the foyer.

For a while, that was fine with me. Obviously, one was ambitious. You wanted to get a better post. The system was the system, and I was not about to buck it. I like parties and people and travel. It was not a bad life.

But with Vietnam I got disenchanted with the Foreign Service. After our Asian post one was usually given a sort of respite, and we were given a post at a university. But Vietnam loomed up immediately. After three months, we had to uproot again—and as usual, I was left to do the packing. I think I had had it. I was just livid.

At first I couldn't go, because there were no wives allowed. Westmoreland had sent wives and dependents away after Tet. In 1970 it was decided that wives could go back. I think it was a great mistake. I can understand that they were trying to give some semblance of normalcy. But what are you going to do with all these women sitting in a war-torn city? Once the wives got there, they weren't very happy, by and large. There were all sorts of things wrong. Many of them discovered their husbands' liaisons with bar girls. And time hung heavy on their hands.

I didn't want to go. But it became very clear that I was expected to. Everybody in the State Department thought I should go. Then I got curious, and I thought, Well, it's a part of the world I've never been in. I can go to Bali. [Laughs.] You talk yourself into these things. Most of my friends were antiwar, and they were horrified. And I didn't approve of what we were doing in Vietnam. A lot of Americans didn't know what the hell war was about, but I did. I spent years in London during World War II. I knew about bombs falling on you. I was torpedoed on the way over. And I'm not a dumb person. I knew about the French in Vietnam. I could see we were being sucked into something we didn't understand. But I guess I was tired of saying no to my husband, so I went.

Saigon is a very attractive city. The people are absolutely charming. There wasn't any great fear. There was always the threat of a *plastique* going off, and there were a few little strange bombings. Nothing to speak of. But the atmosphere—it wasn't quite hopelessness. It was a feeling of, What the hell are we doing here? There were a couple of really gung-ho wives. There always are. But you really had to find things to do, and if you didn't, you were in trouble. You lived inside the compound. It was like living in a country club.

We wives didn't talk much about the war or our presence in Vietnam. There was almost a studied attempt to create the semblance of normalcy. The women, as a group, were extremely supportive. But it was a strange, unsettled way to live—at least I thought so.

So we made ourselves do things. We re-created AWAS—the American Women's Association of Saigon. It had existed before the wives were evacuated, and we decided to revive it. There had to be some kind of structure to hold this situation together. We had about 100 wives of officials in the association. Then there were all these peripheral wives of contractors, like the men who worked for Foremost Dairy. We had strange and wonderful activities. We did Chinese painting and Japanese flower-arranging. The wife who had a house with tennis courts opened her courts two days a week. We went to the commissary and the PX. There was a lot of entertaining, as these VIPs trooped in. And a lot of going on leave. That was the biggest activity. Trips to Bangkok, to Bali, to Jakarta, to Malaysia, to Penang. It was a life you never settled into. Most people didn't bring many possessions. The houses, the furniture, and even the pictures on the wall were government-issue. You were a transient in a way station, waiting for the next thing to happen.

Each wife did what you would expect her to do, based on her personality. Some got very busy. Some really went into Chinese painting. Some did volunteer work in the American hospital. Others taught English to Vietnamese students. Most of us worked to raise money for a home for the "street boys," the orphans who roamed Saigon. Nobody worked in the refugee camps, because it was considered unsafe, and it probably was. We weren't supposed to go out of the city limits. But the association did a lot of raising money. We gave bazaars and teas and clothing drives for the refugees. There was worthwhile stuff going on. There had to be—otherwise you would have lost your mind. I probably shouldn't be facetious and talk about the Chinese painting. I don't know why that one sticks in my mind. We hired this Chinese gentleman, and he'd come to somebody's house and give classes. Everybody produced these awful Chinese paintings. But the seriousness with which we all went at it! I finally gave up the classes, I was so bad.

On the other hand, I was lucky, because I was a good bridge player. I was chosen to go on some trips with the wife of a military commander. When she went on shopping expeditions in Hué, she liked to have people along who played bridge, so several of us would be invited to go. That was when I got to see the country, and my eyes were really opened. If you sat in Saigon, your life was absolutely artificial. You heard about the war, and you heard rumors about this and that. Most of the people who came over from Washington had the party line. There were a few junior officers, the young Turks, who didn't, but most of them got shoved out when it became apparent they weren't going along. So you didn't have much to base a judgment on. But if you got out of Saigon, then you sensed the waste of everything. I'll never forget the first time I saw one of those tank dumps, or whatever they're called. Acres and acres of rusting, broken tanks. It obviously wasn't a place for tank warfare, yet here were these thousands of tanks.

In Saigon you always had the feeling that you didn't know quite what was going to happen. Boy, was it a rumor factory. At one point we decided the wives should know more about what was happening in Vietnam, and we put on a political seminar. The speakers were all Vietnamese. The notion was to get a different point of view. We got the American line in our own homes. So we went around and talked to all these Vietnamese and discovered they were perfectly happy to come and talk to the wives. Then we had a sign-up period. It was overwhelming. Every wife in town wanted to come. We had the meetings once a week for about six weeks. One of the speakers was an army officer. One was a deputy in the Parliament. They were dissidents, mostly. They supported the war, but they were very much against the Thieu government. I was amazed at how forthcoming they were. I don't think anybody in the embassy was particularly happy this was happening, but nobody stopped it. The only interesting thing is that the tapes of the seminars disappeared. They were taken to the embassy to be listened to, and they never reappeared.

The other thing was that the men in the embassy worked such God-awful hours, till eight at night. That left a lot of time hanging. I remember one unhappy wife—and there were many—who had discovered her husband's affair with a bar girl. This devastated her. She started to drink heavily. One night, I got a call from another wife. She said that this woman had locked herself in the bathroom and was weeping hysterically and was going to cut her wrists. I had to rouse the driver at the compound, because none of us drove cars ourselves. I got to this apartment building, and the wife who called met me in the hall. We went up to the apartment. There she was in the bathroom, weeping and wailing and saying, "I'm going to do it, I don't want to live." Her husband was not worth any of this, by the way—that's what was so sad about it. I knocked on her door and told her I was there. She told me to go away. I said, "I don't know why you're doing this. If I were you, I wouldn't want to kill myself, I'd want to kill him." Suddenly the door opened. The light had dawned. We talked her into going to bed. The other wife had some Valium. No fuss was made. And her husband never knew. He was up-country someplace. Soon afterward she went home.

Some women took to their beds. They had all these servants, so they didn't have to do anything. One very senior wife was constantly taking to her bed. It was a real problem, because she was expected to do certain things. People were coming through all the time; there were dinners. So there was some restiveness about her, because she wasn't doing her part. I don't know if she was really ill or not. I used to go have meetings in her bedroom. She had migraines. I think it was just a way of escaping the life there.

My favorite people were the newspapermen. You could have fun with them. The ambassador didn't want to have too much to do with the press, so it fell to the rest of us to take care of them. You had to have some kind of relations with them, if only because they were there asking questions all the time. We felt the best thing to do was to have entertainment. There was a lot of horseplay. The reporters would come back from Laos with the most outrageous stories about these nightclubs. The war there was supposed to be secret, because the CIA was running it. The reporters called it "the no-no war in the never-never land."

Then there were the beaches. The Vietnamese minister of economics used to invite us on these excursions. He had a little plane, the kind where you sit in bucket seats. We'd all troop out to the airport with our baskets and bathing suits. When the plane landed we'd be in an absolute fairyland, the most beautiful beaches you've ever seen. The Japanese ambassador and his wife used to walk up and down the beach, and you could see them saying, When the war is over, Japan will come in here and build hotels. You had a sense they were casing the joint.

One of the great beaches was on Con Son Island, where they had the prison camp with the tiger cages. We'd be having picnics and barbecued shrimp, and right over there were these prisoners being kept in caves. You could see the camp. You could go into the village and buy chopsticks carved by the prisoners. I brought hundreds of chopsticks back to the States, every time I went home.

I was given carte blanche to change the decor of the house. I spent months doing that. I often wonder who's living in it now. It was a French villa that had belonged to a banker, or somebody like that. It had a beautiful swimming pool and gorgeous gardens. Every Sunday there was water polo in the pool, and then a big barbecue.

We had a number-one maid, a number-two maid, a houseboy, and a cook. And endless gardeners. They just kept appearing. The servants would come out and serve drinks by the pool. The barbecue pit was an oil drum cut in half. Charcoal you got at the PX. It was exactly as if you were home, except more servants.

Menu-planning was the thing you looked forward to the most. It became part of this strange way of life. It might occupy you for a whole hour in the morning. Some of my cookbooks, when I pull them down to look up a recipe, I have written in the margin triple or quadruple the quantities, because we were feeding maybe forty people at these open houses. I had this marvelous old French-speaking Chinese cook. He looked like he was eighty, though I imagine he was fifty-eight or so. One of my great pleasures in life was teaching him how to cook American-style. Everybody served either French food, because the cooks were trained that way, or American food, because you could get anything at the PX. I finally realized we were being absolutely stupid. This guy could cook up the most dreamlike Vietnamese meals. But he wanted to learn how to cook American. I taught him chili, casseroles, hamburgers. I just loved seeing him out there flipping the hamburgers. It was fun, I have to admit.

I found Vietnamese women fascinating. Much stronger than the men. The women were often the real breadwinners of the family. They were lawyers and businesswomen and landowners, while the men dabbled in politics. I really admired the women. I had a frank talk once with the wife of a Vietnamese official. She was a business-woman. She made a lot of money. I doubt she was very scrupulous, but she was tough as nails. And boy, she kept that family together, because the husband was a charming, dilettantish type. After that I made it a point to study the whole phenomenon. Among the men, the North Vietnamese were obviously the strong ones. As you got farther south, they got a bit more namby-pamby. Then you got over to Cambodia, and they were even more so. By the time you got to Laos, they were the most feckless people I've ever met. Real push-overs. Laughed a lot. Fighting the no-no war in the never-never land. Our men would go off to inspect the war in their combat boots. When I'd visit Laos, this embassy wife and I used to sit over the breakfast table and howl with laughter as we saw our men off to the no-no war.

Some of the wives didn't feel the way I did, obviously. I was careful who I talked to. I don't know whether they were more loyal spouses or whether they had bought into the Foreign Service so completely that they felt it was wrong to have doubts about official policy. I do know that it was a lonely life. There were some nice and interesting people. But I felt hypocritical.

When our daughter came out—well, first she said she would never come, because she was so violently opposed to the war. She fought with her father every time he was home on leave. But she had a month's vacation, so she deigned to come and visit for Christmas. Of course she had a wonderful time. She's attractive, and she had all these young guys taking her here and there. But she wasn't going to shut her face—until I told her to. She used to sit up arguing with her

father. I didn't see any point in arguing, because I was always told—
and other wives were told the same thing—"You don't know what
you're talking about, because you don't see the cables." That's un-
answerable, of course. It's baloney, but it's what they believed. The
Foreign Service is very structured, and you get a little brainwashed.
I think a lot of the men really believed that what they were doing was
right. What kind of niggling doubts they had, I don't know. I kept
wondering why these men, whom I regarded as intelligent people,
didn't see that it wasn't working.

As a wife, you didn't go around criticizing what was happening. If
you didn't like it, you got out. And that's exactly what I did. I gave
up arguing with my husband. There's no point in going on and on
having the same argument. So when I had exhausted all possibilities
of trips—after I had gone to Calcutta three times, I had gone to Nepal
three times, I had gone to Bali—once I had done that, the only thing
to do was go home. Or sit there and argue and be more and more
unhappy. I got a chance to take a government plane. My mother was
ill, but not drastically. I just told the number-one servant that she
shouldn't be surprised if I didn't come back. She shrugged her shoulders. So I went, and I never came back. I felt it was the more honest
thing to do.

BILL CROWNOVER

*He is a tall, solidly built, dark-haired man in his early forties. He talks
in a great rush, the stories spilling over each other. We are in the
basement of a relative's home in a seedy neighborhood of Brooklyn.*

*"I went into the service in '66. I got drafted. After about three days
I enlisted and went to an electronics school in Fort Monmouth, New
Jersey. Spent a year in Thailand working in microwave communications. Then to Texas. Then to Italy. Left Italy in April of '70, got out
of the army, and saw the ad in September. The ad was for technicians
to go to Vietnam. I said, Yeah, I've never been to Vietnam. Let's check
this out. The people who were advertising were Federal Electric Corporation, over in Paramus. I went in for an interview: Sign on the
dotted line, we'll call you. Bang. I wait and I wait and I wait, never
hear a thing from them. Then I get a call between Christmas and New
Year's: Come on in again. I went down and filled out a little more
paperwork, and they said, 'We're gonna give you a call in about a
week.' Okay, great. On January 2, 1971: 'Your plane is leaving day
after tomorrow.'"*

• • •

It took me about a week to process in, and I ended up going to Tan Son Nhut. I'm standing there, and this guy's got a big board. "What'd you do in the service?" I was a 32-E, which is a fixed plant carrier repairman.

In the military, jobs were specialized, but when I got into FEC that all changed. They said, "Look, it used to take fifty people to run this site. We're doing it with ten. That means you wear all the hats." They also cut down the cost by not paying us much. I started off at under three dollars an hour. Plus they gave you ten dollars a day for living expenses. But you didn't pay any taxes.

I started working as an outage reporter. Whenever there was a circuit out we kept track of it. FEC had cost-plus, but the plus was variable. It seems that the higher your reliability rating was, the more money you got back. So it was very important that we not have too many outages. It was up to us that they had as high a rating as they could get. That's what the operations center was for.

Most of the time it was a case of, "If it's out, fake it. Don't tell us about it, just try to get it fixed." But sometimes you'd have a circuit logged out for days, or even weeks. You'd log it in, call up the subscriber, and have them check it out. It doesn't work. Okay. You log it back out. It was in for one minute, so you don't have a record of channel such-and-such being out for four days and sixteen hours. You can end one record of a log-out and start over again. It's only out for two days and eight hours, and then for another two days and eight hours. It adds up to the same total hours, but nobody looks at it that way.

The shifts were usually twelve hours. You worked three days, three nights, three off. Or two days, two nights, two off. If I was on nights, I'd come home from work in the morning and go straight to the bar. Skip the hotel. Tan Son Nhut is up at one end of Saigon. Halfway back to town was the American Legion Club. My hotel was all the way down on the waterfront, so rather than go down there and come back, I went right to the club. I generally got there about seven-thirty, had breakfast, and then the bar opened at eight. We'd sit there from eight until you got to the point that [imitates drunk with slurred speech] "Oh, in a couple hours gotta get up again. Guess I should get some sleep." But when I was working days I'd come back to the hotel, eat something, and then take off for the bars. I'd be at the bars by nine until whenever the curfew was.

I'd usually have just one meal a day. When I was working nights, I'd just have breakfast. You've got to remember all the calories in the alcohol. That was enough to keep me going. Vitamin deficiencies?

I guess I must have had a few. I always got vitamin C, though. I made a point of that. Somebody turned me on to salty dogs. A salty dog is a screwdriver made with pineapple juice and loads and loads of salt around the edge of the glass. It's bad news after a while, but that was my vitamin C.

I drank just about every day I was in Vietnam. I'd say easily a third of the people I worked with were heavy drinkers. Another third were quiet drinkers. They didn't get that excessive. Probably less than a third didn't drink that much at all. But if you didn't drink, what else was there to do? Go downtown and see a movie? Well, the Vietnamese loved Chinese movies. That's the blood and guts and kung fu. Or you could go back to the airbase, where they had a theater. And then there was the club, but what could you do in the club? Play the slot machines or drink or both.

I drank heavily. About a fifth a day. Which gets expensive downtown. You're talking about anywhere from twenty to twenty-five drinks a night at fifty cents a drink, toward the end. At the NCO club, drinks were a quarter. But I never drank at the military clubs in Saigon, because I'd rather drink downtown.

I drank bourbon, mostly. And the Ba Moui Ba beer. I loved that Ba Moui Ba. There was a week when I drank about half a case a day of that stuff, and one morning I got up, looked at my eyeballs, and they were yellow. I said, "Shit, gotta give up that Ba Moui Ba, I'm getting hepatitis." Yeah, that messed up my drinking for a while. Fucked up my liver. I didn't get hepatitis, but I was getting into alcohol poisoning. Getting cirrhosis. Very serious. I wasn't the only person who ended up like that. But I got off the Ba Moui Ba because it had a lot of formaldehyde in it. American booze was a bit easier on you. I think I should have gone to vodka instead of bourbon. But I liked that bourbon. Sure did.

I usually went to the same bar. It was right around the corner from Tu Do Street. I rarely drank on Tu Do. The GIs drank over there, and I drank at other bars where it was mainly civilians. There was a big separation. The girls were different, too. On Tu Do the girls were frantically hustling, and generally they were of lesser quality. Some of them could barely speak English. Just enough to say, "You buy me one tea," which the GIs might appreciate because they didn't have that much contact with girls, but since I'm down there every night of the week, I'm not going to sit there with someone whose only command of English is "You buy me one tea." And the bars for civilians didn't have the beggars and the people trying to sell you any old piece of junk, shoving it in your face.

The bar I went to was called Mimi's La Flamboyante. I believe

Mimi was half-French. She'd take off for France at least once a year. Owning the bar, she made fairly good money. I imagine she was into a lot of other things, too. She did get closed down once while I was there. They passed these laws that all these establishments were supposed to be closed. Propaganda, I guess it was. We're in a war situation, and we can't have all this frivolity, so all forms of entertainment are closed. They closed the movie theaters. I think dancing was banned the whole time I was there. Jukeboxes were illegal. A puritan society. Of course, none of the places closed. Everybody violated the law. But Mimi probably didn't pay the right person. Somebody screwed up somewhere. She might have pissed off some ARVN officer who was in there. But she had another place two blocks away, and she told everybody, "They closed us down here, that's where we'll be." So we just moved.

The quality of the girls in Mimi's was excellent. She must have had about ten of them. Three or four were half-Vietnamese, half-French. Really nice-looking. And generally well educated. One of them had gone to the university. They spoke English as well as French. These were strictly tea hustlers and that's the end of that.

The point of buying them tea was for conversation. The way it was set up—now, this is by the book—the girls were hostesses, and they were serving you. They were supposed to be on one side of the bar, with you on the other. The bars over there were usually very low. It's not like here, where you sit up on a big stool. You're sitting on a little low chair and the bar is no higher than your waist. The liquor is behind the bar on shelves like in an American bar. The way it would work is that the girl usually sat on your side of the bar. There was a lookout, and if he said, "Hey, somebody's coming," all the girls would suddenly get on the other side of the bar. The law said they were hostesses and had to stay on their side. Again, everybody knows what's going on, but officially this is it.

They got their share of tea out of me. I wouldn't say I was buying every night, but every two weeks or so I'd break down and spring for fifteen dollars' or twenty dollars' worth of tea. I'd say, "Well, give everybody a tea, what the hell." I knew them all and I didn't like to play favorites. But buying teas could get expensive. If you were sitting with a girl, she usually wanted one every fifteen or twenty minutes. If you were a good talker, you might get half an hour, but that was rare. I'd swear some of them watched the clock. I don't know what their quota was, but there was a certain amount of tea they had to push in one night. And since half of that went into their pocket, they were definitely on the lookout for as much as they could get. If you were slow in buying tea and somebody else walked in, the girl would say, "Excuse me," and off she'd go.

If you got there in the middle of the afternoon and there weren't that many people they could hustle tea from, you could sit down and play cards and have a good old time. I played rummy with them, double-deck solitaire, or we'd just sit there and help each other play solitaire.

The girls at Mimi's might take you to their place if you got to know them fairly well. They weren't prostitutes, not in the normal sense of the word. They weren't for hire for anyone who walked in off the street. Even on Tu Do, most times the girl had the final say, unless you went directly to the mamasan and said, "Hey, Mamasan, here's 10,000 P and I want that girl." In Mimi's not even the mamasan could put pressure on the girl. Because she'd just say to Mimi, "Hey, get lost, I'm gonna take a hike. You need me more than I need you." Like I said, they were very nice-looking girls.

I talked to the mamasan about it. She said, "They work here for their tea. What they do on their own time, that's up to them. I don't want it in the bar." Why? "Because say she goes with somebody and she gets all cut up. She's all scars. I'm not going to let her work here all scarred up, and I'm not going to pay. If I told her to go with somebody who did that, she'd come back to me and she'd want me dead. She'd say, 'Look what you did to me. You owe me.' So what the girls do, that's their own affair." She'd tell anybody that asked about it, "You want the girl, you talk to her. Don't talk to me. I have nothing to do with that. And whatever she gets paid, that's hers. Don't come back to me and complain about it."

You might have been able to get one of Mimi's girls for $150, $200. If it was available at all, they might do it for a healthy chunk of money. But it just wasn't their line of work. Of course, most of these girls had one or two special customers. I had semi-regular things with two of them on that kind of basis. I'd stop by the bar and say, "Are you doing anything tonight?" She'd say no, and I'd say, "Okay, I'll see you back at the apartment." She'd say okay and give me the key. I'd make my way down there. And sometime during the night she'd say, "Hey, look, buying tea is great, but it doesn't amount to much. You come up to my place, and I'm paying rent for this place. I need help with the food. There's clothes, laundry. . . ." She had the whole list of things that would make you feel bad. "Here you are, big rich American, living in this fancy hotel, and here I am living in a hovel." They were funny people. Role-playing, I suppose—they want to be one thing, but then again they want to be something else. And the last thing they want to be is a prostitute. So in the morning you just left a certain amount of money, which was to help defray expenses. What you were doing was giving them a gift. But they made sure they got the gift. You didn't dare leave without that gift.

Mostly I had the Honda girls, the cowboys' girls, that I picked up in front of the hotel. Meat on the hoof. The cowboys would come by on their Hondas with their girlfriends and you'd look them over. If you didn't like them you'd send them off and another crew would come around, until you finally found one that you liked. Say curfew was at eleven. At ten-thirty I'd be standing in front of the hotel as the meat market went by, just bullshitting with the cowboys. They were a bunch of crazy individuals. I'd see a girl I liked. "I'll take that one." It usually ran around ten dollars. The girl got five dollars and the guy on the motorcycle got five dollars.

One of the girls was an ex-singer who used to work at a classy bar a little farther downtown, near Cholon. She couldn't work—live entertainment was banned. So she says to me, "What am I going to do? I'm forced to do this for a living." For a while I was going pretty steady with her. I said, "You know, any time you've got nothing else to do, why don't you come on over?" "Well, I can't do that, I've gotta pay him off, too." "Yeah, well, no sweat, no big thing." I went on with her for three or four months. They finally opened up her club again, and she was telling me, "Next week I go back to work." "Oh, great, great." "Come down and see me and I get you A-number-one table and all the food and everything on me." But I never did show up. I said to myself, Well, really, I don't mind patronizing her, but I don't want her patronizing me. [Laughs.]

It's true, it's the Ugly American syndrome. Very common over there. I fell victim to it unintentionally. Like when I'd get in fights. One night I walked into my hotel and I decided, "To hell with this place. It's too far away from the main strip." It was about six blocks away, a long walk. I'd had quite a few drinks and I went up to the night clerk and said, "Okay, make up a bill and I'm leaving in the morning." He started to fill out the bill. I guess I was a little irate about something, I don't know, and I yelled and screamed at him. He's trying to figure out the figures, and he gave me a bill that came to about $150. I said, "You're full of shit, I paid the fucking bill day before yesterday, it shouldn't come to more than about twenty-five dollars." He started saying that all he could do is look at the records as they are right now, and I just hauled off and belted him. So he gave me some little-boy-lost look and said something to me, I don't know what it was, and I ended up pounding the piss out of him. I went up to my room. The next morning I came down and the guy I had beaten up was sitting there with his face all swollen up. I gave him a dirty look and walked out. I came back after work and the manager of the hotel called me over and said, "I think your bill is ready, and unfortunately I don't think you can stay at this hotel anymore." "Oh, fine, hell, I was gonna get the hell out of here anyway." I picked up my bags, which were waiting for me, all packed up—they had taken care of that—and I moved out.

There was another incident that nearly got me seriously hurt. One night I was in front of the hotel looking over the meat wagon, and I ended up with a dog. I mean a super dog. She didn't want to do anything in bed. And of course it's already paid for. In Vietnam, it's always cash first, before anything else. Then she started telling me she's pregnant. I said, "Then what the hell are you doing selling yourself if you can't do anything?" She starts to cry, giving me all this stuff, she needs the money. I said, "You may need the money, but listen, that's not my problem. Get out." "Where am I gonna go?" I said, "Well, shit, don't tell me I'm gonna pay you for nothing and you're gonna sleep in my room and I don't get anything at all out of this deal." Generally we'd spend the whole night, because once there was curfew they can't go back out on the street. It was kind of late, toward curfew time, which is why I'd ended up with her. My usual girls didn't show up. They were already occupied somewhere else. And I must have been in worse shape than I thought I was, because I remember now what she looked like. Oh, man, what a dog this was. I'm not kidding.

Anyhow, I finally got her to get dressed and I got her in a hammerlock and threw her out the door. I don't mean I pushed her out, I mean I threw her out. I got the door locked and she's banging on it, she wants to come back in. I'm saying, "I don't give a shit where you go. Sleep down in the lobby with the clerks. I'm not paying you to get nothing and let you sleep in my bed anyway, with my air conditioning. Fuck you, girl, get going."

Well, that had repercussions later, because it made the cowboys mad at me. I was out drinking at Mimi's and I got all drunked up. I was leaving on vacation in a couple of days. Anyway, who needed an excuse to drink? I didn't. I got good and screwed up. I'm walking back to the hotel on Nguyen Hue Boulevard. Four lanes in the middle, and two islands and two more lanes. I made my way across and I'm crossing between the islands, which had these little kiosks on them, and going across the last lane to my hotel. There are taxis coming by. Now, I'm a New Yorker from way back. You judge the distance and the speed right, and you can practically walk right behind the car as it's going by. Well, this guy swerved toward me and damn near got my toes, so I rapped him on the roof. He stopped and backed up, yapping something at me. I told him to get fucked and keep going, I didn't need any damn taxi. He's yelling at me and he gets out of the cab, and I think, Uh-oh—c'mon, I've taken on a lot of you guys, I'll get you, too. He's saying something to me and I'm saying something to him, and it's getting uglier and uglier. Another guy stands up over here. I said, Ah, shit, now I've got two of them. By this time I've backed up so that the kiosks are over here and the hotel is behind me. I said, "C'mon, I don't give a shit, I'll take you both on." Well, about that time something got me upside the head. I didn't know what the hell happened. So I said, "Well, c'mon, you motherfuckers, I'll still take you on. That little shot in the head, man, that ain't gonna hurt in the least." Then I felt something, bang, in the back. I said, Shit, I know what that is, the motherfuckers are throwing rocks at me. Let 'em throw rocks. I don't give a shit. Then I turned a little bit and out of the corner of my eye I could see about sixteen people behind me. All the cowboys and the girls, motorcycles starting and motorcycles zipping off, and people behind me with sticks and chains. I was only about twenty feet from the hotel, about even with it in the middle of the street. I said, What the hell do I do? So I fake at this guy, and he turns away. I go for the taxi driver but he jumps in the cab and takes off. I start running one way and they all follow me, so I just pull a U-turn and, *pop*, get into the hotel and they can't cut me off. Great. Having a ball.

I said, "Motherfuckers assaulted me out there! Goddamn sons of bitches!" I go to the hotel clerk and tell him I want to call the police, because I don't like being assaulted in the street. He's saying, "What are you talking about? You're the one out there making all the noise." And some guy I vaguely know is standing by the elevator, and he says, "You're bleeding." The only thing that really hurt was my head, where I got hit by a two-by-four. I've got so much alcohol in me that it hurts, yeah, but not that bad. I said, "Well, what the hell is a little blood? I don't see anything." And he said, "No, it's not your head, it's your back." I looked down and said, "Oh, my God." There was blood all the way down my leg. I'm bleeding like a stuck pig. Then look out, here come the MPs. They run me down to the hospital and I get sewed up. I think it was four stitches. Some guy had stabbed me, probably with a stiletto. Shoved it straight in. It felt like a rock but it was bleeding like hell. I'm on the table and the guy looks in and says, "Ah, you're all right. They missed everything. Went right into the fat. But pretty deep." He says, "If you start getting blood in your urine, come on back."

So that's how it was. There were times when I'd say, I know what I'm doing and I still don't care, by God. I *am* an Ugly American. There was the feeling of superiority. Here I am, I've got my job and my money and you've gotta come to me on your hands and knees. It's not really that way, but it's a mental outlook that the American is better than all these Vietnamese. For Christ's sake, the Americans had to come over and help the Vietnamese fight their own goddamn fucking war. It was just a pervasive attitude, you couldn't get away from it, and there were times when you'd have an outbreak. You would get arrogant with them. Like when you started making fun of the way Vietnamese would speak English. Which wasn't fair, because you didn't speak Vietnamese at all, and at least he's trying. I'd say to myself, Yeah, but anybody that's trying to rook an American—and of course any Vietnamese was out to rook an American—the least he could do is speak the language well. I mean, after all, he's getting paid very highly for it. [Laughs.]

I don't regret anything. Well, regret . . . I sometimes say, Gee, I really wish I didn't do that, but it's only a minor regret. I'm sorry I did it. Some of the hard times I gave people. Generally being obnoxious—to girls, hotel employees, taxi drivers, supervisors, guards at the gate. Sometimes you say, Well, could I have done it a little differently?

I think everybody was that way. I'm a fucking American and you're a goddamn gook, so you've got no right to talk to me. Damn silly stupid geeks. Zips. Slopes. Of course, you're in this hazy world, drinking all the time, working all the time, running into the same people all the time. And to you personally as an American it seems the Orientals have their own way of thinking, which they do. They have their own culture, which isn't yours, and you realize, man, they just don't do it this way back in the real world. The terminology, too, will screw you up. "The real world," because you're out here in never-never land, and it doesn't matter what you do in never-never land because it doesn't affect the real world. You very rarely referred to the Vietnamese as Vietnamese. The zips, always the zips. Zips could mean zipper-heads, because someone unzipped his head and dumped all his brains out. Or it could mean zero, which means nothing, which is what they were. The zip mentality. Zip, zip, zip, zip, zip. It was a beautiful word.

BOOK THREE

LIFTOFF

★

BOOK THREE

LEIPOLD

CHRONOLOGY
1970–1975

<u>1970</u>

April 30: American and South Vietnamese troops invade Cambodia to destroy the base areas near the border.

May 4: Four students are shot dead by National Guardsmen at Kent State University. More than 400 college campuses across the U.S. shut down in protest.

May 14: Two students are killed by police at Jackson State College in Mississippi.

October 7: Nixon publicly proposes a "standstill cease-fire," but it is hedged with so many conditions that North Vietnam rejects the idea.

<u>1971</u>

February 8: In a test of Vietnamization, South Vietnamese troops strike into Laos. They are beaten decisively.

April 24: More than 200,000 demonstrators march in Washington.

June 13: *The New York Times* begins publishing excerpts from a massive Pentagon study of Vietnam policy that comes to be known as "The Pentagon Papers."

June: Both the House and the Senate pass nonbinding resolutions calling for withdrawal of all U.S. troops from Vietnam by the end of the year.

October 3: Running unopposed, Thieu is reelected president of South Vietnam.

1972

February 21: Nixon visits China.

March 30: North Vietnam launches a major offensive on three fronts in South Vietnam. After initial advances the attack stalls, thanks largely to bombing by U.S. planes, including B-52s. But the NVA hold Quang Tri until September, and the Viet Cong make big gains in the Mekong delta as ARVN troops are rushed elsewhere. President Nixon orders massive bombing raids on North Vietnam.

May 8: Nixon announces the mining of Haiphong and other ports in North Vietnam.

June 17: The Watergate burglary goes awry and its five perpetrators are arrested, beginning the process that eventually leads to Nixon's downfall.

August 1: Kissinger and Le Duc Tho resume talks in Paris. The North Vietnamese seem to back away from their demand that Thieu resign before a settlement is possible.

August 11: The last U.S. ground combat troops leave Vietnam. Some 60,000 airmen, advisers, and support personnel remain.

October 8: Le Duc Tho makes the proposal that becomes the final outline for a settlement: a cease-fire in place, after which U.S. troops would withdraw and POWs would be repatriated. A "National Council of Reconciliation" would be created to work out a political accord. In late October, President Thieu rejects the deal, largely because it leaves North Vietnamese troops in place in South Vietnam.

November 7: Nixon defeats Senator George McGovern in the U.S. presidential election.

November 20: Kissinger and Le Duc Tho resume talks, but they soon break down in the face of "amendments" to the agreement insisted on by Thieu.

December 18: Nixon orders massive bombing raids on Hanoi and Haiphong. The "Christmas bombing" lasts for eleven days, excluding Christmas day itself.

1973

January 8: Kissinger and Le Duc Tho meet again and eventually make a deal almost identical to the one negotiated in October. Thieu reluctantly goes along.

January 27: The peace accords are formally signed.

February–March: North Vietnam repatriates 590 U.S. POWs.

March 29: Departure of the last U.S. troops in Vietnam. Some 150,000 NVA soldiers remain in the South. Heavy skirmishing continues between them and the South Vietnamese.

June 24: Graham Martin replaces Ellsworth Bunker as ambassador to South Vietnam.

August: Congress votes to prohibit any further U.S. combat role in Vietnam, Cambodia, and Laos.

1974

January–May: Any semblance of a cease-fire in South Vietnam ends.

August 9: President Nixon resigns; Gerald Ford takes office.

August: Father Tran Huu Thanh begins his anticorruption campaign, accusing President Thieu of enriching himself illegally.

December: NVA troops attack in Phuoc Long province.

1975

January 6: The Communists take Phuoc Binh, capital of Phuoc Long province. It is the first time an entire South Vietnamese province has fallen since Quang Tri in 1972.

March 10: General Van Tien Dung begins what is to become the final offensive by attacking Ban Me Thuot in the central highlands. The city falls immediately.

March 14: President Thieu orders his generals to abandon the highlands, setting off a chaotic retreat toward the coast.

March 30: Fall of Danang.

April 1: The evacuation of American civilians in Saigon begins on a small scale and builds up gradually.

April 16: Phnom Penh falls to the Khmer Rouge.

April 21: Thieu resigns.

April 29: The North Vietnamese begin shelling Tan Son Nhut airport, effectively putting an end to the large-scale evacuation of Americans and South Vietnamese.

April 30: The North Vietnamese take Saigon, and the war ends.

14

THE LONG GOOD-BYE

By the time President Richard M. Nixon took the oath of office on January 20, 1969, some 30,000 Americans had died in Vietnam. He had run promising to "de-Americanize" the war and make peace. During his first term, 25,000 more GIs were killed and 100,000 were wounded. The Vietnamese on both sides suffered huge losses. The war expanded into Cambodia, with unimaginable horrors to come. Yet Nixon, in a sense, kept his promise. Our boys did come home. And he made peace—at least for the U.S.

The policy was called "Vietnamization," a polite way of saying "our guns, your bodies." Nixon recognized that the American public was losing patience with the long bloodletting. But for much the same reasons as Eisenhower, Kennedy, and Johnson before him, he would not accept the "loss" of South Vietnam. The only course was to withdraw the troops gradually, do everything possible to give the South a fighting chance, and try to make a deal with the North. That process took four years. The glacial pace caused bitter protest, and Nixon's efforts to stamp it out led to Watergate and his own downfall.

Ironically, as General Elvy Roberts and General John Cushman report in this chapter, the withdrawal began at a time when American troops had driven the enemy from much of South Vietnam. Both men had done previous tours, so they had a basis for comparison; and in 1969–70 they found the country a changed place. Cushman says of the Mekong delta: "The government had control of more territory. The infrastructure of government services was more extensive. . . . By 1970 we had really begun to make pacification work." Roberts is exaggerating, but not outrageously, when he says, "South Vietnam in the fall and winter of 1969 was virtually pacified. The military part of the war was won." One reason for the success was sheer numbers: In June of 1969, U.S. troop strength peaked at 543,000. That many men, with their formidable planes, tanks, and cannon, were bound to have some impact. The Tet offensive had largely destroyed the local guerrillas, and the Phoenix program had started to wreak havoc on the Viet Cong village apparatus. The invasion of Cambodia in 1970, while politically disastrous for Nixon, further set back the Communists' ability to fight.

From the grunts' point of view, of course, things looked different. The Tet offensive was the turning point. While the brass rightly saw it as a major victory, what the grunts saw was an entire nation rising up against them in the night. After Tet, the GIs instinctively knew the war could not be won, and Vietnamization only confirmed that view. The U.S. was headed home; the despised ARVN would fight on if it could; the point now was to avoid becoming "the last GI to die in Vietnam." Morale disintegrated. An anonymous MP stationed at Long Binh remembers near-universal drug use. Pete Mahony, a newly minted lieutenant "advising" a Vietnamese battalion, details the mental gymnastics necessary to avoid thinking about what was going on around him. A 1971 report by Colonel Robert Heinl, entitled *The Collapse of the Armed Forces*, said, "By every conceivable indicator, our army that now remains in Vietnam is in a state approaching collapse, with individual units avoiding or having refused combat, murdering their officers and noncommissioned officers, drug-ridden and dispirited where not near-mutinous."

Even General Cushman, a positive thinker if there ever was one, had his doubts about the long term: "It just seemed to me that Vietnamization was moving awfully fast."

Naturally, the real price for Vietnamization was paid by the Vietnamese. Hugh Manke, an IVS volunteer who spent four years incountry before being kicked out, describes a society "crumbling." Sweeping draft calls, soaring inflation and taxes, higher casualties, more refugees, political unrest, hit squads in the villages, hordes of disabled veterans—the burdens on South Vietnam grew heavier as the Americans left.

Meanwhile, Henry Kissinger played a marathon game of chess with a patient and steely negotiating opponent, Le Duc Tho. Kissinger's position could hardly have been worse: Year by year, his pieces kept vanishing from the board, as public opinion forced Nixon to withdraw more troops. The North Vietnamese knew that all they had to do was stall, and stall they did. Finally, in October 1972, having failed to win a smashing victory with the Easter offensive, Le Duc Tho made his breakthrough offer. The North would agree to let Thieu stay in power pending a political settlement, and would release the American POWs. The U.S., in turn, would bring home its few remaining soldiers and agree to let Communist troops stay in place in the South. Predictably, Thieu balked, sensing that the deal amounted to a death sentence for South Vietnam. When Kissinger presented Thieu's objections, the North recoiled, suspecting a double-cross. Nixon's response was Operation Linebacker II: unleashing the B-52s over Hanoi, Haiphong, and the Red River valley.

Both Americans who approve of the "Christmas bombing" and those who abhor it tend to exaggerate its effects. Dana Drenkowski, who flew an F-4 Phantom escorting the B-52s, thinks the punishment forced North Vietnam back to the table: "Five days later they met in Paris. Twenty days later everything was signed. Sixty days later the POWs came home. All as a result of Linebacker II." But the final treaty hardly differed from the October accords. The real purpose of the bombing campaign may have been to reassure Thieu—a bit of muscle-flexing to show that his big brother would stick by him in future. Nor did the B-52s carpet-bomb Hanoi, as antiwar activists charged. In fact, given the tonnage dropped and the North's fierce antiaircraft defenses, which made accurate bombing more difficult, the bombers were highly precise in hitting military and industrial targets. Telford Taylor, who was in Hanoi, came away convinced that the hospital and neighborhoods he saw leveled were "mistakes." Still, some 1,600 civilians died, according to the North.

So the American war ended with a spasm of firepower and an explosion of patriotism as the POWs came home. The troops went back to the World, too—except for several thousand who stayed on in various civilian guises.

But for Vietnam there was no end. The "leopard spot" arrangement, whereby both sides controlled the territory they held at the cease-fire, guaranteed further fighting. The Americans had urged Thieu to grab as much of the countryside as he could, which left his troops spread thin. The ARVN continued to lose 1,000 killed every month. And while the U.S. poured $2 billion worth of arms and equipment into South Vietnam in just six weeks at the end of 1972, the cutback afterward was drastic: In 1974 the country received only $1 billion in military aid, compared with $30 billion a year at the peak of the American effort.

South Vietnam had not been entirely abandoned. But Thieu and his cohorts could be excused for feeling insecure.

LIEUTENANT GENERAL ELVY B. ROBERTS

He looks patrician: tall, thin, white-haired, blue-eyed, with a kindly face and a soft Southern accent. He wears a dark blue pin-striped suit. But the look is deceptive. He grew up in a little Kentucky town, and he entered West Point in 1939 partly because he couldn't afford medical school. After graduation, infantry school, and airborne training, he parachuted into Normandy on D-Day. When the war ended, he stayed with airborne units. His first Vietnam tour came in 1965, as a brigade commander with the 1st Air Cavalry. He went back in 1968 with the 9th Division, and again in 1969, this time as the 1st Cav commander.

We talk in his corner office on the twentieth floor of a San Francisco skyscraper, commanding a panoramic view of the bay. Insurance is his business now.

I thought Vietnamization was great. Y'see, when we first went in in '65, our mission was to fight a war. We went in to get it over with. As things progressed, it became apparent that we had to help the South Vietnamese stand up on their own two feet. We couldn't stay there forever. It was going to take a lot of time. So I endorsed Vietnamization strongly, and I believe that if we had been able to carry out what was supposed to be the underpinning for the program, it would have succeeded. If we had supplied the South on the scale that was visualized at the time, if we had made it a war they could handle themselves, it would have worked.

So in 1969, my mission was to help Vietnamize the war. My principal effort over a whole 280-mile front of jungle was training and airlifting two ARVN infantry divisions and the ARVN Armored Cavalry Regiment. From October of '69, there were few operations that the 1st Cav launched without the South Vietnamese. We'd provide the lift for them, the artillery support, the gunship support they liked so well. We gave them medical evacuation support. General Dong moved his headquarters right in beside mine. One infantry division's headquarters were some ten kilometers away, and there wasn't a day that we didn't visit back and forth. We began to get a mutual confidence and a mutual understanding, and we got more out of 'em.

It was a totally different war from 1965. When I first went to Vietnam, the South Vietnamese army was losing about a battalion a week. A lot of it was casualties, a lot was desertions. If we hadn't gone in, they wouldn't have survived probably more than a few months. The Viet Cong had a very deep hold. They had control of everything in the countryside. And, of course, the South Vietnamese had been fighting that war for a long time, and they were running out of steam. So it was absolutely essential, if one believed that South Vietnam was worth saving, for U.S. forces to go in.

But by the fall of 1969, we had virtual control of the jungle in some of the roughest areas of Vietnam. We ranged over Tay Ninh province, the Cambodian border, the Parrot's Beak, and north in Phuoc Long province and east to Long Kanh and Binh Long provinces. We went in and rooted out the bunkers, rooted out their command centers, carved out trails, knocked out holes in the jungle where we could deploy people. We'd take people out in small platoons, set 'em down with five days' rations, ammunition, and water, and they'd operate the same way the Viet Cong had been operating. Then I'd pick 'em up, take 'em back, give 'em two days' rest, and send another unit out. I had groups working all over the jungle in War Zones C and D. We did have some casualties from time to time, but compared to what military operations normally are, it was very encouraging.

Our basic mission was Vietnamization. But that's not to say that the 1st Cav didn't have some sharp fights in supporting ARVN units during 1969 and early 1970. We did—and the officers and troops were splendid. I took command in late March, and the Cav had just been moved down from I Corps to work around Tay Ninh and Phuoc Long. This had been Viet Cong territory for a long, long time. The district chiefs were living in bunkers, never getting out. When I first went in, I was shocked by some of the atrocities that the Viet Cong had committed. I personally saw when a village chief's whole family had been strung up and gutted the night before. I went out to visit the district chief, and when I landed, he said, "I'd like to show you something." The family was tied to poles and gutted. Children. Wife. But by the beginning of 1970, the people along the Song Be River were having Sunday picnics in places where we had some very difficult fighting earlier.

The Communists had been so ground down that our area was almost pacified. We could do anything we wanted in the field. The North Vietnamese could not mount a military effort that was worthy of the name. It was pitiful—the people coming down the Ho Chi Minh Trail were just kids, really, fourteen-, fifteen-, sixteen-year-olds. I had my groups out in the jungle, and as soon as these guys would come across the border, we'd grab 'em. Then my people would interview them, and I used to sit in sometimes. I'd ask them how much training they had. They'd say they'd been inducted just a few weeks before they hit out on the trail. They had fired their weapons a few times, not many. They were given a rifle and a bag of rice, and they'd head south. That goes to show that the North Vietnamese were in terrible shape. They had exhausted their reserves in Hanoi. They were hanging on by the skin of their teeth.

We were picking up letter carriers every day coming out of Hanoi and down the trail. And from the spring of 1970 on, all the mail was pleading with the units and the party cadre not to get engaged in military ground action at all. They realized they couldn't sustain it. They were too weak. The letters said, "We're winning the war at the conference table in Paris, so don't fight the Americans."

The military part of the war was won. The situation after Tet was ideal. I never understood why Tet was pictured as a victory for the Communists, which it wasn't at all. It was the greatest defeat. It was just like Hitler's debacle in the Ardennes in 1944. That was pictured at the time to be a great defeat for the U.S. forces, but it turned out to be the key that shortened the war, because the Germans expended all their combat effort in the Ardennes rather than fighting in the homeland. Well, after Tet the North Vietnamese and Viet Cong effort went right down. And the South Vietnamese were starting to get their underpinnings. We trained a whole lot of 'em. Their young captains watched how our company commanders worked, and they learned.

We got the ARVN to be more aggressive. I think they got shamed into it, really. We never completely succeeded, but they improved a great deal. One way was to get them away from their compounds and out into areas where they had to fight. Because if you get a man's back up against a wall, he has to fight. Another way was to get the commanders out in the field. When a South Vietnamese unit would get involved, I'd generally get in my helicopter and go get the division commander or the regimental commander and take him right up to the scene. This was something that early on had never been done. I had 'em right up in these real hostile places where they were surrounded. Many times we had to go in under fire. But he'd see it could be done. We'd land him right in there. They didn't like this very much, but after they got used to it . . . [Laughs.]

I was supposed to leave Vietnam on the first of May, 1970. I had completed my one-year tour, my third year in Vietnam. On the twenty-sixth of April I got word from General Abrams to prepare a plan for the invasion of Cambodia. The order came from Washington. The mission was to destroy the large depots and tunnels that had been built up on the other side of the border, and buy two years of time for the South Vietnamese army, so we could withdraw our troops and let them pull up their bootstraps and fight the war by themselves.

We knew exactly where the depots were. My pilots were a gung-ho bunch, and they'd see these long convoys of trucks coming down on the other side of the Cambodian border. From time to time they'd get an itchy finger and shoot up a few of 'em. Within hours, before I even knew it happened, General Abrams would be on the telephone to me, saying, "Elvy, goddamn it, your people shot up another convoy over there in Cambodia." I'd say, "Really? I don't know anything about it." Well, when it would happen the word would go directly from Cambodia to Hanoi, and directly over to Le Duc Tho in Paris and from him to Kissinger or somebody, to Washington, and it was on the command and control line back to Abrams within two hours. This happened frequently.

So we knew where the big depots were hidden under the trees, and where they were bringing all these trucks in. It was a very simple matter to plan the operation. Since we were Vietnamizing the war, we decided early on that this would be a basically ARVN operation, supported by the 1st Cav. We prepared a plan to go in using the ARVN Airborne Division, the 5th ARVN Mechanized Division, the 5th ARVN Infantry Division, and an ARVN armored cavalry regiment, plus the U.S. 11th Armored Cavalry and my 1st Cav. The initial effort would be made by two brigades of the airborne division. But we didn't have any idea if this plan was going off, because we'd been trying to get authority to go into Cambodia for three or four years without success.

We had a conventional sort of Leavenworth plan, a typical airborne operation. You put the airborne down behind the area and the armor coming in. The mechanized division on one side, another division on the other. Encircle the whole area, seal it off. My armored cavalry regiment, which was attached to the 1st Cav, and the Vietnamese armored cavalry would make a pincer movement. Simple type of thing.

We prepared the plan on Saturday evening, the twenty-sixth of April. Went back the next day and presented it to General Abrams, who approved it. I don't think he had any notion it would be implemented either. [Laughs.] It was sent back to Washington, and I went back to doing what I had been doing, paying no attention to this. My successor had already been named.

About three on Tuesday morning, General Abrams called me on the secure telephone and said, "Elvy, they want to know in Washington whether you will extend your tour in Vietnam." I said, "Well, if they want me to extend, if it's necessary, I would. What's it all about?" He said, "I'll be damned if I know, but it probably has something to do with this plan we sent back there yesterday."

He called back four hours later and said, "Elvy, you are authorized to go over and tell only General Do Cao Tri." He was the III ARVN Corps commander. All the troops I was using were under his command. There were around 50,000 troops all told. I went over and told him we'd been directed to conduct this operation. He liked the plan. He was a real fighter. He was one Vietnamese officer who was really, really good. He was delighted.

Then he said, "When's it supposed to go?" Somewhere in there I had gotten word it was being contemplated for the first of May. He went over and pulled out a drawer and took out a little red book. Looked in it, and said, "General Roberts, I can't go on the first of May. My horoscope says that anything I am involved with on the first four days of May will be an absolute disaster. We'll have to get it postponed to the fifth."

So I got on the secure telephone to Abrams and told him what Do Cao Tri had said. Abrams said, "Well, I'll be damned, they'll never believe this in Washington." About three hours after that, he was on the phone: "Elvy, orders from the highest level that you will go back to Do Cao Tri and tell him that he will go on the first of May. It cannot be postponed."

I went back and told him, "The highest authority of the United States wants you to command this operation, and there cannot be any more delay than the first of May." Tri said to me, "General Roberts, I have great confidence in you. We've worked together, and I know you'll take as good care of my troops as you do your own. I will not command the operation. I will not even go into the operation. But I will turn over all my troops to you. And I'll do nothing. Because anything I do will be a disaster." So I went back, called Abrams. [Laughs.] A few hours later the word came: "By order of Washington, General Roberts will command all the forces, and we will go on the first of May." That's how I ended up in command of the whole Cambodia operation.

Then it really got into high gear. I was like a one-armed paper-hanger, running from here to there to get the logistics tied in, get the senior ARVN commanders tied in, coordinate our units and the South Vietnamese. It was a difficult operation to mount, because normally, when you launch an attack, you concentrate your troops. But we didn't want advance word to leak, which it almost always did. So we didn't brief any of the South Vietnamese troops. The division commanders all knew, and on the day before the operation, the regimental commanders knew. My helicopter commanders knew what was going on. The whole concept of the operation was that no troops would have to concentrate. My pilots were so well trained by this time that we could pick up a company here, a company there, all around, and then mass in the air. So there were very few people who even knew about the operation.

The night before the operation, my chief of staff came in and said, "There's four operations analysis people out there, two from Washington and two from Saigon. They say they've got to talk to you." I told him, "You handle that, I don't have time to talk to these people." He said, "No, they say they can only talk to you, and I can't even be present in the room." So I said, "All right, I'll give 'em fifteen minutes."

They came in, and the message they brought me was that they had war-gamed our operation on the machines. They programed in certain factors and so forth, and every time they had done it, both in Washington and Saigon, it came out that I would lose at least 40 percent of my helicopters. Well, 40 percent of my helicopters, which we were loading with twelve to fifteen ARVN soldiers, that's an awful lot of casualties. So I asked them the parameters they used to come up with this. They told me they knew about all the machine guns and anti-aircraft weapons in the Parrot's Beak area. I said, "What altitude did you program us in at?" By that time the war had ground down to the point where most of the flying was at 1,500 feet, because there was very little resistance and you didn't have to get down at treetop level. They said, "We programed you in at 1,500 feet." The only people that knew we were going in at treetop were my assistant division commander, Bob Shoemaker, and a few others on the division staff. Well, I knew from then on that these people didn't have anything that would influence me. I heard them out, and in fifteen minutes they were on their way. I just said, "We're into this operation, it's been ordered, so we can't back away from it." They thought I was another crazed cavalryman, I suppose.

On May 1 we attacked. And the operation was extraordinarily successful. It was probably the most successful large combat operation that was launched in conjunction with the South Vietnamese, because the security was so good. We used basically all ARVN forces in the initial assaults. We brought a brigade of the 1st Cav in late in the afternoon, just to keep up the pattern that we always worked together. As a measure of the success, there were more people killed on the campus of Kent State on the fourth of May than we lost in the whole operation—Americans, that is. The South Vietnamese had a few more casualties.

It was a walk in the sun. We knew what we were doing, we knew where to suppress the fire, and the fighting capability of the North Vietnamese in that area was nil. All of 'em were units that had been clobbered while they were in South Vietnam and had pulled back to rest. So we met very sparse resistance. It was quickly overrun. Within two days we were deep into the depots. Within three days we were up to the thirty-mile limit that Washington had put on the operation. Then it was just a question of capturing these ragtag units.

Needless to say, I don't think we had any lift helicopters shot down. We may have lost one or two gunships. But it was very, very light, considering the magnitude of the operation. We went in at treetop level, and all their ammunition was being fired at holes in the sky, because they couldn't see us. We just ignored it, and took out the guns later with the ground troops.

We got right into the depots. We found exactly what we had reported to be there. These depots were well shielded with bunkers. Very thick coverings of dirt. Big underground installations. As a result of that operation, we took out weapons, equipment, supplies, anti-aircraft guns, personnel carriers that were stashed over there. Our mission was to buy two years' time, but we actually bought about three years. They couldn't demonstrate any military capability in that area until '73 or early '74. In '74 they really came boiling out in the same old areas, War Zones C and D, and they had some heavy fights around Tay Ninh and Quan Loi.

To make matters worse, in late '73 or early '74 a delegation from Congress went over to assess progress. They came back with a report that there should be no further military equipment or support for South Vietnam. Well, if you bounce that off the fact that the Russians were equipping them with very modern stuff, it was inevitable what was going to happen in '75.

But the Cambodia operation did what it was supposed to. It was an incursion oriented toward the logistics of the North Vietnamese. And also to boost the morale of the ARVNs, give 'em a successful operation that wasn't too costly. One that was supposed to have been directed by them. From that standpoint, it was worth it, it was valid, it was a good operation.

At the time, I knew very little about the reaction in the States. Frank Reynolds, the ABC News guy, spent some time traveling around with me. I think he told me about Kent State. He said the campuses were aflame with the reaction to what was going on. I didn't know the details. And I didn't spend a lot of time worrying about it. As far as I was concerned, I was looking into the eyes of a smashing success.

But y'know, there must be something in the horoscope. I don't believe in horoscopes, but Do Cao Tri took command of the operation on the fifth of May. By that time we had gotten into all the depots, with thousands and thousands of tons of ammunition, weapons, tanks. And the ARVNs were having a heyday. They'd never seen so much stuff. They were doing great. But Tri's horoscope must have been off a little bit. The following February his helicopter was shot down, and he was killed along with his whole staff.

ANONYMOUS

He is a doctor who has just finished his internship. His Greenwich Village apartment has a collegiate feel: magazines scattered about, a softball glove on the couch, and large paintings, reminiscent of Matisse, on the walls. They turn out to have been painted by his mother.

His father is a navy admiral. "The war was a sore point between me and my father. When I was growing up in Washington, there was an Admirals' Row where the kids were divided into two camps—those that were going to be like Daddy, and those that were very involved in getting hip. I was in the latter camp. I was very rebellious. I had nothing but disrespect for the military, for the straight aspects of our society, and for the power structure. So there were arguments. I was an adolescent and I had two older sisters, and we were all antiwar. My father was someone who early in the war was strategically opposed to a land war in Asia, but as it evolved and became less and less popular, he closed ranks with his peers and was very much in favor of it. To this day he will say that he thinks it was one of America's finest hours, the attempt to help the Vietnamese. He was chief of personnel for a while, and he had to have lunch with the wives of prisoners of war. So he was working hard and under a lot of stress. He felt pretty betrayed by his own family.

"That probably had a lot to do with my going into the army. I was in college, and my academic outlook wasn't good because I wasn't doing any work. In December of 1968 I was suspended for 'flagrant academic neglect.' Then I was stuck with: Well, what do you do now? You're going to be reclassified 1-A unless you eat bananas and have a bowel movement on the recruiter's table or something. Or go back to school, which I could have done if I'd stayed at home, and I wasn't into that. So I floundered around and talked to people, and decided that I would embrace a cathartic experience. I would go ahead and get it over with, start as soon as possible.

"After going through basic training they made me a military police-

man, since I didn't have a jail record. I still wonder if my dad had something to do with it, but I don't think it's the sort of thing he would have done. Anyway, they assigned me to guard duty at Fort Holabird in Maryland. And it was boring. *Pretty soon I started feeling, 'Hey, to hell with this.' Because I worked with people that came back from Vietnam, and a lot of them said, 'Fuck this shit, man. I'm putting in to go back over there.' Vietnam was basically more exciting. More free. I think I hungered for that. I certainly had no interest in fighting the Vietnamese.*

"So I volunteered to go to Vietnam. And I was turned down. The provost marshal had decided he didn't have enough MPs. I thought that was totally absurd, that anybody who volunteered to go to Vietnam would be turned down, since there were obviously so many people who didn't want to go. So I called my father and told him I'd volunteered and been turned down. He had dinner with the commanding general of the continental U.S. Army, who pulled the string and had my orders changed."

When we landed, the thing that really struck me, getting out at Bien Hoa, was the appearance of the veterans who were getting ready to leave. I remember a lot of blacks, very tall, they all looked like basketball players. They were all wearing very faded jungle fatigues with a lot of headbands, Black-Power jewelry, incredibly faded jungle boots, and they were all giving dap. *Dap* was the Vietnamese word for beautiful, and it was this way of shaking hands. It's like this. [Demonstrates complicated handshake.] There were about ten guys that were giving this ritualized form of greeting, which I did a lot of in the next seven and a half months. I was just so blown away by these guys, they were so impressive. The most impressive thing, besides the fact that they all looked so physically powerful, was that they all looked so experienced. They all had M-16s slung across their shoulders, and it was like a whole new culture. I had just left a country where everyone is talking revolution, and you walk in and see people like that—it's a long way from the Black Panthers ridiculing the Yalies for playing Frisbee. These guys looked awesome.

Then I was sent up to Long Binh, which I think at that time had 40,000 GIs assigned there and 60,000 Vietnamese that worked there on a regular basis. An enormous base. I walked into our company area, and one of the first things I saw was a big rubber tree with the word REVOLUTION on it in big letters. And there were about thirty dogtags hammered into it. I was impressed. I mean, that's pretty significant, when you realize that it hadn't been taken down.

Long Binh was like a big depot. Mountains of beer cans, mountains of Coca-Cola. A golf driving range, swimming pools, massage parlors, and Chinese restaurants, all done not like a Chinese restaurant in New York but like a Chinese restaurant in suburban Oklahoma. There was a library that was excellent, where you could go and type. I attended the University of Maryland extension, I studied Spanish and Vietnamese. There were NCO clubs where shows would come in to entertain us.

We were MPs, but they didn't need us for police work, so the company was put in charge of guarding and maintaining one part of the perimeter. My job involved getting in a convoy every morning in the dark, driving four miles through the base to the area we were in charge of, then working up there. I quickly got a job working with Vietnamese, old men in their sixties, seventies. They were all carpenters. Occasionally I had to do guard duty, but mostly I worked with these carpenters building bunkers. It typically took us a week to do what you could do in a day. Part of my attitude had to do with the fact that I never felt we would get attacked there, and we never did. I'd heard that in 1968 the base caught some rockets, but I never did see any hostile activity.

I must confess that I had a friend who was a Viet Cong. He was a twelve-year-old street urchin with one arm who was the leader of a pack of kids who lived in a refugee village. They hung out bumming oranges and stuff off GIs. This guy's nickname was Johnson. Don't ask me why. He used to come in my bunker, and I'd buy food that he'd bring me. He would give me shit for having my M-16 too dirty. He would break it down and put it back together. He used to do it very quickly with one hand.

Once we were talking philosophy and politics. I don't remember exactly what it was he said, but I said to him, "Hey, Johnson, you think same-same as Ho Chi Minh." He said, "No bullshit, Ho Chi Minh, Number One." I remember that same day he was walking down the line, and an FNG—which is an acronym for Fucking New Guy— was in this bunker wearing a helmet and flak jacket, which no one else did. This guy locked and loaded, and Johnson turned around and waved his one arm at the guy and said, "Hey GI, you think I'm VC? You bet your ass I'm VC." And gave him the finger and walked on. An interesting twelve-year-old.

I was involved in an orphanage assistance program. We worked to get stuff for this orphanage in a village. We tried to make life a little better for the nuns that were running it. People wrote home and asked for stuff. One of the things that we arranged for was to have a truck that the nuns could bring in and get old stuff that wasn't being used in the depot. And they were stopped—this is what I heard—these nuns were stopped on the way out the gate with a truckload of IBM typewriters, telecommunications equipment, all sorts of stuff, headed straight for the black market. That was the end of our orphanage assistance program.

The other thing I was on was the Human Relations Council, which was basically to try and avoid racial tensions. I made a lot of black friends there, and they called me Professor, I think because I used a lot of polysyllabic terms. They knew I'd been to college, so in a debate, people would go, "Well, we'll ask the Professor." Which, as a nineteen-year-old kid, I loved. So I was put on the Human Relations Council. But I'm afraid it's a disappointing story, because we met with the chaplain about three times, and the only constructive thing that ever came out of it was to get Afro-Sheen products brought into the PX.

I guess I should say that drugs were a big, big part of what was going on when I was there. When I arrived, I walked into my hootch— we were in Quonset huts made out of sheet metal and plywood and screen—and there were two black guys in there. I could tell these guys had been smoking dope. They said, "Sure, it's in the drawer over there." I walked over and opened the drawer and saw nothing but a pack of cigarettes. I said to myself, "Oh, God, these guys are going to mess with me, give me grief because I'm white." But it turned out these were marijuana cigarettes. With filters and little marijuana plants on the papers. Very, very strong pot. I went with them up near a helipad, smoked a few tokes of this stuff, and left them to go and unpack. I was walking through the dark and I hit some barbed wire. All of a sudden, dogs were barking and I heard Vietnamese voices. Lights went on all over the place. I thought it was curtains for sure. But I had just hit the wrong part of the perimeter.

By the end of my year I think everybody in my hootch was doing heroin. You didn't shoot it, you snorted it. I remember being intro-duced to snorting a little heroin, and I did it with some regularity for a couple of months. It was because it was such a surreal environment. And it was part of the cultural thing. The group of people that were doing it—everyone was into music, with incredible tape decks. This didn't just include the school dropouts and the blacks and Chicanos. It included the insurance people from Fort Wayne, Indiana, and the nice kids from everywhere. It was an extension of the whole drug culture of the '60s. You know how army trucks and Jeeps and every-thing will have little slogans stenciled on the front? Back in World War II I'm sure it was BIG MAMA or LAZY HARRIET or something like that. In Vietnam you saw trucks that said PURPLE HAZE or WINDOW-PANE, or some other LSD term. It permeated not just my group of GIs but my entire unit and other units that latter half of 1970.

There was a party for Thanksgiving or Halloween or some damn thing. A company party, where for twelve hours half the company was doing guard duty and the other half was partying. Then we switched. And I honestly remember—this is a military police unit—I remember a keg of beer and a tin of ice, with the commanding officer, the executive officer, a couple of sergeants, and a couple of GIs hanging around it. Then about fifty yards down was everybody else—smoking joints that were laced with opium, snorting smack, taking dimes, or Number 10s, which were barbiturates. The ratio was something that will always stick in my mind—the number of people doing drugs. Near the end of my tour, when everybody was doing heroin, I remember there was a pool of vomit outside our hootch that never dried up completely. Like for days on end. Because heroin makes you vomit.

What was interesting to me about the heroin was that even after doing it regularly for a couple of months, I never had withdrawal. Even though it was so cheap. You could trade a carton of cigarettes for a bag of heroin. And it was relatively pure, so you could really get high. Of course, we were snorting it or smoking it, and you just don't get the same hit you get with a needle. And the astonishing personal thing was that it was limited to Vietnam. I was still doing it when I was on R&R, and even when I got back. I remember walking through the San Francisco airport, smoking a Kool cigarette laced with heroin, just getting blown away. Discharged, $600 in my pocket, back in the World. But then I stopped. When you arrived in the World, it just didn't have a role.

My mother had a friend who was married to someone in the State Department, and this guy was transferred to Saigon about the time I was there. In fact, he was under-ambassador, his name was Sam Berger. I got an invitation to visit them in Saigon, which I had to decline because it was against MACV regulations. Then about a month later, I was out working on the bunkers. Slightly longish hair, slightly unshaven, zip-up boots instead of regulation tie boots, no sign of rank or insignia, just a real slough-ball GI, working in the mud. This guy came up and said, "They want you at HQ." I thought I was getting busted for something. I didn't know what, but it smelled like that. So I got in the Jeep, and we didn't even go to MP headquarters, we went to the actual depot HQ. I'm shitting bricks a little, because I know how unmilitary I appear. I walk into the office, and you're supposed to approach militarily, two steps in front of the officer and say, "Specialist PFC so-and-so reporting, SIR!" I started to do that and before I could even get a salute up, this colonel whips around the table and says, "Hi, I hear you're a friend of Sam Berger's. My name's Jack." And he offers me his Jeep to go to Saigon in.

So I went to Saigon, and I was introduced for about two or three days to this entire society of embassies and businessmen. An international sort of diplomatic thing—Australian, British, French, American. The Cercle Sportif. The games of water polo with French diplomats, one of whom I bashed in the nose accidentally. Cocktail parties at some British manufacturer's house. Swimming parties. People playing tennis. It was all very social and hilarious.

I remember one dinner party at the under-ambassador's house when I tried to talk a bit about what was going on. The drug use, the lack of discipline, the way no one was into fighting. The complete disdain for orders. I mean, if it was an easy order you'd do it, but there were definite troublemakers, and the jail at Long Binh was chock full of people. I remember the poor reception I got from Under-Ambassador Berger when I described how much drug use there was, what morale was like. I thought the dichotomy between life as they were leading it and life as we were leading it ten miles up the road was monstrous, and I wanted to tell them what it was like. I might have been trying to shock him. But he didn't want to get in a big debate with me. He didn't want to hear these things. He didn't hear them. I remember not being taken completely seriously. He's passed away now and that's all over the board, but he must have thought I was just a terribly maladjusted adolescent.

On the day I left Vietnam, there were 200 people in a room waiting to get on the big bird to go back to the World. And we were directed, "Okay, open up all your stuff and spread it out on this platform. We want all your toothpaste containers. Any powder containers, any jars, any liquids. We want all batteries out and up. We want you to disassemble all stereo equipment. It's going to be a major bust." And then they said, "But—there's an amnesty box at the end of the room. Anything that goes in there in the next twenty minutes is amnestied. You won't get prosecuted for it." Well, I have to tell you, that thing was overloaded. It was a two-by-four-foot box, and it was overflowing with drugs. There were weapons in it, too. An amazing amount of stuff. And then, typically army, they never inspected a thing. We just walked right by. The army was proud of its mind games over the enlisted men, and this was a classic example. I have to admit they did it very well.

LIEUTENANT GENERAL JOHN H. CUSHMAN

In January 1970, he was ordered to Vietnam for his third tour (see Chapter 3). The job: deputy senior adviser for IV Corps, the Mekong delta. "I arrived in Can Tho in early March of 1970. Can Tho was the headquarters for all the delta. The senior adviser there was named Hal McCown, who was a major general. I spent about a year as his deputy, and then my name came out on the major generals list. The proposal was that I would become the senior adviser when McCown left. He had a while to go, so I didn't take over until May 1, 1971."

Did you see much difference in the delta from 1964 to 1970?

All the difference in the world. There was a much bigger American effort. Of course, by 1970 there were hardly any U.S. ground troops left in IV Corps. The 9th Division had been there, but under Nixon's drawdown it had just about gotten out. There were only some army aviation, some engineers, and some signal troops. But there were still a lot more Americans around than in 1964. The navy had moved in. The riverine forces had fought with the 9th Division around the Mekong, and there was a navy base at the tip of Ca Mau. And the ARVN presence was stronger. There was far more manpower, more units. The government of Vietnam had control of more territory. Places we couldn't get into in 1964, we could get into. Places that were real outposts in '64, you could go to by road. The infrastructure of government services was more extensive. The roads were much better. And by 1970 we had really begun to make pacification work. We had an enormous pacification effort. We had the Hamlet Evaluation System.

On the other hand, the enemy was stronger. There were main-force North Vietnamese units—and if we'd never had to fight the NVA, we'd never have lost Vietnam. Compared to the first time I was there, when Diem was shot and the whole thing was going to hell in a handbasket, the balance was more favorable to our side. But the progress was to a degree countered by the growth of the enemy. He wasn't giving up. He wasn't fading away. He still had his structure intact—not strong, but it existed.

The name of the game in 1970 was to turn it over to the Vietnamese. We had to get out of there. We knew we were going down to zero, and we had to turn everything over in a very short time. So we had to do it in an intelligent and systematic way, at the same time keeping up our advisory efforts so we could continue to beat the VC back in the countryside and gain more control.

You had to remember that your purpose was to assist. Even Westmoreland's mission was to assist. By and large, Americans aren't very well suited for that mission. To assist somebody you have to understand what he's doing. And it may be that you're much smarter than the person you're assisting, but you still can't do it for him. Let's say you're a duck-hunting guide. The hunter has to rely on you to get him to the blind, get out the duck-calling whistle, make the ducks come in. He can't do any of that. But when the time comes, he's got to shoot the duck. Now, if he works with you long enough, he might learn some of the tricks of the trade. It would have been wonderful if we had advisers at every level in Vietnam who were as qualified as the average northern Canadian duck-hunting guide. The trouble was, they took these people off the street—not off the street so much, but out of the army—put 'em on orders, and said, "Now you're an adviser, go do your job." Sometimes they got a little training. And advisers turned over pretty fast, once a year.

So here's this Vietnamese battalion commander. He's been fighting the VC for ten years. Living in the rice paddies, living in the mountains. Fighting. Lucky to be alive, in his opinion. He's got all these problems on his mind, all these troops he has to take care of. He's not even sure he's going to survive the next day. And here comes this new adviser, some captain fresh out of advisory school. Doesn't know how to live in the rice paddies. Gets diarrhea the first week he's there. Of course, he does know something about helicopters. He might know something about the theory of tactics, and he's smart enough to know when the troops are dogging it. Nonetheless, what you have there is a very interesting situation: an adviser who's got a lot to learn from his counterpart.

It's an art, an absolute art, to be a good adviser. The first thing you have to do is understand the situation. If you don't, you've got to be smart enough not to act like you do. Don't be popping off about it. Find out about your counterpart. See what your leverage is. You can't be a nonentity. You can't just come along with him to run the radio so he can get helicopters. You have to earn his respect. You come with a certain amount of respect attached, because you represent the United States of America, a powerful country with lots of capabilities. And you represent the armed forces of the United States of America, which have a good reputation.

So you don't come in there feeling inferior. When you had something to say that made sense to you, you didn't have to apologize for it. There'd be times when you had to get tough, because he'd be doing something tactically or morally wrong—tolerating dishonesty, putting up with corruption, or not making his troops behave in a disciplined way. Not showing vigor. Good relations weren't the problem. You could have very good relations if you did nothing and arranged to get your counterpart a bottle of whiskey once a week. You had to have a little tension between good relations and getting the job done.

When I got to Can Tho, the corps commander was General Thanh. He was killed and replaced by General Dzu. Then Dzu got moved to another job, and General Ngo Quang Truong came in. He had been a two-star general commanding the 1st ARVN Division. I had worked closely with him when I commanded a brigade of the 101st Airborne Division in the fighting around Hué in Tet 1968. Now he had made his third star and was sent down to be the corps commander.

I was delighted. Truong was one of the finest commanders in the Vietnamese armed forces. When I first knew him, he had been an airborne officer for fifteen years or more. He was in his forties, and he'd been fighting for twenty years. He was a brilliant and shrewd tactician and a scrupulously upright person. He loved his men, took care of them. He was a man of considerable character and presence, though he wasn't an imposing man. He didn't look like much, because he was so slightly built, even for a Vietnamese. But he was good, the best they had. Abrams used to say about Truong, "He could command an American division." That's true. And do a better job of it than many Americans.

Now, the armed forces of the Republic of Vietnam were organized in four levels. There was what you call the hamlet militia, farmers by day and fighters by night. They never went out of the hamlet. The next level was the Popular Force. They were organized into platoons, and the best weapons they had were machine guns. Mostly they had rifles. They never went out of their home district. Then you had the Regional Force, formerly the civil guard. They had company-size units, sometimes battalions. They had officers, and weapons a lot like the regular army. They were supposed to stay in their own province. And then you had the ARVN. They went wherever they were ordered.

One thing we were trying to do was see if we could move RF units from one province to another. The populated provinces had more security because they had more people. They could raise more civil guard companies. In a province like Phuong Dinh, where Can Tho was, they might have twenty companies of RF. They didn't need twenty companies, because there weren't that kind of enemy around.

But out in Chuong Thien, which was really Indian Country, they didn't have enough RF. So we were working very hard to make it possible to transfer those companies. We made our studies and beat the drums, and finally Truong said, "Okay, we'll do it."

By this time Wilbur Wilson, who was retired from the army, was my deputy for CORDS. He was leaning on his province chiefs. But it was a big struggle. It was like taking New York State Police and having them patrol highways in Connecticut. The average province chief looked at these guys as his. He had gotten money from the government, recruited them on the basis that they would stay in the province, and equipped them. He'd gone to a lot of trouble and had them all nicely deployed. Now he's being asked to turn them loose. And it wasn't just the RF. We also wanted to move the PF around inside a province from one district to another. If you take PF from a district that's well-pacified and put them in another district, you can shake loose lots of RF and get them out into other areas. Then the ARVN can go after the enemy in the U Minh forest, where they're dug in deep. So I kept saying, "Let's use these forces. Go out and get rid of these guys. Run 'em out of there. Make the countryside so they can't survive. Get BUSY!"

And Truong would react, "Now, wait just a minute. I've got to consider why these people are here, and how they got there. I've got to talk these folks into this." He didn't resist, but he was cautious. He had to figure out the hows of it. It's easy for an adviser to say, "We ought to do this," but there were lots of feathers to be smoothed over and problems to be addressed. The families of these people. Their enlistment contracts. You had to work it out so they understood why. You had to rotate them so they didn't stay out there forever. You had to give them missions that weren't too tough. You had to pick the right ones the first time, because some of these companies were better than others, just like any units. So you take the good ones. And Truong had to show a lot of leadership. The province chief would say, "I did my job. If they need more RF in Chuong Thien, that's their problem." Truong would say, "Now, wait a minute. It's the country's problem. Can you give me just three companies, and we'll rotate them?" The next day the province chief says, "I'll give you one now, one later, and one real later." "No, no, no." But you couldn't order him to do it because he'd go right through channels to Saigon, and you'd have a problem.

On the other hand, I couldn't let up. I knew this was the right thing to do. I knew it would succeed if we did it. And Truong saw it was the right thing to do. He just had a different timetable. So that's the nature of advising. The relationship had its elements of tension, because we weren't out there making mudpies. It's not like this is a couple of good ol' boys enjoying themselves. We had a tough enemy. We had certain time pressures, too. You can't rush the process of taking over the countryside. You can't go out there and sit in an outpost and say, "Pacified!" On the other hand, we couldn't wait around another ten years. The Americans were pulling out.

Vietnamization was another problem. I could see it was the only way we were going to end up the war. Popular opinion was so much against us that we had to get out. And some very good changes had been made. By this time the ARVN was fighting the main-force units, and the RFs and PFs were taking over the job of securing the countryside. That was a long-overdue reform. Abrams was largely responsible for it. The ARVN finally had their proper job. It was devastating to their morale not to be allowed by the Americans to fight the main force, and to be relegated to supporting pacification. They were unsuited for that. They weren't from the local areas. The RFs and PFs were recruited right in the places they'd be protecting, but the ARVN were transients. Not as bad as the Americans, but still they didn't have the right attitude for pacification. They thought of themselves as fighters.

It just seemed to me that Vietnamization was moving awfully fast. And we had taught the Vietnamese a lot of bad habits. We took over that war, and we tried to mechanize it. So the essential bad habit was that they didn't know how to fight with really good infantry. We had gotten them on a diet where they believed in the helicopter and couldn't operate without it. But we were going to pull our helicopter companies out of there, quite possibly before the VNAF was able to fly those missions. There were going to be helicopters left, but not that many.

Also, they were going to have to get by with a lot less artillery. They shot artillery like it was going out of style. We had taught them to do it like that because that's the way we do it. The American army wastes artillery. And the Vietnamese didn't have to pay for it. I once found a Vietnamese unit firing artillery ammunition so they could get the boxes it came in to make furniture. These 105mm rounds were shipped all the way from the U.S. in boxes. There were two rounds to a box. Each round cost $110, something like that. These were quite good boxes, very useful for building walls, beds, or desks. And I found these guys out in Chuong Thien. I don't remember how I found out, but I did learn that one of my advisers had known about it and permitted it.

I remember one Vietnamese said to me, "It's like a fire department. You've been teaching us to fight fires with a lot of fancy equipment.

Now you're going and taking the gear, and leaving us with a bucket brigade." I've got a memo here I wrote to my advisers, and I talk about how "We must teach them to do more with less. . . . Primitive, austere, and possibly more appropriate measures." Well, that's very easy for me to say. It was true—they had to figure out how to do without all those helicopters. But I suspect Truong was sorry to see the helicopters go. I expect in his heart of hearts he could see the handwriting on the wall.

But Truong had committed himself. He had committed himself for twenty years. He never talked to me about how the Vietnamese could have done better. He never talked to me about how his government was unsatisfactory. He never shared his thoughts about his country or the performance of his seniors or his peers. And he never said he was apprehensive about whether they could make it on their own. That wouldn't be soldierly. He never got angry at me. He was too gentlemanly for that. We had some hot-tempered Vietnamese commanders who would stamp their feet and make a lot of bluster, but he wasn't one of them. And he never complained about the Americans. Never. He would give me to understand things, but he was very reticent with respect to personalities. I considered that a plus, and I was sensitive not to force him into conversations he didn't want. He was so strong a commander and took his position so seriously that he would have looked at it as sharing his command. I always wanted him to know that he was the commander, so I never pushed him.

I did lean on him pretty heavily sometimes. I would tell him things he ought to do. I was probably not as understanding of his problems as he would have liked, and he was probably wondering how he could keep me happy and still do what he needed to do. If he didn't think something could be done as fast as I wanted it done, he'd just nod his head and say something elliptical. I'd come back to it later. He'd do the same. I'd come back to it again, enough times to make him realize I was really serious.

It was a relationship between two generals, two different nationalities, with two different missions. To a degree they coincided, but his loyalty was to his country and his mission. I was a means to be used for that end. It was a subtle thing.

PETE MAHONEY

He was born in 1948 in Brooklyn, the oldest son in a working-class Catholic family. "When I was eighteen I sort of ran away from home. I was going to Providence College. The first semester I made the dean's list, which was a real mistake, because what they did when you made the dean's list was give you unlimited cuts, which I started to use my second semester. I got so far behind that I just dropped out. I was also real itchy, I wanted to get out and be on my own. So I just told my family one night, 'I'm leaving tomorrow morning,' and me and a friend started hitchhiking around the country. We ended up in New Orleans, and I joined the army there.

"There were two reasons, really. Number one, I joined in April 1968, right after the Tet offensive. I had grown up real patriotic—my father was in World War II, belonged to the VFW, so there was the whole working-class patriotic Catholic background. I had the feeling it was only a matter of time before I'd be in the military. And the Tet thing galvanized me. Seeing a lot of guys out there on the front lines getting their asses blown away, I said, Hey, what are you doing with yourself? And I decided to do the honorable thing. Plus I was working in a hamburger stand, which was not the most exciting and romantic life in the world."

After his tour, he helped found Vietnam Veterans Against the War. Later he was one of the Gainesville Eight, a group of antiwar activists who were tried for conspiring to disrupt the Republican National Convention in 1972. Charges were eventually dismissed because of misconduct by the prosecution.

We talk in his office at the Vietnam Veterans Memorial Foundation, which raised the money to build a monument to the vets in downtown Manhattan.

When you get to the reception station, they give you this whole battery of tests, one of which is the test to go to OCS. I passed, and they offered me OCS. Which I wasn't all that enthused about. But they also give you this little card that has pay grades on it. I looked at the pay grade of an E-1 and the pay grade of an O-1, and I said, "Well, okay, I guess I'll try OCS." The other thing was that in terms of proving myself, obviously OCS was one of the toughest things they could offer me. But once I got through it, I was a nineteen-year-old second lieutenant, and I had a feeling of, Well, here I am, now what do I do?

I also went through jump school because I was deathly afraid of heights. At the time, the way I would confront the things I was scared of was by doing them. Plus airborne was seen as the elite, and I wanted to be part of the elite. I applied for the Green Berets but didn't get that.

I finally got my orders for Vietnam, but they sent me over as an adviser. I had mixed feelings about that. On the one hand, I was hoping I could be an infantry platoon leader, because that would really put me out there. But on the other hand, I was not all that confident that I could handle it. I don't think I was a very good officer, and I was very aware of my shortcomings. I'm not the authoritarian type. I'm real easygoing. I was the kind of officer who said, "Hey, guys, do this because blah, blah, blah." So I worried that a group of twenty, thirty, or forty men's lives would depend on the decisions I'd make.

They sent me to three months of adviser school at Fort Bragg and two months of language school. That was interesting. What they do is give you a general overview of Vietnamese history and culture. The big idea was to establish rapport with your counterpart. Which meant developing a relationship with him so you could get him to do the things you wanted him to do. The teaching, at least officially, was to try to overcome some of the racism the Americans had toward the Vietnamese. Treat the guy as an equal. Don't talk down to him. Learn about his customs. Show that you know things about Vietnam, so he'll feel less distant from you. Get this guy to trust you, so he'll be willing to work closely with you.

I was really impressed with the training I got in adviser school. It hooked into my Catholic background—civil rights, treat people as equals, not looking down on the Vietnamese. Vietnamization fit right into my outlook.

At the same time, when you go to a military school there's two levels. There's the official course of instruction, what they're supposed to say. Then there's the underlying level that you get from the guy who's giving the class. Whatever his experience is comes in there. He says, "Well, look, this is the reality of the situation." So the official line was that you should try and leave everything to the South Vietnamese commander. If he needs advice, he should come to you and ask you for it. You shouldn't keep trying to tell him what to do. But the underlying reality level was, Look, if you don't do something aggressive, he's not going to do anything.

The other big thing about advising was resupply. Most South Vietnamese commanders viewed their American counterparts as a way to get supplies that they couldn't get through the ARVN supply system. Their system was extremely rigid because there was so much graft and corruption. In order to get one bullet, you had to show where the bullet you're replacing was expended in combat. But as an American adviser, I could walk into almost any American unit and say, "Hey, I need a couple cases of M-16 rounds," and I could get them without any problems.

So the official line was, Don't give them anything from the American supply system, because we've got to make the South Vietnamese system work. The underlying lesson was that giving supplies was one lever with the South Vietnamese commander. If you want to get them to do something, then you can use the supplies as a bribe.

I went to Vietnam in March 1970. I was assigned to I Corps, in the lowland provinces around Hué. When I first got there I worked in Phu Thu district, which is south of Hué, right across Route 1 from Phu Bai airport. I was assigned to a mobile advisory team, running training classes for Ruff-Puff soldiers.

After I'd been there a few months I was transferred. One problem was that I didn't get along with the district senior adviser. But it had to do with other things. Number one, I had gotten fairly heavily involved in black-market-type stuff. Especially selling cigarettes and beer through my interpreter.

Number two, I wasn't a good leader. When we'd finish our training mission for the day, I'd go, "Okay, we've done our job," rather than looking around for what else we could do. For the most part, the training was finished by one or two in the afternoon. Usually we'd head into the city of Hué and have a good time. Hang out at the central compound, go to the steam bath there. My team got a reputation for being in Hué too much. I had a villa in Hué for three months that I spent $300 a month for. It had a Western toilet. I had a custom-made bed, because the Vietnamese beds were too short for me. Technically, I should have been at the district compound or out somewhere in one of the villages or hamlets. But it was only a twenty- or thirty-minute ride out to the district, so I could spend the night in my villa and go back out. I was like a commuter. I'd commute to the war every day.

And I had a Vietnamese girlfriend. I met her at the steam bath, where she worked. She had just started working there. She was seventeen, and she latched onto me immediately because I was a young American lieutenant, and the Vietnamese assumed that because I was so young and I was an officer, I had to be rich.

So all those things together got me transferred. I was assigned to Phung Dien district, which is the last northern district before you get to Quang Tri province. My new MAT team was advising this RF battalion whose primary mission was to guard the An Lo bridge, which I believe was the largest bridge on Route 1 between Hué and Quang Tri. It had been blown up in Tet of '68, and the Seabees had built a new bridge to the east of the old one. So you could stand in the middle of the bridge and look upstream at the remnant of the old one, and say, If I don't do my job, that's what it's going to look like.

For a month and a half I was the senior adviser on that team. The RF battalion had three companies and a captain in charge, Captain Hieu. The RFs' level of training was a lot lower than the ARVN. Most of these guys were in the RF because they didn't want to be in the ARVN. They were just peasants, mostly, farm boys. When they turned the right age, they put a uniform on and someone put a gun in their hand. Their basic training was only four weeks or something like that.

Captain Hieu was very upper class in certain ways. Delicate hands, delicate features. Very different from the normal Ruff-Puff soldiers. Obviously he had bought his commission, and basically he was there to sit out the war. He didn't want to do anything he didn't have to do. He had fixed up his bunker, it was nice and comfortable for him, and as far as he was concerned he didn't want to leave it, except when he'd go visit his wife in Hué. The bunker was the battalion command post. It was maybe twenty feet square, and at least half of it was his personal quarters. The entire rest of the headquarters staff lived and worked in the other part of the bunker.

Hieu viewed me as a sort of nuisance because I was always trying to get him to come out of his bunker and be more aggressive. There was a whole string of hamlets down the river, so I'd say, "Let's run a surprise mission through the hamlets." He never ran a surprise mission. Or I'd say, "Hey, I can get us helicopter support, let's have an airmobile assault some morning real early. We can get the helicopters here, and we'll put everybody on them and rush them out to an area where we think there might be some Viet Cong, and insert people real quick and see if we can flush them out." He didn't want to do that.

I wanted to do it because I thought that's what my job required, and I wanted a little action. I wanted to get into a fight. I'd been in a training situation the whole time I was in Phu Tu, and although I went out on a couple of ambushes, nothing ever happened. Phu Tu was considered a fairly pacified region, but Phong Dien was not. There was much more contact. I wanted to get a CIB. I was looking to win medals, and I figured, How am I going to win a medal if I don't go out and do something?

Hieu wouldn't really say a whole lot. He'd just shrug his shoulders and say, "Hmmmmmmm, it's too difficult. My men are not trained well enough." I do remember him saying one time, "You Americans, you're all alike. You come here for a year, and you want me to win the war in your year."

So the way I operated as an adviser was pretty much to bribe him to run military operations. He liked to play cards. I got a bottle of cognac from the officers' club, and I played cards with him. And I lost. We played some Vietnamese card game that I had learned from my interpreter. I lost semi-on-purpose. I wasn't playing real hard. And obviously he knew the game a whole lot better than I did, so it wasn't that difficult to lose. After we were both pretty well soused and he had won a lot of hands, I said, "Hey, look, why don't we run an operation? It'll make you look good, it'll make me look good. Why don't we just do it and I'll stop bothering you about it, and everybody will be happy all the way around." So he agreed to do it.

There was the string of hamlets down the river, and a little bombed-out sandy area, a desert-type area, to the north of the hamlets. We swept the battalion through until somebody stepped on a booby trap, and that was the end of the operation. That was it. Then we all went home. Nobody ever said anything, but the implication was, Now the American has gotten his excitement, so let's all go home. It was a booby-trapped bomb, I guess. A dud round that they had rigged back up again. Because the thing exploded, and there was nothing left of the guy that we could find. I wasn't real close to it. I heard it, a big loud boom, and by the time I got there, there was nothing but a crater.

Then a new captain came in to run the MAT team. His name was Stratton. He was pissed off all the time because they had made him an adviser and he wanted to be an infantry company commander. He was a career officer, and they had assured him that being an MAT team leader would count as much in terms of promotional possibilities as being an infantry company commander. Which of course he did not believe, and he was probably right.

He had no conception of trying to establish relations with the Vietnamese. He just came in and wanted to order people around. He was a strict military man, and very stubborn. "This is the way I want it done, so goddamn it, do it this way." That's the way he ran the MAT team, and that's the way he tried to deal with Hieu. He tried to tell him what to do. And Hieu hated him. Hieu would ignore him, just turn around and walk into his private quarters. And Stratton would never cajole him in any way. He wouldn't play the game.

Finally Stratton complained to the district senior adviser, who complained to the district chief, so I think we ran one operation. The district chief got some helicopters and ordered us to make an airmobile assault. It was a big operation. It involved other RFs. They decided we were going to sweep through this group of hamlets. Of course, it became a real joke in terms of actual military maneuvers, because it was supposed to be this really secret thing. We were going to surprise these guys, charge in one morning, but everybody knew it was going to happen, and we ended up just walking down the road through the hamlets.

That was the only operation we had while Stratton was there. Then he left on emergency leave. And during that three weeks I got Hieu to run two operations. The old basic bribery technique. This time it was spare parts for his Jeep. He had gotten this brand-new Jeep, and he really wanted side panels because it was the beginning of the rainy season, so he wanted it to be fully enclosed. I said, "I could probably get those for you, but gee, we haven't run an operation in a long time." Then the Jeep broke—the transmission or something in the drive train. I was able to replace it for him in return for another operation.

Both went the same way—it wasn't planned like that, but we ran the operation until somebody stepped on a booby trap. Most of our operations were run on the western side of Route 1, which ran up the coast north and south. On the far side of it, we were at the beginning of the area called the Street Without Joy. It was all sand and very easy to hide booby traps. I had been wanting to get Hieu to run an operation there, but he didn't want to go near that place, which was obviously a heavily booby-trapped area. And there were probably VC there, which is why he didn't want to go. But we did go there once, and then we tried another sweep through the villages. On the first operation I was fairly close to where the guy got blown up, and my immediate reaction was to run right to the place. I thought later what a dumb thing that was to do, because there could have been more booby traps. And on both of these operations, the guys were killed. I would call in a helicopter, and they would be medevacked out, and that would be it. We'd go home.

One thing that has bothered me since was that I was getting these guys killed every time I'd get Hieu to run one of these classic search-and-avoid missions. I felt, Well, I'm doing my best as an adviser. This is war, and the fact that these guys get killed—well, that's part of what war is all about. It was only later, after I got back and got involved in the antiwar movement, that I began to realize that if I hadn't been there pushing Hieu to run operations, these guys wouldn't have gotten killed. I don't know how the soldiers felt about it. The only place I can remember seeing something would be right at the time a guy had been killed. When everybody's standing around waiting for the helicopter to come and pick up the body. I'm not sure exactly what they were saying, but I could feel the eyes of the soldiers on me. They'd be muttering to themselves.

The scariest time I ever had there was on a night ambush with the

Vietnamese soldiers. At the time there was an order that you always had to have at least two Americans on an operation. The notion behind the order was that if one American got hurt, the other would be able to call in the medevac. But it basically came from mistrust of the Vietnamese. There should always be at least two Americans, so you could cover one another's back, because you couldn't trust the Vietnamese to do that. But I was trying to show by example how to be aggressive, and I was very into this establish-rapport kind of thing. I wanted the South Vietnamese soldiers to feel that I trusted them— I'm a comrade of yours, I'm fighting with you, I trust you and I don't feel I need another American. For the most part the Vietnamese probably weren't even aware of the rule, or if they were it wasn't a big thing with them. The thing that was more on the mind of the South Vietnamese soldiers was the fact that the Americans had totally priced them out of the prostitute market.

The RFs would never go out on an all-night ambush. I would get them to go out, and usually about eleven or twelve, somebody would blow off a couple of rounds, the ambush would be compromised, and we'd have to go back to the compound. At first I would complain to the South Vietnamese guy who was in charge of the ambush, "Why'd that guy shoot?" "Well, he thought he saw something." But it happened every time. I finally realized I wasn't going to change them. That is what they did. And if I could at least get them out there for that time, it was better than nothing.

So this one night we were set up along a road that ran through the middle of the hamlets and down the side of the Song Be River. I guess it was ten, ten-thirty, right at the time when I was thinking, Well, somebody's going to blow off a round pretty soon and we can all go home, when these three guys come walking down the road. We were on the side of the road next to the river, so the river was to our backs. These three guys were not in any way looking to be secretive, they were just walking down the road. It was after curfew and nobody was supposed to be out. And they had weapons. They weren't dressed in fatigues, but here were these guys walking down the road, not clearly identifiable as South Vietnamese soldiers, and carrying weapons. I was scared shitless, because this was the first and only direct confrontation with enemy soldiers I had the entire time.

They were coming from the left, and I was down at the other end of the ambush. They entered and walked all the way through the ambush—and nobody fired. It was almost like I panicked. My head was going, What's going on here? None of these Vietnamese soldiers fired! They're all in this together! I started having all these fantasies, and it was just like [snaps fingers rapidly] going a million miles a second in my mind. I remember thinking very clearly, It's the Vietnamese against the Americans out here now, and you're the only American. I had this incredible feeling of being alone, of being totally isolated, not being near anyone I could depend on. I wasn't actually thinking the South Vietnamese were going to shoot me. But I didn't know what was happening. Just, Why aren't they firing?

I had my 16 on semi-automatic. I jumped up, flipped it on auto, and just sprayed the guys on the road with a magazine. I fired wildly in the general direction of the guys, used up the whole magazine, shot off all eighteen or nineteen rounds. I was a good shot in terms of hitting a target, but I'd never been in a battle situation. I killed two of them, but I was firing in the air by the time I got to where the third guy was, and he ran away. It turned out that one of the guys I killed was an NVA soldier and the other was a VC. So the assumption was that the other was probably an NVA also, and that they had come in for a relief supply mission from out in the mountains and had met the local VC who was bringing them into the village.

When it was over, the South Vietnamese soldiers started slapping me on the back and congratulating me. One came out and shot a couple of rounds into the dead bodies. And things were happening on a million different levels. I was freaked out that I had actually killed two people, for the first and only time in my life. And I was feeling fulfilled as a soldier. On the one hand, it was, What have I fucking done here? I just killed two people! And on the other, it was, Hey, man, you're something else. You just killed somebody, you're a soldier. And on the surface level, I was still shaken by the whole thing. I wanted to say, How come I was the only one who fired? But I never did. I never asked them.

What I did was try to stay absolutely calm and cool and collected, just going about my military business. "You check the bodies for any papers. I'll call in a situation report." Being very unemotionally military about the whole thing, as if I do this every day. I was so caught up in playing that role that I never really dealt with the voice at the back of my mind. And I was feeling proud of myself because these were the first kills we had had in the area since I had been there.

I ended up getting a medal for it, a Vietnamese Cross of Gallantry. Which I always thought was so absurd, because what was so fucking gallant about shooting somebody in an ambush? Like a thug in an alleyway. But the Americans gave the South Vietnamese commander of the ambush a Bronze Star for it—this was part of our motivation factor for the South Vietnamese—so they felt the need to reciprocate and they gave me the Cross of Gallantry. The two of us stood up there and had our medals pinned on.

It's still amazing to me that I never asked those guys why they didn't fire. It may be that underneath I already knew why. Which was that they didn't want to fight a war. They just went out on those ambushes because I more or less forced them to. But they didn't want to kill anybody, they didn't want to confront anybody. Before that time, the ambushes had been a game, and suddenly they were put in a situation where it wasn't a game anymore, but they didn't want to go to the next level.

But I didn't deal with any of that once the evening was over. I just didn't deal with it. I didn't think about it. I didn't even tell the other American advisers that I was the only one who fired. I just completely blocked it out.

That was basically the head I was in—and I think a lot of other guys, too. You just did not deal up front with things, because it made life more difficult. The way I worked in Vietnam was that something I couldn't explain, couldn't understand, or understood in a way that was totally contrary to where I was coming from—*wsssshhhhhht!* I forgot about it.

HUGH MANKE

He is a newly minted lawyer and a bit apologetic about it, in the manner of ex-activists who are nervous at the prospect of making money. We talk in his office, a homey place in downtown New Haven. Pictures of his wife and two young children adorn the desk. He is in his forties, sandy-haired, baby-faced, easygoing. For dinner, we go to the Chez Bach Restaurant, where he chats with the owner in Vietnamese.

He went to Vietnam in 1967 as an IVS volunteer, already uneasy about the American role but looking to see for himself. By 1969, he was running IVS in Vietnam. In 1971 the Thieu government ordered him out of the country. IVS itself only lasted there a few months longer.

The minute Vietnamization began, and the American withdrawal began, the string started running out as far as IVS was concerned. Because stability was not going to exist, and short-term gains were the name of the game. The government had to have some kind of short-term success. The timetable was pretty tight for withdrawal. Not tight enough, of course. [Laughs.] I think it would have been far better to just get out right away. But for the people trying to shore up the government, it was very tight.

The idea was to take American soldiers out of the countryside and substitute them with ARVN soldiers. And in the areas where the ARVN was not very strong, we were going to relocate the people and take them away from the VC. This meant IVS couldn't do what it had set out to do.

Also, everyone knew that the minute you put the ARVN out there, it's an insecure situation. Most of the ARVN units were at 30 percent or 40 percent capacity. When they went out with a division, they really went with one-third of a division. A lot of that was because of desertion. They were not a substitute for American units, that's for sure. I knew by the time I left Vietnam that there was absolutely no chance that Vietnamization would work, and therefore that the war was lost. I thought it was lost after the Tet offensive, but by '71 it was clear that it was gonna be pretty quick. The biggest problem was that the ARVN soldiers were not at all interested in fighting. The kinds of people they were counting on were the people that IVSers knew well: schoolteachers, bureaucrats who were dragged out into the front-line units as low-level officers. Their heart wasn't in it. They were not equipped to fight a conventional war. It was doomed.

So Vietnamization was a horrible experience. It was so destructive. It was worse than the war during the American buildup. They were drafting all these people who were half-hearted to begin with, and poorly trained, to meet a well-trained army. It was a terrible thing when the casualties started coming in.

I had been saying since Tet that an IVS project needed two things to start with: security, and good economic development possibilities. Security had to be the number-one thing, but you needed both. By '70 and '71, there was neither in most of Vietnam. We gradually got shut out of the traditional, mainstream Buddhist villages, because those were major political prizes for both sides, so that's where the fighting was. The work we were doing by 1970 ended up being in the fringe areas of Vietnamese society—the Hoa Hao, who were absolutely independent of everybody, and the Montagnards, whom the Vietnamese didn't care about. In those places, Thieu wasn't going to get any votes anyway, and at that time, vote-getting became very important.

The government had something called the Village Self-Development Program, which was entirely politicized. It wasn't serious economic development. It was meant to manipulate people for short-term gain, to solidify the government. They gave the village chiefs and the hamlet chiefs a pot of money and said, "Here it is, you budget for it and we're gonna monitor to see that you use it for the right purposes."

Now, that's a good idea. I believe in that kind of program Stateside.

Let the local people set their priorities, and let them carry them out. The problem is that the money went to certain political types who were almost all government supporters. You tell your hamlet chief, "Here's 20,000 piasters. You can do what you want with it." He then tells everybody else, "Hey, I've got some money, and you've gotta come to me." That's not real economic development. That's just building political alliances with money.

There were some schoolrooms built, there were some wells dug. But it made it difficult for us to do anything, because the village chief is just doling out money without any idea as to what the long-term benefits are going to be and how to make that money have a ripple effect. If you want to set up a co-op, which is a long-term project, you need to have people making commitments to you. If they can get insecticide free by playing games with the village chief, they're gonna do that. Plus it was taking away from any program that might have someone other than the village chief as the key person. This guy has all the goodies, so he's the key guy, even though it's possible that the guy with real vision and a commitment to stick in there for a long time would be somebody else.

And you had an assassination program that everybody was aware of, for those people who were a threat to your village chief. If a guy couldn't win support because of the money he had, there was the ultimate weapon, which was to bad-mouth your opponent. If he got three bad marks—if the reports were confirmed of three events that were considered indications of his leaning toward the VC—the guy's gone. Liquidated.

So things were so heavily politicized that it was doubtful there was much IVS could do. There was a tremendous American effort to shore up a shaky government and go through fifty years of political development in a matter of months. Because we were obviously heading out.

Plus the political and social turmoil was unbelievable. Starting with the early '70s, when Vietnamization was really starting to roll, the society was crumbling. People were being forcibly relocated, which I thought was horrendous—and if you can't win the insurgency battle out in the villages, you might as well forget it. Because what you're doing is making NLF supporters out of every person you move. You take people away from their ancestral burial grounds and you do tremendous damage to them psychologically. They will never forgive you for it.

Saigon was flooded with refugees. And when peasants come into Saigon, you know there's trouble out in the boondocks. In early '71

I testified before Senator Kennedy's subcommittee on refugees. And I said [reads from testimony]: "In the last six months, 44,000 new refugees have been generated in Military Region 2 alone. In the last three months, over 70,000 new refugees have been registered throughout the country." The highlands basically were being abandoned to the Viet Cong.

I recall there was a study done by some CORDS analyst who was a number-cruncher. He surveyed the Montagnards on how they felt about relocation. [Laughs.] The information was very interesting, because even though it was done by someone who was not a Montagnard and was working with interpreters—so the Montagnards were probably afraid to really tell him the truth—the results were that the vast majority of them wanted to go back where they came from. These people were very unhappy. And it was well known that the Vietnamese were taking title to the lands that were vacated. The Montagnards didn't have things like deeds. They lived as a communal group. But the Vietnamese were taking deeds to their land, which meant they could never go back.

So that's desperation. The government had written off this whole ethnic group, which was one of the bulwarks against the Viet Cong in the highlands. I'm sure the Montagnards had an accommodation with the VC to cover their backsides, but they would not have chosen to go with the VC. They wanted to be independent. But the people who were trying to be politically sensitive were overriden by the military necessities. If you want to win hearts and minds, you don't move these people away. But if you can't keep the Viet Cong from the villagers, you take the villagers away from the Viet Cong.

And in the big cities there was absolute social chaos. You had large numbers of disabled war veterans, who were people that were injured as casualties went up under Vietnamization. You had dragnets to catch the people who were running away from the draft. And then you had tremendous inflation. You had a government that was told they had to start taxing their own people to cover some of the costs of the war. Every time they levied a tax there was this tremendous political fight, and another group was alienated. I remember they had a newsprint tax, and of course all the newspapers thought, This is how they're gonna close us down. So there was a real battle over that.

The students started getting arrested in large numbers in August of 1970. There was a tuition tax, so they rioted. Every time there was an opportunity to have a legitimate complaint, one that didn't look like it was pro-Communist, people came out of the woodwork. It was dangerous to have a pro-Communist or pro-NLF demonstration. But if you went out there against the government because of taxes, or because they weren't giving disabled war veterans enough benefits, that gave it a sense of legitimacy. Then the Cambodian invasion brought out the Buddhist opposition, because the government was in the odd position of supporting Lon Nol. He was considered to be a real bandit.

The disabled veterans got organized in late '69 and early '70. If you were disabled and out of the army, there wasn't much in the way of jobs. You were depending on the government for a pension. They were paying you in currency that was depreciating at a very rapid rate, probably 4 percent or 5 percent a month. And there was no cost-of-living increase. [Laughs.]

Once the disabled veterans' movement started, it was almost an invitation to open anarchy. They were armed. Some of them had M-16s, and a lot were just carrying pistols. It was like the Wild West. You'd hear gunfights in the streets. People would be fighting over prime pieces of land for squatting. But it was clear that some activities were very well organized. They had a leadership structure. They had marches down Tu Do Street. The way I saw the politics of it, they had a great deal of support from the military themselves, who felt they were soon going to be disabled veterans, too. [Laughs.] And from the police, who for the most part were people who had bought their way out of going into the military. Also, the third force seemed to gain favor with these people. We're talking about thousands of these guys in Saigon, maybe tens of thousands. With their families.

Generally they didn't live right in the streets. But if there was a shoulder, like four feet between the edge of a road and a house, that was enough for them to build a little hootch. Suddenly, if you thought you were fronting on a street, you'd see a tin shack put right in front of you. So the streets got narrower and narrower. But the main thing they were after was the public parks. They took over a number of parks in downtown Saigon. They were driven out by force a few times. But they got away with a lot because the local police didn't really want to beat up on these guys. And nothing was worse politically than to have military police come in and beat up on guys in wheelchairs. Eventually the government made major concessions. I think the veterans agreed to leave some of the main parks in return for some housing projects, and maybe increased benefits.

At one point they started coming to the outskirts of Saigon, which was where the IVS headquarters was. It was on an old agricultural station. We had a very large building, which at any one time could house maybe eighty people. We had some small grounds for parking cars, and a really nice front yard of about a quarter acre. Behind us there were fields, about ten acres of empty land. The disabled vets came and set up a city in those ten acres. They had streets. They had their own little political structure, the equivalent of a hamlet chief. They had people there directing traffic, saying, "You take this lot over here, and you take this one over there." Right before my eyes, a new city emerged.

Of course, there was only one public water fountain for something between 1,000 and 2,000 people. And the sewage—right out the back door. It was terrible. The garbage added to the joy. Plus you've got all this pollution from the broken-down Hondas on the streets. And there was open burning of trash.

The problem was that they coveted our quarter-acre front yard. There was no reason why we had to have that quarter-acre sitting there as green space. But we were concerned about the security of our buildings, most of which were easy to get in and out of. We had some thefts. And day by day we were losing bits of our front yard as the disabled veterans encroached, coming from the front road. Finally they busted through an old fence that was about ten feet from the main road. And they kept coming.

The shacks would be thrown up in a matter of hours. It'd be a wooden frame, and then they'd take these sheets of tin that were used to wrap up American containers that came over on ships. Sometimes the tin would be defective Coke cans, so a whole side of a tin shack would be Coke cans. It's a traditional way of claiming land in Vietnam: You stake it out and wait for the shit to hit the fan. If no one comes to challenge you, then it's yours. That's what they were doing in downtown Saigon—and to the IVS house.

We had some confrontations when they started moving into the yard. There was a woman who chased after one IVSer with a large knife and told her never to come back. So we went through the preliminary jousting. Nothing worked. This location was nice. It wasn't a great neighborhood, there were shacks all around us, but it was right on one of the main streets in Saigon, Le Van Duyet. Probably three or four miles down Le Van Duyet was the central marketplace. And the Lambrettas all started their trips to downtown Saigon in our neighborhood. So it was prime turf.

We tried to find out who these people were. We felt if we could get to the leaders, maybe we could negotiate some kind of arrangement. The best thing for us, before it was all taken, would be to cut our losses and draw a line someplace. But we didn't get anywhere gathering any kind of information. So we decided in the middle of the night to take all the junked vehicles that IVS had in its driveway and tow them with our good vehicles into the middle of the yard to make it impossible for these squatters to build a shack during the night. That's when it would happen—you'd hear this *bang-bang-bang*, and you knew. Some IVSers were absolutely driven up the wall by this. They were getting close to violence. That would have been foolhardy. But when someone's sticking it in your eye day after day, you wonder what you ought to do.

We went to the police and they didn't want to do anything. They just said, "You're on your own. These people have serious problems. You just deal with them yourselves." Right.

We finally got a handle on it when they saw that we wouldn't roll over and let them take the entire place. When they saw we were serious, I think we won the admiration of the local disabled war veterans group. They were concerned about the fact that there were free-loaders, people pretending to be disabled veterans who were getting away with things only veterans were supposed to get away with.

Eventually we got to talk to the leader. He had apparently given the green light. So we formed a delegation and were led to him. There were three IVSers, all Americans. I couldn't get anyone else to go. [Laughs.] You have to remember there was acre after acre of shacks in this area. We had to go through two checkpoints to get to him. He had this nice wooden house—shack, rather. He was a heavy dude. He didn't come out to greet us. His gofer led us to his front door, then we were let in the building. It was no bigger than this room. But there was a little room inside that was separate. The guards were all well armed. There were a couple guys at the main door, and a couple at the door of this inner room.

When we went in, this guy was seated behind a really beat-up old table. He had one or two other guys with him. He was unfriendly. We were accustomed to impressing people when we opened our mouths and talked Vietnamese, but this guy—our Vietnamese was terrible as far as he was concerned. He thought we were really the bottom of the barrel. He had a patch over his eye, and he had something wrong with an arm. He didn't shake our hands or anything. It was like going in to see a judge. He's sitting behind a table, you're on this side, and there's no interaction. Just: What do you guys want?

We told him what our problem was. He agreed that if we gave up part of our yard, he would see that the rest was kept for us. So we invited him to our place, but of course he would not dignify us with his presence. He sent some flunky, and we talked about where the line would be. The Vietnamese style of negotiating is very interesting.

They will sometimes go one step forward, and you say, Ah, great. Then they go two steps backward. And you go, Oh, my God, that's not the way you're supposed to do it. Americans do it incrementally. If you want to end up at ten, one person starts out at zero and the other at twenty. The Vietnamese don't do it that way. And they will not enter into a deal unless you go through a ritual. There's nothing as dissatisfying for them as a quick deal. You gotta do a little crying, you gotta do a little moaning, you gotta do a little name-calling, and then you agree on something and you hug each other. It's wonderful.

That's how this deal went. We'd say, "We need this space, we've gotta park vehicles over here. We don't need it for basketball or anything like that, we need it for essential things." He'd say, "Ah, you don't need it. We've got people who are ten to a room that's five feet by ten, and all they're asking you for is another four feet. Have a little heart." We didn't have the greatest bargaining position. We had empty land there, and we didn't have any guns. But they didn't know that. We probably didn't take full advantage of our greatest asset: We could bring the wrath of Richard Nixon down on them. [Laughs.] They were probably worried about that, the tanks rolling in and flattening their houses.

We agreed that the line would involve the relocation of some of these shacks. It was only a matter of three or four feet, but he agreed to get these people to move their shacks. We were really shocked when they actually delivered. And everybody was delighted. The people who had built these tin houses, their whole attitude changed. They suddenly thought we were great people, and they wanted to be good neighbors. They had negotiated a deal they thought was terrific. Of course, we began thinking we might have tried to get a little bit more.

After they moved the houses that had to be moved, we invited them to a *bua thic*, which is like a banquet. This was out in the yard. We didn't invite them into the house. We set up this long banquet table and did it in typical Vietnamese style. A lot of the disabled veterans that were in the hierarchy showed up. We had toasts back and forth, formalized toasts. It was probably the biggest damn thing in their lives, when you come right down to it. Here they are with these Americans, and there were some Chinese and Indian IVSers, all speaking Vietnamese with a funny accent and having a good old time. It was really wonderful. People were hugging each other.

We ended up putting up a wall. The AID people came out and looked at our place and said, "This won't do." They built this wall all around us, so we became one more compound. It was a damn big wall. [Laughs.] I would say it was about eight feet high.

But y'know, that made a great wall for the veterans. They didn't have a tin wall then, they had a concrete wall for the backs of their houses. Not bad, huh?

DANA DRENKOWSKI

Fighter pilot, mercenary, lawyer—he has lived a few lives in his forty-odd years. He is a small man, dark-haired and -eyed, strung tight. His San Francisco apartment is filled with military mementos: models and paintings of planes, a cartoon poster of a mustachioed flyer, a photo album with pictures of him on patrol in an African country he won't name. Even the coffee cups have the insignia of his old fighter squadron. These days he practices law, but military history remains a passion, and he is an aviation editor for Soldier of Fortune.

His father was an air force man, so the Air Force Academy seemed a natural choice for college. He graduated in 1968. "I prepared myself very carefully for a career in counterinsurgency, something similar to what my father had done. Went to pilot training, and in the inimitable ways of the U.S. military, I was assigned to B-52 heavy bombers—the most rigid, hidebound organization you can imagine. I was a square peg in a round hole. But being a good air force man, I was going to make the best of it. I became a co-pilot in B-52s and volunteered for my first tour in Vietnam."

After that tour he wangled a transfer to Tactical Air Command and started flying F-4s. In June 1972—two months after President Nixon resumed the bombing of North Vietnam—he arrived in Danang. "My unit was the 366th Gunfighter Wing. They started in April with about seventy-two or seventy-six airplanes, a three-squadron wing. One squadron of twenty-two transferred out, so that left about fifty-four. By early July, when we moved to Thailand, there were either sixteen or eighteen left. That's how heavy the losses were in that unit."

In Thailand he was transferred to the 432nd TAC Reconnaissance Wing, based at Udorn. He flew 165 missions with the 13th Squadron, about a third of them over the North, in the raids known as Line-backer—which ended in October 1972—and Linebacker II, dubbed by antiwar activists the "Christmas bombing."

We were notified the day before the actual raids, but we didn't know what it was for. We often didn't know what the mission or the target was until they drew the drapes on the maps. I didn't go up on the first night, because I was in the command post. So I didn't know what was going on until the raid was actually launched, and even then I didn't know what the targets were. All I knew was it was going Downtown, which is what we called the Hanoi area. It was also known as Dodge City. We knew it was a big raid, and we knew that usually meant the Red River valley. What we didn't know was the scope of the raid, and we didn't know the B-52s were involved.

We knew we were on the edge of a great air battle, something that hadn't been seen since the wilder days of World War II in Germany and Japan. We worked our tails off in the command post. And just as soon as I could get out of there, I went to the squadron and got myself on the next mission going up north. We were all pretty excited. On that second night, when the curtains drew open on the maps showing the routes going in and the targets in and around Hanoi, there was cheering, shouting, yelling. Guys were eager. For the first time, this was going to be air power the way it was designed to be used. These were the toughest missions we flew, missions where we lost a lot of planes, but morale was extremely high. I suspect it's always that way when you think you're on the winning side.

All the targets were specific: power plants, rail yards, military headquarters. Most of them were targets that had been hit in the previous six months but were now rebuilt because we had given the Vietnamese a resting period. Some were targets that had never been touched before because they were too close to downtown Hanoi. Like the Hanoi power plant, and Radio Hanoi. We were very, very excited about that. Because we figured for once the gloves were really off, and the North Vietnamese were going to see what war was really about.

The first and second nights, our fighters were all outfitted with air-to-air missiles, radar-guided, and four Sidewinder missiles whenever possible. We were carrying no bombs, because our primary job was to make sure the 200 MiGs didn't come up and attack the B-52s. For the next few nights, I flew entirely TAC air superiority. That means taking control of the air over the battlefield.

I remember my first mission. In fact, I've got a tape recording of it. I went up as a wingman. The B-52s got hosed pretty good by the missiles. I think we lost three that night. My job was to close the back door. When the B-52s went in to raid, F-4s went along to escort them. But the F-4s fly at higher speeds and burn up more fuel. After the raid, the escorts would be running out of fuel. They'd race back to the tankers or to base, and other F-4s would move in. So there would be two shifts of F-4s on the strike, and a final shift, which was my job. We came in as the target was being hit and orbited over it for the next twenty to thirty minutes. It was our job to make sure the MiGs didn't try to jump the B-52s from behind as they left.

This time there were only two of us. It was a wild night. I remember coming off the tanker over Laos about twenty-five minutes before I was supposed to be on station. Having to drive into North Vietnam and watching as the first strikes started hitting and the missiles started coming up. I had never seen that many come up before. I counted something like thirty within a few minutes before I stopped counting.

I spent my time trying to stay close to flight lead, because at night you can't see the other airplane very well. We would fly with dimly illuminated panelescent lights, a kind of fluorescent light panel on the side of the aircraft. We'd fly maybe forty or fifty feet away from each other, trying to keep that panel in sight. And what I saw when I got close to Hanoi was not a dark target like so many of them were, but one that looked like the Fourth of July. I saw missiles going off everywhere, bursting in mid-air, cannon shells exploding. It reminded me completely of "The Star-Spangled Banner." The city was supposed to be blacked out, but there were fires and lights from the missiles and guns. Bombs were going off. CBUs would hit near a gunsight, and they'd go off.

On the way in my radar went down. I didn't tell flight lead. I saw my plane as critical to the mission at that point. We were the only two planes scheduled to close the back door on the MiGs. If I called out over the radio to my lead that my radar was down, I would be virtually ineffective as an anti-MiG aircraft. We relied on radar to get the enemy targets, and the radar-guided missiles on the airplane don't work unless your airplane radar works. So I'd be announcing to the North Vietnamese that I was ineffective. Either we'd both have to come back, because the rules were that planes didn't go singly into the Red River valley, or we'd let them know that one of us was not effective. So I didn't announce it.

As soon as we got over our orbit point at the western edge of the Red River valley, we started getting hosed at by SAM missiles. The B-52s had left. They had kicked the hornets' nest, and now we two F-4s were orbiting rather insolently over what was left.

My flight call sign at that point was Olympia. Flight lead was Olympia 1 and I was Olympia 2. As we got into the area, I saw a SAM coming at us off to the right. I took charge of the flight, which was normal procedure. "SAM at three o'clock, take it down, Olympia, take it down!" Then Waco Pete, who was the pilot of Olympia 1—his name was Pete Peters, we called him Waco Pete because he liked to fly old-time Waco aircraft for a hobby—saw where the SAM was coming from. As we maneuvered to avoid it, he started telling me,

"Pull it up, pull it up!" As we went back up, the SAM went under us and exploded beyond us.

It was the first time a SAM had come that close to me. And believe me, it's quite a sight, especially at night, when you see one of those things come roaring by you at Mach 3. Huge plume of flame going right under you. If they get within 600 feet of you and explode, they'll probably get you. And they're very, very difficult to judge at night.

We were just pulling up from that first dodge, when out of the corner of my eye I saw a second one. That was a favorite trick. First they'd fire a SAM at you from one radar site, and then fire a second one behind you while you're busy maneuvering for the first. I happened to glance to my left—I was on the right of flight lead at the time—and I didn't even have time to yell on the radio. All I can hear on my tape recording is my words to my backseater, which were: "Hold onto your shit!" And I immediately went into a snap-roll to an almost inverted position in a full dive. Waco Pete had seen the same SAM, and he rolled in the opposite direction. The SAM went right between us. We were probably within its kill range, but for some reason it exploded a little bit above us.

From that time on I never saw flight lead. We were being hosed so badly by the North Vietnamese triple-A and the SAMs that Waco Pete made a good tactical decision, which was to head north of the valley and orbit over the mountains where the SAMs and triple-A weren't. He'd still be able to intercept any MiGs that came up, but he'd be out of the zone of fire. Our actual orders were to stay in the valley where they could see us on their radar and hear us and know we were up there. What he didn't know was that I didn't have radar, so when he took off, I didn't know it. And he was not going to announce it on the radio for everybody who wanted to listen. So for the next twenty minutes, I was the only aircraft in the Red River valley. Orbiting and looking for Waco Pete. We thought we had just separated visually. We'd periodically turn on our lights, but every time I did that, the Vietnamese who didn't have radar now had a visual target to shoot at.

It seemed like a long time. All the while we were trying to get in contact with our lead, who was somewhere near China, playing it smart.

Finally I left the valley to rejoin. I was feeling mortified that we'd never rejoined our leader. It was considered a major *faux pas* for any fighter pilot to lose his lead, or for a lead to lose his wingman. Well, as it turned out, of 66 two-ship formations that were launched that night, 132 planes came back separately.

As I was coming out of the valley, we were hearing all these radio calls, beepers going off. This is a very eerie and terrifying thing. It's a warbling sound like a cut-off siren. It tells you somebody has just hit the silk. The beeper goes on automatically when a parachute comes out. We were hearing beepers all over, and it was just terrifying, because we knew a bunch of our people were down, and we were trying our best not to join them. At the same time, we were trying to note where the beepers were for rescue operations.

As we were going out of the valley, I heard that a plane was missing. I turned around and headed back to the valley looking for him. Got shot at a few more times. We finally discovered that the airplane we were looking for had actually exited the valley but had lost his radio equipment. So we headed back out. For that night, for going back in, I got a Distinguished Flying Cross.

After that night, we were flying missions around the clock. Some guys flew three to five missions in a day, which was phenomenal. I was lucky to get one or two a day because of my command post duty. Nobody went to the hootches on the other side of the base. We all slept on tables, floors, or under the airplanes while they were getting fixed for the next flight. The gung-ho attitude, the élan, was inspirational.

In fact, I hardly slept at all, other than ten-minute catnaps. I'd work a full eight- or ten-hour shift in the command post and immediately go out and brief for the next flight into North Vietnam. Fly the mission, debrief, take a catnap at the squadron, and be asked ten minutes later to go brief for another flight. Maybe fly the mission, maybe stand by. Then go back to the command post and hold down another eight-hour position. I went for five days without sleep, until one day I actually passed out in an F-4 while refueling from an airborne tanker. The plane broke off the boom and started rolling. My navigator saved my life by taking the airplane and controlling it until I came around. After that mission, I went to the squadron schedulers and said, "Haven't slept in five days. Take me off the schedule for twenty-four hours." And I slept the next twenty-four hours straight.

After five or six days, we were sending up all kinds of broken airplanes. We even sent up one plane with no missiles. Literally defenseless. We knew the North Vietnamese would see the F-4 on radar and assume it was a fully loaded fighter ready to shoot 'em down. We didn't have enough missiles to go around. We were transferring 'em from plane to plane. As one plane broke, they'd take all the missiles off it and put a couple on this plane and a couple on that one.

We hit the MiG bases, but we never went after the MiGs on the ground. This was a bone of contention throughout the war. We were never allowed to hit MiGs on the ground, and we were never allowed to bomb their bases except in the southern portion of North Vietnam. We did not bomb Kep Ha or Phuc Yen or Yen Bai or Gia Lom, which were all MiG bases. By the way, Gia Lom is also the Gia Lom International Airport, the civilian airport. It was knocked out of operation by accident on the first night. F-111s were fragged to go in and hit all the major operating MiG bases that night. The only MiG base not on the list was Gia Lom, because it was considered an international airport, and we weren't supposed to hit it. To us, that was ridiculous. If a MiG launches out of an international airport, it's as deadly to me as one that launches out of Phuc Yen.

Well, as it turned out that night, Gia Lom was the only one that got knocked out of operation. The F-111s missed every one of the MiG bases. They were bombing at night with radar from low altitude at high speed, and in every one of the cases their bombs missed the runways. They had to go in and hit 'em again.

But the B-52s were getting hosed by the SAMs, and the reason was that their tactics were terrible. These tactics were developed after the first raids over South Vietnam, back in the early days of the war. They quickly realized that the B-52s were in absolutely no danger from ground-fired weapons at the altitude they flew, 30,000 to 40,000 feet. The most feared weapon to a B-52 flying over South Vietnam was another B-52. So they developed the sort of tactics you would use if you were a commercial airline operator and had to get twenty or thirty airplanes from point A to point B within twenty or thirty minutes of each other. You just put 'em in a long line. That way they'd be safe. They wouldn't be bumping into each other.

Well, it was obvious after the first night of Linebacker II that things were going badly. In addition to the business about flying in a long line, the B-52s all had this 180-degree or 150-degree turn off target. The B-52's radar-jamming devices are on the bottom of the plane. The jamming goes out somewhat like a cone from under it. As a B-52 turns away from the target area, where the worst threat is, he's also turning the majority of his jamming power away from that target. And this is a time when a B-52 is vulnerable for two reasons. One, he has started a run inbound before releasing the bombs, and he's been on a steady track. No longer does he do even minimal maneuvering. He's supposed to be on the bomb run for thirty seconds. When he gets into the turn, he's at a predictable spot in the sky. Two, he has opened his bomb bay doors, which magnifies a B-52's radar return on a scope. So he's highlighting himself at the same time he's turning away his jamming.

The B-52s would be in cells of three planes. A number of cells all in a row would be called a wave. Each B-52 would have fifteen or twenty seconds between it and the preceding plane in the cell. And between cells there might be thirty seconds. The gaps may have been even longer in these raids, because I talked to a general from the SAC headquarters in Omaha who said they were under orders from Nixon to stretch out the raids as long as possible. Of course, that gave even more of a shooting-gallery effect.

Every night, for five or six nights, they attacked from the north, parallelling Thud Ridge, which was also a bankrupt idea. I'm told the planners had chosen that tactic because the SAMs were less dense in that area. But we knew from the F-4s that the Vietnamese had moved some of their best-shooting SAM operators there. And if you keep attacking from that one point, they'll move mobile SAMs in. Which is what they did.

During those days, we felt a combination of—should I call it revulsion?—at the SAC higher command, which we knew was responsible for the tactics, and exhilaration. We were finally doing the job, but boy, were we doing it in a muddled way. The rail yards at Gia Lom were knocked out, but at the cost of putting out the international airport by mistake, because somebody was dodging SAMs and released his bombs a little late. They went a quarter-mile past the railroad and hit the airport. Of course, we were elated that it was knocked out. Joan Baez and Telford Taylor weren't, because they were in Hanoi, and they were trapped.

All of a sudden we had the standdown for Christmas day. And on the sixth day, the B-52s finally changed their tactics. Somebody took a look at the losses and said, "Boy, we're not going to have any planes left in another four or five days." The losses were going up—something like one or two the first night, three the second night, four the next, six the next. Actually, it's more than that, because those are just the planes lost, as opposed to those that were damaged and weren't flyable.

To us fighter pilots, the loss of so many crews was disturbing, and I found out when I went to U Taphao a couple of months later that the B-52 crews were just furious. They would actually start booing, hissing, or shouting down their commanders when they came up on the stage to give briefings on what tactics and paths to use. The commanders aren't the ones responsible for the tactics either. That goes back to SAC headquarters in Omaha. But nobody was listening to the crews, and the commanders were the only representatives of the hierarchy they could get to. So there was an awful lot of dissension. Two doctors told me they had the equivalent of a mutiny on their hands, because a number of air crews went down and put themselves on sick call. That's the pilot's way of getting out of flying without being court-martialed for refusing to fly.

On the sixth day, they attacked from five different directions and hit dozens of different targets. They no longer tried to stretch out the raids. And some of the first B-52s that came in were carrying loads of CBUs. If you can imagine—these are like shotgun weapons on an F-4, which would carry three or four. Try to imagine hundreds of CBU cases. They had special CBU cases like Sea-Land cargo containers that would go into the bomb bay. It was like an assembly-line production. They could drop those things out and leave a trail about a mile and a half long of nothing but devastation. They used them to target the SAM sites as well as the various triple-A sites that were raising a ruckus.

At the same time, they finally targeted the missile storage facilities. There were 2,400 SAMs at the beginning of the operation. They fired about 1,100 of them. There were about 1,300 left. Well, as this general told me two years later, one of his majors came in looking at aerial reconnaissance photos and said, "Y'know, they don't have all the SAMs on the launch rails. We know they've got 2,400, but they've only got about 150 or 200 at any given time on the rails. So they must be storing them somewhere." Great revelation to SAC. They went through all their photos and found the SAM storage areas.

The fighter pilots knew about the storage areas before the raids began. We'd been asking permission to bomb them since the Linebacker I days. We knew pretty much where they all were. On occasion we'd be allowed to hit them. We'd have to go through channels, and we'd get permission a week or ten days later. Maybe we'd blow up 400 missiles on the spot. Well, the B-52s finally targeted them, and from that time on there were virtually no SAMs.

By the last days there was very little enemy air activity against us. The MiGs stayed on the fields. We apparently holed up so many of their runways that they couldn't launch, even though we hadn't destroyed the MiGs on the ground. The SAMs were nonexistent. Maybe one or two a day would be fired. No resupply was coming down the roads. All that was left was triple-A. And because Hanoi was so isolated, they may have been running low on ammunition. At any rate, if MiGs and SAMs aren't flying, we do all our operations from 15,000 feet and above, where the triple-A is ineffective. It was sort of like flying over the North Bombing Range. [Laughs.] You just fly along in your formations, look around at the countryside, see all the things you didn't have time to look at before.

The B-52s did their job. They did it with losses that we felt were unacceptable, but the B-52s, in spite of poor leadership, did a very professional job.

One thing that really irritated us was what we were reading in the American newspapers. The Left in America, following propaganda from Hanoi, was just railing about these massive casualties in North Vietnam, the thousands of civilians who were deliberately killed in carpet-bombing of the cities. To this day, I still run into people who talk about the carpet-bombing of Hanoi. If they knew anything at all about carpet-bombing they'd never say that. Because the city of Hanoi would have ceased to exist in one or two days had we decided to carpet-bomb it. We bombed one block very near the center of Hanoi, where the power plant was. Most of the bombs stayed in that block. There was some residual damage, which is to be expected when you use an inaccurate weapon like a bomb. But just nine months before that, in April of '72, the North Vietnamese Army surrounded An Loc in South Vietnam and deliberately shelled the city. Artillery is far more accurate than bombs. They randomly shelled this provincial capital and killed over 20,000 civilians. And this hardly got any notice. All we saw in the press were Americans killing thousands of civilians in North Vietnam with terror bombing.

I will grant you we made an effort to psychologically cow the North Vietnamese, which was successful. That was terror, deliberate application of terror. But on military targets. It was just that if you lived anywhere in the Red River valley, you heard all your military bases blow up around you. You heard your rail yards disappear under a wave of bombs. But as far as terror for the sake of killing civilians, we didn't do that.

At first the North Vietnamese were claiming 3,000 civilians dead. This after ten days of the most intensive bombing since World War II. I still thought that was high, because I had heard as low as 2,200, including the military people who were killed. Now the North Vietnamese themselves say 1,700. But even assuming the highest figure they've ever given out is true, that certainly compares favorably with 20,000 or 30,000 killed in one night in Berlin, the tens and tens of thousands in Tokyo—and nobody knows how many in Dresden in the firestorm, because it was full of refugees.

On the eleventh day, we were overjoyed to get an order to download the missiles off the airplanes and upload them with CBUs and fire ordnance, like small mines and firebombs, phosphorus bombs. Mostly CBUs. So we knew our targets were going to be trucks on the roads. We were going to shut down North Vietnam from that time on. For the first time, we were starting to fight like our forefathers in World War II, when General Eaker* gave the order to the 8th Air Force: "Seek and destroy the enemy wherever you find him, in the air or on the ground." That eleventh day we had actually loaded our planes, 100 or 130 F-4s at Udorn. We would have inundated North Vietnam. Nothing would have moved on the roads. Any truck that moved was ours. Any big boat that moved in the rivers was ours. Any ship that moved in and out of Haiphong was ours. And we were ready. I mean, we were really up and prepared.

That was one of the bigger letdowns in the war. We were very disappointed when Nixon ordered the standdown at that point. The Vietnamese had come in and said, "Yes, we'll sign the peace accords." Five days later they met in Paris. Twenty days later everything was signed. Sixty days later the POWs came home. All as a result of Linebacker II. But we wanted them to know that in spite of all the controversy and the disruptions in America over the so-called Christmas bombings, it worked. We now owned the skies and the ground in North Vietnam.

TELFORD TAYLOR

He was the chief prosecutor at the Nuremberg war-crimes trials. We talk in his office at the Columbia University Law School. Now in his eighties, he is a handsome, reserved man who seems to seek, above all, to be judicious.

The origin of my trip to Vietnam was a telephone call from Ramsey Clark, who had come back from such a trip a few weeks or months earlier. He explained to me that there was a way of going to Vietnam, and he told me the reason he was keen on my going. It was because some people who had gone had suffered a good deal of criticism. I think he mentioned Bill Coffin, the former chaplain of Yale Divinity School. Ramsey thought it would be a good thing if other people would go and indicate that it wasn't a thoroughly unrespectable thing to do.

That particular appeal didn't move me much, but it so happens that at that moment I was rather susceptible to the idea of an adventurous trip. Also, I had just written *Nuremberg and Vietnam*. Having ex-

*Major General Ira C. Eaker, best known as commander of the Eighth U.S. Army Air Corps in World War II.

pressed some opinions about the bombing of North Vietnam, I was anxious to see whether what I said was right.

In *Nuremberg and Vietnam*, I said that it was surprising to me that Harrison Salisbury had described the destruction in North Vietnam with such excitement, as if it was something new and horrible. My first point was that anybody who had been through World War II and had seen what happened in England—and of course, much more what happened in Germany—could hardly regard what he was describing as something new. It was entirely in line and rather minor compared with the destruction wrought on those occasions. And second, that as far as war crimes were concerned—well, as far as I knew, and I thought I did know, there weren't any limits on aerial warfare compared to the laws of land warfare. For the obvious reason that from 1899 to 1907, when the laws of war were drafted, there was no military significance to the air except balloons. So I knew of no basis on which one could say that bombing was a war crime.

My conclusions in the book had been antiwar, but I had not participated in what you'd call antiwar activism. I was not going around with Bill Coffin and Dr. Spock preaching the gospel. But I was opposed to the war, yes. I said in the book that I had supported the war up to 1966 or '67, when it began to appear to me that the destruction caused was out of all proportion to the reasons for our enormous investment.

Having indicated to Ramsey Clark that I would consider going, I was told that one had to pay one's own way. Once you got there, they would put you up in a hotel and feed you and show you what they were willing to show you. I called *The New York Times* and they gave me stringer status. And I went to NBC, where I had friends. They made a deal with me that they would give me a camera to take and pay me $750 to bring back film. Well, that came pretty close to covering the cost of the trip.

I made the arrangements, got the tickets, and joined up with Joan Baez and Mike Allen and Barry Romo, who were the other three going. We flew to Copenhagen, then a one-stop flight to Thailand, stayed overnight there, flew the next day to Vientiane, stayed overnight, at which point we picked up the visa into North Vietnam and went on Aeroflot the following day to Hanoi.

We were met at the Hanoi airport by a reception committee. They seemed to be persons in the business of shepherding people around. This was December 18, 1972. We drove in from the airport to the hotel. On the way we passed the railroad yards on the opposite bank of the Red River from the city. They were an utter shambles, obviously not working. Damaged freight cars piled one on the other, and everything higgledy-piggledy. Then, when we came to the river, I looked downriver and saw this big bridge with two spans into the water. So I knew for a fact that railroad communications from Haiphong into Hanoi were not working. We crossed on a pontoon bridge and went to the Hoa Binh Hotel, which means "peace."

The next few days were devoted to sights around Hanoi. Hospitals, schools. But the schools weren't very much in operation. No colleges. There had been a considerable evacuation of Hanoi because of the bombing up to October. The North Vietnamese told us they had evacuated about a third of the population. They had moved the colleges and all higher education out of town. They also told us, which proved not to be the case, that they had moved most of the prisoners out of town, a long way out. We took over a lot of mail for them from their families, and we were expecting to bring mail back. We were also hoping that we'd be able to make contact with the prisoners directly. One of the first things we asked about was if we could see the prisoners. Well, they said they'd think about it. Then after the bombing started, they said it would be much too dangerous, because it was a long way.

Hanoi didn't seem like a city under siege. We didn't see any guns at all, either in the city or outside. When we drove outside the city in the marshlands where the rice was growing, out near the airport, I saw two or three places where heavy tracks went off into a copse. I guess that's where they had a gun. But we didn't see any.

I had a meeting alone with lawyers in Hanoi. But I'd been told by the Ministry of Education that they didn't think much of lawyers. Their ways of settling disputes were much more like arbitration and lay judges. But there were lawyers, most of them French-trained. We had a kind of go-round about whether the American bombing was legal or not. I didn't get anywhere convincing them, nor them convincing me. I told them that as far as I knew, there weren't any established principles about this. They said, "Well, there ought to be."

We also saw the museum where they had collected the horrors— the shell casings, those shattering bullets, things like that. They made a pretty impressive spectacle. But there wasn't any indication of where these things had been picked up. I couldn't tell whether they'd fallen on Hanoi or somewhere else. And of course, shells that spread around little pellets are very good antipersonnel weapons. If you're bombing a gunsite, it's a practical thing to use. On the other hand, to drop one of those into a city would not be rational. But the guides didn't know where they came from. Which from my standpoint made them virtually useless.

The night before we were supposed to start traveling, we were all sitting around watching a film of Jane Fonda and Ramsey Clark looking at bomb damage [laughs], when the siren went off. I spent a good part of the time from 1943 to the end of the war in London, and this was the first time I'd heard an air raid siren since then. The Vietnamese immediately rushed to us and said, "You've got to go to the shelter." Outside the hotel in back there was a concrete-shielded entrance. You went down steps, and it turned so as to eliminate any blast coming in. There were two concrete benches along a long wall. I guess we must have been about fifteen feet underground. Reinforced concrete. It seemed very solid. I was quite happy there on the whole during the bombing. A direct hit, of course, would have done us in, but it didn't seem to me to be very likely.

The other occupants of the hotel included a couple of Polish sailors who came later. They'd been on one of the ships in Haiphong harbor that was hit. There were several Indians who'd been on the Peace Commission. They kept saying to us, time and time again, "Hanoi: easy to come in, hard to get out." [Laughs.] They'd been there a long time. On the top floor of the hotel was the representative of Agence France Presse. His wife was also there. When the bombing started, a *confrère* of his came down from Peking to help report. They were gutsier than the rest of us, because they had to be. They spent a good deal of time at the top of the hotel instead of in the bomb shelter. But things would get to the point where they decided to come down, too.

The shelter also had a rear entrance, and from time to time people who lived around there came in and sat with us. Sometimes there were some kids. But there weren't nearly as many as there would have been if the city was fully populated. And apart from that very fine shelter, the air raid discipline in Hanoi was superb. There were other main shelters on most of the main streets, and lots of little foxhole-type things, maybe five or six feet deep. You could pull a bamboo cover over your head that would help you against blast and fragments. Often the covers were left off, and walking around at night you had to watch your step so you didn't fall into one.

A great deal of the bombing was concentrated right across the river. They hit the airport the first night. Supposedly that was three or four miles away, maybe not that far as the crow flies. They also lambasted the railroad yards again. That was close enough so it made quite a racket. A big B-52 dropping a load of bombs makes an awful impact.

The blast is terrific. And they don't all hit simultaneously. It makes a *b-r-r-r-r-r-r-r* as they hit one after the other, very rapidly, like rolling a snare drum.

The bombing very speedily took a definite form. The B-52s didn't come over except at night. In the daytime, they used occasional runs—but only in good weather—of medium bombers that came in at low altitude and dropped smart bombs. Some of them came close to us, but of course the bombs weren't nearly as heavy, and it wasn't a B-52 load—usually two or three bombs from a flight of two or three airplanes. Hitting specific targets in Hanoi. There would often be a raid around midday. And if you'd had a bad night, it was likely that the morning would be okay at least until lunchtime.

I spent only one whole night in the shelter. That was the night we'd had a farewell party, and the combination of a long period of strain and a great deal of Vietnamese schnapps rather knocked me out. Sound asleep. Usually we'd sit there until the all-clear sounded, and then I'd go to bed. The raid might last an hour and a quarter. Then maybe you'd get another raid at three o'clock and go to the shelter for another half hour. I slept much better upstairs than in the shelter. It took a lot of liquor to knock me out to the point where I could go to sleep on that concrete, or on the bench. [Laughs.]

One thing I found out afterward was that although the North Vietnamese told us the bulk of the prisoners had been taken out of the city, they hadn't at all. They were in the famous Hanoi Hilton, which was not more than a quarter-mile from the railroad station. I'm sure the air force knew that. In bombing so close to the prison, they must have had great confidence in those bombs. A couple of years later, when I went down to Maxwell Air Force Base to give a lecture, I met several of the flyers who'd been prisoners. They told me they remembered the raid perfectly well. They'd seen the three planes come over. They were all out clapping their hands and cheering. Two of those bombs hit the railroad station, and the third one was a little smarter—it flew on and hit the back of the Cuban Embassy.

The bombing changed the atmosphere quite a lot, of course. But the Vietnamese were used to it. I didn't see any sign of rage. They're pretty well-controlled people. They were very solicitous of our comfort. They apologized for the inconvenience in an Oriental way. I think they may have been pleased that we were getting a view of something we'd remember and take back. And I guess it was less of a surprise to them than to us. As soon as the bombing started, there was a renewal of evacuations. The hotel was on a street that was an egress route into the countryside to the west. The next morning and all through our stay, there was a more or less constant procession of bicycles, family wagons, and occasionally automobiles and trucks moving out of town. I was told that by the time we left, two-thirds of the population was gone.

We all became more nervous, no doubt about that. People ask me, "How afraid were you?" Except on one or two occasions, it was not so much a high degree of fright as a constant strain. There were damn near ten days when it didn't let up. You never could tell when a raid was coming, and you had to be ready. The times I felt most nervous were when we were trying to get out of Hanoi. They would tell us, "Tonight a plane's coming in, and you can get out on that back to Laos." Every time we went out we had to drive over the river, and you felt kind of naked out there if a raid came. Sometimes there was a raid on when we were coming back. The flights were called off because of there being an alert. The plane would turn back. So it was the crossings of the river over and back that I found the most trying.

On Sunday, two days after the bombing started, we went to the big cathedral for a night service. That was interesting. The church wasn't full, but there were a lot of people. I've been to churches in Russia, and the people would be mostly old women and old men. This was full of all ages, and they sang very freely and appeared to be devout. It was plain that Catholicism had not been stamped out by any means. And there didn't seem to be any effort to. The priest who conducted the service was a fine linguist—he did everything in four languages: English, Vietnamese, German, and French.

We were there twice. We went again on Christmas Eve. We had been told to assume there would be no bombing, and there wasn't. The cathedral was full. I had expected to hear a lot of Oriental music, but I didn't hear a stick of it the whole time. The two songs they sang in the cathedral on Christmas Eve were the Bach-Gounod "Ave Maria," and "Stille Nacht," which they sang in English. There were quite a few foreigners there, diplomatic representatives and the press. Those two church services and the little service they had in the hotel when we came back were in some ways the most poignant part of the visit. There was a fellowship, a feeling that there were some things we all shared. During the service at the hotel, Joan Baez was singing a setting of the Lord's Prayer. As she was singing it and strumming her guitar, there came a very sudden air raid warning and at the same time the buzz of something over us. Her voice faltered. A Frenchman immediately shouted, "Joan, don't pay any attention, that's just one of those drones. Go on." Her voice picked up, and she went on and followed the song through.

The main feature of the remaining days was the prisoners. They had told us the prisoners were way out of town. Well, we were having an interview with two or three representatives of the Church, and right in the middle, our guide came rushing in sort of breathless and said, "You better come with us immediately. One of your American prisoners has been hurt by a bomb. We want to take you out and show you what happened." Having been told several days earlier that the prisoners were way, way out of town, I was astonished when we all got in the car without any packing. I took a look at the mileage as we started out. We went down the same route we'd been before, but a little farther. We stopped and turned in somewhere. And we'd gone exactly eight kilometers. So it was quite plain I'd been lied to.

This was a place the prisoners referred to as the "Zoo." It was used for those prisoners who were willing to meet with incoming foreigners, especially Americans. Mike Allen had put on his dog collar for the occasion, and Joan had brought her guitar. She was going to sing to them, and he was going to preach.

Only about twenty prisoners were there. Some army, some navy, some marines. Mostly army or navy flyers. It was an area of small huts with beds in them. You could circulate among the huts. We were just milling around, and pretty soon they converged around us. But we weren't given much time to talk to them, not nearly as much as I would have liked.

We had gone out on the information that somebody had been wounded. Well, the wounding consisted of one guy who'd gotten a splinter in his hand. It wasn't even a big splinter. It was a splinter of wood or glass that had cut his hand badly. But since this was said to have taken place during an air raid, as soon as I had a chance to talk to some of them, I said, "Where were you when the bombers came?" The answer was, "We were under the beds." I said, "That's a funny place to be in a bombing. Why weren't you in a shelter?" "Haven't got any shelters." I looked out the door and saw a lot of shelters. "What about those?" They said, "Those are for the guards."

When we went back out, we had an interview with the camp commandant. I immediately raised the question, "Why don't they have shelters?" His reply was, "Well, we abandoned the shelters for them when the bombing stopped." He meant before the renewal of it. I said, "Well, you didn't close up those shelters for the guards." Of course he had no answer. When we went away, I simply rose and stalked off. Didn't shake his hand. This was noted by our guides. And two days later, we had an interview with a man from the press ministry—the propaganda ministry, really. He said they had been slow in getting the security for the prisoners under way, and they had now rectified that.

I didn't know whether he was lying or not. That's one of the things I was able to check up on when I met that fellow at Maxwell. He said it was all perfectly true. At about the middle of that week, they had given the prisoners in the Hanoi Hilton shovels and told them to dig shelters and given them stuff to cover them over. They had shelters from that point on. I was rather pleased that my little demonstration had had some effect.

We didn't spend a lot of time looking at bomb damage, which was one of the things that convinced me the air force was not trying to wipe Hanoi off the map. I confess I'd been a little worried about that. But it seemed apparent to me that when they wanted to bomb right in Hanoi, they used medium bombers. They knocked out the power station. They knocked out the telephone exchange. They knocked out the railroad station, which was already knocked out. What else they could knock out, I don't know. But they were obviously very careful to use the smart bombs on specific targets in Hanoi, and the B-52s for the most part stayed away.

Now, they made some mistakes. Or—I don't know if they were mistakes. Three or four days after the visit to the Zoo, we were taken early in the morning to see the famous Bach Mai hospital, which they told us had been destroyed. And they were right. It had been. I was pretty careful to check up on that. I thought maybe this was damage that had been inflicted before, in the earlier raids. But bombs knock down trees as well as buildings. There were a lot of trees down, and the leaves were green. The soil underneath them was still fresh and moist. So it was obvious it had happened the previous night. There had been a big raid, and we'd heard some big bombs very nearby.

Of course, the construction out there is very light. The air force later contended that the hospital hadn't all been destroyed. There were a certain number of shells of buildings that stood up, which from the air would look like they were still intact. But the blast had gone through the windows and wrecked everything. I didn't see any building that was intact. Everything was swept around and broken all over the place. There was no hospital equipment left. We were taken around by the head of the hospital, who was practically crazy with rage. His whole enterprise was destroyed. He had pride in the hospital, and here it was all gone. It was the first time I'd seen anybody crazy with rage in Vietnam.

The loss of life had not been nearly as great as I expected. They told us they had gotten all the patients underground. There had been enough time to get them all in shelters. But a number of the staff had remained above, and twenty-six of them had been killed. I had no reason to doubt it.

It was a terrible scene. We saw a couple of wounded being carried out. This enormous—for Vietnam—hospital had been gutted. What were they going to do with the patients? I began to wonder when I saw it, because there were a lot of craters. At least two sticks of bombs had been dropped square on that hospital. And I didn't know at the time that there was a small military airfield about a quarter-mile away. Which I think is what they were trying to hit.

There was one other occasion just two days before we got out. Again, there'd been a big, heavy raid. We were taken past the railroad station and down the road to an area where the car stopped. I stared out upon what seemed to be nearly a square mile of utter destruction. It was the so-called Kham Thien, one of what the French would have called "native areas." Very poor, flimsy construction of huts and sheds over a large area. That was flattened, the whole damn thing. There were a lot of very desolate, crying people wandering around. They said the death toll had been around 200 or 300. I had no way of checking it, but there must have been a hell of a lot more people that lived there.

Again, that shook me a little on this business of whether they were really trying to hit Hanoi. But still, after ten days to see just that and the hospital and one other housing district where the damage wasn't anywhere near as bad—that's not a very big amount for ten days of heavy bombing. It couldn't have been that little unless they were trying not to destroy the city. And I couldn't bring myself to believe that they'd targeted the hospital. I simply couldn't. Of course, I got peppered by the left-wing press corps a good deal. "What do you say now about your bombing?" That sort of thing. Which was painful to take. And I had no good answer. I didn't know about the military airfield until I got back.

After the second time our takeoff was aborted because the Peace Commission plane couldn't come in, I said to my companions that it seemed to me that we didn't see an end to this, and I had some classes to teach and some family back home, and I wanted to go back before long. I suggested we go to the Chinese, who had a plane that could get in on a shorter runway. It came in on Tuesday mornings. We had no Chinese visas, so I arranged through the Vietnamese to pay a visit to the Chinese Embassy. They were very nice and gave us the permissions.

So we finally got across the river for the last time and flew to

Nanking. Then to Canton, where we spent the night, and then to Tokyo, and then home.

We had a press conference in Hong Kong, and we got along pretty well in sorting things out. Joan and Mike and Barry were prepared to indulge the suspicion that the air force had bombed the hospital and the city on purpose. I said, "Well, look, if we're going to have a press conference, I see a lot of things we do agree upon. Let's wait till we get back, and then you guys can say whatever you want. But for the time being, let's say the things we can agree upon." So I handled the press conference. We described the bombing. We didn't get into things like whether it had been done on purpose or not. But we made pretty clear that there was a lot of heavy bombing, and a lot of people killed. And we had seen the hospital demolished.

I was satisfied that within the city, they were trying to hit only military targets. The air force general I saw in the Pentagon explained to me that they thought the Bach Mai hospital and the Kham Thien area were probably jettisons. They said the B-52 was a very hard plane to fly when loaded. If one of them got injured and difficult to control, the first thing the crew would do was to get rid of the bombs so they could fly the thing more easily and get home. Their guess was that the big drop near the railroad station was a jettison. They weren't so sure about the hospital, but obviously something had gone wrong. They hadn't intended to hit the hospital, they had intended to hit the nearby airfield.

I made a comment that to use a B-52 dropping from 36,000 feet with no controls on the bomb—I mean, you can't hit a small target with B-52 bombs. It hits a big target. I was critical of that. They didn't have any very good answers. They said it was the only way they could fly in bad weather. They had their reasons.

When I got back I became aware that Washington was getting a very bad press from all this. My own analysis of it is that both sides were eager to get the bombing stopped. It's quite plain that the air force could have done worse if they wanted to. To have bombed the devil out of Hanoi would have been very hard for the Vietnamese to take. But it wasn't done, and I guess we didn't want to do it. Both sides were finding it very hard going.

JOHN PETERKIN

In 1969 and 1970 he served as a district senior adviser in the pacification program (see Chapter 7). By 1972 he was bored with Stateside duty, so he volunteered for reassignment to Vietnam.

• • •

I went back in March 1972. I was assigned to CORDS headquarters as a plans officer. Good assignment. Really good assignment. You lived right there in the city of Bien Hoa, which was off-limits to all military personnel except for those assigned to CORDS HQ. Twenty-five kilometers from Saigon, which you could visit every Saturday or Sunday, whenever you were off. When I first got there, I lived in a compound for military people. But as soon as I arrived, they closed it. With the reduction in personnel, they didn't have enough people to maintain a compound of that size. So they put us on the military airbase. That was good for a while, but the Viet Cong started hitting it with rocket fire, and it became a little precarious to live there. I complained about it. I said, "Look, you wanna keep us here, you better put us in a place where we're not gonna be hit on a nightly basis." So they decided to move us into one of the State Department buildings.

I never realized it, but the State Department lived well. The CIA lived well. They put us in the main building, which was called the White House because it was a lot like the White House in Washington. It was four stories in height, painted white, with a big white fence around it. Well maintained, secure, with everything you needed for an independent lifestyle. The setup would have been cushy even back here. There were one- and two-bedroom apartments with air conditioning, very well furnished. There was a club that had dining-room facilities, entertainment, a bar with a huge selection. It was open for two meals per day, lunch and supper, with table service. There was dancing. You could invite guests, either military or nonmilitary. There was a pool. They had tennis courts. They had a theater, with a movie every night.

So the war became an eight-to-five job. I was an assistant plans officer. We developed plans for policy that had already been established. Part of the job was to meet with our Vietnamese counterparts concerning a plan which was established year by year, part of a five-year plan. The South Vietnamese were afraid the Americans were going to abandon them. In fact, my interpreter asked me, "Are the Americans going to abandon us?" I said, "No, no way." I was giving him a truthful answer, based on my personal feeling and what I knew. I could see things were winding down. But I thought there would always be a military presence, perhaps not the type we have in South Korea, but some type, if nothing more than just an advisory effort. I was wrong, of course. And they were very apprehensive about it. They had no idea we would leave the way we left, that there would be a complete pullout of all military forces. I knew the level of pacification had not reached a point where the Vietnamese were going to be capable of maintaining any momentum.

So I thought the advisers would stay. Then I got orders to work on a plan to reduce the advisory effort down to zero. That was in the last three months prior to the signing of the Paris Peace Accords. We had plans for every contingency in the military. It doesn't mean the plan's going to be instituted. It just means that in the event it becomes necessary, there's a plan which can be executed. It's already thought through, already staffed, already been approved by the commander. We put a plan in place for the withdrawal of the advisers—how it was going to be done, who was going to go first, what would be transferred or destroyed in place. What bases would be turned over to the Vietnamese. But that was just a contingency plan.

Then, some time before the peace accords, we kept getting bits and pieces of information about what would take place. It wasn't anything firm, but it was firm enough that most advisers expected to be leaving the country shortly after the accords were signed. I still thought we would provide material support—weapons, ammunition, and economic support. What's needed to wage war from a defensive standpoint. I suspected the North Vietnamese would stay in place. The VC, I couldn't see how they could stay in place, because they were completely surrounded by South Vietnamese forces. I thought it would be a mop-up operation for the South Vietnamese, and they'd have a DMZ of the type they have in Korea. I knew that if the American advisers weren't there, the support could be eliminated at any time. But I didn't think it would be, mainly because Americans have a sense of doing what's right.

At the end, just prior to the peace accords, we maintained a situation room, which had a map of Military Region 3 with all the provinces and districts and villages and the level of military activity. Right before the signing there was a lot of maneuvering around, villages changing hands overnight. We called it musical villages. They were trying to gain as much territory as possible, because once the accords were signed, everything theoretically had to remain in place.

Just to keep up with the information became a chore, because it changed so often. Not that there were great numbers of people on the Viet Cong side. It's just that they were able to hold small pockets of resistance because it didn't take that much. There wasn't any such thing as holding a position indefinitely, because they didn't have the numbers to do it. They'd hold for two, three days, and if the accords weren't signed in that period of time, they'd disappear into their tunnels. Then they'd pop up somewhere else. And whatever they held on the day the accords were signed would be their in-place position, where they could surface legally and put their flags up, which is what they did. It was a hide-and-seek thing, but it meant the ARVN was going *zoop! zoop!* all over. And they were being worn down.

Right at the end, when we knew the accords were going to be signed and it was just a matter of time, the jockeying for position got even more intense. Day by day, changes were taking place. When each change takes place, there has to be a reaction from the field. More evaluations, more reports. These reports would come through advisory channels, because you couldn't trust the South Vietnamese channels. And you have to be very careful with those reports, because they went to the ambassador and then to Washington. Hell, we'd get a report and within ten minutes the report would change. I'd go to my map and stick a Viet Cong flag there, or take one out and stick a South Vietnamese flag there. It would sound comical if it weren't so serious. Back and forth.

When the accords were finally signed, there was a feeling of relief. We were told hours in advance when the accords would go into effect and the cease-fire would begin, and I would say within an hour or two thereafter everything stopped. No shooting. No sounds of gunfire whatsoever. Quiet.

But the pockets remained. The map looked like a spotted leopard.

Not long after that, I was among the last 2,500 military to go. Everybody was pulled in except for my headquarters. Then the military headquarters pulled out. The civilians remained, and those who were masquerading as civilians.

When I left, we were supposed to gather at Tan Son Nhut airbase. So I took a taxi. Normally the taxi would go right up to the main gate. If they had clearance, they'd go on the base. If they didn't, you could get out and take another taxi, a base taxi. But this fellow let me off a good 150, 200 yards away from the main gate. This was at night. I was in uniform, and I had to run a gauntlet, just about, of Vietnamese who were milling around the gate. These were friendly Vietnamese, supposedly. They were selling things, or just wondering if you had any extra money to give away. The piaster couldn't be reconverted to foreign currency, so you'd give that away. Plus you had military scrip, which you could use in lieu of American money, and once you bought it, you couldn't cash it in. So you had a choice: You could use it to light your cigar, or you'd give it away.

But I had already given all my stuff away. I didn't have a radio to give or anything like that. And I felt a little uneasy—I felt very uneasy, to tell you the truth. I was by myself, and there wasn't another American face in sight. It was like pushing your way through a subway crowd, it was that thick. I'd say there were a couple hundred people there. If they wanted to just attack and strip you, they could have done it right there and probably it wouldn't have been seen. So the idea was to be very tactful. You couldn't just bull your way through, because they realized and you realized you were on your own. There were no American MPs to come to your aid, and the Vietnamese MPs at the gate, whether or not they would have come to your aid is another story. So just diplomatically—"Excuse me, excuse me"—I got through. But I felt uncomfortable, very uncomfortable.

I remember in the last days, we were rushing to meet a deadline prescribed by the peace accords. We had a date when we were supposed to leave the country. We had to destroy in place or turn over to the Vietnamese the equipment and installations and much of the food we had. Television sets, recorders, lots of that stuff was destroyed in place. Some of it was made available to the troops, but nobody wanted to take it home. I could have had one of the latest stereo sets around if I'd wanted one. For free. But I didn't want to be bothered with it. It was stupid on my part. But most of us had already bought the latest stereo equipment at bargain-basement prices. I saw stereo sets in cartons, never opened, they just threw them on the fire. They wouldn't give them to the Vietnamese, so they destroyed them. I don't know why they wouldn't give them to the Vietnamese. Something to do with the law. I think destruction of American property in place was acceptable, but there wasn't any procedure for giving it away. Except for military installations, which were turned over as part of the withdrawal.

It looked good on paper—stand down and turn over the installations to the Vietnamese. But it was ridiculous. The big Olympic-size pool they had at Long Binh became a duck pond. [Laughs.] That was some pool, too. They built that thing to stay there for years, and it would have been there for years, because we expected to have the same sort of arrangement we have in Korea. But they closed Long Binh before I left and turned it over to the Vietnamese.

Sometimes the structures were given away, but even if they were, the Vietnamese didn't actually use them. They would dismantle them piece by piece and either reuse the stuff or sell it. They didn't have any use for these huge military bases, and they couldn't maintain them. It takes money to maintain an installation the size of Long Binh, or the complexes up at Danang.

The Bien Hoa army base was turned over to the Vietnamese, and they took that apart piece by piece. Board by board. The ceremony took place, and practically before it ended, the Vietnamese engineers were there taking the base apart. It looked good on television, the ceremony, but that wasn't the way it happened. Those little fellows could take a base apart in seconds. [Laughs.] Hey, there goes Long Binh, down the road! There goes Bien Hoa army base, down the road!

FRANK SNEPP

His first tour with the CIA in Vietnam ended in 1971 (see Chapter 8). Before long, he was back in-country.

An agency colleague who knew my work during my previous tour called me in and said, "We've just captured the deputy chief of North Vietnam's CIA. Would you like to go back and try to break him?" It was a sensitive case, because the North Vietnamese had recently offered to exchange some of the Americans they were holding for this guy, and the CIA had turned them down in hopes that he would cough up some vital intelligence. But no one had been able to break him. Now that a cease-fire and a prisoner exchange were in the offing, the agency was worried that our refusing the deal might be made public. So in effect we had to prove that the guy was that valuable. I said, "Sure, I'll go." And that took me back to Vietnam from '72 until the end of the war.

I did a creditable job with the prisoner, and after that my responsibilities expanded rapidly. Besides handling other interrogations, I got involved in running an informant network in North Vietnam, and from time to time was brought in to debrief our best agent inside the Communist command in the South. So I had a pretty good view of the waterfront. The way I solidified my position was through a briefing of Ted Shackley, my former station chief, who was now head of the CIA's East Asia Division. He came through on a fact-finding tour, and since I now knew all the euphemisms and could mimic his computerlike delivery, I gave him a briefing with charts and pointers and body counts that was out of his own textbook. Tom Polgar, the new station chief, was so impressed that he soon put me in charge of writing his principal strategic estimates for Washington and briefing just about everybody who came through the embassy.

That gave me even wider contact with the press corps—which was good and bad. By then I had gotten to know many of the big-name journalists who dealt with the embassy regularly and who got under-the-table handouts from the CIA and others. They profited from this arrangement, and sometimes we did, too. Not that any of these guys were working for the CIA. But they knew where the handouts came from, and were aware that anything they told us was apt to find its way into an intelligence report. Even so, there was a gentleman's agreement that nobody got embarrassed. I don't know what these guys were thinking, but I do know that a lot of stuff we handed out showed up pretty much unfiltered in the press. And some of it was classic disinformation, not so much lies as half-truths.

Case in point: Right after the peace accords in '73, the embassy was trying to convince Congress that the Communists were breaking the cease-fire right and left, so we could get additional aid for the South Vietnamese. We did this by playing up the Communist violations and blinking at the South Vietnamese ones, and by exaggerating the Communist buildup in the South. There was evidence that the NVA were constructing some roadways along the western spine of the country, and that they had begun to replace the casualties they suffered in 1972. What we did was to take the evidence and pump it up, to the extent of suggesting that the Communists were building airfields and superhighways in the "third Vietnam." We gave journalists to believe that the replacement troops were not replacements at all, but reinforcements for an already oversized invasion force. Since we had a lock on this kind of intelligence, no journalist could double-check the handouts to see where the poisoned peanuts had been planted. Some of them might try, of course. An industrious reporter might go to his contacts in the British embassy or the Australian or New Zealand embassy and try to confirm what we had told him. What he couldn't know is that we were handing out the same poisoned peanuts to the other embassies. Everybody was getting the same hook, line, and sinker. Few journalists realized the system was so completely wired. That's the way disinformation was generated. And it was very effective. When I got back after the fall of Vietnam, I read back issues of papers and magazines, and sure enough, there was a lot of the material we had handed out.

Besides serving as the station chief's spear carrier, I became close to Ambassador Martin, who spoke with the same Southern accent as I, and hailed from the same somewhat ragged patrician background. I remember one meeting with him which in many ways summed up his views toward the Vietnamese. We had just finished lunch in his villa. It was a Sunday, I believe. He was talking about the way Southerners treat blacks. And he said, in essence, that the South Vietnamese were like the blacks—we had to do a lot of things for them, and show them the way. I was dumbfounded. I sputtered out something like,

"I think probably it would be useful to talk to them about what they could do for themselves, sir. And let them know we can't do everything for them, sir." Always couching it politely.

I should have objected more forcefully. Somebody should have, because Martin's condescension toward the South Vietnamese caused terrible problems. Not only did he pretend we could do more for them than we could; he never leveled with them about what we couldn't do. For instance, he never explained to them that the War Powers Act and the Cambodian bombing ban made it impossible to bring back U.S. forces, let alone the B-52s. As a result, South Vietnam got blindsided. They didn't adjust to the problems of U.S. policy, because they didn't understand them. U.S. purse strings were tightening, but the South Vietnamese left their forces overextended and allowed corruption to continue, to the point that it destroyed their capacity and will to fight.

Not that Martin can be blamed for all this. His kind of paternalism had been around for a long time. Even the Vietnamization program suffered from it. The premise of Vietnamization was that the South Vietnamese were ready to do it on their own. But the truth was that Vietnamization was a mask for our doing it with their bodies.

For all of this, if you had asked me on the day of the cease-fire whether they would survive, I would have answered "Yes." I was convinced an honorable peace was at hand—overly convinced. I remember the day they announced that the Paris Accords were about to be signed. I was interrogating a prisoner. And when I told him about the agreement, he broke down and wept, saying, "It's the happiest day of my life." He might have been speaking for me. I had become so emotionally involved with Vietnam that I couldn't do anything but gild its prospects. One of the first pieces of analysis I wrote after the cease-fire did just that, at least by omission. Supposedly it was to deal with the stability of the Saigon government. I had studied the regime and questioned experts, including a colleague who specialized in South Vietnamese politics. He kept saying, "There's corruption here, there's cronyism." But I knew that wouldn't fly. I told him, "There's no room for pessimism in the front office. It will never get past the ambassador or Polgar."

And it didn't. Every time somebody tried to report on corruption or Saigon's weaknesses, wishful thinking got in the way. The report was "Polgarized," as we used to say in the station—diluted or rewritten so completely that it became just its opposite, a celebration of the government's strengths.

Eventually I realized that Saigon's only real hope was the truth, and I tried to overcome my own wishful thinking. But getting the truth out to Washington was harder than I ever imagined, particularly as the ambassador's optimism increased. At first I figured I could change his mind by being politely deferential. So I became more gentlemanly than Beau Brummel. My fitness reports reflect it: "He defers to his superiors. He's very good in question-and-answer sessions. He never gets too far out in front." I kept thinking, If I play along, I'll be able to make a difference here.

But that wasn't enough. You couldn't just bow and scrape and expect to change everybody's mind. You had to have raw intelligence, and I began looking for it. You shouldn't do that in the spy business. The worst sin you can commit is to search for intelligence to prove a case. But I did it anyway.

As it happened, I didn't have to look far. One day, at the National Interrogation Center, I ran across a major defector from COSVN. For reasons I still don't understand, he quickly became attached to me. This guy was an incredible fount of knowledge about the VC. But he was also a walking tragedy. The Communists had let his wife die in childbirth for lack of proper medicines. He had gone to pieces and decided to defect. Once we developed a rapport, we'd sit around in his cell, just talking. And it quickly became apparent that I'd stumbled onto a mint. Everything I had known about the Communists third-hand became clear second-hand or first-hand. He'd sit there telling me about the guys who headed up the Communist command, what their problems were, what they thought of the South Vietnamese government. The reports I wrote up were so sensational that even Kissinger sent a cable saying they were solid gold.

But nobody drew the logical inferences from the reports. The picture I got from the defector and other sources was that the Communists were not about to be beaten. Nor were they the only ones breaching the cease-fire. The South Vietnamese were doing it, too—and hurting themselves in the process. By pushing out wherever they could and stalling the emplacement of the truce teams, they made it impossible to stabilize any lines of control in the countryside. As long as nobody knew who controlled what, everybody was going to push and shove. No standstill of forces, no cease-fire. And no chance for either side to conserve resources.

You would have thought that territorial control would have been one of the hottest intelligence topics. But actually it was a no-no. We hardly ever put anything about it into channels. At one point Polgar even refused to distribute a map that I drew up showing VC holdings in-country. Why? Because once you acknowledged that the Com-

munists controlled something, you were going to have trouble justifying an additional aid package for Saigon. Say a congressman comes
through and sees that map. He just might figure that instead of asking
for more aid, South Vietnam ought to be thinking about a real cease-
fire. So my map was verboten. I had to keep it hidden in my office.

As for the COSVN defector, his message didn't get through either.
Basically it was that the Communists didn't think the South Vietnamese government could hold. I hoped to use such information to show
that the Communists were standing fast, not weakening. Then maybe
Saigon and Washington would realize that a new round of negotiations
on political issues had to take place. In fact, by mid-1974 the ambassador was about ready to accept that, though for reasons different
from the defector's. Martin and others in the embassy had decided
that the Communists were running out of steam and were looking for
a new cease-fire. But instead of nudging the South Vietnamese toward
the bargaining table, as would seem logical, Martin went to Congress
to plead for a big new aid package. To justify it, he insisted the South
Vietnamese were down to their last bullets. That wasn't true. There
were plenty of supplies if corruption could have been eliminated and
logistics streamlined. Without that, more aid would have been useless
anyway. But Martin demanded the aid. Thieu dug in his heels, thinking
he'd get it. And the NVA got ready for another round of fighting,
which escalated into the final offensive. Meanwhile, the last chance
for patch-up negotiations was lost.

And what of my defector? Through it all he remained so empathetic,
such a marvelous guy. One night, as a reward for everything he'd
done, I took him out for a night on the town to expose him to the
new society that he had committed himself to. Dummy that I am, I
took him to an American eating establishment on Nguyen Hue, a
holdover from the war days, one of the few. There were sweating old
homesteaders, American contractors, wrestling Vietnamese women
around the dance floor. After a while my defector started getting tipsy.
He'd been in the boonies for so long that he wasn't used to booze. I
remember him sitting in his chair weaving. Finally he looked up and
stared hard at these Vietnamese girls, all prim and proper, practically
being raped by the fat old homesteaders, and something came over
him. It was as if a sheet of ice suddenly encased his whole body. He
kept staring for a few minutes, and then he said, "I've made the wrong
choice. We're going to lose." I was so stunned. He just sat there
shaking his head, saying, "I've made the wrong choice." But it was
too late to send him back. We had him. He was in. The Communists
knew he had defected. They probably already knew what he told us,

because they had people in all the camps and interrogation centers. The ultimate horror is that he was left behind. What they did to someone like him, I can only surmise.

KEITH BRINTON AND CLAUDIA KRICH

They met in 1971 at a work camp in Massachusetts sponsored by the Quakers.

KEITH: *"I was raised just north of Philadelphia in a Quaker town. After college, I went into the Peace Corps and worked in the Ivory Coast for two years. When I came back, I wanted to do something else like that. I went to the American Friends Service Committee to find a job in Africa. They had none. But they had a job in Vietnam. So I went as a conscientious objector, and I worked for three and a half years at the Quang Ngai Rehabilitation Center. Came back in mid-1970. Bummed around. Finally applied for a job as a summer counselor at a teenage work camp. I got a look at the paperwork on my co-director, all her social activities and political awareness, and I thought, 'My God, I'm going to have to work with this lady? This is going to be very embarrassing.' I didn't seem to have the same level of background."*

CLAUDIA: *"And of course, I was looking at this guy who spent three years in Vietnam and was in the Peace Corps in Africa. . . . [Laughs.] I was born in 1948 in Los Angeles. My parents were teachers. Liberal. I had a very ordinary American upbringing. By the last year of college, I was well aware of the war and against it. And against Governor REE-gan, as we called him then."*

They were married in 1972. Nine months later, the AFSC asked them to become co-directors of the Quang Ngai center. CLAUDIA: *"I went with the clear understanding that there was peace in Vietnam. This was in April of '73, right after the accords were signed. I had images of spending time on the beaches and rebuilding the country and taking lovely vacations and having a good time. I really thought the war was ending right then. It was a bit of a shock to find out it wasn't."*

When we talk, they live in Woodland, California, a town in the Sacramento valley surrounded by board-flat fields of rice, tomatoes, and fruit trees. He works as a family nurse practitioner; she markets her own invention, a patented fabric baby carrier. Three young daughters keep the house messy and lively.

KEITH: The rehabilitation center was run in the Quang Ngai hospital, in a building that wasn't used by them. Basically we took people who were wounded and healing, and by giving them physical therapy and moving them in special ways, we'd help them gain more use of the wounded limbs than they would otherwise. Sometimes the gain was very dramatic—20 percent recovery without physical therapy, 80 percent with it. That's what convinced AFSC that a rehabilitation center would probably be the most useful project they could do in that area. They built it in 1967 and supplied it with the tools you need to make artificial limbs. There were Westerners there training the Vietnamese until toward the end of the program, say in 1974, when the last foreign physical therapist left and wasn't replaced.

When we were there, we had fifty-five Vietnamese staff. There were about twenty-one making artificial limbs, and about eight in the physical therapy department. There were some carpenters making crutches, and people making wheelchairs. The American team would usually have a doctor, sometimes a nurse, a PT, and so forth.

CLAUDIA: We were always in a fix trying to get a doctor. No Vietnamese doctors would work for us, because we couldn't pay enough. They were also all required to be in the military. So they were spread very thinly. They had their military duty, they had their private practice, where they made money, and they'd put in a couple of minutes a week at the hospital.

KEITH: There were 500 beds, so say maybe 1,000 patients.

CLAUDIA: Two to a bed. Every bed had two at least, going head to toe.

I think about 80 percent of the people we treated were wounded by American-made land mines. There were kids, young people, anyone who walked along, stepped on a mine, and bingo, lost a leg. The mines were almost always left by the South Vietnamese Army. In other words, us. And almost always we had to recut the bone. The hospital would simply cut off the injury, leaving no place to put some skin around the stump of bone. Our staff would do stump-revision surgery to shorten the bone and leave enough skin and fat and tissue there to be able to take the pressure of an artificial limb. It was really stupid, to have to do it twice. But that's how it worked, and we had no control over it.

KEITH: A lot of people were also hurt by what they call unexploded ordnance—things that didn't explode, but did when they were hit by a hoe.

CLAUDIA: We did a lot of burns, too, like white phosphorus burns. Or people were just shot by nervous or tired South Vietnamese troops.

KEITH: Usually our patients would just show up at the center. Sometimes they came right from the hospital. They had recovered from their acute injuries, so they could move to the center and do physical therapy and be fitted for an artificial limb, if that's what they were gonna get.

CLAUDIA: A handful would come to the door every day and apply for admission. They'd be questioned about whether they were military. That was the main question—we didn't take them if they were. But the soldiers wanted to get in anyway, because our service was faster and our limbs were better. Sometimes they'd try to bribe our people, or bully and threaten them.

KEITH: The military could go to any of the rehabilitation centers that the Saigon government was running with American money. I think we would have treated military if they hadn't had any amputee service. But there were five government centers, beautiful ones. With tile walls . . . just beautiful. Much nicer than ours. We had a plain, cement-block building.

So there was no crush of people, but we still had to build a place behind the center to house them. They were being discharged by the hospital, yet they still needed rehabilitation for, say, a month. So they were camping on this big U-shaped porch we had. They'd live in big cardboard boxes. Families and families and families. They'd cook their little meals and come in for daily treatment.

CLAUDIA: There were lots of kids. Y'know, I never understood until I had kids why those parents didn't tell those children, "Don't pick up anything shiny." Most of our kid victims were wounded by playing with some damn thing. One time six kids came in at once. They were out in a field, and they played with a white phosphorus bomb that was sitting there unexploded. And blew themselves up. They were horribly wounded. Why didn't they leave it alone? Because they're kids. They just couldn't resist.

The patients would stay for a long time, sometimes for months. Then they'd suffer the next trauma, trying to go back to the village. They weren't considered freaks at the center. But once they stepped out and back into their villages, or even into the town, they were gawked at. The limbs were pretty much covered. We had shoes that fit over artificial feet, and they all wore pants, men and women. So you couldn't really tell. But when they tried to go back to their villages, they'd have to go by boat, or walk in the sand, or walk up rocky paths. That's when it didn't work. At the center, everything was set up for them. There were ramps and nice toilets. In the villages, there weren't any toilets. You can't stoop if you have two artificial legs and nothing to hold on to.

KEITH: Our best limb-maker was a guy named Quy. He was ingenious in being able to get the alignment just right, and the hinge. Everything had to be equivalent to the other side. Length, too, and that's not that easy. One time a visiting doctor who ran one of the government limb centers was commenting how so-and-so's limb looked pretty good. Quy watched the patient walk back and forth and proceeded to enumerate thirteen points that could be improved. He was in deadly earnest. And so self-confident about it—not arrogant, quite the contrary. Very modestly. "I think we could angle the foot a little bit," things like that. Point after point after point.

CLAUDIA: One thing we did was write long letters and take pictures that we'd try to get published. We also wrote articles. We'd try to show that more military aid wouldn't accomplish anything. We'd send statistical reports on the injuries we were dealing with, and how people got injured. The whole conclusion from our time there was that all the American armament was just too much for the people shooting it. They couldn't handle it. There was too much stuff. They were shooting it off in the fields. They were using it up so they could get next month's quota. They were just shooting like crazy. I think spare parts were lacking here and there. But bullets sure weren't lacking, and cannon shells.

KEITH: Every year, AFSC would produce a flyer that had photographs and little charts showing the number of gunshot injuries, mine injuries, shrapnel, for 1971, 1972, 1973, and so on. This was the number of people who were treated by us. There was a dramatic change: It was getting worse under Vietnamization. There was an increasing number of certain types of injuries. With the peace accords, we didn't see an end of gunshot wounds. By no means. You'd think there'd be less shooting. But more people were hurt after the accords than before.

CLAUDIA: I remember that. It was one of the first things we wrote back, that injuries were actually up, not down. We told people in Quang Ngai about the peace accords. Remember, Keith? They didn't know anything about it.

KEITH: That's right. [Laughs.] They didn't have a text. We ordered some, and I carried one around in my pocket.

CLAUDIA: The press was censored, so we'd show it to people and read it to them. People on our staff didn't know. Neither did the English professor down the street who loved to come over and chat. But the North Vietnamese and the PRG published it till it was coming out of their ears. All their people knew it. They probably knew it by heart and backwards.

KEITH: They read it on Liberation Radio over and over and over. Somebody would read it all the way through, and then start again.

Whereas the newspaper in Quang Ngai may have reported it was signed, but how would anybody know what it said? The soldiers didn't know. How would they learn? Only if they listened to Liberation Radio, and that was dangerous. The government had no interest in telling them that North Vietnamese troops were going to be allowed to stay where they were, and the PRG was going to keep the territory it occupied. That this was not considered South Vietnam, but rather one part of a nation that would eventually be unified. Really, the government had no interest in telling them that. There would have been desertions by the thousands. Or the fact that people could go back to their homelands. Saigon didn't want to breathe that, my God. By bombing the countryside they had accumulated most of the population in their areas. They didn't want to lose that.

CLAUDIA: Another thing we did was take care of people in the prison ward. This was where they kept prisoners from the town prison when they had to be in the hospital. Usually as a result of torture. They were brought from the interrogation center to the hospital and put in the prison ward.

KEITH: It was just a locked ward.

CLAUDIA: So we dealt with a lot of prisoners who were victims of torture. I don't remember a single male torture victim. Maybe they didn't let them out. Or maybe they were in a military hospital. But heck, the woman who died just after we arrived—she was about seventy-five, and she'd been tortured to death. We watched her die. She was shackled to her bed with a chain. I don't know what she died of. She got very thin. Couldn't keep food down. Maybe she died of starvation. She was one of my first memories. She'd been there for months.

I remember writing about those prisoners. Their stories usually went like this: "I was walking through the rice paddy one night, and I was arrested and accused of being a VC. So they tortured me." And who knows? Maybe the seventy-five-year-old woman was part of the Liberation Front. Maybe she wasn't. But if she's walking around at night, it didn't matter.

I remember a young woman with a nursing baby who was taken back and forth. She cried. There was nothing we could do about it. We'd just lose our privileges if we interceded beyond a certain point. We'd take visitors in to see the prisoners and interview them. AP, UPI. They would write stories about it. It was crazy. It's funny how crazy it was. It didn't bother the interrogators that it was being written up. It had no effect on them whatsoever. Nobody ever did anything, nobody ever said, "Hey—"

KEITH: The attitude was, Listen, these people are VC. If they won't tell of their own account, you have to make them tell. Or: This isn't U.S. policy, it's the Saigon government. They're an independent country.

CLAUDIA: It was really low-key. It wasn't like an American prison system at all. But the torture part was very real. We would get permission sometimes to bring them over to our center and treat them there. They would have seizures. They'd be reliving the shock treatments. Flashing lights would set them off. They'd come into the center, and if one of the fluorescent lights wasn't working right, that would set them into a real physical seizure, biting their tongue, thrashing. Several of us would have to get on them and hold them down. This was reliving an experience they'd had with electric shock on some part—on their genitals or their nipples or some other place. They would tell about it, we would write about it, and it would continue.

It was almost always a light that would set them off. It was a new medical area for us. [Laughs nervously.] We didn't know what was doing it.

KEITH: They were beaten a lot, too.

CLAUDIA: That old woman had bruises all over her.

KEITH: There's a saying in Vietnamese that means, We beat you until you admit you're a Communist. Then we beat you until you promise never to be one again.

CLAUDIA: Do you remember Em Huong, Keith? This was a very, very poor country family with the most beautiful girl. She was twelve or fourteen. Her father was extremely humble. He always spoke with a little cigarette butt in his mouth, so he never opened his mouth, and if I couldn't read his lips I couldn't figure out what he was saying. He had this gorgeous daughter who had curly black hair. Wavy, which was unusual. And she had a very low voice, like a movie star.

First we met the two of them. Little by little we learned the story. She was a paraplegic. She'd been wounded in the back in a bombing attack and was paralyzed from the waist down. But she was taking it very well. She was exercising well. She had a spirit that couldn't be matched. The story of their family was that they lived in a little village that was bombed—

KEITH: And she was injured. He was taking her to town for therapy— not the very first time, but he was taking her to town one day, and while absent—

CLAUDIA: The village was bombed again.

KEITH: And his wife and his three other kids were killed. But he didn't know that right away. He came home and found out.

CLAUDIA: So he ended up being the only whole member of his family. Em Huong died, too, but that was much later. I think we learned later on, when we were in Saigon.

KEITH: Being paraplegic, she was susceptible to kidney infections, and she had gotten a disease.

CLAUDIA: We knew she was going to die. How could she live? None of those paraplegics had a long life expectancy. The chances of infection were too great. They need tremendous care. They need to be turned all night long, because they won't turn. They can develop a bedsore in one night. Our staff cleaned bedsores for patients more than anything else they did for them. They would find them in the hospital wards, and the hospital made no attempt to even educate them. They would be lying there perfectly still, and the PT would turn them over and see just massive, deep—a bedsore is an open wound. Like you take a shovel and scoop out a hunk of flesh all the way to the bone. Infected and ugly. They'd infect the blood or the bone, and the patient would die.

The really sad thing about the amputees was the common belief that they were infertile—if you lose a leg, you can't make babies. Of course, direct evidence contradicted that time and time again. But it didn't matter. They were unmarriageable, because they were defective, and they couldn't work adequately. We had many young women, including our cook and our seamstress and our receptionist, who were all considered unmarriageable. Two of them had been engaged and about to get married when they got injured. Both fiancés abandoned them.

I remember one young woman who had been pregnant for the first time, who lost one leg and also the fetus. Her husband had abandoned her. And the fetus was not coming out. It doesn't automatically. They let it stay in there for a long time. I think it was weeks. They just waited until nature took its course. The poor woman had to deal with the fact that she had a dead fetus inside her and lost her husband and lost her leg. She was lying there—and her brother was taking care of her. I have an image of him washing her breasts, because milk was coming out. She was lying there too depressed to move. Just lying there. She wasn't that hurt, but she was miserable. And him taking care of her so lovingly. A beautiful, horrible image.

15

THE FAST EXIT

The final act was played out in just fifty-five days.

On March 10, 1975, General Van Tien Dung of the People's Army of Vietnam attacked the town of Ban Me Thuot in the southern Central Highlands. The South Vietnamese were expecting an offensive somewhere in the region. But Dung had secretly massed three divisions against a regiment of defenders. The battle was over almost as soon as it began.

With Ban Me Thuot lost and other skirmishes flaring around the country, President Thieu took a step he had been considering for months—and one that effectively ended the war. He ordered his generals to withdraw from Kontum and Pleiku in the northern highlands and regroup on the coast. From there, they would try to retake Ban Me Thuot. But there was no planning for the maneuver. Commanders simply jumped in choppers or Jeeps and fled. Soon the retreat turned into chaos, and then into a death march, with tens of thousands of troops and civilians ensnarled on a tiny road through the mountains. Two divisions disintegrated. The panic quickly spread north. Hué was abandoned without a fight, as soldiers from the crack 1st Division threw away their weapons and tried to escape with their families. The final catastrophe came in Danang, the country's second-biggest city, now bloated with 500,000 new refugees. As the NVA cut off escape routes to the south and sent artillery crashing in, riots exploded at the airport, the docks, and the beaches. Of the relatively few refugees who managed to cram themselves on ships and barges, many died of thirst or were murdered by rampaging ARVN deserters. Danang fell on March 30. Nearly half of South Vietnam had been overrun in three weeks. Now Hanoi decided to go for broke.

It is hard to know who was more surprised by the collapse: the northerners, the southerners, or the Americans. But the signs were there. Shep Lowman, who ran the embassy unit that reported on South Vietnamese politics, remembers the grim mood when he came in-country (for his third tour) in 1974. The gloom grew from numerous sources: Watergate, the sharp rise in oil prices, a hostile U.S. Congress, the North's buildup of the Ho Chi Minh Trail, and the corruption rotting the army and government. He did not see the end coming quickly, he says—but he saw it coming.

In keeping with the rest of the war, South Vietnam's final month spawned controversies that retain their bitterness today. Was the evacuation a brilliant success or a fiasco? Was Ambassador Graham Martin a mastermind or a monster? Through 1974, did he and his aides keep Washington in the dark by censoring reports of runaway corruption and plummeting morale—thus setting South Vietnam up for the kill? And at the end, did Martin, hoping against all evidence for a negotiated settlement, refuse to plan a large-scale evacuation until it was far too late?

Martin was a formidable figure who inspired strong feelings, as the speakers in this chapter make clear. There seems no doubt that his reluctance to admit how fast the end was coming contributed to the haphazard quality of the exit. The only halfway efficient evacuation, the airlift run by the Defense Attaché's Office out of Tan Son Nhut, was initiated, promoted, and then speeded up by DAO personnel who often met resistance from the embassy. But whether Martin himself was the villain of the piece is, in a way, irrelevant. On the whole, during the dénouement the Americans treated the Vietnamese much as they had for the previous decade: as secondary players in their own drama. Understandably, the first focus was on getting the Americans out. Unforgivably, it took pressure from low-ranking staff both in Washington and Saigon to force serious planning for the movement of large numbers of Vietnamese. And once the planning was under way, events moved too fast. The decision to transport 10,000 people in a huge airlift was not taken until April 28—and before it could start, the Communists began shelling Tan Son Nhut, wrecking the runways. Most of the Vietnamese with close ties to the Americans—let alone the bulk of military officers and government officials—were left behind.

But it could have been far worse. Martin's refusal to allow an earlier evacuation was only partly based on false hopes. He also was desperate to avoid another Danang in Saigon—a descent into panic and rioting that would have made it impossible even for Americans to escape.

Martin feared that flying out key Vietnamese too soon would unleash the furies. That Saigon did not go haywire on the last days was a great accomplishment. Perhaps the most poignant scene in this chapter is Shep Lowman's account of his gatekeeper role at a safehouse where Vietnamese were assembling for evacuation. He let in those with the proper credentials and said no to the others—who went away politely. Nobody pushed past him, caused trouble, or pulled a gun. In South Vietnam's dying hours, these Saigonese still deferred to a lone American.

The helicopter lift on April 29 was a marvel of organization and courage, a last flaring of the American can-do spirit in Vietnam. And overall, during April the U.S. did spirit some 65,000 people from the country, about 55,000 of them Vietnamese. Thousands more found their own way out shortly before and after Saigon's fall. The numbers are impressive, even if they should have been better.

Still, one is left with a sense of unbalanced risks. Forced to leave behind hundreds of Vietnamese—employees, friends, associates— whom they had promised a ticket out, Alan Carter and Shep Lowman suffered bad dreams for a time and bad consciences forever. But some of those Vietnamese died in "reeducation camps."

And, of course, no American, hearing the news as South Vietnam's fate became clear, could ever have responded with the cry of anguish that ends this book.

SHEP LOWMAN

When I walk in the door, the smells hit me: garlic, frying vegetables, pungent spices. The lady of the house, a slim Vietnamese woman named Hiep, is cooking up a feast, and before the interview begins in earnest, lunch is served. Afterward, dark French coffee and little cakes with nut filling and a cooked egg yolk in the middle. Hiep's husband wields his chopsticks with the expertise of someone who spent more than five years in Vietnam. He explains that the cakes are called banh trung thu: *"We're coming into the autumn moon festival, and they're traditional in Vietnam." He met Hiep in 1966, when he was working in Chau Doc province, and they were married the next year.*

He grew up in Texas and Oklahoma, the son of an oil geologist. In 1957, after graduating from Harvard Law School and working in business for a time, he joined the Foreign Service. "I had a fairly traditional career to begin with—an assignment in Vienna, some work at the State Department, a year of studying economics at Harvard. Then I was

*supposed to go to Geneva. But in the summer of '65 a flyer came across
my desk. They were recruiting people to go to Vietnam on loan to AID
as province representatives. I was ready for an adventure because I had
just gone through a divorce. But in addition—and I swear this is true
and not concocted twenty years later—I really was concerned to find
out whether or not there was any input the United States could make
in a situation where a vulnerable society was under attack by the Communist system."*

*After his last tour ended on April 30, 1975, he spent nearly six years
running the State Department's Indochinese refugee program. Then he
served as deputy chief of mission in Honduras, and now he heads the
Vietnam, Laos, and Cambodia desk in the Bureau of East Asian and
Pacific Affairs.*

My first tour went from 1966 to 1970. I worked in the delta, and then
in Saigon with the pacification program, and then as adviser to the
mayor of Saigon. For the last six months I was in Danang.

It was interesting, and often frustrating. One of the most frustrating
parts of it was the—I guess I'd call it corruption, although that's an
oversimplification. It was partly a value system that was family-based.
You say, Okay, what I have to do is protect my family, take care of
my son. I have to get him a good job. If he's a complete nincompoop,
that's got nothing to do with it. If I've got some influence and his
uncle's got a good position, then he's going to get a job. That's my
value system. I'm not going to worry about the good of the nation.

Then the system was corrupted. Whatever broader-based ethical
values it had began to fade when it became the value system of a
military bureaucracy. If you talk to Vietnamese, they'll say there was
a time when Confucian values and the mandarin system worked. You
have highly educated leaders. They may take from the populace, but
what they give back is an effective administration and some depend-
ability, some predictability in life. When that begins to break down,
you still have people taking, but they're not giving much back, especially in the way of predictability. The officials are being changed
all the time, positions are being bought and sold, and it runs all through
the system. That's one of the things that makes it hard to change.

We did make progress. We made progress in lower-level things, but
not in that basic area. We made big progress in agriculture. We brought
in miracle rice from the Philippines, and rice production per hectare
was tripled. All kinds of farmers' cooperatives were getting started.
Land reform was making strides. People's self-defense was an interesting concept that seemed to be working. And on and on. If you

look at individual, specific programs, you could find lots and lots of things that looked like successes. And yet the place was going to hell. It was going to hell because the kind of basic progress in political maturation seemed to be frozen. It was frozen because progress would have meant the people in power giving up power voluntarily. I'm sure they felt they didn't have to do that because we were going to keep on supporting them.

In 1970 I went back to Washington and worked on the Philippine desk for a while. But in February of 1973, at the time of the peace treaty, they called a number of people back to Vietnam to observe what was going on. Most of them went out to the field. Because my Vietnamese wasn't very good, I stayed in the embassy political section with a little four-man unit, and we put out a daily situation report. And when I left in the summer of '73, I felt pretty good about Vietnam. That's why I disagree a little bit with this idea that the Vietnamese collapsed psychologically because we cut ties with them. Remember, two days before the peace agreement, the Communists launched a whole bunch of limited but sharp attacks to capture strategic points. They assumed that when the cease-fire came, the government wouldn't be able to do anything about it. The South Vietnamese said, "No, we won't accept that." By the time I left there had been sharp fighting, and they had taken back a significant part of the land they lost— without us, and even without our air power. Entirely on their own. So I thought they had a decent chance militarily, and they felt pretty good about themselves. A lot of confidence. People didn't like it that we were gone, but in no way were they showing panic or fear.

I went over to the Philippines for a year. In the summer of '74 I came back to Saigon for the third time, to take over the internal political reporting unit. The mood was much grimmer. People were downcast. They were worried about Watergate, worried about the economy, worried about the Communists. It was startling. I didn't expect it, although I knew the military situation had declined. In 1973 one of my officers had produced a report that he called "The Third Vietnam." It laid out a lot of intelligence about the Communist logistic system in the highlands. The Ho Chi Minh Trail had become an all-weather road. They were building an oil pipeline. We thought, "God, this is the infrastructure for a major invasion." All in violation of the Paris Accords, and nobody was doing anything about it. People knew that we were being more restrictive in our support, and the other side was getting increasingly generous support. The balance was beginning to tilt.

That summer, right after I got back, a Catholic priest by the name

582 | Strange Ground

of Father Thanh started an anticorruption movement. He was somewhere in the northern part of South Vietnam, in Hué or Danang. For
the first time, President Thieu was publicly accused of personal corruption. Thanh said, "It's a corrupt system, and the President is involved, too." That was followed later on by specific charges. I can
remember years before, Hiep, my wife, sitting on the bed sobbing
about corruption and saying, "They're going to destroy my country."
But she would always say that Thieu didn't know the extent of it, or
that he was a captive of the system and he couldn't do anything about
it. Many Vietnamese felt that way. They would excuse him personally.
They had to. He was their leader.

I've always felt that Father Thanh's movement was a traumatic event
in the history of South Vietnam. It came in the context of Watergate.
Nixon had been accused and had fallen. The military situation in
Vietnam was getting worse. As long as Thieu was seen to be successful
in his duty to keep the Americans on board and the Communists at
bay, people weren't going to attack him on the corruption issue. But
when he seemed to be failing, all of a sudden he became vulnerable.
The minute Thanh accused him publicly, everybody believed it. The
emperor had no clothes. Everybody said, "Hey, that's right, he is
corrupt. He has to be. He couldn't sit on top of a system like this and
not be profiting from it. It's perfectly logical."

From that time on, Thieu was totally ineffectual. The movement
had a shattering effect on him. He lost face. For a long time there
was almost no response. He finally made a speech in October, and it
was such a nothing speech that I can hardly remember what he said.
Both in content and delivery it was a complete washout. If you talked
to his closest confidants, they'd say, "He can't make decisions." I was
meeting with opposition figures and his own people, but particularly
with what I call the most moderate opposition, people like former
foreign minister Tran Van Do, and ex-Senator Sung, a newspaper
publisher, and Buu, the labor leader. They all dealt directly with Thieu
on political matters. They were saying, "He's becoming withdrawn."

There was a lot of public protest, and it grew. Protest didn't usually
happen in Vietnam, partly because the government didn't permit a
whole lot, and partly because they were fairly self-disciplined. At
about the same time as the Father Thanh movement, we had a free-
dom-of-the-press thing. Editorial complaints, burning of newspapers
in the streets. There was another priest who insisted that there were
tens of thousands of political prisoners in Vietnam. I suppose those
things were going on because people thought they could get away with
it more easily. Some were serious people. Some were demagogues.
But they were all pushing at the edge of the permissible.

Washington saw all this going on. Things had gotten quite chaotic. There were disorderly street meetings, public denunciations. They asked us for an analysis of what was causing all the problems. The factors we came up with were, first of all, Watergate. A feeling of great concern that Nixon was gone. And they were right to be concerned, because he had been their protector. If he had been the tough political leader that he could be, undamaged by Watergate, he might have fought back when North Vietnam violated the accords. But not Ford, and not the way the country was going. And it was more complicated than that, because Watergate got replicated in this anticorruption campaign.

Then there was the oil shock that happened in 1973, which hurt the economy. ARVN soldiers literally weren't getting enough to eat. Not to say there was malnutrition, but if you want to walk a guy all around on patrol and work him hard as a soldier, and you don't give him the calorie count to support that, his performance goes down. He gets into taking a little from the local people, and that doesn't make him very popular. What happened was the oil shock caused sharp inflation, and the allowances for food didn't go up enough to compensate.

Finally, there was the perception that maybe the United States was going to abandon the South. That was a major factor in the collapse. But it didn't happen when we pulled out our troops, and it didn't happen when we pulled out our air force. It happened when it looked like we were not going to support them politically or with matériel. Then it really began to hit.

I myself became very pessimistic. I didn't think the country was doomed in the near future, but to do the kind of things that were required would have taken a great deal of leadership ability or a resignation. If Thieu didn't resign, he'd have to share power. He'd have to fire a bunch of corrupt people who worked for him as toadies and bagmen. He'd have to take his best commanders and put them in command positions, and forget politics. He'd have to open up the political process to the opposition, make the parliament a real parliament. He didn't show signs of doing any of that. There was talk of a coup, but there had been talk of a coup by Ky for years. I think the embassy discouraged it.

In January the Communists took Phuoc Long province. The situation in Washington was getting worse rather than better. Ford did ask for more aid, but it wasn't very long before people could see he wasn't going to prevail. We had a dreadful time with this congressional delegation that came out in December or January. Bella Abzug running around with her damn floppy hat on. I'll never forget her at Tan Son Nhut airport, raving away at the news media, apparently with zero interest in anything she was seeing. As far as I could tell, they came with their own agenda. They made arrangements ahead of time with their own contacts. They saw the people they wanted to see. Fine, okay, don't let the embassy brainwash you. But most of them weren't interested in seeing any of the moderate or responsible opposition people we wanted them to see. When they left, we had the impression that, well, we failed. There probably isn't going to be another chance. It was the last hope I had, anyway, of getting a turnaround on Capitol Hill.

MONCRIEFF SPEAR

He greets me at the door of his house in Bethesda, just beyond the Washington city line. The house is a big colonial, its front yard a profusion of shrubs and flowers and trees sloping down to Massachusetts Avenue. He is tall, lean, white-haired, and rather formal, a diplomat of the old school, happier talking about the flow of events than about himself. For our interview he has equipped himself with a chronology of his final days in Vietnam.

He was born in 1921 and joined the Foreign Service in 1950. "I had a variety of posts, starting out in Central and Eastern Europe, and back here in the State Department on and off. Then my career sort of drifted off toward Southeast Asia. I served as a special assistant to Ambassador Martin from 1964 to 1967 in Bangkok. After that, I came back to Washington, worked as director of Thai affairs, went to the department's senior seminar on foreign policy, and had my own post in the Bahamas during the transition to independence. As that assignment came to an end, Martin was named ambassador to Saigon and asked if I'd come out and join him. That's how I ended up taking over as consul general in Nha Trang."

He arrived in Vietnam in September 1973.

My area was II Corps, the Central Highlands. It covered about 47 percent of the total area of Vietnam. We had representatives in each of the twelve provinces, sometimes with a staff of a half-dozen Americans or so, and maybe twenty or thirty Vietnamese. I'd say there were probably 100 Americans and maybe 500 or 600 Vietnamese working for us at the time I arrived. We did a good deal of slimming down, but by the end there were still 400 or 500 Vietnamese and about seventy-five Americans.

When I first got in-country I took it at face value that there had been peace accords. But even as I arrived, both sides were making land grabs, and considerable fighting had broken out in Kontum, which was the northernmost province in II Corps, up on the Cambodian border. That's one of the reasons they rushed me out there. The ARVN had pushed the North Vietnamese back across the cease-fire line just a few days before I arrived.

At the time, we thought the South Vietnamese forces were giving a pretty good account of themselves. The cutbacks in military assistance were beginning to be felt—the ARVN were having to ration ammunition and artillery and get over all the wasteful habits that we taught them over the years. I think the thing that hit morale hardest was the cutback in medevac helicopter flights. They'd also had to lay up a lot of aircraft, particularly some of the older ones that had been rushed in when we loaded them down with all kinds of surplus military equipment. But by and large, the ARVN were fighting well.

I'd say maybe 70 percent of the territory in II Corps was held by the government, and maybe 20 percent by the Communists. Big areas in between were no-man's-land. You had the usual pattern of the Communists holding the less-populated areas.

It was not a peacetime situation. It was very confused, with no nice clean lines. The fighting tended to rise and fall. If you try and do a "Who struck John?" and lay the blame for violating the accords, I think it's utterly futile. You find yourself going all the way back to the French war and beyond. I remember once there was a Communist push down out of the coastal areas they occupied in Binh Dinh to try and cut Route 1. That was a clear violation. But when the counter-offensive went rolling back in there, the South Vietnamese were bombing villages that the Communists had held practically since the days of the French. So who was the aggressor?

But during the latter half of '74, in the dry season, the Communists made a distinct effort. There were a series of isolated ARVN mountain outposts up north of Kontum. Very deliberately, those were wiped out. And of course there was the NVA dress rehearsal that took place in January, when they took Phuoc Long province. Phuoc Long bordered on the south side of Region II, right along the Cambodian border. A lot of Montagnard refugees came flowing up out of there, so we went tearing out with our refugee relief people to try and resettle them. That was the first time a provincial capital had fallen to the Communists, so it was quite a blow. And they made no bones about it being a dry run for their winter offensive.

But we thought the ARVN could hold. And our intelligence was pretty good. In January and February of 1975 we got a lot of reports.

There was a rather weak NVA division that had been in Laos that moved into the Pleiku area. As we later discovered, that was to keep the South Vietnamese occupied while the NVA moved their main combat units down around Ban Me Thuot. Then we captured documents indicating that they would try to seize the roads and isolate the highlands from the lowlands. But the plan was for a two-year offensive. They would make major inroads in '75 and finish the job in '76. And finally, the South Vietnamese captured a recon patrol up in the Binh Dinh area and got their plan showing how they were going to interdict Route 19 that ran from Qui Nhon to Pleiku. Later on we got word that they'd try to cut the highway between Nha Trang and Ban Me Thuot as well. So we had pretty good tactical intelligence.

But the NVA had also sneaked another division in, the 316th. Nobody even knew it was in the country until about three days into the battle of Ban Me Thuot. That was very cleverly done. And even though they moved their major forces down, they kept up all sorts of harassing actions around Pleiku. In hindsight you can see that some reports were quite accurate, but they were accompanied by ones that looked equally convincing but weren't true. The usual fog of war.

The first sign of the offensive was when they cut off the two main highways that led up into the highlands. On Tuesday, March 4, they cut Route 19, the northern one that went from Qui Nhon up to Pleiku. They cut that off at the An Khe pass, which was a steep winding road up to the escarpment, where the Viet Minh had won a major victory over the French. The same day they also blocked Route 21. And on Saturday, March 8, the 320th Division, which was one of the major units massed for the attack on Ban Me Thuot, cut Route 14, the main north-south road that ran from Kontum to Pleiku down to Ban Me Thuot and then on down into Quang Duc.

Generally we'd get this information at a morning briefing at ARVN military headquarters in Nha Trang. They'd have a briefing every morning at eight o'clock, and my deputy and I and some of the staff would go over and sit in. In this case they didn't seem alarmed, because they'd had intelligence reports that led them to expect some of this.

On Sunday the ninth, very heavy artillery fire came in on the ARVN province headquarters in Quang Duc. There had been speculation that they might hit there. But General Phu, the corps commander, told me he had reports that the attack would come at Ban Me Thuot that evening. He organized a task force to set up a command down there and begin sending troops down, but that morning, the tenth, the attack began, and within a few hours it had overrun Ban Me Thuot.

We had a provincial representative there, Paul Struharik. Three or four American missionaries and a Fulbright scholar took refuge in his compound, along with an Australian radio broadcaster. That was our first and major concern. We were trying to get a helicopter or a plane in and get them out, but Paul sent word that it wasn't safe, there was firing and artillery going off. So we put one of our propeller aircraft up overhead to maintain contact with him. We had radio contact for about three days until they were finally surrounded and overrun. I went up on one of those flights myself. We were taking turns—various people from the staff at Nha Trang would go up. For the first two or three days we stayed in contact. But by the time I went up we had lost it. Paul's radio batteries had been running down, and contact had been very intermittent. But we were hopeful. We'd go up and circle over the city. You could see the artillery fire coming in from the outskirts. Of course, we had to stay up at about 15,000 feet, because they had these SAM missiles. Whenever we'd try to contact Paul, I'd take a pair of binoculars and spot his compound, and then the plane would dive on down. I remember a distinctly unpleasant feeling of vertigo. We couldn't make any contact. We thought his radio had gone bad, but within a few days the NVA had occupied all of the city, and we had to assume he'd been captured.

On the fourteenth there was the famous meeting of Thieu and his generals at Cam Ranh Bay. They decided to abandon the highlands and retreat down Route 7, an old logging road. There may have been some plan for the retreat at first, but what happened was that everybody just jumped in their vehicles. They didn't even let the province chief up in Kontum know they were pulling out. We heard about it on Saturday morning, the fifteenth. At that point, Phu advised Earl Thieme, the province rep in Pleiku, that he should start evacuating Americans. We had already been telling various nonessential personnel that it might be prudent for them to get going. One of the things you learn is that if you're going to have a good evacuation, the more people you can get out early, before the roof falls in, the easier things are. Some of this, of course, was in the evacuation plans, which we did have and we did use, contrary to what Snepp and others have said. However, we didn't go broadcasting from the rooftops that we were evacuating people, because we didn't want to set off a panic. All during this period we were quietly sluicing people out the back door just as hard and fast as we could. I think the criticism is evidence of our success in keeping our underground evacuation secret.

But we had a very bad time in Pleiku. It was the first example of panic at the airport. All during the day we had American planes flying back and forth, these old C-47s. It had come so suddenly that by the end of the day we still hadn't gotten enough of the Vietnamese staff out. I remember being quite sharp with Earl Thieme at one point, saying, "C'mon, fella, I'm supposed to evacuate Americans." He made the point that you had to keep a certain number of Americans there to act as traffic cops and keep things under control. We did have one plane that was taken over by some Vietnamese deserters at gunpoint. They just walked up to the plane and said, "We're getting on." The pilot very smartly took off with what load he had, and we got word when they were in the air. So the Vietnamese sent out some military police and arrested these guys as soon as they landed.

By the end of the day Thieme hadn't gotten everybody out, so he gave the keys to all the vehicles to the Vietnamese and started putting them on the road following the military forces down Route 7. Then we sent up helicopters the next day to fly along the road and try to pluck our people off as they came down. We got quite a number that way. But it turned out that the city hadn't been overrun, and Thieme and Ed Toll from Kontum started demanding to go back. They were terribly concerned about getting the rest of their staff out. With a little arm-twisting I was persuaded to let them go. They went back to both Kontum and Pleiku, and they got almost everyone else on planes or on the road to the coast. Right after that the Communists did march in, and there was all kinds of shelling and looting in Pleiku. To this day it gives me goose bumps when I realize how close to the edge of that thin ice we were skating.

On Monday, the seventeenth, Thieme and his men were flying all up and down Route 7 recovering their local employees. By this time the head of the retreating column was in Cheo Reo, the capital of Phu Bon province. There were something like 200,000 people on that road, and the ARVN units had lost their military discipline. For one thing, the NVA 320th Division had cut across and was beginning to shell the rear units. There were civilians all mixed in, and very few officers with the troops. It wasn't a matter of one unit setting up a defensive position and the column leapfrogging that, and then falling back. It was: Everybody jump in the car and go. Vehicles would stall and they'd have to be pushed off the road with bulldozers. Pretty soon they started running out of gas. By the time they came through Cheo Reo it was a looting mob. I remember our housekeeper, who was a devout Catholic—her brother was a priest in Pleiku, and he died of starvation up there on the escarpment somewhere, trying to bring his flock down. There were enormous civilian casualties. The bodies were all up through the woods. They didn't have any food, and it took them about a week to get to the coast.

In Cheo Reo the ARVN were looting and taking things at gunpoint and shooting civilians. They tried to loot our compound. We had a fellow named Ed Sprague there, who'd been in the Special Forces. He and his staff held the compound in a series of firefights all through the night until we were able to get helicopters and evacuate them the next morning. But as the first helicopter was coming down, Ed was surrounded by a bunch of soldiers who put guns on him and wanted to hijack the chopper. With some very quick thinking, Ed said, "There's another one right behind. I'll get on this one and we'll radio and have the next one come down and pick you guys up." They let Ed and his people get on the helicopter, and of course he had both of them get away in a rush.

At Song Be the column had to go across a river crossing. The route had been abandoned for years, and there was no bridge. General Chuk and his army engineers brought up a pontoon bridge and put it across, but it took them two or three days, and in the meantime the column was under fire. On the twenty-second I went up there with a *Wall Street Journal* correspondent and some others. We wanted to get up over the fighting and beyond Song Be to see if we could get some refugee supplies in there. But when we landed near the road, a whole gang came running at us, firing in the air and trying to take over the helicopter. So we took off. It obviously wasn't practical to take in supplies, not if we wanted to keep our helicopters.

I remember flying down Route 7 toward Tuy Hoa and watching the refugees coming in there. You could see this endless line of vehicles and people moving along the road at a walk. Very few people made it to the coast out of that column of hundreds of thousands.

At the same time, hundreds of thousands more were coming by ship down the coast from I Corps. The government was talking about relocating as many as a million refugees from I Corps to II Corps. As I evacuated my staff people from the highlands I was sending them down to work on the coast, trying to help the refugees as they came into Cam Ranh Bay.

But things were crumbling all around. Quang Duc province collapsed. One day the province chief, who had given magnificent leadership all through the war, just disappeared and the whole defense fell in. Fighting had broken out in Binh Dinh. The NVA division that had been in the A Shau valley had broken out, and the ARVN 22nd Division had to fall back from the An Khe pass. We had been doing pretty well with our quiet evacuation, but on Friday the twenty-eighth we got word that everything had gone to hell up in Danang, and we should send every helicopter and plane we had to Al Francis, the consul general up there. As it turned out, he had a perfectly ghastly time. The Communists closed in much more quickly up there, and the ARVN got whipsawed with all sorts of contradictory orders. General Truong, the I Corps commander, was first told he should evacuate, and then that he should go back and hold the line. As a result, everything got out of whack. They finally had to evacuate across the beach. Al got on one of these South Vietnamese naval vessels and came down into Cam Ranh. A lot of the refugees came down on MSTS ships, military sea transport, and some horrible things happened. The soldiers would take them over and terrorize the civilians. The American crewmen were all under siege up in the pilot house for the whole trip down.

On the twenty-ninth I flew out to pick up Al Francis on his ship. I had Gerald Ford's photographer with me, David Kennerly. We went out and circled around the ship, and I could see muzzle flashes. Whether they were firing in the air or firing at us I don't know, but I told the pilot to get us back to the landing pad. They brought Al in by cutter. He gave me all sorts of good advice. One thing was to put little hoards of jet fuel for the helicopters away in various places so people didn't know where it was. The other was to work with the local police and promise them that we'd evacuate as many of their people as we had room for, with the idea that this would help keep them in place and keep order during the evacuation. And finally, Al said, "The roof will fall in about twenty-four hours before you think it will." That's just about what happened.

Incidentally, there was a very nasty undercurrent of anti-Americanism going on by this time. The Vietnamese felt with some justification that we had let them down. We got various reports that there was bitter anti-American feeling in the military units, which of course made it difficult to try and work with these people. We tried to explain to them that we weren't very happy about what was going on and what our government had done, and we were out there doing the best we could. Had the aid been voted, or had the United States shown it was not abandoning Vietnam, it might have made a difference. We were worried that the feelings would explode and we'd wind up with a whole lot of American hostages, which is another reason we tried to keep our evacuation effort so quiet. I remember all sorts of high-ranking Vietnamese wives coming around to see if my wife, Lois, had packed up, and what we were doing. Lois had been teaching at the local community college, and they had just had exams. We also had house guests at the time, of all things. So Lois flew the guests down to Saigon and then came back and passed out all the exam papers, just to let the kids know we were still there.

On Monday the thirty-first the aircraft came back from Danang. We ordered our people back from Cam Ranh so we could have them in Nha Trang. At two in the morning on the first we got word that the 22nd Division had abandoned Qui Nhon, up in Binh Dinh, and had been pulled off by three naval vessels. My deputy and I went over to the II Corps briefing, and when we got back we found all our guards waiting in a big crowd. The first of April was payday. We had contracted out payroll services to a private contractor, and the treasurer had taken off. I had to sign a very large promissory note to get enough money to pay off the guards. [Laughs.]

We finally got that mob cleared out and started evacuating again. We'd been sending out local employees, people from the Vietnamese-American Association, and people from the up-country provinces. Plus certain people in the local administration. We'd call them and tell them to drive into the compound with whatever they could carry in suitcases. Then we'd drive them to the airport and fly them down to Saigon. There was a steady steam of airplanes, every hour or so. But by this time we had 600 or 700 people that we'd brought down out of the highlands. They were all in compounds down along the beach. And there were a number of retired Americans around town. We discovered that instead of getting out as we told them to, they were all waiting around for the first of April, which is when their government checks came through. [Laughs.]

At ten-thirty that morning the province chief came in and reported that the VC had blown the provincial jail, and VC sympathizers were roaming around town. I might add that for a couple of days before, Nha Trang had become dangerous to travel through because of what one colleague described as "rattlesnakes"—the armed deserters. They were all over. We had tried to take our friends out to dinner at a nice restaurant one evening, and all sorts of people were coming in and getting fed at gunpoint.

At noon they had to close the main entrance to the airport. We could no longer get through the town. The province chief came to say that he had asked for troops from II Corps to maintain control of the city and was told they didn't have any. At that point we called in the helicopters to move people from the compound out to the airport. There was a big parking lot right by the building, and we used that as a landing pad. There were palm trees in there, so we just hooked up the ambulance and pulled them out of the way. I put my administrative officer in charge of loading people on the planes, and I stayed on the radio. But when the first helicopters came in, we had this mob scene. They all rushed out and we were afraid they'd get cut with the rotors. In one case a helicopter took off and there was this woman still hanging on the skids. The pilot got about one story high and realized what was going on, so he settled back down and she wasn't hurt.

At that point we cleared the compound and started bringing people in small groups through the building. There was a fence between the parking lot and the building, and we kept people behind the fence. That way we could let in one helicopter load at a time. We posted some marine guards and backed them up with some of the AID people who were former military or Special Forces—cool heads. They had shotguns. But we had a lot of people inside by that point. And we kept screening the people outside the compound so we could let in the ones who were ours. There weren't great mobs outside, but one of the compound walls went right back alongside some old buildings, and people were getting in through cracks and crevices.

This went on all morning and afternoon. We got the last of the files and communications destroyed. Around four-thirty a bunch of "rattlesnakes" tried to rush the compound. The marine guards managed to fire over their heads and discourage them. But about this time people started climbing over the walls. It was obvious that we were beginning to run out of people that we could identify as ours. Also, the helicopter pilots started complaining that as they circled over the city to make their landing they were being fired on. So we reversed the landing pattern and had them come in over the beach. But we were losing control, and we'd gotten out most of the people we could identify. Phil Cook, my assistant, was checking people off, and he said, "I think we're getting more interlopers than staff in here." After all, people were bringing in families of ten, and we'd never seen them before.

So Phil Cook and I agreed that I'd go out to the airport and take charge there, and he'd do one last go-round and come out with the last of the marines. I flew to the airport and sent the chopper back. I had a radio, and Phil was saying, "Where's the chopper? We're being fired on." I told him it was making its final approach. That was one of the worst moments I had during the evacuation.

When I got to the airport, we heard that only one more plane would be coming. That was a World Airways jet. It couldn't move off the main runway because it was too heavy. And we didn't have any ramps that were tall enough to reach up to it. Everybody would have to climb up a knotted rope ladder, which was no use to us. We also got orders from the embassy: "Pull the Americans out. No more evacuation. It's over. Take the planes you have there and get out." Well, this meant leaving a fair number of locals, but we didn't have anything to get them out with anyway. So we got all the Americans together, told them what was happening, and made a dash for the planes. We took off leaving about 250 local staff and their families, and 100 other Vietnamese civilians at the airport. That was very disheartening.

The helicopters stayed behind. They were going to try to get our people who were down by the beach, where we seemed to have a little more control. A military transport and a Korean LST had come into the harbor. When I got to Saigon, I was told that the helicopters had tried to land the first couple of times, but they were mobbed and fired on, so they had broken off. I was left with the impression that we had abandoned 700 people on the beaches. It wasn't until three months later, in Washington, that I saw a memo from this MSTS guy saying that they had gotten those 700 people onto the ships.

The people we left at the airport were taken out that night. The chief Vietnamese employee, with a great deal of courage, had gone over to the commanding general of the 6th Air Division. He said, "We've been run out on by our Americans, and we want you guys to get us out." The air force evacuated them to Saigon on military transport planes. The ambassador and I got a very bitter note from the head of the local staff about the way the Vietnamese had been used like a sponge and then squeezed out and thrown away because they were useless. Which I certainly understood, but it was pretty painful to get that kind of note.

What we did for the next week or so was to send planes up on recon over Nha Trang. It stayed as an open city for a day. Then, on April 3, the plane was fired upon, so North Vietnamese forces were in the city. That was the day General Phu was relieved of his command. He had fled Nha Trang without telling anyone, and he committed suicide later down in Saigon.

I left about the fifteenth of April. Ambassador Martin sent me back because they'd set up a task force in Washington and they wanted somebody who'd had firsthand experience. Also I didn't see any point in putting my wife through a second evacuation. And I thought we should get the people who weren't necessary out of there. Until I left we stayed with the Martins, in the guest house at the residence. I remember Lois and Dottie used to go over to the PX and spend hours shopping for almost nothing. At this point it wasn't clear whether we were going to evacuate the people working at the commissary, so Lois went over just to show them we were still around. Just trying gently to give the impression that we had full confidence in the government and the armed forces. Trying to keep the structure together as long as we possibly could.

ALAN CARTER

His office is a light-filled room in an old house perched on top of a hill near Brattleboro, Vermont. It is the headquarters of the Experiment in International Living, which sponsors cross-cultural exchanges. From the window I can see fields sloping down to the other campus buildings, and students sitting at picnic tables in the sun. He has worked here since retiring after twenty-two years in the United States Information Agency, a span that included posts in Pakistan, India, Japan, and Vietnam, as well as a stint in Washington. "I had a nourishing career, and I was a very lucky guy—until Saigon. I moved fast, unusually so, and I retired with the rank of minister, all those nice things." Now about sixty, he gives an impression of good health and energy. The first thing he does on my arrival is to make dinner reservations for me at the best restaurant in town.

He got to Vietnam only eight months before the collapse, but he might have gone earlier. "In the late '60s, a man named Barry Zorthian was assumed to be ending his term as head of JUSPAO. Ellsworth Bunker, our ambassador in Saigon, asked the agency to assign me as Barry's replacement. I was caught in a bind because I didn't want to go. I had some real problems with the U.S. position there. I grew up in an era where everybody said you don't fight land wars in Asia. I also felt that whatever the sins of the North Vietnamese were, and they were many, it was futile to try to implant a democratic organ into a Confucian/Buddhist/mandarin society. That was American macho at its finest, or worst, depending on your point of view. But I had worked for Bunker in India, and my commitment to him was so deep that I couldn't have said no. Luckily the agency said no for me, because they wanted me to go to Japan. After four years there, when they finally assigned me to Vietnam, I had no ideological problem. The peace treaty had been signed. We were presumably in a transition to the kind of program that I felt comfortable with. So I went."

They offered me the job in 1974. I would be minister counselor for public affairs, which means that I'd run the USIS program and would be public affairs adviser to the mission. I wasn't enamored of the idea. At the time, relations between the embassy—Graham Martin in particular—and the press corps were as bad as they had been during the actual war. I was specifically asked by my bosses to try to improve things. Well, that's ridiculous. The USIS's clout in that kind of situation is minimal. Graham Martin was a formidable person, and he had a great alliance of some sort with Henry Kissinger. So here is wonderful Alan Carter, who's going to heal this several-years-long schism between the press and the embassy, under the reign of an ambassador who used the word "treason" in talking about certain reporters. I wasn't very comfortable about the task.

I don't know what was in Martin's mind when he brought me out there. I can only guess. He and I met before I went out. He was on consultation in Washington, so I did the thing one does: Go over and meet the ambassador for whom you'll be working. Martin is a very impressive-looking man. Tall, lean, patrician. Steel-blue eyes. A very bright guy. We were talking, and I said, "Y'know, I don't really understand what you know about me that led you to accept me on your staff. Do you know anything about my background?" He freezes you with those eyes and says, "I know everything about you. Do you think I would have accepted you without knowing everything?" I said, "Then you know I have a particular philosophy and a way of dealing with the press. You know I'm not a yes-man. But I know that you hand-picked most of your chief lieutenants because of their adherence to you and your ways." He said, "Exactly. I've got to have somebody near me who isn't an automatic yes-man." And there was still enough naiveté left in me to think, Well, I can see that, I guess.

I got there in September 1974. And I thought, Okay, let's see if there's any room to ease relations with the press. There was also the other task, the demobilization of the psy-war operation. I wanted to do programing in which American points of view were rationally discussed with important emerging South Vietnamese leadership. Younger people in the press, in the government, in cultural circles. A wide-open, free-ranging discussion. We had a big binational center there that had wonderful facilities—a theater, seminar rooms—so you could have important people sitting around talking about important ideas.

Well, not only was there not time for all that, but the few suggestions I made were not well greeted. USIS had a magazine there that read like the most militant kind of propaganda. I don't remember what it was called. I stopped it and said, "We'll design something more rational." But what's rational? Just converting from one magazine to another provoked a lot of adverse comment, because many of the Americans there were old Vietnam hands. They had an emotional stake, and it was pretty hard to shake them up even though circumstances had changed and U.S. policy had changed. The commitment

they felt—the deep, deep commitment to Vietnam and its final salvation was so great that anything suggesting that their past efforts had
been in vain, well, you're striking at the most difficult chord in a
human being.

We did start a new magazine, but it was a constant battle. "Why
are you doing this? We're still at war." "No, you're not at war. There's
a peace treaty. Remember the decent interval?" But for these people,
the kind of thing I wanted to do was irrelevant. They needed to see
the South Vietnamese government survive. Survival meant military
aid and economic aid, and anything else was irrelevant. They weren't
dealing in the realm of ideas, so to talk about an open exchange of
ideas was unreal to them. Maybe they were right. From their perspective, the only real thing was to get more aid out of the U.S.
government. That was what South Vietnam needed. It didn't need
ideas.

The point is that the embassy was the most emotion-ridden embassy
I have ever seen. There was not much coolness there. I have disagreed
with American policy in other embassies, but I was lucky enough to
work with basically rational people who tried to hold on to objectivity.
Not in Saigon. There was no objectivity there. It was a moral and
political and military crusade. Above all else, a crusade.

I'd been there no more than ten days when I looked up a reporter
whom I had been told was particularly good. I said, "David, you know
what I want to do? I'd like to sit down with eight or ten of the press
guys and listen. Why don't you put together a dinner? Then you can
tell me what your problems are with the embassy." So we spent a
long evening. They had a lot of stuff they were unhappy about. Some
of it I didn't agree with, but much of it I did. For example, the
ambassador had effectively cut off briefings by anyone except him or
his chosen designate. He thought he had sealed off CIA briefings,
military briefings, political briefings. Well, I could understand why he
wouldn't want everybody blabbing, but I could also understand that
the reporters had to get points of view somehow. They also talked
about being denied information they should not have been denied, or
being fed distorted information.

The very next morning I got a summons from Martin. He said, "I'd
like you to give me a memo about your evening last night. I understand
you had dinner with these correspondents." I said, "Yes, that's no
secret." "I want a memorandum of conversation. I want to know what
each of them said, and I want to know what your reply was to each
one of the criticisms, so that I can feel comfortable that you're correctly
representing the embassy's point of view." I said, "I have no intention

of doing that. I'll give you my comments about where I think they were right and wrong, but I will not give you a memorandum in detail. For one, it's bureaucratic. And it's not the way things work best for them or for you." By that I meant, nobody wins that way. Nobody's going to trust me if I come out and say, "I'm open, you tell me, but I'm also going to tell him each thing you said." I'd be dead in the water.

So he said, "I think the only thing I can do then is to deny you the privilege of talking to the press, if you can't play by the rules." I said, "You can't do that. You can send me home, but as long as I'm here you can't deny me meeting with the press." He said, "I'm denying you." I said, "It won't work. I will continue to meet with the press. Or send me home." And there we left it, a stalemate.

Not long after that, two of our consuls were being debriefed by the seniors in the embassy. One was talking about eroding security in the delta, although theoretically the delta had been politically and militarily secured. Well, the ambassador gave that a life span of conversation of about one millisecond. Then a younger person said, "I must say I think one of the things we're doing very badly is the way we're handling the press. I think we have to be more open. I think we have to be more available. I think we have to be more factual." I thought, I can't sit here and not weigh in. So I said, "I know I'm relatively new here, but I'm not so new that I don't know there's a serious problem here. I'd just like to say that what he just said makes a lot of sense, and I think we need to consider it." The ambassador let a decent interval of about two minutes go by. Then he started a long speech about how inevitably newcomers come along, and just as inevitably they know all there is to know, and they speak before they've gotten the feel. I had been there four or five weeks. This was the minor castration operation taking place.

I followed him after the meeting and said, "Mr. Ambassador, I'd like to come to your office." He said, "Sure." I went in and said, "I don't know what you want me to do here, but you've just begun the process of undermining me with all that business about newcomers." He gave me that wonderful fixed stare and said, "You really think I was talking about you? Your ego tells you I was talking about you? I was being very general." I said, "I don't think you were. There's only one person in the room that could have been aimed at." He just said again, "I think your ego is large enough for you to trip over."

So you back out toward the door, bowing a little bit. What can you do? You've made your statement, and it's been turned into you being a damn fool or an egomaniac. My education was rapid. I was taken from kindergarten all the way to my master's degree within a few weeks. It was not a happy time. It's the one chunk of time in government that I regret and resent. I enjoyed every other part of my career. But that one—*blecch*. I've never been dealt with like that, never been surrounded by so much emotion that prevailed over any kind of reason, and never got myself castrated quite as quickly or repeatedly.

As time went on, there was a lot of talk behind closed doors about new infiltration of the Viet Cong into the delta. There was always a long gap between the time that information would come up and the time it would get reported to Washington. The rationale was that we needed to be sure this was not some consul skewing the picture. But it quickly became apparent that there was a reason for holding this information. This was late 1974, and Martin's working premise was that the most immediate need of the Vietnamese was economic aid. That's a perfectly rational position. However, should the U.S. Congress learn that the military situation in the delta, of all places, was starting to unravel, the chances of them voting aid would be dim. I suppose withholding that information is smart political strategy. But it's not the embassy's role to determine that strategy. It's a matter for the White House and the State Department. In my judgment, an ambassador should not make the decision to withhold information so it won't get to Congress.

Well, the stuff surfaced anyway, because there were discussions. Mission council did talk about it sometimes, and I would go to other people and say, "What's the reporting from the delta?" So when the reporters were saying to me, "We're getting warped information out of the embassy," they were right. There was one middle-grade political officer, a good officer, who was being used as the political briefer. He went through anguish because what he knew and what he was told to say were often at odds. Of course the reporters were smelling it, and they had sources in the consulates. Maybe I'm an idealist, but I don't think it's the function of an embassy to manipulate, exploit, and lie to the press and to Congress. I'm not so naive that I think you always tell the press everything. "No comment" is very functional. Most journalists will respect it if you tell them, "Sorry, you're on turf I can't cover now."

By December we were getting nervous about what all this infiltration meant. We had surveillance stuff—photos of the North Vietnamese pipeline being extended south, major movement of their forces along the border, redeployment of some of their tactical air wings. By January that intelligence had taken on some really disturbing tones.

In early March the offensive began, and pretty soon it looked like it could be the final push.

By late March, our assumption was that we probably had until the end of June. Even as April came in, we were still saying, Well, maybe June or July. And six weeks seemed like an infinity. God knows nobody was expecting to evacuate on April 29. But you could sense the mounting fear in the streets. Every day when I'd go to work, the numbers of people hovering around the main gate were increasing. I thought I ought to have a couple of pistols around, just to scare people off and for crowd control if we needed it. I'd talk to my staff, and they were scared. It was a Brechtian scene. I'd get up in the morning—still in early April, now. I lived in a very pleasant villa, and I'd go out on my very lovely patio into the very pleasant morning sun, and I would eat mango or some glorious fruit and have some freshly ground French coffee, and I'd look up at the gate and all these Vietnamese were flowing by on their motor scooters, and the lovely women in the lovely ao dais were going by on their bikes. You knew the whole damn thing was unraveling, and it was like watching old film roll while a new script is being written.

This led to another run-in with Martin. I got a phone call from Washington asking me if I would file a situation report through my own USIS channels—in other words, without showing it to Martin. It's not unusual for USIS posts in that kind of situation to do "atmospherics." But they were really asking me to make sure the ambassador didn't see it. I was told, "State doesn't think it's getting accurate reports. Could you file something?" What they were saying was they didn't trust their own source, the ambassador. That was unusual.

So I sat down and batted out a cable that included the phrase "fear bordering on panic." I suggested it wouldn't take much to spark panic in the streets. And I just sent it out, knowing the ambassador would eventually catch up with it. The next day, a C-5 cargo plane that was taking hundreds of Vietnamese orphans back to the States crashed near the airport. And I got a phone call from Graham. He said, "Y'know, this crash never would have happened if people had talked to me about it. I know enough about the military to know that the C-5 has had problems. I never would have allowed it, but I wasn't consulted. That's what happens when people bypass me and tell Washington that there's fear out here, and Washington chooses to ignore me." I said, "My God, you're suggesting that I'm responsible for that plane crash." He said, "You can read it any way you want. I'm telling you that if I had been consulted . . ."

It was in the second week of April that we got requests for a lot of lists. We were told to compile lists of our staff by alphabetical roster, by seniority, by sensitivity. We also had lists of important Vietnamese contacts, which for us meant people in the Ministry of Information or media people. So we were pumping these lists out, staying up till two or three in the morning, going cockeyed getting lists together. I'd take them to the embassy bleary-eyed in the morning and go back to my compound.

Of course, I was pretty much out of the information loop about the evacuation plans—but I wasn't the only one. A lot of us had no idea what was in the ambassador's mind or what was going over the back channel. For example, one day, on my own compound, which was separate from the embassy, I saw a lot of people going in and out of a Quonset hut we had on the lawn. There was an auditorium in there. I went in the back door and stood there in amazement, because it was a briefing by mission warden, one of the security guys, of the American business community about evacuation plans. He said there'd be helicopter pads at certain sites, and three options: fixed-wing aircraft, helicopters, and the corridor option, going out through the delta to Vung Tau.

The next day I went to the mission council meeting and said, "Why can't we get the same briefing that the American businessmen got?" The administrative officer, who was in charge of mission warden, said, "There was no briefing of American businessmen or anybody else." I said, "Yes, there was, there was a briefing yesterday, and by your people." Joe Bennett, the political officer, sat upright and said, "There was a briefing yesterday?" I said, "Yes, Joe, I sneaked in the back door and listened to it." Joe was Martin's man, but for the first time he exhibited some anger and said, "Well, why can't we be briefed also? We need to know these things."

After that we were suddenly given bits and pieces of the same kind of information. Around mid-April I began holding daily briefings for my senior Vietnamese staff, and I would tell them what I thought was true, just the way it was fed into me. I was smart enough to hedge it a little bit by saying, "I can't guarantee that we can get out, so I won't guarantee that you're going to get out either. But I can guarantee you one thing: When the day comes, we'll do everything humanly possible to take you with us." Which was a lie. It wasn't even intended. Martin planned to get out only a small cadre. He had signaled Washington that he saw no way of taking out these people in the numbers that would be required. Instead, he suggested sending them down the river in tugs and barges, and if they were lucky, they'd get out. By the time Washington ordered him to plan a massive evacuation by air, it was too late. In effect, I was being manipulated to lie to my staff to keep them calm. To this day I can't forgive Martin or myself for that part. I didn't know I was lying, but I can't get over my anger that I was lying to my staff—whether deliberately or not. I was lying to the poor bastards. I was saying, "Hang in there. We're nice folks."

Then I discovered that DAO was getting a lot of people out on fixed-wing aircraft at the airport. I assumed these people were coming off the lists we had been turning in. Except it quickly became obvious that anybody and everybody was climbing on those goddamn planes. The embassy had issued certain certificates that you could sign to get people out. I didn't even know these forms had been issued. When I found out, I went over to the embassy and said, "I want some of the forms." There was a big stack of them in the hall by someone's office. They gave me a few, and I papered a few of my staff.

Here were the embassy people like little vultures, feeding off these papers, getting out friends and girlfriends and boyfriends and uncles and whatevers, and we're sitting over at the USIS compound not knowing these papers even exist.

After that we started serious staff reductions. I got my American staff down to four or five, and my Vietnamese staff down to a core group. I told them, "We'd like you with us all the way through, if you're willing. You're the key people. If we go, you go." The Vietnamese grapevine, which is the fastest form of communication known to man, picked up on all this. We began to get more and more people hovering around the compound gates, looking to see me. People started showing up at my villa.

Somewhere in there, maybe the third week in April, I had to do a TV broadcast. Graham called me in and said the Ministry of Information was asking if we could issue any kind of statement that would calm down the city. Martin and I talked about what the main points should be. Some of them were valid. Yes, we have reduced our American staff, and there are some Vietnamese who've been leaving as well. Two, we have no intention of closing this embassy. We are not evacuating. We are taking prudent measures. Three, Congress was debating an aid bill at that point. Well, that was a fact, but it was misleading, because none of us thought Congress was going to vote any aid. And four, don't be alarmed by the long lines outside the embassy. The lines were out into the street, maybe a block and a half long—mostly Vietnamese, and a few of the resident American colonial types. We said these were just orderly lines of people looking for visas for their wives or relatives. That still bothers me, because it was a half-truth at best, and it got less true as the hours passed.

They videotaped this interview. The answers were carefully written by me, with Martin making only a couple of changes. It was broadcast that night, and the assumption was it would be on that night. But it kept running, and I didn't even know it. I wasn't watching their television. That's my one claim to innocence in that episode. I thought it was a one-night thing—let's hold the hordes off, tell them we're just drawing down our people. But neither the ministry nor Martin had any doubt about their intention to keep running the bloody thing, night after night. Some of the things were true until the last day: We weren't closing the embassy. But this garbage about the lines—by that time we were force-feeding the evacuation channel at incredible speeds with anybody who could get near an airport. The lines were now lines of desperate people looking for desperate ways out.

In the last days, I would wake up in the morning and come home at night to find lines of people at my villa. There might be anywhere from five to fifteen. I'd be having my breakfast, and the guard would come in. He'd say, "I've got eight or nine people waiting outside." I'd say, "All right, send them in and I'll talk to them one at a time." They were very quick conversations. Grown men would come in and say, "Never mind me. Get my family out." I'd say, "I can't. I can't get your families out. Get down to the river. Get out any way you can. Don't go around looking for help." But then some of these grown men would literally get on their knees and beg you to get their fam— [Long pause.]

Can you imagine the humiliation of a grown man having to throw himself on his fucking knees to me just because I've got a title? They didn't know me. They just knew I was some wheel at the embassy. And the same thing would happen when I got to the compound. They would come in. If it was a woman, she would cry. There were men who would break into tears. And we had to confront our own staff, tell them they couldn't bring their whole families. And the Vietnamese, about the family—it's an emotional thing for them. So they would grovel— [Long pause.] You don't like anybody groveling anytime, but when you're telling people— [Long pause.]

If they only knew how idiotic it was, how powerless all of us were, and me in particular, sitting over in my compound.

The ground rules were that a staff member could take out a spouse and children, but the male children had to be under eighteen. So Ken Jackson and I would call our staff in and say, "We're putting you on this list with your wife and your daughter and your fifteen-year-old son. But you can't take your parents, and you can't take your eighteen-year-old son." You don't have to know much about the Vietnamese to know what we were saying. But I thought it was the only fair thing to do. Like a real horse's ass, I assumed that I had to stick to the rules. We had long discussions at the embassy, and the ambassador himself had said, "If you multiply the average employee here by seven average family members, you're talking about getting out 200,000 people. There's no way we can do it." So we agreed on the rules, and I listened. Others were smarter. I was just dumb.

On April 23 we started evacuating our locals, and I moved out almost all my remaining American staff. Around the twenty-sixth, the Vietnamese started gathering at the compound, until pretty soon we had 200-plus there in addition to the staff. We sent out a couple of busloads to the airport on the twenty-seventh. On the twenty-eighth we were loading the first of three buses when the North Vietnamese air force attacked Tan Son Nhut. We immediately closed the gates, and that bus didn't get out.

We had a couple of families show up with their parents. I remember Ken saying, "We're going to have to separate them. How can we face that?" But if we let this one extended family in, how could we say no to the rest? There were three or four who said, "If I have to split my family, I won't go." Ken and I would beg them to think about it carefully. As it turned out, it didn't matter. I remember one man, the most senior of our Vietnamese. He was an older man, quite elegant. He was scheduled to go on the first bus. When the time came, we couldn't find him. I called his house and he said, "I want to go, but my wife has changed her mind. I'm begging her. Send the bus without us." He showed up several hours later with her. We had them loaded on the next bus when the air attack came. That was the end of the fixed-wing evacuation. As far as I know, they never got out.

At midnight on April 29, there was a meeting in the embassy. The decision was made to move 10,000 additional people over the next few days. They told us to come up with priority lists. By this time I was getting famous for being a little bit explosive, and I said, "What are you talking about? We've all given you lists already." And the guy who was supposedly compiling the lists said, "They're a mess. They're chaos. They're just sitting in boxes." So at six the next morning, we were going to reassemble and start putting new lists together.

I got to the embassy that morning, and the ambassador was calling the full mission council into his office, but by name. I just happened to be hovering and saw them going in. I said, "What is this?" Somebody said, "The ambassador is having a meeting of senior people." I said, "I'm inviting myself." We were told that the fixed-wing evacuation was off. The runways were too shot up. The ambassador said, very coolly if a bit dramatically, that he bloody well was going to drive out and look at those runways himself. The tenor of the meeting was, we're in deep-shit trouble but we'll play this out a few more days. Then we dispersed and I went back to my compound.

I got a phone call at eleven from Wolf Lehmann, the deputy chief of mission. He said, "Alan, please come over for a meeting." So I picked up my attaché case and went over. When I got in, people were blowing safes. I said, "What's going on? Where's the meeting?" They said, "There's no meeting. We're evacuating." I said, "For Chrissakes, I've got American staff back at the compound." So Lacy Wright went back in a car to pick them up. Then we all sat in a room at the embassy waiting to go.

We still had maybe 150 Vietnamese staff and their families at the compound. All day long we talked with two of the senior staff on the phone. I was also talking to mission warden, who said, "We'll try to get a bus over there to get your people out. But we're running out of buses. The drivers are starting to desert, and we're not sure what we can do." During that time, I was standing in a hallway and I heard somebody mention a barge. I said, "What barge?" "Oh, you don't know about—" "No, I don't know about the barge. Tell me about the barge." It turned out they had a barge that was picking up people down at the waterfront, and nobody had bothered to tell us. It was supposed to leave at three o'clock. We tried to figure out if we should tell our people to leave the compound and walk to the barge. But it was a few miles, and given what was happening in the streets, we figured they'd never make it in time. And if they did, it would probably be absolute chaos anyhow. As it turned out, the barge didn't leave till five or six, and it left half-empty, so they could have made it.

Finally I told them, "Look, I don't know if this will work, but get out of the compound by fours and fives and go to my house. It's closer to the embassy. If there's transportation, we'll try to get it over to you and get you here." By this time there was no way they could fight their way through the crowds around the embassy. Then we were told that we were next to go on the helicopters. We lined up at the stairway and I went up with four or five people. I got them all in the chopper and then just quietly turned around and went back down the stairs. I never intended to go. My plan was to go back to the office and stay in touch with my staff as long as I could. I hadn't a rational thought in my head about how to get them out, since the buses were disappearing on us, but I thought I ought to try.

Well, while I was on the roof, the staff people got to my house. One of them called the embassy and talked to a marine. The marine said, "Carter and his people have gone already." So they left my house, and by the time I got back downstairs in the embassy, nobody answered the phone at my house. They just decided I had gone off and deserted them. Why shouldn't they decide that? They just dispersed. Most of them got out later. Some of them made it in the next two or three days by boat.

During the last hours in the embassy there was a sense almost of orderliness. People were doing what they had to do—blowing safes, or destroying files, or sitting and waiting to be taken out. Papers were being put into the shredders. And finally, about nine or ten o'clock, we were told we had better start lining up. I was still down in one of the offices phoning around like an automaton. I kept dialing my house and the compound, trying to raise somebody. Then I got in this long line snaking down from the roof. And I ended up in the same helicopter as Martin's secretary, who was carrying his dog. The chopper flew out around eleven. As we got up in the air a little bit, it was like watching a Roman carnival. Two ammo dumps were going off—one just north of the city, and one at the opposite end. So a lot of stuff was flying around in the air, and it looked like fireworks. There were big crowds around the embassy, and in almost every street you could see people in motion. I remember looking down at this near-orgy of light and firecrackers and thousands of people milling around, and turning to somebody and saying, "Well, there are all those wonderful hearts and minds that we won."

We flew out to the *Okinawa* and landed. We were all assigned bunks. I threw my stuff down and went to get some coffee. It turned out I was sitting next to the brother of one of the people in my compound. And I broke into tears. I said, "I couldn't get your brother out."

It took me a long time to get over it. For six or seven months I had nightmares almost every night—and I'm not a nightmare person. I had cold-sweat nightmares about the ones who were left behind. They were always dreams about stranded people. Almost any scenario you can imagine—an island, a prison, a barbed-wire camp. The theme was always the same: I had run away from people who were stranded.

I still feel and I always will feel guilty. I wasn't smart. I didn't give those exit papers to everybody. I didn't say, "I want my people on the next bloody fixed-wing." I sat there and I lied to them, in person and on television. That part was so painful for me. Collectively, all of us at the embassy only got out a third of our staffs. I did no better and no worse than the average. But given the number of other Vietnamese that came out, we did pretty poorly.

Not long after I got back I started working for the refugee task force, and I was put in charge of the camp at Indiantown Gap. That was a partial redemption. I was able to do something for the people who did get out, in terms of making their lives as decent as possible in the camp, and relocating them into homes in the U.S. I went around to all the camps looking for my people. I ran into one former staff person who had gotten out on his own. He made a bitter diatribe against me for having misled them on TV night after night. I said, "What are you talking about?" That was the first I had heard of it. I said, "I didn't know it was on. I thought they just broadcast it one night." If he believed me, he's a fool. It's a foolish story to have to believe. Even though it's true, it's a foolish fucking story.

There were a lot more staff who thought I deserted them. That hurts to this day. I didn't desert them, but they had every reason to think I did. I finally found one of the men I was on the phone with, one of the ones who made it to my house. I convinced him of what happened, because other people could confirm it. I didn't leave on that first helicopter. I did come back down. I did make some effort. It was the most futile effort in the world—I didn't help them at all. But at least they didn't see me as having just cut and run, saying, "Screw you."

SHEP LOWMAN

After the offensive began there really wasn't anything for a political officer to do except stay out of the way. What politicians thought about things at that point didn't matter much. Social reform, political party alignments—too late for all that.

But I was still talking to the politicians. I had lots of meetings with them, saying, "This is a desperate situation. I understand your complaints. I believe many of them are legitimate. But if you don't gather around the President now, I think your country is lost." And they would answer, "No, the only salvation is immediate reform. There's no way to save the country with Thieu. He has to go, and then maybe we can rally people to the defense." But the whole thing was lost anyway, I don't think anything could have saved it.

As we come into the last weeks, it's hard to remember the progression of events. But the basic thing is that we were under orders to get the Americans out of the country. The problem was that a lot of the contractor types who had stayed on had wives or girlfriends without the proper documentation. Or if the wife had documentation, they didn't have all the documents for their kids from a previous marriage. Or if they had all those, they didn't have documents for a